Greg Harvey's Excel® 4.0 for Windows™

Greg Harvey

BANTAM BOOKS

NEW YORK • TORONTO • LONDON • SYDNEY • AUCKLAND

Greg Harvey's Excel® 4.0 for Windows™
A Bantam Book/September 1992

Produced and composed by Parker-Fields Typesetters, Ltd.
Interior design by Nancy Sugihara

ISBN 0-553-35152-4

Bantam Books are published by Bantam Books, a division of Bantam
Doubleday Dell Publishing Group, Inc. Its trademark, consisting of the
words "Bantam Books" and the portrayal of a rooster, is Registered in the
U.S. Patent and Trademark Office and in other countries. *Marca Registrada*,
Bantam Books, Inc., 666 Fifth Avenue, New York, New York 10103.

PRINTED IN THE UNITED STATES OF AMERICA

0 9 8 7 6 5 4 3 2 1

Contents

Part II Advanced Worksheet Techniques 271

7 Customizing the Workspace 273

8 Documenting and Troubleshooting the Worksheet 309

19 Customizing the Toolbars 727

20 Working with Add-in Commands and Functions 757

21 Using Excel with Other Applications 777

Acknowledgments

I want to take this opportunity to thank the many people at Bantam, Microsoft Corporation, Harvey and Associates, and Meade Ink who helped me at every stage of this project. Your many efforts have greatly contributed to the quality of this handbook on Excel 4.0.

At Bantam, thanks to:

Jono Hardjowirogo, senior editor, for all of your encouragement and help in getting this project underway, keeping the project going, and performing the technical edit of this work.

Jean Davis Taft, associate managing editor, for all of your reassurances, general good humor, and hard work overseeing the production of this book, and to Debra Manette for your copy editing.

At Microsoft Corporation, I want to thank:

Kelli West, assistant product manager for Excel 4.0, for all your help in getting me the latest releases of the Beta software and keeping me up to date on all the latest Excel information.

At Harvey and Associates, I want to thank:

Lili Micaela, assistant, for your extraordinary patience, dedication, and excellence in the appendices for this book.

Shane Gearing, associate, for your many contributions to the project, including keeping the software current, creating and printing figures, and doing whatever was needed to help me complete the work. I couldn't have done it without you!

And last but not least, at Meade Ink, I very much want to thank:

Jim Meade, author, for your contribution to chapters 12 to 14 on charts and graphics. Your excellent insight into graphical issues combined with your overall writing talent are responsible for making this section so successful.

Greg Harvey
May 25, 1992
Inverness, California

Introduction

Excel 4.0 for Windows is one of the most significant upgrades to what many already agree was the most complete worksheet program available for Windows. As you will soon discover, version 4.0 offers a host of ease-of-use features designed to make short work of the most commonplace worksheet tasks. For example, you can now move or copy worksheet data by dropping and dragging your selection into place in the worksheet. You can also create a series, such as days of the week, quarters, or months in the year, or fill a particular range with a particular value by dragging a special Fill handle.

Along with the original toolbar introduced in version 3.0 of Excel, Excel 4.0 now supports six other built-in toolbars, all of which enable you to select commonly used commands at the click of a tool. You can display as many of these toolbars as you want on the screen. When displaying a toolbar, you can dock it so that the toolbar remains fixed along one side of the work area; or you can make it into a floating toolbar that you can position and resize in the work area as you want it. In addition to these built-in toolbars, you can create your own toolbars using any of the more than 130 built-in tools included in Excel. Or, you can create custom tools that run macros that you attach to them. You can even import pictures from other compatible graphics programs and paste them on the face of the custom tools that you create.

If the convenience of clicking a tool on a toolbar—instead of selecting a command on the correct pull-down menu—is not enough, Excel 4.0 introduces shortcut menus. Shortcut menus are pull-down menus that are directly attached to specific screen objects, such as the cells in the worksheet, toolbars displayed on the screen, or parts of a chart in the active window. To display the shortcut menu for any one of these objects, you simply click the cell, a toolbar, or an area of the chart with the right mouse button (instead of the usual left one). Excel then displays a pull-down menu containing only those commands that can be applied to the selected object.

Those of you who work with multiple worksheets of a particular type, such as departmental budgets or quarterly sales forecasts, will appreciate the new workbook feature. Workbook lets you bind in a single file all the affiliated worksheets, charts, and macro sheets that you normally use together. That way, all the documents are available as soon as you open the file. This not only makes it easier to open and use the documents, but also to back them up and circulate them to all the other people in your office who must have access to the information.

Excel's new ChartWizard makes charting your worksheet data a snap, even if you've never created a chart from worksheet data before. To create a new chart in your worksheet, you simply select the worksheet data to be charted, click the ChartWizard tool on the Standard toolbar, drag the cross-hair pointer to size and position the chart in the worksheet, and then follow the step-by-step instructions in the ChartWizard dialog box. The ChartWizard not only prompts you for all the necessary information each step of the way, but it also lets you preview how the finished chart will appear. Once you've created your chart in the worksheet with the ChartWizard, you can then use the same tool to modify which data are charted, or to change the titles for the chart. You can also modify the type of chart or add enhancements, such as legends or gridlines, with the tools on the new Chart toolbar. Those tools automatically appear whenever you select the chart in the worksheet or open a chart window.

In addition to these ease-of-use features, Excel 4.0 also greatly enhances the analytical capabilities of the program. The program now lets you save the various print settings and display options that you use in a particular worksheet as a view so that you can reactivate all these settings simply by selecting the name of the view in the Views dialog box. For those of you who need to perform extended what-if analysis on your worksheet models, version 4.0 offers the Scenario Manager. With this feature, you can vary your input values in your model and save the results as a scenario. With the new Report Manager feature you can define the views and/or scenarios that you want used when printing various data as a worksheet report. Then, to print the scenarios using the various print settings, you simply select the name of the report in the Print dialog box.

In addition to the Scenario Manager, Excel 4.0 includes Crosstab ReportWizard. This feature makes it easy to generate various cross-tabulated tables that compare and summarize data stored in various fields of the database. Like the ChartWizard, the Crosstab ReportWizard walks you through each step required to define which data you want to include in the table and how you want the various sets of data compared. After generating the crosstab tables, you can then print them or save them in their own documents to be printed later.

For those of you involved in statistical analysis, Excel 4.0 includes the Analysis Toolpak, a set of sophisticated functions used to perform a wide variety of statistical analyses for financial, engineering, and scientific applications. With the Analysis Toolpak, you have access to diverse statistical functions as those that perform Anova, Histogram, F-Test *t*-Test, Regression, Rank and Percentile, and Fourier analyses.

For those of you who use macros to streamline routine spreadsheet tasks, such as entering, formatting, and printing data, Excel 4.0 offers a few important enhancements. You can now save the macros and have access to them any time you create a new worksheet or edit an existing one in a global macro sheet. All macros saved in the global macro sheet are immediately available each time you start the program. In addition to assigning macros to buttons on particular worksheets, you can now assign your favorite macros to tools and then add these tools to particular toolbars (either the built-in toolbars that come with Excel or custom toolbars that you create yourself). That way, these macros are available in any document as long as their toolbars are displayed. You can run the macros simply by clicking their tools.

All in all, after you've had an opportunity to use this book and experience Excel 4.0, I'm sure you will agree that this version of the program is not only one of the most powerful spreadsheet programs on the market but also one of the easiest to learn and use.

What does this book contain?

Greg Harvey's Excel 4.0 for Windows is organized as follows:

- Part I: "Worksheet Basics" contains six chapters that teach you the fundamentals of working with Excel and creating worksheets. Chapter 1 familiarizes you with the parts of the Excel window, document windows, as well as how to start and exit the program. Chapter 2 introduces you to the basic skills you need to build a new worksheet. Chapter 3 teaches you how to format the data in your worksheet. Chapter 4 covers the process of editing and proofreading the data in your worksheet. Chapter 5 introduces you to building and using formulas and functions in your worksheet. Chapter 6 teaches you how to print the data in your worksheet.

- Part II: "Advanced Worksheet Techniques" teaches you more advanced techniques for working with your worksheets. Chapter 7 teaches you techniques for customizing the Excel workspace, including how to arrange and size document windows, freeze column and row headings on the screen, choose new display options, and save various display settings as views. Chapter 8 introduces you to the various techniques for documenting and troubleshooting your worksheets, including how to annotate and audit your worksheet as well as trap error values and prevent their spread in the model. Chapter 9 teaches you how to use Excel's outlining feature to organize and arrange tables of worksheet data so you can view and print the table displaying various levels of detail. Chapter 10 introduces techniques for working with multiple documents in Excel, including how to use templates to generate new worksheets, consolidate data from various worksheets, and how to link data in different worksheets. Chapter 11 teaches you how to perform in-depth analysis on your worksheet data with the Data Table, Goal Seek, And Solver features as well as with the new Scenario Manager and Analysis Toolpak.

Chapter 12 introduces you to the basics of creating charts, both on the worksheet and in separate chart windows. Chapter 13 teaches you how to enhance and customize the basic charts you create with Excel. Chapter 14 introduces you to working with graphic objects, such as macro buttons and text boxes, as well as shapes you create with Excel's drawing tools, pictures you create with the Camera tool, and images you import from other graphics programs.

Chapter 15 teaches you how to create, maintain, and search databases. Chapter 16 teaches you how to analyze the data you keep in your databases using the built-in database functions and the new Crosstab feature.

Chapter 17 introduces you to command macros—both those that you record and play back and those that you write yourself in macro sheets. Chapter 18 teaches you how to use macros to create custom applications in Excel that use their own menus and dialog boxes.

Chapter 19 teaches you how to customize the built-in toolbars as well as create toolbars of your own. Chapter 20 teaches you how to use add-in macros and create custom functions in Excel. Chapter 21 introduces you to many methods for transferring information between Excel and other programs that you use, including how to exchange data via the Clipboard, how to link data in different applications, and how to import and export documents.

The book concludes with two appendices. Appendix A contains the keystroke shortcuts in Excel grouped by function. Appendix B contains a complete list of the worksheet functions in Excel 4.0. The worksheet functions in Appendix B are grouped alphabetically within the same function categories that the Paste Function dialog box uses.

How to Use This Book

Greg Harvey's Excel for Windows is designed for Excel users at all levels, from the beginner to the more advanced. If you are new to Excel, you will want to pay particular attention to the information in the six chapters in Part I, as this part contains all the fundamentals that you will need to begin creating and working with your own worksheets. If you already have some experience with Excel 3.0, you may only want to browse through the information in Part I to get specific version 4.0 information before you begin reading and using the more advanced and specialized information in the later parts of the book. Look for the ▧ icon next to sections that discuss the new 4.0 features.

Once you've become familiar with the basic worksheet features in Excel, you can use this handbook as a reference to look up and explore more specialized techniques and features as you need them. Remember, you can also find detailed information on keyboard shortcuts and worksheet functions in the two appendices.

Conventions and Icons Used in This Book

This book uses the following icons and typographic conventions to help you quickly identify special information in the text:

- The ▧ icon indicates a tip, which gives you hints on how to get more out of the particular Excel feature being discussed or how to combine particular features with others being discussed in another section of the book.

- *Note* indicates that additional information on the topic or technique being discussed in that section is being provided.

- The ▧ icon indicates an alert. It gives you cautionary information, which is designed to help you avoid pitfalls when using the technique or feature being discussed in that section.

- The ▧ icon indicates a new feature or function first introduced in version 4.0 of Excel.

- The ▧ icon in Appendix B indicates a worksheet or macro function that is attached to Excel as an add-in function.

- Entries that you might type in the Excel formula bar or in a dialog box are indicated in the text with **boldface** type.

- The names of all the files and directories mentioned in the text of the book are indicated in lowercase letters in **boldface** type.

- Range names mentioned in the text of the book are capitalized (although you can enter them in any combination of upper- or lowercase letters).

- The names of the worksheet and macro functions are indicated with all uppercase letters (although you can enter them in any combination of upper- or lowercase letters).

- Obligatory arguments in the worksheet functions in Appendix B are indicated with sans serif type, as are optional arguments in these functions.

Part I

Worksheet Basics

1

Getting Started with Excel

In this chapter you learn how to get started with Excel 4.0 for Windows. You will begin by learning the components of the Excel window along with the different types of objects that can be displayed there. Becoming acquainted with the function of each part of the Excel screen will go a long way toward making you comfortable with the program and efficient in creating and editing your worksheets. After learning how to identify the elements used by Excel, you then will learn how to start Excel and get on-line help whenever you need it. As you will discover, Excel offers extensive on-line help that you can turn to at any time when using the program.

If you are new to Excel for Windows, you should read this chapter with some care before you move on to the next, where you learn how to build a new worksheet. If you've been using Excel 3.0 for Windows and are upgrading to version 4.0, you're already acquainted with most of the material in this chapter. You should, however, read the sections on shortcut menus and the toolbar before moving on. Excel 4.0's shortcut menus provide a brand-new way of selecting commonly used menu commands without using the menu bar. The toolbar, which was first introduced in Excel 3.0, is more versatile in version 4.0, and the Standard toolbar contains several tools that weren't present on the Excel 3.0 toolbar.

Understanding the Excel Window

When you start Excel, the program loads as a full-size program window entitled *Microsoft Excel*. As you can see in Figure 1.1, the program window is composed of several distinct areas, each of which contains its own elements. The Excel window is divided into the following areas:

3

1. The *title bar* at the top of the screen, which contains a Control-menu button, the title of the application (Microsoft Excel), a Minimize button, and a Restore button.

2. The *menu bar*, which contains the pull-down menus that you use to select various Excel commands as you work with the program.

3. The *toolbar*, which contains a series of tools each of which performs a commonly used Excel command when you click its button.

4. The *formula bar*, which has three parts: the first part displays the current cell reference, the second part displays the cancel and enter boxes when you enter or edit data in the current cell, and the third part displays the contents that you are entering or have entered into the current cell.

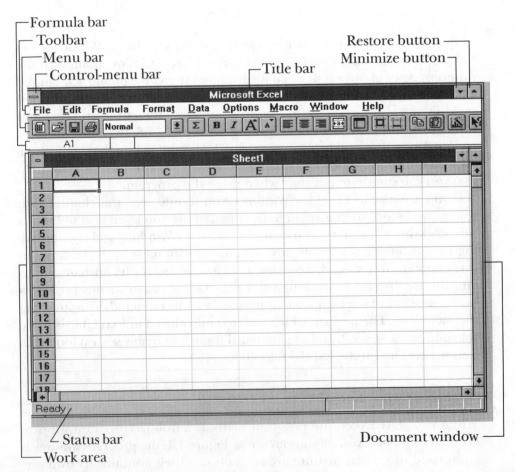

Figure 1.1 The Excel Program Window on Startup

5. The *work area* (between the formula and status bars), which contains all Excel document windows that you have open—normally Excel displays only the active document window in the middle of the work area.

6. The *status bar* at the bottom of the screen, which is divided into two parts: the first part displays messages about the current state of the program or the Excel command you are about to select, while the second part contains five mode indicators that tell you when certain keys, such as the Num Lock, Extend (F8), or Caps Lock keys, or modes are engaged.

The Title Bar

The title bar for the Excel window displays the name of the application (Microsoft Excel) between the program Control-menu button on the left and two sizing buttons on the right. When you click the Control-menu button, the program displays the Control menu shown in Figure 1.2. You can use the options on this menu to resize the Excel window, close the Excel window (and subsequently quit Excel), or switch to another program that you have running.

When you first start Excel, the two sizing buttons on the right side of the title bar are titled Restore and Minimize. You click the Minimize button to

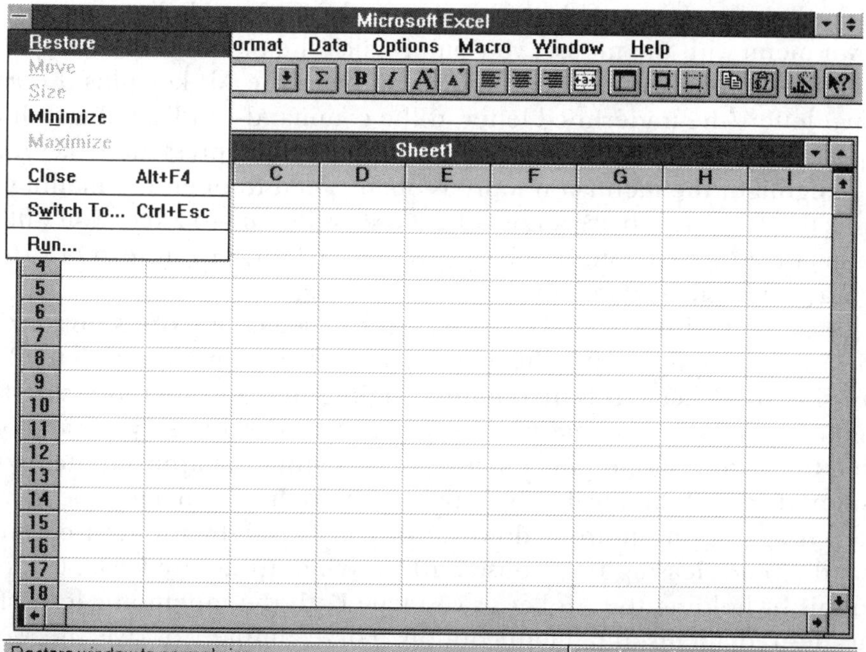

Figure 1.2   The Control Menu for the Excel Window

reduce the Excel window to a program icon on the Windows desktop as shown in Figure 1.3. (This is the equivalent of selecting the Minimize option on the Excel Control menu.) You click the Restore button to reduce the Excel window to a midsize window in the middle of the Windows desktop as shown in Figure 1.4. (This is the equivalent of selecting the Restore option on the program Control menu.)

When the Excel window is reduced to the Excel program icon, you can restore it to full size by double-clicking the icon or by clicking the icon and selecting the Restore option on its Control menu. When the Excel window is reduced to a midsize window, the Restore button on the title bar changes to a Maximize button (shown as a single arrowhead pointing up). You click the Maximize button to restore Excel window to full size. (This is the equivalent of selecting the Maximize option on the program Control menu.)

The Menu Bar

The menu bar contains nine pull-down menus (File through Help) that you use to select the Excel commands you need when creating your worksheets. As with other Windows programs, you can select commands from the pull-down menus with the mouse or the keyboard. To open a pull-down menu with the mouse, you simply click the menu name. To open a pull-down menu with the keyboard, you press the Alt key plus the *mnemonic* letter (the underlined letter in the command—indicated with bold type in this book). Alternately, you can press F10, then press the → key until you highlight the menu you want to open. Then to open the menu, you press the ↓ key. If you are a Lotus 1-2-3 user switching to Excel, you will be happy to know that you can also press the / (slash) key instead of F10 to activate the pull-down menus.

Once a pull-down menu is open, you can select any of its options by clicking the option with the mouse, typing the mnemonic letter, or pressing the ↓ key until the option is highlighted and then pressing the Enter key. As you become more experienced with Excel, you can combine the action of opening a menu and selecting the appropriate menu option from it. When using the mouse, you do this by clicking the menu, then dragging the pointer down until you highlight the desired command; then releasing the mouse button. When using the keyboard, you do this by holding the Alt key as you type both the mnemonic letter for the desired menu and menu option. For example, to save the work you've done on your worksheet by selecting the Save option on the File menu, you can simply press Alt+FS.

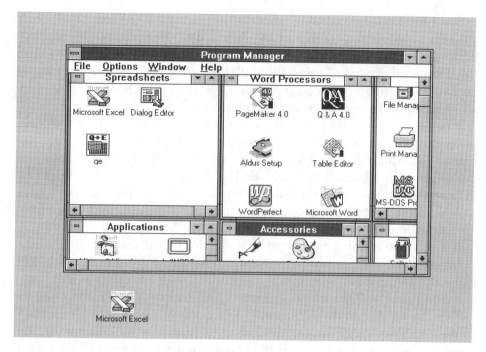

Figure 1.3 Excel Window Reduced to a Program Icon

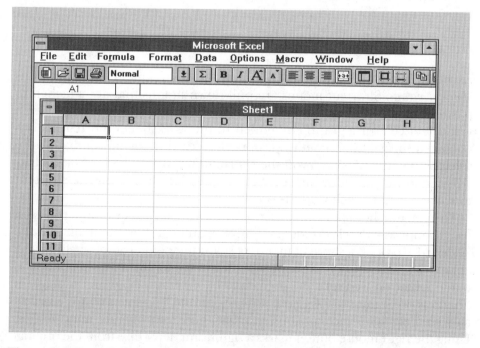

Figure 1.4 Excel Window Reduced to a Midsize Window

Some Excel commands have shortcut keys assigned to them. The shortcut keys assigned to a command are shown after the option on the appropriate pull-down menu. If you prefer, you can use the shortcut keys to select the command instead of using the pull-down menus. For example, to save an Excel document, you can press the shortcut keys Shift+F12 instead of selecting the **S**ave option on the **F**ile menu.

When using the Excel pull-down menus, you will find that after selecting many commands, a dialog box of further options from which you can choose is displayed. (For more information on selecting dialog box options, see "Understanding Excel Dialog Boxes" later in this chapter.) Whenever option names on the pull-down menu are followed by ellipses (...), or three periods in a row, those commands are attached to a dialog box of further options.

If a command appears in light gray on the menu (also referred to as being *dimmed*), the command is not currently available for selection because the conditions under which it operates are not in effect at that time. For example, the **P**aste command on the **E**dit menu remains dimmed so long as the Clipboard remains empty. As soon as you cut or copy some data to the Clipboard (with the **C**ut or **C**opy commands on the **E**dit menu), the **P**aste option appears in normal bold type when you open the **E**dit menu and is available for use.

Shortcut Menus

Excel 4.0 introduces a new way of quickly selecting menu options with its *shortcut menus.* Shortcut menus are pull-down menus that are attached to particular screen elements (referred to as *objects*) such as the toolbar, a worksheet cell, or a graph embedded in the worksheet. Shortcut menus contain a special list of command options related to the object that you've selected. Figure 1.5 shows you the shortcut menu attached to the toolbar (discussed in the following section). Figure 1.6 shows you the shortcut menu attached to each worksheet cell.

To open the shortcut menu attached to a particular screen object, you must use the mouse—Excel provides no way of opening a shortcut menu with the keyboard. To open a shortcut menu, position the pointer somewhere on the appropriate object (such as on the gray area of the toolbar or within or on the border of the desired cell) and then click the *right* mouse button. Normally in Windows programs such as Excel, you use only the left mouse button to select all screen elements such as icons, windows, pull-down menus, and the like. Using the right mouse button marks a significant departure from the original Windows design standards. However, the use of the right mouse button to

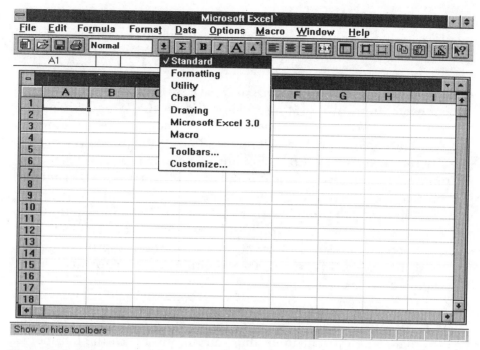

Figure 1.5 Shortcut Menu Attached to the Toolbar

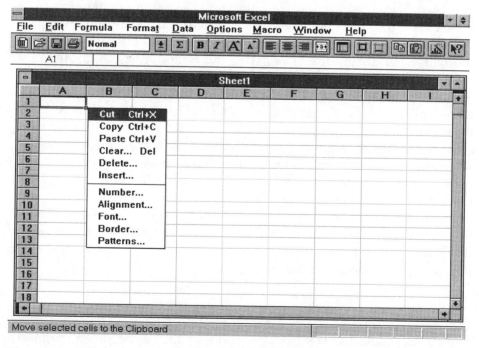

Figure 1.6 Shortcut Menu Attached to Each Worksheet Cell

open pull-down menus attached to particular screen objects is becoming more and more common. With Microsoft's adoption of its use in Excel 4.0, this may well become a new Windows standard.

Tip   If you're left-handed (as I am) and have switched the left and right mouse buttons in the Mouse dialog box in the Windows Control Panel, you currently click the right mouse button to select standard Windows objects such as icons, windows, and pull-down menus. Therefore, to open a shortcut menu, you need to click the *left* mouse button. Everywhere I give the instruction "click the right mouse button," you need to click the left mouse button and everywhere I say "click the left mouse button" or just "click the mouse button," continue to click the right mouse button. I don't expect such contradictory instructions will faze you, as you are probably quite used to making this type of transposition in order to survive in a right-handed world.

The hardest part of using the right mouse button to open a shortcut menu is that you must remember that you still must click the left mouse button to select a command option from the shortcut menu. Switching immediately from the right mouse button to the left mouse button can be somewhat confusing. The easiest way to avoid trouble with this right/left transition is to click the object with the right mouse button to display the shortcut menu, then, without releasing this button, drag down the menu until you highlight the desired command, whereupon you release the right mouse button. Alternately, you can click and release the right mouse button to display the shortcut menu, then select the desired menu command with the keyboard by pressing the ↓ key until you highlight the appropriate option, and then press the Enter key. (Excel doesn't assign mnemonics to the commands on the shortcut menus.)

Despite the strangeness of switching between right and left mouse buttons, you will probably find the use of shortcut menus to be a great time saver. As shortcut menus display their options right next to the selected object, you can choose the desired commands more quickly because you don't have to take the time to open the Excel pull-down menus and select the appropriate commands there.

The Toolbar

The toolbar feature, first introduced in Excel 3.0, has become even more powerful and versatile in version 4.0. The toolbar contains a series of buttons

---

Table 1.1 Tools on the Standard Toolbar

Tool	Function
	New Worksheet
	Open File
	Save File
	Print
Normal	Style Box
Σ	AutoSum
B	Bold
I	Italic
A	Increase Font Size
A	Decrease Font Size
	Left Align
	Center Align
	Right Align
	Center Across Selected Columns
	AutoFormat
	Outline Border
	Bottom Border
	Copy
	Paste Formats
	Chart Wizard
	Help

---

with icons (referred to as *tools*) that can be used to perform common Excel tasks. (Table 1.1 lists the function of each tool on the default, or Standard, toolbar.) To perform the desired task with the toolbar, simply click the appropriate tool with the (left) mouse button.

Unlike Excel 3.0, which limited you to a single toolbar, in version 4.0 you can have multiple toolbars in the Excel window. The program comes with several preconfigured toolbars, which you can display or hide at any time. The easiest way to display a particular toolbar is by selecting it from the shortcut menu. (Figure 1.5 showed you the toolbar options available in this shortcut menu.) You can also display a particular toolbar by selecting it in the Toolbars dialog box that you open by choosing the **T**oolbars option on the **O**ptions pull-down menu.

The toolbar that is automatically displayed at the top of the Excel window when you start Excel 4.0 is now called the Standard toolbar to differentiate it from the other toolbars you can choose and display. Figure 1.7 shows you the Excel window when both the Standard toolbar (at the top) and the Utility toolbar (right below it) are displayed. Note that the Utility toolbar contains fewer tools and therefore is shorter than the Standard toolbar.

Normally, Excel positions each toolbar that you select below any others that are displayed at the top of the Excel window in the area between the

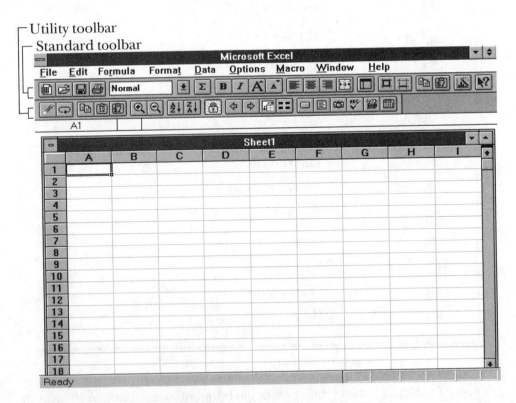

**Figure 1.7   Excel Window with the Standard Toolbar and Utility
        Toolbar Displayed**

menu bar and the formula bar (a condition known as *docking the toolbar*). The only exception to this arrangement is in the case of the Chart toolbar. By default, the program docks the Chart toolbar at the bottom of the Excel window above the status bar any time you display it.

Tip Excel automatically displays the Chart toolbar whenever you select an embedded chart in the active worksheet or open a chart window. As soon as you close the chart window or deselect the embedded chart, Excel automatically removes the Chart toolbar from the bottom of the Excel window.

Also new in Excel 4.0 is the ability to convert any docked toolbar to a "free-floating" toolbar that you can move anywhere you'd like within the Excel work area. To undock a toolbar, simply place the pointer somewhere on the gray area of the toolbar (outside of any tool) and drag the toolbar into the work area. As you drag the pointer, an outline of the toolbar moves with it. Once you've got the outline of the toolbar where you want it to appear, release the mouse button. Excel then redraws the toolbar, this time in its own window, containing a Control-menu button and a title bar with the name of the toolbar. Figure 1.8 shows you the Standard toolbar after it has been undocked and moved to the middle of the work area.

Once you've undocked a toolbar, you can then move its window around the Excel work area by dragging the title bar. You can also modify the shape of the toolbar window. To do this, you position the pointer either on the right edge or on the bottom edge of the toolbar window. When the pointer changes to a double-headed arrow, you then drag the mouse to change the shape of the toolbar. If you've positioned the pointer on the right edge of the toolbar window, drag to the left to make the window narrower and longer or to the right to make the window wider and shorter. If you've positioned the pointer on the bottom edge of the window, you accomplish the same thing by dragging the mouse down or up. Excel increases or decreases the number of rows of tools in the toolbar window to accommodate the change in shape. Figure 1.9 shows you the Standard toolbar after its shape has been modified so that its tools are arranged in three rows.

To return a toolbar window to its docked position, simply double-click on the toolbar. If you have modified the shape of a toolbar before you return it to its docked position, the toolbar automatically resumes this shape the next time you undock it. To remove a toolbar window from the work area without docking it, click the Control-menu button on the toolbar window. If you close a toolbar window without docking it, the toolbar resumes its previous position and shape in the work area the next time it is displayed.

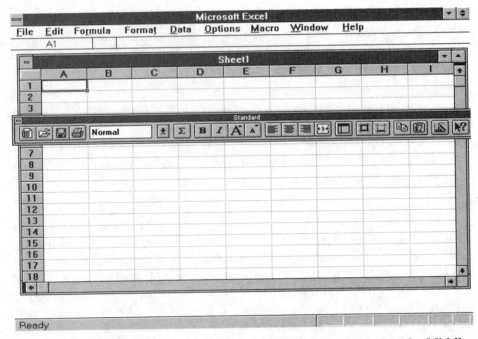

Figure 1.8 Excel Window with Toolbars Undocked and Moved to the Middle of the Work Area

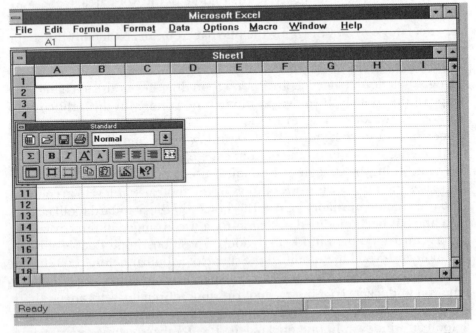

Figure 1.9 Excel Window After Changing the Shape of the Standard Toolbar to Three Rows

Tip In addition to moving and reshaping a toolbar, you can also customize the tools it contains and create new toolbars. For complete information on how to customize Excel toolbars, refer to Chapter 19.

The Formula Bar

The row beneath the toolbar (or toolbars, if you have displayed more than one) is known as the formula bar. This row is divided into three areas. The first area keeps you informed of the position of the *cell pointer* (indicated by heavy border around the edges of the cell) in the worksheet in the active document window by displaying the current *cell reference.*

The cell reference indicates the column and row that contain the cell pointer. Excel can give you this information in two ways. Normally, the column is indicated by letters and the row by numbers, as in *A1*, when the cell pointer is located in the first column (A) of the first row (1). Excel can also indicate the cell reference entirely by numbers (the so-called R1C1 system). When you use this system, the number of the row always precedes the number of the column, as in *R2C1*, when the cell pointer is located in the first column of the second row (also known as B2).

After the cell reference, the formula bar contains an area for the cancel and enter boxes. These boxes automatically appear as soon as you begin entering some data in the current cell. If the current cell already contains data, these boxes appear whenever you select any part of its contents on the formula bar. (You can do this by clicking I-beam pointer in the text or by pressing F2.) You can click the cancel box (the one with the X in it) to abandon a new cell entry or any editing changes made to an existing entry. You can click the enter box (the one with the check mark in it) to complete a new cell entry or any editing changes made to an existing entry.

The third part of the formula bar displays the contents of the current cell. If the current cell is empty, this part of the formula bar is blank. As soon as you begin typing an entry or building a worksheet formula, each part of the entry is displayed in this part of the formula bar. After you complete the entry or formula in a cell, Excel then displays it in the formula bar whenever you position the cell pointer in that cell.

Note: Although cell entries appear both on the formula bar and in the current cell as you type them, they are not actually inserted into the cell until you complete the entry by clicking the enter box, pressing the Enter key, or pressing a direction key such as the ↓ key. For complete information on entering data in a cell or editing an entry, see Chapter 2.

The Status Bar

At the bottom of the Excel window, you find the status bar. As its name implies, the status bar keeps you informed of the current state of the program as you use it. The left side of the status bar displays messages on the current activity or the currently highlighted command. Usually this area contains the word *Ready*, indicating that Excel is ready to accept data in the current cell or some type of command. When you select a pull-down menu or a menu option, this area displays a short description of its purpose. If you're new to Excel, you can use this information on the status bar to help you learn the function of the Excel menu commands.

The right side of the status bar contains five *mode indicators*. These indicators tell you when certain lock keys, such as the Caps Lock, Num Lock, or Scroll Lock, are toggled on. (These keys are called *toggle* keys because you turn them on by pressing the key once; they stay on until you turn them off by pressing the same key again.) In addition to these keys, this area tells you when three other modes are active in Excel. Table 1.2 explains all the mode indicators that appear in this part of the status bar.

Table 1.2 Keyboard Modes Indicated on the Status Bar

Mode	To turn on and off	Function
EXT	Press F8	Extends the range of cells you select with the direction keys.
ADD	Press Shift+F8	Adds the cells you select with the direction keys to the currently selected range even if the cells are nonadjacent to the original range.
CAPS	Press Caps Lock key	Types all letters in uppercase.
NUM	Press Num Lock key	Activates the numeric keypad on the keyboard.
SCRL	Press Scroll Lock key	Freezes the cell pointer in its current position as you scroll the worksheet.
OVR	Press Ins(ert) key	Puts the program in overtype mode so that new text replaces existing text with the characters you add instead of inserting them.

Table 1.2 *(Continued)*

END	Press End key	When combined with an arrow key ($\leftarrow$, $\rightarrow$, $\uparrow$, or $\downarrow$), Excel moves to the first occupied cell adjacent to a blank cell in the direction of the arrow.
FIX	Select **W**orkspace from **O**ptions menu, then select the Fixed Decimal check box	Fixes the placement of the decimal point so that Excel automatically adds the decimal point to the numbers you enter in a cell.

Understanding Excel Document Windows

Excel 4.0 supports several types of document windows: worksheet, chart, macro sheet, workbook, and slides. Except for the chart window, all the other types of document windows use the same set of pull-down menus, the same Standard toolbar, and the same kind of worksheet grid divided into columns and rows. The chart document window, however, uses its own set of pull-down menus, a special Chart toolbar, and does not use any type of gridline. (You will learn all about Chart windows in Chapter 14.)

All Excel document windows, like the Excel window itself, contain their own Control-menu buttons, title bars, and sizing buttons. When you first start Excel, the work area contains a single blank worksheet document window. As shown in Figure 1.10, this worksheet is almost a full-size document window that takes up nearly the entire Excel work area.

Each new document window that is opened in the Excel window is given a temporary name that appears in the title bar. This temporary file name indicates the type of window (Sheet for worksheets, Chart for charts, Macro for macro sheets, Book for workbooks, and Slides for slide sheets) along with a number reflecting the sequence in which each particular type of document was opened. For example, the first worksheet document window opened is named Sheet1; the second, Sheet2; and so on. So too, the first workbook document window that you open is named Book1; the second, Book2; and the like.

Alert! Excel does not renumber document windows. If you close Sheet1 without saving the worksheet, the program does not change Sheet2 to Sheet1. The program does, however, keep track of the last number assigned to a particular type of document window during the work session. If you close the document window containing Book4 and then open a new workbook, the program assigns the name Book5 to this new document window.

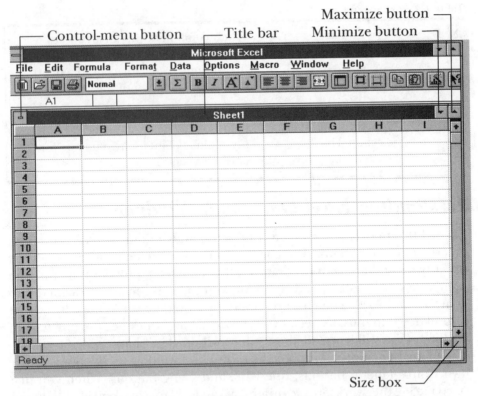

Figure 1.10 Worksheet Document Window that Appears on Excel Startup

You can move and resize document windows just as you can the Excel window. To reduce a document window to an icon in the Excel window, click the window's Minimize button, select the Minimize option on the Control menu, or select the window and press Ctrl+F9. As you can see in Figure 1.11, each type of document window uses a slightly different icon that is also identified by the name in the title bar. To restore a document window that has been reduced to an icon to its former size, you can double-click the icon, select the icon, and choose the **R**estore option on the Control menu, or select the icon and press Ctrl+F5.

You can also increase the size of a document window so that it takes up the entire work area. To do this, you can click the Maximize button on the document window, select the Maximize option on the Control menu, or select the window and press Ctrl+F10. When you make a document window full size, the window's title bar disappears. The name on its title bar is added to the title bar of the Excel window, and the window's Control-menu button and two sizing buttons are added to the menu bar (with the Control-menu button to the left of the menus and the sizing buttons to the right).

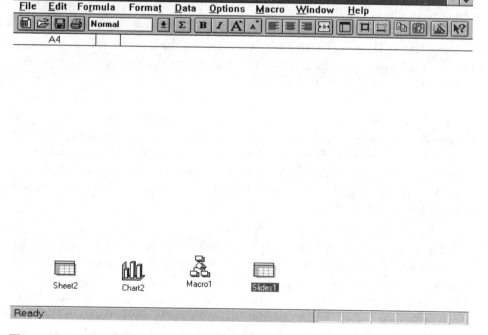

**Figure 1.11 Excel Window with Different Types of Document Windows
Reduced to Icons**

For example, if you are working on a worksheet named **BUDGET.XLS**, the
Excel title bar reads *Microsoft Excel - BUDGET.XLS* when you increase its
document window to full size.

You can also manually size any document window open in Excel. To do
this, click the *size box* (the box in the lower right corner of the document
window), then drag the pointer until the outline of the window is the size
and shape you'd like and release the mouse button.

The Worksheet Grid

The most common type of document window that you will be using in
Excel is the worksheet window. This type of document window contains a
grid composed of columns and rows. The intersection of each column and
row in the worksheet grid is called a *cell*. An Excel worksheet consists of 256
columns and 16,384 rows for a grand total of 4,194,304 cells! The data you
enter for the spreadsheets you create (such as titles, numbers, and formulas) are all entered and stored in individual cells of the worksheet.

As mentioned earlier, each cell is known by referencing to its column
and row position in the worksheet. Normally columns are lettered, starting

with A for column 1, B for column 2, and so on. When the alphabet runs out of new letters at Z for the twenty-sixth column, Excel starts doubling the letters. AA stands for column 27, AB for column 28, and so on, with the last column letters IV for column 256. The rows, on the other hand, are strictly numbered from 1 through 16384. The address of the last cell in any Excel worksheet is therefore IV16384.

> *Note:* Remember that Excel also supports the R1C1 system of cell references whereby both columns and rows are numbered and the row coordinate is listed before the column coordinate. If you were to switch to this system (by selecting **Workspace** option on the **O**ptions menu and then choosing the R1C1 check box), the last cell in the worksheet would be R16384C256.

It has been estimated that a paper worksheet with the same number of columns and rows as an Excel worksheet would measure more than 21 feet across and 341 feet high. As the typical computer monitor usually is able to display no more than about 9 of the total 256 columns and 18 of the total 16,384 rows (or 162 of the total 4,194,304 cells), obviously you can view only a tiny fraction of the total worksheet area at any one time. When you are working with a large worksheet, you will find that you have to move around a great deal to view your data. To lessen the amount of scrolling that you have to do, Excel allows you to split the worksheet window into different "panes" through which you can view different parts of the same worksheet.

You can also reduce the amount of scrolling you have to do by breaking up large spreadsheets into separate (smaller) worksheets. In Excel 4.0, you can then organize these separate worksheets into a workbook. Once these worksheets are added to a workbook, Excel treats each one like a single page of a regular book. (For complete information on creating and using workbooks, see Chapter 10.)

Scroll Bars

Each Excel document window that uses the worksheet grid (that is, worksheet, macro sheet, workbook, and slides windows) contains a vertical and horizontal scroll bar that you can use to bring new parts of the worksheet into view. As Figure 1.12 shows, each scroll bar contains two scroll arrows and a scroll box.

To scroll the worksheet grid a row at a time, click the scroll arrows on the vertical scroll bar (the up arrow to scroll up by a row and the down arrow to scroll down). To scroll the worksheet a column at a time, click the scroll

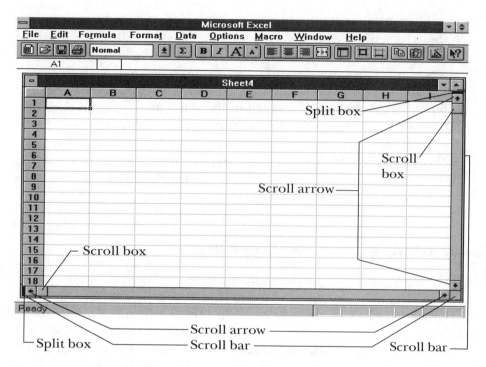

Figure 1.12 Each Worksheet Window Is Equipped with Two Sets of Scroll and Split Bars

arrows on the horizontal scroll bar (the left arrow to scroll left by a column and the right arrow to scroll right).

To scroll the worksheet a screen at a time, click the gray area of the scroll bar between the scroll box and the scroll arrows. To scroll the sheet up or down by a screen, click the vertical scroll bar (above the scroll box to scroll up and below the scroll box to scroll down). To scroll the sheet left or right by a screen, click the horizontal scroll bar (left of the scroll box to scroll left and right of the scroll box to scroll right).

For faster scrolling through a large worksheet, you can drag the scroll box. The position of the scroll box in its scroll bar reflects its relative position in the *active area* of the worksheet. The size of the active area determines how much of the worksheet you scroll when you drag the scroll box to a new position in the scroll bar. For example, if the active area extends to row 50 of the worksheet and you drag the scroll box to the middle of the vertical scroll bar, row 25 will be the first row that appears in the document window. But if the active area extends to row 150, row 75 then will be the first visible row.

Note: The active area of a worksheet is the block of cells that extends from the first cell (A1) over and down to the cell that is located at the intersection of the last column and last row occupied by data. Note that this last cell of the active area may not contain any data. To move the cell pointer directly to the last cell in the active area, you can choose the **S**elect Special command on the Formula bar and then choose the Last Cell option button or simply press Ctrl+End. To bring the last part of the active area into view in the document window, you drag the scroll box in the horizontal scroll bar all the way to the right and the scroll box in the vertical scroll bar all the way down.

Understanding Excel Dialog Boxes

As mentioned earlier in the discussion on the menu bar, all options on the Excel pull-down menus that are followed by ellipses (...) lead directly to the display of *dialog boxes* where you make further command choices. Dialog boxes are special windows that appear in the work area of the Excel window in front of the active document window. Like document windows in Excel, dialog boxes have Control-menu buttons in the upper-left corner (which you can use to move or close the dialog box), and you can move a dialog box within the work area by dragging its title bar. Unlike document windows, however, dialog boxes lack menu bars with pull-down menus, and you cannot change their size.

   In place of pull-down menus, dialog boxes enable you to make command choices through the use of different kinds of boxes and buttons. Most dialog boxes have default options or entries that are used automatically unless you make new choices before you close the dialog box. To close a dialog box and activate your choices (default or ones that you made), you select the OK button. If the OK button has a dark border (which is most often the case), you can also press the Enter key to put your choices into effect. To close a dialog box without putting into effect any new choices you've made, you can double-click the Control-menu box in the upper-left corner, select the Cancel or Close button inside the dialog box, or simply press the Esc key.

   Dialog boxes present an array of options in a single window. Most dialog boxes group related options together. When making selections in a dialog box with the mouse, simply click the option you want to use or, in the case of text entries, modify. When making selections with the keyboard, however, you must sometimes first activate the item that contains the group of options in the dialog box. You can do this two ways: You can press Tab to move to the next item (or Shift+Tab to move to the previous item), or you can press Alt plus the mnemonic letter in the option or item name. When pressing Tab (or Shift+Tab), Excel indicates which item is selected either by highlighting the default entry or by placing a dotted line around the name of the option.

The dialog boxes in Excel use all the standard types of boxes and buttons developed for Windows. The following sections briefly describe how each of these dialog box elements is used in making command choices.

Text Boxes

The *text box* provides a space in which you can type a new entry. Many text boxes already contain default entries. For example, the File **N**ame text box in the File Save As dialog box shown in Figure 1.13 contains a default file name *sheet1.xls* (composed of the temporary filename, Sheet1, plus the extension XLS used for worksheet files).

To enter a new entry in a blank text box, click the box or press Tab until you select it, then begin typing the text. To replace an existing entry, drag

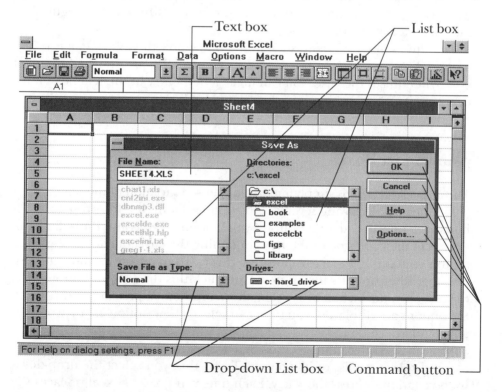

Figure 1.13 The File Save As Dialog Box

the I-beam pointer across the text to select the entire entry or press Tab until you select the text box (to simultaneously select all the characters in the current entry), then type your replacement. Excel replaces the existing entry as soon as you type the first character. To edit an existing entry, click the I-beam pointer at the place in the text that needs changing and make your modifications.

List Boxes

The *list box* provides a list of options from which to choose. If the list box contains more options than can be displayed in its box, the box contains a scroll bar that you can use to bring new options into view. To select an option in a list box with the mouse, simply click the option, and Excel will highlight and place a dotted line around it. To select an option with keyboard, select the list box by pressing Tab or pressing Alt plus the mnemonic, then press the ↓ or ↑ key until you highlight the desired option. You can also select an option if you know its name by typing the first few characters—Excel jumps to the first option in the list box whose name begins with the characters you type.

Note that some list boxes, such as the one below the File **Name** text box in the File Save As dialog box shown in Figure 1.13, are attached to a text box. When this is the case, you can make a new entry in the text box either by typing it or by selecting it in the related list box.

Drop-down List Boxes

The *drop-down list box* is simply a more condensed variation of the standard list box. Instead of displaying several of the options in this list, the drop-down list box shows only the current option (which originally was also the default option). On the right side of the box containing the current choice, there is a button containing an arrow pointing down. To open the list box and display the other options for an item, you click this drop-down button. (You can also open the list box by selecting the item and then pressing Alt+↓.) Once the options are displayed, you then can select a new option as you would in any standard list box.

You can also select a new option in a drop-down list box without opening it and displaying a list of its options. To do this, you select the drop-down list box and then press the ↓ key. Each time you press ↓, Excel replaces the current option in the list box with the next option in the list.

Check Boxes

The *check box* is used to present dialog box options that you can toggle on and off. A check box item consists of a square check box followed by the name of the option. When the check box contains an X, you know that its option is selected. When a check box is blank, you know that its option is not selected.

To select a check box (by placing an X in it) with the mouse, simply click the box. To deselect a check box that you've selected (by removing the X), click the box again. To select or deselect a check box option with the keyboard, press Alt plus the option's mnemonic letter or select the check box option with the Tab key (indicated by a dotted line around the option) and then press the spacebar.

Check boxes are often used in dialog boxes for items that allow you to select several different options at the same time. You can see such a case with the Cells item in the Display Options dialog box shown in Figure 1.14. There check boxes are used to enable you to select multiple display options for the cells in your worksheet at one time.

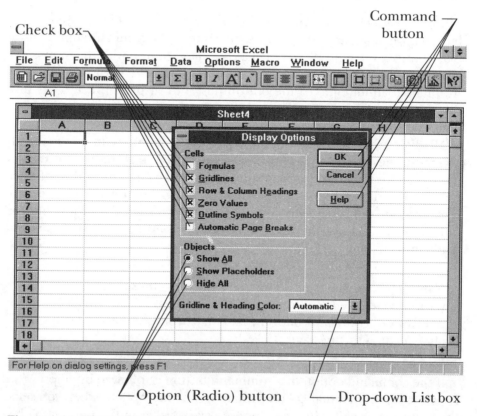

Figure 1.14 The Display Options Dialog Box

Option (Radio) Buttons

The *option button* (also known as a *radio button*) is used in dialog boxes to present items that have mutually exclusive options. The option button consists of a circle followed by the name option. Option buttons are always arranged in groups, and only one of the options in the group can be selected at one time. Excel lets you know which option currently is selected by placing a dot in the middle of its circle. (When an option button is selected, it looks like a knob on an old fashioned radio, thus the name radio button.)

To select an option button with the mouse, you simply click the button. To select an option button with the keyboard, press Tab until you select the first option button in the group, then, if necessary, press the ↓ key until the button for the option you want to use contains a dot. Whenever you select a new option button in a group, Excel automatically deselects the previously selected option button.

Command Buttons

The *command button* is used in a dialog box to initiate an action. The command button is rectangular in shape, and the name of the command option is displayed within the button. To select a command button with the mouse, you click the button. To select a command button with the keyboard, you press Alt plus the mnemonic (if the button has one) or press the Tab key until the button is selected (indicated by a dotted line around the button's name) and press Enter.

All dialog boxes contain some sort of command buttons. The most common ones are the OK and Cancel buttons. You select the OK button when you are finished choosing options in the dialog box and want Excel to close the dialog box and put these options into effect. You select the Cancel command button (sometimes Cancel is replaced by a Close button) only when you close the dialog box without putting any choices you've made into effect.

> *Note:* The simplest types of dialog boxes are those that display only warnings (referred to as *alert boxes*). These types of dialog boxes contain only an OK command button that you select to close the dialog box after reading the message.

If the command option in a command button is followed by ellipses (...), Excel displays a new dialog box containing further options when you select the button. Normally after you choose your options in the new dialog box and select its OK command button, Excel closes this dialog box and returns you to the first dialog box. You must then select the OK button in this dialog box to close the box and put all of your choices into effect.

Starting Excel

You can start Excel from the DOS prompt if Windows is not already running on your computer, or you can start the program from within Windows. To start Excel from the DOS prompt, follow these steps:

1. If the directory containing the Excel 4.0 program files (usually c:\excel) is not current, use the DOS Change Directory command to make it current. For example, if the DOS prompt shows C:\> as the current directory, you would type cd\excel (assuming that Excel is installed in a directory called c:\excel) and press Enter to change the prompt to C:\EXCEL>.

2. Type excel at the C:\EXCEL> prompt and press Enter.

Typing the **excel** startup command at the DOS prompt starts both Windows and Excel. Note that if you added c:\excel to the PATH statement in your **autoexec.bat** file, you don't have to make the c:\excel directory current before typing the **excel** startup command.

STARTING EXCEL FROM THE PROGRAM MANAGER

Microsoft
Excel

If Windows is already running, you can start Excel from the Program Manager in a couple of ways. The simplest way to start the program is by selecting the Microsoft Excel 4.0 group window (if you don't see this group window, choose the Microsoft Excel 4.0 in the Program Manager's **W**indow pull-down menu) and then double-clicking the Microsoft Excel 4.0 program icon. You can also start the program by selecting this program icon and pressing Enter.

You can also start Excel in the Program Manager by entering the Excel startup command in the Run dialog box as follows:

1. Select the **R**un option from the **F**ile menu to display the Run dialog box.

2. Type the **excel** startup command including the path in the **C**ommand Line text box. If you installed the Excel 4.0 program files in the c:\excel directory and didn't add this directory to the PATH command in your **autoexec.bat** file, you would type c:\excel\excel in the Command Line text box. If you did add this directory to the PATH statement, you simply type excel in the **C**ommand Line text box.

3. Select the OK button or press Enter.

When you start Excel with the Run dialog box, you can also specify the worksheet file that you want opened when the program loads into memory. To have Excel open a file when you start the program, enter the Excel startup command in the **C**ommand Line text box, then press the spacebar and type the name of the file you want opened. If the file is not located in the directory containing the Excel 4.0 program files, you must specify the pathname as part of the filename. For example, to open a worksheet file named **budget.xls** located in the directory **c:\accts**, you would enter

excel c:\accts\budget.xls

in the **C**ommand Line text box of the Run dialog box (making sure to separate the Excel startup command from the path and filename with a space).

 Tip If you have a worksheet that you work on almost every time you use Excel, automatically load this file each time you start the program by saving the file in the special **c:\excel\xlstart** directory. On startup, Excel loads any file saved in this directory even when you don't specify the filename as part of the startup command in the Run dialog box or start the program by double-clicking the Excel program icon.

Starting Excel from the File Manager

You can also start Excel from the Windows File Manager as follows:

1. Double-click the **EXCEL** folder icon in the Directory Tree window or click it and then press Enter.

2. Double-click the **EXCEL.EXE** document icon in the C:\EXCEL*.* window or click it and then press Enter.

If you want to open a particular Excel document at the same time you start Excel in the Windows File Manager, simply open the folder that contains the Excel document you want to work on, then double-click the document icon (or click it and press Enter). You can open the following types of documents when starting Excel:

- XLS documents that contain single worksheet files.
- XLT documents that contain worksheet template files.
- XLW documents that contain multiple worksheets organized into a workbook.

Closing Documents and Exiting Excel

When you are finished using Excel, you can quit the program and return to Windows by choosing the Exit option on the File menu or by pressing the shortcut keys Alt+F4. If you have document windows open in Excel when you give this command, the program prompts you to save any documents that contain unsaved changes. Once the Excel window closes, you are returned to place in Windows from which you started the program. If you started Windows from the Program Manager, you will be returned to the Program; if you started Windows from the File Manager, you will be returned to the File Manager.

Getting On-line Help

Excel 4.0 offers excellent on-line help that you can use any time you need information on how to use an Excel command, function, or feature. To get context-sensitive help information on the use of a particular Excel command, press Shift+F1 or click the Get help tool on the Standard toolbar (the last tool with the question mark icon), then select the option on the Excel pull-down menus for which you need information. When you press Shift+F1 or click the Get help tool, Excel adds a question mark (?) to the standard pointer icon to indicate that you will get help when you select the menu option instead of the command itself. To get context-sensitive information about the options in a dialog box, select the Help command button.

To look up information on a particular topic such as printing, or importing and exporting data in Excel, press F1 or select the Contents option on the Help menu. When you do this, the program opens the Microsoft Help Contents in a Microsoft Help Window. The Help contents is divided into three sections: Using Microsoft Excel, Switching from, and Reference. Each section contains various *jump terms* (a jump term is indicated by underlining in the Help window). To view information on a particular topic, you simply click the appropriate jump term.

For example, if you want information on how Excel uses the keyboard, you would click *Keyboard Guide* in the Reference section of the Help Contents. Microsoft Help then displays Keyboard help information in the Help window, which in turn contains a list of all the keyboard topics on which you can get further help. At that point, if you wanted information on the shortcut keys that you can use to format a worksheet, you would then select the *Formatting Keys* jump term, which would display a complete list of the formatting shortcut keys.

When you're finished using on-line help, you can close the Microsoft Excel Help window by choosing the Exit option on its File menu, double-clicking its Control-menu box, or pressing Alt+F4. Remember that you can always obtain a hard copy of the help topic you're viewing by selecting the Print Topic option on the File pull-down menu in the Microsoft Excel Help window.

Tip   If you are using Windows version 3.1, you can keep the Microsoft Excel Help window open on top of the Excel window as you use Excel 4.0. (Normally the Help window disappears as soon as you select any element in the Excel window.) To do this, open the Microsoft Excel Help window by pressing F1 or selecting Contents on the Excel Help menu. Then you choose the Always On Top option on the Help menu within the Microsoft Excel Window. When the Microsoft Excel Help window is open on top of the Excel window, you can move and resize it as necessary to see the contents of your Excel document window, and you can refer to specific help information as you work in Excel.

Navigating On-line Help

Microsoft Help keeps track of each topic that you visit when using on-line help. If you want to review the last help topic you saw, click the Back command button at the top of the Help window. If you want to revisit a topic out of sequence, click the History command and then double-click the jump term in the History dialog box.

You can also search for particular help topics if you're not sure exactly what jump term to select in the Help Contents. To search for help topics, choose the Search option on the Help menu or click the Search command button in the Microsoft Excel Help window, which displays the Search dialog box. You then type a keyword in the text box that contains the insertion point, or you select the keyword from the associated list box below. For example, to display a list of help topics on how to delete cells in Excel, you could type **del** in the text box, whereupon the program would jump to the keywords *deleting buttons* in list box. To display help topics on deleting cells, you would then double-click the keywords *deleting cells* listed right below *deleting buttons* or click *deleting cells* and then click the Show Topics command button.

Figure 1.15 shows the help topics on deleting cells that appear in the lower part of the Search dialog box. To display the help information for either help topic, you can double-click the topic or click the topic and select the Go To command button.

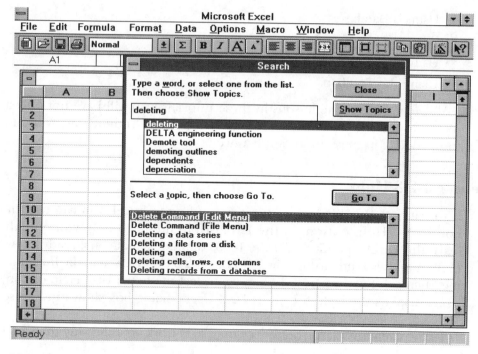

Figure 1.15 Searching for Help Topics on Deleting Cells

Using the On-line Tutorials

The Excel **Help** menu includes two tutorial options, **I**ntroducing Microsoft **E**xcel and Learning Microsoft **E**xcel, that start on-line tutorials which demonstrate the basic capabilities of Excel 4.0. If you are new to spreadsheets in general and Excel specifically, you will find it well worth your while to go through the lessons in both tutorials. The Introducing Microsoft Excel tutorial contains three lessons: The **B**asics, **W**hat's New, and For Lotus 1-2-3 Users.

The Learning Microsoft Excel tutorial contains the following lessons:

- What is Microsoft **E**xcel?
- Using Microsoft Excel **H**elp
- What is a **W**orksheet?
- Using a Worksheet
- What is a **C**hart?
- Using a Chart
- What is a **D**atabase?

- Using a Database
- What is a Macro?
- Using a Macro
- Using the Toolbars

After completing the lessons in these tutorials, you will have not only a good grasp of the capabilities of Excel 4.0 but also a rudimentary working knowledge of its most important features.

Getting 1-2-3 Help

If you are a Lotus 1-2-3 user who is upgrading to Excel, you can use the Lotus 1-2-3 Help option on the Excel Help menu to help you quickly learn the Excel equivalents for the 1-2-3 commands that you already know. (You should also run through the For Lotus 1-2-3 Users lesson in the Introducing Microsoft Excel tutorial.) When you select the Lotus 1-2-3 Help option, Excel displays the Help for Lotus 1-2-3 Users dialog box shown in Figure 1.16.

To display a note at the bottom of the Excel work area showing the Excel

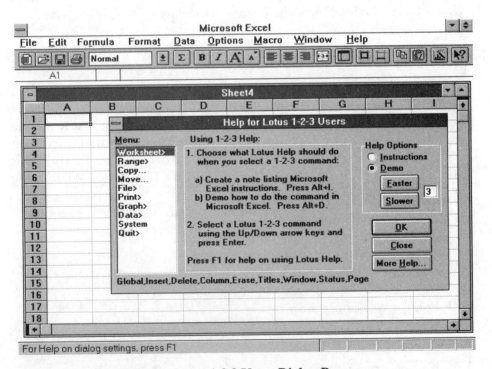

Figure 1.16 The Help for Lotus 1-2-3 Users Dialog Box

equivalent for any 1-2-3 / (slash) command, select the **I**nstructions option button under Help Options, then type the 1-2-3 command-letter sequence or use the arrow keys to highlight the appropriate menu sequence, pressing Enter after each selection. For example, to display a note telling you how to turn on global protection in an Excel worksheet, you would select the **I**nstructions option button, then type **WGPE** to select the Worksheet, Global, Protection, and Enable commands in the **M**enu list box. Excel closes the Microsoft Excel Help window and displays a note at the bottom of the active worksheet window that tells you that the procedure for the 1-2-3 /Worksheet Global Protection Enable command in Excel is to choose Protect Document from the Options menu. When you are ready to remove the note from the work area, simply press the Esc key.

Instead of a note, you can have Excel actually demonstrate its equivalent for a particular 1-2-3 / (slash) command. To do this, you select the **D**emo option button in the Help for Lotus 1-2-3 Users dialog box before you indicate the 1-2-3 menu sequence. For instance, to see a demonstration of the Excel pull-down menu equivalent for the 1-2-3 /Worksheet Global Protection Enable (WGPE) command, you would select the **D**emo option button in the Help for Lotus 1-2-3 Users dialog box before typing **WGPE**. Instead of displaying a note, Excel actually opens the **O**ptions menu, then highlights the **P**rotect Document option and briefly displays the Protect Document dialog box. If you find that the program demonstrates the Excel command sequence too quickly for you to catch everything, select the **S**lower command button beneath the **D**emo option button before you indicate the 1-2-3 menu sequence in the **M**enu list box.

SUMMARY

In this chapter you became acquainted with the function of the basic on-screen components in Excel 4.0. In addition to learning the purpose of each element, you also learned how to start and quit Excel and get on-line help when you need it.

Armed with these fundamentals, you are ready to move on to Chapter 2, where you will learn the skills needed to build worksheets. As part of this process, you will learn how to select cells, move the cell pointer in the worksheet, and enter various kinds of data. You will also get an opportunity to complete a hands-on tutorial that will show you some of the most efficient ways to build a new worksheet in Excel 4.0.

2

Building the Worksheet

This chapter introduces you to the fundamental skills required to build a new worksheet. Here you will learn how to select cells, make cell entries, move around the worksheet, and perform the more basic editing tasks. At the end of the chapter you will find a short tutorial that provides hands-on experience with building and formatting a worksheet. This tutorial is designed to show off several of the new ease-of-use features introduced in Excel 4.0, including the AutoFill, AutoSelect, and AutoFormat features.

If you are a new spreadsheet user, you should pay close attention to the material in this chapter. Regardless of what type of spreadsheets you create with Excel, you will find yourself using all of the techniques for selecting cells, moving around the worksheet, and entering data discussed herein. If you are an experienced Excel user, take time to read at least the sections "Selecting a Range of Data with AutoSelect" and "Entering a Series with AutoFill" that cover the user of the new AutoSelect and AutoFill features. You may also want to do the tutorial, as this will give you some firsthand experience with the new AutoFill, AutoSelect, and AutoFormat features.

Creating a New Worksheet

When you start Excel, the program automatically opens a new worksheet document window named Sheet1 where you can begin creating your spreadsheet. If, later during the same work session, you need to start another worksheet, you can do so by clicking the New Worksheet Tool (the first one) on the Toolbar or by choosing New on the File menu and then selecting the OK command button or pressing Enter.

35

To maximize the number of cells visible in the document window at one time while working on your worksheet, click the Maximize button in the upper-right corner of the worksheet document window. On most monitors you can see columns A through I, a small part of column J, and rows 1 through 20 when you maximize the worksheet document window. Of course, as you build your worksheet and begin customizing the widths of the columns and the heights of the rows to suit the data you enter in the cells, the number of cells visible may increase or decrease. Also, displaying multiple toolbars definitely reduces the number of rows that can be displayed unless you undock them so that they float on top of the worksheet.

Excel's Zoom feature makes it easy to see more data in the active worksheet window. You can magnify or reduce the size of the active worksheet window either by clicking the Zoom in and Zoom out tools on the Utility toolbar or by selecting one of the Magnification options in the Zoom dialog box (opened by choosing Zoom on the Window menu). Figure 2.1 shows you the Magnification option buttons in the Zoom dialog box. Note that these option buttons enable you to increase the magnification 200 percent, which doubles the size of the data in the

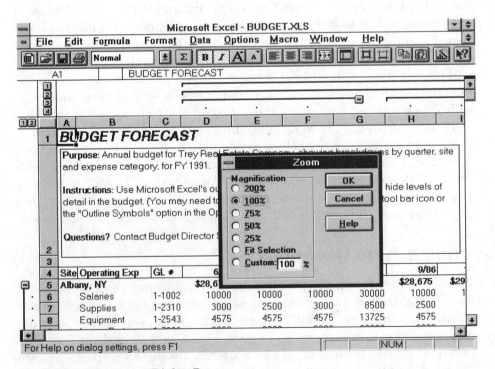

Figure 2.1 The Zoom Dialog Box

worksheet (effectively halving the number of cells visible), as well as to reduce the magnification in increments of 25 percent. If none of these preset magnification factors will do, you can select the Custom option button and enter a percentage between 10 and 400 in the % (percent) text box.

> *Note:* When you choose the Fit Selection option button, Excel chooses the magnification factor necessary to display all of the cells you've selected in the active document window.

Figure 2.2 shows the worksheet **BUDGET.XLS** after reducing the magnification of the worksheet window to 50 percent of normal size. At half normal size, you can now see columns A through P and rows 1 through 25. This reduction was done by clicking the Zoom out tool on the Utility toolbar twice. (The first time reduced the view from 100% to 75%, the second time from 75% to 50%.) This is the equivalent of selecting the 50% option button in the Zoom dialog box. Note that you can see the free-floating Utility toolbar in the lower-right corner of the worksheet window in the figure. The Zoom out tool is the second tool in

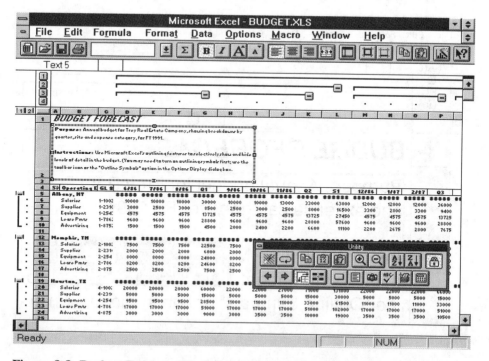

Figure 2.2 Budget Forecast Worksheet Reduced to 50 Percent of Normal

the second row of the Utility window, the one with the minus sign in the magnifying glass. (The Zoom in tool is the first one in the second row with the plus sign in the magnifying glass.)

Figure 2.3 shows you the same BUDGET.XLS worksheet after increasing the magnification to 200 percent of normal size. This increase was done by clicking the Zoom in tool four times. (The first time this increased the view from 25% to 50%, the second time it increased the view from 50% to 75%, the third time it increased the view from 75% to 100%, and the fourth time it increased the view from 100% to 200%.) This is equivalent to selecting the 200% option button in the Zoom dialog box.

You can use the Zoom in and Zoom out tools on the Utility toolbar or the Magnification options on the Zoom dialog box to adjust the size and number of cells visible in the active window while working on your worksheet. You use the Zoom out feature to quickly get an idea of the size and shape of your worksheet and the tables of data it contains, while you can use the Zoom in feature to make it easier to read and verify the data you enter in the cells.

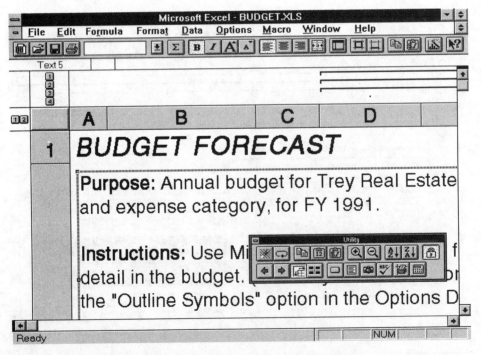

Figure 2.3   Budget Forecast Worksheet Increased to 200 Percent of Normal

Selecting Cells in Excel

If you went through The Basics lesson in the Introducing Microsoft Excel on-line tutorial, you may remember that the first thing you were taught was the general principle of first selecting the item you want to work with before selecting the command you want to perform. Actually, this is a standard way of working, not only in Excel but in all Windows programs that you may use. In Excel, however, you normally apply this principle by selecting the cells in the worksheet that you want to work with before choosing the Excel command that you want to apply to the cells.

In Excel, you can select a single cell, a block of cells (known as a *cell range*), various discontinuous cell ranges (also known as a *nonadjacent selection*). Figure 2.4 shows just such a nonadjacent selection made up of four different cell ranges. (The smallest range is the single cell A1.)

Selecting Cells with the Mouse

Excel offers several methods for selecting cells with the mouse. With each method, you start by selecting one of the cells that occupies the corner of

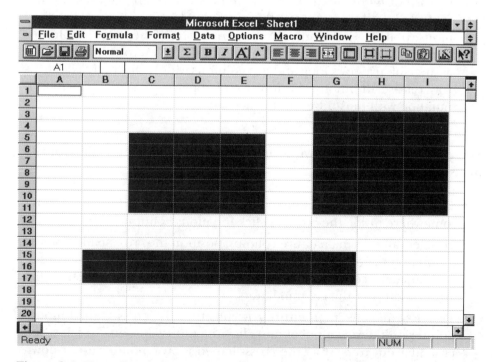

Figure 2.4 Nonadjacent Selection Made Up of Four Cell Ranges

the range you want to select. The first corner cell that you click becomes the *active cell* (indicated by its cell reference in the formula bar), and the cell range that you then select becomes anchored on this cell.

After you select the active cell in the range, you then drag the pointer to extend the selection until you have highlighted all the cells that you want to include. To extend a range in a block that spans several columns, drag left or right from the active cell. To extend a range in a block that spans several rows, drag up or down from the active cell. To extend a range in a block that spans several columns and rows, drag diagonally from the active cell in the most logical directions (up and to the right, down and to the right, up and to the left, or down and to the left). If you ever extend the range too far in one direction, you can always reduce it by dragging in the other direction. If you've already released the mouse button and you find that the range is incorrect, click the active cell again (clicking any cell in the worksheet deselects a selected range and activates the cell you click), and reselect its cells.

Tip   You can always tell which cell is the active cell forming the anchor point of a cell range; it is the only cell within the range that you've selected that is not highlighted, and it is the only cell reference listed on the formula bar. As you extend the range by dragging the cross-shaped mouse pointer, Excel indicates the current size of the range in columns and rows in the formula bar (as in 5R times 2C when you've highlighted a range of five rows long and two columns wide). However, as soon as you release the mouse button, Excel replaces this row-and-column notation with the address of the active cell.

You can also use the following shortcuts when selecting cells with the mouse:

- To select a single-cell range, position the cross-shaped mouse pointer somewhere inside the cell and click the mouse button.
- To select all cells in an entire column, position the cross-shaped mouse pointer on the column letter and click the mouse button. To select several adjacent columns, drag the cross-shaped mouse pointer to the right or left over the column letters.
- To select all cells in an entire row, position the cross-shaped mouse pointer on the row number and click the mouse button. To select several adjacent rows, drag the cross-shaped mouse pointer up or down over the row numbers.

- To select all the cells in the worksheet, click the box at the intersection of row of column letters and column of row numbers (right below the Control-menu button for the worksheet window).

- To select a cell range composed of partial columns and rows without dragging, click the active cell in the range where you want to anchor the range, hold down the Shift key, then click the last cell in the range and release the Shift key. Excel selects all the cells in between the first and the last cell you click. If the range you want to mark is a block that spans several columns and rows, the last cell is the one diagonally opposite the active cell. When using this Shift+click technique to mark a range that extends beyond the screen, you can use the scroll bars to move quickly to the last cell. (Just make sure that you don't release the Shift key.)

- To select a nonadjacent selection made up of several discontinuous cell ranges, drag through the first cell range, then hold down the Ctrl key as you drag through the next range. As long as you keep the Ctrl key depressed, you can continue to select as many discontinuous cell ranges as you want. Once you have marked all of the cell ranges you want included in the nonadjacent selection, you can release the Ctrl key.

Selecting Cells with the Keyboard

Excel also makes it easy for you to select cell ranges with the keyboard by using a technique known as *extending a selection.* To do this, move the cell pointer to the active cell of the range, then press F8 to turn on Extend mode (indicated by EXT on the status bar) and use the direction keys to move the pointer to the last cell in the range. Excel selects all the cells that the cell pointer moves through until you turn off Extend mode (by pressing F8 again).

Tip You can use the mouse as well as the keyboard to extend a selection when Excel is in Extend mode. All you do is click the active cell, press F8, and then click the last cell to mark the range.

You can also select a cell range with the keyboard without turning on Extend mode. Here you use a variation of the Shift+click method by moving the cell pointer to the active cell in the range, holding down the Shift key, and then using the direction keys to extend the range. When you've highlighted all the cells you want to include, you release the Shift key.

To mark a nonadjacent selection of cells with the keyboard, you need to combine the use of Extend mode with that of Add mode. To turn on Add mode (indicated by ADD on the status bar), you press Shift+F8. To mark a nonadjacent selection using Extend and Add mode, you follow these steps:

1. Move the cell pointer to the active cell in the first range you want to select.

2. Press F8 to turn on Extend mode.

3. Use the direction keys to extend the cell range until all cells are highlighted.

4. Press Shift+F8 to turn off Extend mode and turn on Add mode instead.

5. Move the cell pointer to the active cell of the next cell range you want to mark.

6. Press F8 to turn off Add mode and turn Extend mode back on.

7. Use the direction keys to extend the range until all cells are highlighted.

8. Repeat steps 4 through 7 until you have selected all of the ranges that you want included in the nonadjacent selection.

9. Press F8 to turn off Extend mode.

Selecting a Range of Data with AutoSelect

With the *AutoSelect feature*, Excel 4.0 introduces a new method for quickly selecting a range of cells that already contains data. The AutoSelect feature provides a particularly efficient way to select all or part of the cells in a large table of data. The AutoSelect feature automatically extends a selection in a single direction from the active cell to the first nonblank cell that Excel encounters in that direction.

You can use the AutoSelect feature with the mouse or keyboard. To use AutoSelect with the mouse:

1. Click the active cell to anchor the range you are about to select.

2. Position the pointer on the edge of the cell in the direction that you want the range extended. To extend the range up to the first blank cell to the right, position the pointer on the right edge of the cell. To extend the range left to the first blank cell, position the pointer on the left edge of the cell. To extend the range down to the first blank cell, position the pointer on the bottom edge of the cell. And to extend the range up to the first blank, position the pointer on the top edge of the cell.

3. When the pointer changes shape from a cross to an arrowhead, hold down the Shift key and double-click the mouse.

As soon as you double-click the mouse, Excel extends the selection to the first occupied cell that is adjacent to a blank cell in the direction of the edge you double-clicked.

To get an idea of how AutoSelect works, consider how you could use it to select the table in the cell range A3:I8 shown in Figure 2.5. With cell A3 the active cell, you could use the AutoSelect feature to select all the cells in the table in two operations. In the first operation, you would hold down the Shift key and either double-click the right edge of cell A3 to extend the selection right to cell I3 (selecting the range A3:I3) or double-click the bottom edge of cell A3 to extend the selection down to cell A8 (selecting the range A3:A8).

If you selected the cells in the first row of the table (range A3:I3) in the first operation, you would then extend this range down the remaining rows of the table by double-clicking the bottom edge of one of the selected cells. (It doesn't matter which one.) On the other hand, if you started by selecting the cells in the first column of the table (range A3:A8) as shown in Figure 2.6, you would then extend this range across the remaining columns of the table as shown in Figure 2.7 by double-clicking the right edge of one of the selected cells. (Again, it doesn't matter which one.)

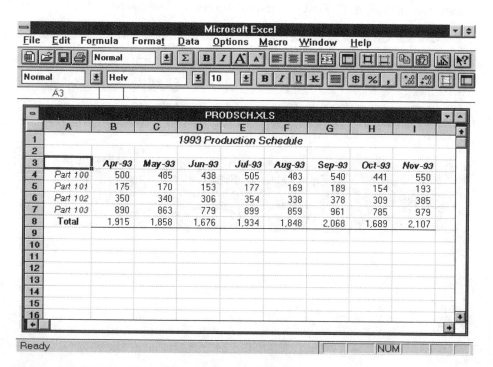

Figure 2.5 Table of Data to Be Selected with AutoSelect

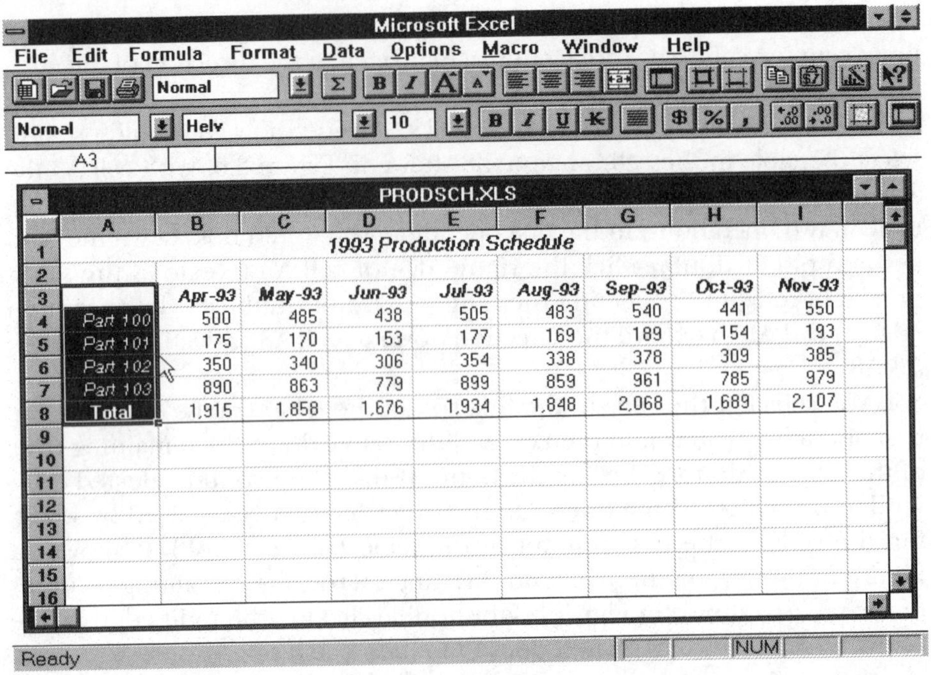

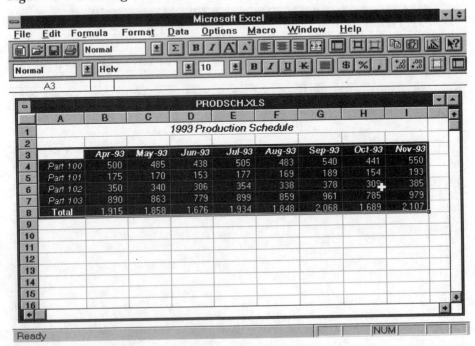

Figure 2.6 Selecting the First Column of Data with AutoSelect

Figure 2.7 Selecting the Remaining Columns of Data with AutoSelect

To use the AutoSelect feature with the keyboard, you press End and one of the four arrow keys as you hold down the Shift key. When you hold down Shift and press End and an arrow key, Excel extends the selection in the direction of the arrow key to the first cell containing a value that is bordered by a blank cell.

In terms of selecting the table of data shown in Figure 2.5, this means that you would have to complete four separate operations to select all of its cells:

1. With the A3 as the active cell, you hold down Shift and press End+↓ to select the range A3:A4. (Excel stops at A4 because this is the first cell containing a value bordered by a blank cell.)

2. Again, you hold down Shift and press End+↓, this time extending the range down to A8 because A8 is now the first cell containing a value bordered by a blank cell. At this point, the cell range A3:A8 is selected.

3. You hold down Shift and press End+→. Excel extends the range only to column B (because B3 is the first cell to the right of the active cell that contains a value and is bordered by a blank cell). At this point, the cell range A3:B8 is selected.

4. Again, you hold down Shift and press End+→. This time Excel extends the range all the way to column I (because cell I3 contains a value and is bordered by a blank cell). Now all of the cells in the table (the cell range A3:I8) are selected.

Selecting Cells with the Goto Feature

While you usually use the Goto feature to move the cell pointer to a new cell in the worksheet, you can also use it to select a range of cells. When you choose the **G**oto command on the Formula menu or press F5, Excel displays a Goto dialog box similar to the one shown in Figure 2.8. To move the cell pointer to a particular cell, you enter the cell address in the **R**eference text box and select the OK button. (Excel automatically lists the addresses of the last four cells or cell ranges you specified in the **G**oto list box.)

Instead of just moving to a new section of the worksheet with the Goto feature, you can select a range of cells by taking these steps:

1. Select the cell onto which the range is to be anchored.

2. Choose the **G**oto command on the Formula menu or press F5 to display the Goto dialog box.

3. Hold down the Shift key.

4. Type the cell address of the last cell in the range in the **R**eference text box. If this address is already listed in the **G**oto list box, you can

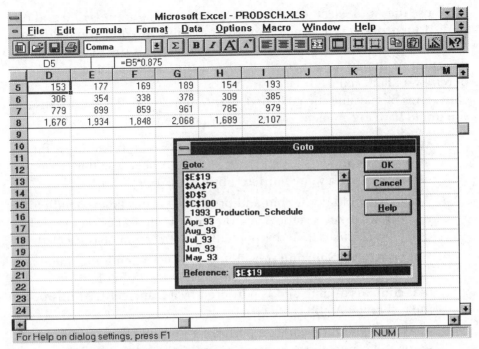

Figure 2.8 The Goto Dialog Box Showing the Addresses of the Last Four Active Cells and All Range Names

enter this address in the text box by clicking it in the list box.

5. Select the OK command button or press Enter to select the range between the active cell and the cell whose address you specified in the Reference text box.

Instead of selecting the anchor cell and then specifying the last cell of a range in the **R**eference text box of the Goto dialog box, you can also select a range simply by typing in the address of the cell range in the **R**eference text box. When you type a range address, you enter the cell reference of the active cell and the last cell in the range separated by a colon. For instance, to select the cell range that extends from cell B2 to G10 in the worksheet, you would type the range address **b2:g10** in the **R**eference text box before selecting the OK button or pressing Enter.

Excel also allows you to assign descriptive names to cell ranges in the worksheet. All such range names are automatically listed in the **G**oto list box of the Goto dialog box. To select the cells in a named range, you only have to double-click its range name in this list box or click it before you select the OK command button. (For complete information on defining range names in a worksheet, see Chapter 3.)

Moving Around the Worksheet

Excel provides several methods for navigating the worksheet. As discussed in Chapter 1, one of the easiest ways to bring new parts of a worksheet into view is with the scroll bars. The only disadvantage to using the scroll bars is that they simply bring new parts of the worksheet into view without changing the position of the cell pointer. This means that if you want to enter data in the new area of the worksheet, you still have to click the cell or drag through the cell range to activate it.

Tip No matter how far away you scroll from the active cell, you can always redisplay the active cell in the document window by selecting the Show Active Cell command on the Formula menu.

As an alternative to the scroll bars, you can use a number of keyboard shortcuts. Each of these shortcuts selects a new cell by moving the Excel cell pointer in it. Table 2.1 summarizes these keyboard shortcuts and what cells they select when you use them.

Table 2.1 Keystrokes for Moving the Cell Pointer

Keystroke	*Movement*
→ or Tab	Next cell to the right
← or Shift+Tab	Next cell to the left
↑	Next cell up
↓	Next cell down
Home	Cell in column A of the current row
Ctrl+Home	First cell (A1) of the worksheet
Ctrl+End or End, Home	Last cell in the active area of the worksheet
PgUp	Cell one screenful up in the current column
PgDn	Cell one screenful down in the current column

Table 2.1   *(Continued)*

Ctrl+ PgUp	Cell one screenful to the left in the current row
Ctrl+PgDn	Cell one screenful to the right in the current row
Ctrl+→ or End→	First occupied cell to the right adjacent to a blank cell
Ctrl+← or End←	First occupied cell to the left adjacent to a blank cell
Ctrl+↑ or End↑	First occupied cell up adjacent to a blank cell
Ctrl+↓ or End↓	First occupied cell down adjacent to a blank cell

The keyboard shortcuts shown in the table also scroll the worksheet, if necessary, to move to and select the cell. For example, if the cell pointer is currently in the last column visible in the worksheet window, and you press Tab or the → key, Excel scrolls the worksheet one column to the right when it selects the next cell over. So too if you press the Home key when the cell pointer is located in a column many columns to the right, Excel scrolls the entire screenful of data when it selects the cell in column A of the current row.

Among the many keystrokes for moving the cell pointer, the ones that combine the Ctrl or End key with an arrow key are among the most helpful for navigating large blocks of cells, such as tables that span more than one screenful, or for moving between tables in a complex worksheet.

Tip   When you use Ctrl and an arrow key to move around a table or between tables in a worksheet, you hold down Ctrl as you press one of the four arrow keys. When you use End and an arrow key, you press *and release* End before you press the arrow key. Pressing and releasing the End key causes Excel to display the END indicator on the status bar, indicating that the program is waiting for you to press one of the four arrow keys. Because you can keep the Ctrl key depressed as you press different arrow keys, the Ctrl+arrow key method provides a faster, less disjointed means of navigating blocks of cells than the End-then-arrow key method.

To get an idea of how these keystrokes can help you navigate blocks of cells, consider how you might use the Ctrl+ arrow keys to navigate the tables shown in Figure 2.9. With A3 the active cell, the first time you press Ctrl+→, the cell pointer moves to the second cell of the first table of sales figures (B3 with *Jan-92*). The second time you press Ctrl+→, the cell pointer jumps to the end of the first row of this table (cell E3 with *Qtr 1*). The third time you press Ctrl+→, the cell pointer moves to the first cell of the second table (cell G3 with *Apr-92*). The fourth time you press this key combination, the cell pointer moves to the end of the first row in the second table (J3 with *Qtr 2*).

With cell J3 active, if you then press Ctrl+↓, the cell pointer jumps to cell J7 (containing Paul's Qtr 2 total of 9,289). When you press Ctrl+↓, the cell pointer jumps to cell J9 in the last row of the table (containing the Qtr 2 grand total of 31,118). You could continue to move around the table in this manner, jumping from corner to corner, by holding the Ctrl key and changing the direction of the arrow you press.

Note that if you press Ctrl and an arrow key and there are no more occupied cells in the direction of the arrow key you pressed, Excel moves the cell pointer to the cell at the very edge of the worksheet in that direction. For example, if the cell pointer is located in cell A12 and there are no more occupied cells in column A, when you press Ctrl+↓, Excel moves the cell pointer to cell A16834 at the bottom of the worksheet.

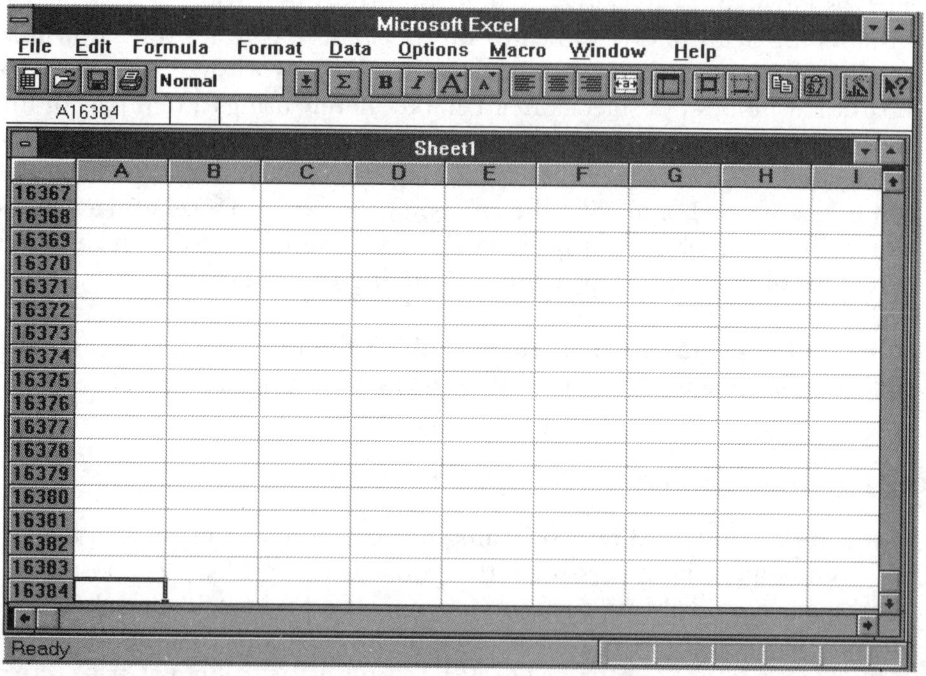

Figure 2.9 Using Ctrl Plus an Arrow Key to Navigate a Table

Moving the Cell Pointer with the Goto Feature

The Goto feature provides the most direct way to move to a distant cell or cell range in the worksheet. Earlier you learned that you can display the Goto dialog box by selecting the **G**oto command on the Formula menu or by pressing F5. To move the cell pointer to a particular cell in the worksheet, you type its cell reference in the **R**eference text box, then select OK or press Enter. Note that when you enter the cell reference, you can type the column letter(s) in upper- or lowercase.

Excel remembers the cell references of the last four cells that you selected and lists them in the **G**oto list box. The address of the very last cell you selected is also automatically entered into the Reference text box. You therefore can return quickly to your previous place in a worksheet by pressing F5 and Enter. Pressing F5 displays the Goto dialog box and pressing Enter selects the previous cell reference.

Using the Scroll Lock Key

You can use the Scroll Lock key to "freeze" the position of the cell pointer in a worksheet as you scroll to new areas in it, using shortcut keystrokes such as PgDn and Ctrl+PgDn. When you press the Scroll Lock key, Excel displays the SCRL mode indicator on the status bar to let you know that scroll lock is engaged. Then, when you scroll the worksheet with the keyboard, Excel does not select a new cell but merely brings a new part of the worksheet into view. For example, pressing the PgDn key when scroll lock is engaged has the same effect as clicking the vertical scroll bar below its scroll box: Instead of moving the cell pointer down one screenful as would normally occur when you press PgDn, Excel simply scrolls up the next screenful of data into view without changing the original position of the cell pointer.

To "unfreeze" the pointer when scrolling the worksheet, you press the Scroll Lock key again and the SCRL indicator disappears.

Using the 1-2-3 Alternate Navigation Keys

If you are a Lotus 1-2-3 user switching to Excel, you can make use of all of the pointer-movement keystrokes that you learned in 1-2-3 by choosing the **W**orkspace command on the **O**ptions menu and then selecting the Alternate Navigation **K**eys check box. Excel already supports most of the pointer-movement keystrokes used by Lotus 1-2-3, such as Ctrl+← and Ctrl+→ to scroll left and right by screenfuls, and PgUp and PgDn to scroll up and down by screenfuls. When you select the Alternate Navigation **Keys** check box in the Workspace Options dialog box, Excel changes the function of the following keystrokes as well:

- Home moves the cell pointer to the first cell (A1) in the worksheet instead of the first cell in the current row.
- Tab moves the cell pointer one screenful to the right (same as Ctrl+→) instead of one cell to the right.
- Shift+Tab moves the cell pointer one screenful to the left (same as Ctrl+←) instead of one cell to the left.

Entering Data in a Worksheet

The cells of your worksheet can accept one of two types of entries: *constant values*, which are the data that you type directly in the cell, or *formulas*, which combine values, cell references, functions, and/or operators that you enter into the cell to produce new values from existing values. Constant values are further subdivided into three major categories: numeric values, dates and times (which are special values), and text (also known as *labels*).

Note: Excel also allows you to enter two other, more uncommon types of values called *logical values* and *error values* as constants in a cell. Normally, logical values result from formulas that contain a logical function or some sort of true-or-false equation and error values result from formulas that Excel cannot calculate successfully. In rare cases, however, you may actually want to enter a logical value (such as TRUE or FALSE) or an error value (such as #N/A) in the active cell, making it a constant. To enter a logical or error value in a cell, you type = followed by the name of the value (in upper- or lowercase letters), as in =#N/A when you want to enter the error value #N/A to indicate that no value is currently available.

A constant value, as the name implies, does not change unless you select the cells that contain the value and edit the value yourself. The results of a formula, on the other hand, are updated automatically whenever you modify any values in the cells on which the formula depends. To enter a constant value in a cell, you simply type the entry in the active cell. To enter a formula in a cell, you must remember to type = (equal sign) before you begin building the formula in the active cell.

Tip Former Lotus 1-2-3 users take note: Excel also recognizes any formula that you begin with + (the plus sign) instead of the more common = (equal sign).

As soon as you type the first character of your entry, Excel activates the formula bar by displaying the cancel and enter boxes in the middle of the formula bar followed by the character you typed and the *insertion point* (the flashing vertical bar). As you continue to type the constant or build your formula, Excel displays your progress both in the formula bar and in the active cell within the worksheet window, as shown in Figure 2.10.

Once you've finished typing your constant value or building your formula, you still have to enter it in the active cell. You can do this in one of several ways: You can click the Enter box (the second one with the check mark in it) on the formula bar, you can press the Enter key, or you can press one of the direction keys. If you click the enter box or press the Enter key, Excel does not move the cell pointer after completing the cell entry. If you press a direction key, such as an arrow key like the ↓ or → key, Excel completes the entry at the same time it selects the next cell in the direction of the arrow.

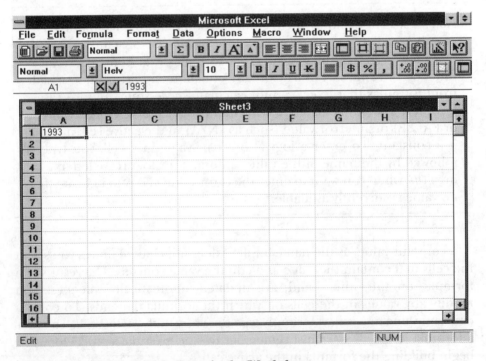

Figure 2.10 Making a New Entry in the Worksheet

Tip If you find that you are about to make an entry in the wrong cell, you can click the cancel button (the first one with the X in it) or press the Esc key to clear the formula bar and prevent Excel from placing the entry in the active cell. Also, Excel automatically will move the cell pointer to the next cell down when you complete an entry if you press Enter by opening the **O**ptions menu and choosing the **W**orkspace option and then selecting the **M**ove Selection after Enter check box in the Workspace Options dialog box.

As soon as you enter your constant or formula in the active cell, Excel deactivates the formula bar by removing the Cancel and Enter boxes. Excel continues to display the entry you made in the cell both in the formula bar and in the cell whenever you select the cell.

Correcting Errors in an Entry

You use the backspace key to correct any typing errors that you make before you complete a cell entry (that is, as long as the Cancel and Enter boxes are still displayed on the formula bar indicating that it is still activated). Pressing the backspace key deletes the character immediately to the left of the insertion point, one character at a time.

If you have already completed an entry before you discover your error, you have a choice: Either you can replace the entry by retyping it (or rebuilding it if the entry is formula), or you can edit it. To edit a completed cell entry, you must reactivate the formula bar and make your corrections there. Excel does not allow you to edit the contents of a cell in the worksheet itself.

To reactivate the formula bar, you can click the I-beam pointer in the formula bar at the place in the entry that needs editing, or you can press F2 (which locates the insertion point at the very end of the cell entry in the formula bar). Table 2.2 shows you the editing keys that you can use to move the insertion point in the entry and delete unwanted characters. To insert new text at the insertion point, you simply start typing. To replace text at the insertion point, you press the Ins(ert) key and begin typing the replacement text. Excel lets you know that you are no longer in Insert mode and that your typing will replace existing characters by displaying the OVR mode indicator (for overtype mode) in the status bar. To return to Insert mode, you press the Ins(ert) key a second time.

When you have finished making your corrections to the cell entry, you can complete the edit by updating the contents of the cell in the worksheet.

Table 2.2 Keys Used to Edit Cell Entries

Key	Function
F2	Reactivates the formula bar and places the insertion point at the end of the current cell entry.
Del	Deletes the character to the immediate right of the insertion point.
Backspace	Deletes the character to the immediate left of the insertion point.
→	Moves the insertion point one character to the right.
←	Moves the insertion point one character to the left.
↑	Moves the insertion point to its previous position in the cell entry.
Home	Moves the insertion point in front of the first character of the cell entry.
End or ↓	Moves the insertion point after the last character in the cell entry.
Ctrl+ →	Moves the insertion in front of the next word in the cell entry.
Ctrl+ ←	Moves the insertion in front of the previous word in the cell entry.
Ins	Toggles Excel in and out of Insert mode.

To do this, click the enter box or press the Enter key. (When editing a cell, you can't use the arrow keys to complete your edits because they are now used to move the insertion point.)

Performing Data Entry in a Selection

You can speed up the process of entering data in a worksheet by preselecting the cells where you need to make entries. When you select a range of cells, Excel restricts data entry to that range. The program also automatically advances the cell pointer when you click the enter box on the formula bar or press the Enter key to complete each cell entry. Excel advances the cell pointer down each row of the column. When the program reaches the cell in the last selected row of the column, the cell pointer advances to the first selected row in the next column to the right. If the range consists of only a single row, Excel advances the cell pointer from left to right across the row.

For example, suppose that you have to enter a table of data that uses three columns and ten rows. To speed up data entry in the worksheet, you select the range A3:C12. When you finish marking this selection, cell A3 is still active. You then type in the entry for A3 and press Enter. When you press Enter, Excel completes the entry in cell A3 and automatically advances the cell pointer down to cell A4. You then continue to enter the data for column A of the table. When you complete the entry in cell A12 by pressing Enter, Excel automatically advances the cell pointer to cell B3 (the top of the second column in the selection). Likewise, when you finish entering the data for column B in cell B12, Excel advances the cell pointer to cell C3 (the top of the last column in the selection). When you finish making the last cell entry for the table in cell C12, Excel returns the cell pointer to cell A3 at the beginning of the selection.

When entering data, you can preselect a nonadjacent selection composed of several cell ranges instead of just a single cell range. When Excel reaches the end of the last range you marked in the selection, the program automatically advances the cell pointer to the first cell of the first range you marked. Excel continues to work through each of the ranges included in your nonadjacent selection.

Table 2.3 shows you the keystrokes that you can use to move within the current selection. You can use these keystrokes to move to a particular cell in the selection that needs data entry or editing or to alter the direction you enter data. For example, to enter data across a row in the current selection, you would press Tab instead of the Enter key to complete each cell entry.

Alert! Be sure that you don't press an arrow key to complete a cell entry within a selection. Pressing an arrow key instead of one of the keys listed in Table 2.3 to complete a cell entry collapses the selection when Excel moves the cell pointer to the next active cell.

ENTERING THE SAME VALUE IN A SELECTION

Excel allows you to enter the same value in all the cells in the current selection. To do this, you mark the cell range or ranges (if you want to enter the same value in a nonadjacent selection) before you type numeric value or text or build the formula that you want to enter. When you're ready to complete the entry in all selected cells, you then press Ctrl+Enter (instead of just Enter).

Table 2.3   Keystrokes for Moving Within a Selection

Keystrokes	Function
Enter	Moves the cell pointer down one cell in the selection when the selection consists of more than one row. Moves one cell to the right when the selection consists of a single row.
Shift+Enter	Moves the cell pointer up one cell in the selection when the selection consists of more than one row. Moves one cell to the left when the selection consists of a single row.
Tab	Moves the cell pointer one cell to the right in the selection when the selection consists of more than one column. Moves one cell down when the selection consists of a single column.
Shift+Tab	Moves the cell pointer one cell to the left in the selection when the selection consists of more than one column. Moves one cell up when the selection consists of a single column.
Ctrl+. (period)	Moves the cell pointer to the next corner of the current cell range.
Ctrl+Tab	Moves the cell pointer to the next range in a nonadjacent selection.
Ctrl+Shift+Tab	Moves the cell pointer to the previous range in a nonadjacent selection.
Shift+BkSp	Reduces the current selection to the active cell.

Figure 2.11 illustrates a situation where you want to enter the heading *Total* in a number of cells in a worksheet table. To accelerate this data entry, you select all the cells that should contain *Total* for the entry as a nonadjacent selection. Then you type **Total** and press Ctrl+Enter to place this text value in each selected cell. Figure 2.12 shows you the worksheet after you press Ctrl+Enter and have input *Total* into the selected cells.

Entering Numeric Values

Most worksheets that you create in Excel require the entry of at least some numeric values. To enter numeric values, you select the cell and then type the numerals 0 through 9. In addition to these ten digits, you may also use the following characters in numeric values:

+ – E e $, . % ( ) /

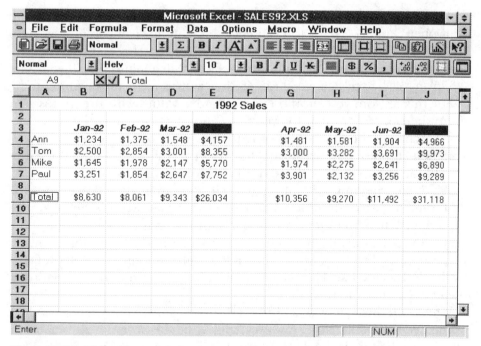

Figure 2.11 Nonadjacent Selection to Contain the Same Text Value

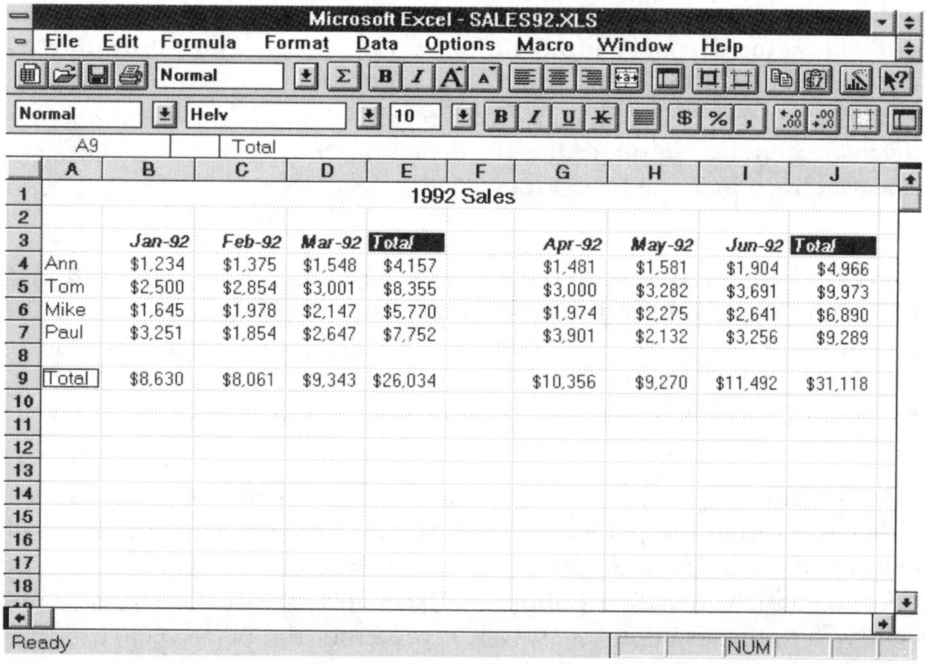

Figure 2.12 The Same Text Value Entered in the Selection with Ctrl+Enter

To enter negative values in a cell, you can start the number with – (minus sign or hyphen), as in – 250, or you can enclose the number in parentheses, as in (250). Note, however, that Excel automatically converts any negative value entered within parentheses to a number prefaced with a minus sign. If you enter (45.75) in a cell, Excel changes it to – 45.75 as soon as you complete the entry.

For this reason, you should enter negative values with the minus sign even when you want them to eventually appear enclosed within parentheses. To change the formatting of negative numbers, you select their cells and then choose a number format that uses parentheses to display negative values. (See Chapter 3 for details on formatting numbers.)

When entering numeric values in a cell, you can include dollar signs ($) and commas (,) as they appear in the printed or handwritten values you are inputting. When you enter a number with commas separating the thousands, Excel automatically assigns a number format to the value that displays commas. Likewise, when you enter a dollar amount in a cell prefaced by the dollar sign, Excel automatically assigns a dollar number format (that includes commas) to the value.

When entering values that contain decimal values, you type a period (.) as the decimal point. Note, however, that while the program automatically adds a zero before decimal values (so that Excel inputs **0.95** in a cell where you enter **.95**), the program always drops trailing zeros after the decimal point (so that the program inputs **45** in a cell where you enter **45.00**). If you don't know the decimal equivalent for a value, you can enter the value as a fraction, as in **4 3/16** (with a space between the 4 and 3) instead of **4.1875**. When you enter the fractional form of a decimal number, Excel inputs the decimal equivalent in the cell, while displaying the fraction by assigning it a special fractional number format.

 Alert! When entering simple fractions such as 3/4 or 5/8 in a cell, you must enter them as mixed numbers preceded by zero, as in **0 3/4** or **0 5/8**. (Be sure to enter a space between the zero and the fraction.) Otherwise, Excel interprets the fraction as a date. For instance, if you enter **3/4** in a cell, Excel displays the date **4-Mar** when you complete the entry.

When entering numeric values that represent percentages in a cell, either you divide the percentage number by 100 and enter the decimal equivalent, as in .25 for 25 percent,, or you enter the number followed by the percent sign, as in 25%. Either way, Excel stores the decimal value in the cell (**0.25** in this example); however, if you enter the percentage with the percent sign, Excel assigns a percentage number format to the display of the value in the worksheet (so that it appears as **25%**).

By default, all numeric values in a new worksheet are right aligned in their cells. If you enter a number that is too long to fit in the width of the cell, Excel automatically converts it into scientific notation. For example, if you enter the value **9876543210987** in the cell of a new worksheet, Excel displays this value in scientific notation as **9.88E+12**. You can also enter numeric values in scientific notation by using the letters **e** or **E** (for *exponent*). For instance, to enter the value of two and a half million in a cell in scientific notation, you would enter **2.5e6**. When you complete the entry, Excel stores the value **2500000** in the cell and displays this value as **2.50E+06** in the worksheet.

FIXING THE DECIMAL POINT IN NUMERIC ENTRIES

Excel can make it easy to input a series of numbers that use the same number of decimal places, such as financial figures that display both dollars and cents, by automatically entering the decimal point for you. To have the program insert the decimal point and fix its position in the numbers you enter, take these steps:

1. Open the **O**ptions menu, then select the **W**orkspace command to display the Workspace Options dialog box.

2. Select the **F**ixed Decimal check box.

3. By default, Excel fixes the decimal place two places to the left of the last digit you input. To change this position, enter the number of places in the **P**laces text box.

4. Click the OK button or press Enter.

After you fix the decimal place in numeric values in this manner, Excel automatically adds the decimal point to any number that you enter—all you do is type the digits and complete the entry. For example, to enter the value **45.99** in a cell after fixing the decimal point at 2 places, you simply type **4599**. When you press Enter or an arrow key to complete this cell entry, Excel inputs **45.99** in the cell.

While the **F**ixed Decimal check box is selected, Excel adds decimal points to all numbers that you enter in any cells of a worksheet. To override this, you must type the decimal point (period) yourself. For instance, to input the value **4599** (instead of 45.99) when the decimal point is fixed at two places, you must enter **4599.** in the cell. When you wish to return to normal data entry for numerical values (where you enter any decimal points yourself), you need to open the Workspace Options dialog box again and deselect the **F**ixed Decimal check box.

Entering Dates and Times

In Excel, as in other popular spreadsheet programs, dates and times are stored as special values. Dates are stored as serial numbers and times are stored as decimal fractions. Excel supports two date systems: the 1900 date system used by Excel for Windows (also used by Lotus 1-2-3 and Quattro Pro), which uses January 1, 1900 as serial number 1, and the 1904 system used by Excel for the Macintosh, which uses January 2, 1904 as serial number 1.

Tip If you use Excel on the IBM-compatible PCs and Macintosh computers in your office, you can switch to the 1904 date system in those worksheets that you create in the Windows version and then transfer to the Macintosh version. (For information on how you do this, see Chapter 21.) To switch to the 1904 date system used by the Excel on the Macintosh, open the **O**ptions menu and choose the **C**alculation command, then select the 1904 Date System in the Calculation Options dialog box.

By storing dates as serial numbers representing the number of days that have elapsed from a particular date (January 1, 1900, or January 2, 1904), Excel can perform arithmetic between dates. For example, you can find out how many days there are between February 15, 1994, and January 11, 1998, by entering **1/11/98** in one cell and **2/15/94** in the cell below and then creating a formula in the cell below that one which subtracts the cell with 2/15/94 from the one containing 1/11/98. Because Excel stores the date 1/11/98 as the serial number 35806 and the date 2/15/94 as the serial number 34380, it can calculate the difference and return the result of 1460 (days).

Alert! When you use a date directly in a formula that performs date arithmetic, you must enclose the date in quotation marks. For instance, if you want to enter a formula in a cell that calculates the number of days between February 15, 1994 and January 11, 1998, you would have to enter the formula **="1/11/98"–"2/15/94"** in the cell.

Times of the day are stored as decimal numbers that represent the fraction of the twenty-four-hour period starting with 0.0 for 12 midnight through 0.999 for 11:59:59 P.M. By storing times as decimal fractions, Excel enables you to perform time calculations such as those that return the elapsed time (in minutes) between any two times of the day.

Although Excel stores dates as serial numbers and times as decimal fractions, luckily, you do not have to use these numbers to enter dates or times of the day into cells of the worksheet. You simply enter dates using any of the date formats used by Excel and times using any of the time formats. Excel then assigns the appropriate serial number or decimal fraction at the same time the program assigns the date or time format you used to store this value. Table 2.4 shows you the formats you can use when entering dates and times in the cells of a worksheet, and the date and time formats that Excel automatically assigns to each of them.

Table 2.4 Date and Time Formats Recognized by Excel

Date and Time Entries	Date or Time Format Assigned by Excel
3/4/93	m/d/yy
4-Mar-93	d-mmm-yy
4-Mar	d-mmm
Mar-93	mmm-yy
5:25 PM	h:mmm AM/PM
5:25:33 PM	h:mmm:ss AM/PM
17:25	h:mm
17:25:33	h:mm:ss

In addition to using the standard date and time formats as shown in the table, you can also vary these formats as follows:

- You can interchange the / (slash) and the – (hyphen) in date formats, as in **3-4-93** instead of the more standard **3/4/93**. (Note that Excel converts 3-4-93 to 3/4/93.)

- For dates in the 21st century, Excel accepts all four digits or just the last two, as in **7/23/2002** or **7/23/02**.

- You can enter a date and time in a single cell if you separate the date and time format with a space, as in **2/19/94 10:15 am**.

- Unless you use am or pm (in lower- or uppercase) in the time format you enter, Excel automatically assigns the decimal fraction using a twenty-four-hour clock. The program uses the decimal fraction 0.09 if you enter the time 3:10 in a cell (the decimal fraction for 3:10 AM) instead using 0.63 (the decimal fraction for 15:10 — the twenty-four-hour clock equivalent of 3:10 PM).

- When using a 12-hour clock, you can abbreviate am as a and pm as p in the time format as in 3:10 p.

Building Simple Formulas

Formulas are, of course, among the most important and common types of cell entry that you use in a worksheet. To indicate that you are building a formula rather than entering some type of constant, you start each formula by typing the equal sign. After you type the equal sign, you are ready to build the rest of your formula. A formula can consist of up to 255 characters in a cell.

Most simple formulas consist of a built-in function, such as SUM or AVERAGE (you will learn about Excel functions in Chapter 5), or a string of numeric values or cell references separated by the following mathematical operators:

- + (plus sign) for addition
- − (minus sign or hyphen) for subtraction
- * (asterisk) for multiplication
- / (slash) for division
- ^ (caret) for exponentiation (raising a number to a power)

For example, to create a formula in cell B3 that multiplies the value in cell A3 by 50, you would enter the formula

    =A3*50

in this cell. To enter this formula, you select cell B3 and then type the entire formula in the formula bar, or you can just type = (equal sign) and then select cell A3 with the mouse or keyboard (which places the cell reference A3 in the formula bar) before you type *50. This latter method of directly selecting any cells that you reference to in a formula is called *pointing*. Pointing is, in fact, the preferred way of inserting cell references in a formula because there is much less chance of indicating the wrong cell reference. If you type in cell references, you can easily make a typo in a cell address. Just by looking at the result that Excel displays in the cell, you may not be aware of your mistake. If you physically move the cell pointer to the cell that contains the value you want used in the formula, you are much less likely to select the wrong cell and thereby insert an incorrect cell reference.

Tip The word *Point* appears at the beginning of the status bar when you click a cell. Press a direction key after typing an operator in a formula. Select the cell whose cell reference you want to add to the formula and type the next operator. Point then changes to Enter on the status bar.

When you enter the formula =A3*50 in B3, if cell A3 contains the value 2, cell B3 displays the result 100 in the worksheet. If you edit the value in A3 and change it from 2 to 3, Excel recalculates the value in B3 and displays the new result of 150. This ability to recalculate a formula when you change the value in one of its cell references is one of the major benefits of using a spreadsheet over some sort of calculator. When you use a calculator, you must input all numerical values in your formulas. If one or more of the values used in your formulas change, you must re-input the entire formula to obtain the new result. In an Excel worksheet, if you build formulas using cell references, you have only to edit those cells whose values change to update the results of your formulas.

ORDER OF PRECEDENCE

Many formulas that you create will perform more than one mathematical operation. When a formula contains a series of operations, as in

=A3+B3/B4

Excel performs each operation in the left-to-right direction according to the *order of precedence* shown in Table 2.5. For example, if cell A3 currently contains the number 2, B3 contains the number 6, and B4 contains the number 3, in essence, Excel would be evaluating the following formula:

=2+6/3

which would produce a result of **4**. Because division has precedence over addition, the program first performs the division operation of B3/B4 (or 6/3=2) before it performs the addition by adding the value in A3 to the result (2+2).

To alter the usual order of precedence in a formula, you enclose the operation you want performed first in a pair of parentheses. For example, to have Excel perform the addition before the subtraction operation in the sample formula, you would enclose the addition operation in parentheses, as follows;

=(A3+B3)/B4

Table 2.5   The Order of Precedence in Formulas

Operator	Function
: (colon)	Cell range
space	Intersection
' (apostrophe)	Union
– (minus sign or hyphen)	Negation
%	Percent
^ (caret)	Exponentiation
* and /	Multiplication and division
+ and –	Addition and subtraction
&	Concatenation (joining text strings)
=, <, >, <=, >=, and < >	Comparison: equal to, less than, greater than, less than or equal to, greater than or equal to, not equal to

Assuming that cells A3, B3, and B4 still contain the values 2, 6, and 3, respectively, this formula would now return a result of **2.666667** instead of **4**. This is because the parentheses in the formula cause Excel to perform the addition of A3+B3 before it divides the result by the value in B4 (6+2=8, then 8/3=2.666667).

If necessary, you can alter the usual order of precedence in a formula by nesting multiple pairs of parentheses. Excel always performs the operation on the innermost pair of parentheses first and works its way outward. If you enter the formula

   =(A2+(C2–C3))*B5

in a cell, Excel subtracts C2–C3 first, adds the result to A2, and then multiplies that result by the value in B5. When nesting parentheses, be sure that your parentheses are balanced, that is, you have entered a right parenthesis for each left parenthesis that you use. If they aren't balanced, Excel displays an alert dialog box saying "Parentheses do not match." When you select OK to close this alert box, the program returns you to the formula bar so that you can edit the formula, while at the same time it attempts to show you where the right parenthesis belongs. You can insert the parenthesis at the place suggested by the highlighting in the formula bar or move it as required.

ERRORS IN FORMULAS

If Excel can't calculate a formula that you enter in a cell, the program displays an *error value* in the cell as soon as you complete the formula entry. Excel uses several error values, all of which begin with the number sign (#). Table 2.6 shows you the error values in Excel along with the meaning and the most probable cause for its display. To remove an error value from a cell, you must discover what caused the value to appear and edit the formula so that Excel can perform the desired calculation.

Table 2.6   Error Values in Excel

Error Value	Meaning
#DIV/0	Division by zero—this error value appears if the division operation in your formula refers to a cell that contains the value 0 or is *blank*.
#N/A	No value is available—this is an error value that you can enter manually into a cell to indicate that you don't yet have a necessary value.
#NAME?	You used a name that Excel doesn't recognize—this error value appears when you incorrectly type the range name, refer to a deleted range name, or forget to put quotation marks around a text string in a formula (causing Excel to think you're referring to a range name).
#NULL!	This error value appears when you specify an intersection of two ranges whose cells do not actually intersect—because the space is the intersection operator, this error will occur if you insert a space instead of a comma (the union operator) between ranges used in function arguments.
#NUM!	Problem with a number in the formula—this error can be caused by an invalid argument in an Excel function or a formula that produces a number too large or too small to be represented in the worksheet.
#REF	Invalid cell reference—this error occurs when you delete a cell referred to in the formula or when you paste cells over the ones referred to in the formula.
#VALUE!	This error value appears when you use the wrong type of argument in a function or the wrong type of operator—this error is caused most often by specifying a mathematical operation with one or more cells that contain text.

If a formula in your worksheet contains a reference to a cell that returns an error value, that formula returns that error value as well. This can cause error values to appear throughout the worksheet, making it very difficult to discover which cell contains the formula that caused the original error value so that you can fix the problem. In Chapter 8 you will learn techniques to help you locate errors as well as to prevent their spread to other cells in the worksheet (a technique known as *error trapping*).

Entering Text

A *text entry* is any cell entry that Excel does not interpret as a numeric value, formula, date, time, logical value, or error value. A text entry in a cell can consist of letters, numbers, punctuation, and other special characters that you can produce with the keyboard, up to 255 characters maximum.

By default, a text entry is left aligned in the cell where you enter it. If the text entry is longer than will fit in the cell and the cells in the columns to the immediate right are blank, the extra characters "spill over" to the neighboring cells. Despite this ability to display extra characters in blank cells to the right, you must remember that only the cell that was active when you made the text entry actually contains that entry. This means that to edit a long text entry, you must select the cell that contains the entry and then activate the formula bar. Figure 2.13 shows long text entry in cell A3 whose display spills over to cell G3.

If you later make some type of entry in one of the "spillover" cells displaying part of a long text entry, this new cell entry truncates the display of the long text entry. In Figure 2.14, you can see this effect. There the number 10 has been entered into cell B3, truncating the display of the long text entry in cell A3 so that you can now see only the characters that will fit within the width of the cell. Note that the cell entry in B3 has had no effect on the contents of A3 (indicated by the appearance of the complete text in the formula bar).

To redisplay a long text entry whose display is truncated in a worksheet, you can widen its column until the characters are displayed (the easiest way to do this is by double-clicking the right border of the column letter) or by using the text wrap feature so that the text is displayed on multiple lines within the current cell. (To do this, you select the cell, then open the **Format** menu and choose the **Alignment** option and select **Wrap Text** check box. For more about aligning cell entries, see Chapter 3.) Figure 2.15 shows the long text entry in cell A3 redisplayed in the worksheet after widening column A with the Best Fit feature (that is, double-clicking the right border of column letter A).

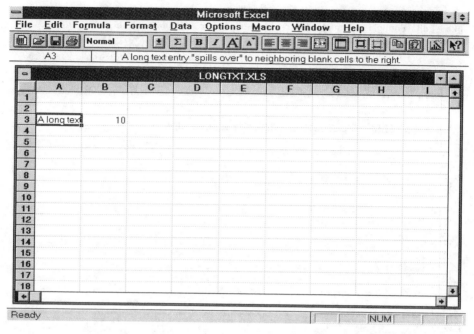

**Figure 2.13 Worksheet with Long Text Entry that Spills Over to
Neighboring Cells**

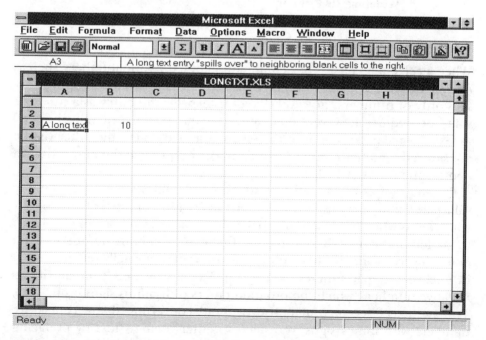

Figure 2.14 Worksheet with a Truncated Long Text Entry

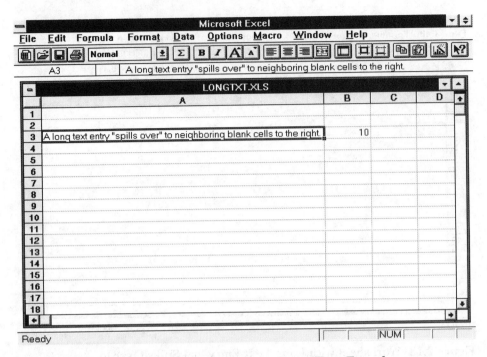

Figure 2.15 Worksheet After Redisplaying a Long Text Entry by Widening Its Column

ENTERING NUMERIC VALUES AS TEXT

When a cell entry consists of a combination of letters and numbers, such as **AB1002** or **1002AB**, Excel interprets the entry as text. When a cell entry consists only of numbers, however, Excel interprets the entry as a numeric value. Sometimes, however, you may want to enter a numeric value in a cell as text. To make Excel interpret a cell entry as text that would otherwise be considered a numeric value (or formula), you preface the entry with an apostrophe ('), as in '**61045**.

For an example of a situation in which you would want to enter numeric values as text in a worksheet, consider the creation of a telephone log for your clients where you want the area codes to appear in a separate column to the left of the one where you enter the main telephone numbers. If you enter the area codes in their column as you would normally see them, that is, enclosed in parentheses as in (213), Excel interprets your entries as negative numbers, which the program enters with minus signs, as in –213. To have Excel accept your entries without converting them to negative numbers with minus signs, you need to enter them as text by prefacing each entry with an apostrophe, as in '(213).

> **Note:** When you preface a cell entry with an apostrophe to have Excel input it as text, the apostrophe does not appear in the cell display in the worksheet, only on the formula bar when the cell is active. To display an apostrophe at the beginning of an entry within a cell, you must enter two apostrophes in a row.

TEXT ENTRIES IN FORMULAS

Although most formulas in a worksheet perform mathematical calculations, Excel is also capable of performing a special "joining" calculation between text entries called *concatenation*. To join two text entries into a single text entry, you use **&** (ampersand) instead of + (plus sign) as the operator in the formula. For instance, if cell A4 contains the city of Berkeley, B4 contains the state abbreviation of CA, and C4 contains the zip code of 94704 (entered as a text entry by typing '94704), and you enter the formula

   =A4&B4&C4

in cell E4, Excel joins each text entry to create the new concatenated text entry of

   BerkeleyCA94704

(with no spaces between the joined text entries) in the cell. If the purpose of your concatenation formula is to create a composite entry containing the city, state, and zip code for use in a mailing label, you would want to edit the formula in E4 to

   =A4&", "&B4&" "&C4

to add the requisite comma between the city and state as well as the needed spaces in the new concatenated text entry. By joining a comma and space between A4 and B4 and a space between B4 and C4, Excel returns the more legible result of

   Berkeley, CA 94704

in cell E4.

ENTERING A SERIES WITH AUTOFILL

Excel 4.0 makes it a snap to enter almost any series of sequential numbers, dates, times, or text strings in your worksheet with its new *AutoFill feature*. The AutoFill feature uses the cells you initially select to figure out intelligently what kind of series to create. Then, to enter the series, you extend the initial selection by dragging the *fill handle* in the appropriate direction

(such as to the right to extend the series to the columns on the right or down to extend the series to the rows below).

The fill handle (see Figure 2.16) appears only when you position the cross-shaped mouse pointer on the lower-right corner of the cell pointer on top of the tiny square (divided into four quarters) that you see there. When you drag the fill handle, Excel allows you to drag in only one plane at a time. This means that you can extend the series or fill the range to the left or right of the selected cells, or above or below the selected cells, but you cannot extend the series or fill the range in two directions simultaneously (such as down and to the right by dragging the fill handle diagonally).

Tip   If your cell pointer doesn't have this tiny square and the fill handle doesn't appear when you place the pointer on the lower-right corner of the cell, the Cell **D**rag and Drop check box is not selected in the Workspace Options dialog box. Open the **O**ptions menu, choose the **W**orkspace option, and click the Cell **D**rag and Drop check box to activate the Drag and Drop and AutoFill features. (Drag and drop allows you to copy and move cells by dragging the arrowhead pointer—see Chapter 3 for details.) When you close the Workspace Options dialog box by selecting OK or pressing Enter, you will then see the tiny square in the lower-right corner of the cell pointer where you position the cross-shaped mouse pointer when you want to display the fill handle.

When you release the mouse button after extending the range with the fill handle, Excel either creates a series in all of the cells you selected or fills the entire range with the initial value. Figures 2.16 and 2.17 demonstrate how this works. Figure 2.16 shows the range of initial values selected in column A that you want to extend with the AutoFill feature. In Figure 2.17, you can see the results of extending the range by dragging the fill handle to the right to column H.

Note that the AutoFill feature created an extended series from the initial values in the entries in the cell range A2:A12, but filled the range only with the initially selected values in the cell range A14:A16.

When you select an initial value such as a date, time, day, year, and the like, the AutoFill feature uses that value to determine the elements in the series and how they should be incremented. All of the series created in Figure 2.17 are incremented by 1 unit in each succeeding cell in the range (one month, one hour, one year, one quarter, and one number).

You can also use the AutoFill feature to create an extended series that is incremented by some other factor. To do this, simply enter two sample values in the worksheet that demonstrate the increment to use in the series and then

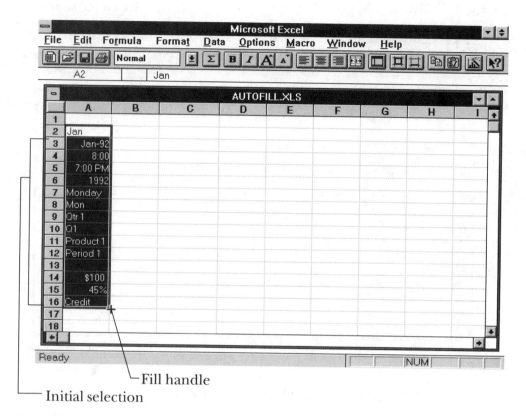

Fill handle

Initial selection

Figure 2.16 Selecting the Initial Values for AutoFill

select these values in the initial selection, which you extend with the fill handle.

Figures 2.18 and 2.19 illustrate how this works. In Figure 2.18, the initial values are entered in column A in the cell range A3:A14 and the values showing the next increment in the series are entered in column B in the cell range B3:B14. This entire range (A3:B14) is selected as the initial selection. Figure 2.19 shows you the resulting extended series created when you extend the series to column G with the fill handle. Note the different increments applied to each series created with the AutoFill feature.

> *Note:* You can also create a series by using the options in the Series dialog box (opened by choosing the Series option on the **D**ata menu), although in most cases you can enter any linear series you need solely with the AutoFill feature. To create a best-fit trend based on exponential growth, however, you must use the Series dialog box. See the TREND and GROWTH functions in Appendix B for more information on this type of series.

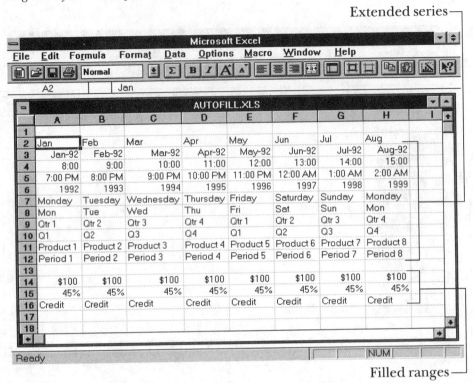

Figure 2.17 Extended Series and Fill Ranges Created with the AutoFill Feature

Building Your First Worksheet

For your first worksheet, you will create a simple sales table that calculates projected sales for a series of stores in the first quarter of 1993. In doing this exercise, you will get some experience with entering data, building simple formulas, using the AutoFill feature to create a series and copy formulas, and using the AutoFormat feature to apply sophisticated formatting to the entire table in one operation. You will also get experience with saving and printing your completed sales table. Because Excel 4.0 offers so many ease-of-use features that automate most of the repetitive tasks involved with building a new worksheet, your projected sales table will be completed in no time at all, even if you've never used a spreadsheet program before in your life.

ENTERING AND EDITING THE WORKSHEET TITLE

To get started, you need to start Excel, open a new worksheet document, and enter the title for your new worksheet:

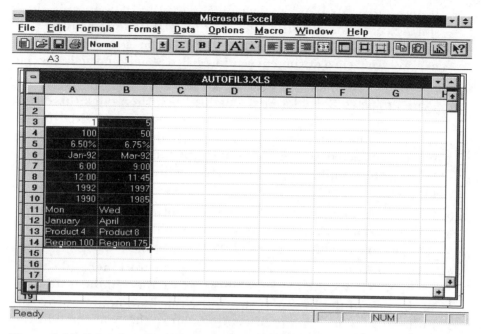

Figure 2.18 Selecting the Initial Values Showing the Series Increments for AutoFill

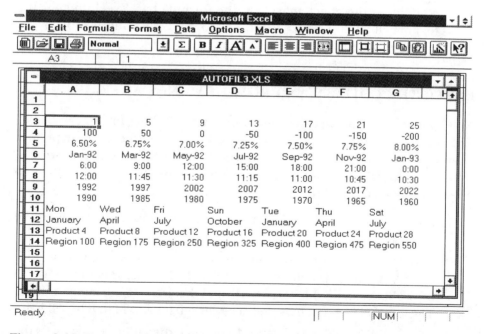

Figure 2.19 Extended Series Using Various Increments Created with the AutoFill Feature

1. If necessary, start Windows by typing **win** at the DOS prompt, then start Excel by locating the Microsoft Excel 4.0 group window and double-clicking the Microsoft Excel 4.0 program icon. Excel opens a new worksheet in a document window called **Sheet1** and activates cell A1 where you will enter the title for the worksheet.

2. Type **Projected Sales for First Quarter 1993,** then click the enter box or press the Enter key to insert this worksheet title in cell A1. If you make a mistake when typing this title, press the Backspace key to delete your errors and retype the necessary characters. When you complete this text entry, note how this title spills over into cells B1 and C1.

3. Click cell B1 to make this cell active. The formula bar is empty when you select cell B1. Although the text entry spills over into this and the next cell, the cell entry exists only in cell A1.

4. Click cell A1 to make the cell containing the worksheet title active again, then click the I-beam pointer before the *S* in the word *Sales* in the title of the formula bar. Doing this both activates the formula bar and inserts the insertion point so that you can edit the worksheet title.

5. Type **Store** and press the spacebar, then click the enter box (the one containing the check mark) on the formula bar. Excel updates the text in cell A1 and displays your edited worksheet title as soon as you click the enter box.

ENTER THE COLUMN AND ROW HEADINGS AS SERIES

Now you are ready to enter the column and row headings for the sales table. The column headings will extend across row 3 and indicate the time periods (January, February, and so on). The row headings will extend down column A and indicate the store numbers. You can use the AutoFill feature to enter both types of headings:

1. Click cell B3, then type **January** and click the enter box or press the Enter key.

2. Position the cross-shaped mouse pointer on the lower-right corner of cell B3. When the pointer changes to the fill handle, drag the handle to the right to extend the range to D3 and then release the mouse button. The AutoFill feature enters February in cell C3 and March in cell D3.

3. Click cell E3, then type **Quarter 1** and click the enter box or press the Enter key.

4. Click cell A4, then type **Store 1** and click the enter box or press the Enter key.

5. Position the cross-shaped mouse pointer on the lower-right corner of cell A4. When the pointer changes to the fill handle, drag the handle down to extend the range to A8 and then release the mouse button. The AutoFill feature enters a series of store numbers in the selected range.

6. Click cell A9, then type **Total** and click the enter box or press the Enter key.

Your worksheet should now look like the one shown in Figure 2.20.

ENTERING THE JANUARY SALES

January represents the base month in your projected sales worksheet. Your projected sales figures for the rest of the first quarter will be based on the January sales figures for each of the five stores:

1. Click cell B4, then drag the cross-shaped mouse pointer down until you have selected the range B4:B8.

2. Type **125000** in cell B4, then press Enter.

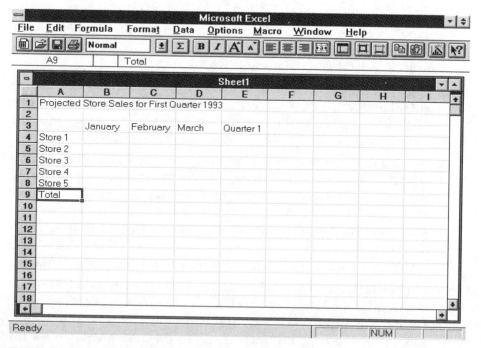

Figure 2.20 Projected Sales Worksheet with Column and Row Headings

3. Type **150600** in cell B5, then press Enter.

4. Type **145500** in cell B6, then press Enter.

5. Type **112000** in cell B7, then press Enter.

6. Type **221500** in cell B8, then press Enter.

7. Click cell C4 to activate this cell and deselect the cell range A4:A8.

BUILDING AND COPYING YOUR FIRST FORMULAS

You've now completed all the data entry required for your sales table. To finish the table, you need only to build and copy the formulas that calculate projected sales for each month, the monthly totals for all five stores, and the quarterly totals for each store. You'll start by building the formula in cell C4 to calculate projected sales in February for Store 1, which you can then copy for the other stores. This formula will calculate a modest 1.5 percent increase in sales in February by multiplying the January sales figure by the constant 1.015:

1. With C4 the active cell, type = to begin the formula, then click cell B4. When you click cell B4, Point appears on the status bar, a moving dotted line (called a *marquee*) appears around cell B4, and the formula =B4 appears in cell C4 and in the formula bar.

2. Type * (asterisk) to insert the multiplication operator in the formula. The marquee disappears around cell B4 and the formula =B4* appears in cell C4 and the formula bar.

3. Type **1.015**, then click the enter box or press the Enter key. The result, **126875**, appears in cell C4, while the complete formula, =B4*1.015, appears in the formula bar. Now you are ready to use the AutoFill feature to copy this formula down the column.

4. Position the cross-shaped mouse pointer on the lower-right corner of cell C4. When the pointer changes to the fill handle, drag the handle down to extend the range to C8, and then release the mouse button. The AutoFill feature fills the extended range with copies of the original formula you built in cell C4, thus calculating projected sales in February for the remaining four stores. Now you are ready to build a formula in cell D4 that calculates a 2 percent increase of February sales in March.

5. Click cell D4, then type =, click C4, then type *1.02 and click the enter box or press the Enter key. Excel displays the result of **129412.5** in cell D4 and the formula =C4*1.02 in the formula bar. Next you need to use AutoFill to copy this formula down the March column for the other stores.

6. Position the cross-shaped mouse pointer on the lower-right corner of cell D4. When the pointer changes to the fill handle, drag the handle down to extend the range to D8 and then release the mouse button. The AutoFill feature fills the extended range with copies of the original formula you built in cell D4, thus calculating projected sales in March for the other four stores.

7. Click cell B9 to make it active.

Your worksheet should now look like the one shown in Figure 2.21.

USING THE AUTOSUM TOOL

Next you need to create and copy the formulas that will calculate the monthly and quarterly totals for your sales table. To do this, you use the AutoSum Tool on the Standard toolbar (the tool with Sigma to the right of the Style drop-down list box). The AutoSum Tool uses the SUM function, one of the most commonly used worksheet functions. When you click the AutoSum Tool, Excel not only enters the SUM function in the current cell but also automatically selects the cell range containing the values you most likely want totaled. Most of the time, Excel selects the correct range. On the

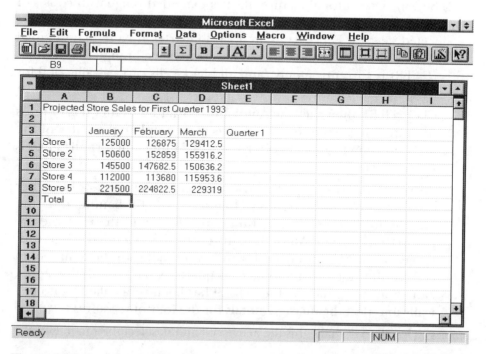

Figure 2.21 Projected Sales Worksheet with First Quarter Sales

rare occasion when the program has not selected correctly, you can modify the selection before you complete the entry of the SUM function in the cell.

To see how this works, use the AutoSum Tool to calculate the total January sales for all stores:

1. With B9 the active cell, click the AutoSum Tool on the Standard tool-bar. Excel enters the formula =SUM(B4:B8) in cell B9 and on the formula bar. The program also indicates the selected range of cells to be totaled by placing the marquee around them in the worksheet and highlighting the range **B4:B8** in the formula itself on the formula bar. If this cell range were incorrect, you could now modify it in the worksheet or the formula bar. As it is correct, go ahead and complete the entry in B9.

2. Click the enter box or press the Enter key. Excel displays the total **754600** in cell B9 and the formula with the SUM function =SUM(B4:B8) in the formula bar. Now you're ready to copy this formula across the row for the other months.

3. Position the cross-shaped mouse pointer on the lower-right corner of cell C9. When the pointer changes to the fill handle, drag the handle right to extend the range to cell E9 and then release the mouse button. The AutoFill feature fills the extended range with copies of the SUM function formula you built in cell C9, thus totaling the projected sales for February, March, and Quarter 1. Note that the total displayed in cell E9 is 0. This is because the cell range that it totals (E4:E8) is currently empty (and all blank cells carry a value of 0 for calculating purposes).

4. Click cell E4, then click the AutoSum Tool and the enter box or press the Enter key. Note that as soon as you complete the entry of the SUM function formula in cell E4, the SUM function formula in E9 is recalculated.

5. Position the cross-shaped mouse pointer on the lower-right corner of cell E4. When the pointer changes to the fill handle, drag the handle down to extend the range to cell E8 and then release the mouse button. The AutoFill feature fills the extended range with copies of the SUM function formula you built with the Sum tool in cell E4, thus totaling the projected quarterly sales for all five stores. Note that the grand total in cell E9 has been recalculated automatically to reflect the quarterly totals for the four other stores.

6. Click cell A3 to make this the active cell and deselect the range E4:E8.

Your sales worksheet should now look like the one in Figure 2.22.

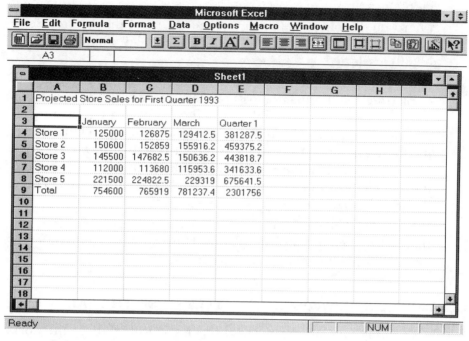

Figure 2.22 Sales Worksheet After Building and Copying the Formulas

FORMATTING THE SALES TABLE

Although your sales worksheet contains the correct sales data, the table it-self is not that easy to read. To put the finishing touches on the sales table and make it more legible, you will use Excel's new AutoFormat command. With this powerful new command, you can select sophisticated formatting for all the text and numbers in your sales table in a matter of seconds. All you have to do is select the table of data to be formatted before you select one of the predefined table formats. To select the sales table in your work-sheet, use Excel's new AutoSelect feature:

1. With cell A3, the active cell, hold down the Shift key and position the cross-shaped mouse pointer on the bottom edge of this cell. When the pointer changes to an arrowhead, double-click the bottom edge of cell A3. The AutoSelect feature extends the selection to A9 when you double-click the bottom edge of cell A3.

2. With the cell range A3:A9 selected and the Shift key still depressed, position the pointer on the right edge of one of the selected cells. (It doesn't matter which one.) When the pointer changes to an arrow-head, double-click the right edge of one of the cells, then release the

Shift key. The AutoSelect feature extends the selection to column E when you double-click the right edge of one of the selected cells. With a couple of double-clicks, the entire sales table (cell range A3:E9) is selected.

3. Open the Format menu, then select the AutoFormat command to display the AutoFormat dialog box. The AutoFormat dialog box offers fifteen predefined Table Formats that you can apply to your selection. To get an idea of what type of formatting each uses, click the format in the Table Format list box. Excel then shows a preview of the formatting in the Sample box to the right. Figure 2.23 shows the Sample box with the Financial 3 Table Format selected. This is the table format you will apply to your sales table.

4. Double-click Financial 3 in the Table Format list box or click it and then select the OK button. Instantly, Excel applies several different kinds of formatting to the sales format!

CENTERING THE WORKSHEET TITLE OVER THE SALES TABLE

For the finishing touches to your worksheet, you will boldface the worksheet title and center it over the sales table. In Excel 4.0, you can center a cell entry over selected columns by selecting the cells and then clicking the Center Across Selected Columns Tool (the one with the **a** between a left and right arrow). Go ahead and bold and center the worksheet title:

1. Click cell A1 to select the worksheet title and deselect the sales table.

2. Click the Bold tool on the Standard toolbar (the one with **B** next to the Sum button).

3. Drag the cross-shaped mouse pointer to extend the selection to cell E1 (cell range A1:E1), then click the Center Across Selected Columns Tool (the one immediately to the right of the Right align text tool).

4. Click cell A1 to make this the active cell and deselect the cell range A1:E1.

Your worksheet should look like the one shown in Figure 2.24.

SAVING AND PRINTING THE SALES WORKSHEET

Now that you have finished the worksheet, it's time to save your work on disk. If you have a printer connected to your computer, you can also print your work:

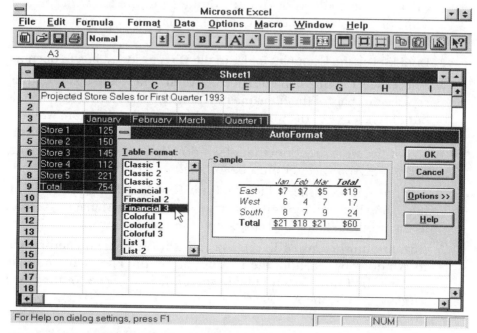

**Figure 2.23 Selecting the Financial 3 Table Format in the AutoFormat
Dialog Box**

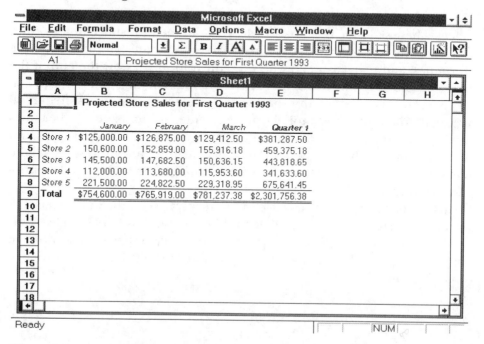

Figure 2.24 Completed Projected Sales Worksheet

1. Click the Save File Tool (the third one from the left with the disk icon) on the Standard toolbar. Excel displays the File Save As dialog box.

2. Double-click the Examples folder in the **D**irectories list box to open it.

3. Select **sheet1** in the filename **sheet.xls** in the File**N**ame text box, then replace this part of the filename by typing **q1sale93** and select the OK button. Excel saves the worksheet in the Examples directory with the filename **Q1SALE93.XLS** and this filename now appears in the title bar of the worksheet document window. If you want to print your worksheet, your printer must be installed for Windows already.

4. To print your worksheet, click the Print Tool. Excel displays the Printing dialog box and sends the print job to the Print Manager. As soon as the Printing dialog box closes, you can return to work.

5. If you're finished using Excel, you can exit the program and return to Windows by selecting the Exit option on the File menu, double-clicking the Control-menu box in the upper-left corner of the Excel window, or pressing Alt+F4.

SUMMARY

In this chapter you learned the basic skills necessary to create a new worksheet. These skills include how to select cells in the worksheet, how to enter various types of data (including numeric values, dates and times, simple formulas, and text), as well as how to edit your entries. At the end of the chapter, you got some hands-on experience with creating a new worksheet. As part of this exercise in creating the projected sales worksheet, you learned how to use the AutoFill feature to enter column and row headings and to copy formulas, how to use the AutoSum Tool to total columns and rows of numbers, how to use the AutoSelect feature quickly to select all the cells in a table, and how to use the AutoFormat command to apply sophisticated formatting to the selected table.

In the chapter ahead, you will learn more ways to edit the worksheets that you have created. There you will learn how to insert and delete cells, rows, and columns in a worksheet, cut and paste data to new parts of a worksheet, find and replace data in a worksheet, and even spell-check the entries in your worksheet.

3

Formatting the Worksheet

Formatting is the process by which you determine the final appearance of the worksheet and the data it contains. Excel's formatting features give you a great deal of control over the way the data appears in your worksheet. To all types of cell entries, you can assign a new font, font size, or font style such as bold, italic, underlining, strikeout, or color. You can also change the alignment of entries in the cells in a variety of ways, including the horizontal alignment, the vertical alignment, or the orientation, and you can wrap text entries in the cell or center them across the selection. To numerical values, dates, and times, you can assign one of the many built-in number formats or apply a custom format that you design. To the cells that hold your entries, you can apply different kinds of borders, patterns, and colors. And to the worksheet grid itself, you can assign the most suitable column widths and row heights so that the data in the formatted worksheet is displayed at its best.

In this chapter you will learn how to make all of these kinds of formatting changes. As you will soon discover, Excel 4.0 makes formatting the worksheet a pure joy. This version of the program offers a host of ease-of-use features designed to make changing the appearance of the data and the cells in a worksheet as direct and effortless as possible. Among the new ease-of-use formatting features in version 4.0, you will find a variety of formatting tools on the Standard and Formatting toolbars along with the powerful AutoFormat feature. You will also find that Excel 4.0 has added new vertical and orientation options to the customary horizontal and text wrap alignment options.

Assigning and Removing Formatting

Of all worksheet procedures, formatting may best exemplify the general working principle in Excel of making a selection before you choose the command to perform. When formatting, you always select the cell, cell range, or nonadjacent selection before you choose the formatting command to apply it. For example, to change the font for a group of cells in the worksheet, you select those cells before you choose the desired font, size, style, and color for the cells in the Font dialog box.

To remove formatting from cells, you select the cells then press the Del (Delete) key or choose the Clear option on the Edit menu. Excel displays the Clear dialog box, similar to the one shown in Figure 3.1. You then select the Formats option button in the Clear dialog box and choose OK or press Enter to remove the formatting assigned to the selected cells without deleting their entries.

Tip   Excel enables you to format more than one worksheet at a time with its Group Edit feature. This feature is perfect for formatting a group of worksheets that share the same structure, such as budgets, profit and loss statements, and the like. For complete information on how to use the Group Edit feature, see Chapter 10.

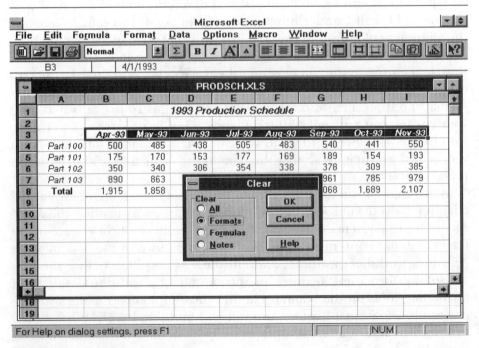

Figure 3.1 The Clear Dialog Box

Formatting Data with the Toolbars

In Excel 4.0 you can do much of the formatting for your worksheet with the tools on the Standard and Formatting toolbars. Figure 3.2 indicates the formatting tools on the Standard toolbar, and Table 3.1 summarizes their usage. In addition to the group of formatting tools on the Standard toolbar, Excel offers a whole series of formatting tools on the Formatting toolbar, shown in Figure 3.3. As you can see from this figure, some of the formatting tools in the Standard toolbar are duplicated in the Formatting toolbar, including the Style box, Bold tool, Italic tool, and AutoFormat tool. Table 3.2 summarizes the functions of the other tools that are unique to the Formatting toolbar.

Tip See Chapter 19 for information on how you can customize these toolbars. There you will find suggestions on ways you can eliminate the duplication in the Standard and Formatting toolbars by removing duplicated tools and adding new ones.

Assigning Number Formats

When you enter numeric values in a cell or a formula that returns numeric values, Excel automatically applies the General number format to your entry. The General format displays numeric entries more or less as you enter them. The format does, however, make a number of changes to your numeric entries. It:

- Drops any trailing zeros from decimal fractions, so that **4.5** appears when you enter **4.500** in a cell.

- Drops any leading zeros in whole numbers, so that **4567** appears when you enter **04567** in a cell.

- Inserts a zero before the decimal point in any decimal fraction without a whole number, so that **0.123** appears when you enter **.123** in a cell.

- Truncates decimal places in a number to display the whole numbers in a cell when the number contains too many digits to be displayed in the current column width and converts the number to scientific notation when the column width is too narrow to display all integers in the whole number, so that **7890123** appears when you enter **7890123.45** in a cell using the default column width, but **7.89E+08** appears when you enter **789012345.67** in that cell.

Remember that you can always override the General number format when you enter a numeric value by entering the characters used by the

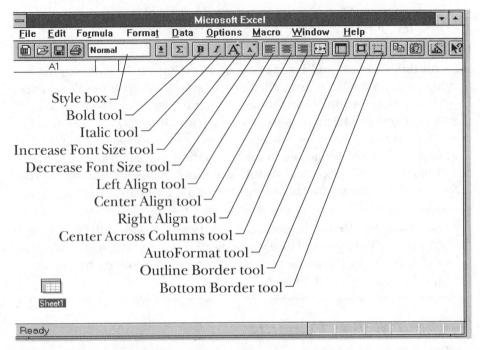

Figure 3.2 The Standard Toolbar

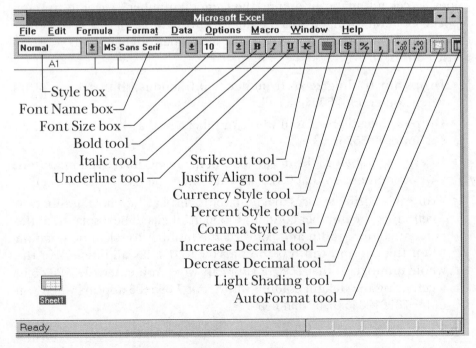

Figure 3.3 The Formatting Toolbar

Table 3.1 The Formatting Tools on the Standard Toolbar

Tool	Function
Style box	Applies the cell style you select in the drop-down list box to the current selection. Creates a new style using the formatting of the current selection when you enter a new style name in the text box. (See "Formatting with Styles" later in this chapter.)
Bold tool	Applies the bold style to the current selection. If the selection is already bold, clicking this tool removes the bold style.
Italic tool	Applies the italic style to the current selection. If the selection is already italic, clicking this tool removes the italic style.
Increase Font Size tool	Increases font in the current selection to the next larger size. Hold down the Shift key when you click this tool to decrease the font to the next smaller size.
Decrease Font Size tool	Decreases the font size in the current selection to the next smaller size. Hold down the Shift key when you click this tool to increase the font to the next larger size.
Left Align tool	Horizontally aligns the contents of the selection with the left edge of their cells.
Center Align tool	Horizontally centers the contents of the selection within their cells.
Right Align tool	Horizontally aligns the contents of the selection with the right edge of their cells.
Center Across Columns tool	Centers the entry in one cell horizontally across the columns selected to the right.
AutoFormat tool	Formats the table around the active cell with the last table format selected. Hold down the Shift key when you click this tool to choose the next Table Format.
Outline Border tool	Adds a light line border around the outside edges of the selected cells.
Bottom Border tool	Adds or removes a light line border on the lower edge of each selected cell.

Table 3.2   Unique Tools on the Formatting Toolbar

Tool	*Function*
Font Name box	Applies the font you select in the drop-down list box to the current selection.
Font Size box	Applies the font size you select in the drop-down list box to the current selection.
Underline tool	Applies the underline style to the current selection. If the selection is already underlined, clicking this tool removes the underline style.
Strikeout tool	Applies strikeout (a line through the middle) to the current selection. If the strikeout is already displayed in the strikeout text, clicking this tool removes the strikeout style.
Justify Align tool	Justifies wrapped text in the active cell with the left and right borders of that cell by spreading out the words with extra spaces.
Currency Style tool	Applies the $#,##0.00_);[RED]($#,##0.00) format codes to the current selection to display their values in the Currency format with two decimal places.
Percent Style tool	Applies the 0% format codes to the current selection to format their values as percentages with no decimal places.
Comma Style tool	Applies the #,##0.00_);[RED](#,##0.00) format codes to the current selection to format their values in the Number format with commas separating thousands with two decimal places.
Increase Decimal tool	Adds one decimal place to the number format in the current selection each time you click the tool. Hold the Shift key down when you click this tool to reduce a decimal place to the number format.
Decrease Decimal tool	Reduces one decimal place from the number format in the current selection each time you click the tool. Hold the Shift key down when you click this tool to add a decimal place to the number format.
Light Shading tool	Applies light shading pattern to the current selection.

Format Codes (shown in Table 3.3) of one of the other number formats. For example, to enter the value 2500 and assign it the Currency number format that displays two decimal places, you enter $2,500.00 in the cell.

Note that although you can override the General number format and assign one of the others to any numeric value that you enter into a cell, you cannot do this when you enter a formula into a cell. For instance, even if you enter $500.00 in cell A10 and 10 in cell B10 and then build the formula =A10*B10 in cell C10, Excel still displays the result 5000 in this cell using the General format. There are two ways to display this calculated result in cell C10 as $5,000.00. You can make this cell active and then assign the Currency number format that displays two decimal places by clicking the Currency Style tool in the Formatting toolbar, or you can select the $#,##0.00_);($#,##0.00) format codes in the Number Format dialog box.

Table 3.3 Excel's Built-in Number Formats

Category	Format Codes	Usage
All	General	Default format that drops leading zeros from whole numbers and trailing zeros from decimal numbers. Also automatically adds a leading zero to the left of the decimal point for decimal fractions and converts the value to the Scientific format when the number is too long to be displayed in the cell.
Number	0	Displays numbers with no decimal places, as in 6790 when you enter 6789.567.
	0.00	Displays numbers with two decimal places, as in 6789.57 when you enter 6789.567.
	#,##0	Displays numbers with commas separating thousands and no decimal places, as in 6,790 when you enter 6789.567.

Table 3.3   *(continued)*

#,##0.00	Displays numbers with commas separating thousands and two decimal places, as in **6,789.57** when you enter **6789.567**.
#,##0_);(#,##0)	Displays numbers with commas separating thousands and no decimal places, as in **6,790** when you enter **6789.567**. Displays negative values in parentheses, as in **(6,790)** when you enter **–6789.567**. Also places a blank space the width of the right parenthesis at the end of positive numbers so that they align with negative numbers in this format.
#,##0_);[RED](#,##0)	Same as preceding comma format except that negative values appear in red as well as in parentheses on a color monitor.
#,##0.00_);(#,##0.00)	Displays numbers with commas separating thousands and two decimal places, as in **6,789.57** when you enter **6789.567**. Displays negative values in parentheses, as in **(6,789.57)** when you enter **–6789.567**. Also places a blank space the width of the right parenthesis at the end of positive numbers so that they align with negative numbers in this format.

Table 3.3 *(continued)*

	#,##0.00_);[RED](#,##0.00)	Same as preceding comma format except that negative values appear in red as well as in parentheses on a color monitor.
Currency	$#,##0_);($#,##0)	Displays numbers with currency symbol ($ by default), commas separating thousands, and no decimal places, as in $6,790 when you enter 6789.567. Displays negative values in parentheses, as in ($6,790) when you enter −6789.567. Also places a blank space the width of the right parenthesis at the end of positive numbers so that they align with negative numbers in this format.
	$#,##0_);[RED]($#,##0)	Same as currency format above except that negative values appear in red as well as in parentheses on a color monitor.
	$#,##0.00_);($#,##0.00)	Displays numbers with currency symbol ($ by default), commas separating thousands, and two decimal places, as in $6,789.57 when you enter 6789.567. Displays negative values in parentheses, as in ($6,789.57) when you enter −6789.567. Also places a blank space the width of the right parenthesis at the end of positive numbers so that they align with negative numbers in this format.

Table 3.3   *(continued)*

	$#,##0.00_);[RED]($#,##0.00)	Same as currency format above except that negative values appear in red as well as in parentheses on a color monitor.
Date	m/d/yy	Displays date serial number in format 4/1/93.
	d-mmm-yy	Displays date serial number in format 1-Apr-93.
	d-mmm	Displays date serial number in format 1-Apr.
	mmm-yy	Displays date serial number in format Apr-93.
	m/d/yy h:mm	Displays date serial number and time decimal fraction in format 4/1/93 19:05.
Time	h:mm AM/PM	Displays time decimal fraction in format 7:05 PM using a 12-hour clock.
	h:mm:ss AM/PM	Displays time decimal fraction in format 7:05:25 PM using a 12-hour clock.
	h:mm	Displays time decimal fraction in format 19:05 using a 24-hour clock.
	h:mm:ss	Displays time decimal fraction in format 19:05:25 using a 24-hour clock.
	m/d/yy h:mm	Displays date serial number and time decimal fraction in format 4/1/93 19:05.
Percentage	0%	Multiplies numbers by 100 and displays the result with no decimal places and the percent sign (%).

Table 3.3 *(continued)*

	0.00%	Multiplies numbers by 100 and displays the result with two decimal places and the percent sign (%).
Fraction	# ?/??	Displays decimal number as a fraction with a single digit in the numerator of the fraction, as in **3 1/2** when you enter **3.489**.
	# ??/??	Displays decimal number as a fraction with up to two digits in the numerator of the fraction, as in **3 22/45** when you enter **3.489**.
Scientific	0,00E+00	Displays numbers in scientific notation, as in **1.50E+03** when you enter **1500**.

Note: The Number Format that you assign to cells with numeric values in the worksheet affects *only* the way they are displayed in their cells, not their underlying values. For example, if a formula returns the value **3.456789** in a cell and you apply a number format that displays only two decimal places, Excel displays the value **3.46** in the cell. If you then refer to the cell in a formula that multiplies its value by 2, Excel returns the result **6.913578** instead of **6.92**, which would be the result if Excel were actually multiplying **3.46** by **2**. If you want to modify the underlying value in a cell, you use ROUND function. (See Chapter 5 for details.)

You can select any of the built-in number formats by selecting the cells to be formatted, then opening the Number Format dialog box shown in Figure 3.4. You can open this dialog box by choosing the **N**umber command on the Forma**t** pull-down menu or by clicking one of the selected cells with the *right* mouse button, then dragging down to the Number option on the shortcut menu. As you can see from the figure, this dialog

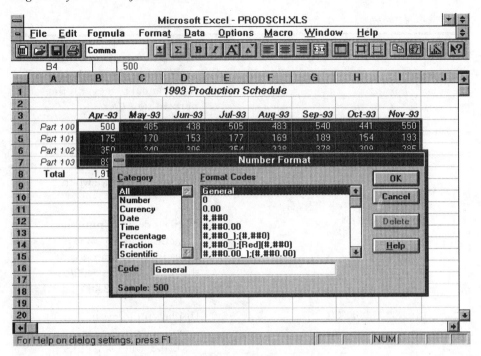

Figure 3.4   The Number Format Dialog Box

box contains two list boxes: the **C**ategory list box, which displays the available number format categories followed by the **F**ormat Codes list box, which displays all the format codes available in each current category.

The first category in the **C**ategory list box is called All. This category displays the format codes for all the built-in number formats. When you select another number format category in the **C**ategory list box, Excel displays only the format codes for that type of value. When you create custom number formats (see "Creating Custom Formats"), their format codes are added to the bottom of the All list box as well as to the bottom of the category of number format to which they belong.

When you choose a set of format codes for the current selection in the **F**ormat Codes list box, Excel displays those codes in the Code text box near the bottom of the dialog box. On the line below after **Sample**, the program also shows you how the value in the active cell of the selection will appear if you apply those format codes to it. You should always check the value in the Sample line of the dialog box to make sure you've correctly chosen the desired number format before you select the OK button or press Enter to apply that format to the current selection.

Assigning Number Formats with the Formatting Toolbar

If you want to assign a currency, percentage, or number format that uses commas to a selection in your worksheet, you don't have to use the Number Format dialog box at all: You can assign these formats simply by displaying the Formatting toolbar and then clicking the appropriate format tool (Currency Style tool, Percent Style tool, or Comma Style tool).

When you mark a selection and then click the Currency Style tool, Excel applies the $#,##0.00_);[RED]($#,##0.00) Currency format codes to its values. When you make a selection and then click the Percent Style tool, Excel applies the 0% Percentage format codes to its values. When you make a selection and then click the Comma Style tool, Excel applies the #,##0.00_);[RED](#,##0.00) Number format codes to its values.

If you find that you want to display fewer or more decimal places in the Currency, Percentage, or Number type formats that you apply to cells (with the Currency Style tool, Percent Style tool, or Comma Style tool or in the Number Format dialog box), you can change the number of decimal places with the Increase Decimal tool or the Decrease Decimal tool on the Formatting toolbar. Each time you click the Increase Decimal tool, Excel adds one decimal place to the number format applied to the current selection; each time you click the Decrease Decimal tool, Excel removes one decimal place from it.

Tip If you find that you have added too many decimal places to your number format with the Increase Decimal tool, you can remove decimal places simply by holding down the Shift key as you click the same tool. So too, if you find that you have removed too many decimal places from the number format with the Decrease Decimal tool, you can add decimal places by holding down the Shift key as you click this tool.

Creating Custom Formats

Although Excel provides a wide variety of built-in number formats, you still may find situations where you need to create your own formats. For example, if you're building a worksheet where you have to input a series of telephone numbers, you would want to create a special number format that automatically encloses the area code in parentheses, separates the area code from the main number with a space, and puts a dash between the prefix and the rest of the telephone number. That way, when entering your telephone numbers in the worksheet, you only have to type the digits of the numbers. Excel adds the necessary punctuation for separating the numbers when you apply your custom number format to their cells. For instance, you can enter the digits 8005551234 in a cell and

(800) 555–1234

will appear in the cell when you apply your custom telephone number format to it.

To create a custom format, you must open the Number Format dialog and enter the format codes for the custom format in the **Code** text box. You can do this by selecting an existing format in the **Format** Codes list box and then editing its formatting codes, or by typing in the format codes from scratch. Format codes can use any of the symbols shown in Table 3.4.

Table 3.4 Symbols Used in Custom Number Formats

Symbol	Usage
General	Displays the number in General format.
0	Digit place holder that inserts zero in the display if the value lacks another digit for that position in the number format. For example, the format 0.000 would display the value .456 as **0.456**, and the format 0.0000 would display .456 as **0.4560**. If the value contains more digits to the right of the decimal point than zeros in the format, Excel rounds the value. For instance, the format 0.00 would display the value .456 as **0.46**.
#	Digit place holder that does not insert any character in the display if the value lacks a digit for that position in the number format. Use this symbol to indicate the position of the separator symbols, such as the , (comma) as in #,###, when you don't want zeros displayed for missing digits in the number.
?	Digit place holder that works like the 0 except that it inserts a space for insignificant zeros to the left or right of the decimal point so that the decimal points align. For example, the format #.?? aligns the values 4.2 and 3.25 in their cells because it adds a trailing space to the first value.
. (period)	Decimal point that determines how many digits appear to the left and right of this point in the number format. If the format contains only #s to the left of this symbol, Excel begins numbers smaller than 1 with a decimal point. To ensure that all such numbers begin with 0 to the left of the decimal point, use 0 as the first place holder to the left of the decimal point instead of #.

Table 3.4 *(continued)*

%	Percentage indicator. Multiplies the value by 100 and inserts the % symbol at the end of the number.
, (comma)	Thousands separator. If the format contains a comma surrounded by 0s or #s as in #,###, Excel separates each group of thousands (thousands, hundred thousands, millions, and so on) with a comma. If the format contains a comma followed by digit place holders, Excel scales the number by a thousand. For instance, the format 0.0 would display **250000** as **250.0** and **12500** as **12.5**.
E– E+ e– e+	Scientific format. If the format contains 0 or # to the right of an E–, E+, e–, Excel displays the value in scientific format and inserts an E or e. The number of 0s or #s to the right determines the exponent's number of digits. E– or e– places a minus sign by negative exponents. E+ or e+ places a minus sign by negative exponents and a plus sign by positive exponents.
$ – + / ( ) : space	Displays any of these characters as typed in the format. To display other characters, precede each character with a \ (see below) or enclose the characters in quotation marks. (See "*text*" below.)
\ (backslash)	Displays the character that follows the backslash in the format (without displaying the backslash). This is the same as enclosing the character in quotation marks. (See "*text*" below.) Excel inserts the backslash for you when you enter the following characters: ! ^ & ' ' ~ { } < >
*	Repeats the next character in the format enough times to fill the cell. You can use only one * (asterisk) in a custom format.
_ (underline)	Inserts a space equal to the width of the character that follows the underline in the format. For example, in the built-in format $#,###0.00_), the characters _) insert a space equal to the width of a right parenthesis at the end of positive values so that their decimal points align with negative values enclosed in parentheses.
"*text*"	Displays whatever text you enclose between the quotation marks, as in the number format "Acct. No." 00000, which enters the text **Acct. No**. in front of the digits you enter.

Table 3.4   *(continued)*

@	Text place holder. If there is text in the cell, this text is inserted in the custom format at the place where the @ character appears.
m	Displays the month as a number without leading zeros (as in 2-15). If the m immediately follows h or hh in the format, Excel displays the minute instead of the month.
mm	Displays the month as a number with leading zeros (as in 02-15). If the mm immediately follows h in the format, Excel displays the minute instead of the month.
mmm	Displays the abbreviation of the month (Jan–Dec).
mmmm	Displays the full name of the month (January–December).
d	Displays the day as a number without leading zeros (1–31).
dd	Displays the day as a number with leading zeros (01–31).
ddd	Displays the abbreviation of the day (Sun–Sat).
dddd	Displays the full name of the day (Sunday–Saturday).
yy	Displays the year as a two-digit number (99–00).
yyyy	Displays the year as a four-digit number (1999–2000).
h	Displays the hour as a number without leading zeros (0–23).
hh	Displays the hour as a number with leading zeros (00–23).
m	Displays the minute as a number without leading zeros (0–59).
mm	Displays the minute as a number with leading zeros (00–59).
s	Displays the second as a number without leading zeros (0–59).
ss	Displays the second as a number with leading zeros (00–59).
AM/PM am/pm or A/P a/p	Displays the hour using a twelve-hour clock. Excel displays AM, am, A, or a for times from midnight until noon and PM, pm, P, or p for times from noon until midnight. If the format contains time symbols without using one of these AM or PM symbols, Excel uses a twenty-four-hour clock.
[BLACK]	Displays the characters in the cell in black.
[BLUE]	Displays the characters in the cell in black.
[CYAN]	Displays the characters in the cell in cyan.
[GREEN]	Displays the characters in the cell in green.

Table 3.4 *(continued)*

[MAGENTA]	Displays the characters in the cell in magenta.
[RED]	Displays the characters in the cell in red.
[WHITE]	Displays the characters in the cell in white.
[YELLOW]	Displays the characters in the cell in yellow.
[COLOR n]	Displays the color that corresponds to n, the number of the color (between 1 and 16) in the color palette. See Chapter 7 for information on creating a custom color palette.

When you create a custom format, each format can have up to three number sections and a fourth text section. Each section of the format is separated by a semicolon as follows:

Positive format;negative format;zero format;text format

The first format you list affects only positive values in the selection, the second format affects only negative values, and the third affects only zero values. If you have only two number sections in your format, as in

$* #,##0.00;$* −#,##0.00

the first section affects positive and zero values, while the second section affects negative values. If you have only one section in your format, as in

??/???

positive, negative, and zero values all use the same format.

The fourth section in the format, if included, affects only text in the cell. If your format doesn't include a text section, text entries are not affected by the format. If you do include a text section, you can refer to any text in the cell with the @ symbol (the text place holder). That way, if there is text in the cell, it is displayed in the cell along with the standard text in the text format section. For example, suppose you create this number format

#,##0.00"CR";#,##0.00"DB";0.00_D_B;**@

so that positive values are followed by CR (for credit), negative values are followed by DB (for debit), zero values are aligned on the decimal point, and text entries are prefaced by a string of asterisks. (The first asterisk tells Excel to repeat the asterisk that follows.) Figure 3.5 shows what happens when you apply this custom format to a series of cell entries. In this figure cell B7, which contains the text entry **Account Closed**, is active. Notice how

![Microsoft Excel screenshot showing ACCTS93.XLS spreadsheet]

	A	B	C	D	E	F
1				1993 Accounts		
2						
3		*Apr-93*	*May-93*	*Jun-93*	*Jul-93*	*Aug-*
4	*Account 100*	500.00CR	485.00CR	437.50CR	505.00CR	482.50C
5	*Account 101*	175.00DB	169.75CR	153.13DB	176.75DB	168.88D
6	*Account 102*	350.00CR	339.50DB	306.25CR	353.50CR	337.75C
7	*Account 103*	Account Closed	0.00	0.00	0.00	0.00
8	**Total**	675.00CR	315.25CR	590.63CR	681.75CR	651.38C

Figure 3.5 Custom Format with Positive, Negative, Zero, and Text Format Sections

the text format section of this custom format adds a string of asterisks in front of this text.

Adding Colors to Custom Formats

When creating custom formats, you can assign colors to any of the sections in the format. By designating different colors to different types of cell entries, you can effectively emphasize various areas in the worksheet on the screen if you have a color monitor or in print if you have a color printer. For example, you can use a specific color to indicate all subtotals and totals in a worksheet, negative values, or even values above or below a particular target. (See "Creating Conditional Formats" later in this chapter.)

Tip Excel also allows you to assign colors directly to particular fonts selected with the Font dialog box or to the fonts used in a style. (See "Changing the Font Color" and "Formatting with Styles" later in this chapter.) The colors assigned by number formats to a cell range, however, override any colors assigned to the fonts used in those entries.

To assign a color to a section of a format, you enter the name of the color (in upper- or lowercase) enclosed in square brackets, as in [CYAN] or [red] at the beginning of the appropriate format section. You can also insert a color from the color palette by entering [COLOR*n*], where *n* is a number between 1 and 16, representing the order of the color on the color palette. (See Chapter 7 for more information on the color palette and how you can customize its colors.) For example, the twelfth color on the default color palette is a light brown. To use this color in a custom format, you would enter [COLOR12] at the start of the pertinent section.

Colors can be used in combination with other format symbols, as in

[BLUE]#,##0.00"CR";[RED]#,##0.00"DB";[GREEN]0.00;[MAGENTA]**@

which adds blue, red, green, and magenta colors to the other formatting assigned to each format section, or alone, as in

[BLUE];[RED];[GREEN];[MAGENTA]

which creates a custom format that simply adds the colors blue, red, green, and also adds colors to the positive, negative, zero values, and text in what otherwise uses the General number format.

Creating a Hidden Format

Unlike some other spreadsheet programs, Excel does not offer a built-in hidden format that you can use when you don't want certain ranges of data to be displayed in the worksheet. You can, however, easily create a custom *null format* that hides the display of any or all types of data in their cells. To create a null format, you enter only a semicolon for the particular format section whose data you don't want to appear in the worksheet. For example, to hide all values (positive, negative, and zero) but continue to display any text entries, your custom format consists of a single semicolon, as in

;

To create a custom null format that applies a comma format to positive and negative values but hides all zero values and text entries in the worksheet, your custom format would look like this:

#,##0_);(#,##0);;

To create a custom null format that hides the display of all types of data (negative, positive, and zero values *and* text), you would create this custom format:

;;;

(three semicolons in a row).

When you apply a custom null format to data in your worksheet, the type of data affected is no longer displayed in the selected cells. You can, however, still see the contents of a cell that's been hidden with a null format on the formula bar when you make that cell active. To have hidden cell entries displayed once again in the worksheet, select the cells and then choose a nonnull number format for them in the Number Format dialog box.

 Alert! Be careful when editing a worksheet that contains entries hidden with a custom null format. It is easy to delete hidden cell entries when copying or moving ranges in the worksheet if any of the ranges you're pasting overlay your hidden cells.

Creating Conditional Formats

When you create a custom format, the first section indicates how to display positive values (>0), the second section indicates how to display negative values (), and the third section how to display zero values (=0). You can also create *conditional formats* that make the formatting dependent on other values in the cells you're formatting. For example, if you create the conditional format

[>5000][CYAN]#,##0.00;[<–100][RED]#,##0.00;[COLOR13]#,##0.00

Excel assigns the color cyan to all values in the selection greater than 5000, the color red to all values less than –100, and the color 13 (purple on the default palette) to all values in between (that is, values 5000 or less and –100 or greater). In this custom format, the first and second sections contain the conditional values that determine the upper and lower range of the values and how they are to be formatted. All values that fall in between this upper and lower range are formatted according to the third section of the custom format.

You can also create custom formats that use only one conditional value. This type of conditional format consists of two sections: The first section contains the conditional value that specifies the formatting for all values that meet this condition, while the second section formats all entries not formatted by the first section. For example, you could create a conditional format that automatically converts grams in quantities of 1000 or greater to kilograms by dividing by 1000 and appending *kg* to the entry as follows:

[>999.99]#,##0.00,_k"kg";##0_k_g"g"

This custom format scales any value in the selection that is greater than 999.99 by 1000, then adds a space the width of the letter *k* and the letters **kg**.

For all other values in the selection (that is, those 999.99 or less), the format simply appends spaces the width of *kg* and the letter **g** (for gram) to them.

Selecting Fonts

In Excel, you can assign any of the fonts you've installed for your printer to cells in a worksheet. Along with selecting a new *font* (also known as a *typeface*), you can choose a new font size (in points), assign a font style (such as bold, italic, underline, or strikeout), as well as change the color of the font.

Tip If you keep the Formatting toolbar displayed somewhere on the screen as you're formatting your worksheet, you can always tell the font and font size of the active cell by looking at the font name displayed in the Font Name box and point size displayed in the Font Size box.

Selecting Fonts with the Formatting Toolbar

In Excel 4.0, you can change the font, font size, and font style with the Formatting toolbar. The only aspect you can't change is the color of the font— you must do this in the Font dialog box as described in the following section. To change the font with the Formatting toolbar:

1. If the Formatting toolbar is not currently displayed, position the pointer on the Standard toolbar, click the right mouse button, and drag down to the Formatting option on the shortcut menu. To undock the Formatting toolbar, double-click it.

2. Select the cell, cell range, or nonadjacent selection that you want to apply the new font, size, or style to.

3. To assign a new font to the selection, Select the name of the font in the Font Name drop-down list box in the Formatting toolbar.

4. To assign a point size to the selection, select the size in the Font Size drop-down list box in the Formatting toolbar.

5. To assign a new style to a selection, click the appropriate tool in the Formatting toolbar: click the Bold tool (the one with **B**) to bold the selection, the Italic tool (the one with *I*) to italicize the selection, the Underline tool (the one with the U̲) to underline the selection, or the Strikeout tool (the one with the K̶ with a line through it) to add the strikeout attribute to the selection.

Note that you can remove an existing font style from a selection by clicking the same Style tool. For example, if you want to remove the bold style from headings in a worksheet, select their cells, then simply click the Bold tool in the Formatting toolbar. All of the style tools act like toggles that turn on and off their particular attribute.

Selecting Fonts with the Font Dialog Box

You can also select a new font, font size, font styles, and even a font color for your selection in the Font dialog box. To open the Font dialog box, select the Font command on the Format pull-down menu or by clicking one of the selected cells with the *right* mouse button, then dragging down to the Font option on the shortcut menu. Figure 3.6 shows you the Font dialog box that appears when a cell that uses the Normal or default font is active (indicated by the X in the Normal Font check box). In this figure, the current Font is Helv (for Helvetica), the Font Style is Regular, the Font Size is 10 (points), and the Color is Automatic.

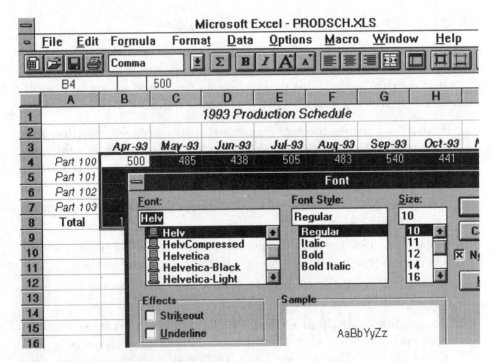

Figure 3.6   The Font Dialog Box

> *Note:* The Automatic color in Excel always refers to the Window Text color that is currently selected in the Windows Color dialog box. This color corresponds to black unless you change it by opening the Control Panel in the Windows Main Group window, then opening the Color dialog box and specifying a new Window Text color for the color scheme you choose.

To change the font for the current selection in the Font dialog box, select the font in the **F**ont list box. The Sample box in the Font dialog box previews the appearance of each font that you select in the Font list box. It also indicates whether the font you've selected is a printer or screen font. (Printer fonts are indicated in the Font list box by a printer icon in front of the font name.) If the font you select is a printer font, Excel chooses the closest matching screen font to display the text in the worksheet. If the font is a screen font, Excel chooses the closest matching printer font when you print the worksheet.

To change the size of the font, select one of the sizes displayed in the **S**ize list box. You can also select a new point size by selecting the current entry in the **S**ize text box and typing in its replacement. If you're using a Post-Script printer such as an Apple LaserWriter, you can type in a point size even if that size is not one of the options listed in the **S**ize list box.

To select a new font style, select the desired option from among those available for the font you've selected (such as Bold, Italic, or Bold Italic) in the Font Style list box. To add underlining or the strikeout attribute to the font, select the **U**nderline or Stri**k**eout check box under Effects.

To change the color of the font, open the **C**olor drop-down list box, then drag to the color you want to assign. The **C**olor list box contains color bars for all of the 16 colors on the current color palette plus the Automatic option (whose color is determined by the Window Text setting in Windows).

When you've finished making all of your changes in the Font dialog box, check the Sample box. When the text in the Sample box appears in the font you want, select the OK button or press Enter to close the Font dialog box and apply the font and selected attributes to the current selection.

Tip When you change the color of a font in the Font dialog box, that color is associated with the font only for the current selection. The next time you select the same font, the color defaults back to the Automatic setting (black, in most cases). If you want a particular font (such as Times Roman) to appear in a certain color (such as dark blue) in all the cells where the font is used, create a style (see "Formatting with Styles" later in this chapter) that uses both the desired font and color, then apply this style to all cells that should use this combination.

Using Borders and Shading

Excel makes it easy to add borders and various shading patterns to cells in the worksheet. You can use the borders to outline tables of data, to emphasize particularly important cells, or to underscore rows of key data. You can also apply various shading patterns to cells to draw attention to significant aspects of the worksheet.

When adding borders and shading, you can make your job a great deal easier by removing the light-gray gridlines used on the screen to indicate the cells in the worksheet. To remove these gridlines, choose the **D**isplay command on the **O**ptions menu and remove the X from the **G**ridlines check box under Cells before you select the OK button in the Display Options dialog box. If you want to print the worksheet with the cell gridlines (and whatever borders you've designated) or redisplay the cell gridlines on the screen as you work, open the Display Options dialog box and reselect the **G**ridlines check box. To print the worksheet without redisplaying the cell gridlines on the screen, choose the Page Se**t**up command on the **F**ile menu and select the Cell **G**ridlines check box instead, then print the worksheet. (See Chapter 6 for information on printing a worksheet.)

Applying Borders to a Selection

You can apply two kinds of borders with the Standard toolbar. Use the Outline Border tool to draw a light line around the outside edges of the cells in the current selection. Use the Bottom Border tool to draw a light line on the bottom edge of the cells in the current selection (in effect, underlining the cells). If you want to use other line weights or colors in your borders or apply the borders to other edges of the cell selection, you use the options in the Border dialog box as follows:

1. Select the cells, cell range, or nonadjacent selection to which you want to apply the borders.

2. Choose the **B**order command on the Forma**t** menu to display the Border dialog box or click one of the selected cells with the *right* mouse button, then drag down to the Border option on the shortcut menu.

3. Click the option in the Border placement box indicating where you want the borders applied. Select the **O**utline option to place a border line around the perimeter of the current selection. Select the **L**eft, **R**ight, **T**op, or **B**ottom option to place border lines on the designated edges of all cells in the selection.

4. To change the line weight or style of the current Border placement option, click the type of line under Style. Excel places a heavy border around the line style you select in the Style box and displays that line style in the currently selected Border placement option.

5. To change the color of the currently selected Border placement option, click the **C**olor drop-down list button, then drag to the color you want to use (this list box contains selections for all sixteen colors in the current color palette plus the Automatic option) and release the mouse button.

6. Repeat steps 3 to 5 until you have defined all of the borders you want to apply to the current cell selection.

7. If you want to shade the selection with a light-gray shading at the same time you apply the borders, select the **S**hade check box.

8. Click the OK button or press Enter to apply the borders to the current selection.

Figure 3.7 shows an example of what you can do with borders. There you see a table of data that has been formatted with three different line styles. (The cell gridlines have been removed to make the borders easier to see.)

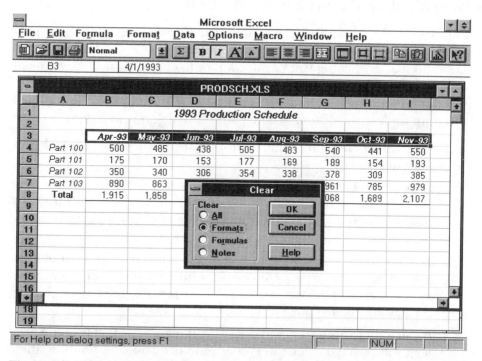

Figure 3.7 Different Borders Applied to a Single Cell Selection

A heavy border has been placed around the perimeter of the entire table, a double line has been placed between each column of data, and a light single line has been placed between each row within the table.

I applied all three border styles to this data table in one operation using the Border dialog box. After selecting the cell range B2:J9, I opened the Border dialog box and selected the heavy line Style for the **O**utline Border option, the double line Style for the **R**ight Border option, and the single line Style for the **B**ottom Border option.

> *Note:* When two different edges of cells within a selection form a common border (for example, the border where the right edges of the cells abut the left edges of the cells on the right in the selection) and you apply two different line styles to these edges (a heavy line style for the Right Border option and a light line style for the Left Border option), Excel displays whichever style is most dominant. Line styles are ranked from the most to the least dominant in the following order: double line, heavy line, medium line, light line, long dash line, short dash line, dotted line, and, finally, no line.

Applying Shading Patterns to a Selection

You can use the Light Shading tool on the Formatting toolbar to apply light-gray shading to the current selection. You can also use this tool to remove this type of shading from a selection or to convert some other type of shading selected with the Patterns dialog box (discussed below) to light-gray shading. If you want to apply some other pattern or color to your cell selection, you use the options in the Patterns dialog box as follows:

1. Select the cells, cell range, or nonadjacent selection to which you want to apply the shading.

2. Choose the **P**atterns command on the Format menu to display the Patterns dialog box, or click one of the selected cells with the *right* mouse button, then drag down to the Patterns option on the shortcut menu.

3. To change the shading pattern, click the **P**attern drop-down button, then drag to the new pattern you want to assign and release the mouse button. The pattern you select appears in the Sample box in the Patterns dialog box.

4. If you want to assign a new color to the lines or dots that form the pattern you selected, click the **F**oreground drop-down list button, then drag to the new color you want to assign (this list box contains selections

for all sixteen colors in the current color palette plus the Automatic option) and release the mouse button.

5. If you want to assign a new color to the background of the pattern you selected, click the **B**ackground drop-down list button, then drag to the new color you want to assign (this list box contains selections for all sixteen colors in the current color palette plus the Automatic option) and release the mouse button.

6. Check the pattern and color combination you've defined in the Sample box. If the pattern in the Sample box appears as you want, select the OK button or press Enter to close the Patterns dialog box and apply the pattern and colors to the current selection.

Changing or Removing Borders and Patterns

If, upon applying new borders to a selection, you discover that you don't like them, you can remove them with the **U**ndo Border command on the **E**dit menu (Alt+BkSp or Ctrl+Z), provided that you choose this command before you edit another part of the worksheet. In the same manner, you can remove the shading you've just applied to a selection with the **U**ndo Patterns command on the **E**dit menu (Alt+BkSp or Ctrl+Z).

If the **U**ndo Border or **U**ndo Patterns command is no longer available on the **E**dit menu, you must reselect the cells and open the Border and/or Patterns dialog box to remove their borders or shading. You also must use these dialog boxes when you want to change the borders or patterns for a selection.

Should you want to change or remove the *borders* assigned to a selection:

1. Select the cells, range, or nonadjacent selection whose borders are to be modified or removed.

2. Choose the **B**order option on the Format menu. The Border dialog box opens, showing the current line styles assigned to each Border placement option. If different line styles have been applied to common borders within the current selection, the box for the Border placement option representing those common borders is shaded gray.

3. To change the line style and/or color for a Border placement option, click the new line weight and type and select the new color in the Sty**l**e box, then click the Border placement option that you want to apply it to. To remove the borders from a particular Border placement option, click the no line style (the empty rectangle in the lower-right corner of the Sty**l**e box), then click the Border option to

apply it. (You can also click the option box to clear the current line style—in the case of gray-shaded option boxes, you must click the box twice.)

4. When you've finished changing or removing the borders for your selection, click OK or press Enter to put your changes into effect in the worksheet.

Should you want to change or remove the *shading* applied to a selection:

1. Select the shaded cells, range, or nonadjacent selection whose pattern is to be modified or shading removed.

2. Choose the **P**atterns option on the Format menu. The Patterns dialog box opens, showing the current shading pattern and foreground and background colors. If all the cells in the current selection don't share the same pattern or colors for a particular Cell Shading option, the text box for that drop-down list box is shaded gray.

3. To change the pattern, click the **P**attern drop-down list button, then drag to the new pattern and release the mouse button. To remove the current shading pattern, select the None option in the drop-down list box.

4. To change the foreground color of pattern, click the Foreground drop-down list button, then drag to the new color and release the mouse button.

5. To change the background color of pattern, click the Background drop-down list button, then drag to the new color and release the mouse button. Note that if you're about to remove the shading from the current selection by choosing None for the **P**attern option, you don't have to bother with resetting the **F**oreground and **B**ackground color options. Excel automatically resets both these options to the default of Automatic as soon as you select the OK button.

6. Click the OK button or press Enter to put your changes into effect in the current selection.

Tip To quickly remove a pattern and colors from a cell selection when the Formatting toolbar is displayed, click the Light Shading tool twice in a row: The first time converts the currently applied patterns and colors to light gray, the second time removes the light-gray shading from the selection.

Changing Column Widths and Row Heights

Excel sets the column width and row height in a new worksheet based on the width of the characters and point size of the font used in the Normal style. (See "Formatting with Styles" later in this chapter for more information on the Normal style.) When you vary fonts and font sizes in the cells of your worksheet, you often have to modify the widths of the columns to accommodate the change in the display of your cell entries.

Remember that although Excel displays text entries that don't fit within the current column width in the blank cells to the right, the program truncates the display of text in its cell if the cell to the immediate right is occupied. To redisplay the entire text entry in the worksheet (and subsequently in any printout you make), you must widen the column sufficiently (or reduce the font size so that all the text can be displayed in the current width).

With numeric values in the General format that are too wide to be displayed in the current column width, Excel either truncates the display of their decimal places or converts them to scientific notation. If you apply a number format other than General to the cells and their values can't be displayed within the current column width, Excel displays a series of number signs in the cells (# # # #), as shown in Figure 3.8. The formatted values are redisplayed only when you widen the column, as shown in Figure 3.9.

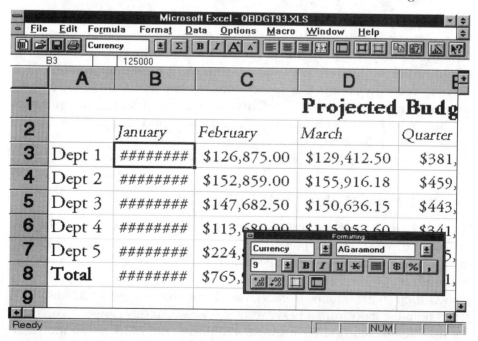

Figure 3.8   Column with Formatted Values Too Long to Display

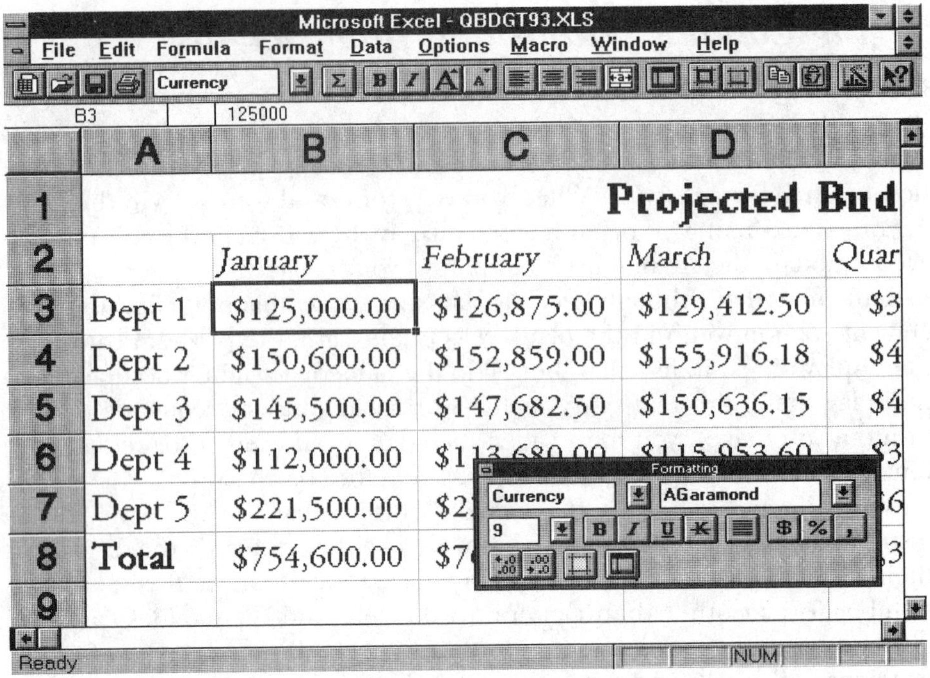

Figure 3.9   Formatted Values Displayed After Widening the Column

Fortunately, unlike columns, Excel automatically adjusts the height of the rows to accommodate changes you make to the font and font sizes of cell entries within them. The program automatically increases the row height sufficiently to display the largest font you may use in any row. If you later decrease the point size of the largest font in the row, Excel subsequently reduces the height of that row. You can, however, override the row height set by Excel for any row in a worksheet and set a new row height of your own. In doing so, however, you must take care that you don't make the row so short that it cuts off the display of some of your cell entries.

Changing Column Widths and Hiding Columns

You can change column widths directly with the mouse or with the options in the Column Width dialog box. To change the width of a column with the mouse, you position the cross-shaped pointer on the borderline dividing one column from the next within the gray area displaying the column letters. The pointer then changes shape from a cross to a double-headed arrow with each arrow pointing away from a heavy vertical line. When this happens, you drag the double-headed pointer until the column is the width you want, then you release the mouse button. As you drag, Excel displays a dotted line representing the column separator (shown in Figure 3.10). You drag the column separator toward the column letter to make the column narrower, while you drag the column separator away from the column letter to make it wider.

To adjust the widths of multiple adjacent columns, drag the cross-shaped pointer across the column letters to select the columns. Then position the pointer on a border of one of the selected columns and drag the double-headed pointer to change the width as described above. To adjust the widths of nonadjacent columns, hold down the Ctrl key as you click the column letters of the discontinuous columns you want to adjust, then position the pointer on a border of one of the selected columns and drag the double-headed pointer in the appropriate direction.

ADJUSTING THE COLUMN TO BEST FIT

Rather than manually determining the width for the column, you can have Excel do it for you automatically. Simply position the cross-shaped mouse pointer on the right border within the gray area containing the column letter and double-click the mouse when the pointer changes to a double-headed arrow. Excel then modifies the column width to fit the column's widest cell entry.

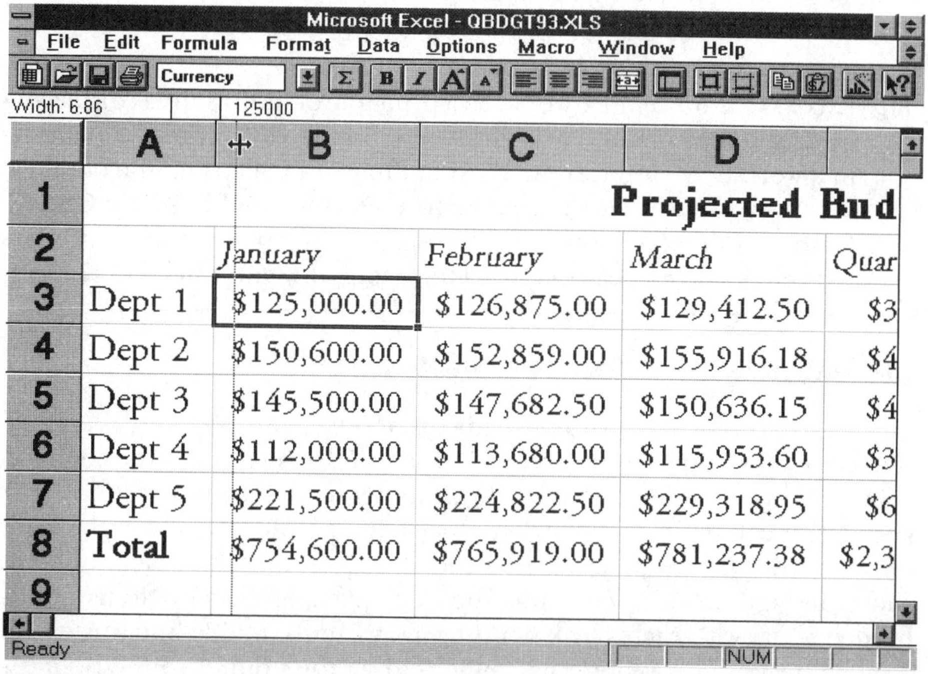

Figure 3.10 Changing the Column Width with the Mouse

As you work with Excel, you will soon find that being able to select the Best Fit option simply by double-clicking the right column border takes the drudgery out of adjusting column widths when formatting your worksheets.

HIDING A COLUMN

The maximum width of a column is 255 characters. (This corresponds to the longest possible entry you can make in a cell.) The minimum width of a column is 0 characters. A hidden column in a worksheet is one that is 0 characters wide. To hide a column, you drag its column separator to the left until you've positioned it somewhere in front of the column separator for the previous column, then release the mouse button (see Figure 3.11). As soon as you release the mouse button, you will notice that the letter of the hidden column is missing at the top of the worksheet. (For example, when you hide column C, the column letters go A, B, D, and so on, as shown in Figure 3.12.)

Although none of the data appears in a hidden column, the data remains a part of the worksheet. This means that you can hide a column containing values referred to in formulas elsewhere in the worksheet without affecting the formulas in any way. (This would not be the case if you deleted the column.) Thus you can hide columns that must be used in calculations but that you would prefer not to appear in printed reports.

Tip Excel's Outline feature works on a principle of hiding and redisplaying groups of columns and rows that correspond to different outline levels in a worksheet (referred to as expanding and collapsing the outline). If your worksheet uses a suitable format, you should use the Outline feature to simplify hiding and redisplaying related columns and rows in the worksheet. See Chapter 9 for details on Outlining a worksheet.

REDISPLAYING A HIDDEN COLUMN

To redisplay a hidden column with the mouse, you position the cross-shaped pointer within the gray area just slightly to the right of the common column border between what are now nonsequential column letters. (For instance, if column C is hidden, you place the pointer slightly to the right of the border between columns B and D, which now abut each other, as shown in Figure 3.13.) This time the pointer changes shape to a double-headed arrow with each arrow pointing away from a double line (instead of a single heavy line). When this happens, drag the pointer to the right. As you do, the column separator for the hidden column appears as a dotted

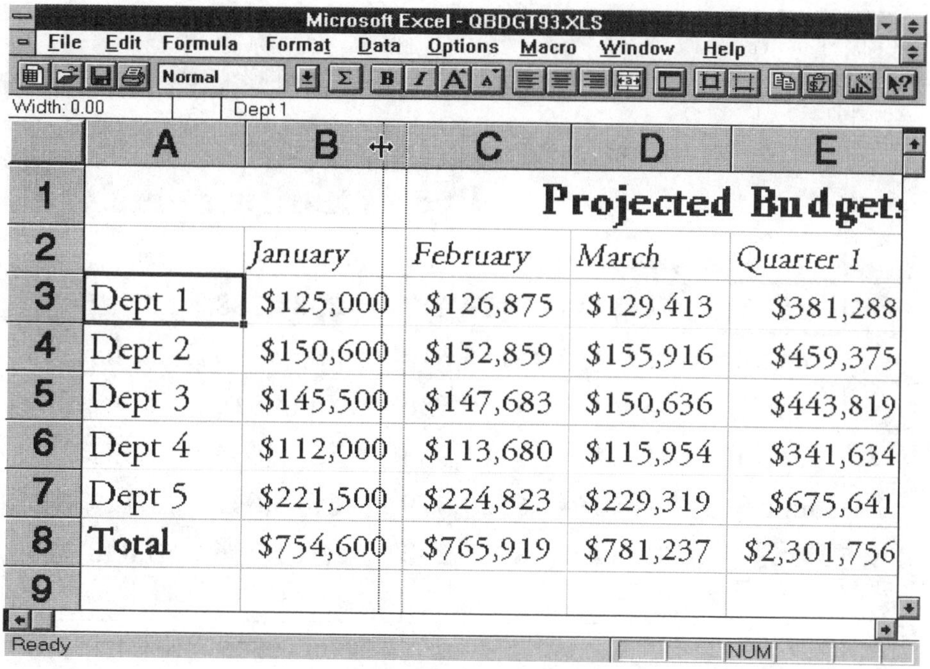

Figure 3.11 Hiding a Column with the Mouse

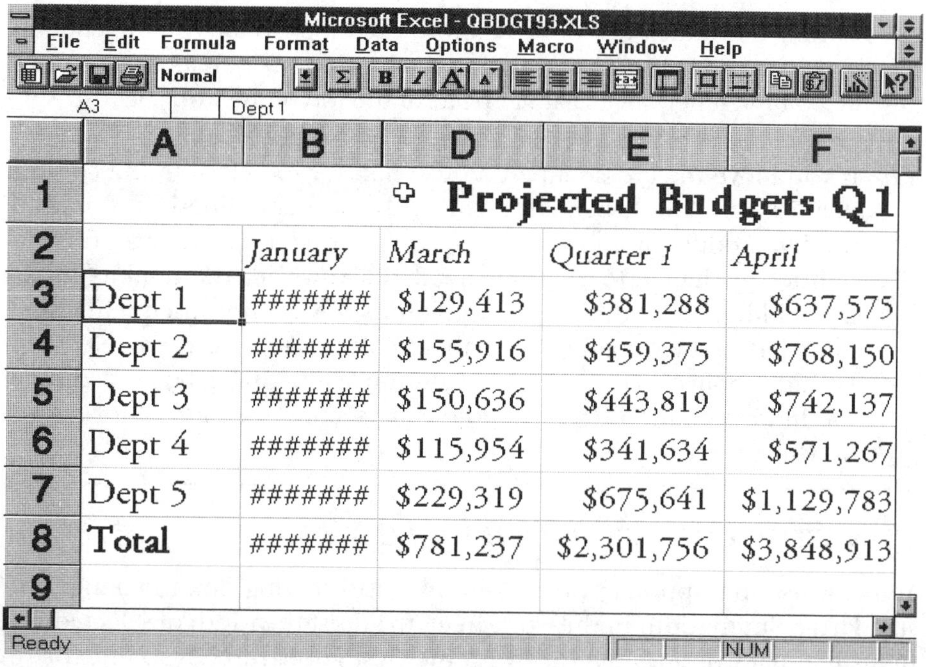

Figure 3.12 Worksheet After Hiding Column C

Microsoft Excel - QBDGT93.XLS					

File   Edit   Fo**r**mula   Format   **D**ata   Options   **M**acro   **W**indow   **H**elp

Normal

Width: 4.00   Dept 1

	A	B	D	E	F
1			**Projected Budgets Q1**		
2		January	March	Quarter 1	April
3	Dept 1	#######	$129,413	$381,288	$637,575
4	Dept 2	#######	$155,916	$459,375	$768,150
5	Dept 3	#######	$150,636	$443,819	$742,137
6	Dept 4	#######	$115,954	$341,634	$571,267
7	Dept 5	#######	$229,319	$675,641	$1,129,783
8	Total	#######	$781,237	$2,301,756	$3,848,913
9					

Ready   NUM

Figure 3.13   Redisplaying a Hidden Column with the Mouse

line running down the worksheet. When you've widened the column enough, release the mouse button. Excel redisplays the column with all of its entries, and the column letter once again appears at the top of the worksheet.

Tip If you move the cross-shaped mouse pointer too close to the column divider, the double-headed arrow with the heavy line in the middle used to modify column widths appears. If you have trouble getting the pointer to change to a double-headed arrow with the double line in the middle, select the adjacent columns now with nonsequential column letters by dragging over their column letters, then select the **U**nhide command button in the Column Width dialog box to redisplay the hidden column. (See the following section for more information on using the Column Width dialog box.)

USING THE COLUMN WIDTH DIALOG BOX

You can use the options in the Column Width dialog box to change the standard column width in the worksheet, to adjust the width of selected columns manually or automatically with the Best Fit feature, or to hide or redisplay selected columns. Figure 3.14 shows you the Column Width dialog

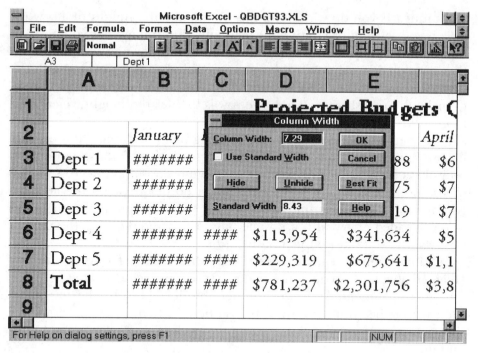

Figure 3.14 The Column Width Dialog Box

box that appears when you choose the Column Width command on the Format Excel pull-down menu. Remember that you can also open this dialog box simply by clicking a column letter with the *right* mouse button and then dragging down the shortcut menu to the Column Width option before you release the button.

To make the columns you've selected a specific nonstandard width, you select the Column Width text box, then enter the number of characters in the new column width (between 0 and 255) and select OK. To let Excel determine the most appropriate width of the selected columns given their longest cell entries, click the Best Fit command button instead.

To hide all of the columns you've selected, you click the Hide command button in the Column Width dialog box. To restore the display of hidden columns, select the now nonsequential columns in the worksheet, open the Column Width dialog box, and then click the Unhide command button.

Changing Row Heights and Hiding Rows

Although you will need to modify the height of rows much less often than you do the width of columns in a worksheet, Excel does allow you to change the row height and hide and redisplay rows in a worksheet using the same techniques as you do with columns. To change the height of a row (or rows if you select more than one) manually with the mouse, you position the cross-shaped pointer within the gray area displaying the numbers on the lower dividing line and drag the double-headed pointer with the heavy line in the middle. Drag downward to make the row taller or upward to make the row shorter. When the row is the desired height, release the mouse button.

Note that you can also hide a row by dragging the row separator up until it is within the previous row and then releasing the mouse button. To redisplay a hidden row with the mouse, you must position the cross-shaped mouse pointer slightly below the common border between the adjacent rows now with nonsequential row numbers. When the pointer changes to a double-headed arrow with a double line in the middle, drag the pointer down before you release the mouse button.

As with columns, you can also modify the display of rows in the Row Height dialog box. To open this dialog box, choose the **R**ow Height option on the Format menu. You can also open this dialog box by clicking one of the row numbers with the right mouse button, then dragging down the shortcut menu to the Row Height option before you release the mouse button.

Aligning Worksheet Data

You can use Excel's Alignment commands to change the way cell entries are displayed within their cells. In Excel 4.0, alignment refers both to the horizontal and vertical placement of an entry within its cell boundaries as well as to the orientation of the text. As you recall, horizontally, Excel automatically right aligns all numeric values and left aligns all text values in their cells (referred to as General alignment). Vertically, Excel aligns all types of cell entries with the bottom of their cells.

Excel offers you the following horizontal alignment choices:

1. **General** (the default) to right align a numeric value and left align a text entry in its cell.

2. **Left** to left align any type of cell entry in its cell.

3. **Center** to center any type of cell entry in its cell.

4. **Right** to right align any type of cell entry in its cell.

5. **Fill** to repeat any type of cell entry until its characters fill the entire cell display. When you use this option, Excel automatically increases or reduces the repetitions of the characters in the cell as you modify the width of its column.

6. **Justify** to spread out a text entry with spaces so that the text is aligned with the left and right edges of its cell. If necessary to justify the text, Excel automatically wraps the text onto more than one line in the cell and increases the height of its row. If you use the Justify option on numeric values or formulas, Excel left aligns the values in their cells just as if you had selected the Left align option.

7. **Center across selection** to center a text entry over selected blank cells in columns to the right of the cell entry.

For text entries in the worksheet, you can also join the Wrap Text option to any of the horizontal alignment choices. When you select the **W**rap Text option, Excel automatically wraps the text entry to multiple lines within its cells while maintaining the type of alignment you've selected (something that automatically happens when you select the **J**ustify alignment option).

In addition to the seven horizontal alignment choices, Excel offers these vertical alignment options:

1. **Top** (the default) to align any type of cell entry with the top edge of its cell.

2. **Center** to center any type of cell entry between the top and bottom edges of its cell.

3. **Bottom** to align any type of cell entry with the bottom edge of its cell.

Finally, as part of its alignment options, Excel 4.0 now lets you alter the *orientation,* or the way an entry reads in its cell. In addition to the normal text orientation, Excel now allows you to choose between a Rotated Vertical, Rotated Up, and Rotated Down orientation option. (See "Changing the Orientation of Entries" later in this chapter for more information.)

Modifying Alignment with the Toolbars

You can change the horizontal alignment of selected cell entries to Left, Center, Right, or Center across columns using the Standard toolbar or to Justify using the Formatting toolbar. To use the Left Align tool, Center Align tool, or Right Align tool on the Standard toolbar, select the cells whose entries you want to align and then click the appropriate tool. Figure 3.15 shows you examples of left-, center-, and right-alignment in various cell ranges.

To use the Center Across Columns tool on the Standard toolbar, make the cell with the entry you want to center (normally a text entry, such as the heading for a table or the worksheet) the active cell, then extend it to the right until you've extended it to all the blank cells within which the entry should be centered, then click this tool. To use the Justify tool on the Formatting toolbar, make the cell with the text entry you want left- and right-justified the active one, then click this tool. Figure 3.16 shows you examples of a text entry that has been centered across columns and one that has been justified in its cell.

Using the Alignment Dialog Box

You must use the Alignment dialog box when you need to use the other horizontal alignment options (such as **F**ill to fill a cell selection with an entry or General to return a selection to the default alignment), add the **W**rap Text option to the current type of horizontal alignment, or any of the vertical alignment and orientation options. Figure 3.17 shows you the options in the Alignment Dialog box. To open this dialog box, select the cells you want to align, then choose the **A**lignment option on the Format pull-down menu or click one of the selected cells with the *right* mouse button and drag down to the Alignment option on the shortcut menu, then release the button.

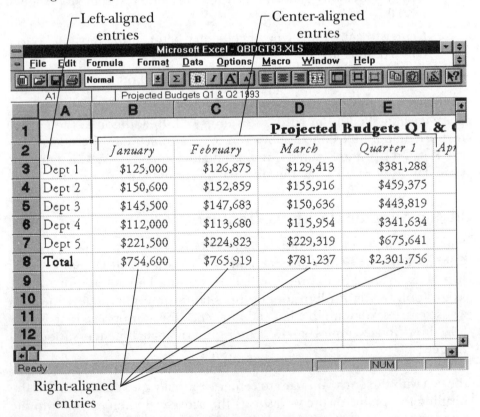

Figure 3.15 Left-, Center-, and Right-Aligned Cell Entries

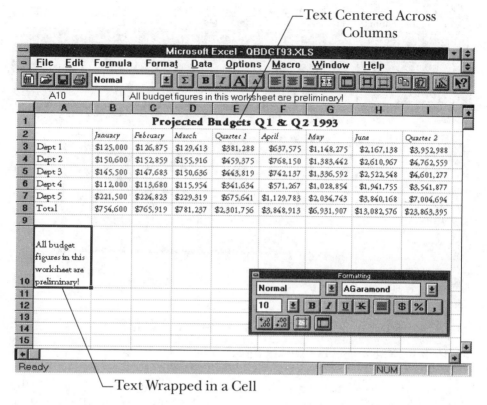

Text Centered Across Columns

Text Wrapped in a Cell

Figure 3.16 Centering Text Across Columns and Justifying Text in a Cell

WRAPPING TEXT IN A CELL

You can use the **Wrap Text** check box in the Alignment dialog box to have Excel create a multiline entry from a long text entry that would otherwise spill over to blank cells to the right. In creating a multiline entry in a cell, the program also automatically increases the height of its row if that is required to display all of the text.

To get an idea of how text wrap works in cells, compare Figures 3.18 and 3.19. Figure 3.18 shows you three long text entries that spill over to succeeding blank cells to the right. Figure 3.19 shows you these same entries after they have been formatted with the Wrap Text option. The first long text entry in cell A2 uses General alignment (same as Left for text) with the Text Wrap option. After using the Wrap Text option, Excel displays this label on three lines, all of which are aligned with the left edge of the cell. The second long text entry in cell A4 uses Justify with the Wrap Text option. Note how Excel puts extra spaces between the words in this cell to justify the first three lines of text with both the left and right edges of the

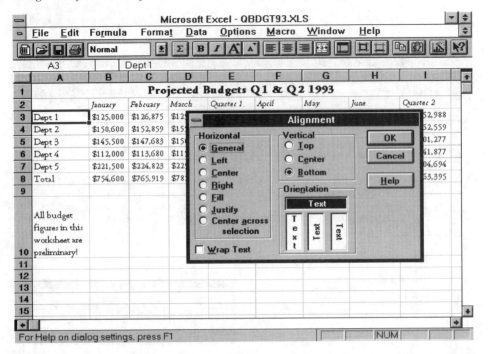

Figure 3.17 The Alignment Dialog Box

cell. The third long text entry in cell A6 uses Center alignment with the Wrap Text option. There Excel creates a six-line text entry with the text of each line centered between the left and right edges of the cell.

When you create multiline text entries with the Wrap Text option, you can decide where each line breaks by inserting a new paragraph. To do this, you put Excel in Edit mode by clicking the insertion point in the formula bar at the place where a new line should start and press Alt+Enter. When you press the Enter key to return to Ready mode, Excel inserts an invisible paragraph marker at the insertion point that starts a new line both on the formula bar and within the cell with the wrapped text. If you ever want to remove the paragraph marker and rejoin text split on different lines, you click the insertion point at the beginning of the line you want to join on the formula bar and press the Backspace key. You can also indent text within a cell by inserting a tab. To do this, you position the insertion point at the beginning of the entry in the formula bar, then press Ctrl+Tab.

Centering and Wrapping Text Across Several Columns

While Excel normally wraps a long text entry within a single cell, you can also have Excel wrap a long text entry across several columns. To do this,

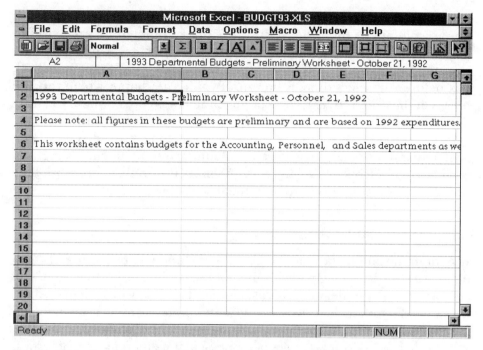

Figure 3.18   Long Text Entries that Spill Over to Blank Cells

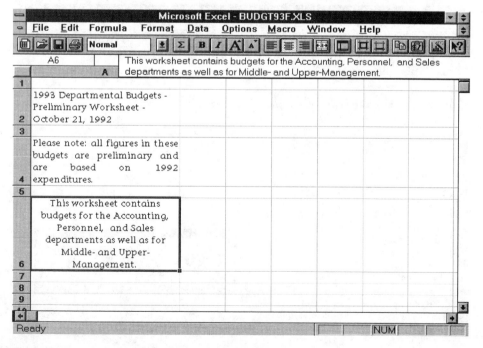

Figure 3.19 Long Text Entries Wrapped in Their Cells

make the cell with the long text entry the active one and extend the selection to columns to the right until you've marked the entire range within which the text should be centered. Open the Alignment dialog box, then click the Center across selection option button and the Wrap Text check box before you select the OK button. If you're not happy where the line breaks in the centered text, you can force the line to break where you want by inserting a paragraph marker in the long text entry as described above.

Figure 3.20 shows you an example where a long text entry has been centered and wrapped across several columns. Note that a new paragraph was inserted in front of *October* in the formula bar so that the entire date would appear together centered on the second line.

Changing the Vertical Alignment

It's not until you increase the height of a row that you notice that the cell entries are vertically aligned with the bottom of their cells. In version 4.0, you can change this default vertical alignment to **T**op, which aligns cell entries with the top of their cells, or to Center, which centers them between the top and bottom edges of their cells. Figure 3.21 illustrates the possible vertical alignments with examples of entries that use different types of vertical

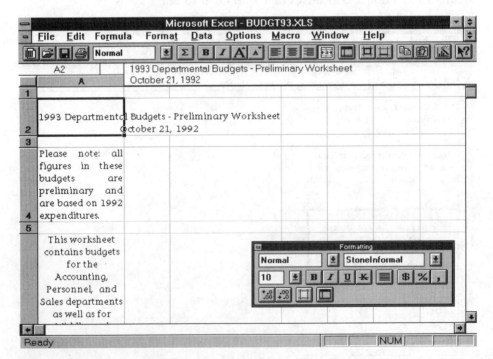

Figure 3.20 Centering and Wrapping Text Across Several Columns

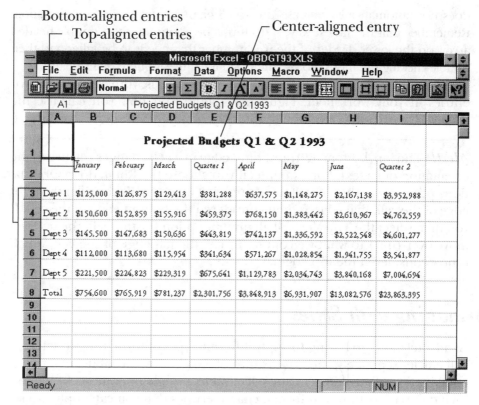

Figure 3.21 **Using Different Types of Vertical Alignments**

alignment. Note in this figure how you can combine various horizontal and vertical alignments with the Wrap Text option.

CHANGING THE ORIENTATION OF ENTRIES

Excel makes it easy to change the orientation of the characters in a cell entry. To do so, select the cells whose orientation you need to change, open the Alignment dialog box, and then double-click the Text option that matches the direction you want to use (normal text, Rotated Vertical, Rotated Up, or Rotated Down) in the **O**rientation box or click the Text option and select OK. Note that you can't change the orientation of wrapped text entries—the Orientation options in the Alignment dialog box are unavailable (indicated by the dimming of **O**rientation) whenever the **W**rap Text check box is selected.

After changing the orientation of entries in a selection to something other than the normal horizontal left-to-right, you will have to increase the height of their rows in order to display them in the worksheet. Unfortunately, Excel does not automatically increase the row height to suit the new orientation. Remember that the fastest way to do this is by positioning the double-headed arrow on the lower divider of the row number that needs to be taller and then double-clicking the mouse to use the Best Fit feature to increase its height.

Figure 3.22 illustrates the different orientations you can choose for entries in your worksheet. Figure 3.23 shows you how you can use the Rotated Up orientation option to vary the column headings in a worksheet.

Alert! The top, bottom, left, and right edge in a cell changes relative to the orientation of its text. For example, if you choose the Rotated Up Orientation option where the characters run up what we normally consider the right edge of the cell, that edge is then considered the bottom edge of the cell. If you then select the **T**op Vertical alignment option for this cell, the text will move over (up?) to what we commonly call the left edge of the cell, which is now considered the top edge.

Formatting with Styles

As an alternative to having to apply different types of formatting to selected cell entries separately, the *Style* feature of Excel offers the ability to apply a combination of attributes to any selection in a single operation. A style can include up to six different format characteristics that you can apply to a selection of cells, including

1. The number format to be applied to numeric values.
2. The font, font size, font style, or color to be applied to any type of cell entry.
3. The horizontal and vertical alignment and/or orientation to be applied to any type of cell entry.
4. The type of border to be applied to the cells.
5. The shading patterns to be applied to the cells.
6. The protection status to be applied to the cells. (Cells can be locked or unlocked and the contents of locked cells can be hidden or unhidden on the formula bar. See Chapter 5 for complete information on protecting a worksheet.)

When creating a style for your worksheet, you can include any combination of these six formatting characteristics that provides the most effective formatting. Formatting your worksheet with Style offers the following advantages over formatting it with separate Excel format commands:

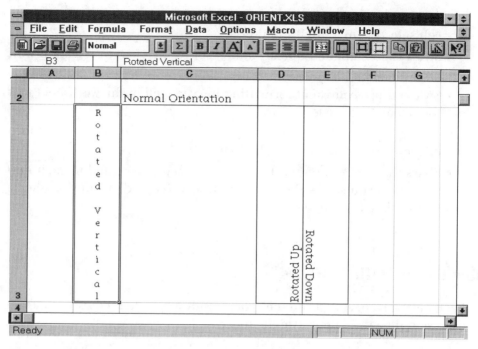

Figure 3.22 Using Different Types of Orientation

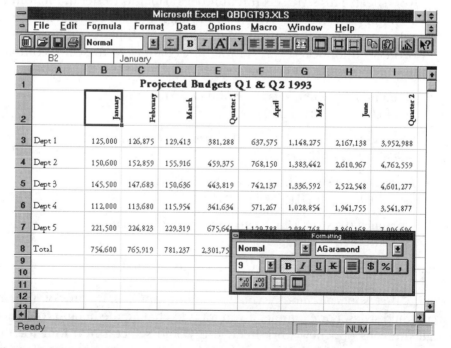

Figure 3.23 Worksheet with Column Headings Rotated Up

- Styles allow you to apply many different types of formatting to a cell selection in a single operation.

- Styles can be applied quickly and easily to the current selection with the Style drop-down list box on the Standard or Formatting toolbar.

- Styles ensure consistent formatting in every cell in the worksheet that uses a particular style.

- Changes you make to a style are immediately and globally put into effect in every cell that uses that style.

- Styles that you use regularly don't have to be re-created in each new worksheet you start—they can be merged (copied) from worksheets you've already created.

Using the Predefined Styles

Each new worksheet that you start comes with six predefined styles that you can use right away. These styles include:

1. **Normal** style, which is the default style applied to all cells in a new worksheet. This style sets the number format to General, the font to 10-point Helv(Helvetica), horizontal alignment to General and vertical alignment to bottom aligned, borders and shading to none, and protection to locked (preventing any changes to the cell's contents when the worksheet is protected).

2. **Comma** style, which sets the number format to #,##0.00_);[RED](#,##0.00).

3. **Comma** (0) style, which sets the number format to #,##0_);[RED](#,##0).

4. **Currency** style, which sets the number format to $#,##0.00_);[RED]($#,##0.00).

5. **Currency** (0) style, which sets the number format to $#,##0_);[RED]($#,##0).

6. **Percent** style, which sets the number format to 0%.

Note that you can modify the formatting applied by any of the six predefined styles. For example, if you want to change the default font used in all the cells of a new worksheet, you would select a new font for the Normal style. (See "Modifying a Style" later in this chapter for details.)

Defining a Style by Example

By far the easiest way to create a new style is by example. When you create a style by example, you choose a cell that already displays all of the formatting attributes (applied separately using the techniques discussed throughout this chapter) that you want in the new style. Then you click the name of the current style in the text box of the Style drop-down list box in the Standard or Formatting toolbar, replace it with the name for your new style, and press Enter. As soon as you press Enter, Excel creates a new style containing the formatting attributes of the active cell and adds it to the list of styles. Note that if neither the Standard nor the Formatting toolbar is displayed, you can open the Style dialog box by choosing the **S**tyle option on the Forma**t** menu, then entering the new style name in the **S**tyle Name text box before you select the OK button.

Tip When defining a style by example, select only one cell that you know contains all of the formatting characteristics that you want in the new style. That way you avoid the potential problem of selecting cells that do not share the exact same formatting. If you select cells that use different formatting when defining a style by example, the new style will contain only the formatting that all cells share in common.

Using the Style Dialog Box to Create a Style

You can also create styles from scratch by defining each of their formatting characteristics in the Style dialog box as follows:

1. Open the Style dialog box by choosing the **S**tyle option on the Format menu.

2. Type a name for the new style you are defining in the **S**tyle Name text box.

3. Click the **D**efine >> command button. Excel redraws the Style dialog box to include a Style Includes box with six check boxes and a Change box with six command buttons, as shown in Figure 3.24.

4. To include a particular formatting attribute in the style, make sure that its check box is selected in the Style Includes area, then select the corresponding command button in the Change area and make all necessary modification in the dialog box that appears.

5. When you've finished assigning the formatting attributes you want in the new style, click the OK button or press Enter to add the style to the worksheet. When you've finished assigning the formatting attributes

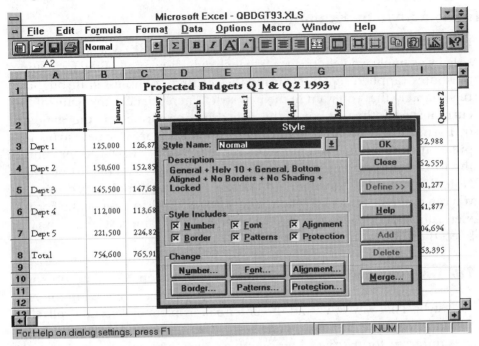

Figure 3.24 Options in the Style Dialog Box After Selecting Define >> Button

you want in the new style, click the OK button or press Enter to add
the style to the worksheet.

Applying Styles to Cells

To use any of the styles in your worksheet, select the cells you want to apply
the style to, then click the style name in the Style drop-down list box on the
Standard or Formatting toolbar. Excel formats the selection according to
the attributes of that style, and the style name appears in the Style box on
the Standard toolbar (and the Formatting toolbar when it's displayed). You
can also apply a style to a selection by choosing the **Style** command on the
Format pull-down menu, then selecting the style in the **Style** Name drop-
down list box before you select OK if neither the Standard nor the Formatting toolbars are displayed in you worksheet.

Sometimes after applying a style to cell selection, you may find that you
want override the style's formatting attributes for just some of the cells. For
example, after applying a style to all the column headings in a table that
italicizes their text, you may want apply light shading and bold to just the
last column heading, which contains the label *YTD Totals*. When you need
to override a style you've applied to a cell, you simply select the cell and then

select the appropriate formatting commands as described earlier in this chapter. If you later modify a style that you've overridden in certain cells, Excel makes the necessary formatting changes in all cells that use the style (including those where the style has been overridden) while still retaining any attributes that you applied afterward. For example, if you change the column heading style so that the font no longer uses the italic style, Excel changes all column headings to normal Roman style while still retaining the light shading and bold in the label in the last column containing *YTD Total.*

Modifying a Style

Excel makes it easy to modify the formatting attributes of a style in your worksheet. You can modify any of the predefined styles as well as any of those that you create yourself. If you no longer need a particular style in your worksheet, Excel allows you to delete it. The only exception to this is the Normal style—although you can modify the characteristics of the Normal style, Excel will not allow you to delete it as this is the default style applied to all "otherwise unformatted" cells in the worksheet.

To modify a style, you follow these steps:

1. Open the Style dialog box by choosing the **S**tyle option on the Forma**t** menu.

2. Select the name of style to modify in the **S**tyle Name text box.

3. Click the **D**efine >> command button.

4. To remove a particular formatting attribute from in the style, remove the X from its check box in the Style Includes area. To delete the style completely from the worksheet, click the **D**elete command button. To modify a particular formatting attribute without eliminating it, select the corresponding command button in the Change area and make all necessary modification in the dialog box that appears.

5. When you've finished changing the formatting attributes you want in the new style, click the OK button or press Enter to add the style to the worksheet.

After modifying a style, Excel changes the attributes in all cells in the active worksheets that use that style.

Merging Styles from Other Worksheets

All styles that you create are saved along with the data and formatting in the worksheet when you save the file. The only styles, however, that are available when you begin a new worksheet are the six predefined styles provided by Excel. If you have created styles in another worksheet that you would like to use in the current worksheet, you can copy them as follows:

1. Open the worksheet document containing the styles you want to copy and use.

2. Make active the document window that contains the worksheet where the styles are to be copied.

3. Open the Style dialog box by choosing the **St**yle option on the Format menu.

4. Click the **D**efine >> command button.

5. Click the **M**erge command button in the extended Style dialog box to open the Merge Styles dialog box.

6. Double-click the name of the worksheet file containing the styles you want to copy in the Merge Styles From list box or click the filename and select the OK button or press Enter. If the worksheet file you selected contains styles with the same names as the styles defined in the active worksheet (such as the six predefined styles), Excel displays an alert box that asks you if you want merge the styles that have the same names.

7. Click the Yes command button or press Enter to have Excel replace all styles in the active worksheet with those that have the same name in the worksheet file you copying from. Select the No command button if you don't want the styles in the active worksheet to be overwritten, in which case Excel merges on the styles with unique names from the other worksheet.

After merging styles from another open worksheet, you can close that worksheet and begin using the merged styles, which now appear on the Style drop-down list boxes in the Standard and Formatting toolbars as well as the Style Name drop-down list box in the Styles dialog box.

Tip If you frequently use custom number formats in worksheets, you should create styles for each format and apply them to your values with the Style drop-down list box on the Standard or Formatting toolbar. By creating styles for custom number formats, you not only make it applying them in a worksheet easier (they are often difficult to locate in the **F**ormat Codes list box in the Number Format dialog box), but you can then make them available in a new worksheet by merging them from an existing worksheet.

Formatting a Table Automatically

Last in our discussion of formatting worksheets, but certainly not least, is the new AutoFormat feature. If you performed the tutorial at the end of Chapter 2, you already have a good idea of how powerful and easy this exciting new feature is. The AutoFormat feature enables you to apply complex formatting to any range of data with no more effort than locating the cell pointer in one of the cells of the table and then clicking the Auto-Format tool (available on both the Standard and Formatting toolbars).

Although the AutoFormat feature is set up for standard tables that use column and row headings, you can use it to format any range of data. You cannot, however, use this feature to format a single cell or a nonadjacent selection. If you position the cell pointer on a cell that is not adjacent to other occupied cells and you try to use AutoFormat, Excel displays an alert box indicating that the program could not detect a table around the active cell. If you try to use AutoFormat when discontinuous cell ranges are selected, Excel displays an alert box indicating that you can't use this command with a multiple selection.

The AutoFormat feature offers you a choice between fifteen different predefined range formats. When you click the AutoFormat tool, Excel applies the last range format used or the so-called Classic 1 range format (the first one in the Table Format list) if you have not yet used the AutoFormat feature. To select another range format with the AutoFormat tool, you hold down the Shift key when you click the tool. This causes Excel to apply the next range format in the Table Format list to the current selection. You can keep selecting new range formats in the list by holding down the Shift key as you continue to click the AutoFormat tool. This is a very convenient way to cycle through the list of range formats until you decide which one looks best.

You can also select a range format from the AutoFormat dialog box (shown in Figure 3.25). To open this dialog box, choose the AutoFormat command on the Format menu. Then click the name of the format in the Table Format list box. As you select a new range format, Excel gives you an idea of how its formatting will look in the worksheet by applying the range format to the sample table in the Sample box. When you've selected the range format you want to use in your worksheet, select the OK button or press Enter to apply its formatting to the current selection. Figures 3.26, 3.27, and 3.28 show you the same data table using the Financial 1, List 1, and 3D Effects 2 range formats, respectively.

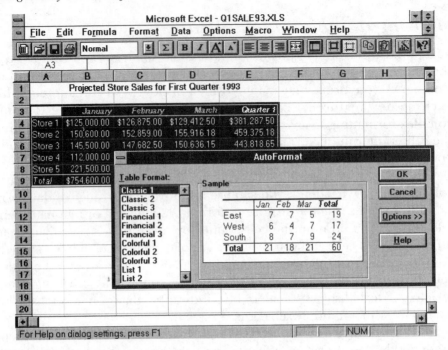

Figure 3.25 The AutoFormat Dialog Box

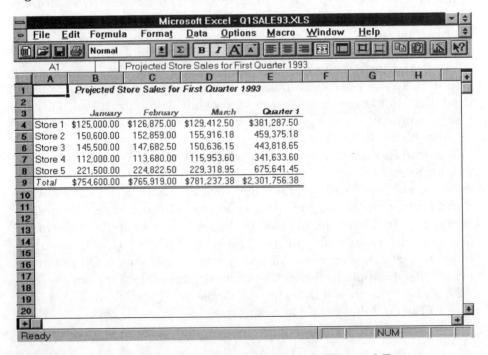

Figure 3.26 Data Table Formatted with the Financial Range 1 Format

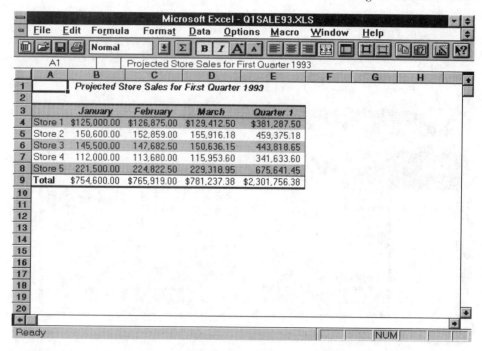

Figure 3.27 Data Table Formatted with the List 1 Range Format

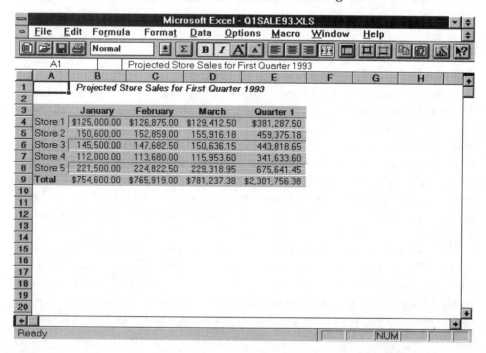

Figure 3.28 Data Table Formatted with the 3D Effects 2 Range Format

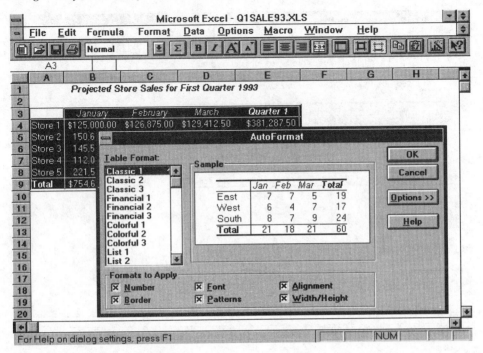

Figure 3.29 AutoFormat Dialog Box with Formats to Apply Check

Modifying a Range Format

Although Excel does not allow you to add range formats to the Table Format list, you can make modifications to any of the predefined range formats in the AutoFormat dialog box. To do this, open the AutoFormat dialog box, then click the **O**ptions >> command button. Excel extends the AutoFormat dialog box to a Formats to Apply section containing the six check boxes shown in Figure 3.29. To modify a range format, select it in the **T**able Format list box, then select or deselect the appropriate check boxes in the Formats to Apply box to add or delete particular format attributes. Excel updates the sample table to show you what affect your change has on the current format.

When you're finished modifying the range format, select the OK button or press Enter to apply the modified range format to the current selection. Note that unlike with styles, Excel applies the formatting changes made to a range format only to the current selection—the program does not modify the formatting for any tables previously formatted with that range format.

SUMMARY

In this chapter you learned how to format data so that your worksheet looks its best. As you now realize, Excel 4.0 offers a host of powerful and easy-to-use formatting features designed to make short work of complex formatting.

In the next chapter you will learn the necessary editing procedures that enable you to modify the layout and contents of your worksheet. As part of this process, you will learn how to use the Undo feature; delete cells, columns, and rows from a worksheet; and copy and move data ranges.

4

Editing the
Worksheet

Creating a worksheet is almost never a one-time experience. Some of the worksheets that you will create with Excel will require routine changes on a regular basis, while others will require more radical changes only once in a while. Regardless of the extent of the changes and their frequency, you can be sure that sooner or later, most of the worksheets you create in Excel will require editing.

In Chapter 2 you learned how to make simple editing changes in a worksheet by modifying the contents of a cell on the formula bar. In this chapter you will learn how to make more complex editing changes in your worksheets. Among the editing techniques you will learn are how to; use the Undo feature; move and copy data; insert and delete new cells, columns, and rows; as well as to move and copy, search and replace, and spell-check data in a worksheet.

If you are new to Excel for Windows, you will need to know all of the features and techniques covered in this chapter as you will use many, if not all, on a regular basis no matter what kinds of worksheets you create. If you've been using Excel 3.0 and are upgrading to version 4.0, you are already familiar with most of the material in this chapter. You should, however, be aware of the new editing features that are covered herein. These include copying and moving data with the Drag and Drop feature, filling a range with the AutoFill feature instead of the Fill Down and Fill Right commands, and spell checking the worksheet with the Spelling command.

Using the Undo Command

As with other Windows programs, you can use Excel's Undo command to recover from potentially costly editing mistakes that would require data reentry or extensive repair operations. The most important thing to remember about the Undo command is that you must use it right away after the mistake happens, *before you select another Excel editing or formatting command.*

You can select the Undo command either by choosing the **Undo** option on the **Edit** menu or by pressing Alt+BkSp (Backspace) or Ctrl+Z. Excel then reverses the effect of the last edit you made in the worksheet. For example, if you edit a cell entry and erase some of its text in error, selecting Undo restores the characters you just erased to the formula bar. If you delete a group of cells by mistake, selecting Undo restores both their contents and formatting to the worksheet.

Tip If the Utility toolbar is displayed, you can select the Undo command to reverse your latest editing change in the worksheet by clicking the Undo tool. You click the Undo tool a second time if you want to restore the editing change.

The Undo command can do more than just restore deleted cell entries to a worksheet. For instance, if you move a group of cells to a new area of the worksheet, selecting Undo restores the cells to their original location. So too, if you change the formatting for a cell selection, such as assigning a new font or number format or changing the alignment, you can use Undo to restore the selection to its previous formatting.

When you make an editing change in the worksheet, the Undo option on the **Edit** menu actually changes to reflect the action you just took. For example, if you delete a group of cells with the **Clear** command on the **Edit** menu (or by pressing the Delete key) and then open the **Edit** menu, the **Undo** command will appear as

Undo Clear   Ctrl+Z

indicating that you can reverse the Clear command and restore the deleted entries (and any formatting) with Undo. If you then apply new formatting to the selection, such as assigning a new alignment, and then open the **Edit** menu, the Undo command now appears as

Undo Alignment   Ctrl+Z

indicating that you can reverse the Alignment command you just used and restore the previous alignment to the selection with Undo.

Some actions in the worksheet have no effect on the current status of the Undo command. For example, you can make a new cell active or select a new range of cells without changing what command is reversible. Thus if you delete a cell range, then make a new cell active in another part of the worksheet, you can still restore the deleted cell range. (If you open the **Edit** menu, **Undo** Clear would continue to appear as the command name.)

You need to be aware that not all Excel commands can be reversed with the Undo command. For example, commands that make changes on the disk, such as the **Save** and **Delete** commands on the **File** menu, can't be reversed. If you select an Excel command whose effects are irreversible, the command name changes to Can't Undo, which appears dimmed on the **Edit** menu.

The Undo feature works by storing a "snapshot" of the worksheet in the memory of your computer at each stage in its editing. Sometimes, if you attempt a large-scale edit in a worksheet, Excel determines that there is not sufficient free memory to hold a snapshot of the worksheet in its current state and complete the planned editing change as well. For instance, this can happen if you try to cut and paste a very large range in a big worksheet. In such a case, Excel displays an alert box that indicates that there is not enough memory and asks you if you want to continue without Undo. If you then select the **Yes** option, Excel completes the planned edit but without the possibility of your reversing its effects with Undo. Before you take such an action, you should consider how much time and effort would be required to restore the worksheet to its previous state manually if you make a mistake in carrying out your editing change.

Using the Redo Command

After you use the Undo feature to reverse an editing change, the **Undo** command on the **Edit** menu changes name again, this time to Redo (**u**) followed by the name of the latest type of editing, such as Redo (**u**) Clear. The (u) in the command name indicates that the mnemonic letter remains *u* whether the command is called Undo or Redo.

You use the Redo command to restore the worksheet to the condition it was in before you selected Undo. You can select the Redo command by choosing Redo on the **Edit** menu with the mouse or by pressing Alt+EU, Alt+BkSp, or Ctrl+Z.

You can use the alternation between Undo and Redo to toggle between a before-and-after view of the worksheet. For example, suppose you make a change to an entry in a cell that is referred to in formulas throughout a table in a worksheet. As soon as you enter the new value in this cell, Excel recalculates the table and displays the new results. To view the previous version of the table before you made this latest change, once again you would use the Undo command. After checking some values in the original table, you could restore the newest version of the table with the Redo command. You could then continue in this manner as long as you wanted, switching between "before" and "after" versions with the Undo/Redo combination.

Using the Repeat Command

The Repeat command provides an easy way to repeat a particular editing change in the worksheet. The Repeat command is especially useful when using commands such as Insert and Delete (for inserting or deleting a range of cells, rows, or columns) or Cut and Copy (cutting and pasting cells), which don't work with nonadjacent selections.

Like Undo, the Repeat command name changes to reflect your latest command selection. For example, if, after applying a style to a cell selection, you open the Edit command, you will see the commands

Undo Style   Ctrl+Z

Repeat Style

at the top of the pull-down menu. If you then select the **R**epeat Style command from the **E**dit menu, Excel applies whatever style you last used to the current cell selection.

Also like Undo, the Repeat command repeats only the last command you used, and the command changes each time you select another Excel command that is repeatable. (Note that Excel can repeat most of its commands, including all editing and formatting commands.) If you select a command that Excel can't repeat, the **R**epeat command name changes to Can't Repeat on the **E**dit menu and appears dimmed.

Unfortunately, Excel for Windows provides no shortcut keys for selecting the **R**epeat command from the **E**dit menu. You can, however, display the Utility menu and use its Repeat tool (shown in Figure 4.1) to make it easier to repeat your last editing or formatting command in the worksheet.

Deleting Data and Cells

Excel allows you to delete the data in a cell and leave the cell intact or to delete the cell (which naturally deletes any data it contains) and adjust the worksheet. Figures 4.2, 4.3, and 4.4 illustrate the very important difference between deleting the data in the cells and deleting the cells themselves.

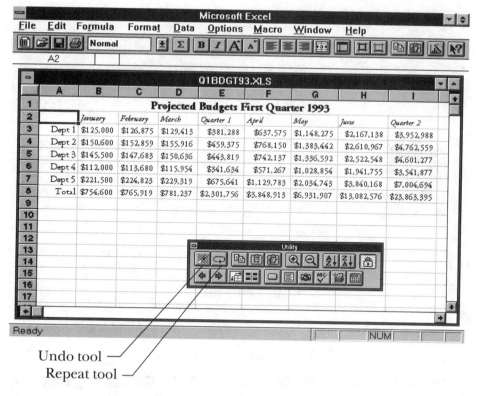

Undo tool

Repeat tool

Figure 4.1 The Utility Toolbar

In Figure 4.2, the cell range A3:A8 containing the row titles is selected for deletion. Figure 4.3 shows you this range after deleting the data in these cells. Note that the cell range now appears empty but that the rest of the table in the worksheet remains undisturbed. Figure 4.4 shows the same range after deleting the cell range A3:A8 instead of just deleting the data in this range. This time Excel not only deletes the row headings from the worksheet but also moves the entries from the first column of the table to the left to fill in the gaps made when the cell range A3:A8 was deleted from the worksheet (subsequently misaligning the data by moving them under the wrong column headings).

As you can see from this example, you delete the contents of a selection of cells when you want merely to empty their cells without disturbing the structure of the worksheet. You delete the cells themselves when you want to delete the contents as well as their structure. As you can see, Excel adjusts the worksheet to fill in the gaps.

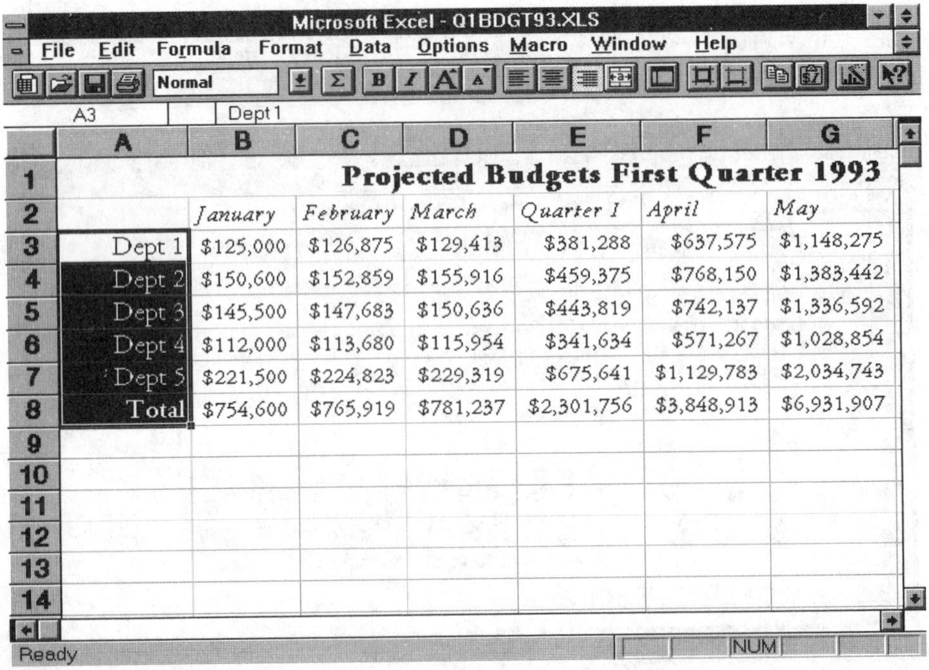

Microsoft Excel - Q1BDGT93.XLS

File Edit Formula Format Data Options Macro Window Help

Normal

A3 | Dept 1

	A	B	C	D	E	F	G
1				*Projected Budgets First Quarter 1993*			
2		*January*	*February*	*March*	*Quarter 1*	*April*	*May*
3	Dept 1	$125,000	$126,875	$129,413	$381,288	$637,575	$1,148,275
4	Dept 2	$150,600	$152,859	$155,916	$459,375	$768,150	$1,383,442
5	Dept 3	$145,500	$147,683	$150,636	$443,819	$742,137	$1,336,592
6	Dept 4	$112,000	$113,680	$115,954	$341,634	$571,267	$1,028,854
7	Dept 5	$221,500	$224,823	$229,319	$675,641	$1,129,783	$2,034,743
8	Total	$754,600	$765,919	$781,237	$2,301,756	$3,848,913	$6,931,907
9							
10							
11							
12							
13							
14							

Ready | NUM

Figure 4.2 Worksheet with Cell Range to Be Deleted

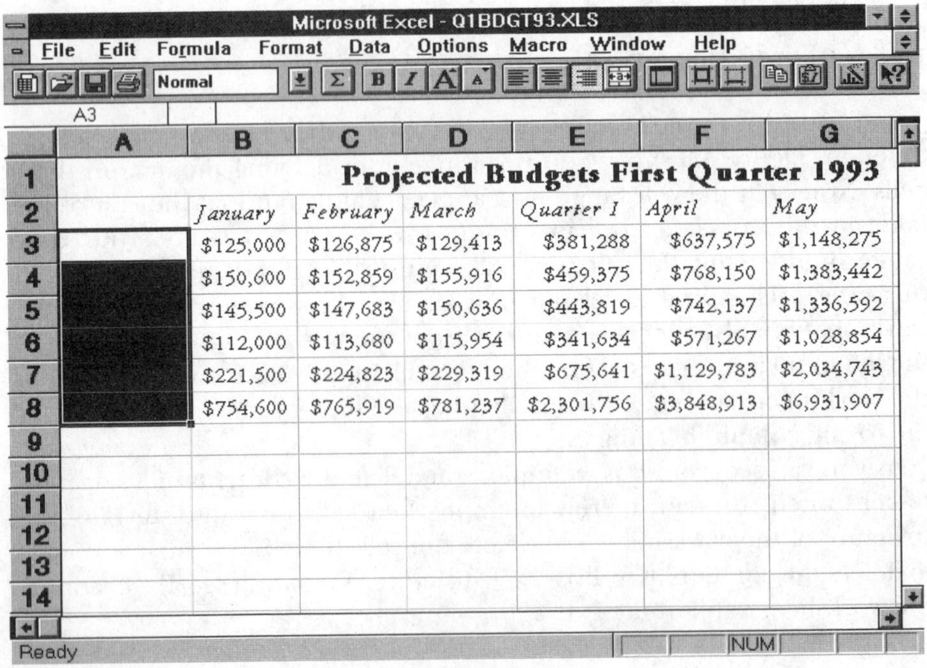

Microsoft Excel - Q1BDGT93.XLS

File Edit Formula Format Data Options Macro Window Help

Normal

A3

	A	B	C	D	E	F	G
1				*Projected Budgets First Quarter 1993*			
2		*January*	*February*	*March*	*Quarter 1*	*April*	*May*
3		$125,000	$126,875	$129,413	$381,288	$637,575	$1,148,275
4		$150,600	$152,859	$155,916	$459,375	$768,150	$1,383,442
5		$145,500	$147,683	$150,636	$443,819	$742,137	$1,336,592
6		$112,000	$113,680	$115,954	$341,634	$571,267	$1,028,854
7		$221,500	$224,823	$229,319	$675,641	$1,129,783	$2,034,743
8		$754,600	$765,919	$781,237	$2,301,756	$3,848,913	$6,931,907
9							
10							
11							
12							
13							
14							

Ready | NUM

Figure 4.3 Worksheet After Deleting the Data

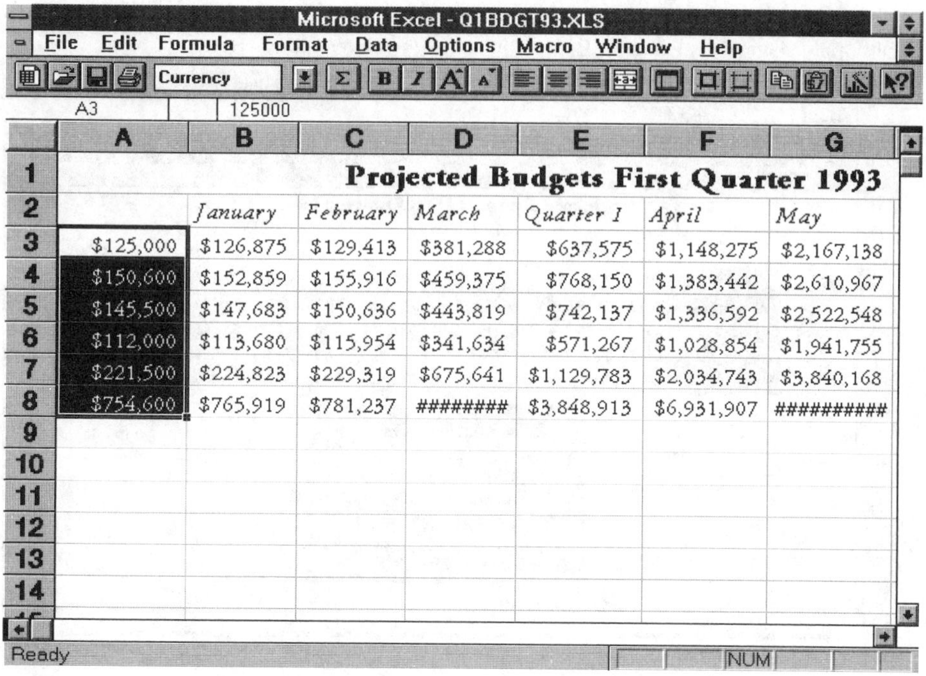

Figure 4.4 Worksheet After Deleting the Cell Range

Using the Clear Command

You use the Clear command on the Edit menu (or press the Delete key) to delete the contents of a cell selection without disturbing the structure of the worksheet. You can use the Clear command on cell ranges, ranges of columns or rows, or a nonadjacent selection of cells, columns, or rows. When you select the Clear command, Excel displays the dialog box shown in Figure 4.5.

To clear all entries in the current cell selection without removing the formatting or notes (for information on adding notes to cells, see Chapter 8) you've assigned to the cells, select the OK button or press Enter when the Formulas option button is selected. To delete the formatting from a selection but leave the entries and notes intact, select the Formats option button before selecting OK. To remove all notes that you've added to cells in the selection without removing them, select the Notes option button. To delete everything from the cells (entries, formatting, and notes) and make them completely empty once again, select the All option button.

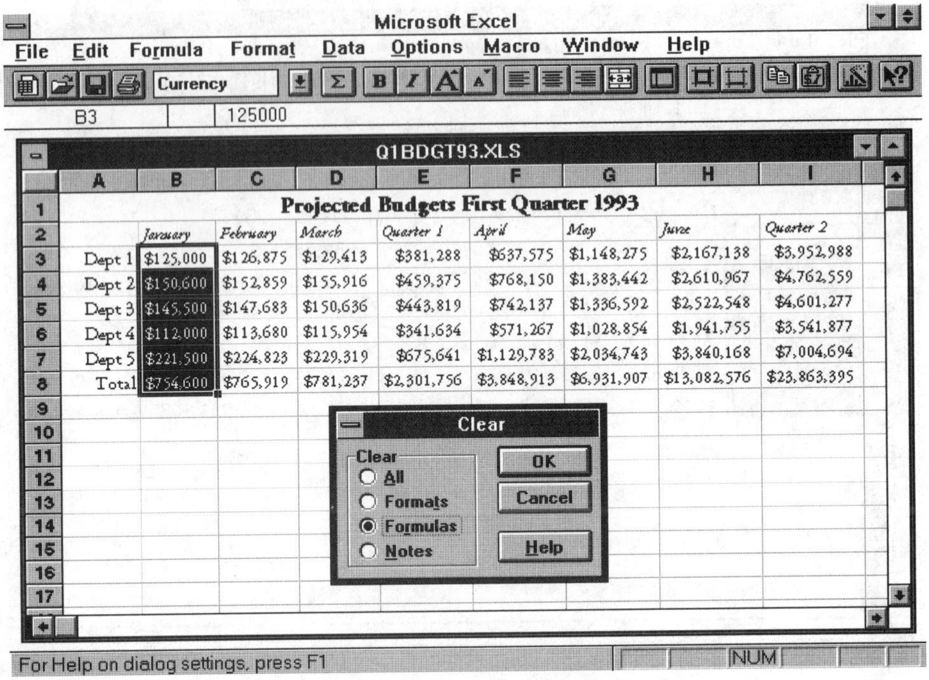

Figure 4.5   The Clear Dialog Box

Note: If you press the Backspace key instead of the Delete key, Excel deletes the contents of the active cell only (instead of displaying the Clear dialog box), while at the same time activating the formula bar. If you pressed this key by mistake, press the Esc key to return the cell entry to the active cell and deactivate the formula bar.

Using the Delete Command

You use the **D**elete command on the **E**dit menu to delete both the contents and the structure of a cell selection. Because Excel adjusts the structure of the worksheet when you use Delete, you cannot use this command on a discontinuous range of cells, columns, or rows. If you try to use the Delete command to remove a nonadjacent selection, Excel displays an alert box that says you can't use this command on a multiple selection.

If you choose the **D**elete option on the **E**dit menu when a single cell or cell range is selected, Excel displays a Delete dialog box similar to the one shown in Figure 4.6. If you've selected a cell range in a single column, the Shift Cells **L**eft option button will be selected. If you accept this option, Excel deletes the cells in the selected rows, while shifting to the left cells in the same rows in columns on the right. Figures 4.6 and 4.7 demonstrate how this works. In Figure 4.6 the cell range B4:B8 is selected before opening the Delete dialog box. In Figure 4.7 you see the result of deleting this cell range with the Shift Cells **L**eft option. As you can see, Excel shifts all the cells in the table one column to the left. The figures that were previously under the *May-93* column heading in column C have now moved left to column B, the figures that were under the *Jun-93* column heading have moved and are now under *May-93*, and so on to the right for each column of figures in rows 4 through 8.

If you've selected a single cell or a cell range that extends several columns before you open the Delete dialog box, the Shift Cells **U**p option button will be selected. If you use this option, Excel fills the gap made by the deletion by moving up cells from below.

If you would prefer to delete the entire row (or rows) in the current cell selection from the worksheet, select the Entire **R**ow option button in the Delete dialog box. To delete the entire column (or columns) in the current cell selection from the worksheet, select the Entire **C**olumn option button instead. Be very judicious in your use of the Entire **R**ow and Entire **C**olumn options. Bear in mind that they cut out entire rows (extending all the way from column A through column IV) and entire columns (extending all the way from row 1 through row 16384) and that *all* entries, not just the ones

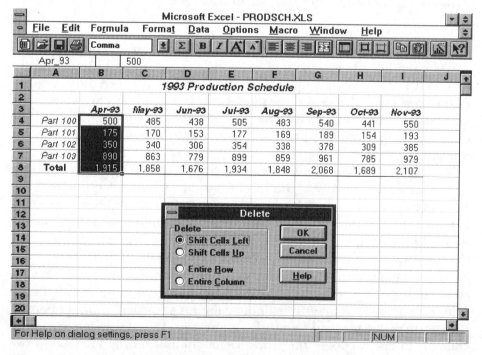

Figure 4.6 Deleting a Cell Range with the Shift Cells Left Option

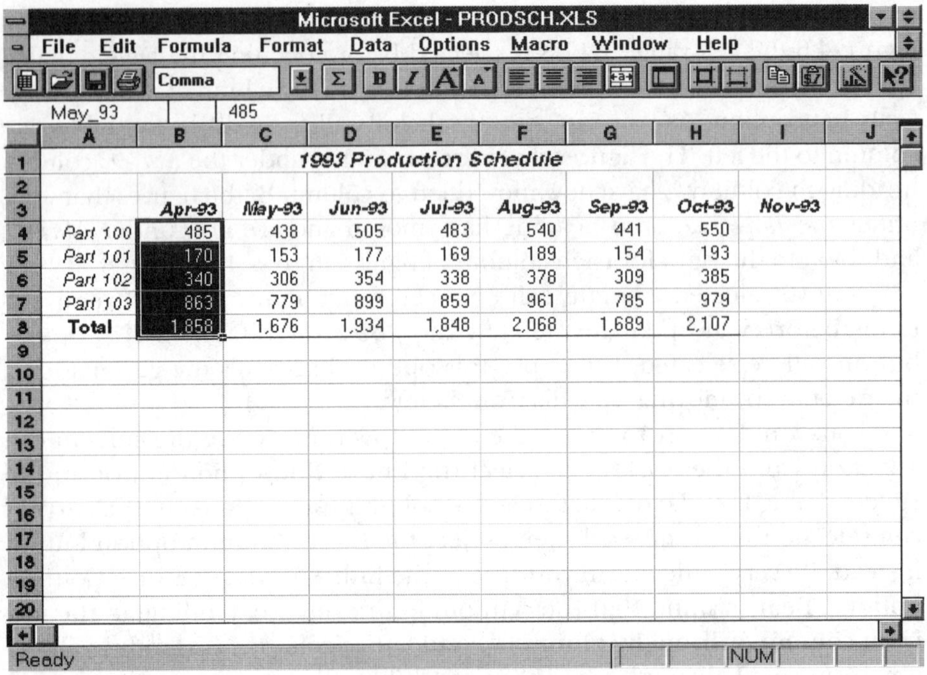

Figure 4.7   Worksheet After Deleting Cell Range B4:B8

you see on the screen, in the selected rows and columns will be erased.

When editing a worksheet that you didn't create, do not use the Entire **R**ow and Entire **C**olumn options in the Delete dialog box immediately. First review the entire worksheet to make sure that, in selecting them, you won't delete some vital data. To locate entries in columns to the right, use Ctrl+→ to jump from range to range. To locate entries in rows lower in the worksheet, use Ctrl+↑.

If you want to delete entire rows and columns from a worksheet (and you know that it's safe to do so), you can bypass the Delete dialog box entirely. To select a single row or column, simply click the row number or column letter to select the entire row or column and then choose the **D**elete option on the **E**dit command. To select a range of rows or columns, drag through the row number or column letters before choosing the Delete command.

When entire rows or columns are preselected and you choose the Delete command, Excel deletes the selected rows or columns and automatically shifts remaining rows up or remaining columns to the left without opening the Delete dialog box and requiring you to select OK. If you delete rows or columns in error, choose the **U**ndo Delete option on the **E**dit menu (or press Alt+BkSp or Ctrl+Z) to restore them.

Alert! When editing a worksheet with formulas that refer to individual cell references, take care that you don't inadvertently delete any of these cells. Doing so will cause Excel to recalculate those formulas and return #REF! error values. Note that if you use a built-in function in a formula and specify a cell range rather than a series of cell references as the function argument (see Chapter 5 for details), Excel does not return #REF! error values if you delete some of the cells in the range. Instead of an error value, the program simply adjusts the range address in the formula and recalculates the new result. For example, if you enter the formula =SUM(A6:A8) in cell A9 and then delete row 7 from the worksheet, Excel changes the formula to =SUM(A6:A7) and shifts it up to cell A8 where the recalculated result will appear. If you had entered either =SUM(A6,A7,A8) or =A6+A7+A8 in cell A9 instead, cell A8 would contain #REF! upon the deletion of row 7.

Inserting Cells, Columns, and Rows

In editing a worksheet, you will sometimes find that you need to insert new cells to accommodate new entries that you didn't anticipate when you created the worksheet. Excel's Insert command on the Edit menu makes it easy to add new cells to any part of a worksheet. You can use this command whenever you need to expand tables of data without having to be concerned about mistakenly replacing the existing cell entries.

As you would expect, the Insert dialog box (shown in Figure 4.8) contains options just opposite to those used by the Delete command. Whereas the Delete dialog box contains option buttons for shifting existing entries either up or to the left to fill in any potential gaps in the worksheet, the Insert dialog box contains option buttons for shifting existing entries down or to the right to accommodate the added cells.

Figure 4.8 shows a situation where you insert new cells with the Shift Cells Right option so that you can add quarterly totals to an existing table. Figure 4.9 shows you the worksheet after inserting the new cells in the range E3:E8 and shifting the columns from *Jul-93* through *Nov-93* to the right.

To insert a partial row or column, select the cell or cell range where you want new cells added, then choose the Insert command on the Edit menu. To add new cells to the current selection and shift existing cell entries to columns to the right, choose the Shift Cells Right option button in the Insert dialog box before you select OK. To shift the existing entries to rows below when the new cells are added, select the Shift Cells Down option button.

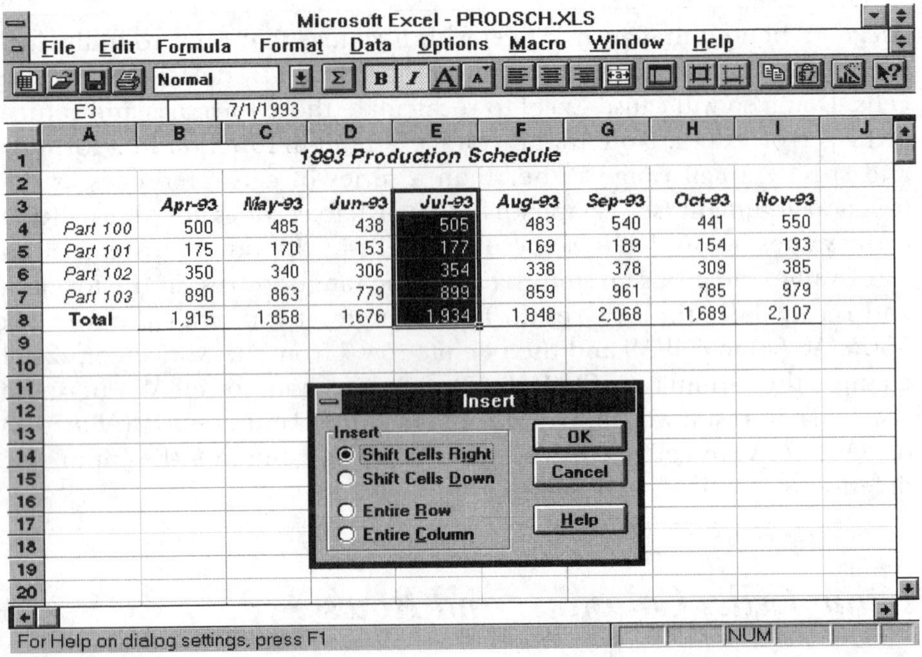

Figure 4.8   Inserting New Cells with the Shift Cells Right Option

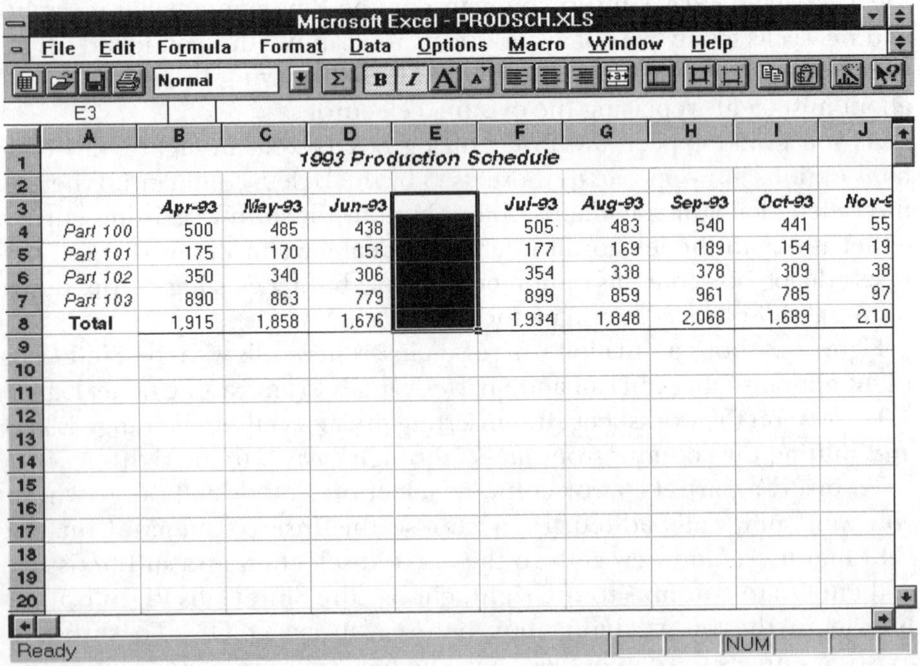

Figure 4.9   Worksheet After Inserting New Cells

To insert complete rows to the current cell selection (and shift existing entries in the rows down), choose the Entire **R**ow option button. To insert complete columns to the current cell selection (and shift existing entries in the columns to the right), choose the Entire **C**olumn option instead.

As with the Delete command, when inserting entire rows and columns, you can bypass the Insert dialog box by selecting the range of rows and columns before you choose the **I**nsert command on the **E**dit menu. Also, before adding new rows and columns into an unfamiliar worksheet, you should examine unseen regions to the right (Ctrl+→) and below (Ctrl+↑) to make sure that you won't be splitting up any existing tables of which you were unaware.

Note too that the Insert command works like the Delete command in that you cannot use it to insert new cells into a nonadjacent selection.

Moving and Copying Cells

Moving and copying are among the most common editing tasks that you will perform in worksheets. Excel 4.0 offers two basic methods for moving or copying a cell selection in a worksheet: You can use the new Drag and Drop feature to drag them to the new area, or you can cut or copy the contents of the cells to the Clipboard and then paste them into the desired area of the worksheet.

For situations where you need only to copy entries across or down cells in the worksheet, Excel offers you two more alternatives: You can select the cells to be copied and use the new AutoFill feature to extend the selection left or down by dragging the mouse, or you can select the range to fill (including the cells to be copied) and then choose either the Fill Ri**g**ht or Fill Do**w**n commands on the **E**dit menu.

Moving and copying data to new areas in a worksheet is basically a very straightforward procedure. There are, however, a few things you need to keep in mind when rearranging cell entries in a worksheet:

- When you move a cell, Excel moves everything in the cell, including the contents, its formatting, and any note assigned to the cell. (See Chapter 8 for information on adding notes to cells.) When you copy a cell, however, Excel copies only the contents and the formatting.

- If you move or copy a cell so that it overlays an existing entry, Excel replaces the existing entry with the contents and formatting of the cell you're moving or copying. This means that you can replace existing data in a range without having to clear the range before moving or copying the replacement entries. It also means that you must take care not to overlay any part of an existing range that you don't want replaced with the relocated or copied cell entries.

- When you move cells referred to in formulas in a worksheet, Excel automatically adjusts the cell references in the formulas to reflect their new locations.

- When you copy formulas that contain cell references, Excel automatically adjusts the cell references in the copies to reflect the change in position of the copied formulas. Excel creates "relative" cell references.

This last point warrants a closer look at how and why Excel normally adjusts cell references in copied formulas before we examine the various techniques for moving and copying data.

Copying Formulas in the Worksheet

After inputting the headings and initial values in a new table, you commonly build the first formula and then copy it to all the other cells that perform the same type of calculation. In fact, copying formulas in a worksheet is so common an activity that most people don't even give it a second thought.

If you completed the tutorial at the end of Chapter 2, you had a couple of opportunities to perform just this kind of thing when you created the worksheet with projected sales for the first quarter in 1993 (shown again in Figure 4.10). The first time occurred when you used the AutoSum tool in cell B9 to build the first formula for totaling the January sales and then used the AutoFill feature to copy this SUM formula to cells C9 through E9. The second opportunity occurred when you used the AutoSum tool in cell E4 to total the quarterly sales for the first store and then used the AutoFill feature to copy this SUM formula down the column to cells E5 through E8.

When you copied the first formula in cell B9 to cells C9 through E9, Excel automatically adjusted the cell references in range used in the SUM function in each copy you made. The program does this because the cell references in the range in the SUM function are *relative cell references*. All relative cell references are adjusted when you copy their formulas: The column letters in the cell references are adjusted when you copy left or right across the columns, and row numbers are adjusted when you copy up or down the rows. (Both column letters and row numbers are adjusted if you copy in two directions, for example, to the right and down.)

If you open this worksheet, you can see how this works for yourself.

1. Start Excel from the Program Manager, then choose the **O**pen option on the **F**ile menu or click the Open File tool (the second one from the left) on the Standard toolbar.

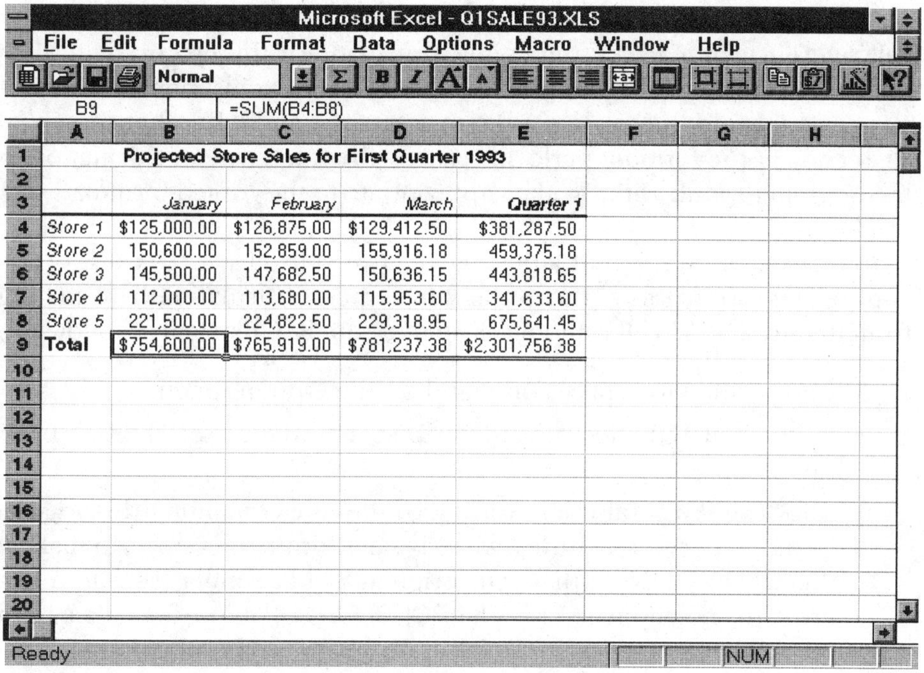

Figure 4.10   First Quarter 1993 Projected Sales Worksheet

2. Double-click the **examples** folder in the **D**irectories list box to open this directory, then double-click the **q1sale93.xls** file in the File **N**ame list box to open this worksheet.

3. When your worksheet opens, click cell B9 to make this cell active (the one with your first SUM formula to total January sales). Notice that the contents of this cell on the formula bar is =SUM(B4:B8).

4. Click cell C9 to make this cell active (the one with the first copy of the SUM formula to the right). Notice that the contents of this cell on the formula bar is =SUM(C4:C8). When Excel copied this formula to the column on the right, the program automatically adjusted the column reference in the range in the SUM function to match its new column (C).

5. Click cell E4 to make this cell active (the one with your original SUM formula to total the quarterly sales for the first store). Notice that the contents of this cell on the formula bar is =SUM(B4:D4).

6. Click cell E5 to make this cell active (the one with the first copy of this SUM formula down the rows). Notice that the contents of this cell on the formula bar is =SUM(B5:D5). When Excel copied this formula down the row, the program adjusted the row reference in the range in the SUM function to match its new row (5).

Although you can easily verify that Excel did indeed adjust the relative cell references in each of the copies you made of the two original SUM formulas, you may still wonder why these kinds of adjustments are necessary. By adjusting the relative references in a formula, Excel ensures that each copy of the formula performs exactly the same type of calculation as the original formula with the data appropriate to the copied formula's new cell location.

You can easily verify that adjusting relative cell references causes each copy of the formula to perform the same type of calculation by switching from the normal A1 cell reference system to the R1C1 system as follows:

1. Choose the **W**orkspace command on the **O**ptions menu.

2. Select the R1C1 check box under Display and then select OK or press Enter.

3. Click cell R4C5 (also known as E4), the one containing the original formula for summing the quarterly sales for the first store, to make it the active cell. Note that your original SUM formula (shown in Figure 4.10) now appears as **=SUM(RC[–3]:RC[–1])** on the formula bar. In the R1C1 system, this formula says "sum the cell range that extends from the cell that is three columns to the left of the current cell (–3) to the cell that is one column to the left of the current one (–1)."

4. Click cell R5C5 (E5), the cell containing the first copy of this formula to make this cell the active one. In the R1C1 notation system, you can verify that this copy of the original SUM formula is also **=SUM(RC[–3]:RC[–1])**, identical to the original formula in the cell above.

5. Click cell R9C2 (otherwise known as B9), the cell with the formula for summing January sales, to make this cell the active one. In R1C1 notation, this SUM formula now appears as **=SUM(R[–5] C:R[–1]C)** on the formula bar. This formula says "sum the cell range that extends from the cell five rows above the current cell (–5) down to the one that is one row up from the current cell (–1)."

6. Click cell R9C3 (C9) to make the cell containing the first copy of the formula the active one. This copy of the SUM formula also appears as **=SUM(R[–5]C:R[–1]C)**, on the formula bar.

7. Switch back to the standard A1 cell notation system by choosing the **W**orkspace command on the **O**ptions menu and then clicking the R1C1 check box to deselect it before you select OK or press Enter. The active cell address changes back to C9 and the formula on the formula bar appears as **=SUM(C4:C8)**.

In the R1C1 notation system, relative column and row cell references in formulas always are stated in terms of the number of cells from the active one, and these numbers appear in brackets after the R or C. The lack of any number after the R or C notation indicates no adjustment from the current row or column. Positive row numbers indicate the number of rows below the current row, while negative numbers indicate the number of rows above. Positive column numbers indicate the number of columns to the right of the current column, while negative numbers indicate the number of columns to the left.

USING ABSOLUTE AND MIXED CELLS REFERENCES

Most of the time, relative cell references are exactly what you need in the formulas you build, allowing Excel to adjust the row and/or column references as required in the copies you make. In some circumstances, however, Excel should not adjust one or more parts of the cell reference in the copied formula. This occurs, for example, whenever you want to use a value in a cell as a constant in all of the copies you make of a formula.

Figure 4.11 illustrates just such a situation. There you want to build a formula in cell B12 that calculates what percentage Store 1's January sales

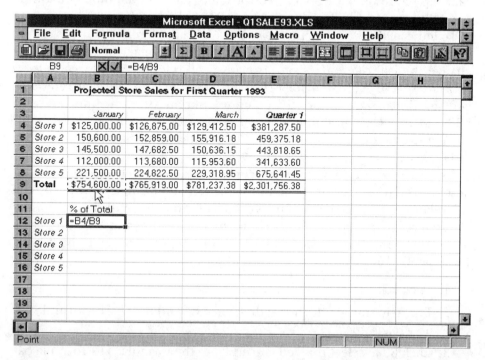

Figure 4.11   Building a Formula to Calculate the Percent of Total Monthly Sales

(cell B4) represents of the total January sales (cell B9). Normally, you would create this formula

    =B4/B9

with all relative cell references in cell B12. However, because you want to copy this formula down the column to the range B13:B16 to calculate the percentages for the other four stores (Store 2 through Store 5), you need to alter the relative cell references in the last part of the formula in cell B9 so that this cell reference with the January sales total remains unchanged in all your copies.

You can start to understand the problem caused by adjusting a relative cell reference that should remain unchanged by just thinking about copying the original formula from cell B12 down to B13 to calculate the percentage for Store 2. In this cell you want the formula to be

    =B5/B9

so that Excel divides the January sales for Store 2 in cell B5 by the January sales total in B9. However, if you don't indicate otherwise, Excel will adjust both parts of the formula in the copies so that B13 will incorrectly contain

    =B5/B10

which would result in the #DIV/0 error value caused by attempting to divide Store 2's January sales by the empty cell B10 (which carries a zero value).

To indicate that you don't want a particular cell reference (such as cell B9 in the example) to be adjusted in the copies that you make of a formula, you change the cell reference from a relative cell reference to an *absolute cell reference*. In the A1 system of cell references, an absolute cell reference contains dollar signs before the column letter and the row number, as in **$B$9**. In the R1C1 notation, you simply list the actual row and column number in the cell reference, as in **R9C2**, without placing these numbers in brackets.

If you realize that you need to convert a relative cell reference to an absolute reference as you're building the original formula, you can convert the relative reference to absolute by selecting the cell and then choosing the **R**eference option on the Formula menu (or pressing F4). To get an idea of how this works, follow along with the steps for creating the correct formula **=B4/$B$9** in B12:

1. Click cell B12 to make it active.

2. Type **=** to start the formula, then click B4 and type **/**. The formula bar now reads **=B4/**.

3. Click B9 to select this cell and add it to the formula. The formula bar now reads **=B4/B9**.

4. Choose **R**eference on the Formula menu (this option appears only when building a formula) or press F4. The formula bar now reads **=B4/$B$9**. When you choose the **R**eference command or press F4, Excel changes only the cell reference of the active cell.

Like it or not, you won't always anticipate the need for an absolute value until after you've built the formula and copied it to a range. Figure 4.12 shows just such a situation. There I created the formula **=B4/B9** in cell B12 and forgot to change the relative reference B9 to the absolute reference $B$9 before copying this formula down the column to the range B13:B16. As you can see, all of the results in the copies of this formula are incorrect and most return error values.

To remedy this problem, you have to edit the original formula in B12, change the relative reference B9 to absolute $B$9, and then make the copies again:

1. With cell B12 active, click the I-beam pointer somewhere in the cell reference B9 (before the B, between the B and 9, or after the 9) in the formula bar (or you can also press F2).

2. With the formula bar still active, choose the **R**eference option on the Formula menu or press F4. Excel changes **B9** to **$B$9** in the formula bar.

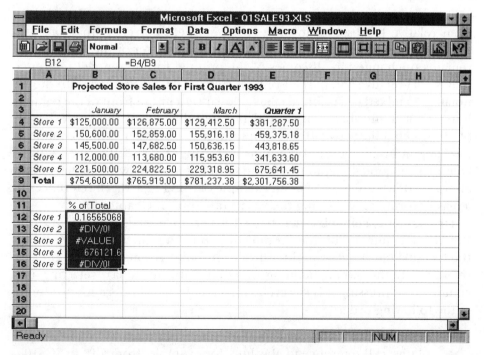

Figure 4.12 Worksheet with Errors in Copied Formulas

3. Press Enter to insert this edited formula into cell B12.

4. Recopy the edited formula in cell B12 to the cell range B13:B16. (You'll learn specifically how to do this in the sections ahead.)

Note that you can also type the dollar sign before the column letter and/or row in a cell reference when editing a formula on the formula bar, although using the Reference command or pressing the F4 key is considerably faster and easier.

Tip You can make an exact copy of a formula in another cell without using absolute references. To do this, make the cell with the formula you want to copy the active one, use the I-beam pointer to select the entire formula in the formula bar by dragging over it, and choose the **C**opy command on the **E**dit menu (or press Ctrl+Ins or Ctrl+C). Then click the cancel box to deactivate the formula bar, select the cell where you want the exact copy to appear, and choose the **P**aste command on the **E**dit menu (or press Shift+Ins or Ctrl+V). Excel pastes an exact duplicate of the original formula into the active cell without adjusting any of its cell references (even if they are all relative cell references).

Some formulas do not require you to change the entire cell reference from relative to absolute in order to copy them correctly. In some situations, you need only to indicate that the column letter or the row number remains unchanged in all copies of the original formula. A cell reference that is part relative and part absolute is called a *mixed cell reference.* In the A1 notation, a mixed cell reference has a dollar sign just in front of the column letter or row number that should not be adjusted in the copies, as in $C10, which adjusts row 10 in copies down the rows but leaves column C unchanged in all copies of columns to the right, or C$10, which adjusts column C in copies to columns to the right but leaves row 10 unchanged in all copies down the rows. (For an example of using mixed cell references in a master formula, see "Using the PMT Function" in Chapter 5.)

To change a cell reference from relative to mixed, you can use the **R**eference command on the Formula menu or the function key F4. When the formula bar is active and the insertion point is somewhere in the cell reference (either when building or editing the formula), selecting this command or pressing this key cycles through each cell reference possibility in the following order:

1. The first time you select the Reference command, Excel changes relative cell reference to absolute, for example, from C10 to $C$10.

2. The second time you select the Reference command, Excel changes the absolute reference to a mixed reference where the column is relative and the row is absolute, as in C$10.

3. The third time you select the Reference command, Excel changes the mixed reference where the column is relative and the row is absolute to a mixed reference where the row is relative and the column is absolute, as in $C10.

4. The fourth time you select the Reference command, Excel changes the mixed reference where the row is relative and the column is absolute back to a relative reference, as in C10.

If you bypass the type of cell reference you want to use, you can return to it by continuing to select the Reference command (pressing F4 is easier) to cycle through the variations again until you reach the one you need.

Tip You can use the Reference command or F4 key to change a relative reference to an absolute or mixed reference only when using the A1 notation system. This command won't work when you have switched Excel to the R1C1 notation system.

Moving and Copying with Drag and Drop

The Drag and Drop feature provides the newest and quickest way to move or copy a range of cells in the worksheet. To move a range, you simply select the cells, position the pointer on any one of the edges of the range, then drag the range to its new position in the worksheet and release the mouse button.

The only thing you need to be mindful of when using Drag and Drop is that you must position the pointer on one of the edges of the cell range *and* wait until the pointer changes shape from a white cross to an arrowhead pointing up toward the left before you begin dragging the range to its new position in the worksheet. Also, when positioning the pointer on an edge of the range, avoid the lower-right corner. Locating the pointer there transforms it into the fill handle (a black cross) used by the AutoFill feature to extend the cell range rather than move the range.

As you drag a cell range using the Drag and Drop feature, Excel displays only the outline of the range. When you have positioned the outline of the range so that it surrounds the appropriate cells in a new area of the worksheet, simply release the mouse button. Excel moves the selected cells (including the entries, formatting, and notes) to this area. Remember that if the outline of the range encloses any existing data, it will be replaced when you complete the move by releasing the mouse button.

Figures 4.13 through 4.15 illustrate how easy it is to move a cell range with the Drag and Drop feature. In Figure 4.13, I selected the cell range F2:I8 as the range to move and positioned the pointer on the lower edge of the selected cell range. Note that the pointer has now assumed the shape of an arrowhead, indicating that dragging will move the selected range. Figure 4.14 shows the new location of the cell range, right before releasing the mouse button to drop the range into this new location in the worksheet. Figure 4.15 shows the moment after releasing the mouse button, right after Excel has moved the selected cell to the chosen location.

You can use the Drag and Drop feature to copy cell ranges as well as move them. To modify Drag and Drop so that the feature copies the selected cells rather than relocating them, you must remember to hold down the Ctrl key when you position the pointer on one of the edges of the selected range (remember to avoid that lower-right corner!). Excel indicates that Drag and Drop will copy instead of move the range by changing the pointer from the white cross to an arrowhead with a small plus sign next to it. (Figure 4.16 shows you this pointer shape.) When the pointer assumes this shape, you simply drag the outline of the selected cell range to the desired position and release both the Ctrl key and the mouse button.

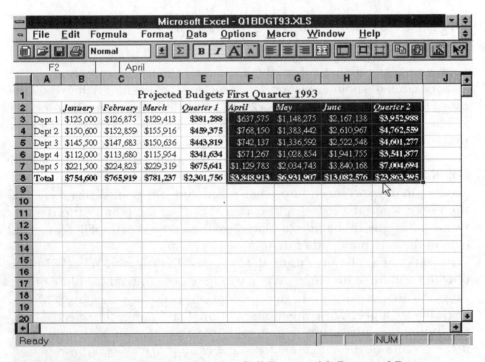

Figure 4.13 Getting Ready to Move a Cell Range with Drag and Drop

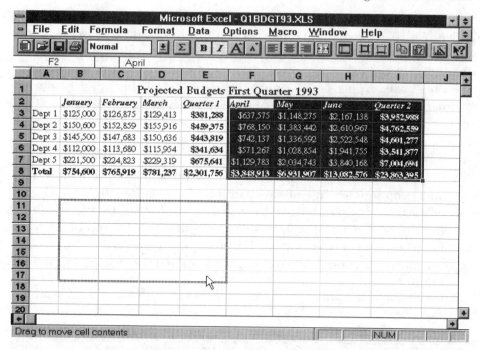

Figure 4.14   Selecting the New Cell Range Location with Drag and Drop

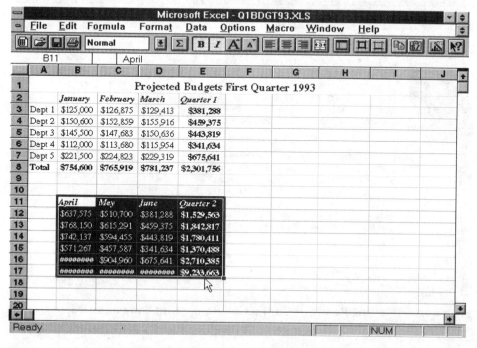

Figure 4.15   Worksheet After Moving a Cell Range with Drag and Drop

Figures 4.16 and 4.17 illustrate copying with the Drag and Drop feature. In Figure 4.16, I selected the cell range A3:A8 (to copy it down to the range A12:A17), then held down the Ctrl key and positioned the pointer on the right edge of the cell range. When the pointer assumed the shape of an arrowhead with a plus sign, I dragged the outline of this range so that it enclosed the cell range A12:A17. Figure 4.17 shows the worksheet after completing this copy operation by releasing the Ctrl key and the mouse button.

Tip To insert the worksheet data that you are moving or copying with Drag and Drop into a range of data and have Excel adjust the existing cell entries, rather than replace them, hold down the Shift key as you drag the arrowhead pointer. Instead of dragging the outline of the cell range, you will be dragging an I-beam shape that marks the place where the moved or copied data will be inserted when you release the mouse button.

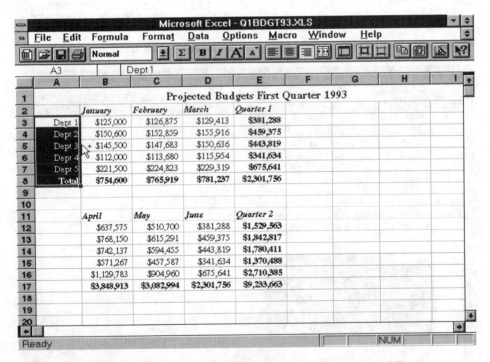

Figure 4.16   Getting Ready to Copy a Cell Range with Drag and Drop

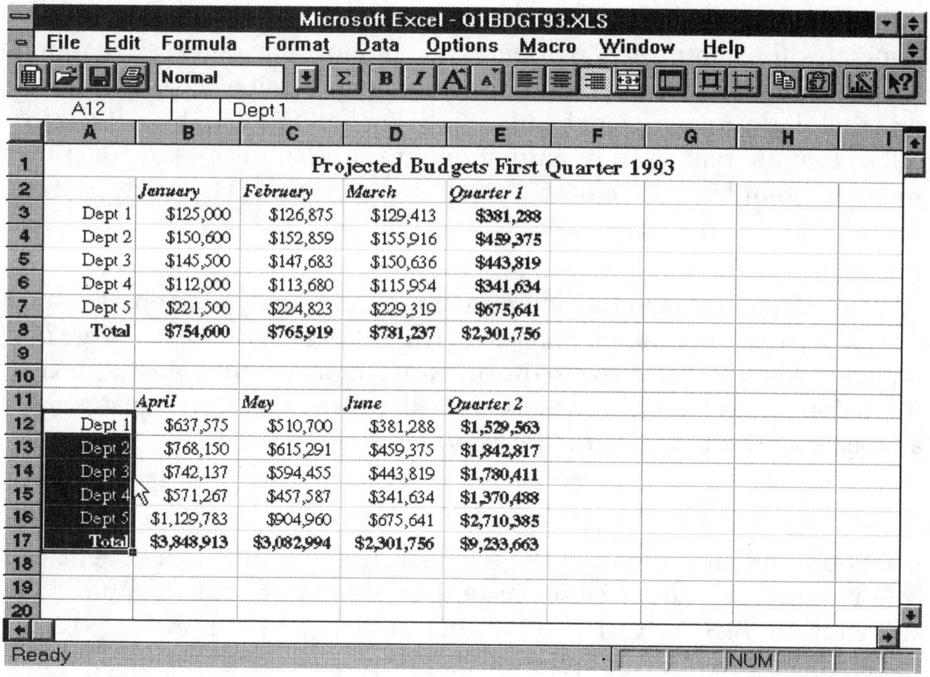

	A	B	C	D	E
1		Projected Budgets First Quarter 1993			
2		*January*	*February*	*March*	*Quarter 1*
3	Dept 1	$125,000	$126,875	$129,413	**$381,288**
4	Dept 2	$150,600	$152,859	$155,916	**$459,375**
5	Dept 3	$145,500	$147,683	$150,636	**$443,819**
6	Dept 4	$112,000	$113,680	$115,954	**$341,634**
7	Dept 5	$221,500	$224,823	$229,319	**$675,641**
8	**Total**	**$754,600**	**$765,919**	**$781,237**	**$2,301,756**
9					
10					
11		*April*	*May*	*June*	*Quarter 2*
12	Dept 1	$637,575	$510,700	$381,288	**$1,529,563**
13	Dept 2	$768,150	$615,291	$459,375	**$1,842,817**
14	Dept 3	$742,137	$594,455	$443,819	**$1,780,411**
15	Dept 4	$571,267	$457,587	$341,634	**$1,370,488**
16	Dept 5	$1,129,783	$904,960	$675,641	**$2,710,385**
17	**Total**	**$3,848,913**	**$3,082,994**	**$2,301,756**	**$9,233,663**

Figure 4.17 Worksheet After Copying a Cell Range with Drag and Drop

Moving and Copying Data with the Clipboard

Even now that Drag and Drop is available, you may still prefer to use the more traditional Cut and Paste feature when moving or copying cells in a worksheet. Cut and Paste uses the Clipboard (a special area of memory shared by all Windows programs), which provides a temporary storage area for the data in your cell selection until you paste the selection into its new position in the worksheet.

You select the cells and then choose the Cu**t** command on the **E**dit menu (or the shortcuts Shift+Del or Ctrl+X) when you want to move a cell selection to a new place in the worksheet with the Clipboard. You choose the **C**opy command on the **E**dit menu (or the shortcuts Ctrl+Ins or Ctrl+C) when you want to copy the cell selection instead. In either case, Excel displays a marquee around the cell selection and the message

Select destination and press ENTER or choose Paste

appears on the status bar. To complete the move or copy operation, you simply select the cell where you want the first cell of the relocated or copied selection to appear and press the Enter key or choose the **P**aste command on the **E**dit menu (or the shortcuts Shift+Ins or Ctrl+V).

When you choose the Paste command or press the Enter key, Excel completes the move or copy operation, pasting the range as required, starting with the active cell. When selecting the first cell of a paste range, be sure that there are sufficient blank cells below and to the right of the active cell so that the range you're pasting doesn't overlay any existing data that you don't want Excel to replace.

Alert! In Excel you don't have to select the entire paste range before you select the Paste command to complete a move or copy operation. If you do select the paste range rather than just its first cell, you must select a range that is identical in size and shape to the one you cut or copied to the Clipboard. If you don't, Excel displays an alert box with the message Cut and paste areas are different shapes, and you will have to reselect the paste range.

If you find that you moved the selection to the wrong area or replaced cells in error, choose the **U**ndo Paste command on the **E**dit menu (or the shortcuts Alt+BkSp or Ctrl+Z) to restore the range to its previous position in the worksheet. (The marquee will reappear around the cell range so that you can still move it after you designate a new paste area.)

When you complete a Copy and Paste operation by choosing the Paste command (as opposed to pressing the Enter key), Excel copies the selected cell range to the paste area in the worksheet without removing the marquee from the original range. This allows you to continue to paste the selection to other areas in the worksheet without having to recopy the cell range to the Clipboard. If you don't need to paste the cell range elsewhere on the worksheet, you can press Enter to complete the copy operation. If you don't need to make further copies but you choose the Paste command, you can remove the marquee from the original selection simply by pressing the Esc key.

Of course, if you ever discover that you've copied the range in error after selecting the Paste command, you can restore the worksheet to its previous state with the Undo command.

Note: As soon as you complete a Cut and Paste or Copy and Paste operation, Excel clears the Clipboard of all worksheet data. Up to that time, you can examine the contents of the Clipboard and even paste your worksheet data into other programs. See Chapter 21 for information on examining the contents of the Clipboard and pasting it into other applications.

USING THE INSERT PASTE COMMAND

When you use the Cut and Paste method to move or copy worksheet data via the Clipboard, you can have Excel paste the data into a new area of the worksheet without replacing existing data by choosing the Insert Paste command on the **E**dit menu instead of the **P**aste command (or pressing Enter).

When you select the **I**nsert Paste command after selecting the first cell of the paste range, Excel displays the Insert Paste dialog box (shown in Figure 4.18). This dialog box contains two option buttons: Shift Cells **R**ight and Shift Cells **D**own. To have Excel paste the selection in the designated paste area and move existing cells to columns to the right, select the Shift Cells **R**ight before you choose OK or press Enter. To have the program paste the selection and move existing cells to rows below, select the Shift Cells **D**own option instead.

In Figures 4.18 and 4.19, you can see how the Insert Paste command works. In Figure 4.18 I selected the range B10:B15 and copied it into the Clipboard with the Cut command on the **E**dit menu, then I selected cell E3 (the first cell of the paste range) and chose the **I**nsert Paste command on the **E**dit menu. Figure 4.19 shows you the result of completing this move using the Shift Cells **R**ight option. There you can see how Excel shifted the existing cells to the right when moving the Q1 totals to the paste range.

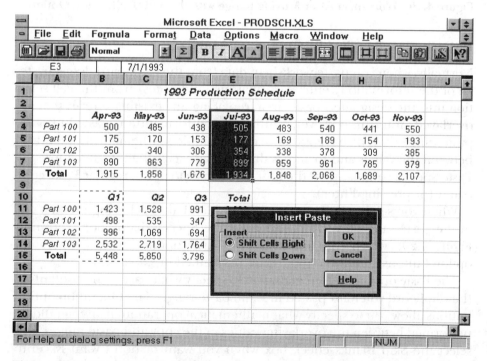

Figure 4.18 Moving a Range with the Insert Paste Command

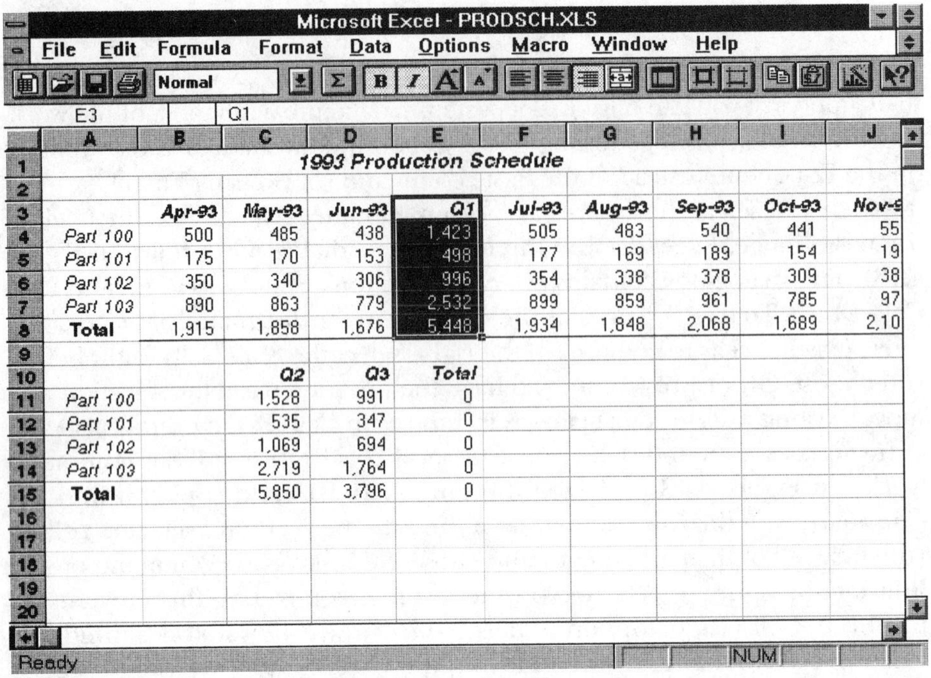

Figure 4.19   Worksheet After Moving Range with the Shift Cells Right Option

USING THE PASTE SPECIAL COMMAND

Normally, when you paste worksheet data from the Clipboard, Excel pastes all of the information (entries, formatting, and notes) from the cell selection into the designated paste area, replacing any existing entries that are overlayed. You can, however, control what information is pasted into the paste range and/or have Excel perform simple mathematical operations between the values and formulas that overlay each other, if you choose the Paste Special command on the Edit menu instead of the regular Paste command (or pressing Enter).

When you select the Paste Special command after selecting the first cell of the paste range, Excel displays the Paste Special dialog box (shown in Figure 4.20), which contains a series of Paste option buttons, Operation option buttons, and two check boxes (explained in Table 4.1).

The Paste option buttons allow you to specify what part of the contents of the Clipboard you want pasted into the paste range. The Operation option buttons allow you to specify what mathematical operation, if any, should be performed between the overlaying values in the copy and paste ranges. You select the Skip **B**lanks check box when you want or don't want Excel to replace existing entries in the paste range with overlaying blank cells in the

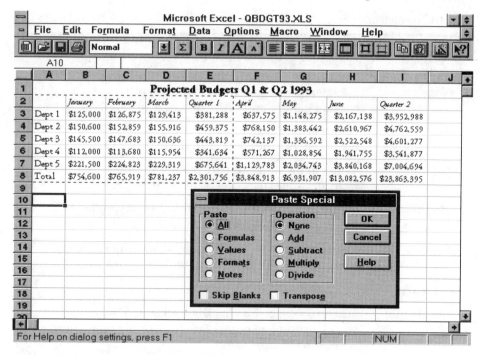

Figure 4.20   The Insert Paste Dialog Box

Table 4.1   The Paste Special Options

Option	Function
Paste Option Buttons	
All	Pastes all types of entries (numeric values, formulas, and text), their formats, and notes from the selection in the paste area.
Formulas	Pastes only the entries (numerical values, formulas, and text) from the selection in the paste area.
Values	Pastes only numerical values and text from the selection in the paste area. *Converts any formulas to their current values before pasting them as numerical values into the worksheet.*
Formats	Pastes only the formats from the selection in the paste area.
Notes	Pastes only the notes from the selection in the paste area.

Table 4.1 *(continued)*

Operation Option Buttons	
None	Values in the range you are pasting replace any existing values they overlay in the paste range.
Add	Values in the range you are pasting are added to any existing values they overlay in the paste range.
Subtract	Values in the range you are pasting are subtracted from any values they overlay in the paste range.
Multiply	Values in the range you are pasting are multiplied to any existing values they overlay in the paste range.
Divide	Values in the range you are pasting are divided by any existing values they overlay in the paste range.
Check Boxes	
Skip Blanks	When you select this check box, blanks in the range you are pasting do not replace the existing values they overlay in the paste range.
Transpose	When you select this check box, Excel inverts the range you are pasting in the worksheet so the top row of the relocated or copied range appears down the left column in the paste range and entries in the left column of the relocated or copied range appear in the top row of the paste range.

copy range. You select the Transpose check box when you want to invert the copy range so that its orientation is reversed in the paste range, as shown in Figure 4.21.

You can select two of the Paste Special options, **V**alues and Formats, directly from the Standard or Utility toolbar. Both of these toolbars have a Copy tool and a Paste Formats tool. In addition, the Utility toolbar also has a Paste Values tools.

You can click the Copy tool to copy the contents of the current cell selection to the Clipboard. Then click the Paste Formats tool when you want to paste only the formatting from the Clipboard into the paste range. To paste only the values into the paste range, you hold down the Shift key as you click the Paste Formats tool on the Standard toolbar (it then changes to the Paste Values tool), or you can click the Paste Values tool if the Utility is displayed.

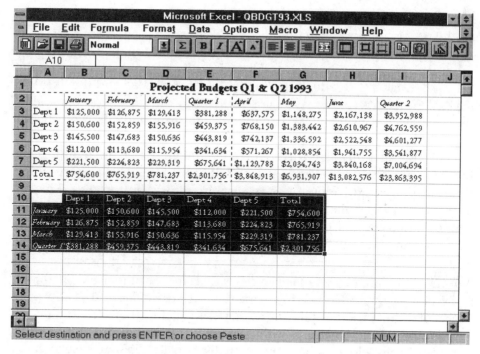

Figure 4.21   Transposing the Copied Range in a Worksheet

Tip   To replace a range of formulas in a worksheet to their currently calculated values, select the cell range with the formulas, click the Copy tool, then hold down the Shift key and click the Paste Formats tool on the Standard toolbar or the Paste Values tool on the Utility toolbar. Excel then replaces the formulas with their calculated values and you can press Esc to remove the marquee from the selected cell range. To replace a single formula with its calculated value, make the cell active, then press F2 to activate the formula bar, F9 to calculate the formula and return the current value, and Enter to replace the formula with the calculated value in the current cell.

Copying with AutoFill

Earlier in the chapter we examined how Excel adjusts the cell references in the copies you make of the formulas in the worksheet. In that discussion I pointed out that it is quite common to build a master formula at the beginning of a row or at the top of a column in a table of data and then copy that formula to the other cells in the table that perform the same type of calculation. Technically, such copies are known as *one-to-*

many copies because you are copying the contents of a single cell range to all the other cells in a selection.

In Chapter 2 you were introduced to Excel's new AutoFill feature. There you learned that you can use AutoFill to create a series of entries such as the Quarter 1, Quarter 2, Quarter 3, and so on, or Jan, Feb, Mar, and the like. You may also remember, however, using AutoFill in the tutorial at the end of that chapter to copy the SUM formulas in your projected sales worksheet.

You can use the AutoFill feature to make one-to-many copies of a formula by selecting the formula, then dragging the fill handle (the black cross in the lower-right corner of the cell) to extend the cell range down or to the right. When you release the mouse button, Excel makes copies of that formula to each cell that you selected with the fill handle. The program naturally adjusts all relative cell references in the master formula and leaves all absolute cell references unchanged.

Note: Remember, if you select a cell with a label or numeric value that Excel recognizes as belonging to a series, such as Product 1, 01/11/93, or Saturday, the program fills out the series in each cell of the extended range. If you select a cell with a label or value that Excel doesn't recognize as belonging to a series, such as Total, 1,500, or Assets, the program copies the entry in each cell of the extended range. Only when the active cell contains a formula does Excel copy that formula to each cell of the extended range.

Copying with Fill Right and Fill Down

Before the advent of the AutoFill feature in Excel 4.0, you had to use the Fill Right or Fill Down commands on the **E**dit menu to make one-to-many copies in a worksheet. You can still use these commands to copy a label, value, or formula to a selected range. To copy an entry across a row, you make its cell the active one, then extend the range to the right. When you've selected all the cells where you want to make copies, you choose the Fill Right command on the **E**dit menu or press Ctrl+R. To copy an entry down a column, you make its cell the active one, then extend the range down. When you've selected all the cells where you want to make copies, you choose the Fill Down command on the **E**dit menu or press Ctrl+D.

Locating and Replacing Data in the Worksheet

No discussion of editing the worksheet would be complete without including the Find and Replace features in Excel. You can use the Find feature to quickly locate each and every occurrence of a specific *string* (a series of characters) in a worksheet. For example, suppose that your normal discount rate is 18 percent but you know that your worksheet contains a few formulas that use a discount rate of 20 percent. Now, in looking over the data, you can't immediately tell which cells in the Discount Rate column use the normal 18 percent rate and which use the irregular 20 percent. You can use the Find command to locate those cells for you immediately by searching the table for the string 20%, as shown in Figures 4.22 and 4.23.

You can use the Replace feature to update a worksheet. Again, referring to the discount example, suppose that you need to increase your normal discount rate from 18 percent to 20 percent. Instead of painstakingly editing each formula that uses the 18 percent value, you would use the Replace feature to update the table automatically by searching its formulas for the string 18% and then replacing each occurrence of this value with 20%, as shown in Figure 4.24.

USING THE FIND COMMAND

To use the Find command to locate information in your worksheet, follow these steps:

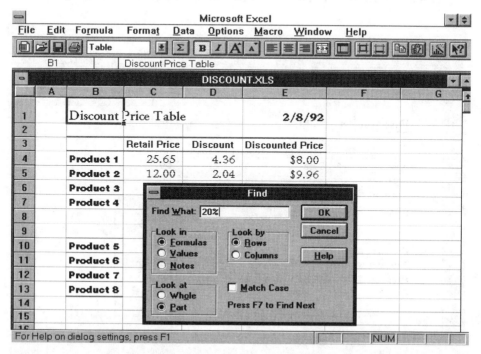

Figure 4.22   Using the Find Command to Locate Formulas with a 20% Discount Rate

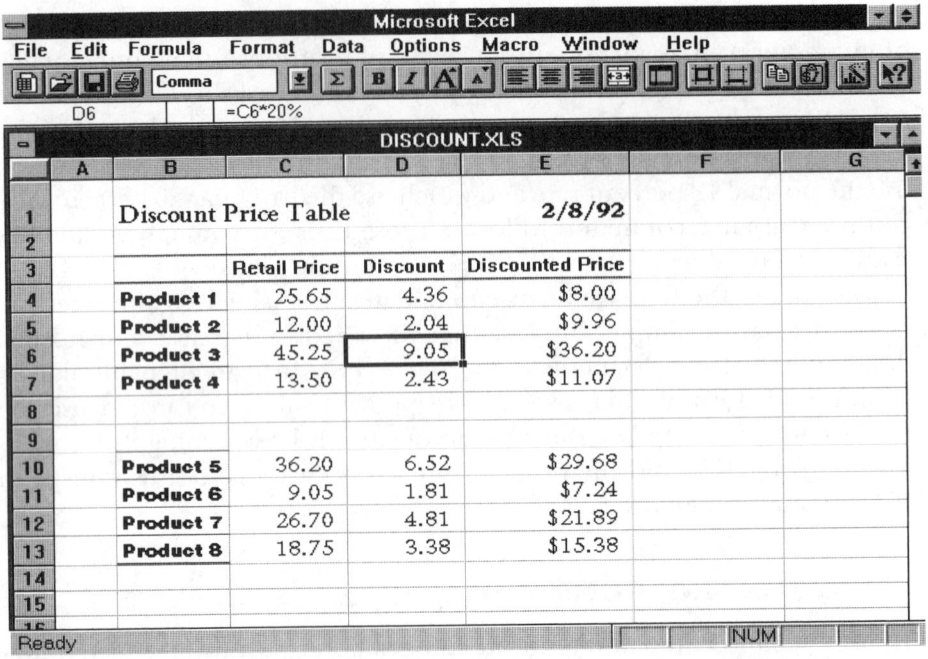

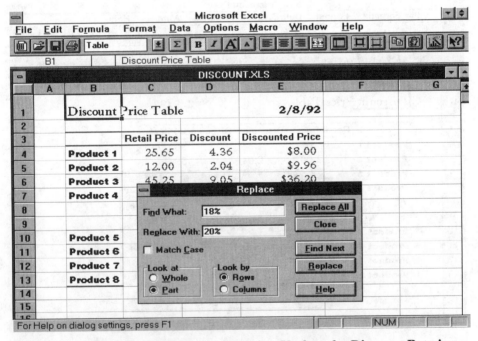

Figure 4.23   Locating the First Formula with a 20% Discount Rate

Figure 4.24   Using the Replace Command to Update the Discount Rate in Formulas from 18% to 20%

1. To search the entire worksheet, select a single cell. To restrict the search to a specific cell range or nonadjacent selection, select all the cells to be searched.

2. Choose the **Find** command on the Formula menu or press Shift+F5. Excel displays the Find dialog box similar to the one shown in Figure 4.22.

3. Type the search string you want to locate in the Find **What** text box. When entering the search string, you can use the question mark (?) or asterisk (*) wildcards to stand in for any characters you're unsure of. Use the question mark to stand for a single character, as in **Sm?th**, which will match either *Smith* or *Smyth.* Use the asterisk to stand for multiple characters, as in **9*1**, which will locate *91, 94901,* or even *9553 1st Street.* To search for a wildcard character, precede the character with a tilde (~), as in **~*2.5** to locate formulas that multiply by the constant *2.5.*

4. By default, Excel will use the **Formulas** option in the Look in box to locate the search string in the contents of each cell as entered on the formula bar. To have Excel locate the search string in the contents of each cell as displayed in the worksheet, choose the **Values** option button. To have Excel locate the search string in the notes you've added to cells, choose the **Notes** option.

5. By default, Excel uses the **Rows** option in the Look by box to search across the rows in the worksheet or current selection (that is, to the right and then down from the active cell). To have Excel search down the columns (that is, down and then to the right from the active cell), choose the **Columns** option button instead.

6. By default, Excel uses the **Part** option in the Look at box, meaning that the program considers any occurrence of the search string even when it is a part of another string to be a match. Thus when the search string is **25**, cells containing *25, 15.25, 25 Main Street,* and *250,000* are all considered matches. To restrict the search to whole-word occurrences, choose the **Whole** option button, in which case, only the cell containing *25* would match the search string **25**.

7. By default, Excel ignores case differences between the search string and the contents of the cells being searched so that *Assets, ASSETS,* and *assets* all match the search string **Assets**. To restrict the search to exact case matches, select the **Match Case** check box, in which case only the cell containing *Assets* would match the search string **Assets**.

8. After you've entered the search string and changed all the search options you want, select the OK button or press Enter to begin the search and

locate the first occurrence of the search string in the worksheet or the current cell selection. Excel closes the Find dialog box and locates the first match to your search string in the specified search direction by making that cell the active one. If no cell in the worksheet or selected range matches your search string, Excel displays an alert box with the message **No match** instead.

Excel retains your search string and search conditions even after closing the Find dialog box. To repeat the search and locate a subsequent occurrence in the worksheet or cell selection without reopening the Find dialog box, you press F7. To repeat the search and locate a previous occurrence, you press Shift+F7.

USING THE REPLACE COMMAND

The Find command is sufficient if all you want to do is locate an occurrence of a search string in your worksheet. Many times, however, you will also want to change some or all of the cells that match the search string. For those situations, you use the Replace command to locate the search string and replace it with some other string.

To search and replace information in your worksheet, follow these steps:

1. To search and replace the entire worksheet, select a single cell. To restrict the search and replace the operation to a specific cell range or nonadjacent selection, select all the cells to be edited.

2. Choose the Replace command on the Formula menu. Excel displays the Replace dialog box similar to the one shown in Figure 4.24.

3. Type the search string you want to locate in the Find What text box. When entering the search string, you can use the question mark (?) or asterisk (*) wildcard in the search string just as you do in the Search dialog box.

4. Type the replacement string in the Replace With text box. Enter this string *exactly* as you want it to appear in the cells of the worksheet. Use uppercase letters where uppercase is to appear, lowercase letters where lowercase is to appear, and the question mark and asterisk only where they are to appear. (They don't act as wildcard characters in a replacement string.)

5. Make any necessary changes to the Look at, Look by, and Match Case options for the search string. (These work just as they do in the Search dialog box.)

6. To search and replace on a case-by-case basis (the safest way to use

the Replace command), choose the Find Next command button. Then, when Excel locates the first occurrence of the search string, choose the **R**eplace command button to replace it. To skip the occurrence without replacing it and find the next occurrence, choose the Find Next button again. To replace globally all matches to the search string in the worksheet or cell selection, choose the Replace **A**ll command button or press Enter.

7. When you're finished replacing entries on a case-by-case basis, click the Close button or press Esc to abandon the search and replace the operation and close the Replace dialog box (when you globally replace the search string, Excel automatically closes the Replace dialog box after replacing the last search string match).

Spell Checking the Data

In previous versions of Excel, you had to edit spelling errors manually in the worksheet or use the Replace command to find and correct them. Of course, this required you to identify all spelling errors in your worksheet and know what corrections needed to be made. Excel 4.0 has added a new Spelling command that takes this kind of guesswork out of spell checking your worksheet. You can use the **S**pelling command on the **O**ptions menu to check the spelling of selected text on the formula bar, selected cell entries, or the entire worksheet.

In checking the spelling, Excel looks up each word in the Excel Dictionary. If the word is not found there (as is often the case with less-common last names, abbreviations, acronyms, and technical terms), the program displays a Spelling dialog box similar to the one shown in Figure 4.25. You can then choose to add the unknown word to a custom dictionary with the **A**dd button so that Excel will know the word the next time you spell check the worksheet, ignore the word this one time only and continue spell checking with the **I**gnore button, or ignore all occurrences of the unknown word in the worksheet or cell selection and continue spell checking with the Ignore All button.

As long as the **A**lways Suggest check box is selected in the Spelling dialog box, Excel attempts to suggest the correct spelling in the Change **T**o text box and displays other possible spellings in the Suggestio**n**s list box. To replace the unknown word listed after Not in Dictionary with the word displayed in the Change **T**o text box, choose the **C**hange command button. To replace this and all subsequent occurrences of the unknown word, choose the Change All button instead.

If the word in the Change **T**o text box is not correct and you know how the word should be spelled, you can type in the replacement in the Change

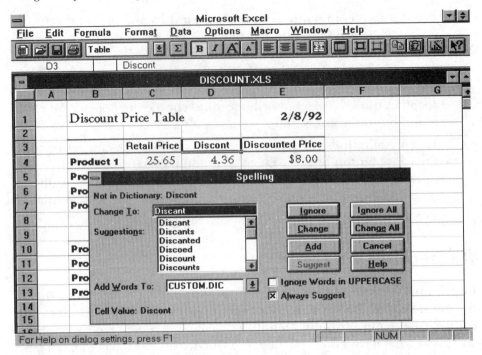

Figure 4.25   The Spelling Dialog Box

To text box or enter the word there by selecting it in the Suggestions list box. After entering the correct spelling in the Change **T**o text box, you can have Excel replace the unknown word in the active cell with it by choosing the **C**hange or Change **A**ll command button.

Tip   To have Excel ignore acronyms in your worksheet, select the Ignore Words in UPPERCASE check box when the program opens the Spelling dialog box to suggest a replacement for the first acronym it locates in the worksheet or cell selection.

Excel spell checks the entire worksheet when only a single cell is active at the time you choose the **S**pelling command on the **O**ptions menu. To spell check a portion of the worksheet, select the range or nonadjacent cell selection before you choose the Spelling command. To spell check just the entry in the active cell, activate the formula bar and then choose the Spelling command.

When Excel finishes checking the worksheet, cell selection, or contents of the formula bar, the program displays an alert box that indicates that the spell checking has been completed.

CREATING A NEW CUSTOM DICTIONARY

You can use the **A**dd command button in the Spelling dialog box to add unknown words to a custom dictionary. By default, Excel adds words to a custom dictionary file named **cust.dic**. This file is located in the **\msapps\proof** subdirectory of your **windows** directory. If you want you can create other custom dictionaries to use when spell checking your worksheets (although you can use only one custom dictionary at a time). To create a new custom dictionary, follow these steps:

1. Choose the **S**pelling command on the **O**ptions menu.

2. When Excel locates an unknown word that you want to add to a new custom dictionary, select **CUSTOM.DIC** in the Add **W**ords To drop-down list box and edit this filename or replace it entirely with a filename of your own (retaining the **DIC** extension).

3. After changing the dictionary filename in the Add **W**ords To drop-down list box, select the **A**dd command button. Excel displays an alert box indicating that the dictionary you designated does not yet exist and asks if you want to create it.

4. Select the **Y**es command button in the alert box to create the new custom dictionary. Excel adds the unknown word to your new dictionary and its filename is displayed as the current dictionary in the Add **W**ords To drop-down list box. To change back to the **CUSTOM.DIC** or any other custom dictionary that you've created, select the dictionary in the Add **W**ords To drop-down list box.

Alert! When you add a word to a custom dictionary, Excel adds it exactly as it appears after Not in Dictionary in the Spelling dialog box. If the word is entered in all lowercase letters, Excel recognizes it in subsequent spell checks no matter what case is used. If the word is capitalized or uses all uppercase letters, Excel does not recognize the word when it appears in the worksheet in all lowercase letters.

SUMMARY

In this chapter you learned how to perform a wide variety of common worksheet editing tasks. These tasks included how to recover from errors with the Undo function; repeat a task with the Repeat command; insert and delete cells, columns, and rows in a worksheet; copy formulas using relative and absolute references; as well as how to copy and move, find and replace, and spell check data in a worksheet.

In the chapter ahead you will learn more about performing calculations with Excel. There you will learn how to use the built-in functions, how to name ranges and use range names in formulas, how to build array formulas, how to protect your worksheets, and how to maintain control when formulas are recalculated.

5

Calculating the Worksheet

In Chapter 2 you were first introduced to building and using simple formulas in your worksheet. In this chapter you will learn about building more complex formulas and calculating the worksheet. Specifically, you will learn how to name cell ranges and use range names in formulas, build array formulas, use Excel's worksheet functions in formulas, control when the worksheet is recalculated, and protect your worksheet to prevent any further changes to your formulas.

Of the topics related to calculating worksheets, the subject of worksheet functions is without a doubt the most extensive. As you will soon learn, Excel offers literally hundreds of specialized functions that make it easy to perform all types of complex calculations. Excel's worksheet functions fall into categories as diverse as financial, statistical, mathematical and trigonometric, and lookup and reference, to name a few. (See Appendix B for a complete function reference.) You will also find that if Excel does not include a built-in worksheet function for the specialized calculations that you want to perform, you can create your own custom functions. (See Chapter 20 for information on creating custom functions.)

Naming Ranges

Thus far, all the formulas we've examined have used a combination of numerical constants and cell references (both relative and absolute and using the A1 and R1C1 notation). While cell references provide a convenient method for pointing out the cell location in the worksheet grid, they are not at all descriptive of their function when used in formulas. Fortunately,

179

Excel makes it easy to assign descriptive names to the cells, cell ranges, constants, and even formulas that make their function in the worksheet much more understandable.

To get an idea of how names can help document the purpose of a formula, contrast this formula for computing the sale price of an item that uses standard cell references

   =B4*$B$2

with the following one that performs the same calculation but also uses range names

   =Retail_Price*Discount_Rate

Obviously, the function of the second formula is much more comprehensible, not only to you as the worksheet creator but also to anyone else who has to use it.

Range names are not only extremely useful for documenting the function of the formulas in your worksheet but also enable you to find and select cell ranges quickly and easily. This is especially helpful in a large worksheet that you aren't very familiar with or use intermittently. Once you assign a name to a cell range, you can locate and select all the cells in that range with the Goto dialog box. Simply choose the **G**oto command on the Formula menu (or press F5) and then double-click the range name in the Goto list box or click and select OK. Excel then selects an entire range and, if necessary, shifts the worksheet display so that you can see the first cell in that range on the screen.

Defining a Range Name

To name a cell, cell range, or nonadjacent selection, mark the cell selection and then choose the **D**efine Name command on the Formula menu. When you select this command, Excel displays the Define Name dialog box similar to the one shown in Figure 5.1. If Excel can identify a label in the cell immediately above or to the left of the active one, the program inserts this label as the suggested name in the **N**ame text box. The program also displays the cell reference of the active cell or the range address of the range or nonadjacent selection that is currently marked (using absolute references) in the **R**efers to text box below.

To accept the suggested name and assign it to the cell references displayed in the Define Name dialog box, select the OK button or press Enter. If Excel is unable to suggest a name or you don't want to use the suggested name, type a new range name in the **N**ame text. (It is automatically selected when you open the Define Name dialog box.) If you need to, you can also

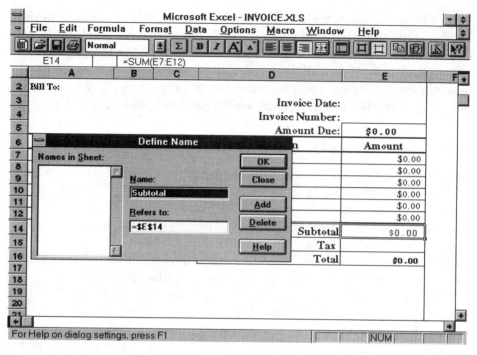

Figure 5.1 The Define Name Dialog Box

modify the cell references in the **R**efers to text box by selecting this box and editing the cell addresses. When editing the contents of the **R**efers to text box, be very careful not to delete the equal sign (=) at the beginning of the box. If you do, you must retype this sign before you click the OK button or press Enter.

When entering a range name in the **N**ame text box, you need to keep in mind certain naming restrictions:

- You must begin the name with a letter of the alphabet rather than a number or punctuation mark.

- You must not use spaces in the name—in place of spaces, use an underscore between words in a range name, as in *Qtr_1.*

- The name must not duplicate a cell reference using either the A1 or R1C1 notation system.

- The name must be unique in the worksheet.

If you choose the OK command button or press OK after verifying or editing the range name or cell address, Excel assigns the range name and then closes the Define Name dialog box. If you want to define other range names before closing the dialog box, select the **Add** command button instead. This adds your first name to the **Name** text box and allows you to define another by typing in the new range name in the **Name** text box, then select the **R**efers to text box and designate the new cell, cell range, or nonadjacent selection. You can enter the appropriate cell references by pointing to them or by typing their addresses in this text box.

NAMING CONSTANTS AND FORMULAS

In addition to naming cells in your worksheet, you can also assign range names to the constants and formulas that you use often. For example, if you are creating a worksheet to generate sale invoices, you can assign the state sales tax rate to the range name *tax_rate*. Then you can use this range name in any formula that calculates the sales taxes.

Figure 5.2 illustrates how you would assign a constant value to the range name *Tax_Rate*. There you see the Define Name dialog box after entering **Tax_Rate** as the name in the **Name** text box and the constant (=7.5% in this example) in the **R**efers to text box. After assigning this constant percentage rate to the range name *Tax_Rate* in this manner, you can apply it to any formula by typing or pasting in the name (see the next section), as in

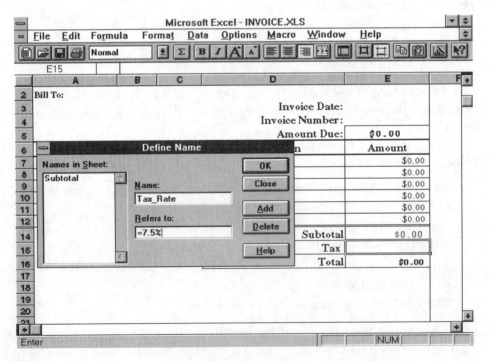

Figure 5.2 Assigning a Range Name to a Constant

Figure 5.3, where the formula in cell E15 (to which the range name *Tax* has been given) is

=Subtotal*Tax_Rate

Here *Subtotal* is the range name given to cell E14, which calculates the subtotal for the invoice.

In addition to naming constants, you can also give a range name to a formula that you use repeatedly. When building a formula in the **R**efers to text box of the Define Name dialog box, keep in mind that Excel automatically applies absolute references to any cells that you point to in the worksheet. If you want to create a formula with relative cell references that Excel will adjust when you enter or paste the range name in a new cell, you must use the **R**eference command on the Formula menu or press F4 to convert the current cell reference to relative or type the cell address in without dollar signs.

PASTING NAMES IN FORMULAS

Once you've assigned a name to a cell or cell range in your worksheet, you can then use the **P**aste Name command on the Formula menu to paste the

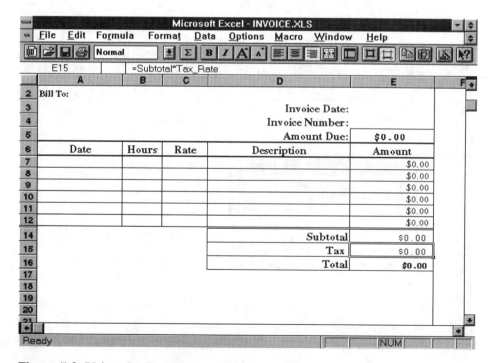

Figure 5.3 Using the Range Name in a Formula

name into the formulas that you build. For example, in the sample invoice shown in Figure 5.3, after assigning the name *Subtotal* to cell E14 and the name *Tax* to cell E15, you can create the formula that totals the invoice in cell C16 (to which the range name *Total* has been assigned) with the **Paste** Name command by following these steps:

1. Make cell C16 the active one.

2. Type = (equal sign) to start the formula.

3. Choose the **P**aste Name command on the Formula menu.

4. Double-click the name **Subtotal** in the Paste **N**ame list box, or click it and then click the OK button or press Enter. The formula now reads =Subtotal on the formula bar (as shown in Figure 5.4).

5. Type + (plus sign).

6. Choose the **P**aste Name command on the Formula menu.

7. Double-click the name **Tax** in the Paste **N**ame list box or click it and then click the OK button or press Enter. The formula on the formula bar now reads =Subtotal+Tax.

8. Press Enter to complete the formula and insert it into cell C16 (as shown in Figure 5.5).

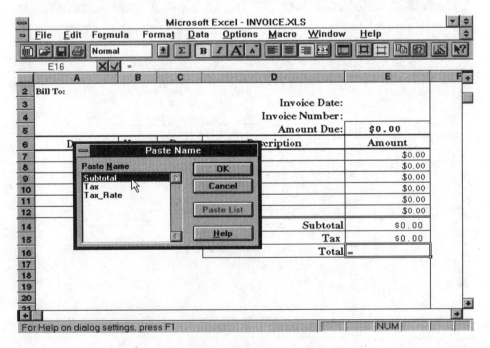

Figure 5.4   Pasting Names in a Formula

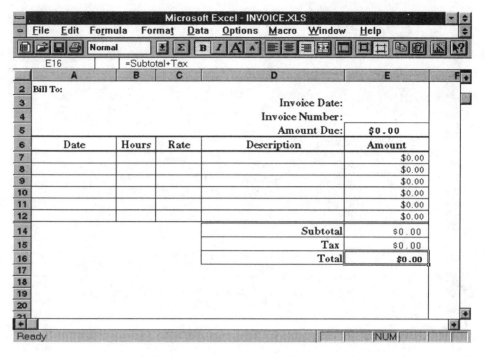

Figure 5.5 Completed Formula Using Range Names

CREATING NAMES FROM COLUMN AND ROW HEADINGS

You can use the Create Names command on the Formula menu to assign existing column and row headings in a table of data to the cells in that table. When using this command, you can have Excel assign the labels used as column headings in the top or bottom row of the table, the labels used as row headings in the leftmost or rightmost column, or even a combination of these headings.

For instance, the sample worksheet in Figure 5.6 illustrates a typical table layout that uses column headings in the top row of the table and row headings in the first column of the table. You can assign these labels to the cells in the table using the **C**reate Names command as follows:

1. Select the cells in the table, including those with the column and row labels you want to use as range names. (In this example, you would select the range B3:E8.)

2. Choose the **C**reate Names command on the Formula menu. Excel displays the Create Names dialog box, which contains four check boxes: **T**op Row, **L**eft Column, **B**ottom Row, and **R**ight Column. The

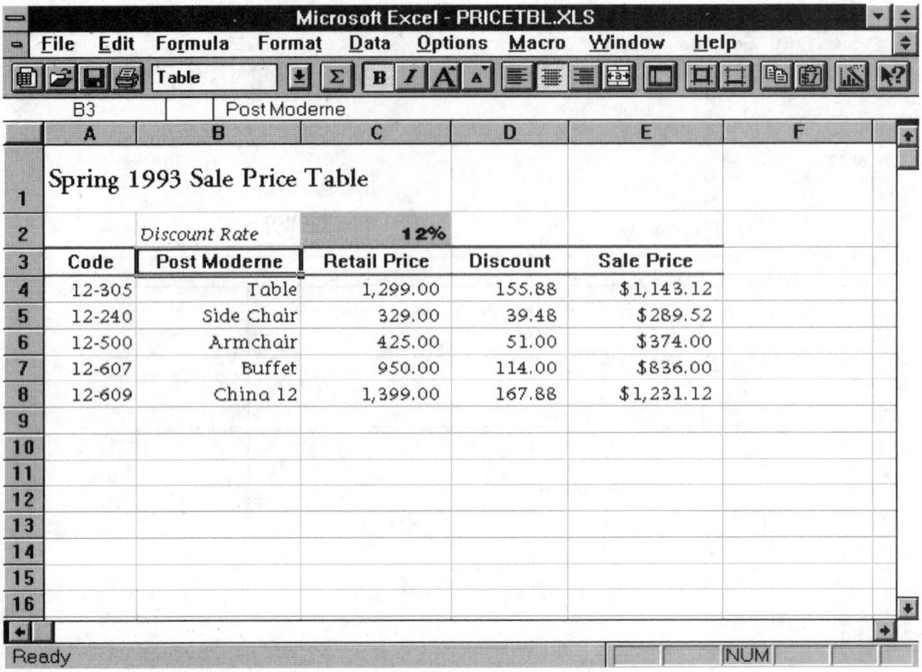

	A	B	C	D	E
1	Spring 1993 Sale Price Table				
2		Discount Rate	12%		
3	Code	Post Moderne	Retail Price	Discount	Sale Price
4	12-305	Table	1,299.00	155.88	$1,143.12
5	12-240	Side Chair	329.00	39.48	$289.52
6	12-500	Armchair	425.00	51.00	$374.00
7	12-607	Buffet	950.00	114.00	$836.00
8	12-609	China 12	1,399.00	167.88	$1,231.12

Figure 5.6 Sample Worksheet with Sale Price Table

program selects the check box or boxes in this dialog box based on the arrangement of the labels in your table. In this example (as shown in Figure 5.7), Excel selects both the **T**op Row and **L**eft Column check boxes because the table contains both column headings in the top row and a row heading in the left column.

3. After selecting (or deselecting) the appropriate Create Names in check boxes, select the OK button or press Enter to assign the range names to your table.

If you select both the **T**op Row and **L**eft Column check box in the Create Names dialog box, Excel assigns the label in the cell in the upper-left corner of the table to the entire range of values in the table (one row down and one column to the right). In our example, Excel assigns the name *Post_Moderne* (the name of the furniture collection) to the cell range C4:E8. Similarly, the program assigns the column headings to the appropriate data in the rows below and the row headings to the data in the appropriate columns to the right. Thus the name *Retail_Price* is assigned to the cell range C4:B8 and the name *Table* is assigned to the cell range C4:E4.

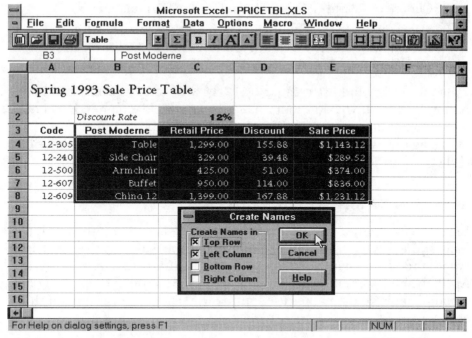

**Figure 5.7 Assigning Names to the Sale Price Table with the Create Names
Command**

PASTING A LIST OF NAMES

After assigning existing labels as range names, all of the new names appear
in the Names in **S**heet list box when you next open the Define Name dialog
box and in the Paste **N**ame list box when you open the Paste Name dialog
box. If you need to verify the extent of the cell selection assigned to a name
or want to select the named range, open the Goto dialog box by choosing
the **G**oto command on the Fo**r**mula menu or pressing F5 and double-clicking the name in the **G**oto list box. Excel then selects all the cells in the
worksheet to which that name is assigned.

To obtain a complete list of the names used in your worksheet and their
locations, you use the Paste **L**ist command button in the Paste Name
dialog box as follows:

1. Select a blank cell of the worksheet where you want the list of names
   to begin. This cell will form the upper-left corner of the table listing
   the names. When selecting this cell, make sure you choose one in an
   area where there is no danger of replacing existing data in the column to the right or rows below. The list of names uses two columns
   (one for the name and one immediately to the right for the range
   address) and as many rows as there are names in the worksheet.

2. Choose the **P**aste Name command on the Formula menu.
3. Select the Paste **L**ist command button. Excel pastes the list of names, starting with the active cell. (Figure 5.8 shows the list for the sample worksheet with the sale prices.)

Be aware that the list created by Excel with the Paste **L**ist command button is static. If you add more names to it or delete names, Excel does not automatically update the list. The only way to bring it up-to-date is by replacing the list in the worksheet, using the Paste **L**ist button as described earlier.

APPLYING NAMES TO FORMULAS

Excel does not automatically replace cell references with the descriptive names you assign to them either with the Define Name or Create Names command. To replace cell references with their names, you use the **A**pply Names command on the Formula menu. You can use this command to apply all the names used in the worksheet or just some of them as follows:

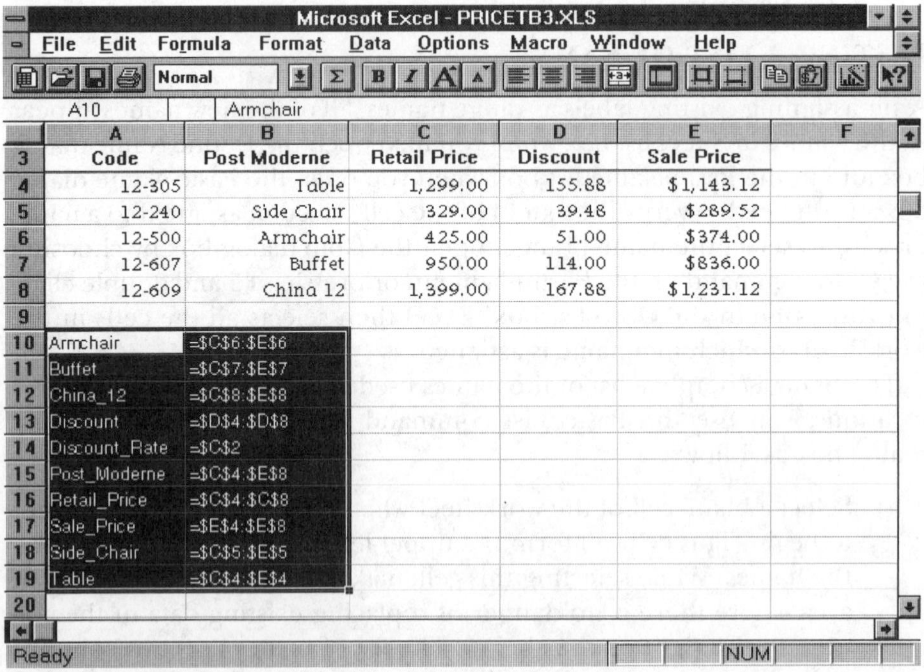
Microsoft Excel - PRICETB3.XLS
File Edit Formula Format Data Options Macro Window Help
Normal
A10 Armchair
A B C D E F
3 Code Post Moderne Retail Price Discount Sale Price
4 12-305 Table 1,299.00 155.88 $1,143.12
5 12-240 Side Chair 329.00 39.48 $289.52
6 12-500 Armchair 425.00 51.00 $374.00
7 12-607 Buffet 950.00 114.00 $836.00
8 12-609 China 12 1,399.00 167.88 $1,231.12
9
10 Armchair =$C$6:$E$6
11 Buffet =$C$7:$E$7
12 China_12 =$C$8:$E$8
13 Discount =$D$4:$D$8
14 Discount_Rate =$C$2
15 Post_Moderne =$C$4:$E$8
16 Retail_Price =$C$4:$C$8
17 Sale_Price =$E$4:$E$8
18 Side_Chair =$C$5:$E$5
19 Table =$C$4:$E$4
20
Ready
NUM

Figure 5.8 Pasting a List of Names in the Worksheet

1. To replace cell references in a particular range of the worksheet, select that range. To apply names to all cells in the worksheet, select any single cell.

2. Choose the **A**pply Names command on the Formula menu. Excel displays the Apply Names dialog box, similar to the one shown in Figure 5.9, displaying a list of all the names assigned in the current worksheet in the Apply **N**ames list box.

3. Select all of the names that you want to apply to the selected range or worksheet in the Apply Names list box. To select multiple nonadjacent names in a list box, hold down the Ctrl key as you click the name (or press the spacebar if using the keyboard). To select a range of names, click the first name then hold down the Shift key when you select the last name.

4. By default, Excel selects the **I**gnore Relative/Absolute check box, meaning that the program replaces cell references with the names you've selected regardless of what type of reference you've used in your formulas. If you want Excel to replace only those cell references that use the same type of references as are used in your names (absolute for absolute, mixed for mixed, and relative for relative), deselect

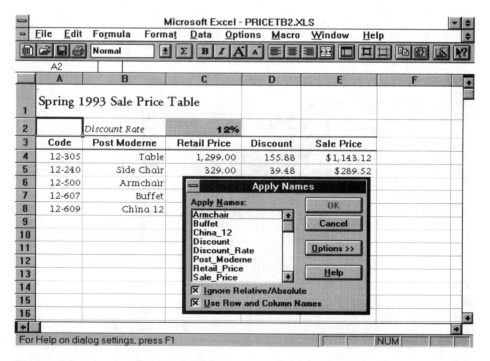

Figure 5.9 The Apply Names Dialog Box

this check box. Most of the time, you will want to leave this option check box selected because Excel automatically assigns absolute cell references to the names you define and relative cell references to the formulas that you build.

5. By default, Excel selects the **U**se Row and Column Names check box, meaning that the names created from row and column headings with the Create Names command will appear in your formulas. Deselect this option if you don't want these row and column names to appear in the formulas in your worksheet. The Apply Names dialog box contains some additional options (shown in Figure 5.10) pertaining to the appearance of names created from row and column headings. These options are not visible until you select the **O**ptions command button.

6. To have Excel display the column name even when the formula is in the same column as the heading used to create the column name, select the **O**ptions command button, then deselect the Omit **C**olumn Name if Same Column.

7. To have Excel display the row name even when the formula is in the same row as the heading used to create that row name, select the **O**ptions command button, then deselect the Omit **R**ow Name if Same Row.

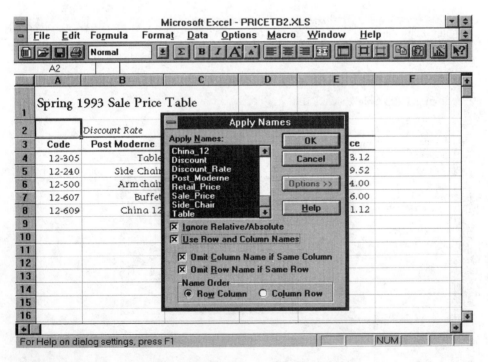

Figure 5.10 The Apply Names Dialog Box with Options

8. By default, Excel displays the row name before the column name when both names are displayed in your formulas (as is the case when you select either of the check boxes in steps 6 or 7). To reverse this order and place the column before the Row, select the Column Row option button (which deselects the Row Column option button).
9. When you've finished selecting the names to use and appropriate options in the Apply Names dialog box, select the OK command button or press Enter to replace the cell references in the selected range or worksheet with the designated names.

Figure 5.11 shows you the sample worksheet with the sale price table after applying all the range names using the default options (that is, with the Ignore Relative/Absolute and Use Row and Column Names check boxes selected). As you can see, Excel has replaced all of the cell references in the formula in the active cell E4. In place of the formula

=B4–C4

the formula bar now contains

=Retail_Price–Discount

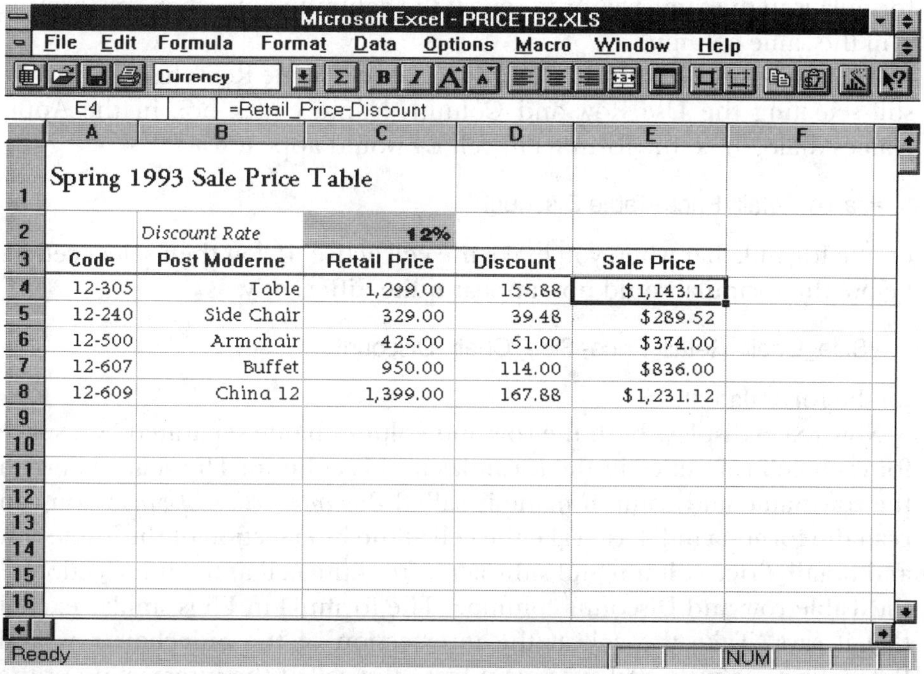

	A	B	C	D	E	F
1	Spring 1993 Sale Price Table					
2		Discount Rate	12%			
3	Code	Post Moderne	Retail Price	Discount	Sale Price	
4	12-305	Table	1,299.00	155.88	$1,143.12	
5	12-240	Side Chair	329.00	39.48	$289.52	
6	12-500	Armchair	425.00	51.00	$374.00	
7	12-607	Buffet	950.00	114.00	$836.00	
8	12-609	China 12	1,399.00	167.88	$1,231.12	
9						
10						
11						
12						
13						
14						
15						
16						

Figure 5.11 Sale Price Table After Applying Names to Formulas

If you moved the cell pointer to cell D4, you would see that this formula now appears as

    =Retail_Price*Discount_Rate

instead of

    =B4*$B$2

as it was before using the Apply Names command.

There's only one problem with applying names using the default settings. The problem begins to show up as soon as you select cell E5. Although this formula subtracts cell D5 from C5, its contents now appear as

    =Retail_Price−Discount

Thus it is identical in appearance to the contents of cell E4 above (and, in fact, identical in appearance to cells E6, E7, and E8 in the cells below).

The reason the formulas all appear identical (although they're really not) is because we selected the Omit **C**olumn Name if Same Column and Omit **R**ow Name if Same Row check boxes. When these settings are used (as they are by default whenever you select the **U**se Column and Row Name check box), Excel does not bother to repeat the row name when the formula is in the same row or to repeat the column name when the formula is in the same column.

If you were to deselect the Omit **R**ow Name if Same Row check box while still selecting the **U**se Row and Column Name check box in the Apply Names dialog box, the formula in cell E4 would appear as

    =Table Retail_Price−Table Discount

on the formula bar when you make the cell active. If you then select cell E5 below, the formula would now appear quite differently, as

    =Side_Chair Retail_Price−Side_Chair Discount

on the formula bar.

Now Excel displays both the row and column name separated by a space for each cell reference in the formulas in this column. The space between the row name and column name is called the *intersection operator.* You can read the formula in E4 as "Take the cell at the intersection of the Table row and Retail_Price column and subtract it from the cell at the intersection of the Table row and Discount column." The formula in E5 is similar except that it says "Take the cell at the intersection of the Sidechair row and Retail_Price column and subtract it from the cell at the intersection of the Sidechair row and Discount column."

Editing Names

You can edit the names you assign to your worksheet with the Define Name command or Change Name command. The Define Name command enables you to modify the cell references assigned to the name or to delete the name altogether. The Change Name command enables you to assign a new name to the same cell selection or delete it as well. Unlike the Define Name command, the Change Name Command always warns if the name you are about to delete is currently in use in formulas in the worksheet.

Alert! Be careful that you don't delete a range name that is already used in formulas in the worksheet. If you do, Excel returns the #NAME! error value to any formula that refers to the name you deleted.

To modify the cell references for a name with the Define Name command, follow these steps:

1. Choose the **D**efine Name command on the **F**ormula menu.
2. Select the name whose references you want to change in the Names in **Sh**eet list box. Excel inserts the name you selected in the Name text box.
3. Select the **R**efers to text box to adjust the cell references as required. (You can edit the contents or replace them by pointing to the new cell range or typing the range address.)
4. Select the OK button or press Enter.

USING THE NAME CHANGER ADD-IN MACRO

Before you can use the Change Name command, you must open the **changer.xla** file. This file contains the Name Change Add-in macro sheet. This sheet runs the macro that adds the change name capability and attaches the Change Na**m**e command to the Formula menu. (For more on customizing Excel with add-in macros, see Chapter 20.)

To rename or delete a name with the Change Name command, follow these steps:

1. Open the Formula menu and choose the Change Na**m**e command. (This command appears between the **C**reate Names and **A**pply Names commands if the Name Change Add-in macro is running.)
2. If this command is not displayed on the Formula menu, close this menu and select the **O**pen command on the **F**ile menu instead (or

click the Open file tool on the Standard toolbar or press Ctrl+F12). Double-click the library folder in the **D**irectories list box to open this directory, then double-click changer.xla in the File **N**ame list box to open this macro sheet and run this add-in macro. After you open this file, you can now select the Change Name command on the Formula menu. If this file does not appear in the File **N**ame list box when you select the c:\excel\library directory, you have to run the Excel Setup program to install it.

3. After selecting the Change Name command, Excel opens the Re-name a Name dialog box. To rename a name, select it in the **F**rom list box, then select the **T**o text box, type the new name, and select the **R**ename command button. As soon as you select the **R**ename button, Excel replaces every occurrence of the old name in the worksheet and then updates the name in the **F**rom list box of the Rename a Name dialog box. You can continue to modify the range names or you can delete them.

4. To delete a name, select the name you want to remove in the **F**rom list box, then select the **D**elete command button. If the name is al-ready used in formulas in the worksheet, Excel displays an alert box asking if you want to delete the name anyway. (Remember, if deleted names are referred to in formulas, those formulas will return #VALUE! error values.) To go ahead and delete the name, select the OK button. To retain the name, select the Cancel button instead.

5. When you are finished renaming and deleting names in the work-sheet, select the **C**lose command button to close the Rename a Name dialog box and return to your worksheet.

Tip   The Change Na**m**e command continues to be available on the Formula menu only until you exit Excel. If you don't want to have to open the **changer.xla** file manually each time you start Excel, use the Windows File Manager to move this file from the **c:\excel\library** directory to the **c:\excel\xlstart** directory. That way Excel automatically opens this add-in macro each time you start the program.

Building Array Formulas

As noted earlier, many worksheet tables use a master formula that you copy to adjacent cells using relative cell references (the so-called one-to-many copy). In some cases, you can build the master formula so that Excel per-forms the desired calculation not only in the active cell but in all the other cells to which you would normally copy the formula. You do this by creating an *array formula*. An array formula is a special formula that operates on a range of values. If this range is supplied by a cell range (as is often the case), it is referred to as an *array range*. If this range is supplied by a list of numerical values, it is known as an *array constant*.

Although the array concept may seem foreign at first, you are really quite familiar with arrays because the Excel worksheet grid with its column-and-row structure naturally organizes your data ranges into arrays. This is illustrated in Figure 5.12, which contains two different-size arrays of numerical values. The first array is a three-by-two array in the cell range B2:C4. This array is a three-by-two array because it occupies three rows and two columns. The second array is a two-by-three array in the cell range F2:H3. It uses two rows in three columns. If you were to list the values in the first three-by-two array as array constants in a formula, they would appear as

{1,4;2,5;3,6}

There are several things of note in this expression. First, the array is enclosed in a pair of braces ({}). Second, columns within each row are separated by commas (,) and rows within the array are separated by semicolons (;). Third, the constants in the array are listed across each row and then

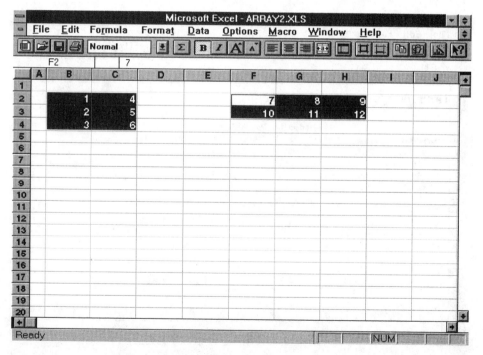

Figure 5.12 Worksheet with Two Different-size Arrays

down each column, *not* down each column and across each row.

The second two-by-three array would appear as

{7,8,9;10,11,12}

if you entered its values as array constants in a formula. Note again that you list the values across each row and then down each column, separating the values in different columns with commas and the values in different rows with a semicolon.

The use of array formulas can significantly reduce the amount of formula copying that you have to do in a worksheet by producing multiple results throughout the array range in a single operation. In addition, array formulas use less computer memory than standard formulas copied in a range. This can be important when creating a large worksheet with many tables; it may mean the difference between fitting all of your calculations on one worksheet or having to split your model into several worksheet files.

To get an idea of how you build and use array formulas, consider the sample worksheet shown in Figure 5.13. It is designed to compute the biweekly wages for each employee. It does this by multiplying each employee's hourly rate by the number of hours worked in each pay period. Instead of creating the formula

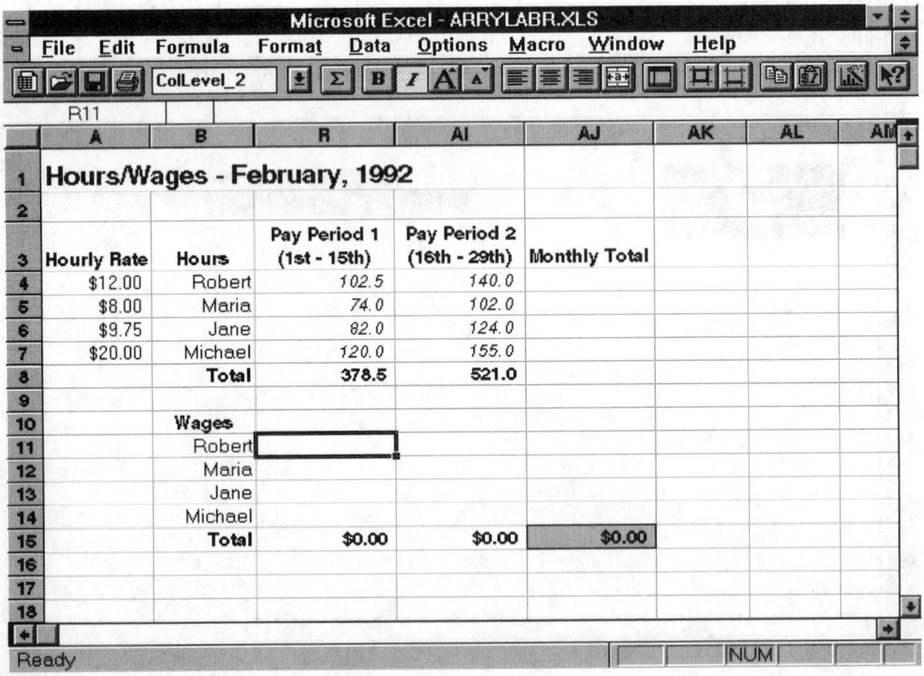

Figure 5.13 Hourly Wage Worksheet

=A4*R4

in cell R11 and then copying it down to cells R12 through R14, you can create the array formula

={A4:A7*R4:R7}

in the array range R11:R14. This formula multiplies each of the hourly rates in the four-by-one array in the range A4:A7 with each of the hours worked in the four-by-one array in the range R4:R7. This same formula is entered into all cells of the array range (R11:R14) as soon as you complete it in the active cell R11. To see how this is done, follow the steps required to build this array formula:

1. With cell R11 the active cell, select the array range R11:R14, then type = (equal sign) to start the array formula, as shown in Figure 5.14. You always start an array formula by selecting the cell or cell range where the results are to appear. Note that array formulas, like standard formulas, begin with the equal sign.

2. Select the range A4:A7 that contains the hourly rate for each employee as shown, then type an * (asterisk for multiplication) and select the range R4:R7 that contains the total number of hours

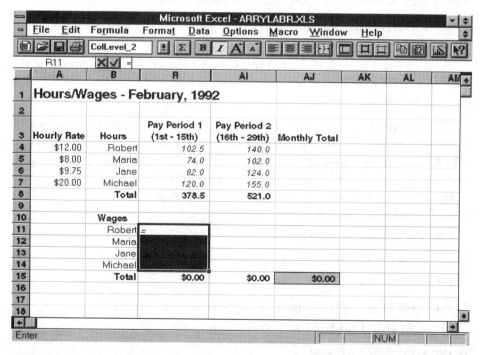

Figure 5.14 Selecting the Array Range and Starting the Array Formula

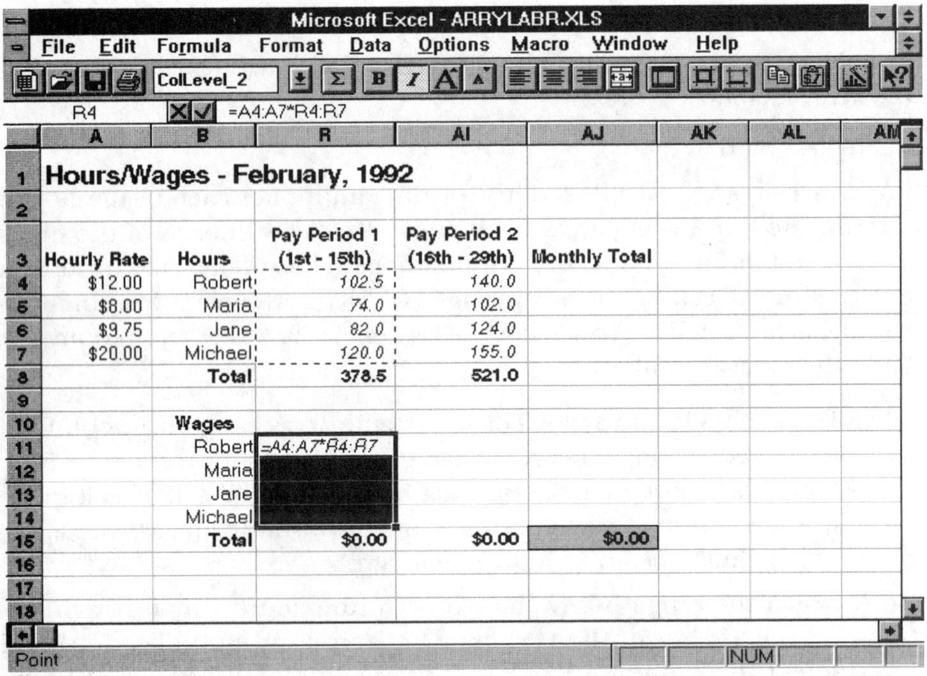

Figure 5.15 Selecting the Ranges for the Array Formula

worked during the first pay period, as shown in Figure 5.15.

3. Press Ctrl+Shift+Enter to insert the array formula in the array range, as shown in Figure 5.16. When you press Ctrl+Shift+Enter to complete the formula, Excel inserts braces around the formula, {=A4:A7*R4:R7}, and copies it into each cell of the array range R11:R14.

When entering an array formula, you must remember to press Ctrl+Shift+Enter instead of just the Enter key; as this special key combination tells Excel you are building an array formula, so that the program knows to enclose the formula in braces and copy it to every cell in the array range.

Figure 5.17 shows you the February wage table after completing all of the array formulas. I entered the array formula

{=A4:A7*AI4:AI7}

in the array range AI11:AI14, the array formula

{=R4:R7+AI4:AI7}

in the array range AJ4:AJ7, and the array formula

{=R11:R14+AI11:AI14}

in the array range AJ11:AJ14.

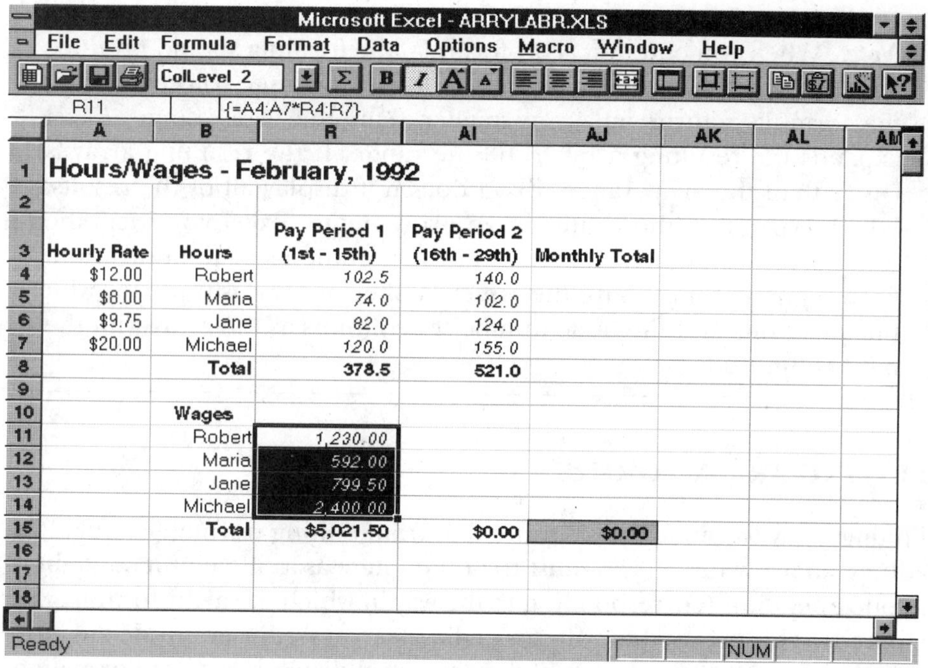

	A	B	R	AI	AJ	AK	AL
1	Hours/Wages - February, 1992						
2							
3	Hourly Rate	Hours	Pay Period 1 (1st - 15th)	Pay Period 2 (16th - 29th)	Monthly Total		
4	$12.00	Robert	102.5	140.0			
5	$8.00	Maria	74.0	102.0			
6	$9.75	Jane	82.0	124.0			
7	$20.00	Michael	120.0	155.0			
8		Total	378.5	521.0			
9							
10		Wages					
11		Robert	1,230.00				
12		Maria	592.00				
13		Jane	799.50				
14		Michael	2,400.00				
15		Total	$5,021.50	$0.00	$0.00		

Figure 5.16 Completed Array Formula in the Array Range

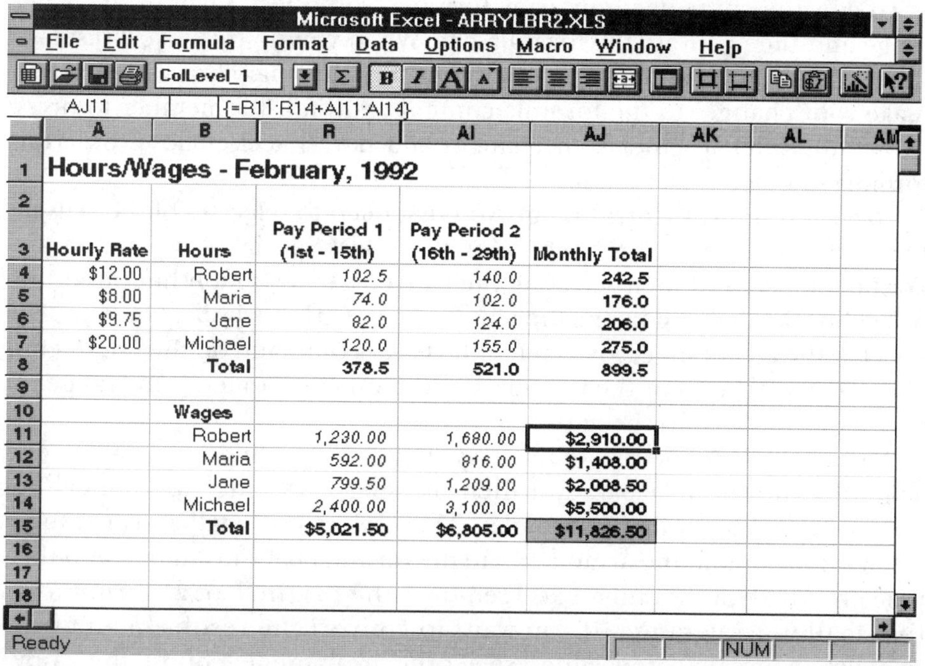

	A	B	R	AI	AJ	AK	AL
1	Hours/Wages - February, 1992						
2							
3	Hourly Rate	Hours	Pay Period 1 (1st - 15th)	Pay Period 2 (16th - 29th)	Monthly Total		
4	$12.00	Robert	102.5	140.0	242.5		
5	$8.00	Maria	74.0	102.0	176.0		
6	$9.75	Jane	82.0	124.0	206.0		
7	$20.00	Michael	120.0	155.0	275.0		
8		Total	378.5	521.0	899.5		
9							
10		Wages					
11		Robert	1,230.00	1,690.00	$2,910.00		
12		Maria	592.00	816.00	$1,408.00		
13		Jane	799.50	1,209.00	$2,008.50		
14		Michael	2,400.00	3,100.00	$5,500.00		
15		Total	$5,021.50	$6,805.00	$11,826.50		

Figure 5.17 Hourly Wage Worksheet with Array Formulas

> **Note:** When you enter an array formula, the formula should produce an array with the same dimensions as the array range you selected. If the formula returns an array smaller than the array range, Excel expands the resulting array to fill the range. If the resulting array is larger than the array range, Excel does not display all of the results. When expanding the results in an array range, Excel considers the dimensions of all the arrays used in the arguments of the operation. Each argument must have the same number of rows as the array with the most rows and the same number of columns as the array with the most columns.

EDITING ARRAY FORMULAS

Editing array formulas differs somewhat from editing normal formulas. In editing an array range, you must treat the range as a single unit and edit it in one operation (corresponding to the way in which the array formula was entered). This means that you can't edit, clear, move, insert, or delete individual cells in the array range. If you try, Excel displays an alert box telling you that you cannot Change part of an array.

To edit the contents of an array formula, you select a cell in the array range and then activate the formula bar. When you do this, Excel displays the contents of the array formula without the customary braces. After you make your changes to the formula contents, you must remember to press Ctrl+Shift+Enter to enter your changes and have Excel enclose the array formula in braces once again.

To clear or move an array range, you first need to select all of the cells in the range. You can do this by choosing the **S**elect Special command on the **F**ormula menu and then selecting the Current **A**rray option button in the Select Special dialog box or simply by pressing Ctrl+/ (slash). Once you've selected the array range, you can use the Cl**ea**r command on the **E**dit menu to delete its contents or the Cut and **P**aste commands to move the range to a new area of the worksheet.

You can reduce the size of an array range by selecting the array range, activating the formula bar, and then pressing Ctrl+Enter to reenter the array formulas as ordinary formulas. Then select the smaller array range you want to contain the array, activate the formula bar once more, and this time press Ctrl+Shift+Enter. Excel reenters the original array formula in the smaller array range. If you want to convert the results in an array range to their calculated values, select the array range, choose the **C**opy command on the **E**dit menu, then, without changing the selection, choose the Values option in the Paste Special dialog box. As soon as you convert an array range to its calculated values, Excel no longer treats the cell range as an array.

Using Functions

Excel offers hundreds of built-in worksheet functions designed to make it easier to perform all kinds of specialized calculations. A *function* is a predefined formula that performs a standard computation each time you use it. All you have to do is supply the values that the function computes (referred to as the function's *arguments*). As with simple formulas, you can enter the arguments for most functions either as numerical constants, such as **5** or **215.75**, or, as is more common, as a cell reference, such as **E24**, **B5:C10**, or a defined range name such as **Subtotal** or **Qtr_2** that contains a constant or a formula.

You can use functions alone or combine them with other mathematical operators in formulas. It is even possible in some cases to nest functions so that the result of one function works as an argument of another.

Excel divides its wide variety of worksheet functions into different categories according to the type of operation each performs:

- Financial
- Date and time
- Mathematical and trigonometric
- Statistical
- Lookup and reference
- Database
- Text
- Logical
- Information
- Cross-tab add-in

Regardless of which category a function falls into, each worksheet function has its own sequence, or *syntax*, that you must follow when you use it. (See Appendix B for a complete list of Excel's worksheet functions and their syntax arranged alphabetically by category.) As with simple formulas, you preface all functions with the equal sign (=). The syntax of a function then includes the name of the function followed by any arguments it requires enclosed in parentheses. For instance, to return the integer portion of a numerical value, you use the INT function, which follows this syntax:

```
=INT(number)
```

where *number* is the value or the cell range that contains the value(s) whose integer you want computed.

Many functions use more than one argument. When a function uses multiple arguments, you separate each argument with commas. For example, to round a value to a specific precision, you use the ROUND function, which follows the syntax

```
=ROUND(number,num_digits)
```

where *number* is the value or cell range that contains the value(s) you want rounded and *num_digits* is the number of digits that value(s) should be rounded to.

A few worksheet functions take no argument whatsoever. When you use a function that takes no arguments, you still must enter a pair of parentheses after the function name. For example, you use the NOW function to insert the current date and time in a cell that follows the syntax

```
=NOW( )
```

ENTERING FUNCTIONS

You can enter worksheet functions by typing them in the formula bar or by using the Paste Function command on the Formula menu. When you type in a function, you must remember to start by typing = (equal sign) before the function name and avoid entering spaces between the equal sign, function name, parentheses, or arguments of the function. When typing the function name, you can use upper- or lowercase letters. (By convention, functions are shown in all uppercase letters in your Excel documentation as well as in this book.) If you enter the function name in lowercase letters or a combination of upper- and lowercase letters, Excel automatically converts the function to all uppercase as soon as you enter it in a cell. If you make a typing mistake when entering the function name, Excel inserts the #NAME? error value in the cell and the function name remains in the case you used when entering it in the formula bar. Simply correct the function name and then reenter the formula.

After you enter the equal sign, function name, and the left parenthesis, you can point to any cell or cell range you want to include in the first argument instead of having to type in the cell references. If the function takes more than one argument, you can point to the cells or cell ranges you want to use after you type the , (comma) to complete the first argument. Regardless of how you designate the arguments (either by pointing or typing), remember to enter a right parenthesis to finish off the function before you enter it in its cell. (Actually, Excel 4.0 accepts any otherwise correct function that lacks the final parenthesis; however, omitting the parenthesis is a very bad habit as other spreadsheet and database programs are not so forgiving.)

Tip Former Lotus 1-2-3 users take note: Excel recognizes functions that start with @ instead of =. If you forget and type @sum(A5:A25) instead of =sum(A5:A25), the program will accept and correctly calculate your formula. (In addition, the program will automatically convert your @ sign to an = sign on the formula bar.)

By far the easiest way to enter a function in the worksheet is with the Paste Function command. This is especially true when you're first learning a function, because the Paste Function command can actually show you the function's syntax by pasting the function with a list of its arguments into the formula bar. You then replace the list of arguments with the actual values or cell references that the function should use in its computations. As an added benefit, Excel even inserts the equal sign before the function when you select it in the Paste Function dialog box, eliminating the need for you to remember to type this character.

To see how easy it is to paste a function in the worksheet, follow these steps for pasting the MAX function in the house sales worksheet shown in Figure 5.18. The MAX function is a statistical function that returns the highest value from a list of values. In this case, the MAX function will return the highest selling price in cell C12 as follows:

1. Make cell C12 the active cell.

2. Choose the Paste Function command on the Formula menu. Excel displays the Paste Function dialog box shown in Figure 5.19. This dialog box contains two list boxes: the Function Category and the Paste Function list box. By default, All is selected as the category in the Function Category list box so that the Paste Function list box contains an alphabetical listing of every worksheet function. If you know the category of the function you want to use, you can select it in the Function Category list box to restrict the list of functions in the Paste Function dialog box to just those ones. If you don't know the category, leave All selected when you choose the function name in the Paste Function list box.

3. Click the ABS function in the Paste Function list box or press the Tab key to select it, then type m. Excel jumps to the MATCH function (the first one that begins with the letter *m*).

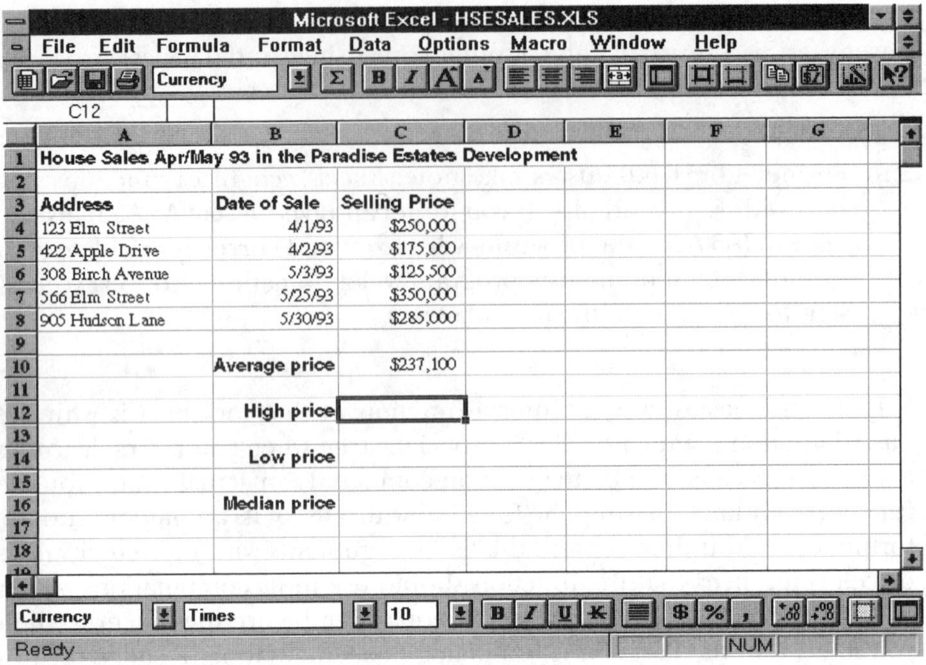

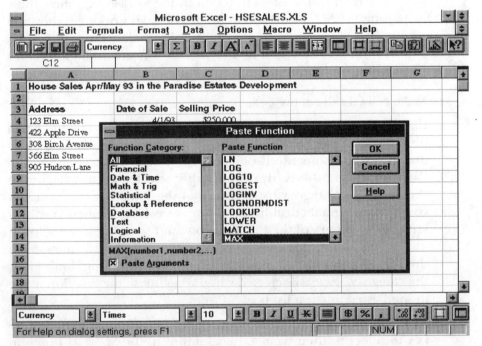

Figure 5.18 Sample House Sales Worksheet

Figure 5.19 Choosing the MAX Function in the Paste Function Dialog Box

4. Click the down scroll arrow or press the key until you can see the MAX function (right below the MATCH function).

5. Double-click the MAX function to close the Paste Function dialog box and paste this function onto the formula bar. Because the Paste Arguments check box is selected, Excel includes a list of the MAX function arguments in the formula bar. When you paste a function into the formula bar with a list of its arguments, you must replace the list with the actual arguments that should be used in the calculation.

6. The first argument *number1* is already selected in the formula bar. Replace this by selecting the cell range C4:C8 (as shown in Figure 5.20). You can find the average for a series of numbers. In this example, however, you only need the average of the scores entered in the range C4:C8. Although you don't need to define a second argument for the MAX function, you do have to delete the rest of the argument list (,*number2*,...) before you enter this function in C12. If you don't, Excel displays an **Error in formula** alert box when you press Enter.

7. Select the text ,number2,... in the formula bar, then press the Del key to remove these characters. The function should now appear as =MAX(C4:C8) in the formula bar.

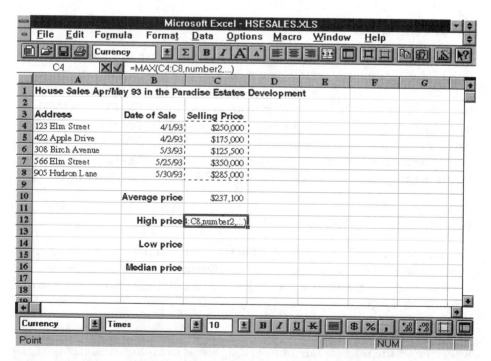

Figure 5.20 Selecting the Argument for the MAX Function

8. Press the Enter key to insert the MAX function in cell C12.

Excel returns the $350,000 as the highest sales price.

To avoid errors in the formula, you constantly have to take great care that all of the text in the argument list is not replaced. You may soon want to start pasting functions in the worksheet without a list of their arguments. To do this just deselect this Paste **Arguments** check box in the Paste Function dialog box. After selecting the function in the Paste Function list box, Excel displays the syntax of the function right above the Paste **Arguments** check box. You can review the arguments used by the function in this area of the Paste Function dialog before you close the dialog box and insert the function (without arguments) in the formula bar.

In the next few sections of this chapter, I'll introduce you to a few of the more important worksheet functions that you are likely to use. These functions fall into categories of Financial, Mathematical, Statistical, Text, Logical, and Lookup functions. Keep in mind that this function overview provides an introduction to only a small percentage of functions available in Excel 4.0. For a complete list of the worksheet functions along with their syntax, you need to refer to Appendix B, "Excel's Worksheet Functions" as you build your worksheets.

Financial Functions

The first group of functions that we will examine are the Financial functions. These functions enable you to perform a wide variety of common business calculations, including such things as calculating the present, future, or net present value of an investment with the PV, FV or NPV function; the payment, number of periods, or the principal or interest part of a payment on an amortized loan with the PMT, NPER, IPMT or PPMT functions; the rate of return on an investment with the RATE, IRR, or MIRR functions; or depreciation with the SLN, DDB, SYD, and VDB functions.

USING THE PV, NPV, AND FV FUNCTIONS

The PV, NPV, and FV functions enable you to determine the profitability of an investment. The PV, or present value, function returns the present value of an investment, the total amount that a series of future payments is worth presently. The syntax of PF function is

=PV(rate,nper,pmt,fv,type)

where *rate* is the interest rate per period, *nper* is the number of periods, *pmt* is the payment made each period. The *fv* and *type* arguments are optional in the function. The *fv* argument is the future value or cash balance you want to have after making your last payment. If you omit the *fv* argument, Excel assumes a future value of zero (0). The *type* argument indicates whether the payment is made at the beginning or end of the period. Enter 0 (or omit the type argument) when the payment is made at the end of the period, and use 1 when it is made at the beginning of the period.

Figure 5.21 contains several examples using the PV function. All three PV functions use the same annual percentage rate of 7.25 percent and a term of 10 years. Because we are assuming that the payments are made monthly, each function converts these annual figures into monthly ones. For example, in the PV function in cell E3, the annual interest rate in cell A3 is converted into a monthly rate by dividing by 12 (A3/12), and the annual term in cell B3 is converted into equivalent monthly periods by multiplying by 12 (B3*12).

Note that although the PV functions in cells E3 and E5 use the *rate, nper,* and *pmt* ($218.46) arguments, their results are slightly different. This is caused by the difference in the *type* argument in the two functions: The PV function in cell E3 assumes each payment is made at the end of the period (the *type* argument is 0 whenever it is omitted), while the PV function in cell

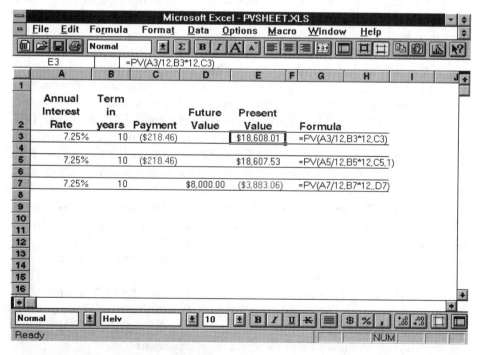

Figure 5.21 Using the PV Function

E5 assumes each payment is made at the beginning of the period (indicated by a *type* argument of 1). When the payment is made at the beginning of the period, the present value of this investment is $0.49 higher than when the payment is made at the end of the period, reflecting the interest accrued during the last period.

The third example in cell E7 in Figure 5.21 uses the PV function with an *fv* argument instead of the *pmt* argument. In this example, the PV function tells you that you would have to make monthly payments of $3,883.06 for a 10-year period to realize a cash balance of $8,000, assuming that the investment returned a constant annual interest rate of 7.25 percent. Note that when you use the PV function with the *fv* argument instead of the *pmt* argument, you must still indicate the position of the *pmt* argument in the function with a comma (thus the two commas in a row in the function) so that Excel doesn't mistake your *fv* argument for the *pmt* argument.

The NPV function calculates the net present value based on a series of cash flows. The syntax of this function is

=NPV(rate,value1,value2,...)

where *value1, value2,* and so on are between 1 to 13 value arguments representing a series of payments (negative values) and income (positive values), each of which is equally spaced in time and occurs at the end of the period. The NPV investment begins one period before the period of the value1 cash flow and ends with the last cash flow in the argument list. If your first cash flow occurs at the beginning of the period, you must add it to the result of the NPV function rather than include it as one of the arguments.

Figure 5.22 illustrates using the NPV function to evaluate the attractiveness of a five-year investment that requires an initial investment of $30,000 (the value in cell G3). The first year you expect a loss of $22,000 (cell B3), the second year a profit of $15,000 (cell C3), the third year a profit of $25,000 (cell D3), the fourth year a profit of $35,000 (cell E3), and the fifth year a profit of $40,000 (cell F3). Note that these cell references are used as the *value* arguments of the NPV function. Unlike when using the PV function, the NPV function doesn't require an even stream of cash flows. The *rate* argument in the function is set at 8% (percent). In this example, this represents the discount rate of the investment, that is, the interest rate you might expect to get during the five-year period if you put your money into some other type of investment, such as a money-market account. This NPV function in cell A3 returns a net present value of $31,719, indicating that you can expect to realize about $1,719 more from investing your $30,000 in this investment than you would from investing the money in a money-market account at an interest rate of 8 percent.

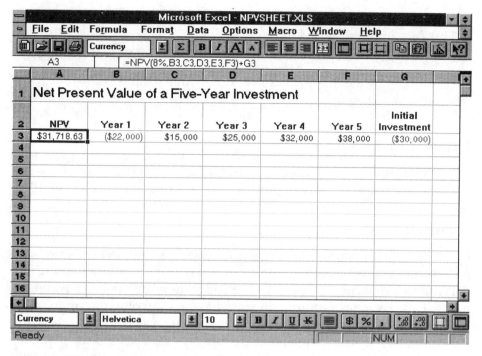

Figure 5.22 Using the NPV Function

The FV function calculates the future value of an investment. The syntax of this function is

=FV(rate,nper,pmt,pv,type)

The *rate, nper, pmt,* and *type* arguments are the same as those used by the PV function. The *pv* argument is the present value or lump-sum amount for which you wish to calculate the future value. As with the *fv* and *type* arguments in the PV function, both the *pv* and *type* arguments are optional in the FV function. If you omit these arguments, Excel assumes their values to be zero (0) in the function.

You can use the FV function to calculate the future value of an investment such as an IRA (Individual Retirement Account). For example, assume that you establish an IRA at age 43 and will retire 22 years later at age 65 and that you plan to make annual payments into the IRA at the beginning of each year. If you assume a rate of return of 8.5 percent a year, you would enter the FV function

=FV(8.5%,22,–1000,,1)

in your worksheet, and Excel would indicate that you could expect a future value of $64,053.66 for your IRA when you retire at age 65. If you had established the IRA a year prior and the account already has a present value of $1,085, you would amend the FV function to

=FV(8.5%,22,–1000,–1085,1)

Excel would indicate that you could expect a future value of $70,583.22 for your IRA at retirement.

USING THE PMT FUNCTION

The PMT function calculates the periodic payment for an annuity, assuming a stream of equal payments and a constant rate of interest. The PMT function follows the syntax

=PMT(rate,nper,pv,fv,type)

where *rate* is the interest rate per period, *nper* is the number of periods, *pv* is the present value or the amount the future payments are worth presently, *fv* is the future value or cash balance you want after the last payment is made (Excel assumes a future value of zero when you omit this optional argument as you would when calculating loan payments), and *type* is the value 0 for payments made at the end of the period or the value 1 for payments made at the beginning of the period. (If you omit the optional type argument, Excel assumes the payment is made at the end of the period.)

The PMT function is often used to calculate the payment for mortgage loans that have a fixed rate of interest. Figure 5.23 shows you a sample worksheet that contains a table using the PMT function to calculate loan payments for a range of interest rates (from 6.50% to 7.75%) and principals ($350,000 to $359,000). The table uses the initial principal that you enter in cell B2 and copies it to cell A7 and then increases it by $1,000 in the range A8:A16. The table uses the initial interest rate you enter in cell B3 and copies it to cell B6, and then increases this initial rate by a quarter of a percent in the range C6:G6. The term in years in cell B4 is a constant factor that is used in the entire loan payment table.

To get an idea of how easy it is to build this type of loan payment table with the PMT function, follow these steps for creating it in a new worksheet:

1. Enter the titles Loan Payments in cell A1, Principal in cell A2, Interest Rate in cell A3, and Term (in years) in cell A4.

2. Enter $350,000 in cell B2, enter 6.50% in cell B3, and enter 30 in cell B4.

3. With cell B6 active, build the formula =B3. By copying the value entered into cell B3 with the formula =B3 instead of with the Copy and Paste commands, you ensure that the value in B6 will immediately reflect any change you make in cell B3.

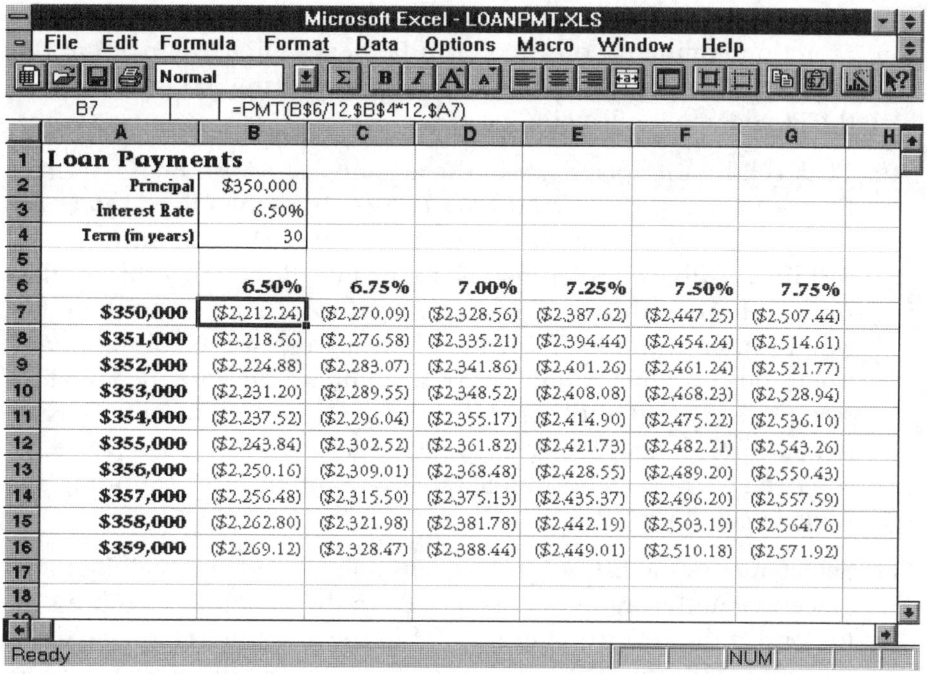

	A	B	C	D	E	F	G
1	**Loan Payments**						
2	**Principal**	$350,000					
3	**Interest Rate**	6.50%					
4	**Term (in years)**	30					
5							
6		**6.50%**	**6.75%**	**7.00%**	**7.25%**	**7.50%**	**7.75%**
7	**$350,000**	($2,212.24)	($2,270.09)	($2,328.56)	($2,387.62)	($2,447.25)	($2,507.44)
8	**$351,000**	($2,218.56)	($2,276.58)	($2,335.21)	($2,394.44)	($2,454.24)	($2,514.61)
9	**$352,000**	($2,224.88)	($2,283.07)	($2,341.86)	($2,401.26)	($2,461.24)	($2,521.77)
10	**$353,000**	($2,231.20)	($2,289.55)	($2,348.52)	($2,408.08)	($2,468.23)	($2,528.94)
11	**$354,000**	($2,237.52)	($2,296.04)	($2,355.17)	($2,414.90)	($2,475.22)	($2,536.10)
12	**$355,000**	($2,243.84)	($2,302.52)	($2,361.82)	($2,421.73)	($2,482.21)	($2,543.26)
13	**$356,000**	($2,250.16)	($2,309.01)	($2,368.48)	($2,428.55)	($2,489.20)	($2,550.43)
14	**$357,000**	($2,256.48)	($2,315.50)	($2,375.13)	($2,435.37)	($2,496.20)	($2,557.59)
15	**$358,000**	($2,262.80)	($2,321.98)	($2,381.78)	($2,442.19)	($2,503.19)	($2,564.76)
16	**$359,000**	($2,269.12)	($2,328.47)	($2,388.44)	($2,449.01)	($2,510.18)	($2,571.92)
17							
18							

Figure 5.23 Loan Payment Table Using the PMT Function

4. With cell C6 active, build the formula =B6+.25%. By adding a quarter of a percent to the interest rate of the value in B6 with the formula =B6+.25% in C6 rather than creating a series with the AutoFill or Data Series commands, you ensure that the value in cell C6 will always be one-quarter of a percent larger than any value entered in cell B6.
5. With cell C6 still active, drag the fill handle until you extend the selection to the right to cell G6, then release the mouse button.
6. With cell B7 active, build the formula =B2. Again, you use the formula =B2 to copy the initial principal to cell A7 rather than the Copy and Paste commands to ensure that A7 will always have the same value as cell B2.
7. With cell A8 active, build the formula =A7+1000 . Here too you use the formula =A7+1000 rather than creating a series with the AutoFill or the Data Series commands so that the value in B8 will always be 1000 greater than any value placed in cell A7.
8. With cell A8 still active, drag the fill handle until you extend the selection down to A16, then release the mouse button.

9. With cell B7 active, begin the PMT function by choosing the **Paste Function** command on the **Formula** menu, click Financial in the Function Category list box, then double-click the PMT function in the Paste Function list box.

10. Click cell B6 to replace *rate* in the argument list with B6, then press F4 twice to convert the relative reference B6 to the mixed reference B$6 (column relative, row absolute), then type /12. You need to convert the relative cell reference B6 to the mixed reference B$6 so that Excel will not adjust the row number down each row of the table when you copy the PMT formula but will adjust the column letter when you copy the formula across its columns. Because the initial interest rate entered in B3 (and then brought forward to cell B6) is an *annual* interest rate, and you want to know the *monthly* loan payment, you need to convert the annual rate to a monthly rate by dividing the value in cell B6 by 12.

11. Select **nper** in the list with the I-beam pointer and click cell B4 to replace *nper* in the argument list with B4 in the function, then press F4 to convert the relative reference B4 to the absolute reference $B$4, then type *12. You need to convert the relative cell reference B4 to the absolute reference $B$4 so that Excel adjusts neither the row number nor the column letter when you copy the PMT formula down the rows and across the columns of the table. Because the term in B3 (and then brought forward to cell B6) is an *annual* period, and you want to know the *monthly* loan payment, you need to convert the yearly periods to monthly periods by multiplying the value in cell B4 by 12.

12. Select **pv,fv,type** with the I-beam pointer and click A7 to replace *pv,fv,type* in the argument list with A7, then press F4 three times to convert the relative reference A7 to the mixed reference $A7 (column absolute, row relative). You need to convert the relative cell reference A7 to the mixed reference $A7 so that Excel will not adjust the column letter when you copy the PMT formula across each column of the table but will adjust the row number when you copy the formula down across its rows.

13. Press Enter to insert the formula =PMT(B$6/12,$B$4*12,$A7) in cell B7.

14. Drag the fill handle on cell B7 until you extend the fill range down to cell B16, then release the mouse button.

15. Drag the fill handle until you extend the fill range B7:B16 to the right to cell G16, then release the mouse button.

Once you've created a loan table like this, you can change the beginning principal or interest rate as well as the term to see what the payments would be under various other scenarios. (For information on how to control the recalculation of this table, see "Recalculating the Worksheet" later in this chapter. For information on how to protect the formulas in this worksheet, see "Protecting the Worksheet," also later.)

Mathematical Functions

The Mathematical functions are placed in the Math & Trig category and are grouped together with the Trigonometric functions on the Paste Function dialog box. While the trigonometric functions are primarily of use to engineers and scientists, the mathematical functions provide you with the ability to manipulate any type of values. This category of functions includes SUM, the most commonly used of all functions; functions such as INT, EVEN, ODD, ROUND, and TRUNC, which round off the values in your worksheet; functions such as PRODUCT, SUMPRODUCT, and SUMSQ, which you can use to calculate the products of various values in the worksheet, and the SQRT function, which you can use to calculate the square root of a value.

The SUM function uses the syntax

=SUM(number1,number2,...)

where the *number* argument is between 1 and 30 values that you want to sum. To sum a selection of cells with this function, you simply paste in the SUM function and then replace the argument list by selecting the appropriate cell range. For example, to total a range of values in the cell range A3:A25 in cell A26, you can paste the SUM function =SUM(number1,number2,...) in cell A26, then select the arguments number1,number2,... with the I-beam pointer and replace this list by selecting the cell range A3:A25 with the white-cross pointer before you press the Enter key. To sum a nonadjacent selection such as the ranges B4:C4, F4:F8, and D12:D16, you would follow the same technique, except to replace the list of arguments in the SUM function, you would hold down the Ctrl key as you select each range with the white-cross pointer. Each time you finish dragging through one range and relocate the pointer to start selecting the next range, Excel automatically inserts a comma in the cell references in the SUM arguments and displays the address of the newest anchor cell. When you've finished selecting all the discontinuous ranges you need to sum, you can press Enter to have Excel calculate the total and remove the marquees from the various ranges in the document window.

Greg Harvey's Excel 4.0 for Windows

Tip By far the easiest way to select the SUM function is with the AutoSum tool on the Standard toolbar. To use this tool, select the cell where the total is to appear, then click the AutoSum tool. Excel pastes the SUM function complete with the cell range it thinks you want summed. If the program's selection is inaccurate, you can replace the incorrect range by pointing to the correct range.

The functions INT, EVEN, and ODD all take a single argument, number, as in

=INT(number)

where *number* is the value you want rounded off to display only the integer portion. The EVEN and ODD function works much like the latter except it rounds off the number to the nearest even or odd integer.

You use the ROUND function to round up or down fractional values in the worksheet. Unlike when applying a number format to a cell, which affects only the number's display, the ROUND function actually changes the way Excel stores the number in the cell that contains the function. The ROUND function uses the syntax

=ROUND(number,num_digits)

where the *number* argument is the value you want to round off and the *num_digits* is the number of digits you want the number rounded to. If the *num_digits* argument is 0 (zero), Excel rounds the value to the nearest integer. If the *num_digits* argument is a positive value, Excel rounds the number to the specified number of decimal places. If the *num_digits* argument is a negative value, Excel rounds the number to the left of the decimal point.

The TRUNC function uses the same arguments as the ROUND function. It converts a decimal number to an integer by truncating the decimal part of the value specified as the *number* argument. The *num_digits* argument indicates the precision of the truncation. Note that the TRUNC function works like the INT function except that the latter rounds the number to the nearest integer based on the fractional part while the former simply drops the fractional part.

The SQRT function returns the square root of the number you specify as its argument so that

=SQRT(20)

returns 4.472135955. If you only want to use the integer portion of the square root, you can combine the INT function with the SQRT function, as in

=INT(SQRT(20))

which returns 4. Note that in this example, you actually place the SQRT function argument with its number argument inside the INT function and use the entire SQRT function as the INT function's argument. This arrangement whereby you use one function as an argument of another is referred to as *nesting functions.*

If you want to round off a square root to a particular decimal place rather than just use the integer portion, you can nest the SQRT function inside the ROUND function, as in

=ROUND(SQRT(20),5)

which rounds the square root of 20 to the five decimal places and returns 4.47214.

Statistical Functions

Excel includes one of the most complete sets of statistical functions available outside of a dedicated statistics software program. These functions run the gamut from the more ordinary AVERAGE, MAX, and MIN functions to the more specialized CHITEST, POISSON, and PERCENTILE functions. We'll look at the more commonplace statistical functions of AVERAGE, MAX, MIN, and MEDIAN.

All four of these statistical functions use the same arguments as the SUM function. For example, if you paste the AVERAGE function into the formula with its argument list, it will appear as

=AVERAGE(number1,number2,...)

where the *number* arguments are between 1 and 30 numeric arguments for which you want the average. Figure 5.24 illustrates how you might use the AVERAGE, MAX, MIN, and MEDIAN functions in a worksheet. This example uses these functions to compute a few statistics on the selling prices of homes in a particular neighborhood. These statistics include the average, highest, lowest, and median selling price for the homes sold in April and May of 1993. All of the statistical functions in this worksheet use the same *number* argument, that is, the cell range C4:C8.

The AVERAGE function computes the *arithmetic* mean of the values in this range by summing them and then dividing them by the number of values in the range. This AVERAGE function is equivalent to the formula

=SUM(C4:C8)/COUNT(C4:C8)

which uses the SUM function to total the values and another statistical function called COUNT to determine the number of values in the list. The MAX and MIN functions simply compute the highest and lowest values in

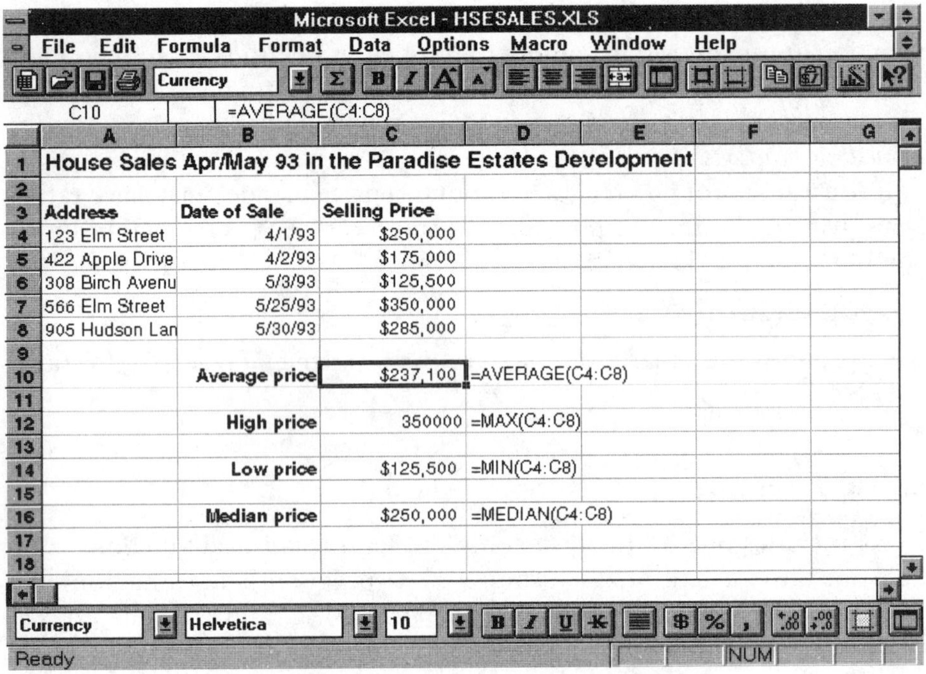

Figure 5.24   Worksheet Using Common Statistical Functions

the cell range used as the *number* argument. The MEDIAN function computes the value that is in the middle of the range of values, that is, the one where half the values are greater and half are less. This is why the median sales price (in cell C16) differs from the average sales price (in cell C10) in this worksheet.

> ***Note:*** In addition to the statistical worksheet functions, Excel offers a complete set of special analysis tools called the Analysis ToolPak. These tools can analyze data tables using such things as Anova, F-Test, rank and percentile, t-Test, and Fourier analysis. For more information on using the Analysis ToolPak, see Chapter 20.

Text Functions

There are two types of text functions: Functions such as VALUE, TEXT, and DOLLAR, which convert numeric text entries into numbers and numeric entries into text, and functions such as UPPER, LOWER, and PROPER, which manipulate the strings of text themselves. Most often you need to use the text functions only when you work with data from other programs. For example, you might purchase a target client list on disk, only to discover that the information has been entered in all-uppercase letters. In order to use this data with your word processor's mailmerge feature, you would use Excel's PROPER function to convert the entries so that only the initial letters of each word are in uppercase.

Text functions such as the UPPER, LOWER, and PROPER all take a single *text* argument that indicates what text should be manipulated. The UPPER function converts all letters in the *text* argument to uppercase. The LOWER function converts all letters in the *text* argument to lowercase. The PROPER function capitalizes the first letter of each word as well as any other letters in the *text* argument that do not follow another letter—all other letters in the *text* argument are changed to lowercase.

Figure 5.25 illustrates a situation where you would use the PROPER function. There both last and first name text entries have been made in all-uppercase letters. Follow the steps for using the PROPER function to convert these text entries to the proper capitalization:

1. With cell C3 active, choose the Paste Function command on the Formula menu, then click **Text** in the Function **C**ategory and double-click **PROPER** in the Paste Function.

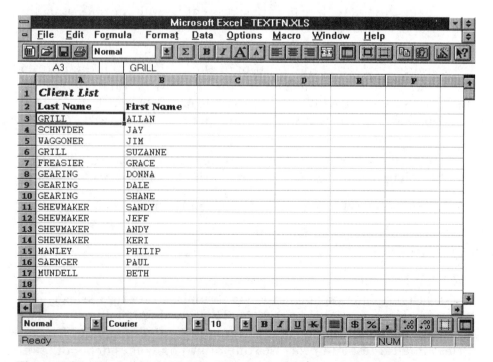

Figure 5.25 Worksheet with Text Entries in All-Uppercase Letters

2. Click cell A3 to replace text with A3 as the argument of the PROPER function on the formula bar, then press Enter.

3. Drag the fill handle in the lower-right corner of cell C3 to the right to cell D3, then release the mouse button to copy the formula with the PROPER function to the column to the right.

4. Drag the fill handle in the lower-right corner of cell D3 down to cell D17, then release the mouse button to copy the formulas with the PROPER function down. The cell range C3:D17 now contains first- and last-name text entries with the proper capitalization. Before you replace the all-uppercase entries in A3:B17 with these entries, you need to convert them from formulas to their calculated values. This will replace the formulas with the text as if you had typed each name in the worksheet.

5. With the cell range A3:D17 still selected, choose the **C**opy command on the **E**dit menu.

6. Without selecting any other cell, select the Paste **S**pecial command on the **E**dit menu, then click the **V**alues option button in the Paste Special dialog box and choose OK or press Enter. You have replaced the formulas with the appropriate text. Now you are ready to move this range on top of the original range with the all-uppercase entries. Doing this will replace the uppercase entries with the ones using the proper capitalization.

7. With the cell range A3:D17 still selected, position the white-cross mouse pointer on the bottom of the range. When the pointer changes to an arrowhead, drag the cell range until its outline encloses the range A3:B7, then release the mouse button. Excel displays an alert box asking if you want the program to overwrite the non-blank cells in the destination.

8. Select the **Y**es button in the alert dialog box to replace the cells with the all-uppercase text entries with entries with proper capitalization.

Your worksheet will now look like the one in Figure 5.26.

Logical Functions

The logical functions are a small but powerful group that you can use to add decision-making capabilities to the formulas in your worksheet. This group includes the IF, OR, AND, NOT, TRUE, and FALSE functions. The principle function in the Logical category is the IF function, which performs a logical test and processes one of two outcomes depending on whether or not the test is true or false. The IF function uses the syntax

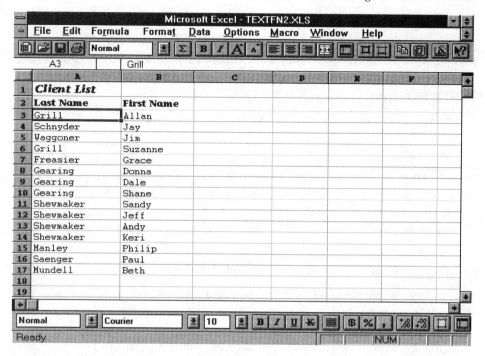

Figure 5.26 Worksheet with Proper Capitalization

=IF(logical_test,value_if_true,value_if_false)

where *logical_test* is any value or expression that can be evaluated to either
TRUE or FALSE, *value_if_true* is the value to be used when the *logical_test* is
TRUE, and *value_if_false* is the value to be used when the *logical_test* is
FALSE.

The *logical_test* argument in the IF function sets up the conditional test
that determines which value is used. To set up the conditional test, this
argument must include one of the following logical operators:

=Equal to

>Greater than

<Less than

>=Greater than or equal to

<=Less than or equal to

< >Not equal to

When the condition is true, the IF function returns the *value_if_true* argument. When the condition is false, the IF function returns the *value_if_false*
argument. For example, when you enter the IF function

=IF(B30>50,1.5,2)

in your worksheet, the function returns 1.5 in the cell when the value in B30 is greater than 50 and returns 2 when the value in B30 is less than or equal to 50.

When you use the IF function, the arguments can include other Excel functions, as in

=IF(SUM(A3:A10)<=1500,0,SUM(A3:A10))

where the IF function returns 0 (zero) in the cell when the sum of the range A:A10 is 1,500 or less, but otherwise returns the sum of the range A3:A10.

You can also have the IF function return a different label depending on the outcome of the conditional test performed by the *logical_test* argument. To do this, you enter the text (enclosed in quotation marks) or the address of the cells that contain text as the *value_if_true* argument and/or the *value_if_false* argument, as in

=IF(MIN(A3:A10)<0,"Negative Value",MIN(A3:A10))

This inserts the text **Negative Value** in the cell when the lowest value in the cell range A3:A10 is less than zero but otherwise will return the minimum value.

Figure 5.27 illustrates a couple of uses for the IF function in a worksheet table that computes monthly sales and the salespersons' commissions. The commission rates in column C are determined by the monthly sales in column B. When a salesperson sells more than $25,000 in the month, the commission rate is set at 7 percent. Otherwise, the commission rate is set at 5 percent. This is computed by the formula

=IF(April_Sales>25000,0.07,0.05)

in the cell range C3:C6 where April_Sales is the name given to the corresponding sales figure in column B.

This sample worksheet also uses the IF function in column F of the table to indicate whether or not a particular salesperson is over or under his or her monthly quota, as shown in column E. This is accomplished by the formula

IF(April_Sales>Quota,"Over","Under")

in the cell range F3:F6, where April_Sales is the name given to the corresponding sales figures in column B and Quota is the name given to the corresponding quota figures in column E.

THE TRUE AND FALSE LOGICAL FUNCTIONS

The TRUE and FALSE logical functions are among the few functions that require no argument. They follow the syntax

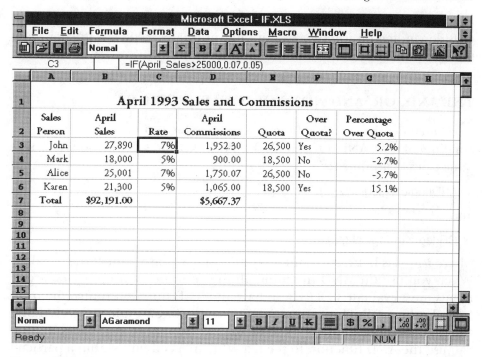

Figure 5.27 Sample Worksheet Using the IF Function

=TRUE( )

or

=FALSE( )

If you were to enter the TRUE and FALSE functions by themselves in two different cells of a worksheet, the TRUE function would return the logical value of 1, indicating true, and the FALSE function would return the logical value of 0, indicating false.

You can enter the true and false logical values of 0 or 1 directly in an Excel worksheet by typing **TRUE** or **FALSE** in a cell: You don't have to enter =TRUE( ) or =FALSE( ). Excel includes these functions to be compatible with other spreadsheet programs, such as Lotus 1-2-3, that do require an equivalent TRUE or FALSE function to enter the true or false values in a worksheet.

In Excel, for example, if you wanted the formulas in column F to return the logical true or false values instead of the text Over or Under, you could create the formulas as

IF(April_Sales>Quota,TRUE( ),FALSE( ))

or

IF(April_Sales>Quota,TRUE,FALSE)

in the cell range F3:F6. Either way, Excel would return either 1 or 0 in the cells depending on whether or not the April_Sales value was greater than the Quota value.

THE AND, OR, AND NOT LOGICAL FUNCTIONS

Excel includes three logical functions that enable you to create compound conditional tests: AND, OR, and NOT. The AND and OR functions take the same types of arguments:

    AND(logical1,logical2,...)

and

    OR(logical1,logical2,...)

where *logical* is between 1 and 30 conditions that are either true or false. When you use the AND function, all the conditions in the *logical* arguments must evaluate to TRUE to have the AND function return the true logical value of 1. This means that if any condition evaluates to FALSE, the AND function returns the false logical value of 0. For example, you can use the AND function to see if a value in a cell falls within a particular range, as in

    =AND(E10>=500,E10<=1000)

This returns the logical true value only when the value in E10 is between 500 and 1000, inclusive.

When you use the OR function, the function returns the true logical value if any condition in the logical arguments evaluates to TRUE. The function returns the false logical value only when all the conditions evaluate to FALSE. For instance, you can use the OR function to see if a value in a cell is any one of a list of values, as in

    =OR(State="CA",State="OR",B2,State="WA")

This returns the logical true value if the entry in the cell named State is CA for California, OR for Oregon, or WA for Washington.

The NOT function takes only a single logical argument. Its syntax is

    =NOT(logical)

where logical is a condition that is either true or false. The NOT function reverses the value of its logical argument. For instance, you could use the NOT function when you want to find out when a cell contains anything except for a particular entry, as in

    =NOT(State="CA")

This returns the logical true value if the entry in the cell name State is anything but CA for California.

The AND, OR, and NOT functions are often nested within the IF function to expand or reverse the *logical_test* argument. For example, you could use the AND example quoted earlier as the condition in an IF function to list values only when they are between 500 and 1000, inclusive, as in

=IF(AND(E10<500,E10>1000),E10, "Value Outside Target Range"

This inserts the value in E10 only if it falls within the target range. Otherwise, the function inserts the text entry **Value Outside Target Range**.

You could use the earlier OR function example as the condition of an IF function to enter the label **Western Region** in a cell only when the entry in a cell name State is either CA for California, OR for Oregon, or WA for Washington, as in

=IF(OR(State="CA",State="OR",State="WA"),"Western Region"," ")

Note that this IF function uses a space enclosed in quotation marks as the *value_if_false* argument to enter a space in the cell so that it appears blank for any other state.

So too, if you were a company operating solely in California, you could use the earlier NOT function example as the condition of an IF function in a tax column to determine how to fill in a cell that contains the sales tax in an invoice, as in

=IF(NOT(State="CA"),0,Subtotal*.075)

This uses 0 as the sales tax when the state code in the cell named State is anything but CA for California. When the State is CA, the formula then multiplies the value in the cell named Subtotal by $7\frac{1}{2}$ percent to compute the local sales tax.

Note: You can combine the IF function with a group of functions in the Information category known collectively as the IS functions (because each one starts with IS, as in ISBLANK, ISERR, ISLOGICAL, and so on) to determine the type of entry in a cell. See Appendix B for information on how to use the IS functions. See Chapter 8 for information on using them to perform error trapping in the worksheet.

Lookup Functions

The last functions that we'll examine in this chapter are the Lookup functions HLOOKUP and VLOOKUP. These functions are located in the Lookup & Reference category in the Paste Function dialog box.

They are part of a powerful group of functions that can return values by looking them up in tables. The VLOOKUP function searches vertically (top to bottom) the leftmost column of a lookup table until the program locates a value that matches or exceeds the one you are looking up. The HLOOKUP function searches horizontally (left to right) the topmost row of a lookup table until it locates a value that matches or exceeds the one you're looking up.

The VLOOKUP functions follows the syntax

```
=VLOOKUP(lookup_value,table_array,col_index_num)
```

The HLOOKUP follows the nearly identical syntax of

```
=HLOOKUP(lookup_value,table_array,row_index_num)
```

In both functions, *lookup_value* is the value you want to look up in the lookup table, *table_array* is the cell range or name of the lookup table, *col_index_num* is the number of the column whose values are compared to the *lookup_value* in a vertical table, and *row_index_num* is the number of the row whose values are compared to the *lookup_value* in a horizontal table. When entering the *col_index_num* or *row_index_num* arguments in the VLOOKUP or HLOOKUP functions, you must enter a value greater than zero that does not exceed the total number of columns or rows in the lookup table.

You can use the VLOOKUP and HLOOKUP functions to look up text or values in a lookup table. In either case, the text or numeric entries in the *comparison range* (that is, the leftmost column of a vertical lookup table or the top row of a horizontal lookup table) must be unique, and they must be arranged in ascending order (alphabetical order for text entries, lowest-to-highest order for numeric entries).

> **Note:** For information on how to sort your worksheet data in ascending order with Excel's Data Sort command, see Chapter 15.

Figure 5.28 shows you how you can use the VLOOKUP function to return either a 15% or 20% tip from a tip table, depending on the pretax total of the check. Cell F5 contains the VLOOKUP function

```
=VLOOKUP(Pretax_Total,Tip_Table,IF(Tip_Percentage=0.15,2,3))
```

which returns the amount of the tip based on the tip percentage in cell F3 and the pretax amount of the check in cell F4.

To use this tip table, you enter the percentage of the tip (15% or 20%) in cell F3 (named Tip_Percentage) and the amount of the check before tax in cell F4 (named Pretax_Total). Excel then looks up the value you enter in the Pretax_Total cell in the first column of the lookup table, which includes the cell range A2:C101 and is named Tip_Table. The program moves down the values in the first column of Tip_Table until it finds a match. Then the program uses the *col_index_num* argument in the VLOOKUP function to determine which tip amount from that row of the table should be returned in cell F5. If, as in Figure 5.28, Excel finds that the value entered in the Pretax_Total cell does not exactly match one of the values in the first column of Tip_Table, the program continues to search down the comparison range until it encounters the first value that exceeds the pretax total (8.00 in cell A10 in this example). Excel then moves back up to the previous row in the table and returns the value in the column that matches the *col_index_num* argument of the VLOOKUP function.

Note that the tip table example in the figure uses an IF function to determine the *col_index_num* argument for the VLOOKUP function in cell F5. The IF function determines the number of the column to be used in the tip table by matching the percentage entered in Tip_Percentage (cell F3) with 0.15. If they match, the function returns 2 as the *col_index_num* argument, and the VLOOKUP function returns a value from the second column (the 15% column B) in Tip_Table. Otherwise, the IF

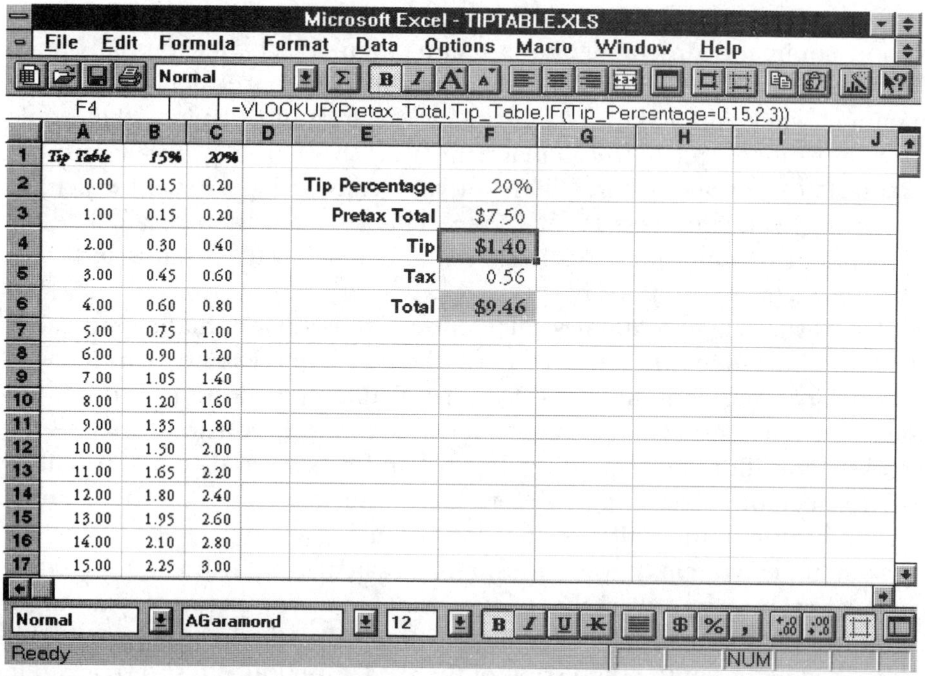

	A	B	C	D	E	F
1	*Tip Table*	*15%*	*20%*			
2	0.00	0.15	0.20		Tip Percentage	20%
3	1.00	0.15	0.20		Pretax Total	$7.50
4	2.00	0.30	0.40		Tip	$1.40
5	3.00	0.45	0.60		Tax	0.56
6	4.00	0.60	0.80		Total	$9.46
7	5.00	0.75	1.00			
8	6.00	0.90	1.20			
9	7.00	1.05	1.40			
10	8.00	1.20	1.60			
11	9.00	1.35	1.80			
12	10.00	1.50	2.00			
13	11.00	1.65	2.20			
14	12.00	1.80	2.40			
15	13.00	1.95	2.60			
16	14.00	2.10	2.80			
17	15.00	2.25	3.00			

Figure 5.28 Using the VLOOKUP Function with a Tip Table

function returns 3 as the *col_index_num* argument and the VLOOKUP function returns a value from the third column (the 20% column C) in Tip_Table.

Recalculating the Worksheet

Normally, Excel recalculates your worksheet automatically as soon as you change any entries, formulas, or names on which your formulas depend. This system works fine as long as the worksheet is not too large or does not contain tables whose formulas depend on several values.

When Excel does calculate your worksheet, the program recalculates only those cells that are affected by the change you've made. Nevertheless, in a complex worksheet that contains many formulas, recalculation may take several seconds. (During this time, the pointer changes to an hourglass and Recalc followed by the number of cells left to be recalculated appears on the left side of the formula bar.) Because Excel recalculates dependent formulas in the background, you can always interrupt this process and make a cell entry or choose a command. As soon as you stop making entries or selecting commands, Excel resumes recalculating the worksheet.

To control when Excel calculates your worksheet, you choose the Calculation command on the Options menu, then select the Manual option button under Calculation. After switching to manual recalculation in this manner, when you make a change in a value, formula, or name that would usually cause Excel to recalculate the worksheet, the program displays Calculate on the status bar. When you are ready to have Excel recalculate the worksheet, you press F9 or Ctrl+=. The program then recalculates all dependent formulas and open charts, and the Calculate status indicator disappears from the status bar.

After switching to manual recalculation, Excel still automatically recalculates the worksheet whenever you save the file. When you are working with a very large and complex worksheet, recalculating each time you want to save your changes can be quite time consuming. If you want to save the worksheet without first updating dependent formulas and charts, you need to deselect the Recalculate Before Save check box under the Manual option button in the Calculations Options dialog.

Sometimes you may want to switch recalculation from automatic to manual even when a worksheet is not very large. For example, you might want to switch to manual recalculation when using the loan payment table described earlier in the discussion of the PMT function and shown again in Figures 5.29 and 5.30. Remember that this loan payment table depends on three inputs: Amount of the loan in cell B2, the annual interest rate in B3, and the term in years in cell B4. Because you are apt to change more than one of these values (such as the initial interest rate and term) before you want to view the range of payments, using manual recalculation enables you to make these changes without being distracted by Excel's recalculating the payments after each modification.

Figure 5.29 shows you the loan payment worksheet after switching to manual recalculation and changing the annual interest rate in cell B3 from $6\frac{1}{2}\%$ to 5% and the term from 30 to 15 years. Note the **Calculate** indicator on the status bar in this figure, indicating that the payments in the table are not up-to-date. Figure 5.30 shows you the same worksheet after using the Calculate **N**ow command (initiated by pressing F9 or Ctrl+=). The payments are now correct in the table and the **Calculate** indicator has disappeared.

Automatic and manual are by no means the only recalculation options available in Excel. Table 5.1 explains each of the options that appears in the Calculation Options dialog box.

Circular References in Formulas

A *circular reference* in a formula is one that depends, directly or indirectly, on its own value. The most common type of circular reference occurs when you mistakenly refer in the formula to the cell in which you're building the formula itself. For example, suppose that cell B10 is active when you build the formula

    =A10+B10

As soon as you press Enter or an arrow key to insert this formula in cell B10, Excel displays an alert box that says **Cannot resolve circular references.** As soon as you press Enter or click OK to close this alert box, the program inserts 0 in the cell with the circular reference and the indicator **Circular** followed by the cell address with the circular reference appears on the status bar.

Excel is not able to resolve the circular reference in cell B10 because the formula's calculation depends directly on the formula's result—each time the formula returns a new result, this result is fed into the formula, creating a new result. This type of circular reference sets up an endless loop that continuously requires recalculating and can never be resolved.

Not all circular references are unresolvable. Some formulas contain a circular reference that eventually can be resolved after many recalculations of its formula. Each time the formula is recalculated with a new value in the circular reference, the results in each cell get closer and closer to the correct ones.

Microsoft Excel - LOANPMT.XLS

File   Edit   Formula   Format   Data   Options   Macro   Window   Help

Normal

B4   15

	A	B	C	D	E	F	G	H
1	**Loan Payments**							
2	Principal	$350,000						
3	Interest Rate	5.00%						
4	Term (in years)	15						
5								
6		**6.50%**	**6.75%**	**7.00%**	**7.25%**	**7.50%**	**7.75%**	
7	**$350,000**	($2,212.24)	($2,270.09)	($2,328.56)	($2,387.62)	($2,447.25)	($2,507.44)	
8	**$351,000**	($2,218.56)	($2,276.58)	($2,335.21)	($2,394.44)	($2,454.24)	($2,514.61)	
9	**$352,000**	($2,224.88)	($2,283.07)	($2,341.86)	($2,401.26)	($2,461.24)	($2,521.77)	
10	**$353,000**	($2,231.20)	($2,289.55)	($2,348.52)	($2,408.08)	($2,468.23)	($2,528.94)	
11	**$354,000**	($2,237.52)	($2,296.04)	($2,355.17)	($2,414.90)	($2,475.22)	($2,536.10)	
12	**$355,000**	($2,243.84)	($2,302.52)	($2,361.82)	($2,421.73)	($2,482.21)	($2,543.26)	
13	**$356,000**	($2,250.16)	($2,309.01)	($2,368.48)	($2,428.55)	($2,489.20)	($2,550.43)	
14	**$357,000**	($2,256.48)	($2,315.50)	($2,375.13)	($2,435.37)	($2,496.20)	($2,557.59)	
15	**$358,000**	($2,262.80)	($2,321.98)	($2,381.78)	($2,442.19)	($2,503.19)	($2,564.76)	
16	**$359,000**	($2,269.12)	($2,328.47)	($2,388.44)	($2,449.01)	($2,510.18)	($2,571.92)	
17								
18								

Ready   Calculate   NUM

Figure 5.29   Loan Payment Worksheet in Need of Recalculation

Microsoft Excel - LOANPMT.XLS

File   Edit   Formula   Format   Data   Options   Macro   Window   Help

Normal

B4   15

	A	B	C	D	E	F	G	H
1	**Loan Payments**							
2	Principal	$350,000						
3	Interest Rate	5.00%						
4	Term (in years)	15						
5								
6		**5.00%**	**5.25%**	**5.50%**	**5.75%**	**6.00%**	**6.25%**	
7	**$350,000**	($2,767.78)	($2,813.57)	($2,859.79)	($2,906.44)	($2,953.50)	($3,000.98)	
8	**$351,000**	($2,775.69)	($2,821.61)	($2,867.96)	($2,914.74)	($2,961.94)	($3,009.55)	
9	**$352,000**	($2,783.59)	($2,829.65)	($2,876.13)	($2,923.04)	($2,970.38)	($3,018.13)	
10	**$353,000**	($2,791.50)	($2,837.69)	($2,884.30)	($2,931.35)	($2,978.81)	($3,026.70)	
11	**$354,000**	($2,799.41)	($2,845.73)	($2,892.48)	($2,939.65)	($2,987.25)	($3,035.28)	
12	**$355,000**	($2,807.32)	($2,853.77)	($2,900.65)	($2,947.96)	($2,995.69)	($3,043.85)	
13	**$356,000**	($2,815.23)	($2,861.80)	($2,908.82)	($2,956.26)	($3,004.13)	($3,052.43)	
14	**$357,000**	($2,823.13)	($2,869.84)	($2,916.99)	($2,964.56)	($3,012.57)	($3,061.00)	
15	**$358,000**	($2,831.04)	($2,877.88)	($2,925.16)	($2,972.87)	($3,021.01)	($3,069.57)	
16	**$359,000**	($2,838.95)	($2,885.92)	($2,933.33)	($2,981.17)	($3,029.45)	($3,078.15)	
17								
18								

Ready   NUM

Figure 5.30   Loan Payment Worksheet Recalculated with Calculate Now

Table 5.1 Calculation Options in Excel 4.0

Option	Usage
Automatic	Calculates all dependent formulas and updates open or embedded charts every time you make a change to a value, formula, or name. This is the default setting for each new worksheet that you start.
Automatic Except Tables	Calculates all dependent formulas and updates open or embedded charts but does not calculate data tables created with the **Data Table** command. (See Chapter 11 for information on creating data tables.) To recalculate data tables when this option button is selected, choose the Calc **Now** (F9) command button in the Calculations Options dialog box or press F9 in the worksheet.
Manual	Calculates open worksheets and updates open or embedded charts only when you choose the Calc **Now** (F9) command button in the Calculations Options dialog box or press F9 or Ctrl+= in the worksheet.
Recalculate Before Save	When this check box is selected, Excel calculates open worksheets and updates open or embedded charts when you save them even when the **Manual** option button is selected.
Calc Now (F9)	Calculates all open worksheets (including data tables) and updates all open or embedded charts.
Calc Document	Calculates only the active worksheet (including data tables) and updates only charts on the worksheet or open charts that are linked to the active worksheet.
Iteration	When this check box is selected, Excel sets the iterations (the number of times that a worksheet is recalculated), when performing goal seeking (see Chapter 11) or resolving circular references to the number displayed in the Maximum Iterations text box.
Maximum Iterations	Sets the maximum number of iterations (100 by default) when the **Iteration** check box is selected.
Maximum Change	Sets the maximum amount of change to the values during each iteration (0.001 by default) when the **Iteration** check box is selected.

Table 5.1 *(Continued)*

Update **R**emote References	Calculates formulas that include references to other applications. (See Chapter 21.) When this check box is deselected, these formulas use the last value received from the other program.
Precision as Displayed	When this check box is selected, Excel changes the values in cells from full precision (15 digits) to whatever number format is displayed so that the displayed values are used in calculations.
1904 **D**ate System	When this check box is selected, Excel changes the starting date from which all serial numbers in dates are calculated from January 1, 1900, to January 2, 1904.
Save External **L**ink Values	When this check box is selected, Excel saves copies of values contained in an external file that is linked to your Excel worksheet. To reduce the amount of disk space required for this copy or to reduce the amount of time that it takes to open this external document, deselect this check box.
Alternate **E**xpression Evaluation	When this check box is selected, Excel allows you to open Lotus 1-2-3 worksheets without losing or changing its data by evaluating text strings to 0, Boolean expressions to 0 or 1, and database criteria according to 1-2-3's rules.

Figure 5.31 illustrates the classic example of a formula using a circular reference that ultimately can be resolved. There you have an income statement that includes bonuses equal to 20 percent of the net earnings entered as an expense in cell B12 with the formula

=–B17*0.2

This formula contains a circular reference because it refers to the value in B17, which itself indirectly depends on the amount of bonuses. (The bonuses are used as an expense in the formulas that determine the amount of net earnings in cell B17.)

To resolve the circular reference in cell B12 and calculate the bonuses based on net earnings in B17, you simply need to select the Iteration check box in the Calculations Options dialog box (unless the Manual option button is selected; then you must press F9 or Ctrl+= as well). Figure 5.32

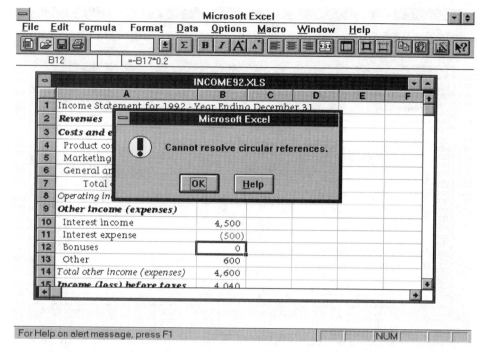

Figure 5.31 Income Statement with Bonus Formula Containing a Circular Reference

shows you the income statement worksheet after selecting the **I**teration setting to resolve the circular reference in the formula in cell B12 and calculate the bonuses for 1992.

Protecting the Worksheet

After you've completed your formulas, checked them out, and completed the formatting for your worksheet, you may want to protect the cells from any further changes. You can do this with the **P**rotect Document command on the **O**ptions menu. When you select this command, Excel displays the Protect Document dialog box shown in Figure 5.33. As you can see from this figure, you can protect cells and objects (meaning graphic objects such as embedded charts) as well as windows in the active worksheet.

By default, Excel assigned a "locked" status to all cells and graphic objects in a worksheet. This locked status takes effect in the current worksheet as soon as you select the Cells or Objects protection in the Protect Document dialog box. After you activate cell and/or object protection, Excel will not allow you to make any changes to the locked cells or objects in the worksheets. This includes formatting, relocating, or deleting them.

	A	B	C	D	E	F
1	Income Statement for 1992 - Year Ending December 31					
2	**Revenues**	50,250				
3	**Costs and expenses**					
4	Product costs	(12,175)				
5	Marketing and sales	(20,785)				
6	General and administrative	(17,850)				
7	Total costs and expenses	**(50,810)**				
8	*Operating income (loss)*	(560)				
9	**Other income (expenses)**					
10	Interest income	4,500				
11	Interest expense	(500)				
12	Bonuses	(587)				
13	Other	600				
14	*Total other income (expenses)*	4,013				
15	**Income (loss) before taxes**	3,453				
16	Provision (benefit) for taxes	(518)				
17	*Net earnings (loss)*	2,935				

Cell reference: B12   =-B17*0.2

Figure 5.32 Income Statement After Using the Iteration Setting to Resolve the Circular Reference

Note that if you select the Windows check box in the Protect Document dialog box, Excel prevents you from opening, resizing, or closing any panes in the active worksheet window. (See Chapter 10 for information on how you split the document window into separate panes.)

Locked cells, objects, or windows remain protected in a worksheet only until you unprotect the document by choosing the Un**p**rotect Document command on the **O**ptions menu. To prevent an unauthorized person from using this command to unprotect the worksheet, you can assign a password in the Protect Document. Then only the people who know the password can ever unprotect the worksheet and make any modifications to its cells, objects, or windows (depending on which of the three options you use).

Tip You can also password protect a worksheet so only those who know the password can open the file and/or save changes to the worksheet. See Chapter 10 for information on restricting access to your Excel files.

To assign a password, type the password in the **P**assword text box exactly as you want it. Keep in mind that Excel distinguishes between uppercase and lowercase letters in a password so that the password dtD (don't tell

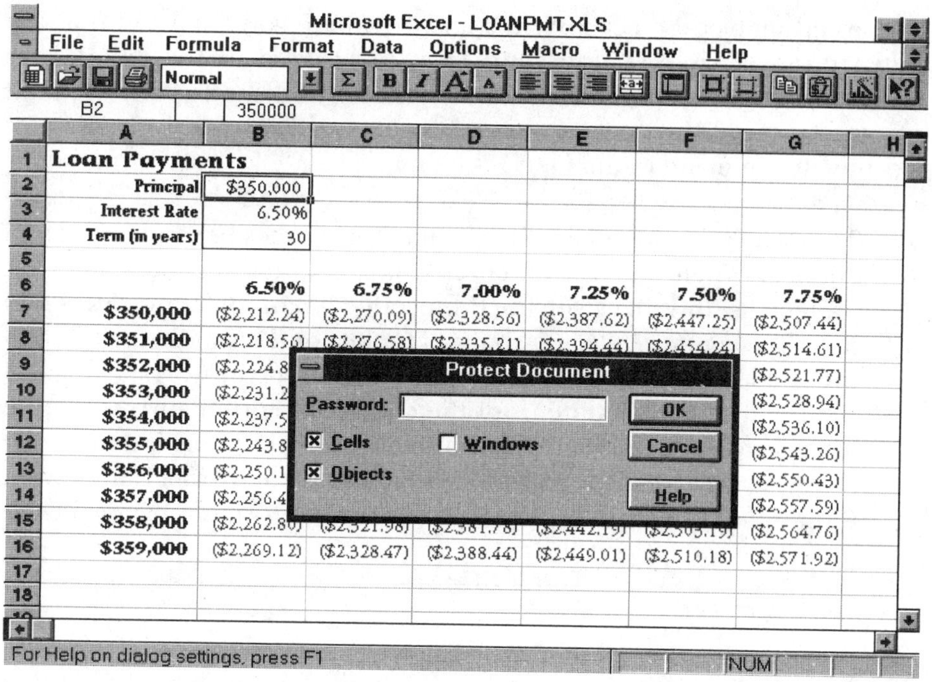

Figure 5.33 The Protect Document Dialog Box

Dad) does not match the password **dtd**. As you type the password, Excel masks each character in the Password text box with an asterisk. When you select the OK command button or press Enter, Excel displays the Confirm Password dialog box where you must reenter the password exactly as you first typed it. Upon successfully duplicating the password and selecting OK or pressing Enter, Excel assigns the password to the Unprotect Document command. This means that you must be able to successfully reproduce the password before you can unprotect the worksheet to make changes to its locked cells, objects, and/or windows. If you forget your password, you will not be able to unprotect the document and will remain prevented from making any modifications to it.

Sometimes you will want to leave some cells unlocked in a protected worksheet so that you can still change their values without being able to modify other parts of the worksheet (such as the dependent formulas). To do this, you must select the cells, cell range, or nonadjacent range and choose the Cell Protection command on the Format menu and clear the Locked check box in the Cell Protection dialog box. Note that you must unlock the cells you still want access to before you protect the worksheet with the **Protect** Document command in the **O**ptions menu.

For example, in the loan payment worksheet shown first in Figure 5.23, you would unlock the cells B2, B3, and B4 where you need to input the initial principal, interest rate, and term to be used in the table. After unlocking these cells with the Cell Protection command on the Format menu, you could then protect the rest of the worksheet with the **P**rotect Document command in the **O**ptions menu.

Tip   The Cell Protection dialog box contains two check boxes: **L**ocked and **H**idden. When the **L**ocked check box is selected for a cell and you protect the worksheet with the **P**rotect Document command, Excel will not allow you to make any changes to the contents of the cell. When the **H**idden check box is selected and you protect the worksheet, Excel will not display the contents of the cell on the formula bar when the cell is active. You can use this setting along with a custom hidden format (see Chapter 4 for information on creating a hidden format) to prevent the display of a cell's contents either on the formula bar or in the worksheet when the cell is active.

SUMMARY

In this chapter you learned more about how Excel calculates the worksheet. Specifically, you learned how to assign names to values used in formulas in your worksheet to make them easier to understand and locate. You then learned how to build array formulas to reduce the size of a worksheet and the amount of memory it takes to load it. You also learned how to use several types of worksheet functions in your formulas, making it easy to perform complex and specialized calculations. Finally, you learned how to control when and how your worksheet is recalculated as well as how to protect the worksheet from any further changes.

In the next chapter you will learn how to print your worksheet. Specifically, you will learn how to print all or part of a worksheet; set up reports with headers, footers, and titles; change the margins and page breaks; and use the Print Preview command to see exactly how your report will print before you actually send it to the printer.

6

Printing the Worksheet

Printing the worksheet is one of the most important tasks you will be doing with Excel. Fortunately, Excel makes it easy to produce professional-looking reports from your worksheets. In this chapter you will learn how to select the printer you want to use; print all or just select parts of the worksheet; change your page layout and print settings, including the orientation, paper size, print quality, number of copies, and range of pages; set up reports using the correct margin settings, headers and footers, titles, and page breaks; and how to use the Print Preview feature to make sure that the pages of your report are the way you want them before you print them.

The printing techniques in this chapter focus primarily on printing the data in your worksheets. Of course in Excel, you can also print macros in your macro sheets and charts in your chart windows. Not surprisingly, you will find that most of the printing techniques you learn for printing worksheet data in this chapter also apply to printing macros or charts in their respective windows. For specific information on printing macros see Chapter 17, and for specific information on printing charts see Chapter 12.

Selecting the Printer

Windows allows you to install more than one printer for use with your applications. If you have installed multiple printers, the first one installed becomes the default printer that is used by all Windows applications, including Excel. If you get a new printer, you first must install it in Windows before you can select and use it in Excel. To install the printer:

1. Start Windows, then locate the Control Panel icon in the Main group window and double-click it to open the Control Panel window.

2. Locate the Printers icon in the Control Panel window and double-click it to open the Printers dialog box.

3. Click the **A**dd Printer command button to redraw the Printers dialog box with the **L**ist of Printers list box, as shown in Figure 6.1.

4. Click the name of the printer you want to install in the List of Printers list box, then click the Install command button.

5. Insert the Windows Setup Disk 5 or a disk with the driver for the printer you are adding in drive A, then click the OK button in the Control Panel-Printers dialog box or press Enter. If you use drive B to load Windows disks on your computer, change A:\ to B:\ in the text box before you select OK. Windows will then copy the necessary printer driver and add the printer to the Installed **P**rinters list box.

6. The list of installed printers will include the printer name along with its port (as in **PCL/HP LaserJet on LPT1**). To change the port setting, click the **C**onfigure command button and choose the correct port in the Ports list box of the Printers-Configure dialog box.

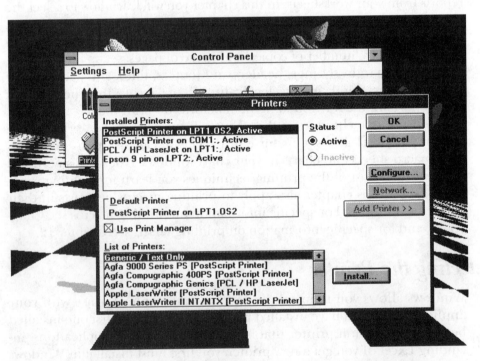

Figure 6.1　Adding a New Printer in the Windows Printers Dialog Box

7. Sometimes the printer you add is listed as inactive under Status. To put the printer on active status, click the **Active** option button.

8. If you want to make the printer you've added the default printer for printing in all Windows applications such as Excel, double-click the printer in the Installed Printers list box so that it appears in the Default Printer box.

9. Once you've finished changing the settings for your new printer, click the OK button or press Enter to save your changes, close the Printers dialog box, and return to the Control Panel window. Then double-click the Control-menu button on the Control Panel window to close this window and return to the Windows Program Manager, from where you can start Excel.

To select a new printer to use in printing your Excel worksheets, you follow these steps:

1. Start Excel or make the Excel program window active, then choose the Page Setup command on the **File** menu.

2. Click the Printer Setup command button in the lower-right corner of the Page Setup dialog box. Excel opens the Printer Setup dialog box similar to the one shown in Figure 6.2.

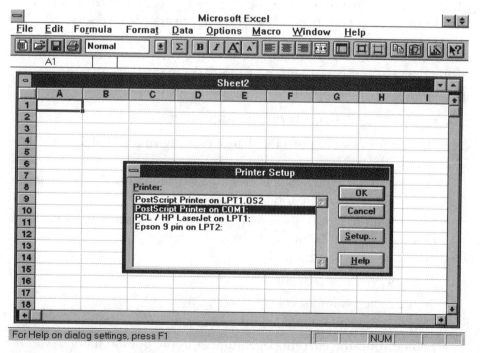

Figure 6.2   Selecting a New Printer in the Printer Setup Dialog Box

3. Click the printer you want to use in the **P**rinter list box of the Printer Setup dialog box.

4. If you want to change any of the default settings for the printer you've selected (see "Changing the Printer's Default Settings" later in this chapter), change the settings in the printer's dialog box and click OK or press Enter to return to the Printer Setup dialog box.

5. Select the OK button or press Enter in the Printer Setup dialog box to finish selecting your printer.

Keep in mind that the printer you select in Excel becomes the current printer for all Windows applications that use that printer with the Windows printer driver. This means that if you change from a laser printer to a dot-matrix printer to print a rough draft of a worksheet and then forget to change back to the laser printer, the dot-matrix printer will be the selected one when you open an application such as Word for Windows.

Printing Worksheet Data

The easiest way to print your worksheet is by clicking the Print tool on the Standard toolbar. When you click this tool, Excel prints the entire worksheet using the default print settings for the printer you've selected. (You also can print the entire worksheet by opening the Print dialog box by choosing **P**rint on the **F**ile menu or pressing Ctrl+Shift+F12 and then selecting the OK command button or pressing Enter.) For most printers, the default print settings used in printing your worksheet are as follows:

- Paper Size is set to letter ($8\frac{1}{2}$ x 11 inches).
- Orientation is set to portrait (that is, printing runs parallel to the short edge of the paper).
- Margins are set to 0.75 inch in from the left and right edge of the paper, and 1 inch in from the top and bottom edge.
- Order is set to Down, then over (meaning lower sections of the print range are printed before sections to the right).
- Scaling is set to 100% (actual size).
- The cell gridlines are printed.
- Starting Page Number is 1.
- Header prints the filename in the top margin.
- Footer prints the current page number in the bottom margin with the word *Page*, as in **Page 1**, **Page 2**, and so on.

- Worksheet data is printed without its notes.
- Prints 1 (one) copy of the report.
- Print Quality is set to High.

Excel prints the worksheet via the Windows Print Manager. During the time Excel is sending the print job to the Print Manager, Windows displays a Printing dialog box that keeps you informed of its progress by displaying the current page being sent as well as the total number of pages in the print job (as in **Page 2 of 3**). Windows continues to display the Printing dialog box until the entire print job has been sent to the Print Manager, whereupon the Printing dialog box closes and you are free to resume your work in Excel.

To terminate the printing before the entire print job has been sent to the Print Manager, you simply click the Cancel button in the Printing dialog box. If you aren't able to cancel the printing before that box closes, you must activate the Print Manager window and cancel the printing from there.

To activate the Print Manager application window, reduce the Excel program window to an icon by clicking the Minimize button in its upper-right corner, then double-click the Print Manager icon on the bottom of the desktop to open the Print Manager window (as shown in Figure 6.3).

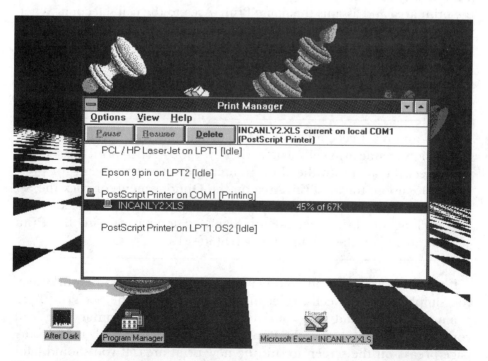

Figure 6.3   Terminating an Excel Print Job in the Print Manager Window

Once this window is open, you can cancel the print job by selecting the job in the window and then clicking the **D**elete command button. Windows then displays an alert dialog box asking you to confirm your termination of the printing. Select the OK command button to have Windows remove the print job from the print queue (that is, the list of print jobs).

After deleting the print job, you can minimize the Print Manager window and return to Excel by double-clicking its program icon at the bottom of the Windows desktop. (If the Program Manager window is open, don't do this; if you do, Windows will try to start Excel a second time.) If the Print Manager window is empty after you delete your Excel print job, you can close that window by double-clicking its Control-menu button before you return to Excel.

Printing Part of a Worksheet

Excel makes it easy to print only part of a worksheet, such as a particular cell range or nonadjacent selection. You simply select the cell range or nonadjacent selection as you would normally and choose the Set Print Area command on the Options menu, or you can click the Set Print Area tool if the Utility toolbar is displayed. Excel then makes the current selection the print area and assigns the name Print_Area to the cell selection. When you set a print area with the Set Print Area command or tool, Excel displays the page breaks for the Print_Area on the screen with dotted lines along the cell borders. To print the Print_Area, you then click the Print tool on the Standard toolbar or choose the Print command on the File menu (Ctrl+Shift+F12) and select OK in the Print dialog box.

Tip If your worksheet contains a section of data that you reprint frequently, assign a name to its cells. Then, whenever you need to print this section, select the area with the **G**oto command on the **E**dit menu (or press F5), choose the Set Print **A**rea on the **O**ptions menu or click the Set Print Area tool on the Utility toolbar, and print the cell selection by clicking the Print tool on the Standard toolbar or with the **P**rint command on the **F**ile menu (Ctrl+Shift+F12).

If you then want to print another cell selection in the same worksheet, you simply select the cells, reset the Print_Area with the Set Print Area command or tool, and print your new selection with the Print tool or Print command. When you reset the Print_Area, Excel immediately redraws the page breaks on the screen to suit the new print area. If you should later want to print the entire worksheet, you select all the cells by clicking the button in the upper-left corner of the worksheet window at the intersection of the row of column letters and the column of row numbers before you choose the Set Print Area command or tool. This resets the Print_Area to the entire worksheet, which you then can print with the Print tool or the Print command.

Printing the Formulas in the Worksheet

When you print a worksheet, Excel prints the entries exactly as they appear in their worksheet cells. As a result, when you print a section of a worksheet that contains formulas, the printout shows only the results of the calculations performed by the formulas, not the contents of the formulas themselves. In addition to a printout showing the results, you may also want to print a copy of the worksheet showing the formulas by which these results were derived. You can then use this printout when double-checking the formulas in the worksheet to make sure that they are designed correctly. (For more ideas on how to troubleshoot your worksheet, see Chapter 8.)

To print a copy of the worksheet with the formulas displayed in the cells, follow these steps:

1. Choose the **D**isplay command on the **O**ptions menu.

2. Select the Formulas check box under Cells in the Display Options dialog box, then select the OK button or press Enter. When the Formulas check box is selected, Excel displays the entry in each cell in the worksheet as it appears on the formula. This means not only do formulas appear as entered in the worksheet but also that all values (text and numeric) appear without their formatting.

3. If necessary, widen the columns in the worksheet to display all of the formulas in their cells.

4. Print the worksheet or cell selection as you normally would. If you only need to print an area of the worksheet, designate that section as the Print_Area (as outlined earlier) before you choose the Print tool or the **P**rint command on the **F**ile menu.

5. After printing the formulas in the worksheet, choose the **D**isplay command on the **O**ptions menu and deselect the Formulas check box before you select OK or press Enter. Excel returns the worksheet display to normal so that only the results of formulas are displayed in the cells and all entries are displayed with their formatting.

Tip To help you identify the cell reference of each formula in your print-out, print the version of the worksheet that displays the formulas in the cells with the column letters and row numbers on the top row and leftmost column of each page. To do this, you need to open the Print dialog box by selecting the **P**rint command on the **File** menu or pressing Ctrl+Shift+F12 (you can't use the Print tool), choose the Page **S**etup command button, and select the Row & Column Headings check box in the Page Setup dialog box. Then choose the OK button in the Page Setup and Print dialog box or press Enter twice to start the printing.

Changing the Printer's Default Settings

When you select a new printer, Excel uses the default settings for its printer driver in printing your worksheets. In most cases, you can modify these default settings if you find that they routinely do not suit your needs. Keep in mind, however, that changes that you make to the default printer settings in Excel affect the printing of all documents that use that printer, even documents created with other Windows applications. In other words, if you change the default orientation from portrait to landscape in Excel, this will also become the default orientation when you next print a document in Word for Windows using that printer!

To modify the default settings for your printer in Excel, follow these steps:

1. Choose the Page Setup command on the **File** menu to open the Page Setup dialog box.

2. Select the Printer Setup command button in the lower-right corner of the Page Setup dialog box.

3. With your printer selected in the **P**rinter list box, select the **S**etup command button in the Printer Setup dialog box. Excel displays the dialog box for your printer with the default options that you can modify. The options displayed vary according to the capabilities of the printer you've selected. They can include such things as the model of the printer (some drivers are used by more than one type of printer), orientation of the page (Portrait or Landscape), paper size, scaling (PostScript printers can scale the size of the printing), and the number of copies. Figures 6.4 and 6.5 show two very different dialog boxes. The first is the one that appears when an HP LaserJet is the current printer, and the second is the box that appears when an Epson dot-matrix printer is the current printer.

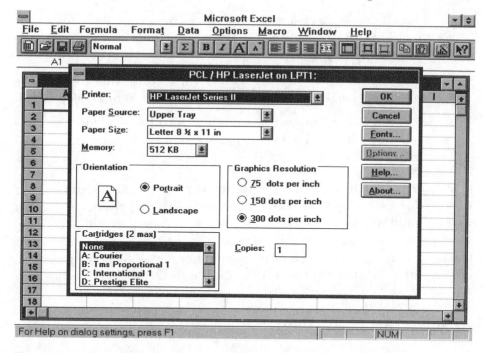

Figure 6.4   The PCL/HP LaserJet Default Settings Dialog Box

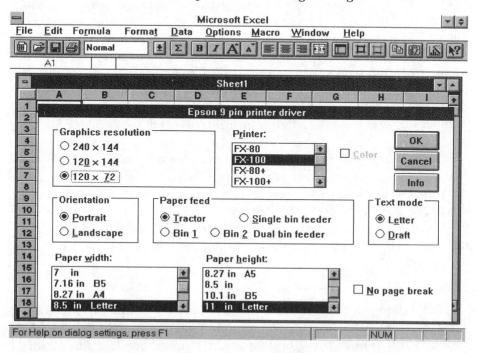

Figure 6.5   The Epson 9 Pin Printer Driver Default Settings Dialog Box

4. Make all necessary changes to options in the dialog box, then select the OK button or press Enter to close this box and return to the Printer Setup dialog box.

5. Select the OK button or press Enter a second time to close the Printer Setup dialog box and return to the Page Setup dialog box.

6. Select the OK button or press Enter a third time to close the Page Setup dialog box and put your changes to the default printer settings in effect.

Keep in mind that changes you make to the printer default settings affect all worksheets and other documents printed with that printer from that time on, until you once again modify that default setting as outlined above. To change a page layout or print setting for a particular printout without making the change in the new printer default, you modify the setting in the Page Setup or Print dialog box as described in the next several sections.

Modifying the Page Setup

Instead of changing printer default settings, you can modify the page setup settings for just the worksheet you are printing. For example, when printing a worksheet that is much wider than it is tall, you would modify the page setup settings to fit more worksheet data on each page and reduce the number of total pages. You can do this by selecting a larger paper size, changing the orientation of the page from portrait to landscape, reducing the size of the margins, or even scaling the printing to fit the data on a set number of pages (assuming that your printer is capable of making all these changes).

You can use the options in the Page Setup dialog box (shown in Figure 6.6) to make changes to the layout of the printed page (including such things as the page orientation, paper size, margin settings, and the like). You open this dialog box by choosing the Page Setup command on the **F**ile menu or by selecting the Page **S**etup command button in the Print dialog box. The next few sections explain the page setup options found in the Page Setup dialog box.

Note: When printing a chart in a chart window (as opposed to a chart placed in the worksheet), Excel displays a Page Setup dialog box with slightly different printing options at the bottom. See Chapter 12 for more information on creating and printing charts.

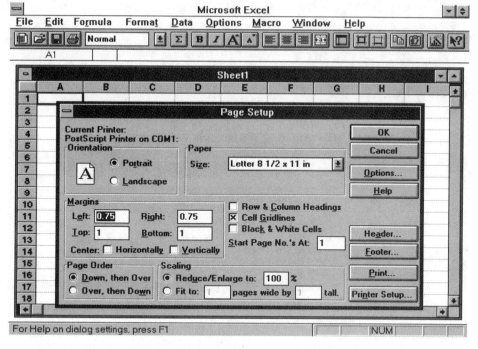

Figure 6.6   The Page Setup Dialog Box

Changing the Orientation

The normal orientation of printing on a page is the *portrait mode*, whereby the printing runs parallel to the short edge of the paper as in the sample page shown in Figure 6.7. Many printers are also capable of orienting text to the *landscape mode*, whereby the printing runs parallel to the long edge of the paper, as in the sample page shown in Figure 6.8.

To change the orientation from the default of portrait mode to land-scape mode, select the Landscape option button in the Page Setup dialog box (which automatically deselects the Portrait button). The dialog box shows the change in orientation by redrawing the page around the letter *A* so that the long side is parallel to the base of this letter.

Selecting the Paper Size

Almost all printers can use different paper sizes even when they aren't able to switch between portrait and landscape mode. The most common paper sizes include:

- Letter 8½ x 11 in

Page 1 of 1

Hours/Wages -
February, 1992

	Pay Period 1 (1st - 15th)	Pay Period 2 (16th - 29th)	Monthly Total
Hours			
Robert	*102.5*	*140.0*	**242.5**
Maria	*74.0*	*102.0*	**176.0**
Jane	*82.0*	*124.0*	**206.0**
Michael	*120.0*	*155.0*	**275.0**
Total	**378.5**	**521.0**	**899.5**
Wages			
Robert	*1,230.00*	*1,680.00*	**$2,910.00**
Maria	*592.00*	*816.00*	**$1,408.00**
Jane	*799.50*	*1,209.00*	**$2,008.50**
Michael	*2,400.00*	*3,100.00*	**$5,500.00**
Total	**$5,021.50**	**$6,805.00**	**$11,826.50**

Figure 6.7 Page Printed in the Portrait Orientation

February, 1992 - Monthly Labor Report *Page 1*

Hours/Wages -
February, 1992

	1	2	3	4	5	6	7	8
Hours								
Robert	5.5	8	8	7	0	10	10	5.5
Maria	6	0	4	8	8	0	8	6
Jane	4	0	4	5	8	8	10	4
Michael	10	10	10	4	5	8	8	10
Total	**25.5**	**18**	**26**	**24**	**21**	**26**	**36**	**25.5**
Wages								
Robert	66.00	96.00	96.00	84.00	0.00	120.00	120.00	66.00
Maria	48.00	0.00	32.00	64.00	64.00	0.00	64.00	48.00
Jane	39.00	0.00	39.00	48.75	78.00	78.00	97.50	39.00
Michael	200.00	200.00	200.00	80.00	100.00	160.00	160.00	200.00
Total	**$353.00**	**$296.00**	**$367.00**	**$276.75**	**$242.00**	**$358.00**	**$441.50**	**$353.00**

Page 2 of 7

Figure 6.8 Page Printed in the Landscape Orientation

- Legal $8\frac{1}{2}$ x 14 in
- A4 210 x 297 mm
- B5 182 x 257 mm

To select a new paper size, you select the size in the Paper Size drop-down list box. If no new paper sizes are available in this box, you need to change the default paper size from the Printer Setup dialog box. (See "Changing the Printer's Default Settings" earlier in this chapter.)"

Setting the Margins

The default margin settings are displayed in the Margins area of the Page Setup dialog box. Normally, Excel leaves a three-quarter-inch margin on the left and right and a one-inch margin at the top and bottom of each page. To change the margin settings for your printout, select the appropriate text box (**Left**, **Right**, **Top**, or **Bottom**) and enter the new value. (All margins are measured from the edge of the paper.)

Tip You can change the margins as well as the widths of the columns by using the Margins buttons and then dragging them to new positions in Print Preview. (See "Using Print Preview" later in this chapter for details.)

Centering the Printing on the Page

Excel offers two centering options that you can use when the worksheet data that you are printing does not use sufficient columns or rows to fill up the entire page. Select the Center Horizontally check box to center a narrow report between the left and right margins on each page, or select the Center Vertically check box to center a short report between the top and bottom margins.

Selecting the Page Order

When printing more worksheet data than will fit on a single page (which is most of the time), Excel pages the Print_Area so that data in rows below the first range of the Print_Area is printed before columns to the right. In Excel 4.0, you can reverse this order so that data in columns to the right of the first range in the Print_Area prints before rows below by selecting the Over, then Down option button under Page Order (which automatically deselects the default Down, then Over option button).

Scaling the Printing

Laser printers can scale the size of the printing so that you can enlarge or reduce the size of the print on each page. To reduce or enlarge the size of the printing by a fixed percentage, select the Reduce/Enlarge to percentage text box and enter a new percentage (with the default value of 100 representing the actual size of the text and graphics in the Print_Area). For example, to reduce the size of the printing by half (thereby cutting the number of pages in half), you would enter 50 in the percentage text box. To double the size of the printing on each page (thereby effectively doubling the number of pages), you would enter 200 in the percentage text box.

If you don't know the percentage you want to decrease the size of the printing, but you do know the maximum number of pages you want to use, you can have Excel figure out the scaling percentage for you. Simply select the Fit to option button in the Scaling area, then enter the total number of pages across in the first text box (in front of *pages wide*) and the total number of pages down in the second text box (in front of *tall*) . By default, Excel prints all of the data in the Print_Area on a single page when you select the Fit to option button (1 page wide by 1 page tall). If, for instance, you want to reduce the width of a large Print_Area so that its columns all fit on three pages and the length so that its rows all fit on two pages, you would enter 3 in the first text box and 2 in the second text box. Excel would then compute the percentage to reduce the printing so that Print_Area used three pages across and two pages down.

After using use the Fit to option to reduce the printout so that it fits on a fixed number of pages, you must select the Reduce/Enlarge to option button when you once again want to print your worksheet data at full size. When you click this option button, Excel displays in its text box the reduction percentage that the program last used in printing the worksheet with the Fit to option. To return to printing actual size, be sure to replace the last-used value in this percentage text box with the 100.

Other Page Setup Options

The Page Setup dialog box also includes several other miscellaneous page layout options. You select the Row & Column Headings check box when you want to print the column letters and row numbers of each cell included in the Print_Area. You deselect the Cell Gridlines check box when you don't want Excel to print the gridlines for each (which is the default). Figure 6.9 shows a printout with both the row and column headings and cell gridlines. Figure 6.10 shows the same printout, this time with neither of these elements.

	A	B	C	D	E
1				**Please Make Checks Payable To:** **Harvey & Associates** **P.O. Box 1175** **Point Reyes Station, CA 94937** **(415) 555-9999**	
2	**Bill To:**				
3				**Invoice Date:**	
4				**Invoice Number:**	
5				**Amount Due:**	$0.00
6	**Date**	**Hours**	**Rate**	**Description**	**Amount**
7					$0.00
8					$0.00
9					$0.00
10					$0.00
11					$0.00
12					$0.00
13					$0.00
14					$0.00
15					$0.00
16					$0.00
17					$0.00
18					$0.00
19					$0.00
20					$0.00
21					$0.00
22					$0.00
23					$0.00
24					$0.00
25					$0.00
26					$0.00
27					$0.00
28					$0.00
29					$0.00
30					$0.00
31					$0.00
32					$0.00
33					$0.00
34				**Subtotal**	$0.00
35				**Tax**	$0.00
36				**Total**	**$0.00**
37					
38					
39				*Thank you for your patronage!*	
40					

Figure 6.9   Printout with Row and Column Headings and Cell Gridlines

			Please Make Checks Payable To:	
			Harvey & Associates	
			P.O. Box 1175	
			Point Reyes Station, CA 94937	
			(415) 555-9999	

Bill To:

			Invoice Date:	
			Invoice Number:	
			Amount Due:	$0.00

Date	Hours	Rate	Description	Amount
				$0.00
				$0.00
				$0.00
				$0.00
				$0.00
				$0.00
				$0.00
				$0.00
				$0.00
				$0.00
				$0.00
				$0.00
				$0.00
				$0.00
				$0.00
				$0.00
				$0.00
				$0.00
				$0.00
				$0.00
				$0.00
				$0.00
				$0.00
				$0.00
				$0.00
				$0.00
				$0.00
			Subtotal	$0.00
			Tax	$0.00
			Total	$0.00

Thank you for your patronage!

Figure 6.10   Printout Without Row and Column Headings and Cell Gridlines

Alert! The display of cell gridlines in the worksheet window (controlled by the **G**ridlines check box in the Display Options dialog box) has no effect on whether or not they are printed. If the Cell **G**ridlines check box in the Page Setup dialog box is not selected, cell gridlines will not appear in your printout even when they are visible on the screen.

Normally, when you assign colors to the cells of a worksheet (see Chapter 7), Excel prints them as patterns on a black-and-white printer. If you want to print the patterns in black and white, you select the Black & White Cells check box (which is normally not selected).

By default, Excel starts numbering the pages in your report with 1 (page numbers automatically appear in the report footer—see "Adding a Header and Footer to the Report" later in this chapter). To start the page numbers with some other number, select the Start Page No.'s At text box and enter the appropriate starting number there.

Modifying the Print Settings

After you finish making your changes to the page layout in the Page Setup dialog box, you can open the Print dialog box by selecting the **P**rint command button. The Print dialog box (shown in Figure 6.11) contains a number of print settings that you can change before you send your print job to the printer. The next few sections explain each of the print setting options found in this box.

Selecting the Page Range

By default, Excel prints all of the pages required to print the entire Print_Area. Sometimes, however, when reprinting a report, you may find that you need to reprint only a particular page or range of pages. When this is the case, you select the **P**ages option button (which automatically deselects the **A**ll option button) and enter the starting and ending page in the **F**rom and **T**o text boxes. Note that to print a single page, you enter the same page number in both boxes.

Changing the Print Quality

The setting in the Print **Q**uality drop-down list box controls the output quality of your printer. Many printers can print at different resolutions. For example, many dot-matrix printers can print either in draft mode (lower

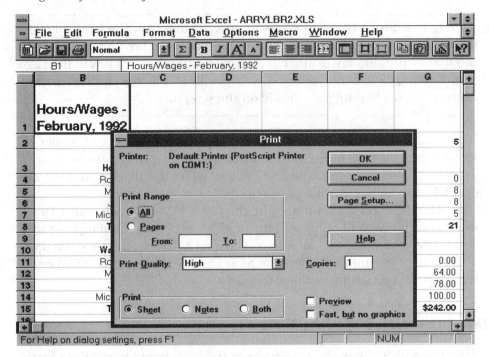

Figure 6.11 The Print Dialog Box

resolution but faster printing) or in near-letter-quality mode (higher resolution but slower printing). Also, most laser printers are capable of printing
in three different qualities: High, Medium, and Low.

If you want to speed up the printing of a draft printout, select a lower
resolution option in the Print **Q**uality drop-down list box. Then, when you're
ready to print a final printout, select a higher resolution option in this box.

Other Printing Options

By default, Excel prints only the worksheet data (including any charts that
you've placed in the worksheet and included in the Print_Area). If you want to
print the notes that you've added to cells (see Chapter 8 for information on
how to annotate your worksheet) along with your worksheet data, you need to
select the **B**oth option button under Print. If you want to print only the notes
in the worksheet, select the Notes option button instead. When you use the
Both option, Excel prints all of the notes on separate pages after printing the
worksheet data and charts in the Print_Area. The notes appear in the order of
their occurrence in the Print_Area but without any cell references. If you want
to see the location of the note in the printout (which is most often the case),

you need to select the Row & Column Headings check box in the Page Setup dialog box before you print with the Notes or **B**oth option.

Select the **C**opies text box when you want Excel to print more than one copy of your report, and enter the number of copies you want printed there. When you have Excel print more than one copy of a report, the program automatically collates the pages of each copy for you.

You can select two more printing options in the Print dialog box. Select the Preview check box when you want Excel to initiate the Print Preview feature (see "Using Print Preview" later in this chapter) when you select the OK button or press Enter, instead of sending the print job directly to the printer. That way, you can proof the pages on screen before you send the report to the printer. Select the Fast, but no graphics check box when your Print_Area includes charts or other graphic objects (which can take a long time to print) and you need just a draft printout containing the worksheet data.

Printing Larger Worksheets

Excel offers several report-writing capabilities that you can use when printing larger worksheets that require several pages. In such situations, you can specify header or footer text that should appear in the top and bottom margins of each page of the report as well as specify rows and columns of data that should appear as the report titles on each page. Excel also enables you to insert your own page breaks in the report so that you can avoid awkward breaks that would otherwise split up tables or ranges that should appear together on a page.

> *Note:* The Print Report command on the File menu has a specialized use. It is used to print different views or scenarios of your worksheet data. To learn how to create views in Excel with the Views command and print reports, see Chapter 7. To learn how to set up different what-if scenarios with the Scenario Manager command and print reports, see Chapter 11.

Adding a Header and Footer to the Report

A *header* is text that appears at the top of each page of your report. The default header in the printout centers the name of the file you are printing (such as **BUDGET92.XLS**) between the left and right margins. The top of the first line of header text is positioned one-half inch down from the top of the page. A *footer* is text that appears at the bottom of each page of your report. The default footer used by Excel centers the current page number with the word *Page* (as in **Page** 1) between the left and right margins. The baseline of the first line of footer text is positioned one-half inch up from the bottom of the page.

When defining a header or footer for your report, you separate the header or footer text into three sections: A left-aligned section where the text is indented one-half inch from the left edge of the paper, a centered section where the text is centered between the left and right edges of the paper, and a right-aligned section where all the text is indented one-half inch from the right edge of the paper. When defining each section of the header or footer, you must take care that the text does not overlap text in another section. (You can use Print Preview to make sure that this is not the case—see "Using Print Preview" later in this chapter.) To prevent the overlapping of text in different sections, you can insert a paragraph return with Alt+Enter to start a new line of text in the section (just as you do to start a new line on the formula bar).

When entering the text for your header and footer, you can use the various tools in the Header or Footer dialog box to format the text with a different font, font size, or bold or italic attribute as well as to insert codes that insert the page number, date, time, or the name of the file you are printing. Table 6.1 shows you these tools and the codes they insert and

Table 6.1 Header and Footer Tools and Codes

Tool	Tool Name	Code	Function
A	Font tool	N/A	Displays the Font dialog box so that you can assign a new font, font size, or attribute to selected section of the header or footer.
#	Page Number tool	&P	Inserts the current page number.
	Total Pages tool	&N	Inserts the total number of pages in the report.
	Date tool	&D	Inserts the current date, as in 3/4/93.
	Time tool	&T	Inserts the current time, as in 9:05 AM.
	Filename tool	&F	Inserts the filename of the active document, as in BUDGET92.XLS.

explains their function in the header and footer.

To define a header for your report, follow these steps:

1. Choose the Page Setup command on the **File** menu.

2. Select the **Header** command button in the Page Setup dialog box. Excel opens the Header dialog box shown in Figure 6.12. Note that the Center section list box already contains the code **&F** that prints the filename.

3. Enter the text that you want to appear in each section of the header. To insert a code at the insertion point, click the appropriate tool. To start a new line in a section, press Alt+Enter. To format the text or code, select the characters and/or the code with the I-beam pointer, then click the Font tool and select the font, font style, font size, and effects you want to apply to the selection in the Font dialog box (shown in Figure 6.13). If you don't want a header in your report, select the **&F** in the **C**enter section and press the Delete key to remove it. Remember that you can mix text and codes in your header. For instance, you could enter **Page &P of &N pages** to have text such as *Page 1 of 5 pages* appear in the header or **Report Date: &N** to have text such as *Report Date: 4/12/93* appear in the header.

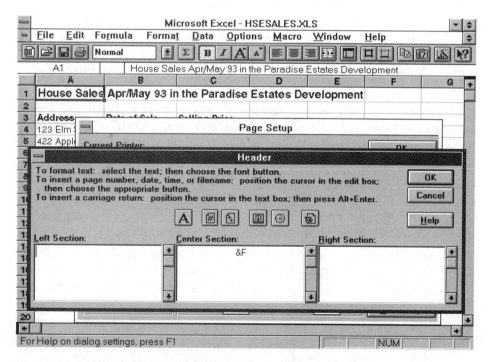

Figure 6.12 The Header Dialog Box

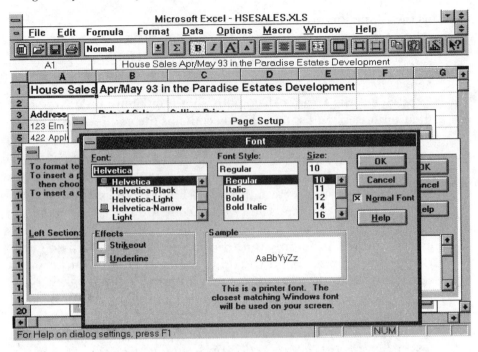

Figure 6.13 The Font Dialog Box for Formatting a Header or Footer

4. When you've finished defining and formatting each section of the header, click the OK command button or press Enter to close the Header dialog box and return to the Page Setup dialog box.

5. To print the report, select the **P**rint command button in the Page Setup dialog box. To preview your header before you send the report to the printer, select the Preview check box and then select OK or press Enter in the Print dialog box. If you're not ready to print your report, select the OK button in the Page Setup dialog box to return to your worksheet.

To define a footer for your report, you follow almost identical steps:

1. Choose the Page Setup command on the **F**ile menu.

2. Select the **F**ooter command button in the Page Setup dialog box. Excel opens the Footer dialog box shown in Figure 6.14. Note that the **C**enter section list box already contains the code **Page &P** that prints the current page number as in *Page 2*.

3. Enter the text that you want to appear in each section of the footer. To insert a code at the insertion point, click the appropriate tool. To start a new line in a section, press Alt+Enter. To format the text or

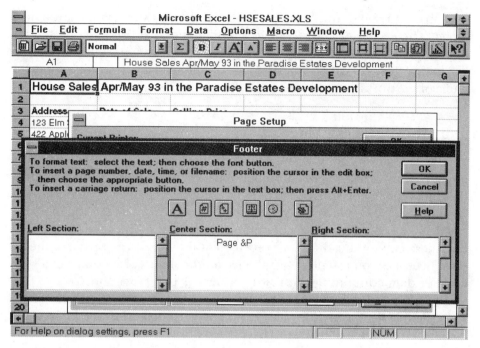

Figure 6.14   The Footer Dialog Box

code, select the characters and/or the code with the I-beam pointer, then click the Font tool and select the font, font style, font size, and effects you want to apply to the selection in the Font dialog box (shown in Figure 6.13). If you don't want a footer in your report, select the **Page &P** in the **C**enter section and press the Delete key to remove it. Remember that you can mix text and codes in your footer. For instance, you could enter Preliminary Report Printed @ &D &T to have text such as *Preliminary Report Printed @ 6/6/93 3:05 PM* appear in the footer or Printout of Worksheet &F to have text such as *Printout of Worksheet BUDGET92.XLS* appear there.

4. When you've finished defining and formatting each section of the footer, click the OK command button or press Enter to close the Footer dialog box and return to the Page Setup dialog box.

5. To print the report, select the **P**rint command button in the Page Setup dialog box. To preview your footer before you send the report to the printer, select the Preview check box and then select OK or press Enter in the Print dialog box. If you're not ready to print your report, select the OK button in the Page Setup dialog box to return to your worksheet.

Figure 6.15 shows you a sample printout that uses both a header and a footer. The header displays the page number and total page numbers in the upper-right corner (**Page &P of &N**). The footer displays the date and time in the lower-left corner (**Printed: &D &T**), Confidential! in the center, and the name of the worksheet file (**Document: &F**) in the lower-right corner.

Defining the Titles for the Report

You can designate columns and rows to be used as column and row titles in larger reports consisting of a number of pages. When you define print titles for your report, you must designate entire columns or rows that are adjacent to each other. Normally you select the row or rows at the top of a long table of data containing the column headings as the Titles for Columns so that these column headings are repeated at the top of each page of the report. Likewise, you usually select the leftmost column or columns in a wide table of data containing the row headings as the Titles for Rows so that these headings are repeated at the left edge of each page of the report.

To define the print titles for your report, choose the Set Print Titles command on the **O**ptions menu. Excel then opens the Set Print Titles dialog

---

February, 1992 Pay Periods   *Page 1*

**Hours/Wages -
February, 1992**

	Pay Period 1	Pay Period 2	
Hours	**(1st - 15th)**	**(16th - 29th)**	**Monthly Total**
Robert	102.5	140.0	242.5
Maria	74.0	102.0	176.0
Jane	82.0	124.0	206.0
Michael	120.0	155.0	275.0
Total	**378.5**	**521.0**	**899.5**
Wages			
Robert	1,230.00	1,680.00	$2,910.00
Maria	592.00	816.00	$1,408.00
Jane	799.50	1,209.00	$2,008.50
Michael	2,400.00	3,100.00	$5,500.00
Total	**$5,021.50**	**$6,805.00**	**$11,826.50**

Printed: 2/21/92 10:19 AM   Confidential!   Document: ARRYLBR2.XLS

Figure 6.15   Sample Printout with Header and Footer

box where you can define the print titles for the columns in your report, print titles for the rows in your report, or print titles for both. To define the print titles for your columns, select the Titles for **C**olumns text box, then click the white-cross mouse pointer in the row in your worksheet that contains the column headings to be used. To define adjacent rows as the print titles, click the top row, then drag the pointer down to include the adjacent rows below. The Titles for **C**olumns text box displays the range of the row(s) you select (as absolute values) so that if you select only row 2, you will see $2:$2 and if you select rows 2 and 3, you will see $2:$3 in the text box.

To define row titles for your report, you select the Titles for **R**ows text box, then select the column or adjacent columns in the worksheet that contain the row headings to be displayed on each page. Excel displays the absolute cell range of the column or adjacent columns you select in the Titles for **R**ows text box so that if you select only column A for your row titles, you will see $A:$A, but if you select the columns A and B, you will see $A:$B in the text box.

 Tip Excel 3.0 users take note: You no longer have to exclude cells in the columns and rows of your print titles from the Print_Area range to prevent Excel from printing your column and row titles twice on the first page. Excel 4.0 is smart enough to exclude the cells in the print titles from the Print_Area automatically.

Figures 6.16 (a and b) and 6.17 (a and b) show examples of the two different types of print titles. In Figure 6.16, the column headings in rows 1 and 2 are designated as the column print titles so that the column headings are repeated at the top of the second page of this report. In Figure 6.17, the row headings in column B are designated as the row print titles so that they are repeated in the left column of the second page of this report.

After you define print titles for your report, Excel displays the print titles on the screen with dotted lines (same as those used for page breaks—see below) that separate the column and rows used as print titles from the rest of the Print_Area in the worksheet. To redefine or clear print titles, open the Set Print Titles dialog box and modify or delete the row or column range displayed in the Titles for **C**olumns and/or Titles for **R**ows text boxes.

Controlling Page Breaks

Excel automatically pages the cell ranges in the Print_Area (according to the settings in the Page Setup dialog box) whenever you print your worksheet or preview the printout with the Print Preview feature (discussed below).

Accounts Database

Account Number	Last Name	First Name	Street Address	City	State
1173073	King	Anne	1912 Meridian Street	Indianapolis	IN
5564320	Jackson	William	314 Crayton Drive	Seattle	WA
4587979	Wulf	Shane	9220 Franklin Road	Memphis	TN
6178812	Micaela	Lili	1912 Branford Drive	San Diego	CA
1020886	Marleston	Thomas	9257 Kinsey Avenue	Orlando	FL
7993805	Cranston	Barry	1637 Ellis Parkway	Chicago	IL
5129488	Smith	Margaret	2548 North Point	Cincinnati	OH
7456362	Pryor	Aaron	1247 College Avenue	Bloomington	IN
7949146	Mansfield	James	1811 Fulton Street	Flagstaff	AZ
4114529	Adams	Karen	626 Keystone Way	Newport Beach	CA
5564320	Thomas	Brian	314 Crayton Drive	Seattle	WA
1338822	Schnyder	Jay	1256 Williamsburg	Atlanta	FL
4253520	Grill	Alan	1710 Delaware	Lexington	KY
9714927	Harrington	James	1945 Danbury Court	Port Huron	MI
1020886	Tuke	Samuel	246 First Avenue	Fort Worth	TX
4211820	Wright	Amy	6327 Arlington	Des Moines	IA
7089277	Holland	Mark	316 Atwood Terrace	Miami	FL
4638409	Englert	Michael	397 Drexel Boulevard	Boston	MA
1173073	King	Anne	1912 Meridian Street	Indianapolis	IN
5564320	Jackson	William	314 Crayton Drive	Seattle	WA
4587979	Wulf	Shane	9220 Franklin Road	Memphis	TN
6178812	Micaela	Lili	1912 Branford Drive	San Diego	CA
1020886	Marleston	Thomas	9257 Kinsey Avenue	Orlando	FL
7993805	Cranston	Barry	1637 Ellis Parkway	Chicago	IL
5129488	Smith	Margaret	2548 North Point	Cincinnati	OH
7456362	Pryor	Aaron	1247 College Avenue	Bloomington	IN
7949146	Mansfield	James	1811 Fulton Street	Flagstaff	AZ

Figure 6.16a Sample Printout with Column Print Titles

Accounts Database

Account Number	Last Name	First Name	Street Address	City	State
4114529	Adams	Karen	626 Keystone Way	Newport Beach	CA
5564320	Thomas	Brian	314 Crayton Drive	Seattle	WA
1338822	Schnyder	Jay	1256 Williamsburg	Atlanta	FL
4253520	Grill	Alan	1710 Delaware	Lexington	KY
9714927	Harrington	James	1945 Danbury Court	Port Huron	MI
1020886	Tuke	Samuel	246 First Avenue	Fort Worth	TX
4211820	Wright	Amy	6327 Arlington	Des Moines	IA
7089277	Holland	Mark	316 Atwood Terrace	Miami	FL
4638409	Englert	Michael	397 Drexel Boulevard	Boston	MA

Page 2 of 4

Figure 6.16b Sample Printout with Column Print Titles

Hours/Wages -
February, 1992

	1	2	3	4	5
Hours					
Robert	5.5	8	8	7	0
Maria	6	0	4	8	8
Jane	4	0	4	5	8
Michael	10	10	10	4	5
Total	25.5	18	26	24	21
Wages					
Robert	66.00	96.00	96.00	84.00	0.00
Maria	48.00	0.00	32.00	64.00	64.00
Jane	39.00	0.00	39.00	48.75	78.00
Michael	200.00	200.00	200.00	80.00	100.00
Total	$353.00	$296.00	$367.00	$276.75	$242.00

Printed: 2/21/92 11:32 AM	Confidential!	Document: ARRYLBR2.XLS

Figure 6.17a Sample Printout with Row Print Titles

**Hours/Wages -
February, 1992**

	6	7	8	9	10
Hours					
Robert	10	10	5.5	8	8
Maria	0	8	6	0	4
Jane	8	10	4	0	4
Michael	8	8	10	10	10
Total	26	36	25.5	18	26
Wages					
Robert	120.00	120.00	66.00	96.00	96.00
Maria	0.00	64.00	48.00	0.00	32.00
Jane	78.00	97.50	39.00	0.00	39.00
Michael	160.00	160.00	200.00	200.00	200.00
Total	$358.00	$441.50	$353.00	$296.00	$367.00

Page 1 of 7

Figure 6.17b   Sample Printout with Row Print Titles

Sometimes Excel places a page break so that it splits apart ranges of data that need to appear together or separates headings from the data they identify. In such cases, you can insert your own page break with the Set Page **B**reak command on the Options menu.

Tip If you don't see dotted lines representing the page breaks on your screen after printing or previewing your worksheet, chances are that the Automatic Page **B**reaks check box in the Display Options dialog box is not selected. To display page breaks on the screen, you need to choose the **D**isplay command on the **O**ptions menu, then select the Automatic Page **B**reaks check box.

To insert a page break at a particular row in the worksheet report, position the cell pointer in the first column of that row in the Print_Area range, then choose the Set Page Break command. For example, Figure 6.18 shows an automatic page break inserted by Excel at the top of row 40 of the worksheet that separates the *Regional Ratio Analysis* heading from most of the ratio tables below and splits the rows of the *Gross Profit on Sales* data table roughly in half. To have Excel print this heading and keep this table

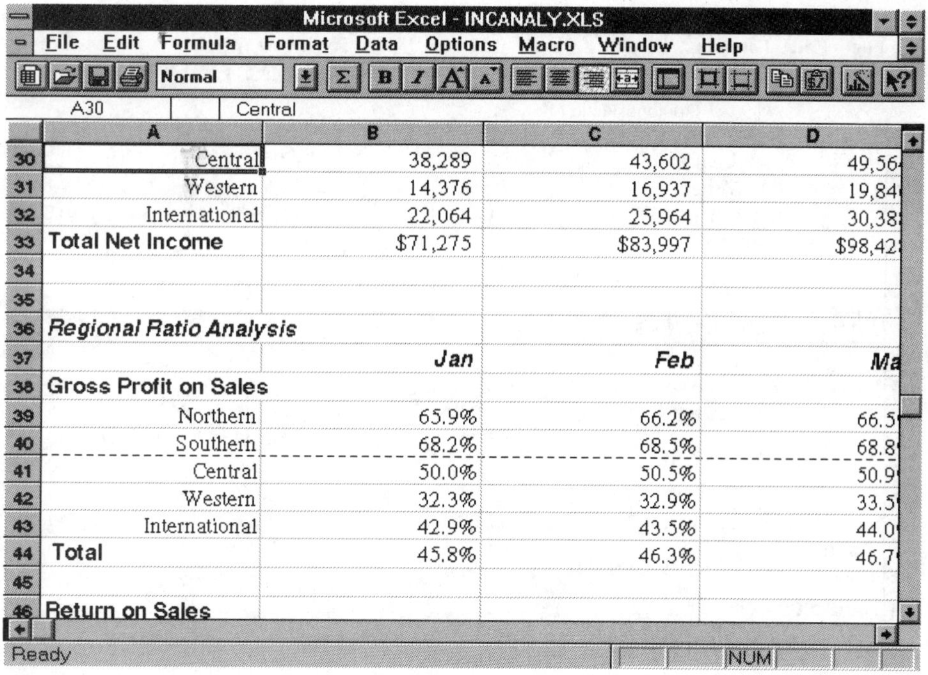

Figure 6.18 Sample Report with Automatic Page Break

together on the following page, you can insert a page break at the top of row 36. To do this, you position the cell pointer in cell A36 (the first column of the Print_Area) and then choose the Set Page **B**reak command on the **O**ptions menu. Figure 6.19 shows you the result. Excel redraws the manual page break at the top of row 36, ensuring that the row with the heading will appear with the table rows on the following page.

To insert a page break at a particular column and row in the worksheet report, position the cell pointer in the cell in the Print_Area whose left border marks the new vertical page break and whose top border marks the new horizontal page break. Figures 6.20 and 6.21 illustrate how this works. In Figure 6.20, Excel has inserted an automatic page break at the top of row 30 and along the left edge of column G. This page break puts the April sales figures in column F on a different page from the rest of the second-quarter figures and puts the first three rows of net income expenses on a different page from the last two rows. You can remedy this bad page break by positioning the cell pointer in cell F26 and then selecting the Set Page **B**reak command on the **O**ptions menu. Excel then inserts a manual page break at the top of row 26 and along the left edge of column F. This causes Excel to print all the net income figures together on pages 2 and 4 of the

Microsoft Excel - INCANALY.XLS

File	Edit	Formula	Format	Data	Options	Macro	Window	Help

Normal

A36 | Regional Ratio Analysis

	A	B	C	D
30	Central	38,289	43,602	49,56
31	Western	14,376	16,937	19,84
32	International	22,064	25,964	30,38
33	**Total Net Income**	$71,275	$83,997	$98,42
34				
35				
36	*Regional Ratio Analysis*			
37		Jan	Feb	Ma
38	**Gross Profit on Sales**			
39	Northern	65.9%	66.2%	66.5
40	Southern	68.2%	68.5%	68.8
41	Central	50.0%	50.5%	50.9
42	Western	32.3%	32.9%	33.5
43	International	42.9%	43.5%	44.0
44	**Total**	45.8%	46.3%	46.7
45				
46	**Return on Sales**			

Ready   NUM

Figure 6.19   Sample Report After Modifying the Vertical Page Break

Microsoft Excel - INCANLY2.XLS

File	Edit	Formula	Format	Data	Options	Macro	Window	Help

Normal

G30 | =G6-G14-G22

	A	C	D	E	F	G	
1	*Regional Income*						
2	**Sales**	Feb	Mar	Qtr 1	Apr	May	
3	Northern	$33,370	$36,707	$100,412	$40,377	$44,415	
16	**Total Cost of Goods Sold**	$238,722	$260,207	$717,940	$283,626	$309,152	$
17							
18	**Operating Expenses**						
19	Northern	$23,036	$24,649	$69,214	$26,374	$28,220	
20	Southern	17,062	18,257	$51,265	19,535	20,902	
21	Central	29,483	31,547	$88,583	33,755	36,118	
22	Western	17,259	18,467	$51,856	19,760	21,143	
23	International	34,626	37,050	$104,037	39,644	42,419	
24	**Expenses**	$121,466	$129,969	$364,955	$139,067	$148,802	$
25							
26	**Net Income**						
27	Northern	($938)	($228)	($2,700)	$611	$1,598	
28	Southern	(1,568)	(1,142)	($4,630)	(630)	(23)	
29	Central	43,602	49,564	$131,455	56,249	63,740	
30	Western	16,937	19,846	$51,159	23,144	26,880	
31	International	25,964	30,388	$78,416	35,397	41,063	
32	**Total Net Income**	$83,997	$98,428	$253,700	$114,772	$133,257	$
33							
34							
35	*Regional Ratio Ana*						

Ready   NUM

Figure 6.20   Sample Report with Automatic Page Break

	Microsoft Excel - INCANLY2.XLS							
	File **Edit** **Formula** **Format** **Data** **Options** **Macro** **Window** **Help**							
	Normal	Σ B *I* A A						
F26								

	A	C	D	E	F	G	
1	*Regional Income*						
2	Sales	*Feb*	*Mar*	*Qtr 1*	*Apr*	*May*	
3	Northern	$33,370	$36,707	$100,412	$40,377	$44,415	
	Total Cost of						
16	Goods Sold	$238,722	$260,207	$717,940	$283,626	$309,152	
17							
18	Operating Expenses						
19	Northern	$23,036	$24,649	$69,214	$26,374	$28,220	
20	Southern	17,062	18,257	$51,265	19,535	20,902	
21	Central	29,483	31,547	$88,583	33,755	36,118	
22	Western	17,259	18,467	$51,856	19,760	21,143	
23	International	34,626	37,050	$104,037	39,644	42,419	
24	Expenses	$121,466	$129,969	$364,955	$139,067	$148,802	
25							
26	Net Income						
27	Northern	($938)	($228)	($2,700)	$611	$1,598	
28	Southern	(1,568)	(1,142)	($4,630)	(630)	(23)	
29	Central	43,602	49,564	$131,455	56,249	63,740	
30	Western	16,937	19,846	$51,159	23,144	26,880	
31	International	25,964	30,388	$78,416	35,397	41,063	
32	Total Net Income	$83,997	$98,428	$253,700	$114,772	$133,257	
33							
34							
35	*Regional Ratio Ana*						

Ready — NUM

Figure 6.21   Sample Report after Modifying the Vertical and Horizontal Page Break

report and print the April sales figures together with the rest of the second-quarter sales figures on pages 3 and 4 of the report.

To remove a page break that was inserted in the worksheet with the Set Page **B**reak command, you need to position the cell pointer in the row or column of the manual page break and choose the Remove Page **B**reak command (which replaces the Set Page **B**reak command) on the **O**ptions menu. You can tell a manual page break from an automatic one in the worksheet window because a manual page break uses a dotted line with smaller breaks in each line; its dotted line appears somewhat darker than the one used to represent automatic page breaks.

To remove a horizontal page break, position the cell pointer in the row that has the manual page break on the top edge in any column and choose the Remove Page **B**reak command. To remove a vertical page break, position the cell pointer in the column that has the manual page break on the left edge of the column in any row and choose the Remove Page **B**reak command. To remove a horizontal and vertical page break in one operation, position the pointer in the cell that has the horizontal manual page break on the top edge of the cell and the vertical manual page break on the left edge of the cell, then choose the Remove Page **B**reak command.

Using Print Preview

Excel's Print Preview can save you countless trips to the printer, not to mention piles of wasted paper, resulting from printing errors that you didn't catch before you sent your report to the printer. By previewing selected pages of a report, you can usually spot any trouble areas that need fixing before you send the print job to the printer.

In Print Preview, text as well as graphics elements assigned to the cells in the Print_Area appear exactly as they will appear in the printout. Unlike the standard on-screen view of the worksheet, Print Preview shows you the headers and footers you've defined for the report, and allows you to page through the report a page at a time so that you can check the page breaks. If you find any errors when previewing a report, you can fix them before you send the job to the printer. If you don't find any problems, you can send the job on to the printer directly from Print Preview.

To open the Print Preview window from the worksheet, you choose the Print Preview command on the **F**ile menu. If the Print dialog box is open, you can open the Print Preview window by selecting the Preview check box before you choose OK or press Enter. When you first open the Print Preview

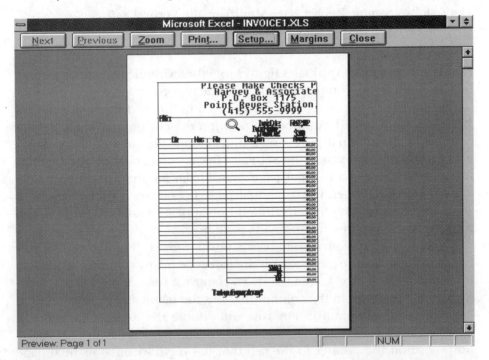

Figure 6.22   Print Preview Window with the First Page of a Report in Full-Page View

window, the window displays a full-page view of the first page of the report (similar to the one shown in Figure 6.22). Note that depending on your monitor's capability, some of the text may look somewhat jammed. To increase the page size to 100 percent, click the **Z**oom button at the top of the window. To zoom in on a particular part of the page (such as the header or footer, for instance), position the pointer on the part you want to zoom in on and click the mouse button. When you position the pointer somewhere on the page, it automatically assumes the shape of a magnifying glass.

When the page is enlarged to 100 percent (as shown in Figure 6.23), you can use the scroll bars to bring new parts of the page into view in the Print Preview window. If you prefer using the keyboard, you can press the ↑ and ↓ keys or PgUp and PgDn to scroll up or down the page, and ← and → or Ctrl+PgUp and Ctrl+PgDn to scroll left and right. You can press the Home key to position the left edge of the page on the screen and the End key to position the right edge. You can also press Ctrl+Home to position the upper-left corner of the page on the screen, Ctrl+End to position the lower-right corner on the screen, and Ctrl plus an arrow key (←, → ,↑, or ↓) to position the left, right, top, or bottom of the page on the screen from whatever part of the page is displayed.

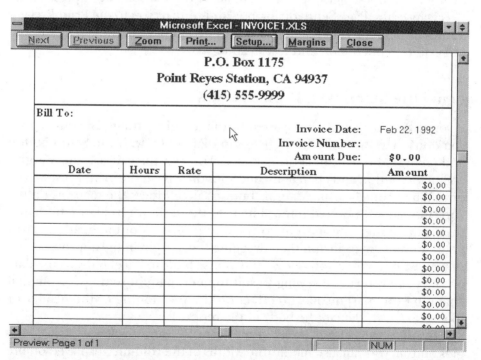

Figure 6.23   Print Preview Window with Part of the First Page of a Report in 100% View

When you want to return to the full-page view, click the arrowhead pointer a second time somewhere on the page or click the **Z**oom button.

If your report has more than one page, you can view succeeding pages by clicking the **N**ext command button on the top of the Print Preview window. If you want to review a page that you've already seen, you can click the **P**revious command button until the page is displayed in the Print Preview window.

Changing the Setup Options from Print Preview

If, while previewing a report, you identify a problem with the page setup, you can open the Page Setup dialog box by selecting the **S**etup command button and fix the problem without having to close the Print Preview window. For example, suppose that you open the Print Preview window only to discover that the report will print the cell gridlines and the row and column headings (neither of which you want in this particular report). To remove these elements from the report, you click the **S**etup button to open the Page Setup dialog box and then deselect the Row & **C**olumn Headings and the Cell **G**ridlines check boxes. Then, when you choose OK or press Enter, Excel closes the Page Setup dialog box and returns you to the Print Preview window, where the program redraws the current page of the report without cell gridlines or column and row headings.

Changing the Margins in Print Preview

If you detect page problems caused by the margin settings for your report, you don't have to open the Page Setup dialog box with the Setup button and change the margin settings there. You can instead use the **M**argins command button and change the margins directly in the Print Preview window. When you click the **M**argins button, Excel draws the margins on the current page with dotted lines, similar to those shown in Figure 6.24. You then can change the margins by positioning the double-headed arrow pointer on the margin and then dragging the margin in the appropriate direction with it. When you release the mouse button, Excel redraws the data on the page you're previewing to suit the new margin settings. (Note that changing the margins has no effect on the positioning of the header or footer text, only data in the body of the report.)

After displaying the margins in the Print Preview window with the **M**argins button, you can also modify the widths of the columns displayed on the current page (whether or not the cell gridlines are displayed). Excel represents the column borders on that page with short column handles at the

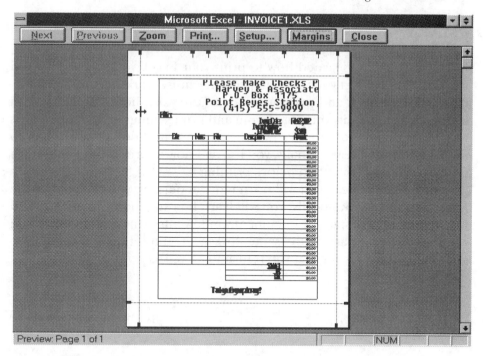

Figure 6.24   Print Preview Window After Selecting the Margins Button

top of the Print Preview window. To change a column width, position the pointer on the handle of the column you want to increase or decrease, then drag the handle with the double-headed pointer in the appropriate direction. When you are finished modifying the margins or column widths, you can remove the on-screen markers by selecting the **Margins** command button again.

Printing from Print Preview

When you finish previewing the report and are satisfied that it is ready to print, you can send the print job to the printer by clicking the **Print** command button. Excel sends your report to the Print Manager without opening the Print dialog box (as if you had clicked the Print tool on the Standard toolbar in the worksheet window). If you discover some problems that can't be fixed with the **Setup** or **Margins** buttons because they require you to edit the worksheet, you can return to the worksheet window by choosing the **Close** command button. Then, after fixing the problems, you can return to Print Preview and verify your changes before you print the report with the **Print** command button.

SUMMARY

In this chapter you learned how to print your Excel worksheets. First you learned how to select your printer, print the entire worksheet using the default print settings, and print just part of the worksheet. After that, you learned how to modify the page layout and print settings and set up reports with headers and footers and row and column print titles, as well as how to modify bad page breaks. Finally, you learned how to proof your report with the Print Preview command before printing it.

In the chapter ahead you will learn more about how you can control the Excel workspace. Specifically, you will learn how to modify the display and workspace options, split the document window into panes within which you can view different parts of the same worksheet, and set up and save different views of a worksheet that you return to as well as print.

Part II

Advanced Worksheet Techniques

7

Customizing the Workspace

Up to now, you have learned to work with Excel pretty much as the program is configured at installation. In this chapter you will learn how you can customize the way your worksheets are displayed in the Excel workspace. We start by looking at ways that you can change the program's default display and workspace options. Then you will learn how you customize the color palette and apply different colors to different parts of the worksheet display.

After that, you will learn techniques for displaying different parts of a large worksheet on the screen. First you will learn how to open different document windows on the same worksheet and then arrange them in the Excel work area. Next you will learn how you can split a single document window into panes and then freeze the panes so that certain parts of the worksheet (such as column and row headings) remain displayed as you scroll new data into view.

Finally you will learn how to create and save different views of a single worksheet. These views can include different display options, colors, and print settings. After creating a view, you can then reuse it at any time when working with the worksheet. You also will learn how you can create and save a report that automates the printing of different views of your worksheet. That way you can have Excel print different parts of the worksheet in a specified order or have the program print the same parts of the worksheet using different print settings.

Modifying the Display Options

You can control which items are displayed in your worksheet with the options in the Display Options dialog box (shown in Figure 7.1) opened by choosing the **D**isplay command on the **O**ptions menu. The display options in this box are divided into two groups: Cells and Objects. The options under Cells control the display of the cells and their contents. The options under Objects control the display of graphic objects placed in the worksheet, which can include charts, text boxes, and other types of line graphics that you can add.

When you start a new worksheet, Excel automatically displays the cell gridlines between the columns and rows of the worksheet, the row and column headings identifying the cells, all zero values entered into the cells, outline symbols when you create an outline (which allow you to expand or collapse the various levels of the outline—see Chapter 9 for details), and all graphic objects in the worksheet.

We've already discussed the use of Formulas and the Automatic Page **B**reaks option in Chapter 6. Remember that you select the Formulas check box when you want to display the contents of each cell (without its formatting) in the worksheet, and you select the Automatic Page **B**reaks to display

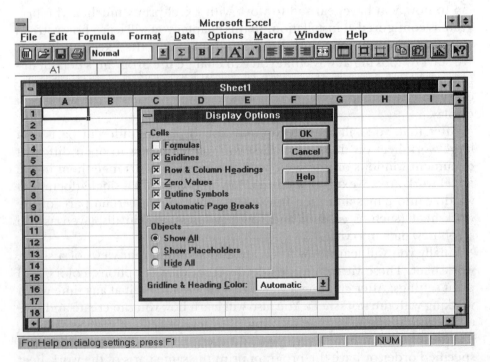

Figure 7.1   The Display Options Dialog Box

the page breaks used in printing your reports as dotted lines on the screen. You can use the Formulas option when you want to print the formulas in your worksheet, and you can use the Automatic Page Breaks option to see where the page breaks occur as you modify your worksheet.

As you're creating and editing a worksheet, you will undoubtedly want to have Excel display the cell gridlines and column and row headings to help you identify cell locations. Once you've finalized the worksheet, however, you may want to remove these items from the screen to maximize the area of the worksheet that you can view. To remove the cell gridlines, clear the **G**ridlines check box. To remove the row numbers and column letters from the worksheet display, clear the Row & Column **H**eadings. Remember that removing the cell gridlines from the worksheet display does not affect their printing. To remove the gridlines from a printout, you must clear the Cell Gridlines check box in the Page Setup dialog box.

The **Z**ero Values check box in the Display Options dialog box controls whether or not zeros appear in the cells of your worksheet. Sometimes you may want to suppress the display of zeros in a printout so that you can concentrate only on the cells that contain values. To remove the display of all zeros in a worksheet (whether entered as constants or resulting from the computation of formulas), clear the **Z**ero Values check box. Excel no longer displays zeros in the worksheet (thereby eliminating them from all printouts), although zeros and the formulas that evaluate to zero still appear in the formula bar when you make its cell active.

The **O**utline Symbols check box controls whether or not Excel displays the Row and Column Level bars with their various outline symbols on the screen (to the left and above the worksheet window) when you create an outline in a worksheet. (You learn how to do this in Chapter 9.) After setting up your outline, you can use this option to remove these bars and their symbols so that you can display more of the worksheet data on the screen.

You can choose from three Object options in the Display Options dialog box. By default, the Show **A**ll option button is selected, meaning that Excel displays as they will be printed all graphic objects such as the charts, text boxes, and line drawings that you place in the worksheet. (See Figure 7.2.) If you're working with a large worksheet that contains many such graphics, you can speed up the screen response time somewhat by selecting either the **S**how Placeholders or Hi**d**e All option button. When you choose the **S**how Placeholders, Excel shows only the location of graphic objects such as charts and text boxes in the worksheet with gray-shaded rectangles (as shown in Figure 7.3). Using placeholders for graphic objects speeds up screen operations because the program doesn't have to take the time to draw any of these graphics details in the worksheet.

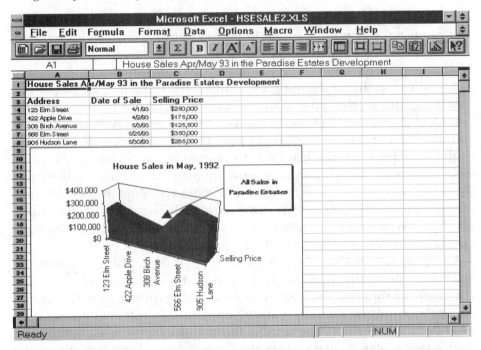

Figure 7.2   Sample Worksheet Displaying All Graphic Objects

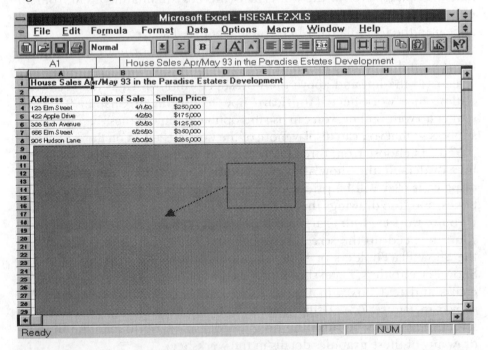

Figure 7.3   Sample Worksheet Displaying Placeholders for Graphic Objects

To remove all graphics objects (charts, text boxes, and line drawings) from the worksheet display, you choose the Hide All option button. Note that when this option has been activated, you cannot select any graphic object for editing. You can edit the contents of a graphic object or delete it from the worksheet only when the Show All or Show Placeholders option is selected.

The Gridline & Heading Color drop-down list box enables you to change the color of the column letters and row numbers as well as the color of the dotted lines that show the cell gridlines. By default, Excel uses the Automatic color selection (which uses black for the row and column text and gray for the gridlines). To select another color from the color palette for these screen elements, open the Gridline & Heading Color drop-down list box and then drag to the new color in the list box. (See "Customizing the Colors in the Worksheet" later in this chapter for information on creating custom colors for the color palette.)

Tip When you assign new colors to gridlines and row and column headings in a worksheet with the Gridline & Heading Color option, Excel changes these colors only in the active worksheet. This means that you can assign distinct colors to various types of worksheets to differentiate them from one another. (Color assignments made with the Gridline & Heading Color check box are saved with the worksheet.) For example, you could make budget worksheets blue, income statements red, and so on.

Modifying the Workspace Options

You can also control several default settings for your worksheet with the options in the Workspace Options dialog box (shown in Figure 7.4) opened by choosing the Workspace command on the Options menu. We already discussed the use of the first option in this dialog box, that of the Fixed Decimal option, in Chapter 2. Remember that you can use this option to enter automatically the decimal in your numeric entries. (See "Fixing the Decimal Point in Numeric Entries" in Chapter 2 for details.)

Some of the Display options in the Workspace Options dialog box are also already familiar. You know that you select the R1C1 check box when you want Excel to use the R1C1 system of cell references rather than the usual A1 system of references. By default, the Status Bar, Scroll Bars, Formula Bar, and Note Indicator check Display boxes are all selected. You're acquainted with all of these screen elements except for the note indicator, which is a small dot (red on a color monitor) that appears in the

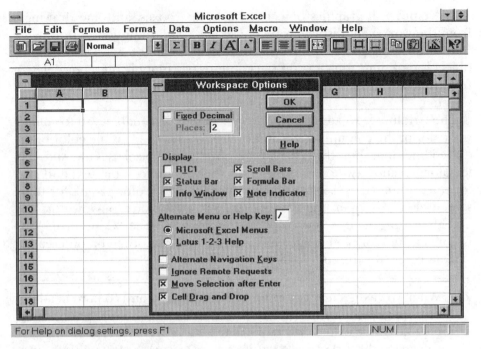

Figure 7.4   The Workspace Options Dialog Box

upper-right corner of a cell when the cell contains a note. (See Chapter 8 for information on using notes.) To suppress the display of any of these elements in the worksheet (status bar, scroll bars, formula bar, or note indicator), simply clear its check box in the Workspace Options dialog box. Figure 7.5 shows you a sample worksheet after removing the formula bar, scroll bars, and status bar from its display. Note how much more of the worksheet is visible on the screen once you remove these parts of the window.

Using the Info Window

The Info Window check box enables you to open a separate information window that can give you all sorts of information about the active cell. To open the Info window, select the cell you want information about, then open the Workspace Options dialog box with the Workspace command on the Options menu and select the Info Window option. Excel then opens a full-size information window that shows you the address of the active cell, its contents (following Formula), and the contents of any note attached to the cell, such as the one shown in Figure 7.6.

When the Info window is active, the Excel menu bar changes so that it contains only five menus: File, Info, Macro, Window, and Help. You can use

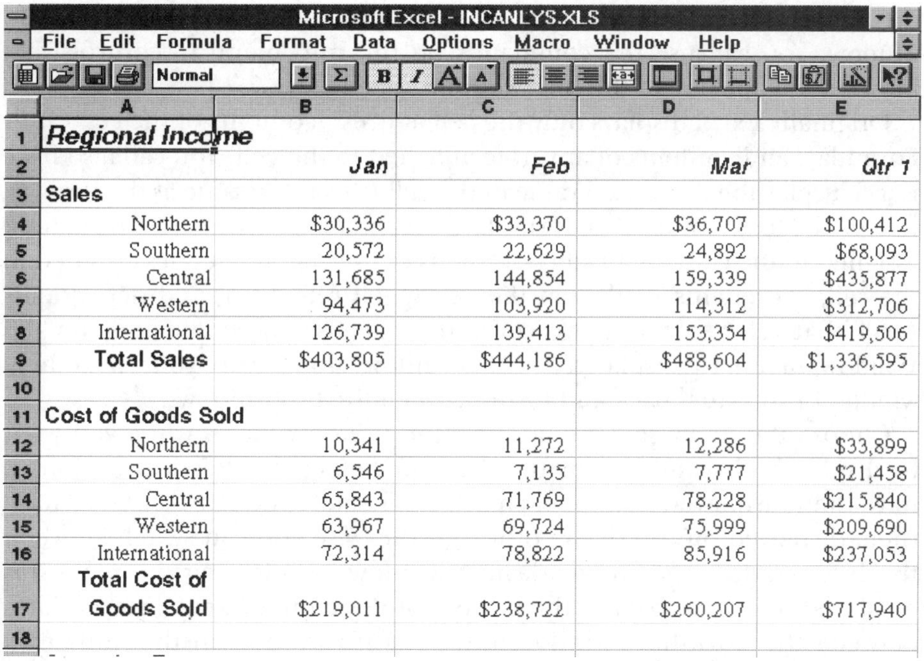

	A	B	C	D	E
	Microsoft Excel - INCANLYS.XLS				
	File Edit Formula Format Data Options Macro Window Help				
1	*Regional Income*				
2		*Jan*	*Feb*	*Mar*	*Qtr 1*
3	Sales				
4	Northern	$30,336	$33,370	$36,707	$100,412
5	Southern	20,572	22,629	24,892	$68,093
6	Central	131,685	144,854	159,339	$435,877
7	Western	94,473	103,920	114,312	$312,706
8	International	126,739	139,413	153,354	$419,506
9	**Total Sales**	$403,805	$444,186	$488,604	$1,336,595
10					
11	**Cost of Goods Sold**				
12	Northern	10,341	11,272	12,286	$33,899
13	Southern	6,546	7,135	7,777	$21,458
14	Central	65,843	71,769	78,228	$215,840
15	Western	63,967	69,724	75,999	$209,690
16	International	72,314	78,822	85,916	$237,053
17	**Total Cost of Goods Sold**	$219,011	$238,722	$260,207	$717,940
18					

Figure 7.5   Sample Worksheet Without Formula Bar, Scroll Bars, or Status Bar

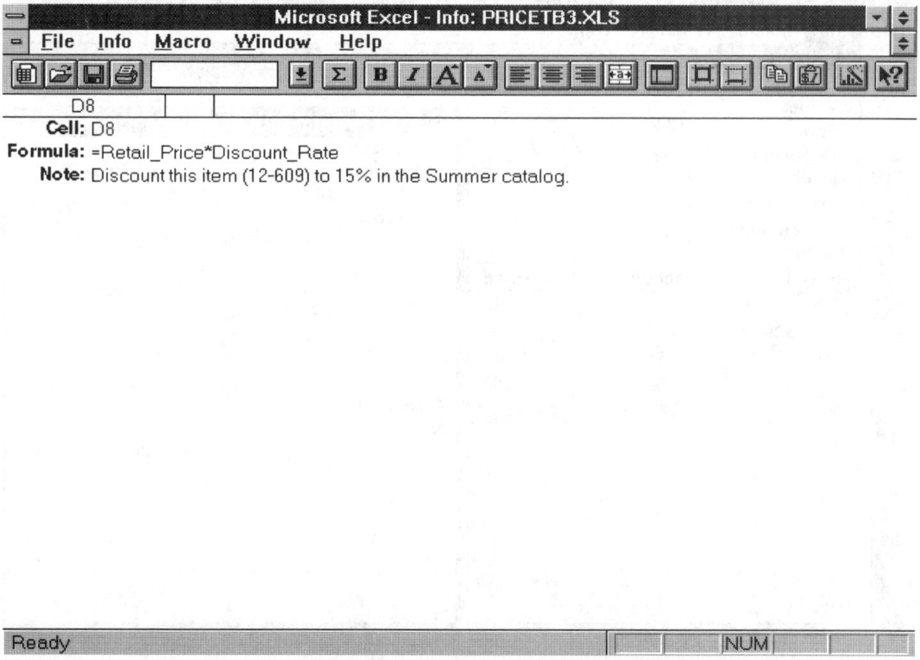

Microsoft Excel - Info: PRICETB3.XLS

File   Info   Macro   Window   Help

D8

Cell: D8
Formula: =Retail_Price*Discount_Rate
   Note: Discount this item (12-609) to 15% in the Summer catalog.

Ready   NUM

Figure 7.6   Full-size Info Window

the **Print** command on the **File** menu to print the contents of the Info window. You can use the commands on the **Info** menu to control what information appears in the Info window. (See Figure 7.7.)

Originally Excel displays only the cell address, contents of the cell (after Formula), and contents of any note attached to the cell. You can also have Excel display the calculated value in the cell (this is the same as the formula unless the cell contains a formula), information about the formatting assigned to the cell, the protection status of the cell, the names assigned to the cell, precedents (cells that the active cell refers to), and dependents (cells that refer to the active cell). You can use the commands on the **Window** menu to display the Info window along with your worksheet window or to switch back and forth between the two windows.

Choose the **Arrange** command on the Window menu when you want to display both windows on the screen. (Select the **Vertical** option to have them displayed next to each other, or select the **Horizontal** to have them displayed on top of the other.) Otherwise you can switch between the Info window and the worksheet window by selecting the name (as displayed in its title bar) at the bottom of the menu. Excel differentiates between the worksheet window and the Info window in the pull-down menu by prefacing the document name with *Info*. If the active worksheet

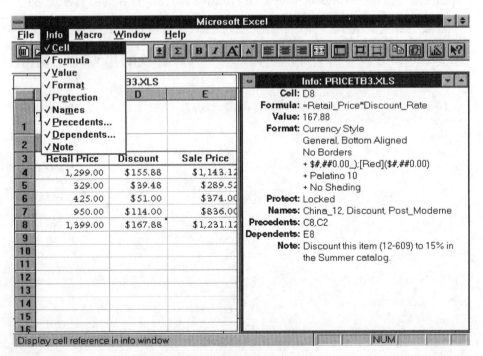

Figure 7.7   Tiled Info Window Showing All Information

is named PRICETBL.XLS, the associated Info window will be called Info: PRICETBL.XLS in the Window pull-down menu.

Figure 7.7 shows the Info Window alongside a worksheet window when all of the Info menu options have been selected. When you use this arrangement, you can immediately see the information in the Info window on each cell that you select in the worksheet window.

Note: You can use the statistics listed in the Info window to help you identify and locate errors when troubleshooting your worksheet. See Chapter 8 for more information on using the Info window when auditing the worksheet.

To close the Info window when you no longer need to get information about cells in your worksheet, choose the Close option on the File menu or double-click the Control-menu box in the upper-left corner of the Info window. Then you can restore the worksheet window to full size by clicking the Maximize button in the upper-right corner of the Excel window. Note that as soon as you close the Info window, Excel deselects the Info Window check box. Also, the next time you open the Info window, you will find that Excel has returned to the default settings (full-size window showing only the cell address, contents, and note attached to the active cell).

Other Workspace Options

The Workspace Options dialog box contains two options: Alternate Menu Key or Help Key and Alternate Navigation Keys. By default, Excel uses the / (slash key) as the alternate key for displaying either the Excel pull-down menu (if the Microsoft Excel Menus option button is selected) or displaying the Help for Lotus 1-2-3 Users dialog box (if the Lotus 1-2-3 Help option button is selected). If you wish, you can enter a new alternate menu or help key by replacing the / (slash) in the text box. If you are a 1-2-3 user who is just switching to Excel and would rather have 1-2-3 Help displayed than the Excel menus when you press the / (slash) key, select the Lotus 1-2-3 Help option button (which automatically deselects the Microsoft Excel Menus option button). You can also select the Alternate Navigation Keys check box to have Excel respond to the pointer-movement keystrokes used by Lotus 1-2-3. (See "Using the 1-2-3 Alternate Navigation Keys" in Chapter 2 for more information.)

There are three more check box items in the Workspace Options dialog box: Ignore Remote Requests, Move Selection after Enter, and Cell Drag and Drop. You can select the Ignore Remote Requests check box if you don't want Excel to stop processing your worksheet data and respond to remote requests from other Windows applications linked to your worksheet. (See Chapter 21 for information on how to link information between Excel and another Windows application.) You can deselect the **M**ove Selection after Enter check box if you don't want Excel to move the pointer to the next cell down when you press the Enter key. After clearing this check box, pressing the Enter key when the formula bar is activated will complete a cell entry without moving the pointer from the active cell.

> *Note:* Excel continues to move the cell pointer to the next cell in a cell selection when you press Enter even after you deselect the **M**ove Selection after Enter check box in the Display Options dialog box.

The last check box, Cell **D**rag and Drop, determines whether or not Excel's drag and drop facility for moving and copying data is turned on or off. If you find that the white-cross pointer doesn't change to the arrowhead when you position it on one of the four cell borders, the drag and drop feature is turned off. To turn it back on, you need to open the Workspace Options dialog box and select the Cell **D**rag and Drop check box.

Customizing the Colors in the Worksheet

Excel offers a default color palette of sixteen colors that you can apply to various parts of the worksheet display. You can assign these colors to the number formats, fonts, borders, or patterns that you apply to selected cells in the worksheet or to the cell gridlines and row and column headings in the entire worksheet. If you have a color monitor, you can see the colors you apply to various parts of the worksheet on the screen. If you have a color printer, you can print the colors as well.

> *Note:* To assign a new color to a number format, you must enter the appropriate color format code in a custom format. (See "Creating Custom Formats" in Chapter 3.) To assign a new color to a font, border, or pattern in selected cells, open the appropriate dialog box with its command (**F**ont, **B**order, or **P**atterns) on the Format menu, then choose the desired color in the drop-down list box. To assign a new color to the cell gridlines and column and row headings in the worksheet, open the Display Options dialog box, then choose the desired color in the Gridline & Heading Color drop-down list box.

Depending on your hardware, you may have a choice of displaying 16 or 256 different colors on your color monitor, depending on the display setting used by Windows. You change this display setting by double-clicking the Windows Setup program icon in the Main group window located in the Windows Program Manager to open the Windows Setup window. Then you choose the **C**hange System Settings command on the **O**ptions menu to open the Change System Settings dialog box. The **D**isplay drop-down list box shows the current display. To see what other display options are available and, perhaps, change the display used by Windows, click the drop-down button and drag to the new display setting (as shown in Figure 7.8). After selecting a new display setting, choose the OK button to close the Change System Settings dialog box and return to Windows Setup. To close this window, double-click the Control-menu box or select the **C**lose option on the Control menu (Alt+F4).

You can customize the colors in the default Excel color palette (described in the following section) and then apply these custom colors to the fonts, borders, or patterns in a cell selection or the gridlines and row and column headings in the worksheet. You can also customize the color scheme used by Windows to display the Excel program and its document windows. (See "Customizing the Windows Color Scheme" later in this chapter.)

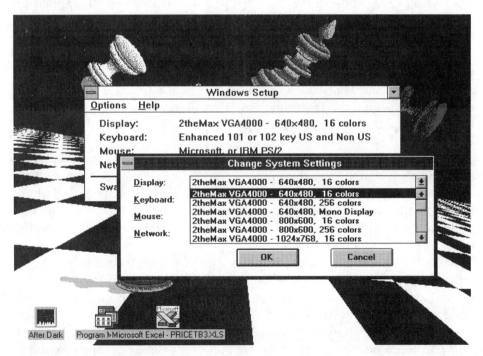

Figure 7.8 Selecting a New Display Setting

Customizing the Excel Color Palette

To customize the Excel color palette, you choose the Color Palette command (the dimmed option if you have a monochrome display setting selected in Windows) on the **O**ptions menu. Excel then opens the Color Palette dialog box (shown in monochrome in Figure 7.9). This dialog box shows each of the sixteen colors on the current palette. To customize a color, you click the color you want to modify, then choose the **E**dit command button. Excel then opens the Color Picker dialog box showing the current settings for the selected color (similar to the one shown in Figure 7.10).

Tip The colors in the Color Palette dialog box are counted from 1 through 8 down the first column and 9 through 16 down the second column. These numbers can be used with the [color] format code to assign a particular color when creating custom number formats. (See "Creating Custom Formats" in Chapter 3.) For instance, to assign light gray from the default color palette to a number format, you would use the code [COLOR 15] in the custom number format.

The Color|Solid box shows the current color as it would be applied to shading patterns (the Color side) and to text and lines (the Solid side). To modify the selected color, you can adjust the hue, saturation (abbreviated "Sat"), or luminosity (abbreviated "Lum") values or you can adjust the red, green, or blue values. You change these values by clicking the up or down arrows next to the **H**ue, **S**at, **L**um, **R**ed, **G**reen, or **B**lue text boxes or by clicking or dragging the Hue and Saturation Color Cursor (the cross in the large color square) or the Lumination Color Cursor (the arrowhead on the right side of the color bar).

As you adjust the values of these color components, Excel shows you the effect of your changes on the current color in the Color|Solid box. The Color side of the box shows you the patterned color that will be used when you apply the custom color to shading patterns in the worksheet, while the Solid side shows you the solid color that will be used when you apply the custom color to text and lines.

When the custom color is the way you want it to appear in the worksheet, select the OK button to close the Color Picker dialog box and return to the Color Palette dialog box. Once there, you can select another color and customize it in the same manner. When you're finished customizing the color palette, click the OK button or press the Enter key to close the dialog box and return to your worksheet. From then on, the color palette displays the custom colors whenever you select an Excel command that uses the color palette.

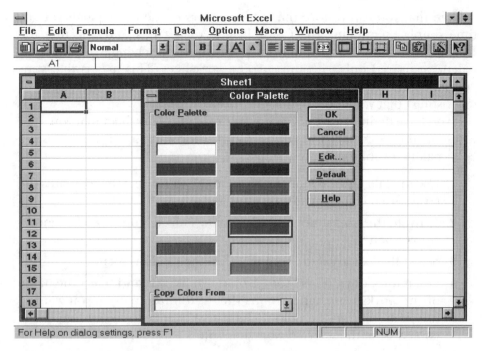

Figure 7.9 The Color Palette Dialog Box

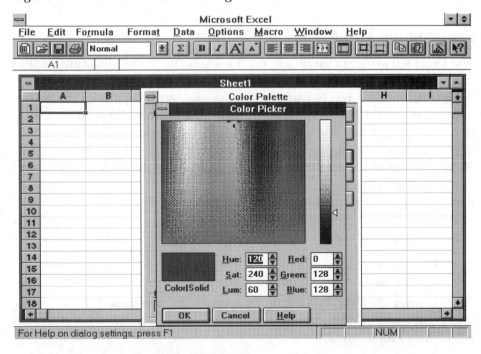

Figure 7.10 The Color Picker Dialog Box

Note that you can restore the default colors to the color palette at any time simply by opening the Color Palette dialog box and selecting the **D**efault command button. Also, keep in mind that changes to the color palette are saved only with the current worksheet. This means that your custom colors are not available automatically in any other worksheet (new or existing) that you open.

If you have defined a set of custom colors in one worksheet that you want to use in the worksheet you're working on, you can copy the customized color palette by following these steps:

1. Use the **F**ile Open command to open the worksheet that contains the customized color palette you want to use.

2. Activate the worksheet into which you want to copy the customized color palette.

3. Select the Color Pal**e**tte command on the **O**ptions menu.

4. Open the **C**opy Colors From drop-down list box and select the name of the worksheet that contains the customized palette you want to use. The colors in the Color **P**alette area change to the custom colors copied from the selected worksheet file.

5. Click the OK command button or press Enter.

Customizing the Windows Color Scheme

The Excel 4.0 program window is, on the whole, fairly colorless (gray being the predominate color). If you want, you can customize the default Windows color scheme by choosing new colors for various parts of the active and inactive windows on the screen, including the colors for the application workspace, title bars, scroll bars, as well as the window frame and borders. Windows allows you to save your customized color schemes. This allows you to use a special color scheme for each application that you run. For instance, you can have a color scheme that you use only when running Excel and another quite different one that you use when you run Word for Windows.

To create a custom color scheme for Excel, you follow these steps:

1. Double-click the Control Panel program icon in the Main group window of the Windows Program Manager.

2. Double-click the Color icon (the one with the crayons) in the Control Panel window to open the Color dialog box similar to the one shown in Figure 7.11.

3. Press the ↓ key to cycle through the preconfigured selections in the

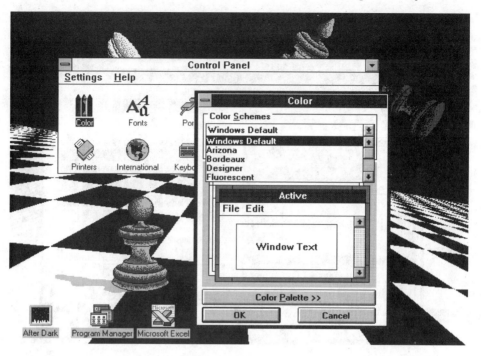

Figure 7.11   Selecting a New Color Scheme in the Color Dialog Box

Color **S**chemes drop-down list box. Windows previews each color scheme you select in the drop-down list box in the sample windows located below the Color **S**chemes area.

4. If you locate a color scheme that you want to use as is, select the OK button or press Enter to close the Color dialog box and put the selected color scheme into effect. If you don't find a color scheme that you want to use as is, select a close design that you can modify, then select the Color **P**alette command button. Windows expands the Color dialog box to include a Screen **E**lement drop-down list box and a **B**asic Colors and **C**ustom Colors palette, as shown in Figure 7.12.

5. Select the part of the screen whose color you want to modify either by clicking the area in the sample color scheme in the left part of the Color dialog box or by selecting the part by name in the Screen **E**lement drop-down list box.

6. Click the color you want to assign to the selected screen element in the **B**asic Colors palette. If you want to use a custom color, click the **D**efine Custom Colors command button to open the Custom Color Selector dialog box (which is almost identical to the Color Picker dialog

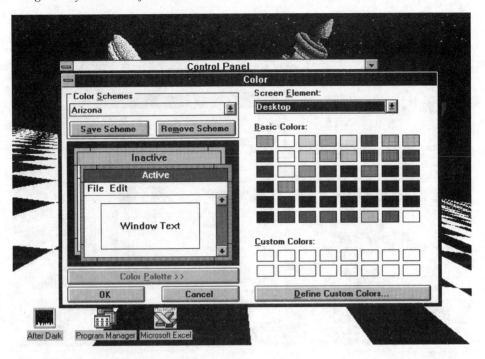

Figure 7.12   The Expanded Color Dialog Box

box in Excel), then define the custom color and choose the **Add Color** command button. You can continue to define the custom colors you want to use in the new color scheme. When you've finished defining your custom colors, select the **C**lose command button to close the Custom Color Selector dialog box and return to the Color dialog box.

7. Continue to select the screen elements you want to modify and the colors you want to apply to them as described in step 6.

8. When you have your color scheme exactly the way you want it, select the S**a**ve Scheme command button in the Color **S**chemes area, then enter a descriptive name for your new color scheme (such as Excel 4.0) in the text box in the Save Scheme dialog box and choose OK.

9. Select the OK command button in the Color dialog box or press Enter to close the Color dialog box, save your new color scheme, and put the new colors into effect. Then choose the **C**lose command on the Control Panel's Control menu or double-click its Control-menu button to close the Control Panel window.

Tip When designing a color scheme for Excel, choose a bright color for the Window Frame as this color not only highlights the borders of all the open document windows but also the borders of all bars (scroll bars, status bar, and so on), buttons (drop-down list buttons, scroll arrows, and the like), and boxes (style, font, font size, and so on) displayed on the screen. Also, all custom color schemes that you create are saved in the **control.ini** file in the **\windows** directory. If you want to use your custom color schemes on another computer running Windows, copy this file into the new computer's **\windows** directory.

Opening Up Multiple Windows on a Worksheet

Back in our initial discussion of the worksheet grid in Chapter 1, we discussed the enormous size of the Excel worksheet when compared with the limited view of the worksheet afforded by the monitor. In Chapter 2 you learned how to use the **Z**oom command on the **W**indow menu to surmount this problem by reducing the magnification so that you can display more worksheet cells on the same screen. The biggest drawback to this method is that as the magnification decreases, so does the legibility of the data until the cell entries simply become placeholders that are too small to read. Also, this method can show you only a single area of data in adjacent cells. You cannot use it to display two discontinuous data ranges that are located in distant parts of the same worksheet.

By opening different windows on the same worksheet, you can overcome both these limitations. When you open a new document window on the same worksheet, you can display two separate areas on the same screen without having to reduce the magnification so much that you can no longer read their data.

To open a new window on the same worksheet, you choose the **N**ew Window command on the **W**indow menu. Excel immediately opens up a second full-size document window containing the same worksheet. The only discernible difference between the first and second document windows is in their title bars, where Excel appends window numbers to the document name. This means, for example, that if you open a second document window on the worksheet named BUDGET92.XLS, the title bar of the first document window will appear as

BUDGET92.XLS:1

while the title bar of the second document window will appear as

BUDGET92.XLS:2

You can continue to use the **N**ew Window command to open new windows on the same worksheet; the maximum number of windows is determined by the amount of computer memory available. Although normally you can open many document windows on the same worksheet, more than four windows on the same worksheet usually is not practical (two are usually the most manageable). This is because the more document windows you open, the smaller each window will be and the more limited the area it can show when you display all the windows in the Excel work area.

Arranging Windows in the Work Area

At full size, two, three, or four different document windows are of no more help than one document window is in displaying different parts of the same worksheet on the screen. To display more than one document window in the Excel work area, you choose the **A**rrange command on the **W**indow menu to open the Arrange Windows dialog box (shown in Figure 7.13).

By default, the **N**one option is selected in the Arrange Windows dialog box, meaning that Excel overlaps the open document windows except for parts of their title bars (an arrangement also known as *cascading*) when you reduce the size of the active document window by clicking the Restore

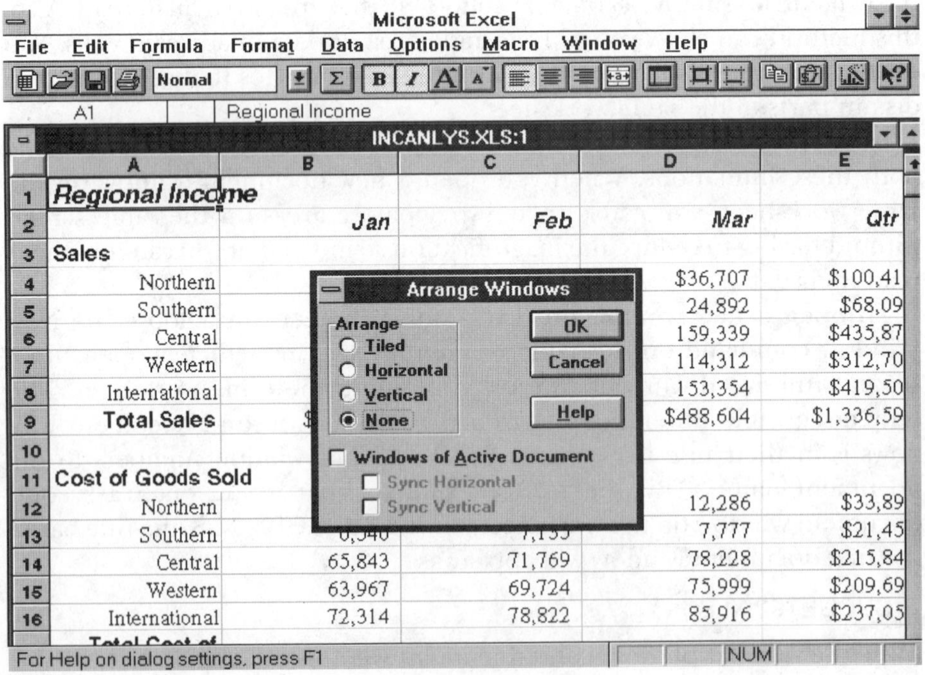

Figure 7.13   The Arrange Windows Dialog Box

button or by selecting the **R**estore command on the document's Control menu (Ctrl+F5).

Figure 7.14 illustrates this default arrangement. In this figure, four document windows have been opened on the same worksheet named **INCAN-LYS.XLS**. Note that the active worksheet window **INCANLYS.XLS:4** (the last one opened in this case) appears on the top of the stack. To make one of the other document windows active and bring the window to the top of the stack, select the number of the window you want to activate in the **W**indow pull-down menu, click its title bar in the work area, or press Ctrl+F6 until the document window appears on the top of the stack.

The Arrange Windows dialog box also contains three different Arrange options that you can use when you want to see all of the open windows in the Excel work area but you don't want them to overlap each other. You choose the **T**iled option when you want Excel to arrange the windows side by side starting with the active window and continuing in the order in which the new windows were opened (from most recent to least recent), as illustrated in Figure 7.15. You choose the **H**orizontal option when you want the document windows arranged one on top of the other, as illustrated in Figure 7.16. You choose the **V**ertical option when you want the document windows arranged one next to the other, as illustrated in Figure 7.17.

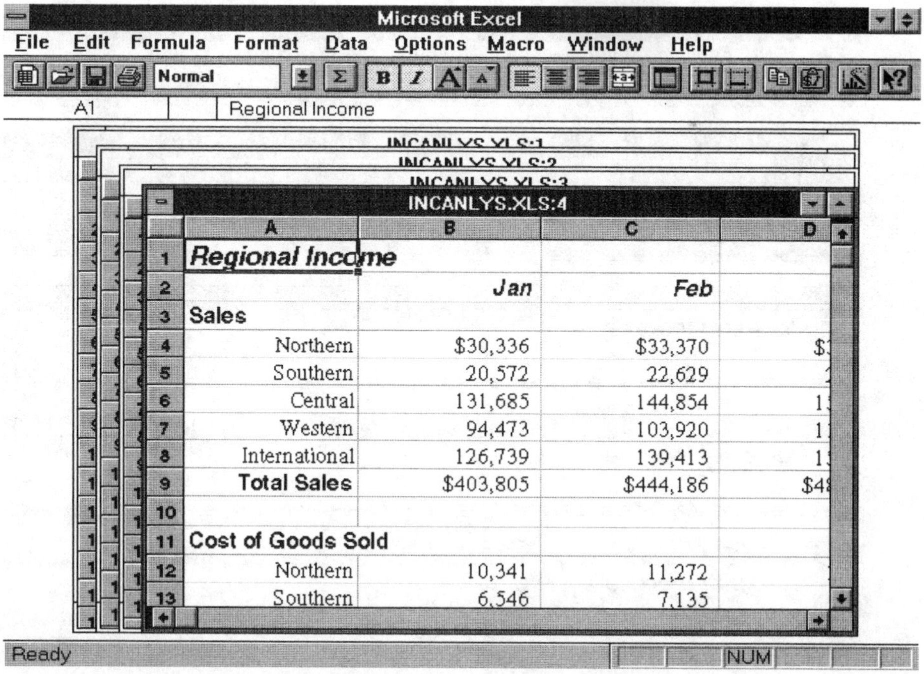

Figure 7.14   Sample Worksheet with Cascading Windows

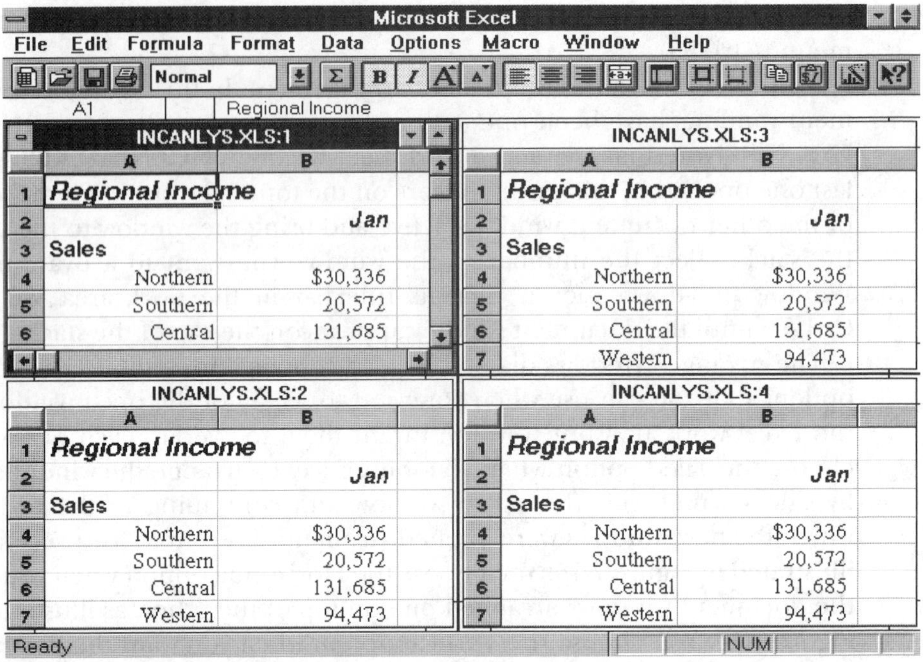

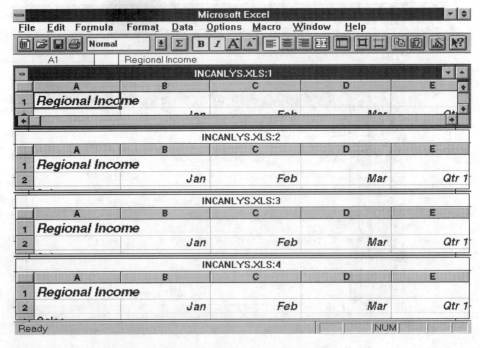

Figure 7.15   Sample Worksheet with Tiled Windows

Figure 7.16   Sample Worksheet with Horizontal Windows

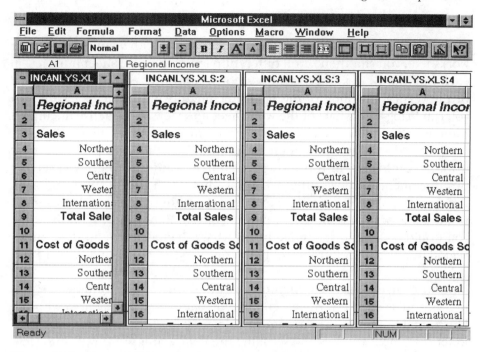

Figure 7.17   Sample Worksheet with Vertical Windows

After arranging your document windows with one of these options, you can make any of the displayed windows full size (by making the window active and then double-clicking its Maximize button) without losing the underlying window arrangement. This means that as soon as you use the Restore button to reduce the full-size document window, Excel places the window in its original position in the tiled, horizontal, or vertical window arrangement.

Tip When you select the Tiled, Horizontal, or Vertical arrangement options, Excel arranges the open document windows in the order they were opened from most recent to least recent, which corresponds to descending numerical order (as in **BUDGET.XLS:4**, **BUDGET.XLS:3**, **BUDGET.XLS:2**, **BUDGET.XLS:1**). To arrange the windows in ascending numerical order (as in **BUDGET.XLS:1**, **BUDGET.XLS:2**, **BUDGET.XLS:3**, **BUDGET.XLS:4**), activate each open document window in most-to-least-recent order by selecting its number on the Window menu in descending order (as in **BUDGET.XLS:3**, **BUDGET.XLS:2**, and **BUDGET.XLS:1** when **BUDGET.XLS:4** is active), then select the desired arrangement option in the Arrange Windows dialog box.

DISPLAYING DIFFERENT PARTS OF A WORKSHEET

Once you've arranged the document windows that you've opened on your worksheet, you can then scroll different parts of the worksheet into view in each window. By default, Excel does not synchronize either the horizontal or the vertical scrolling of the open document windows. This means that you can bring a new part of the worksheet into view in the active document window without likewise changing the view in the other open windows.

Figure 7.18 shows an example of scrolling two different parts of a wide worksheet into view in two vertical document windows. There you see the two document windows after arranging them with the **Vertical** option in the Arrange Windows dialog box, then activating the second document window and scrolling the sales totals in column P into view. With this view, you would be able to see immediately what effect a change in the January regional sales in column B would have on the yearly totals in column P.

Figure 7.19 illustrates an example of scrolling two different parts of a long worksheet into view in two horizontal document windows. In this figure, you see the two document windows after arranging them with the **Horizontal** option in the Arrange Windows dialog box, then activating the lower document window and scrolling the net earnings in row 21 into view.

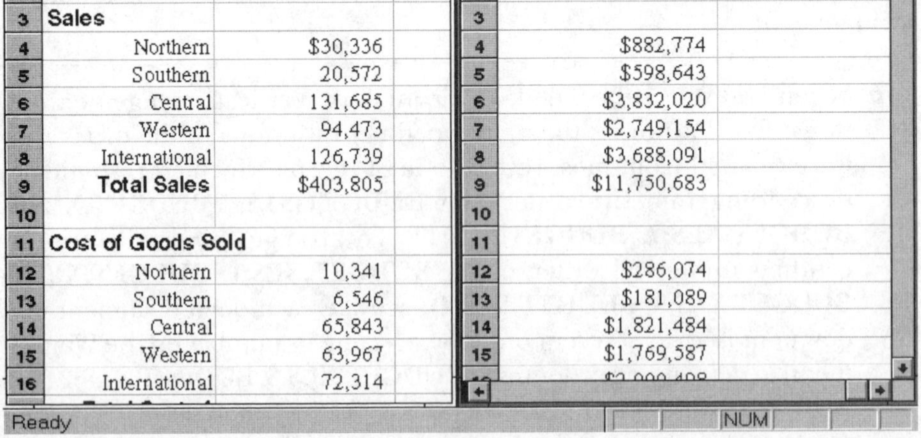

Figure 7.18   Viewing Different Parts of a Worksheet with Vertical Windows

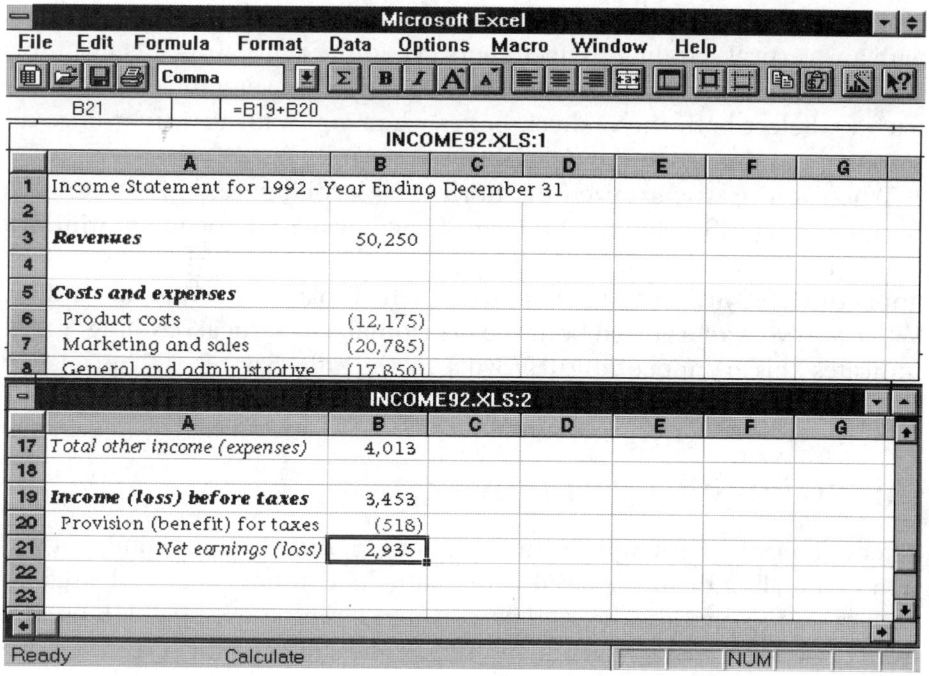

Figure 7.19 Viewing Different Parts of a Worksheet with Horizontal Windows

With this view, you would be able to see immediately what effect a change in the revenues in cell B3 would have on the net income in cell B21.

SYNCHRONIZING DOCUMENT WINDOWS

Sometimes you may want to synchronize the scrolling of open document windows, at least until you have brought a particular section of the worksheet into view in each window. To do so, you choose the **Arrange** command on the **Window** menu where you then select the Windows of **Active** Document check box. As soon as you select this check box, the **S**ync Horizontal and Sy**nc** Vertical check boxes become available. (The synchronization options are only available when working with document windows on a single worksheet, not when working with document windows containing different worksheet files.)

Select the **S**ync Horizontal check box to synchronize horizontal scrolling in all open document windows with any horizontal scrolling that you perform in the active worksheet window (either with the horizontal scroll bar or pointer-movement keys such as Ctrl+→). Select the Sy**nc** Vertical check box to synchronize vertical scrolling in all open document windows with any vertical scrolling that you perform in the active worksheet window (either with the vertical scroll bar or pointer-movement keys such as Ctrl+↓). Select both these check boxes when you want to synchronize all scrolling movements in the open document windows.

When you've synchronized the horizontal scrolling, Excel indicates this by appending [HSync] to the title bar of each displayed document window. When you've synchronized the vertical scrolling, Excel indicates this by appending [VSync] to the title bar of each displayed document window. When you've synchronized both the horizontal and vertical scrolling, Excel indicates this by appending [HVSync] to the title bar of each displayed document window.

HIDING DOCUMENT WINDOWS

After opening and arranging your document windows, you may find that you don't want all of them displayed at the same time in the Excel work area. In such cases, you can close the windows you aren't using and leave only those you need displayed. That way you not only reduce the clutter on the screen but can also increase the size of the document windows that remain in view.

To hide a document window, you activate the window (by clicking its title bar or pressing Ctrl+F6) and choose the **Hide** command on the **Window** menu. Excel then removes the window from the Excel work area without resizing or rearranging the other open windows. To modify the arrangement of the windows still open so that you can fill in the gap and take advantage of the space, you need to open the Arrange Windows dialog box and select the appropriate Arrange option again.

> **Note:** The window numbers of hidden windows no longer appear at the bottom of the **Window** menu. Excel does, however, still keep track of the assigned window numbers. If you open a new document window on the same worksheet, the program assigns the next available number, counting the numbers given to the hidden windows.

You can redisplay a hidden document window at a later time by choosing the **Unhide** command on the **Window** menu. (This command is available only when you have hidden one or more document windows.) When you choose the **Unhide** command, Excel displays the Unhide dialog box containing a list box with all of the hidden windows. Double-click the name of the document window you want to redisplay or click the name and select the OK button. Excel redisplays the selected document window in the

Excel work area in its original position and size. If you modified the arrangement for the unhidden windows, the unhidden window may now overlap other windows in the display. In such cases, you need to rearrange all the open windows with one of the options in the Arrange Windows dialog box.

CLOSING DOCUMENT WINDOWS

When you no longer need multiple document windows displayed in your worksheet and are ready to return to a single-window display, you can do so by closing all but one of the open document windows. To close a document window, activate the window, then double-click its Control-menu button, choose the **C**lose option on the Control menu, or press Ctrl+F4. As you close document windows, Excel automatically renumbers the windows, if necessary, to close any gaps in the numbering sequence. (Thus if you close window 1 when windows 2 and 3 are still open, the program renumbers them to 1 and 2, respectively.)

When you have closed all but one of the document windows (it doesn't matter in what sequence you close them), you can restore the last remaining document window to full size by clicking its **M**aximize button, selecting the Maximize command on its Control menu, or pressing Ctrl+F10. If you want the worksheet to appear in a full-size document window the next time you open the file, be sure to select the **A**rrange command on the **W**indow menu and choose the **N**one option button in the Arrange Window, then save the worksheet. Otherwise, the document window will assume its previous size and position in the Excel work area when you next open the file.

Splitting a Worksheet Window into Panes

Many times you can set up the view you want of different parts of the same worksheet by splitting the document window into separate panes instead of actually opening new document windows for the worksheet. When you divide a single document window into panes rather than open multiple document windows, you can see more of the worksheet; window panes don't require screen space to display the document windows' title bar and repeat the worksheet's row and column headings, as document windows do. You can split any document window horizontally, vertically, or both horizontally and vertically.

To split a window horizontally, you drag the *horizontal split bar* (the black bar located above the up scroll arrow on the vertical scroll bar) down until you reach the row border in the worksheet where you want the document window divided. To split a window vertically, you drag the *vertical split bar* (the black bar located in front of the left scroll arrow on the horizontal scroll bar) to the right until you reach the place in the worksheet's column border where you want the document window divided. To split a window both horizontally and vertically, position the cell pointer in the cell whose top border marks the place where you want the horizontal division to take place and whose left border marks the place where you want the vertical division to take place, then choose the **S**plit command on the **W**indow menu. (You can also drag the horizontal and vertical split bars to create both horizontal and vertical window panes.)

Excel displays the borders of the window panes you create in the document window with a gray bar that ends with the vertical or horizontal split bar. To modify the size of a pane, you position the white-cross pointer on the appropriate dividing bar, then, as soon as the pointer changes to a double-headed arrow, you drag the bar until the pane is the correct size and release the mouse button.

When you split a window into panes, Excel automatically synchronizes the scrolling depending on how you split the worksheet. When you split a window into two horizontal panes as shown in Figure 7.20, the worksheet window contains a single horizontal scroll bar and two separate vertical scroll bars. This means that all horizontal scrolling of the two panes is synchronized, while vertically scrolling of each pane remains independent.

When you split a window into two vertical panes as shown in Figure 7.21, the situation is reversed. The worksheet window contains a single vertical scroll bar and two separate horizontal scroll bars. This means that all vertical scrolling of the two panes is synchronized, while horizontal scrolling of each pane remains independent.

When you split a window into two horizontal and two vertical panes as shown in Figure 7.22, the worksheet window contains two horizontal scroll bars and two separate vertical scroll bars. This means that vertical scrolling is synchronized in the top two window panes when you use the top vertical scroll bar and synchronized for the bottom two window panes when you use the bottom vertical scroll bar. Likewise, horizontal scrolling is synchronized for the left two window panes when you use the horizontal scroll bar on the left and synchronized for the right two window panes when you use the horizontal scroll bar on the right.

To remove all panes from a window when you no longer need them, you simply choose the Remove **S**plit command on the **W**indow menu. You can also remove individual panes by dragging the gray dividing bar for either the horizontal or the vertical pane until you reach one of the edges of the document window.

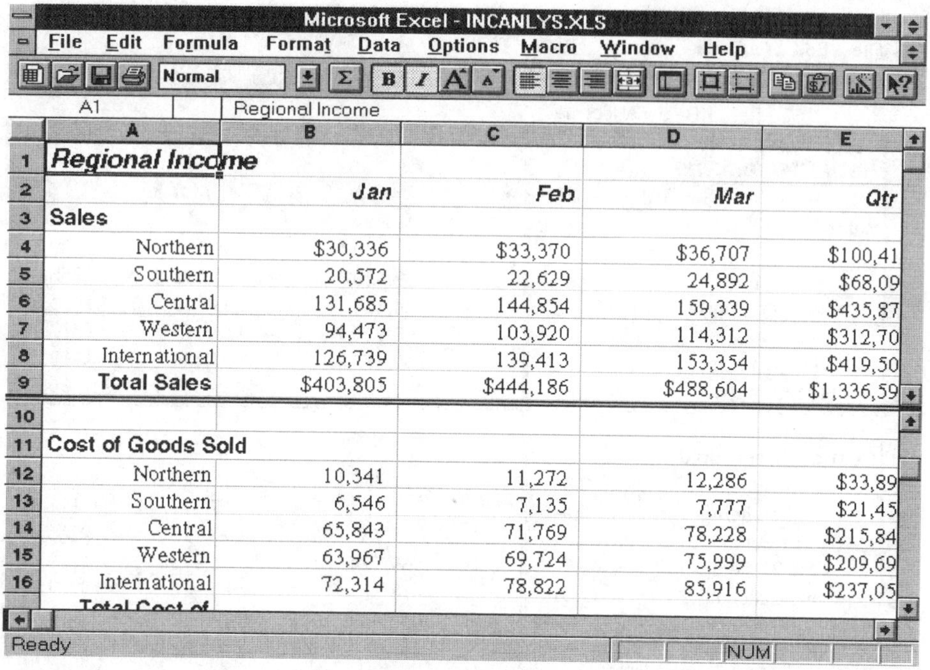

Microsoft Excel - INCANLYS.XLS				
File Edit Formula Format Data Options Macro Window Help				

A1 | Regional Income

	A	B	C	D	E
1	*Regional Income*				
2		*Jan*	*Feb*	*Mar*	*Qtr*
3	**Sales**				
4	Northern	$30,336	$33,370	$36,707	$100,41
5	Southern	20,572	22,629	24,892	$68,09
6	Central	131,685	144,854	159,339	$435,87
7	Western	94,473	103,920	114,312	$312,70
8	International	126,739	139,413	153,354	$419,50
9	**Total Sales**	$403,805	$444,186	$488,604	$1,336,59
10					
11	**Cost of Goods Sold**				
12	Northern	10,341	11,272	12,286	$33,89
13	Southern	6,546	7,135	7,777	$21,45
14	Central	65,843	71,769	78,228	$215,84
15	Western	63,967	69,724	75,999	$209,69
16	International	72,314	78,822	85,916	$237,05
	Total Cost of				

Ready | NUM

Figure 7.20 Sample Worksheet with Horizontal Window Panes

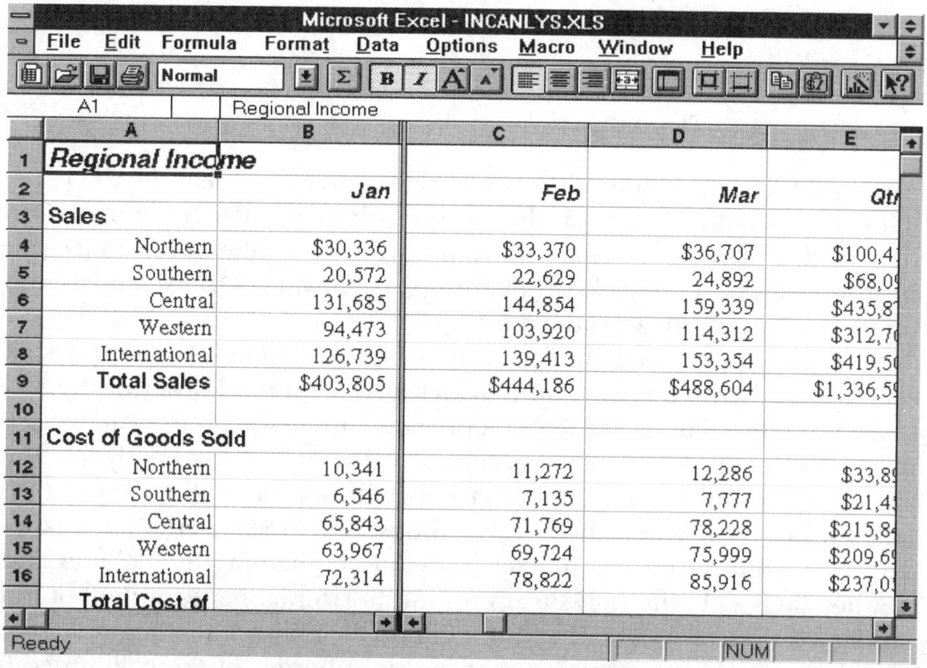

Microsoft Excel - INCANLYS.XLS				
File Edit Formula Format Data Options Macro Window Help				

A1 | Regional Income

	A	B	C	D	E
1	*Regional Income*				
2		*Jan*	*Feb*	*Mar*	*Qtr*
3	**Sales**				
4	Northern	$30,336	$33,370	$36,707	$100,4
5	Southern	20,572	22,629	24,892	$68,09
6	Central	131,685	144,854	159,339	$435,8
7	Western	94,473	103,920	114,312	$312,7
8	International	126,739	139,413	153,354	$419,50
9	**Total Sales**	$403,805	$444,186	$488,604	$1,336,59
10					
11	**Cost of Goods Sold**				
12	Northern	10,341	11,272	12,286	$33,89
13	Southern	6,546	7,135	7,777	$21,4
14	Central	65,843	71,769	78,228	$215,84
15	Western	63,967	69,724	75,999	$209,69
16	International	72,314	78,822	85,916	$237,0
	Total Cost of				

Ready | NUM

Figure 7.21 Sample Worksheet with Vertical Window Panes

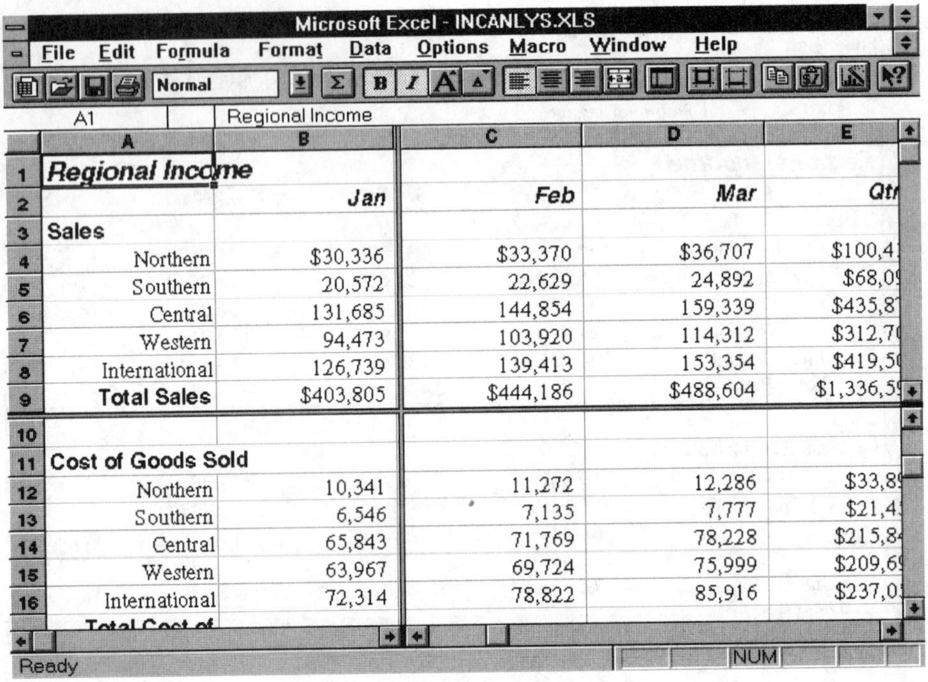

Figure 7.22 Sample Worksheet with Horizontal and Vertical Window Panes

Freezing Panes in the Window

After splitting a document window into panes, you can freeze the top pane, left pane, or both the top and left panes with Freeze Panes command on the Window. This allows you to keep a worksheet's column headings, row headings, or column and row headings displayed on the screen as you scroll new parts of the worksheet into view.

To freeze a horizontal pane with the column headings, you simply split the worksheet into two horizontal panes at the bottom border of the row containing the column headings before you choose the Freeze Panes command. To freeze a vertical pane with your row headings, you simply split the worksheet into two vertical panes at the right border of the column containing the row headings before you choose the Freeze Panes command. To freeze both horizontal and vertical panes containing the column and row headings, split the worksheet into two horizontal panes at the bottom border of the row containing the column headings and then split the worksheet into two vertical panes at the right border of the column containing the row headings before you choose the Freeze Panes command.

When you choose the **Freeze Panes** command on the **Window** menu, the gray bar dividing the window into panes becomes a simple border line. After freezing panes in the document window, you can scroll new parts of the worksheet into view without losing the titles displayed in the frozen panes. Figures 7.23 through 7.25 demonstrate how this works. In Figure 7.23 I created a horizontal pane at the bottom border of row 2 and a vertical pane along the right border of column A and then froze both of them with the **Freeze Panes** command. Figure 7.24 shows this same worksheet after vertically scrolling the sheet up to bring the net income figures in rows 27 through 33 into view. Note how the column headings (January, February, and March) within the frozen horizontal window pane remain displayed in this figure. Figure 7.25 shows this same worksheet after horizontally scrolling to the right to bring the second quarter figures in columns F through I into view. Note how the Regional titles in column A within the frozen vertical window pane remain displayed in this figure.

To unfreeze the panes, you choose the Unfreeze Panes command on the **Window** menu. This allows you to modify the size of the window panes or remove them from the worksheet display. If you want to unfreeze and remove all window panes at the same time, you can choose the Remove Split command on the **Window** menu instead.

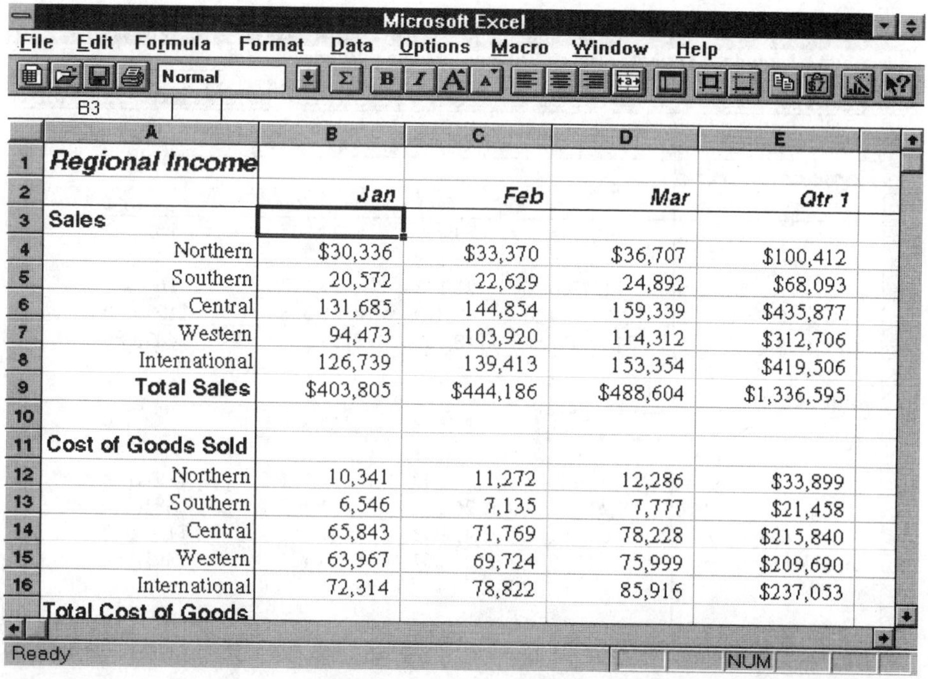

Figure 7.23 Sample Worksheet with Frozen Horizontal and Vertical Panes

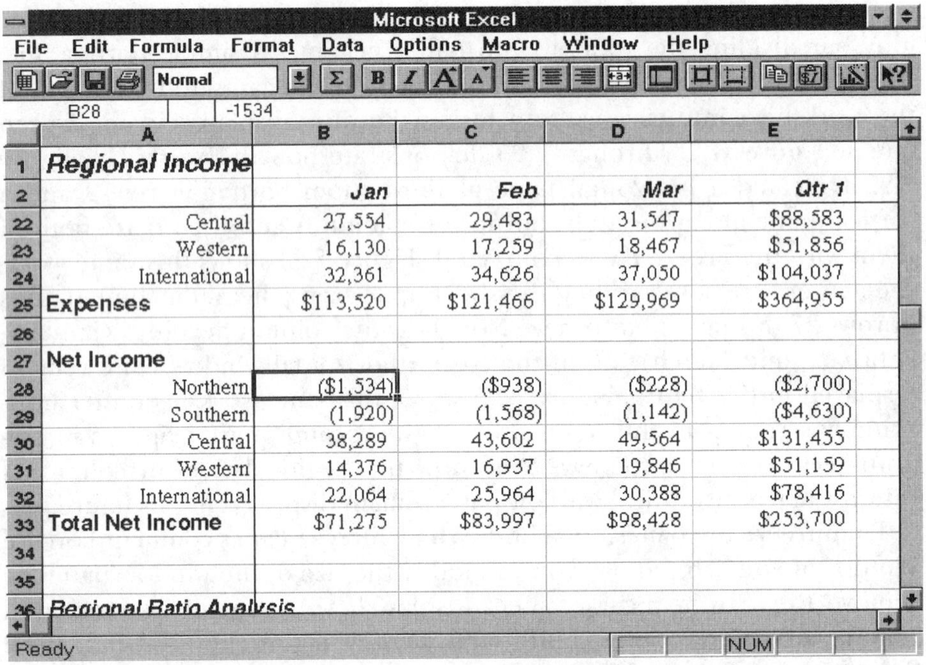

Figure 7.24　Vertically Scrolling the Sample Worksheet with Frozen Panes

	A	B	C	D	E
1	*Regional Income*				
2		Jan	Feb	Mar	Qtr 1
22	Central	27,554	29,483	31,547	$88,583
23	Western	16,130	17,259	18,467	$51,856
24	International	32,361	34,626	37,050	$104,037
25	Expenses	$113,520	$121,466	$129,969	$364,955
26					
27	Net Income				
28	Northern	($1,534)	($938)	($228)	($2,700)
29	Southern	(1,920)	(1,568)	(1,142)	($4,630)
30	Central	38,289	43,602	49,564	$131,455
31	Western	14,376	16,937	19,846	$51,159
32	International	22,064	25,964	30,388	$78,416
33	Total Net Income	$71,275	$83,997	$98,428	$253,700
34					
35					
36	Regional Ratio Analysis				

B28 = -1534

Figure 7.25　Horizontally Scrolling the Sample Worksheet with Frozen Panes

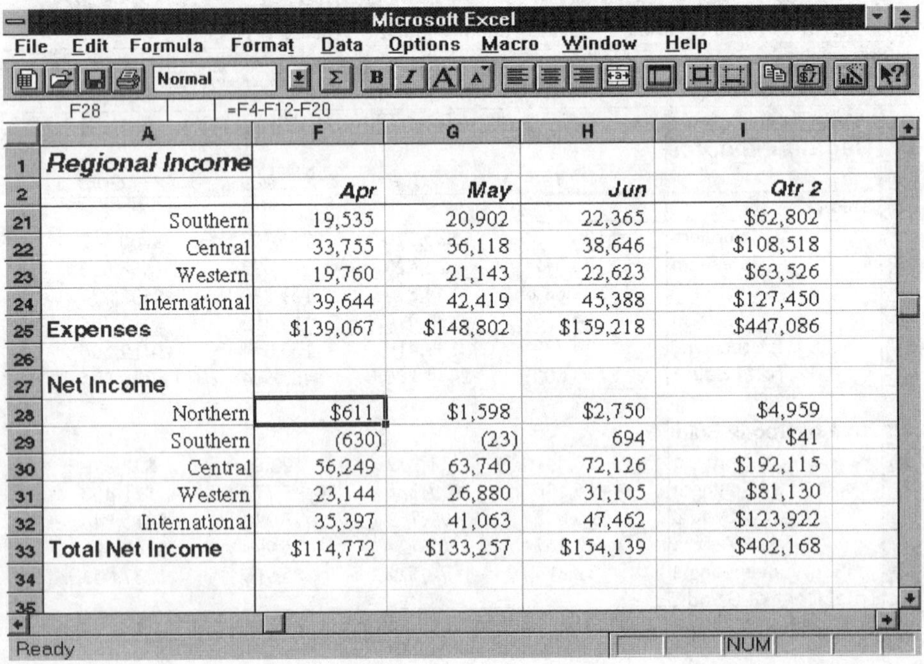

	A	F	G	H	I
1	*Regional Income*				
2		Apr	May	Jun	Qtr 2
21	Southern	19,535	20,902	22,365	$62,802
22	Central	33,755	36,118	38,646	$108,518
23	Western	19,760	21,143	22,623	$63,526
24	International	39,644	42,419	45,388	$127,450
25	Expenses	$139,067	$148,802	$159,218	$447,086
26					
27	Net Income				
28	Northern	$611	$1,598	$2,750	$4,959
29	Southern	(630)	(23)	694	$41
30	Central	56,249	63,740	72,126	$192,115
31	Western	23,144	26,880	31,105	$81,130
32	International	35,397	41,063	47,462	$123,922
33	Total Net Income	$114,772	$133,257	$154,139	$402,168

F28 = =F4-F12-F20

Setting Up Views of the Worksheet

While creating and editing a worksheet, you may find that you need to modify the worksheet display many times as you work with the document. For example, you may find at some point that you need to reduce the magnification of the worksheet display to 75 percent. At another point, you may need to return to 100 percent magnification and hide different columns in the worksheet. At some later point, you may have to redisplay the hidden columns and then divide the worksheet window into panes that you freeze on the screen.

With Excel's **View** command on the **W**indow menu, you can save any of these types of changes to the worksheet display. That way, instead of having to take the time to manually set up the worksheet display you want, you can have Excel re-create it for you by simply selecting the view. When you create a view, Excel can save any of the following settings: The current cell selection, print settings (including different page setups), column widths and row heights (including hidden columns), display settings (both those in the Display Options dialog box and the display settings in the Workspace Options dialog box), as well as the current position and size of the document window and the window pane arrangement (including frozen panes).

Tip Excel cannot create a view that uses separate document windows opened on the same worksheet (only one that uses the panes in the worksheet window). If you want to be able to use the document windows you've opened the next time you use the worksheet, save the worksheet using the desired document window arrangement right before you close the worksheet or exit Excel.

To create a view of your worksheet, follow these steps:

1. Make all of the necessary changes to the worksheet display so that the worksheet window appears exactly as you want it to be each time you select the view. If you will be adding this view to a report (see "Creating a Report Using Different Views," which follows), also select all of the print settings in the Page Setup dialog box that you want used in printing the view.

2. Choose the **View** command on the **W**indow menu to open the Views dialog box (shown in Figure 7.26).

3. Select the **A**dd command button in the Views dialog box to open the Add View dialog box.

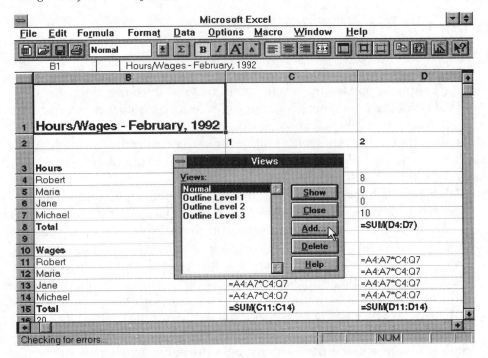

Figure 7.26   The Views Dialog Box

4. Enter a unique descriptive name for your view (following the same rules that you use when assigning range names) in the **N**ame text box.

5. If you want to include print settings and hidden columns and rows in your view (as is the case if you're going to include the view in a report), leave the **P**rint Settings and Hidden **R**ows & Columns check boxes selected when you choose the OK button. If you don't want to include these settings, clear either one or both of these check boxes before you select the OK button.

6. To create other views for the worksheet, repeat the entire procedure outlined in steps 1 through 5.

7. To save the views that you created with the worksheet, save the file with the **F**ile **S**ave command.

After you create your views, you can display the worksheet in that view at any time while working with that worksheet. To display a view, you follow these steps:

1. Choose the **V**iew command on the **W**indow menu to open the Views dialog box.

2. Double-click the name of the view that you want to use in displaying your worksheet in the **V**iews list box or select the name and then choose the **S**how command button.

Creating a Report Using Different Views

After creating views of your worksheet, you can use them in setting up reports. By adding them to a report, you can print the views in a specific sequence in a single printing operation. In addition, each view of the worksheet that you include in the report can use its own print settings, including different page set-ups and headers and footers (provided, of course, you leave the **P**rint Settings check box selected when you create the views).

For example, you can set up a report in two sections so that the first section uses a view that prints the worksheet data normally and the second section uses a view that prints the formulas in the cells and adjusts the column widths to suit their wider display. You can also have Excel print the first section with normal data in portrait mode and then print the second section with the formulas in landscape mode.

To create a report using the views that you added to a worksheet, you follow these steps:

1. Choose the Print **R**eport command on the **F**ile menu to open the Print Report dialog box shown in Figure 7.27.

2. Select the **A**dd command button to open the Add Report dialog box shown in Figure 7.28.

3. Enter a name for your report (again, following the rules for naming cells) in **R**eport Name text box.

4. Define the first section of the report by selecting the view you want to use in the **V**iew drop-down list box. (The current view of the worksheet is used by default.) If you want to print a scenario along with the view you selected in this section of the report (see Chapter 11 for details on creating scenarios), select the scenario you want used in the **S**cenario drop-down list box (the current scenario is used by default), then select the **A**dd command button. If you want to use a view only in the first section of the report, leave the **S**cenario option set to [Current] and simply choose the **A**dd command button after selecting the view you want to use. Excel adds the view and/or scenario you selected to the Current **S**ections list box.

5. Repeat the procedure outlined in step 4 to define each of the sections you want in your report.

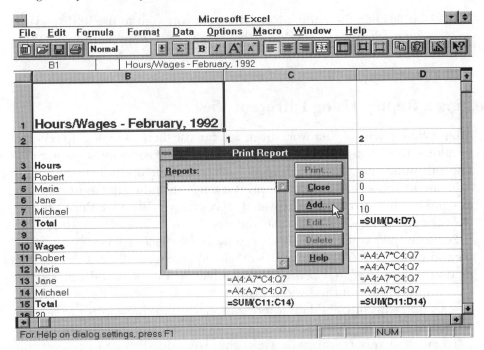

Figure 7.27   The Print Report Dialog Box

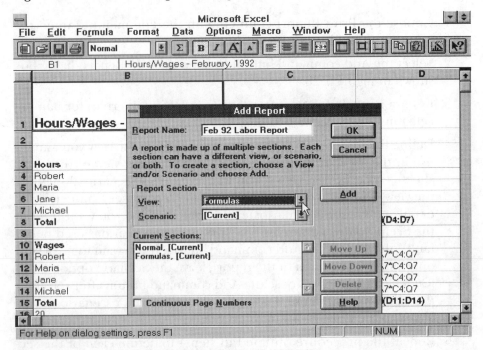

Figure 7.28   The Add Report Dialog Box

6. If you want your report to use continuous numbering, click the Continuous Page **N**umbers check box—otherwise Excel renumbers each section that uses page numbering in its header or footer.

7. When you have your report defined as you want it, choose the OK command button or press Enter to close the Add Report dialog box and return to the Print Report dialog box.

8. To print your report, select the **P**rint command button. If you want to print your report at a later time, choose the Close button.

9. To save the report you defined, save the worksheet with the File **S**ave command before you close the file or exit Excel.

After creating a report for a worksheet, you can print it at any time by opening the Print Report dialog box with the Print **R**eport command on the **F**ile menu, then double-clicking the name of the report in the **R**eports list box or selecting the name and then choosing the **P**rint command button. Excel then displays a Print dialog box that contains a **C**opies text box. To print a single copy of the report, choose the OK button or press Enter. To print multiple copies, enter the number to print in the **C**opies text box, then choose OK or press Enter.

To edit a report that you've added to a worksheet, select the report in the Print Report dialog box, then choose the **E**dit command button. To add a new section to the report, select the view in the **V**iew drop-down list box (and/or scenario in the **S**cenario drop-down list box) and choose the **A**dd button. To delete a section from the report, select the section in the Current **S**ections list box, then click the Delete command button. To change the printing order of a section, select the section in the Current **S**ections list box, then click the Move **U**p or Move **D**own command button until the section is positioned correctly in the list box. (Sections print in top-to-bottom order in the list box.) When you've finished making changes to your report, choose the OK button or press Enter.

SUMMARY

In this chapter you learned several more advanced techniques for controling the worksheet display. Specifically, you learned how to customize the Excel workspace by modifying the display and workspace options. You also learned how to customize the color palette and apply your colors to the worksheet. Next you learned how to open multiple windows on a worksheet and create window panes so that you can display different parts of the same worksheet on the screen. Finally you learned how to create views that save specific display settings as part of your worksheet and how you can use these views in a report.

In the next chapter you will learn advanced techniques for documenting and auditing your worksheets. Among these techniques you will learn how to attach notes (text or sound) to individual cells, set up original formulas that prevent error values from spreading throughout your worksheet, examine the relationship between the input values and formulas in your worksheet, and locate and track the changes you make to your worksheet.

8

Documenting and Troubleshooting the Worksheet

Verifying the accuracy of the worksheet is one of the more important tasks in its creation, a task that is unfortunately too often overlooked. With all the sophisticated formatting tools offered by Excel 4.0, you can easily get caught up in the process of making your worksheets look good at the expense of making sure that they are 100 percent accurate. As a result, you can end up creating a professional-looking worksheet that, while superficially appearing quite impressive, contains results based on faulty or incomplete underlying assumptions.

When speaking of errors in the worksheet, we are really talking about two different types: Formulas that return error values in the cells as opposed to formulas that return incorrect results. The first type of error is much easier to catch than the second type. For example, if you create a formula that uses a blank cell as the divisor, the formula returns the #DIV/0! error value, which alerts you to this problem right away. But if you create a formula that simply uses the wrong nonblank cell as the divisor (let's say your formula divides by the value in cell B4 when you should have had it divide by the value in cell C5), the formula merely returns the (incorrectly) calculated value to the cell. The only way you will recognize that such a formula result is in error is if you have made a mental estimate of the right answer and you notice that the result is not what you had expected.

Although the first type of error is certainly more conspicuous in the worksheet than the second type, it also can be harder to eradicate. This is because in a worksheet model that uses calculated values in further formula calculations, a single error value returned from one formula will spread immediately to all the formulas that refer to it (either directly or indirectly). As a result, if you don't catch the error value at the source, you are presented with a worksheet full of formulas giving you identical error values with no clue as to which one is the cause. In a complex worksheet model, you may have to spend a great deal of time reviewing the formulas in order to track and eliminate the source of error values.

In this chapter you will learn several techniques for documenting and troubleshooting the worksheets you build. Documenting the worksheet can help you avoid errors in formulas that return incorrect results. As you will see, you can add comments that annotate areas of the worksheet or notes to individual cells. You can use these comments or cell notes to document the underlying assumptions of the formulas in your worksheet or to remind yourself of missing data or data that still requires further verification. You can also use cell notes as markers that indicate the location of the master formulas (the ones you copy many times) or array formulas that need verifying before you distribute the worksheet.

Troubleshooting the worksheet includes a number of different methods for locating and correcting errors of both types. In this chapter you will learn how to track the relationship between formulas and the cells to which they refer, locate any deviations between ranges in the worksheet when they should be similar, and locate the error values. In addition, you will learn how to use three add-in macros, Document Summary, Worksheet Auditor, and Worksheet Comparison, to help you document your worksheet file and locate and eliminate various problems.

Because the best defense is a good offense, at the end of the chapter you will learn how to create formulas that prevent error values from spreading throughout a worksheet. By trapping errors at their source before they can spread, you can save yourself from having to spend time looking for their cause, and you will also know right where to go when you are ready to eradicate them.

Adding Comments with Text Boxes

You can add commentary directly to your worksheet with text boxes. A *text box* is a graphic object into which you can type notes that explain your data or remind you of things you still need to do. You can place a text box anywhere in a worksheet, and you can also add an arrow from the text box that points to the data to which your note refers. Because the text box is a graphic object that is not part of the worksheet grid, its borders can straddle columns and rows in the grid, and you can move and resize it around the worksheet as required. A text box is, however, an opaque graphic; if you move the box on top of cell entries in the worksheet, it will obscure the data in the cells below.

To add a text box to your worksheet, you use the Text Box tool , which is found on both the Drawing and the Utility toolbar. (If you use the Drawing toolbar, however, you also have access to the Arrow tool.) When you click the Text Box tool to add a text box, the pointer changes from the white cross to a crosshair shape (using thinner lines than the fill handle) with which you draw the boundaries of the box. To do this, position the crosshair pointer in what will be the upper-left of the text box, then drag the pointer diagonally to what will become the lower-right corner of the box. As you drag, Excel shows you the size and shape of the text box with dotted lines. When you have adjusted the size and shape the way you want it, release the mouse button. If you want your text box to be square, you hold down the Shift key as you drag. (This constrains the shape of the text box to a square, allowing you to concentrate on sizing the box.)

Tip You can review the comments you add to your worksheet in text boxes by using the **Objects** option in the Select Special dialog box. After selecting all the graphic objects in the worksheet with this command, press Tab or Shift+Tab to move to the next or previous object in turn.

Entering Text in a Text Box

As soon as you release the mouse button to draw your text box, Excel positions the insertion point inside the borders of the box in the upper-left corner. You then can begin typing the text of your comment. Excel uses the font and font size assigned to the Normal style in your worksheet and left aligns the text in the box. When you reach the right edge of the box, the program automatically wraps the text to the beginning of a new line. If your comments require more lines than the height of the box can accommodate, Excel scrolls the lines of text up. Lines at the top of the box are no longer displayed in the text box, although you can later increase the height of the text box to display all of the lines. When you are finished entering the text, click the white cross pointer in a cell of the worksheet. Figure 8.1 shows you a sample text box with several lines of text.

If you want to change the font for your text before you begin entering it in a text box, choose the new font and/or font size in the Font dialog box (opened by choosing the Format **F**ont command) or with the Font Name box or Font Size box in the Formatting toolbar. If you want to add an attribute to a section of the text you've entered, such as bold or italic, select the text with the I-beam pointer, then select the style in the Font

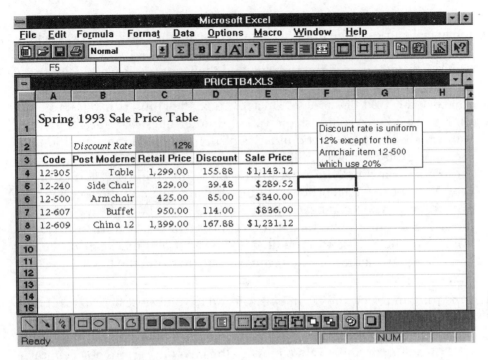

Figure 8.1 Sample Text Box

dialog box or click the Bold, Italic, Underline, or Strikeout tool in the Formatting toolbar.

If you want to change the alignment of the text in the text box, choose the **Text** command (this command replaces **Alignment** when a text box is selected) on the Format menu to open the Text dialog box (shown in Figure 8.2). This dialog box contains text alignment and orientation options (similar to those found in the Alignment dialog box). In addition, the dialog box contains an **Automatic Size** check box that you can select when you want Excel to resize the text box automatically to suit the orientation options that you choose as well as any subsequent edits you make to the text. The dialog box also contains a **Patterns** and a **Font** command button that you can use to open the Patterns and Font dialog box, respectively.

Editing Text in a Text Box

After placing a text box in your worksheet, you can edit its contents by first clicking the arrowhead pointer somewhere in the box to select it (Excel shows that a box is selected by redrawing its borders with a thicker, dotted line and placing sizing handles around the perimeter), then clicking the

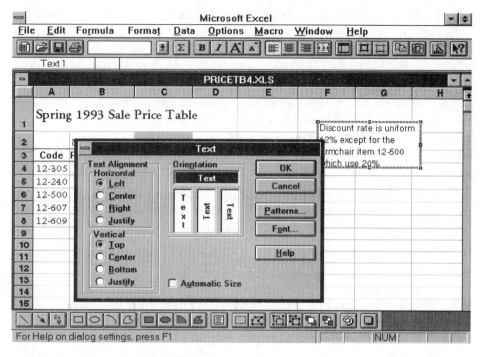

Figure 8.2   The Text Dialog Box

I-beam pointer somewhere in the text to locate the insertion point or dragging the I-beam pointer over the text you want to edit. Once the insertion point is located in the text, you can edit the text just as you edit text on the formula bar.

If you change the orientation of the text so that it uses the Rotated Vertical, Rotated Up, or Rotated Down orientation, Excel temporarily changes the text orientation to normal as soon as you position the insertion point somewhere in it by clicking the I-beam pointer. After you finish editing the text in the normal orientation, the program returns the text to the currently selected orientation as soon as you deselect the text box by clicking the pointer in a cell of the worksheet or by pressing the Esc key.

To delete a text box, you simply click the arrowhead pointer somewhere in the box to select it, then press the Backspace or Delete key.

Adding an Arrow from a Text Box

As mentioned earlier, you can have Excel draw an arrow from your text box to the data or the area of the worksheet that you are describing. To draw an arrow from a text box, you click the Arrow tool on the Drawing toolbar, then position the crosshair pointer on the border of the text box where the arrow should come from and drag the pointer until you have positioned it where the arrowhead should appear. As you drag, Excel displays a line starting at the first point you click and extending to the current position of the crosshair pointer. When you release the mouse, Excel draws the arrowhead at the end of the line with a pair of sizing handles at either end. To deselect the arrow and remove the sizing handles, click the pointer in the worksheet somewhere outside the arrow. Figure 8.3 shows you a typical arrow drawn from a text box to point out the cell described in its comment.

 Alert!   When drawing the arrowhead, always take care that you are dragging the crosshair pointer away from, not toward, the text box. Otherwise, the arrowhead will appear pointing to the text box instead of pointing to the place in the worksheet you want to call attention to.

By default, Excel draws the arrow with a solid black line ending in a filled triangular arrowhead. To modify the arrow you've drawn, double-click its line somewhere to display the Patterns dialog box shown in Figure 8.4. To customize the line, choose the pattern you want in the **Style** drop-down list

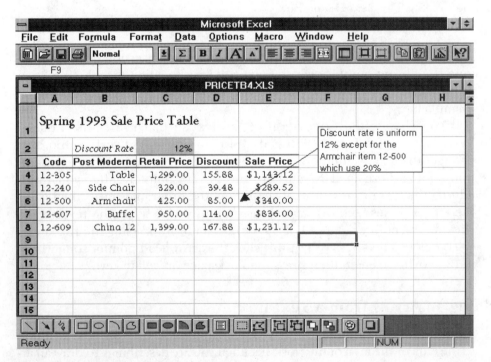

Figure 8.3   Sample Text Box with Arrow

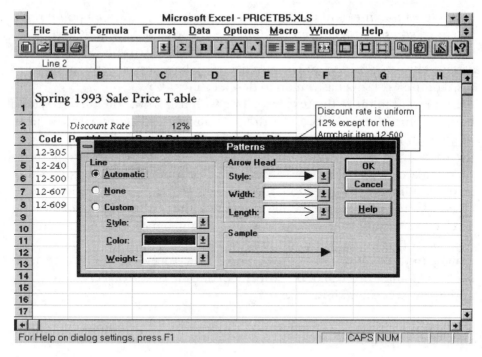

Figure 8.4   The Line and Arrowhead Patterns Dialog Box

box, the color you want in the **C**olor drop-down list box, and/or the
thickness of the line in the **W**eight drop-down list box. To modify the
appearance of the arrowhead, choose the pattern you want in the St**y**le
drop-down list box, the arrowhead width you want in the Wi**d**th drop-down
list box, and the arrowhead length you want in the **L**ength drop-down list
box. To remove the line (arrowhead and all) without deleting it from the
worksheet, select the **N**one option button. As you make changes to the
options in the Patterns dialog box, Excel shows the effect on the selected
arrow in your worksheet in the Sample box.

Moving a Text Box

You can resize or move a text box in the worksheet easily. To move the text
box to a new location, click the box to select it, then position the arrowhead
pointer somewhere on one of the borders of the box and drag its outline to
the new position before you release the mouse button. When you have the
box where you want it, click the white-cross pointer in a cell of the worksheet to place the text box and deselect it.

The technique for moving an arrow is the same as for moving the text
box. Click the arrow to select it (indicated by sizing handles at the arrowhead

and start of the line), then drag the arrow with the arrowhead pointer. As you drag, you see only the line without the arrowhead. However, as soon as you release the mouse button, Excel redraws the arrowhead. To set the arrow in its new position and remove its sizing handles, click the pointer in a cell of the worksheet as you do to deselect a text box.

If you want to move the text box along with its arrow, you need to select both graphic objects before you drag the arrowhead pointer to the new position in the worksheet. To do this, you use the Selection tool [⊡] on the Drawing toolbar. When you click this tool, Excel changes the pointer shape to a crosshair that you can use to select both the text box and the arrow by dragging a selection rectangle large enough to enclose both objects. When you release the mouse button after enclosing the objects in a selection rectangle, Excel displays the sizing handles in both graphic objects. At that point, when you drag either object, both move together as a single unit. When you have the text box and arrow successfully relocated, click the pointer in a cell of the worksheet outside of the objects to deselect both the text box and its arrow.

Sizing a Text Box

To modify the size of a text box, click the box to select it, then position the pointer on the appropriate sizing handle. When the pointer changes to a double-headed arrow, drag it to increase or decrease the size of the box. Drag the sizing handles in the middle of the borders to change the width or height of the box by modifying the position of a single side. Drag the sizing handles at the corners of the text box to change both the width and height of the box by modifying the position of two intersecting sides.

You can modify the length of an arrow in a similar fashion. Select the arrow, then drag one of the two sizing handles. Drag the sizing handle away from the handle on the opposite end to make the arrow longer, and drag the sizing handle toward the one on the opposite end to make the arrow shorter. In addition to modifying the length of an arrow, you can modify its direction by dragging the sizing handle at the tip of the arrowhead around the handle at the start of the line (so that it acts like the hand of a clock rotating around the center).

Modifying the Borders and Fill of a Text Box

Normally, text boxes use a simple, single-line black border on all four sides. If you want, you can modify the borders of a text box and/or assign a fill pattern or color to it with the options in the Patterns dialog box (shown in

Figure 8.5). To open the Patterns dialog box, you can simply double-click the text box, or you can select the **P**atterns command from either the Objects shortcut menu (displayed by positioning the pointer on a *border* of the text box, then clicking the *right* mouse button) or the Forma**t** pull-down menu.

To customize the border lines, choose the pattern you want in the **S**tyle drop-down list box, the color you want in the **C**olor drop-down list box, and/or the thickness of the line in the **W**eight drop-down list box. To modify the fill in the text box, choose the pattern you want in the **P**attern drop-down list box, the foreground color in the **F**oreground drop-down list box, and the background color you want in the **B**ackground drop-down list box.

You can use the Sha**d**ow and **R**ound Corners check boxes to create more impressive-looking text boxes. Select the Sha**d**ow check box to add a drop shadow to a text box, which adds a thicker border on the right and bottom side to give the box a three-dimensional appearance. Select the **R**ound Corners check box to have Excel draw the box with rounded corners. Of course, you can combine the drop-shadow and rounded corners effect, as shown in Figure 8.6, by selecting both of these check boxes.

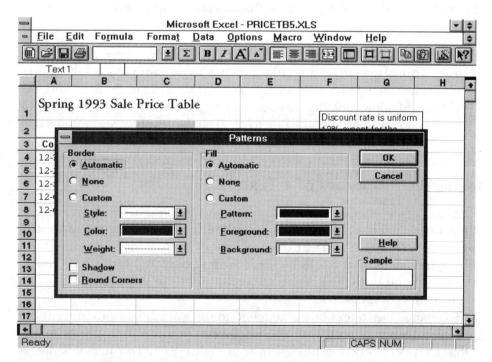

Figure 8.5   The Text Box Patterns Dialog Box

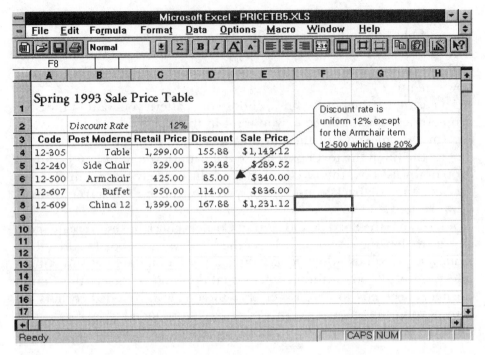

Figure 8.6   Text Box with Rounded Corners and Drop Shadow

Tip You can also convert a regular text box to one with a drop shadow by clicking the text box you want to convert to select it, then clicking the Drop Shadow tool ◨ in the Drawing toolbar. As soon as you click the pointer outside of the box to deselect the text box, you will see that Excel has added a drop shadow to it.

Changing the Properties of a Text Box

You can decide whether or not the comments you add in text boxes should be printed, sized, or moved as part of the worksheet. By default, Excel prints a text box as part of the worksheet (assuming, of course, the Print_Area includes the cells beneath the text box) and moves and resizes the box as you move and resize the cells under the upper-left and lower-right corners of the box.

To change how a text box is attached to the worksheet or to prevent the box from being printed with the worksheet, you use the options in the Object Properties dialog box (shown in Figure 8.7). To open this dialog box, select the text box, then choose the Object Properties command on

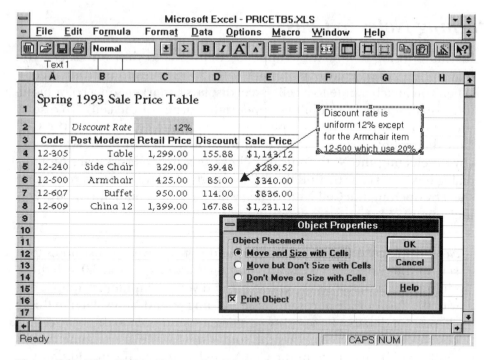

Figure 8.7   The Object Properties Dialog Box

the Objects shortcut menu (displayed by positioning the pointer on a *border* of the text box, then clicking the *right* mouse button) or on the Forma**t** pull-down menu.

This dialog box contains three Object Placement options. By default, the Move and **S**ize with Cells option button is selected, meaning that the text box changes position and size along with underlying cells under the box's upper-left and lower-right corner. Select the **M**ove but Don't Size with Cells option button when you want the text box to move with the cells under the box's upper-left corner but not change size. Select the **D**on't Move or Size with Cells option button when you want the text box to remain stationary and maintain its current size regardless of changes to the underlying cells.

Sometimes you may not want the text box to appear in a printout. In such cases, you deselect the **P**rint Object check box in the Object Properties dialog box. If you've drawn an arrow from the text box and you want both the arrow and the text box to be omitted from the printout, be sure to select *both* graphic objects before you open the Object Properties dialog box and clear the **P**rint Object check box. If you select just the text box without the arrow, the arrow will be printed along with your worksheet data.

Attaching Notes to Cells

Instead of using text boxes to append comments to your worksheet, you may prefer to add your comments by attaching notes to individual cells. When you attach a note to a cell, Excel displays a marker (on a color monitor, a small square in red in the upper-right corner of the cell). To display the text of the note, you simply double-click the cell to open the Cell Note dialog box. If you've turned off the note indicator in the worksheet (by deselecting the **N**ote Indicator check box in the Workspace Options dialog box), you can still find the cell locations of all the notes in your worksheet by opening the Cell Note dialog with the **N**ote command on the Formula menu.

> *Note:* In Excel 4.0 you can attach sound notes as well as text notes to cells in your worksheet if you are running Windows version 3.0 with the Multimedia Extensions or version 3.1 and your computer is equipped with the appropriate hardware. (See "Adding Sound Notes" later in this chapter for details.) If you add a text and a sound note to the same cell, double-clicking the cell plays the sound note while at the same time displaying the text note in the Cell Note dialog box. If you add only a sound note to a cell, double-clicking the cell plays back the note without opening the Cell Note dialog box.

One of the advantages of adding your comments with text notes rather than with text boxes is that you can print just the notes. To print only the notes in a worksheet, you choose the **P**rint command on the **F**ile menu (or press Ctrl+Shift+F12) and then choose the N**o**tes option button in the Print area. If you want to print your worksheet along with the notes, you choose the **B**oth option button instead. To have Excel print the cell reference above each note so that you know its location in case you want to edit or delete it, select the Page **S**etup command button in the Print dialog box and select the Row & **C**olumn Headings check box in the Page Setup dialog box. Then choose the OK command button in both the Page Setup and Print dialog boxes to begin the printing.

Adding Text Notes

To add a text note to a cell in your worksheet, you follow these steps:

1. Make the cell active to which you want to attach the text note.
2. Choose the **N**ote command on the Formula menu to open the Cell

Note dialog box (shown in Figure 8.8).

3. Type the text of the note in the **Text** Note list box. When your text reaches the right edge of the text box, Excel automatically wraps the text to a new line. If you want to start a new line before the text reaches the right edge, press Alt+Enter. When entering the text of the note, you can use the same editing techniques you do when making a cell entry in the formula bar.

4. If, after you finish entering the text for the first note, you want to add a note to another cell, select the **A**dd command button to add the first note to the Notes in **S**heet list box. Select the **C**ell text box and click the cell or type the reference of the cell, then select the **T**ext Note list box and replace the text of the existing note with the text of the new note. When you've finished entering and editing the text of the new note, select the **A**dd button. Note that if you click the cell to add its reference to the **C**ell text box, Excel enters the absolute cell reference in the text box (as $F$1). Also, if you press Tab after selecting the cell reference, Excel not only selects the **T**ext Note but all of the text of the previous note so that you can replace it as soon as you start typing the text of the new note.

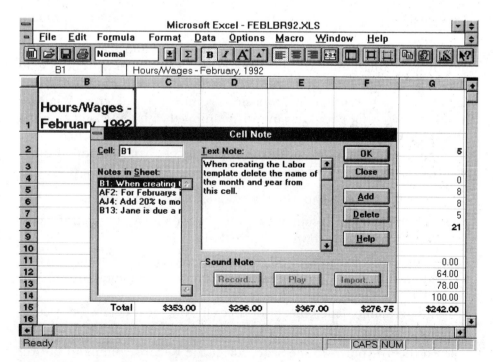

Figure 8.8   The Cell Note Dialog Box

5. Repeat the procedure outlined in step 4 as necessary to add all of the notes that you want to various cells in the worksheet.

6. When you've finished adding all the notes you want in the worksheet at this time, choose the OK button or press Enter. (If you added the last note with the **Add** command button, you can also choose the Close command button.)

 Alert! Excel allows you to add a note only to a single cell. If you select a multicell range or nonadjacent selection or enter a name assigned to such a range or selection, Excel displays an alert box warning "Reference must be to a single cell on the active sheet" (when you select the **Add** command button). To annotate a multicell range or nonadjacent selection, attach the note to the first cell of the range or selection.

After adding a note to a cell, you can open the Cell Note dialog box and display, edit, or delete the note's text simply by double-clicking the cell. (Remember that Excel places a small rectangle in the upper-right corner of the cell as a note indicator.)

Adding Sound Notes

 In addition to text notes, Excel 4.0 is able to record and play back sound notes provided that you have all of the necessary equipment. To be able to create and use sound notes in your Excel worksheets, you must be running Windows 3.0 with Multimedia Extensions version 1.0 or later, or Windows 3.1. In addition, your computer must be equipped with some kind of sound board, and, of course, you must have some sort of microphone attached.

Assuming that you have the necessary equipment, you can add a sound note to a cell by following these steps:

1. Make the cell active to which you want to attach the text note.

2. Choose the **Note** command on the Formula menu to open the Cell Note dialog box (shown in Figure 8.8).

3. To use a prerecorded sound or message that has been stored in a disk file for the sound note, choose the **Import** command button, then select the file containing the sound in the File **Name** list box of the Import Sound dialog box by double-clicking the filename or by clicking it and then selecting the OK button or pressing Enter.

4. To record your own message, select the **Record** command button to open the Record dialog box. Then click the Record icon to start

recording the sound note message in your microphone. The slider bar in the Record dialog box informs you of the length (in seconds) of your message. If you need to pause in the recording of your message, click the Pause icon. Then click the Record icon when you are ready to resume. When you have finished recording your message (up to 1 minute and 18 seconds long), click the Save command button to close the dialog box and return to the Cell Note dialog box. (You can also click the Stop icon and then choose the Save button.)

5. To listen to your sound note (either the prerecorded message you imported or the one you just recorded) in the Cell Note dialog box, select the **P**lay command button. If there are problems with the quality of the sound or with the message you recorded, click the Erase command button and then import or record the message again (as outlined in step 3 or 4).

6. When you are satisfied with your note, select the **A**dd command button if you want to record another note (sound or text). Otherwise, select the OK command button or press Enter.

Excel indicates the addition of a sound note with an asterisk (*) after the cell reference in the Notes in **S**heet list box in the Cell Note dialog box. The program indicates the addition of a sound note to a cell in the worksheet with the same cell indicator used to denote a text note. When you double-click a cell that contains a sound note, Excel automatically plays the message using the speaker in your computer (or any external speakers, if you have added them to your system).

To delete a sound note from a cell, select the cell, open the Cell Note dialog box, and choose the **D**elete command button. To replace a sound note, choose the **E**rase command button and then rerecord your message.

Although a cell can contain only one sound note, you can add both a text and a sound note to the same cell. To add a text note to a cell with a sound note, select the cell, then open the Cell Note dialog box, select the **T**ext Note dialog box, and type the text of your note and choose the **A**dd or OK command button. When you double-click a cell with both a sound and text note, Excel plays back the sound note and displays the Cell Note dialog box showing the text note in its **T**ext Note list box.

Browsing Through the Notes in a Worksheet

One of the most compelling reasons for using cell notes to document your worksheet is the ease with which you can review notes that are widely dispersed. By using the Select Special command (a very powerful command for troubleshooting the worksheet about which you will learn more later in this chapter) and the Info Window, you can browse through the notes in a worksheet quickly. To see how you do this, follow these steps:

1. Choose the **W**orkspace command on the **O**ptions menu to open the Workspace Options dialog box.

2. Select the Info **W**indow check box in the Display area, then choose the OK button or press Enter. Excel opens a full-size Info Window containing Cell, Formula, and Note information on the active cell.

3. Choose the **A**rrange command on the **W**indow menu to open the Arrange Windows dialog box.

4. Select the **V**ertical option button in the Arrange area, then choose the OK button or press Enter. Excel places the Info Window for the active worksheet to the immediate left of the worksheet window.

5. Make the worksheet window active by clicking it or selecting its name on the **W**indow menu.

6. Choose the **S**elect Special command on the **F**ormula menu to open the Select Special dialog box (shown in Figure 8.9), then select the OK command button or press Enter to accept the default option of **N**otes. When you use the default **N**otes option, Excel selects all cells in the worksheet that have notes attached to them, and the Info Window shows you the text of the note in the first cell in the selection (as shown in Figure 8.10).

7. Press the Tab key to go to the next note in the selection or press Shift+Tab to go to the previous note. When you select the next or the previous note, you can read its text in the Info Window. If you come upon a note that you want to print, make the Info Window active, then select **P**rint command on the **F**ile menu. After printing the note, you can create the worksheet window again and continue browsing with the Tab and Shift+Tab keys.

8. When you are finished browsing through your notes, select the Info Window and double-click its Control-menu button to close this window, then click the Maximize button in the worksheet window to make it full size, and finally, open the Arrange Windows dialog box (by choosing the **W**indow **A**rrange command) and choose the **N**one option button followed by OK.

9. Click a cell in the worksheet to deselect the current selection of all cells that have notes attached to them.

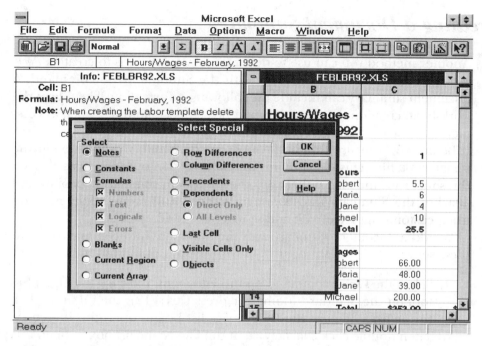

Figure 8.9   The Select Special Dialog Box

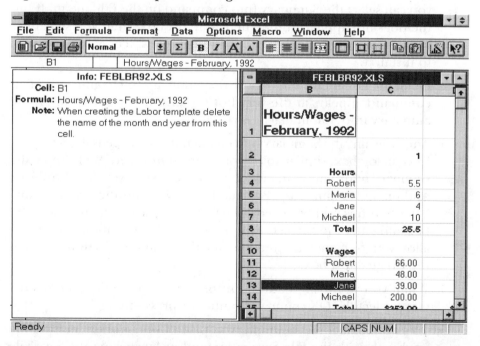

Figure 8.10   Browsing Through Cell Notes with the Select Special Command and Info Window

Creating a Document Summary

Another method you can use to document a worksheet is to create a *document summary* for your worksheet with the Summary **I**nfo command. A document summary can include the following information: The title of the worksheet, creation date, revision number, subject, author, as well as comments on the contents and purpose of the worksheet.

Before you can use the Summary **I**nfo command, you must open the summary.xla file. This file contains the Summary Info Add-in macro sheet; this sheet runs the macro that adds the document summary capability and attaches the Summary Info command to the **E**dit menu. (For more on using customizing Excel with add-in macros, see Chapter 20.)

To add a document summary with the Summary **I**nfo command, follow these steps:

1. Select the **O**pen command on the **F**ile menu (or click the Open file tool on the Standard toolbar or press Ctrl+F12), then double-click the library folder in the **D**irectories list box to open this directory. Then double-click summary.xla in the File **N**ame list box to open this macro sheet and run this add-in macro. After you open this file, you can select the Summary Info command on the **E**dit menu. If this file does not appear in the File **N**ame list box when you select the c:\excel\library directory, you have to run the Excel Setup program to install it.

2. Open the **E**dit menu and choose the Summary Info command. (This command appears at the very bottom of the Edit menu when the Summary Info Add-in macro is running.)

3. After selecting the Summary Info command, Excel opens the Summary Info dialog box, similar to the one shown in Figure 8.11. Enter the summary information in any or all of the text boxes (**T**itle, **S**ubject, **A**uthor, and **C**omments). By default, Excel makes the revision number **1.0**. If this number needs to be changed, select the **R**evision text box and enter the correct revision number. Note that Excel does not allow you to change the creation date that is automatically inserted in the **C**reated text box.

4. When you've finished adding information to the document summary, select the OK command button or press Enter.

5. To save the document summary as part of your worksheet, save the worksheet with the **F**ile **S**ave command or by clicking the Save File tool on the Standard toolbar.

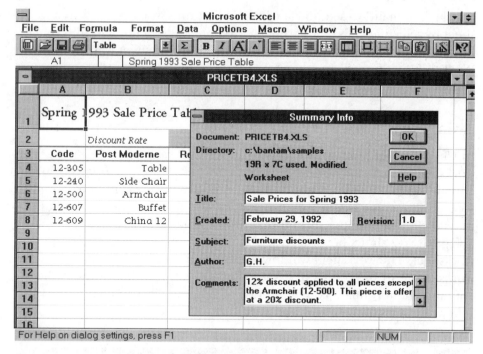

Figure 8.11   The Summary Info Dialog Box with Sample Document Summary

After saving a document summary with the worksheet, you can open and review the statistics in the Summary Info dialog box by choosing the Summary Info command on the Edit menu. (Assuming, of course, that the Summary Info Add-in macro is running.)

Tip   The Summary Info command is available on the Edit menu only until you exit Excel. If you don't want to have to open the summary.xla file manually each time you start Excel, use the Windows File Manager to move this xla file from the c:\excel\library directory to the c:\excel\xlstart directory. That way, Excel automatically opens this add-in macro each time you start the program.

Troubleshooting the Worksheet

Excel offers several excellent techniques and tools for locating problems and errors in a worksheet. In the next several sections, we shall look at the most common of these methods for checking your worksheets and validating their formulas and results. We start by looking at two simple techniques for checking formulas and results. Then we take another look at the Select

Special command to see how it can help you find discrepancies in a work-sheet by selecting cells of a particular type or cells that contain differences. Finally, we look at two more add-in macros, the Worksheet Auditor and the Worksheet Comparison, that can help you locate inconsistencies and changes that might be the result of worksheet errors.

Displaying Formulas and Their Results in the Worksheet Window

In Chapter 6 on printing, we looked at how you can print a version of the worksheet with formulas that you can then compare to a standard printout containing the calculated values. You can also make these kind of compari-sons on the screen by opening two windows on the worksheet: one that dis-plays the results and the second that displays the formulas.

Figure 8.12 shows how this type of arrangement would look in a typical worksheet. The worksheet window on top contains the normal view of the worksheet with the results of each formula. The worksheet window below contains the formulas. To get an idea of how easy it is to create this view, follow the steps for setting it up:

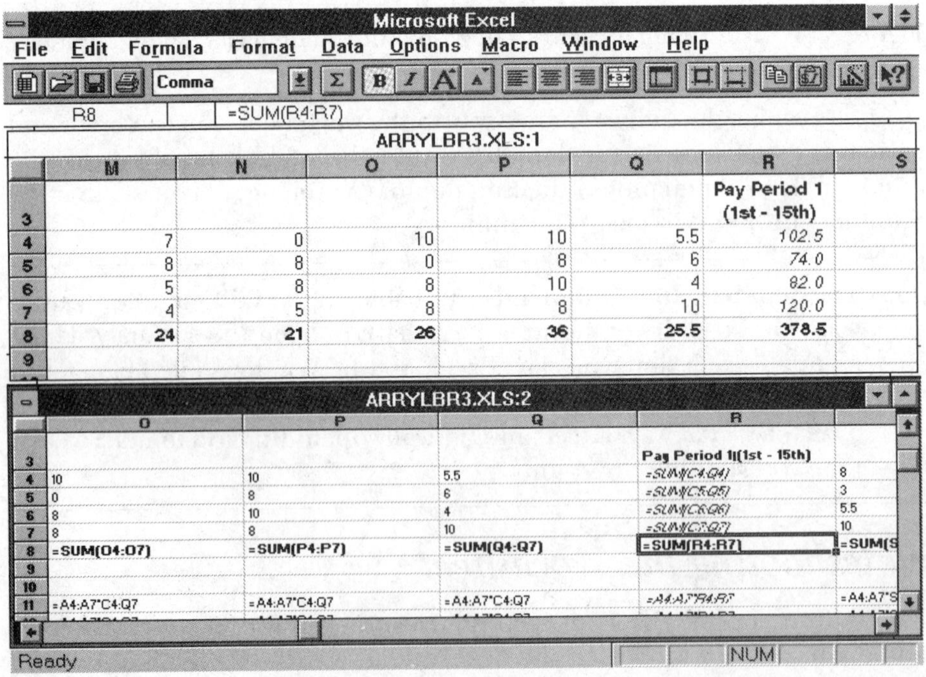

Figure 8.12   Sample Worksheet with Results and Formulas Worksheet Windows

1. Choose the **New** Window command on the **Window** menu.

2. Select the first worksheet window (the one that ends in :1) in the **Window** menu.

3. Choose the **Arrange** command on the **Window** menu, then choose the Horizontal option button and choose OK or press Enter.

4. Scroll to the area of the worksheet containing the formulas you want to check.

5. Click the second worksheet window to make it active, then scroll to the same area in the worksheet as is on display in the window above.

6. Press Ctrl+' (the grave accent on the key with the ~[tilde]) to display the formulas in the lower worksheet window. (You can also do this by choosing the Formulas check box in the Display Options dialog box.) The Ctrl+' keystroke shortcut is a toggle—you can switch back to the normal view of the formula results by pressing it a second time.

7. Choose the **Zoom** command on the **Window** menu, then reduce the magnification in the lower window that displays the formulas by selecting the **75%** option button and choosing the OK option.

8. When you're finished comparing formulas and results, double-click the Control-menu button in the lower window to close this window, then click the Maximize button in the worksheet window above. Finally, open the Arrange Windows dialog box and select the **None** option button before selecting OK or pressing Enter.

Checking Intermediate Results in a Formula

Sometimes you may find that a particular formula is not returning the expected result and yet you are unable to pinpoint the error either in its logic or in the arguments assigned to its function(s). In such cases, you can try calculating just part of the formula to see what intermediate result it is using in calculating the final answer. By doing this, you may be able to find out at exactly what point the error in logic or function arguments occurs so that you can fix that part of the formula.

To view intermediate results in a formula, you need to select the cell that contains the formula, activate the formula bar, and then use the I-beam pointer to select just the section of the formula whose results you want to check. Once you've highlighted the section of the formula, you press F9, the Calc Now key, to display the result of the formula for just the part you selected. When selecting a part of the formula, you must be sure that you have selected a complete function, argument, or section that Excel *can* calculate by itself.

Figures 8.13 and 8.14 illustrate how this works. In Figure 8.13 the formula bar has been activated when cell E3 containing the formula

=IF(OR(A3="John",A3="Alice"),26500,18500)

is active, and the *logical1* argument of the OR function

A3="John"

has been selected with the I-beam pointer. To see whether or not Excel is evaluating this argument as true or false, you press the F9 (Calc Now) key.

Figure 8.14 shows you the result. According to Excel, cell A3 is equal to John because the *logical1* argument of the OR function is evaluated as TRUE. After calculating the first argument, you can continue checking the formula by calculating the *logical2* argument by selecting just

A3="Alice"

in the formula and then pressing F9. When you have finished checking the intermediate results of a formula, press the Esc key or click the cancel box to restore the formula to its original form. Then, if necessary, you can edit its contents as you would any other formula in the worksheet.

When checking calculations with the Calc Now key, you can verify what values Excel has assigned to the names used in a formula as well as the

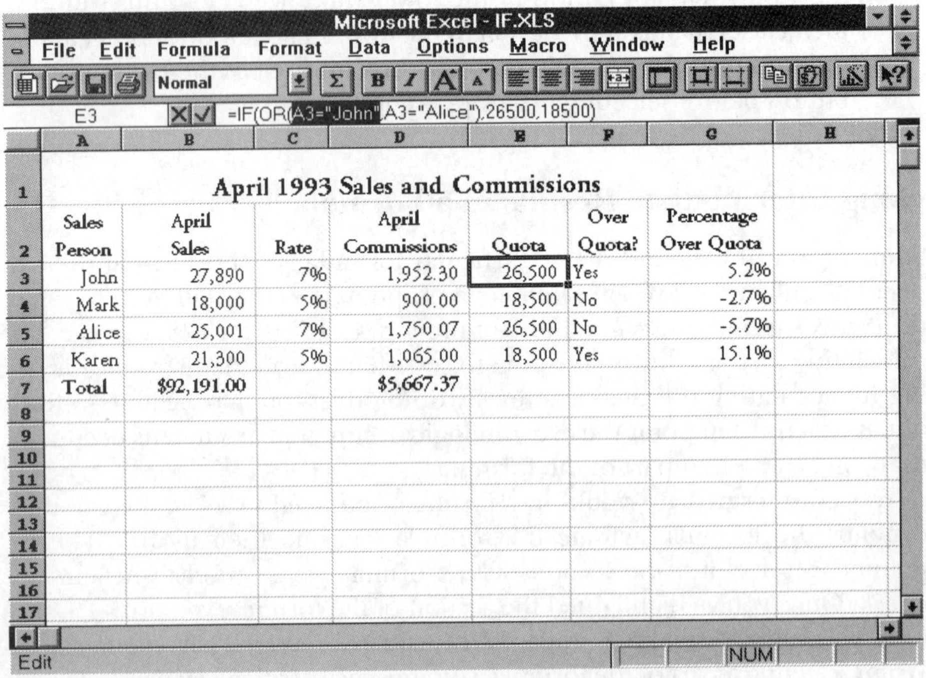

Figure 8.13   Selecting the *Logical1* Argument of an OR Function

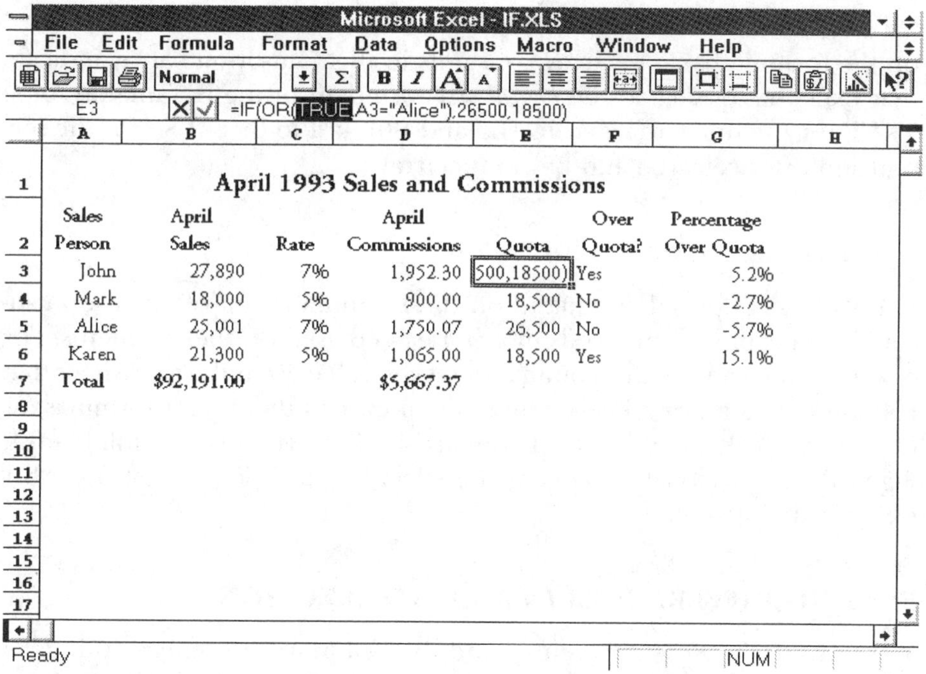

Figure 8.14   Calculating Only the *Logical1* Argument of an OR Function

results of intermediate calculations. For example, the formula in F3 is

   =IF(April_Sales>Quota,"Yes","No")

April_Sales is a name that has been assigned to the column of April sales
(cell range B3:B6) in the table. To verify that these values are being used
correctly when Excel evaluates the *logical_test* argument of the IF function,
you would select the April_Sales in the formula in the formula bar and
then press F9. When you do, the program displays the values assigned to
the range name April_Sales as a four-by-one array with the following array
constants:

   =IF({27890;18000;25001;21300}>Quota,"Yes","No")

Remembering that the semicolons between the values indicate new rows
in the array, you can verify that these are the values in the cell range
B3:B6.

   If you then select the complete *logical_test* argument of the IF function,
that is,

   {27890;18000;25001;21300}>Quota

and press F9, the formula changes to

=IF({TRUE;FALSE;FALSE;TRUE},"Yes","No")

on the formula bar. The array constants in this four-by-one array indicate that Excel has evaluated the *logical_test* argument of the IF function to be TRUE for the first and last cells (B3 and B6) and to be FALSE for the second and third cells (B4 and B5) in the array.

Using the Select Special Command

Excel's **S**elect Special command on the Formula menu offers a sophisticated means of selecting cells in a worksheetbased on their contents. For example, you can use this command to select all cells in the worksheet that contain formulas, or all cells that contain entries that aren't formulas, or even all the cells that don't yet contain anything (that is, are still blank). Figure 8.15 shows you the options in the Select Special dialog box and Table 8.1 explains their usage.

FINDING DIFFERENCES IN A CELL SELECTION

You can use the Row Differences and the Column Differences options in the Select Special dialog box to quickly locate cells that do not conform to

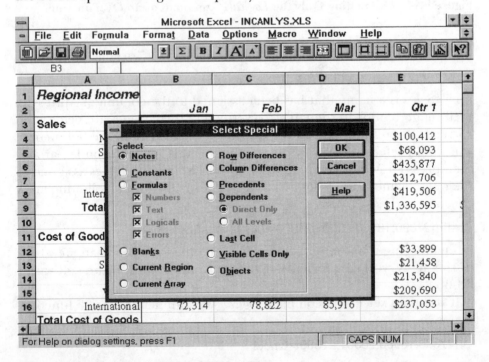

Figure 8.15   The Select Special Dialog Box

Table 8.1   Selection Options in the Select Special Dialog Box

Option	Usage
Notes	Selects all cells that contain notes. You can use this option to help you locate, read, and print all notes in the worksheet.
Constants	Selects all cells that contain constants of the types enumerated in the selected check boxes below. (See Numbers, Text, Logicals, and Errors later in this table.) Constants are the text and values that you enter into the cells that do not change when the worksheet is recalculated.
Formulas	Selects all cells that contain formulas resulting in the types of values enumerated in the selected check boxes below. (See Numbers, Text, Logicals, and Errors later in this table.) Formulas are expressions whose calculated results are displayed in the cells of the worksheet. Formula results change when the values on which they depend are modified and the worksheet is recalculated.
Numbers	Selects numerical constants or formulas that return numbers.
Text	Selects text entered in cells or formulas that return text.
Logicals	Selects logical constants or formulas that return either the logical TRUE or FALSE value.
Errors	Selects error value constants or formulas that return an error value.
Blanks	Selects all cells in the active area of the worksheet that are blank.
Current Region	Selects all cells in the contiguous block of cells bounded by blank rows, blank columns, or worksheet borders of which the active cell is a part.
Current Array	Selects all cells in the array of which the active cell is a part. You also can choose this option by pressing Ctrl+/.
Row Differences	Selects all cells in the rows of the current selection that do not match the pattern of the cells in the same column as the active cell. You also can choose this option by selecting the cells and pressing Ctrl+\.

Table 8.1   *(continued)*

Column Differences	Selects all cells in the columns of the current selection that do not match the pattern of the cells in the same row as the active cell. You also can choose this option by selecting the cells and pressing Ctrl+Shift+\ .
Precedents	Selects the cells that feed into the value in the active cell. Choose the Direct Only option button to select only those cells that directly refer to the active cell. Choose the All Levels option button to select direct precedents of the active cell plus all the cells that feed into these precedents.
Dependents	Selects the cells that depend on the value in the active cell. Choose the Direct Only option button to select only those cells that depend directly on the active cell. Choose the All Levels option button to select direct dependents of the active cell plus all the cells that depend on these dependents.
Last Cell	Selects the last cell in the active worksheet area (that is, the cell at the intersection of the last used row and column in the worksheet). You also can choose this option by pressing Ctrl+End.
Visible Cells	Selects all cells in the current selection except for those that are in hidden columns or rows.
Objects	Selects all graphic objects in the worksheet (not just the current selection), such as charts, text boxes, and macro buttons.

the prevailing pattern in a cell selection. For example, suppose that you have inadvertently replaced a formula with a constant (a not-all-that-unusual error) in one of a range of formulas that sums your quarterly totals. You can use the Column Differences option to have Excel find the cell that contains the constant instead of a formula.

Figures 8.16 and 8.17 illustrate just such a situation. In the sample worksheet shown in Figure 8.16, column E contains the SUM function formulas that return the first-quarter totals. To ensure that all the cells in this column actually contain SUM formulas, you select the range E4:E17 before choosing the Column Differences option in the Select Special dialog box. Because E4 is the active cell when you choose the Column Differences option, Excel compares the contents of each cell in the column range E4:E17 with that of cell E4. From the formula bar and the Info

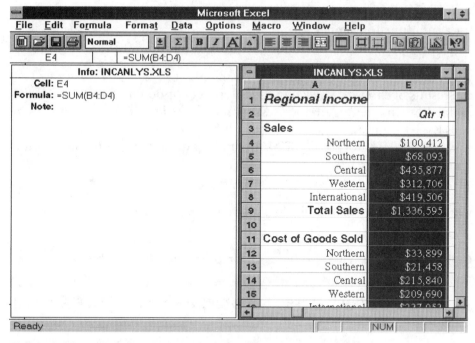

Figure 8.16 Using the Column Differences Option to Find Inconsistencies in a Cell Selection

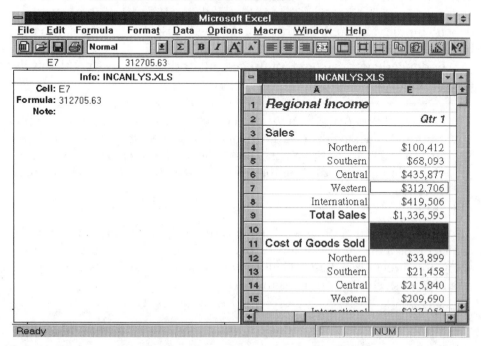

Figure 8.17 Sample Worksheet with the Column Differences

Window shown in the figure, you can see that the program will be looking for a sum function similar to

   =SUM(B4:D4)

when making the comparisons in the range E4:E17. Figure 8.17 shows you the results of choosing the Column Differences option in the Select Special dialog box. In the range E4:E17, Excel has located three inconsistencies in cells E7, E10, and E11. As you can see in the Info Window shown in that figure, cell E7 does not fit the SUM function pattern because it contains the constant

   312705.63

instead of the anticipated SUM function

   =SUM(B7:D7)

Cells E10 and E11 have also been selected because they are blank.

LOCATING PRECEDENTS AND DEPENDENTS OF THE ACTIVE CELL

You can use the **Precedents** and **Dependents** options in the Select Special dialog box when troubleshooting a worksheet to display either all of the cells that feed into the formula in the active cell or all of the cells that depend on the value in the active cell. When you use these options, you can have Excel display only direct precedents (with the Direct Only option button) or dependents or all levels of precedents or dependents (the All **Levels** option button).

Tip   In Excel 4.0 you can select the direct precedents of the active cell simply by double-clicking the cell. This works in all cases except when you have attached a note to the cell, in which case double-clicking will play back the sound message and/or display the note in the Cell Note dialog box as usual.

Figures 8.18 and 8.19 show you the differences between selecting only direct precedents and all levels of precedents for a formula. Figure 8.18 shows the direct precedents of cell E9, which contains the first-quarter total of all regions. This cell contains the formula

   =SUM(E4:E8)

Therefore, Excel selects the cell range E4:E8 as the direct precedents of this cell.

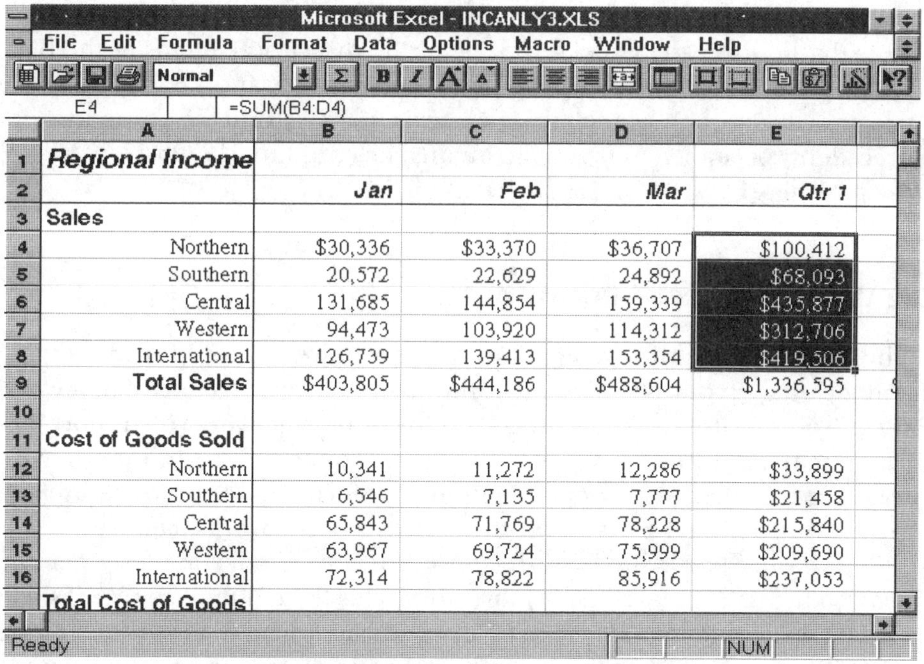

Microsoft Excel - INCANLY3.XLS

File Edit Formula Format Data Options Macro Window Help

Normal

E4   =SUM(B4:D4)

	A	B	C	D	E	
1	**Regional Income**					
2		*Jan*	*Feb*	*Mar*	*Qtr 1*	
3	Sales					
4	Northern	$30,336	$33,370	$36,707	$100,412	
5	Southern	20,572	22,629	24,892	$68,093	
6	Central	131,685	144,854	159,339	$435,877	
7	Western	94,473	103,920	114,312	$312,706	
8	International	126,739	139,413	153,354	$419,506	
9	**Total Sales**	$403,805	$444,186	$488,604	$1,336,595	
10						
11	Cost of Goods Sold					
12	Northern	10,341	11,272	12,286	$33,899	
13	Southern	6,546	7,135	7,777	$21,458	
14	Central	65,843	71,769	78,228	$215,840	
15	Western	63,967	69,724	75,999	$209,690	
16	International	72,314	78,822	85,916	$237,053	
	Total Cost of Goods					

Ready   NUM

Figure 8.18   Sample Worksheet Showing the Direct Precedents of Cell E9

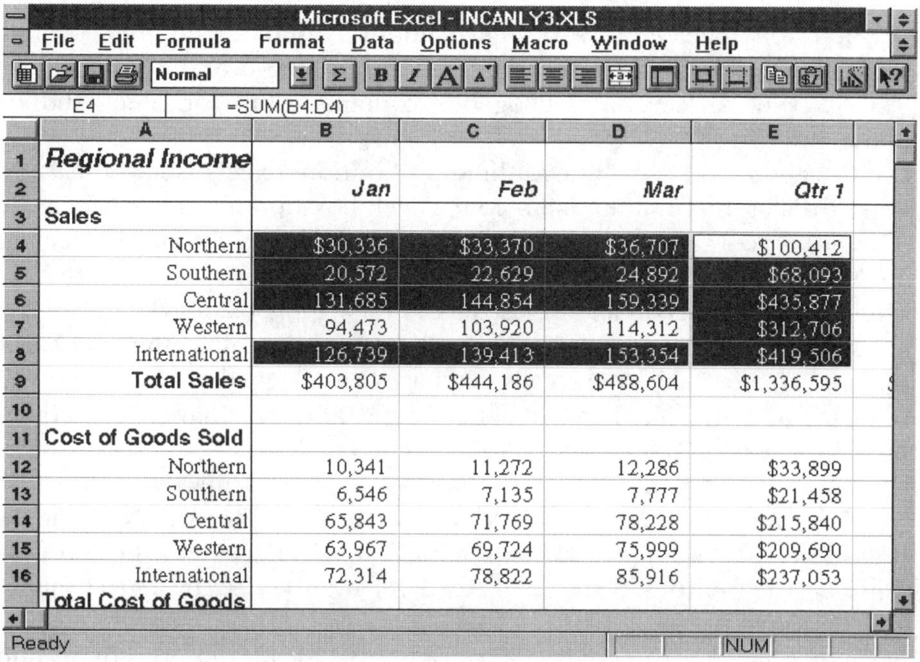

Microsoft Excel - INCANLY3.XLS

File Edit Formula Format Data Options Macro Window Help

Normal

E4   =SUM(B4:D4)

	A	B	C	D	E	
1	**Regional Income**					
2		*Jan*	*Feb*	*Mar*	*Qtr 1*	
3	Sales					
4	Northern	$30,336	$33,370	$36,707	$100,412	
5	Southern	20,572	22,629	24,892	$68,093	
6	Central	131,685	144,854	159,339	$435,877	
7	Western	94,473	103,920	114,312	$312,706	
8	International	126,739	139,413	153,354	$419,506	
9	**Total Sales**	$403,805	$444,186	$488,604	$1,336,595	
10						
11	Cost of Goods Sold					
12	Northern	10,341	11,272	12,286	$33,899	
13	Southern	6,546	7,135	7,777	$21,458	
14	Central	65,843	71,769	78,228	$215,840	
15	Western	63,967	69,724	75,999	$209,690	
16	International	72,314	78,822	85,916	$237,053	
	Total Cost of Goods					

Ready   NUM

Figure 8.19   Sample Worksheet Showing All Levels of Precedents of Cell E9

Figure 8.19, on the other hand, shows all levels of precedents for cell E9. Note that in this case, Excel selects all of the direct precedents in the B, C, and D columns for the SUM formulas for E4, E5, E6, and E8. Note that the program has not, however, selected cells B7, C7, or D7. These are not precedents of cell E7, as this cell contains the constant 312705.63 instead of the formula =SUM(B7:D7), as shown in Figure 8.17.

Using the Worksheet Auditor

The Worksheet Auditor command offers a powerful tool for identifying and locating errors as well as any other types of inconsistencies in a worksheet. You can use the Worksheet Auditor to produce an error report, display a map showing the types of entries in your worksheet, interactively trace the precedents and dependents in your formulas, or produce a report giving you compiled statistics on the contents of the worksheet.

Before you can use the Worksheet Auditor command, you must open the audit.xla file in the c:\excel\library directory. This file contains the Worksheet Auditor Add-in macro sheet that runs the macro which adds the auditing capabilities and attaches the Worksheet Auditor command to the Formula menu. (For more on using customizing Excel with add-in macros, see Chapter 20.)

When you select the Worksheet Auditor command on the Formula menu, Excel displays the Worksheet Auditor dialog box shown in Figure 8.20. As you can see, this dialog box contains four Worksheet Auditor option buttons.

If you choose the Generate Audit Report option, Excel displays the Audit Report dialog box that contains four check box options, all of which are selected. If you choose the OK button or press Enter without deselecting any of these check boxes, Excel generates a report in a new worksheet window that reports on all of these facets. (See Table 8.2 for details.)

Figure 8.21 shows you a sample audit report using all of the check box options. The top table shows cells that have been flagged on the worksheet, while the bottom table shows all of the range names that have been defined but have not been referred to in the worksheet.

You can use the Map Worksheet option to create a new window with a map indicating the location and type of each entry in the worksheet. Figure 8.22 shows you a sample worksheet map. Note that Excel uses the abbreviation T for text entries, F for formulas, 9 for numbers, L for logical values, and # for error values.

You can use the Interactive Trace option to locate the precedents and dependents for a particular cell. To use this option, select the cell that you

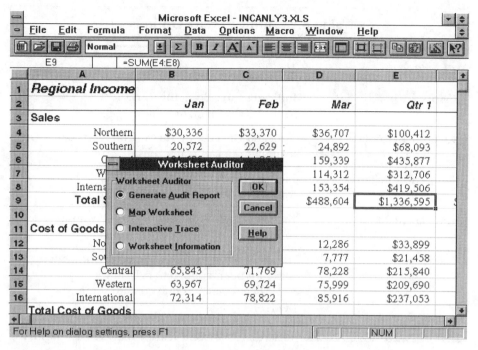

Figure 8.20   The Worksheet Auditor Dialog Box

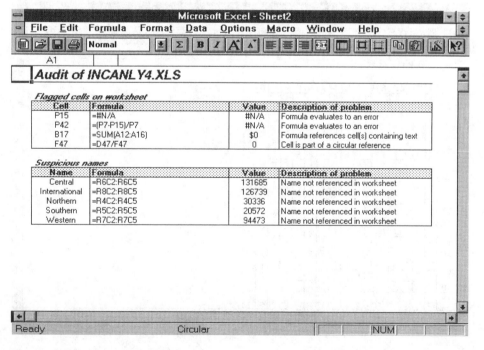

Figure 8.21   Sample Audit Report

Table 8.2 Audit Report Options

Check Box	Usage
Errors	Indicates the cells in the worksheet whose formulas return error values.
References to **B**lanks	Indicates the cells in the worksheet whose formulas refer to blank cells.
References to **T**ext	Indicates the cells in the worksheet whose formulas refer to cells with text entries.
Circular References	Indicates the cells in the worksheet whose formulas contain circular references.
Names	Indicates names that have been defined but have not been applied to cells in the worksheet or names that contain some type of error.

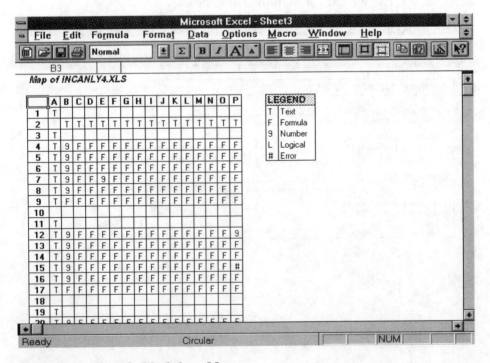

Figure 8.22 Sample Worksheet Map

want to trace, then choose the Interactive **T**race option in the Worksheet Auditor dialog box. When you do, Excel automatically splits the screen into two vertical windows. An Info Window appears on the left and the worksheet window appears on the right (as shown in Figure 8.23). The Trace dialog box also appears near the bottom of the Info Window. To have Excel select the precedents or dependents of the active cell, choose the **Prece**dents or **D**ependent command button. Then you can use the **N**ext or Pre**v** command buttons (under Go to sibling) to make the next or previous precedent or dependent cell in the selection the active one. After making a new cell active, you can then trace its precedents or dependents with the **P**recedents or **D**ependent command button.

To retrace your moves in the worksheet as you examine the precedents or dependents of different cells, choose the **B**ack or **F**orward command buttons. To change the active cell to one outside of the selected precedents or dependents, choose the **R**eset Active Cell command button, then type the cell reference in the **R**eference text box (Excel won't allow you to point to the cell) or select a named cell or cell range in the Goto list box before you choose the OK button. When you have finished tracing the precedents or dependents and are ready to close the Trace dialog box and Info Window, choose the **E**xit Trace command.

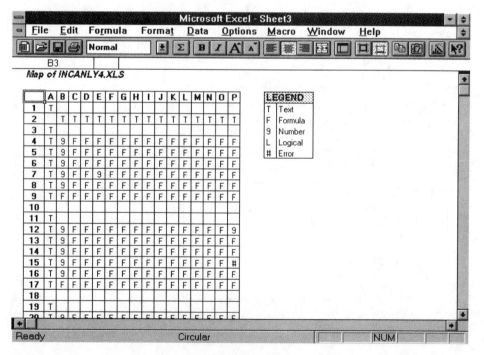

Figure 8.23 Using the Interactive Trace Option

You can use the Worksheet Information to produce a report similar to the one shown in Figure 8.24. A Worksheet Report contains two tables. The top table gives you information about the document, including changes that have been made since you last saved the file. The bottom table gives you information about the worksheet, including the size of the active area and the number and percentages of different types of cells.

Tip The Worksheet Auditor command is available on the Formula menu only until you exit Excel. If you don't want to have to open the audit.xla file manually each time you start Excel to have access to this tool, use the Windows File Manager to move this xla file from the c:\excel\library directory to the c:\excel\xlstart directory. That way Excel automatically opens this add-in macro each time you start the program.

Comparing Versions of a Worksheet

The last method for troubleshooting the worksheet is to use the Compare command to compare different versions of a worksheet to identify and locate all of their differences. When you compare versions of a worksheet, Excel

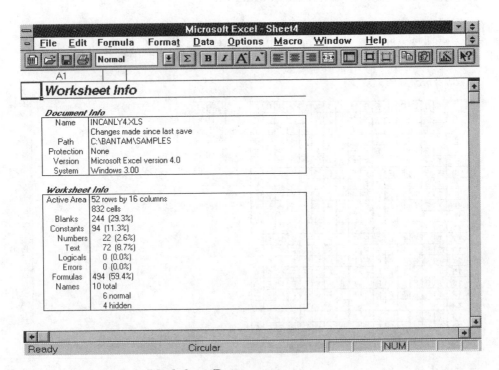

Figure 8.24 Sample Worksheet Report

creates a comparison report in a new worksheet window that shows you, by cell reference, all the differences between the two versions. You can use this comparison report to decide which is the most recent and/or complete of the documents when you have more than one version on your disk.

Before you can use the Compare command, you must open the **compare.xla** file in the **c:\excel\library** directory. This file contains the Worksheet Comparison Add-in macro sheet; this sheet runs the macro that adds the auditing capabilities and attaches the Compare command to the Formula menu. (For more on using customizing Excel with add-in macros, see Chapter 20.)

To compare two versions of a worksheet file, follow these steps:

1. Open both worksheet files that you want to compare with the **File Open** command.

2. Choose the Compare command on the Formula menu to open the Worksheet Comparison dialog box. If the Compare command does not appear on this menu, you need to open **compare.xla** in the **c:\excel\library** directory.

3. Select the name of the worksheet file you want compared to the worksheet that appears in the active window in the Compare to sheet list box, then choose the OK command button or press Enter. Excel then compiles a report in a new worksheet window similar to the one shown in Figure 8.25.

Trapping Errors in Formulas

Having discussed several techniques for finding error values once they occur in the worksheet, it is now time to discuss how you can use the ISERR and ISERROR functions to prevent error values from showing up and spreading throughout the worksheet. Figure 8.26 illustrates a common problem. There you see the labor worksheet template (see Chapter 10 for information on how to create templates) with the percent of sales formulas entered in row 18. In the formula bar shown in the figure, you see that the master formula for computing the percentage of sales that goes to pay wages in cell C18 is

=C15/C17

This formula has been copied across row 18. As long as the daily sales totals in the cells in row 17 are missing (this information will come from an associated monthly sales worksheet when this worksheet has been completed—see Chapter 10 for information on linking worksheets), the formulas in row 18

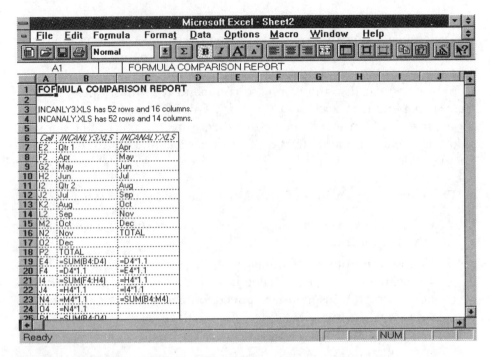

Figure 8.25 Sample Worksheet Report

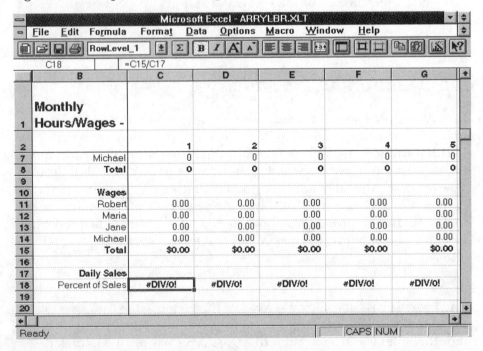

Figure 8.26 Sample Worksheet with #DIV/0! Errors

will continue to return #DIV/0! errors. Remember also that these error values will spread to any formula that uses any of these cells as either direct or indirect precedents.

To prevent the error values from being displayed and spreading throughout the worksheet template, you can use the ISERR or ISERROR function as the *logical_test* argument of an IF function to trap error values at the source. For example, if you edit the formula in cell C18 to

=IF(ISERR(C15/C17),0,C15/C17)

Excel returns 0 in the cell when the division of C15/C17 results in the #DIV/0! error value (or any other error value except #N/A). Otherwise, the formula returns the actual result of the division of C15/C17. This happens because the ISERR function evaluates the *logical_test* argument as TRUE when the division results in an error value (other than the #N/A value). When the IF condition is TRUE, 0 (zero) is entered in cell C18. When the division C15/C17 does not return any error value (except #N/A), the *logical_test* argument of the IF condition evaluates as FALSE, and Excel returns the result of this division.

If there is a chance that one of the cells that feeds into a formula will contain the #N/A error value, you use the ISERROR function in the IF function's *logical_test* argument rather than ISERR. Unlike ISERR, the ISERROR function evaluates as TRUE when any error value, including #N/A, is returned by the calculation specified as its *value* argument.

Referring back to our earlier example, if cell C18 contains the formula

=IF(ISERR(C15/C17),0,C15/C17)

and you then enter the #N/A error value with the formula

=#N/A

in one of the daily hours cells—let's say in cell C7 for Michael—Excel returns #N/A in cell C18 despite your attempts at error trapping. However, if you edit the IF function to use ISERROR in the *logical_test argument as in*

=IF(ISERROR(C15/C17),0,C15/C17)

Excel returns 0 even when the #N/A spreads from cell C7 to cell C15, as shown in Figure 8.27.

You can also nest the ISERROR function inside the IF function to perform error trapping with calculations that use some kind of built-in function. For example, cell R15 in this sample worksheet template contains the SUM function

=SUM(C15:Q15)

Because C15 contains the #N/A error value, this SUM function now also

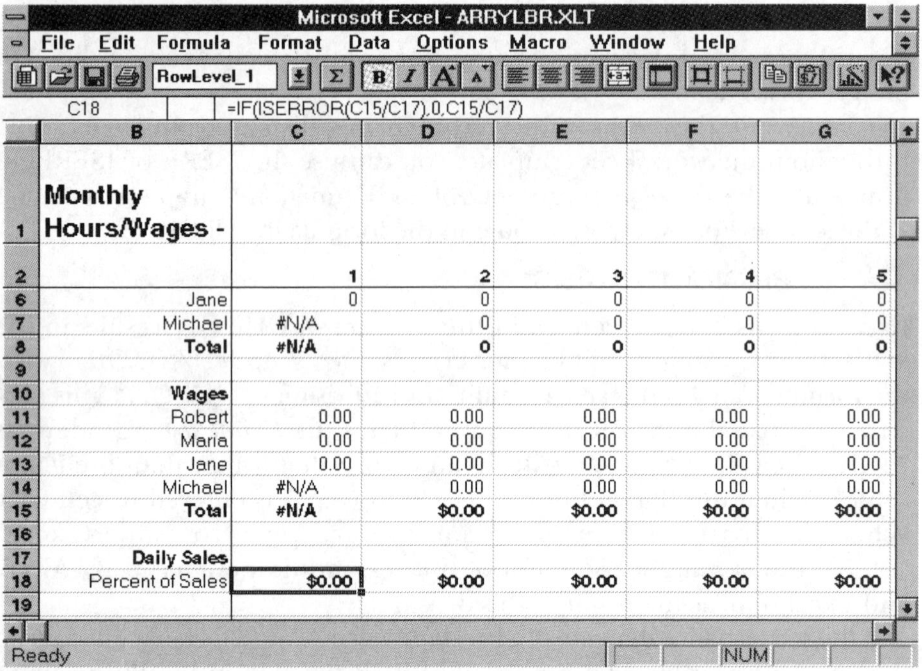

Figure 8.27 Sample Worksheet with Error Trapping Formulas

returns the #N/A error value. To trap this error, you would modify this formula in cell R15 as follows

=IF(ISERROR(SUM(C15:Q15)),0,SUM(C15:Q15))

Error trapping makes formulas such as this long and complex. To make the process of nesting a built-in function such as SUM within the ISERROR and IF functions a great deal easier, edit the formula with the following steps:

1. Make cell R15 active, then click the insertion point between the = and **SUM** in formula in the formula bar.

2. Type **if(iserror(** to insert these characters between = and the SUM function.

3. Press the End key to move the insertion point to the end of the formula, then type **),0,** (You use a close parenthesis to close off the ISERROR function, a comma to start the second argument, a zero as the TRUE argument, and a comma to start the third argument.)

4. Use the I-beam pointer to highlight the entire function **SUM(C15:Q15)** in the formula.

5. Press Ctrl+C to copy this text to the Clipboard.

6. Click the insertion point at the end of the formula on the formula bar (after the last comma), then press Ctrl+V to copy the SUM function as the third (FALSE) argument from the Clipboard.

7. Type) to close off the IF function, and press the Enter key to enter the entire edited formula in cell R15.

SUMMARY

In this chapter you learned many techniques for documenting and troubleshooting your worksheet. First you learned how to add comments to your worksheet with text boxes. Next you learned how to attach text and/or sound notes to individual cells of the worksheet. Finally you learned how to add a document summary to your worksheet with the Summary Info command.

You also learned a number of methods for troubleshooting and verifying the contents of your worksheets. First you learned how to set up two windows on your worksheet so that you can compare side by side the formulas in your cells to the calculated results. Next you learned how to pinpoint calculation errors in a formula by selecting and calculating intermediate values. Then you learned how to use the Worksheet Auditor and Worksheet Comparison add-in macros to create several types of diagnostic reports as well as to trace interactively the precedents and dependents for your formulas. Finally you learned how to use the ISERR and ISERROR to trap error values so that they are not displayed in the original cells in the worksheet and do not spread to other cells as well.

In the chapter ahead you will learn how to use Excel's outlining feature. Spreadsheet outlining is a unique Excel feature that can help you quickly and efficiently organize tables that use multiple time periods and multiple data groupings.

9

Outlining Worksheet Data

Excel's Outline feature is truly unique; to date, it is not shared by any other spreadsheet program. First introduced in version 3.0, the Outline feature enables you to control the level of detail displayed in a table in a worksheet. After outlining a table of data, you can condense the table's display when you want to use only certain levels of summary information, and you can just as easily expand the outlined table to display various levels of detail data as needed. As you shall see, being able to control which outline level is displayed in the worksheet makes it easy to print summary reports (with various levels of data) as well as to chart just the summary data.

In this chapter you will learn how to set up your worksheet for outlining, create outlines, apply automatic styles to your outlines, adjust the outline levels, create views and reports that use different outline levels, and copy or chart only the displayed cells in an outline.

Understanding Worksheet Outlining

Even if you don't have reason to create outlines in your job, you probably remember creating outlines for papers that you wrote when you were in school. In a standard word processing outline you organize your outline topics in a vertical hierarchy, whereby subordinate topics are placed below and indented in from major topics. Each outline level is assigned a different numbering style that is used for each topic at that level (as in I, A, 1, a, and so on).

Just as a word processing outline organizes your thoughts hierarchically, a worksheet outline manages the data in a table in an hierarchical fashion.

However, unlike a word processing outline, which organizes all outline levels vertically, the outline levels in a worksheet outline can extend both vertically (in the rows) and horizontally (across the columns). In fact, Excel can outline up to eight different vertical and horizontal levels in a worksheet table. In the worksheet outline, the summary rows and columns in the table are analogous to the major headings in a word processing outline, while the rows and columns of the table containing the detail or supporting data are analogous to the subordinate topics. Also, whereas a word processing outline uses different numbering styles to denote the different levels in the outline, a worksheet outline simply uses different level symbols (1, 2, 3, and so on up to 8).

Figure 9.1 shows you the first part of a worksheet table that is arranged perfectly for outlining. This table contains the annual sales for a record store. In the rows, the sales data is arranged by musical category (Rock, Jazz, Classical, and Other) and by the type of media (compact disc, cassette tape, or records). Across the columns, the sales data is arranged by month (Jan through Dec—although you can only see Jan through Jun in the figure) and by quarter (Qtr 1, Qtr 2, Qtr 3, and Qtr 4—although you can only see the Qtr 1 and Qtr 2 columns in the figure). As you would expect, all the

	A	B	C	D	E	F	G	H	I	J
1	G & S Records - 1993 Annual Sales by Media and Category									
2		Jan	Feb	Mar	Qtr 1	Apr	May	Jun	Qtr 2	Jul
3	Compact Disc Sales									
4	Rock	1230.00	1512.90	1860.87	4603.77	1722.00	1739.22	1756.61	5217.83	1600.08
5	Jazz	1575.00	1937.25	2382.82	5895.07	2205.00	2227.05	2249.32	6681.37	2048.89
6	Classical	560.00	688.80	847.22	2096.02	784.00	791.84	799.76	2375.60	728.49
7	Other	899.00	1105.77	1360.10	3364.87	1258.60	1271.19	1283.90	3813.68	1169.49
8	Total CD Sales	4264.00	5244.72	6451.01	15959.73	5969.60	6029.30	6089.59	18088.48	5546.95
9	Cassette Tape Sales									
10	Rock	950.00	969.00	988.38	2907.38	1235.00	1543.75	1929.69	4708.44	1678.83
11	Jazz	1200.00	1224.00	1248.48	3672.48	1560.00	1950.00	2437.50	5947.50	2120.63
12	Classical	350.00	357.00	364.14	1071.14	455.00	568.75	710.94	1734.69	618.52
13	Other	750.00	765.00	780.30	2295.30	975.00	1218.75	1523.44	3717.19	1325.39
14	Total Cassette Sales	3250.00	3315.00	3381.30	9946.30	4225.00	5281.25	6601.56	16107.81	5743.36
15	Record Sales									
16	Rock	500.00	490.00	480.20	1470.20	750.00	715.00	700.70	2165.70	929.50
17	Jazz	389.00	381.22	373.60	1143.82	583.50	556.27	545.14	1684.91	723.15
18	Classical	950.00	931.00	912.38	2793.38	1425.00	1358.50	1331.33	4114.83	1766.05
19	Other	258.00	252.84	247.78	758.62	387.00	368.94	361.56	1117.50	479.62
20	Total Record Sales	2097.00	2055.06	2013.96	6166.02	3145.50	2998.71	2938.74	9082.95	3898.32
21	Total Sales	9611.00	10614.78	11846.26	32072.04	13340.10	14309.26	15629.89	43279.24	15188.63

Figure 9.1   Record Store Sales Table Arranged by Category and Quarter

types of sales are totaled in the last row of the table (row 21) and all sales made in the year are totaled in the last column (column R—not visible in the figure).

In a worksheet outline using this data arrangement, you will have three vertical (row) levels and three horizontal (column) levels. Vertically (in the rows), the highest summary level is that of the total sales for all types of media and categories of music (in row 21). The intermediate summary level is that of the total sales for each type of media (in rows 8, 14, and 20). The detail level is that of the sales for each music category for each type of media (rows 4 through 7, 10 through 13, and 16 through 19). In a word processing outline, the vertical levels of your worksheet outline would appear as:

I. Total Sales
   A. Total CD Sales
      1. Rock
      2. Jazz
      3. Classical
      4. Other
   B. Total Cassette Sales
      1. Rock
      2. Jazz
      3. Classical
      4. Other
   C. Total Record Sales
      1. Rock
      2. Jazz
      3. Classical
      4. Other

Horizontally (across the columns), the summary level is that of the total annual sales for all four quarters (in column R). The intermediate summary level is that of the total sales for each quarter (in columns E, I, M, and Q). The detail level is that of the sales for each month (columns B through D, F through H, J through K, and M through P). In a word processing outline, the horizontal levels of your worksheet outline would appear as:

I. Annual Total
   A. Qtr 1
      1. Jan
      2. Feb
      3. Mar

    B. Qtr 2
        1. Apr
        2. May
        3. Jun
    C. Qtr 3
        1. Jul
        2. Aug
        3. Sep
    D. Qtr 4
        1. Oct
        2. Nov
        3. Dec

If you compare these word processing outlines with the arrangement of the data they describe in the worksheet shown in Figure 9.1, you will immediately notice a structural anomaly between the two. In the word processing outline, the headings at the highest levels (I) are placed at the top of the outlines. In the worksheet, however, the highest-level summary row and column are actually located at the bottom and far right of the table. So too, in the outlines, the headings at the intermediate levels (A, B, C, and so on) are placed above their subordinate levels. In the worksheet, these intermediate summary totals are actually located below and to the right of their detail data.

In fact, the word processing outline that describes the vertical arrangement of the three levels of data in the worksheet table uses a structure that is a mirror image (rotated up 180 degrees) of the arrangement of the rows in the worksheet itself. The word processing outline that describes the horizontal arrangement of the three levels of data in the table uses a structure that is a transposition (rotated 90 degrees counterclockwise) of the arrangement of the columns in the worksheet itself.

The reason that worksheet outlines often seem "backward" when compared to word processing outlines is that, most often, to calculate your summary totals in the worksheet, you naturally place the detail levels of data above the summary rows and to the left of the summary columns that total them. When creating a word processing outline, however, you place the major headings above subordinate headings, while at the same time indenting each subordinate level, reflecting the way we read words from left to right and down the page.

> *Note:* Actually, you can usually help yourself visualize the structure of the worksheet outline that you are about to create and understand its level numbers by "reading" the various summary and detail levels of data in the table backward—columns from right to left and rows from top to bottom.

Creating the Outline

To create an outline from a table of data, you select the table cells to be included in the outline, and then choose the **O**utline command on the Formula menu to display the Outline dialog box shown in Figure 9.2. If you want to outline all the data in the worksheet (assuming that the worksheet consists of a single table of data), you can make any cell active before you select the **O**utline command.

By default, Excel assumes that summary rows in the selected data table are below their detail data and summary columns are to the right of their detail data, which is normally the case. If, however, the summary rows are above the detail data and the summary columns are to the left of the detail data, Excel can still build the outline. Simply clear the Summary rows **below**

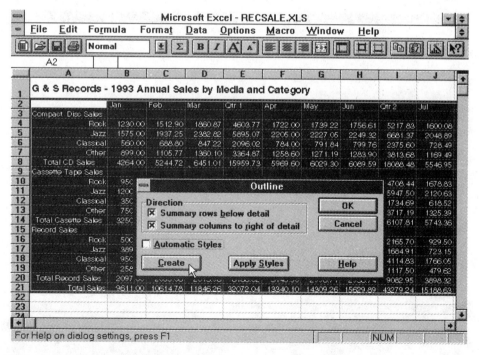

Figure 9.2 The Outline Dialog Box

the detail and/or Summary columns to the right of the detail check boxes in the Direction section. Also, you can have Excel automatically apply styles to different levels of the outline by selecting the **A**utomatic Styles check box. (For more information on these styles, see the next section.) To have Excel create the outline, select the **C**reate command button. (If you select the OK button, the program simply closes the dialog box without outlining the selected worksheet data.)

If you've arranged the summary rows and columns above and to the right of the detailing data (as in the table shown earlier in Figure 9.1) and the Utility toolbar is visible, you can create your outline simply by clicking the Show Outline Symbols tool (shown in Figure 9.3) on the Utility toolbar. When you do this, Excel displays an alert box telling you that the program is unable to display the outline symbols as no outline exists and asks if you want to create one. To create your outline, you simply select the OK command button. To close the alert box without outlining the selected data, choose the Cancel button.

Figure 9.4 shows you the first part of the outline created by Excel for the Record Sales worksheet. Note the various outline symbols Excel added to the worksheet when it created the outline. Figure 9.4 identifies these outline symbols and Table 9.1 explains their functions.

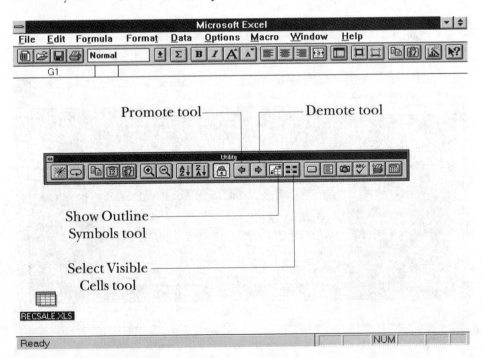

Figure 9.3 The Outlining Tools on the Utility Toolbar

Row Level symbols
Column Level symbols
Column Level bar
Collapse symbols

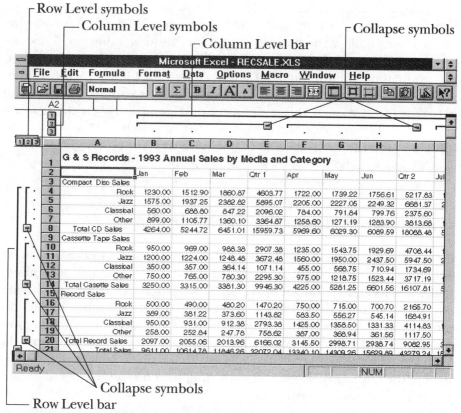

Collapse symbols
Row Level bar

Figure 9.4 Sample Record Sales Worksheet After Outlining

Table 9.1 The Outline Symbols

Symbol	Function
Row- and column-level symbol (1, 2, 3, and so on up to 8)	Click the button with the number of the row or column level you want displayed throughout the outline. When you click a row- or column-level symbol, Excel displays the level and all levels above it in the worksheet display.
Row- and column-level bar	Click the row or column bar to hide the display of the detail rows or columns the level bar includes (the same as clicking the collapse button—see below).
Expand (+) symbol	Click this button to expand the display to show the detail rows or columns that have been collapsed.
Collapse (–) symbol	Click this button to condense the display to hide the detail rows or columns that are included in its row- or column-level bar.

Alert! You can have only one outline per worksheet. If you've already outlined one table and then try to outline another table on the same worksheet, Excel will display the "Modify existing outline?" alert box when you choose the Outline command. If you choose the OK command button, Excel will add the outlining for the new table to the existing outline for the first table (even though the tables are nonadjacent). To create separate outlines for different data tables, you need to place each table on a different worksheet. You can then save these worksheets with the outlined data tables together in a workbook file. (See Chapter 10 for details.)

Applying Automatic Styles to the Outline

You can apply predefined row- and column-outline styles to the worksheet with the Outline command. To apply these styles when creating the outline, be sure to select the Automatic Styles check box before you choose the Create command button in the Outline dialog box. If you didn't apply the outline styles when you created the outline (as is the case when you create the outline with the Show Outline Symbols tool on the Utility toolbar), you can do so afterward by selecting all the cells in the outlined table of data, then opening the Outline dialog box (by selecting the Outline command on the Formula menu) and choosing the Apply Styles command button.

Figure 9.5 shows you the sample Record Store dialog box after applying the automatic row and column styles to the worksheet. In this example, Excel applied two row styles (RowLevel_1 and RowLevel_2) and two column styles (ColLevel_1 and ColLevel_2) to the worksheet table. (You can see the style name RowLevel_1 in the Style box of the Standard toolbar in the figure.)

The RowLevel_1 style is applied to the entries in the first-level summary row (row 21) and bolds the font. (In this example, the font is Helvetica assigned by the Normal style.) The ColLevel_1 style is applied to the data in the first-level summary column (column R) and it, too, simply bolds the font. The RowLevel_2 style is applied to the data in the second-level rows (rows 8, 14, and 20), and this style adds italics to the font. The ColLevel_2 style is applied to all second-level summary columns (columns E, I, M, and Q), and it also italicizes the font.

After applying the automatic outline styles to your worksheet outline, you can modify the formatting of the row- and column-level styles. Unfortunately, unlike when redefining built-in styles such as the Normal, Comma, Currency, or Percent styles, Excel does not automatically update the formatting of the data that currently uses a particular outline style. This means

Microsoft Excel - RECSALE.XLS

File   Edit   Formula   Format   Data   Options   Macro   Window   Help

RowLevel_1

A21 | Total Sales

	A	B	C	D	E	F	G	H	
2		Jan	Feb	Mar	*Qtr 1*	Apr	May	Jun	*Qtr 2*
3	Compact Disc Sales								
4	Rock	1230.00	1512.90	1860.87	*4603.77*	1722.00	1739.22	1756.61	*52*
5	Jazz	1575.00	1937.25	2382.82	*5895.07*	2205.00	2227.05	2249.32	*66*
6	Classical	560.00	688.80	847.22	*2096.02*	784.00	791.84	799.76	*23*
7	Other	899.00	1105.77	1360.10	*3364.87*	1258.60	1271.19	1283.90	*38*
8	*Total CD Sales*	*4264.00*	*5244.72*	*6451.01*	*15959.73*	*5969.60*	*6029.30*	*6089.59*	*180*
9	Cassette Tape Sales								
10	Rock	950.00	969.00	988.38	*2907.38*	1235.00	1543.75	1929.69	*47*
11	Jazz	1200.00	1224.00	1248.48	*3672.48*	1560.00	1950.00	2437.50	*59*
12	Classical	350.00	357.00	364.14	*1071.14*	455.00	568.75	710.94	*17*
13	Other	750.00	765.00	780.30	*2295.30*	975.00	1218.75	1523.44	*37*
14	*Total Cassette Sales*	*3250.00*	*3315.00*	*3381.30*	*9946.30*	*4225.00*	*5281.25*	*6601.56*	*161*
15	Record Sales								
16	Rock	500.00	490.00	480.20	*1470.20*	750.00	715.00	700.70	*27*
17	Jazz	389.00	381.22	373.60	*1143.82*	583.50	556.27	545.14	*18*
18	Classical	950.00	931.00	912.38	*2793.38*	1425.00	1358.50	1331.33	*41*
19	Other	258.00	252.84	247.78	*758.62*	387.00	368.94	361.56	*11*
20	*Total Record Sales*	*2097.00*	*2055.06*	*2013.96*	*6166.02*	*3145.50*	*2998.71*	*2938.74*	*90*
21	**Total Sales**	**9611.00**	**10614.78**	**11846.26**	**32072.04**	**13340.10**	**14309.26**	**15629.89**	**432**
22									
23									

Ready   NUM

Figure 9.5   Record Store Sales Table with Outline Styles

that you must manually reapply each redefined outline style to the cell entries in the outline level to have your changes take effect. This, of course, diminishes their usefulness in formatting the worksheet table.

Displaying Different Outline Levels

The real effectiveness of creating an outline becomes apparent only when you start using the various outline symbols to change the way your worksheet data is displayed in the table. By clicking the appropriate row- or column-level symbol, you can immediately hide detail rows and columns to display just the summary information in the table. For example, Figure 9.6 shows you the Record Sales table after clicking the number 2 row-level button and the number 2 column-level button. There you see only the first- and second-level summary information, that is, the quarterly and yearly totals for each type of media as well as the quarterly and yearly totals for all types of sales.

Figure 9.7 shows you the same table, this time after clicking the number 1 row-level button and the number 1 column-level button. There you see only the first-level summary for the column and the row, that is, the grand total of the annual record store sales. To expand this view horizontally to

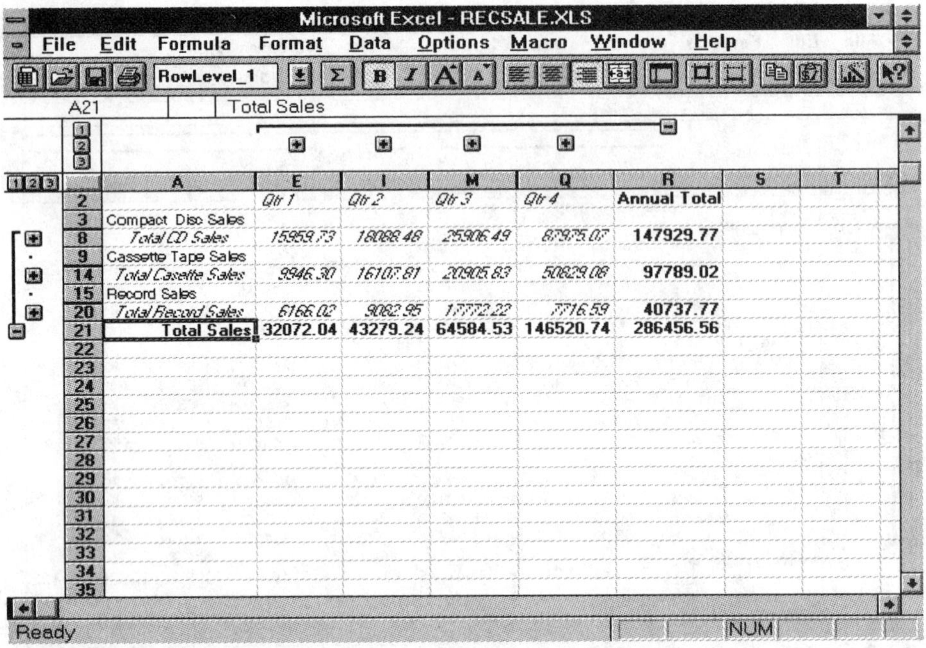

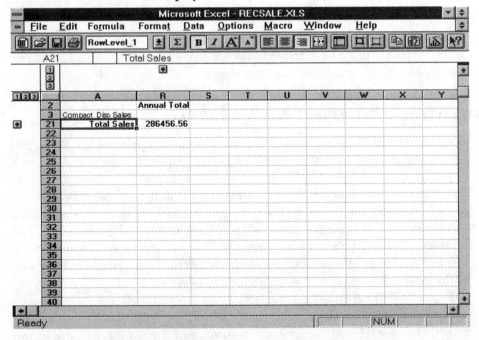

**Figure 9.6   Record Sales Table with First- and Second-level Summary
Information Displayed**

**Figure 9.7   Record Sales Table with Only First-level Summary
Information Displayed**

see the total sales for each quarter, you would simply click the number 2 column-level button. To expand this view even further horizontally to display each monthly total in the worksheet, you click the number 3 column-level button. So too, to expand the outline vertically to see totals for each type of media, you would click the number 2 row-level button. To expand the outline one more level vertically so that you can see the sales for each type of music as well as each type of media, you would click the number 3 row-level button.

When displaying different levels of detail in a worksheet outline, you can use the collapse or expand symbols along with the row-level and column-level buttons. For example, Figure 9.8 shows you another view of the Record Sales outline. There, in the horizontal dimension, you see all three column levels have been expanded, including the monthly detail columns for each quarter. In the vertical dimension, however, only the detail rows for the record sales have been expanded. The detail rows for CD and cassette tape sales are still collapsed. To create this view of the outline, you simply click the number 2 row-level button, then click the expand symbol

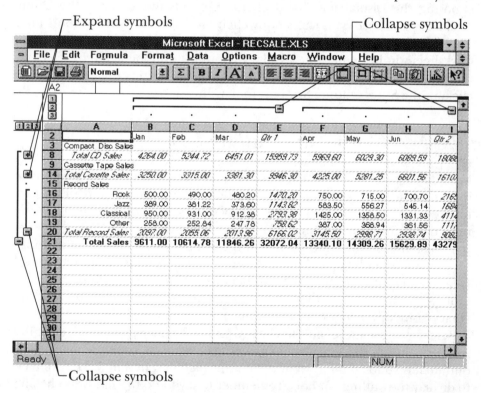

Figure 9.8   Record Sales Table Expanded to Show the Record Sales Detail Rows

(+) located to the left of the Total Record Sales row heading. When you want to view only the summary-level rows for each media type, you can click the collapse symbol (–) to the left of the Total Record Sales heading or you can click its level bar (drawn from the collapse symbol up to the first music type to indicate all the detail rows included in that level).

 Alert! Excel adjusts the outline levels displayed on the screen by hiding and redisplaying entire columns and rows in the worksheet. Therefore, keep in mind that changes you make that reduce the number of levels displayed in the outlined table also hide the display of all data outside of the outlined table that is in the affected rows and columns.

After selecting the rows and columns you want displayed, you can then remove the outline symbols from the worksheet display to maximize the amount of data displayed on the screen. To do this, you deselect the **O**utline Symbols check box in the Display Options dialog box (opened by choosing the **D**isplay command on the **O**ptions menu) or, if the Utility toolbar is displayed, you can simply click the Show Outline Symbols tool. Then, when you need to change outline levels which are displayed in the worksheet window, you can redisplay the outline symbols again by selecting the **O**utline Symbols check box in the Display Options dialog box or by clicking the Show Outline Symbols tool again.

Manually Adjusting the Outline Levels

Most of the time Excel correctly outlines the data in your table. Every once in a while, however, you will have to manually adjust one or more of the outline levels so that the outline summary's rows and columns include the right detail rows and columns. To adjust the levels of a worksheet outline, you must display the Utility toolbar and use the Promote and Demote tools. The Promote tool ⬅ assigns selected rows or columns to a higher-level (that is, one with a lower-level number) in the outline, while the Demote tool ➡ assigns selected rows or columns to a lower level in the outline (that is, one with a higher-level number).

Before you use these tools to change an outline level, you must select the rows or columns that you want to promote or demote. To select a particular outline level and all the rows and columns included in that level, you need to display the outline symbols (remember that you do this easily by clicking the Show Outline Symbols tool on the Utility toolbar), then hold down the shift key as you click its collapse or expand symbol. Note that when you click an expand symbol, Excel selects not only the rows or columns visible at that level but all the hidden rows and columns included in that level as well. If you want to select only the visible rows in that level, you need to click the Select Visible Cells tool . If you want to select only a particular detail or summary row or column in the outline, you can click that row number or column letter in the worksheet window, or you can hold down the shift key and click the dot (period) to the left of the row number or above the column letter in the outline symbols area.

> ***Note:*** If you select only a range of cells in the rows or columns (as opposed to entire rows and columns) before you click the Promote or Demote tool on the Utility toolbar, Excel displays the Promote or Demote dialog box, which contains a **R**ows and **C**olumns option button (with the **R**ows button selected by default). To promote or demote columns instead of rows, click the **C**olumns option button before you select OK. To close the dialog box without promoting or demoting any part of the outline, choose the Cancel button.

To see how you can use the Promote and Demote tools to adjust outline levels, consider once again the Record Store worksheet outline. When Excel created this outline, the program did not include row 3 (which contains only the row heading *Compact Disc Sales*) in the outline. As a result, when you collapsed the rows by selecting the number 1 row-level button to display only the first-level Total Sales summary row (as shown earlier in Figure 9.7), this row heading remained visible in the table, even though it should have been included and thereby hidden along with the other summary and detail rows.

You can use the Demote tool to move this row (3) down a level so that it is included in the first level of the outline. You simply click the row number 3 to select the row, then click the Demote button on the Utility toolbar. Figure 9.9 shows you the result of doing this. Notice how the outside level bar (for level 1) includes this row. Now when you condense the outline by clicking the number 1 row-level button, the heading in row 3 will be hidden as well (as shown in Figure 9.10).

Some worksheet tables are best outlined manually from start to finish with the Demote tool. Figure 9.11 shows you just such a case with the monthly hours and wages table. While Excel can automatically outline the rows of this table correctly by creating two summary levels (one for hours and the other for wages), the program is not nearly so successful in outlining the columns. This is because for the most part, the column headings in row 2 consist solely of numbers (representing the day of the month), and Excel does not know where to create the summary columns in this series.

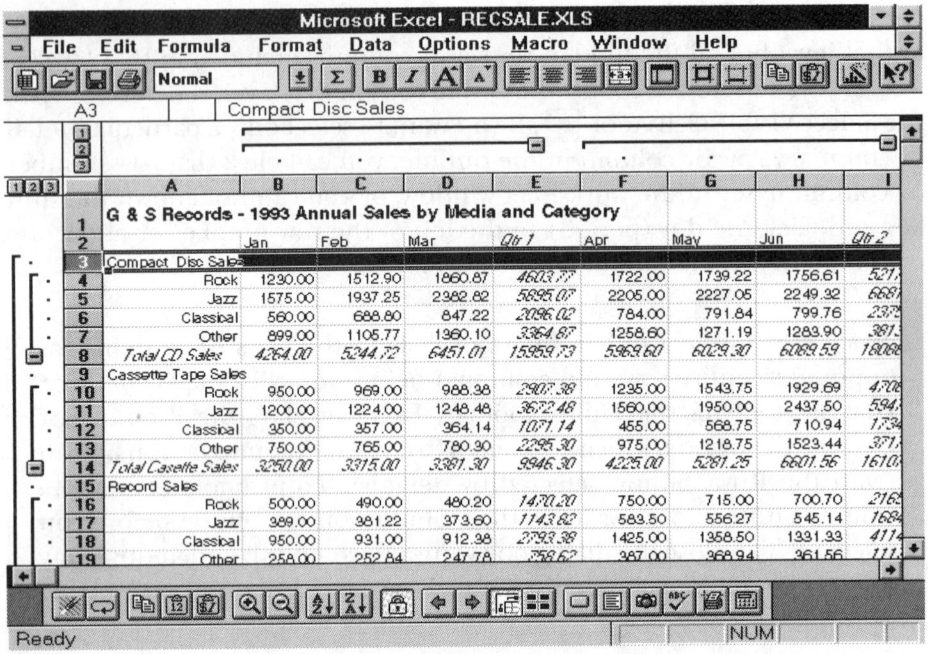

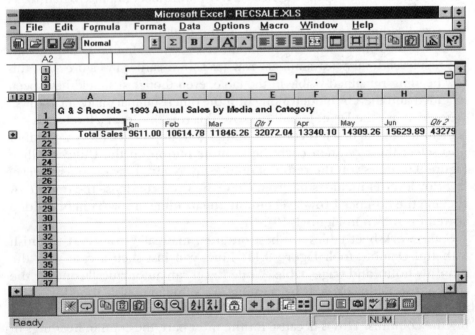

Figure 9.9   Record Sales Table After Demoting Row 3

Figure 9.10   Record Sales Table After Selecting the Number 1 Row-Level Button

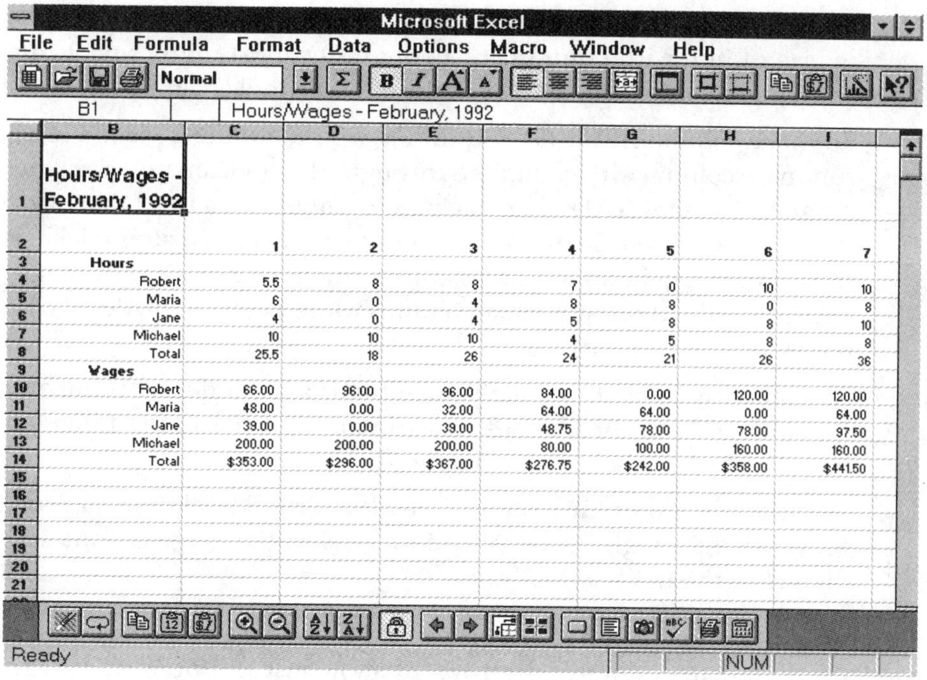

Figure 9.11 Monthly Hour and Wage Table

Because the employees are paid biweekly, the day numbers run in two sequences, the first from 1 to 15 in columns C through Q and the second from 16 through 31 in columns S through AH. Column R contains the totals of the hours and wages for the first pay period of the month. Column AI contains the totals of the hours and wages for the second pay period of the month, and column AJ contains the monthly totals. In the worksheet outline, the first-level summary column should be the monthly total column (AJ) with all the columns to the left (C through AI) subordinate. The second-level summary columns should be the first and second pay periods (columns R and AI). Columns C through Q should be the detail columns subordinate to the first pay period column (R), and columns S through AH should be the detail columns subordinate to the second pay period column (AI).

To get an idea of how you manually create an outline with the Demote tool on the Utility toolbar, follow these steps:

1. To make column AJ with the monthly total the first-level summary column with columns C through AI subordinate, you select the range of columns C:AI, then click the Demote tool.

2. To make column R with the first pay period totals a second-level summary column with columns C through Q subordinate, select the range of columns C:Q, then click the Demote tool again.

3. To make column AI with the second pay period totals a second-level summary column with columns S through AH subordinate, select the range of columns S:AH, then click the Demote tool a third time. Figure 9.12 shows you the worksheet outline at this stage after clicking the number 2 column-level button to condense the outline so that it shows only the three summary columns without any of the detail columns.

4. To make row 14 with the daily wage totals a second-level summary row with rows 10 through 13 subordinate to it, select the range of rows 10:13, then click the Demote tool.

5. To make row 8 with the daily hour totals a second-level summary row with rows 4 through 7 subordinate to it, select the range of rows 4:7, then click the Demote tool.

Figure 9.13 shows you the worksheet outline after clicking the number 1 row-level button to condense the rows to show just the hour and wage summary rows without any detail rows.

Figure 9.12   Monthly Hour and Wage Table Outline Showing Summary Columns

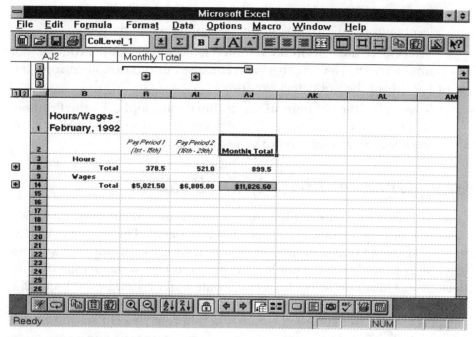

Figure 9.13 Monthly Hour and Wage Table Outline Showing Summary Rows

 Tip When creating an outline manually with the Demote tool, always work from the highest (and most inclusive) outline level to the lowest (and most specific) outline level. You can have Excel automatically apply the predefined row- and column-level styles as you define your levels by selecting the Automatic Styles check box in the Outline dialog box before you begin creating the outline. Also, if your summary rows are above instead of below the detail rows, deselect the Summary rows **b**elow the detail check box. Likewise, if your summary columns are to the right instead of to the left of your detail columns, deselect the Summary columns to the **r**ight of the detail check box.

Removing an Outline from the Worksheet

To delete an outline from your worksheet, you use the Promote tool on the Utility toolbar. Note that removing the outline does not affect the data in any way—Excel merely removes the outline structure. To delete an outline from your worksheet, you follow these steps:

1. If necessary, display the Utility toolbar and click the Show Outline Symbols button to display the outline symbols.

2. Display all the levels in the outline by clicking the lowest number row-level button and the lowest number column-level button.

3. Select all of the rows in the outlined table and click the Promote tool until all of the row-level bars and collapse buttons disappear from the left side of the worksheet window.

4. Select all of the columns in the outlined table and click the Promote tool until all of the column-level bars and collapse buttons disappear from the left side of the worksheet window.

Creating Different Views of the Outline

Once you've created an outline for your worksheet table, you can create views that display the table in various levels of detail. Then, instead of having to display the outline symbols and manually click the appropriate row-level buttons and/or column-level buttons to view a particular level of detail, you can simply select the appropriate outline view in the Views dialog box.

Figures 9.14 through 9.16 illustrate how different views of an outline can be used. In Figure 9.14 you see a Views dialog box (for specific information on how to set up views of a worksheet, see Chapter 7) that contains three normal views at different Zoom percentages (100%, 90%, and 75%) along with six different outline views that display various combinations of row and column levels. Currently this figure uses the Normal_90 view, which displays the worksheet outline with all levels of summary and detail rows and columns at 90 percent magnification.

Figure 9.15 shows you the worksheet after selecting the RowLvl_2 ColLvl_3 outline view, a view that displays the monthly summary sales information for each type of media. Figure 9.16 shows you the worksheet after selecting the RowLvl_3 ColLvl_2 outline view. This view displays the quarterly sales totals for each type of media and each type of music.

As you can see from these examples, by creating views of your outlined worksheet, you give yourself immediate access to a variety of different levels of detail and summary information without ever having to display the outline symbols.

Tip When creating views of outlined worksheet data, be sure that you leave the Hidden **R**ows & Columns check box selected in the View Includes section of the Add View dialog box. Also, leave the **P**rint Settings check box selected if you intend to add the outline view to a report. (See the next section.)

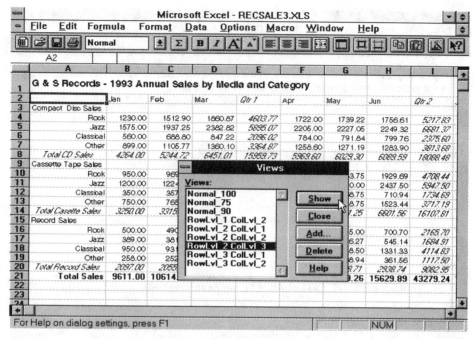

Figure 9.14 Choosing a New Outline View for the Record Sales Worksheet

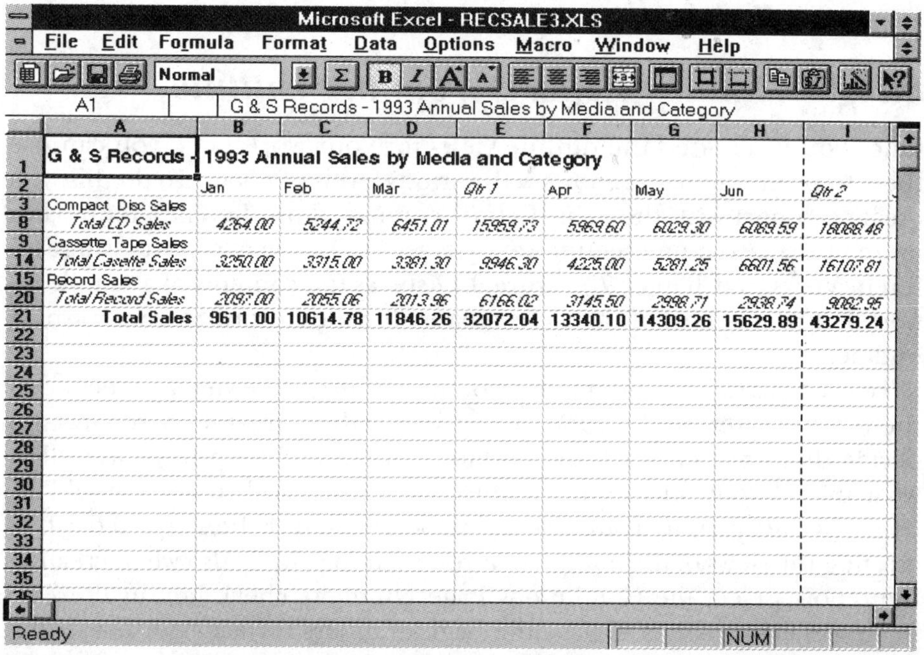

Figure 9.15 RowLvl_2 ColLvl_3 Outline View for the Record Sales Worksheet

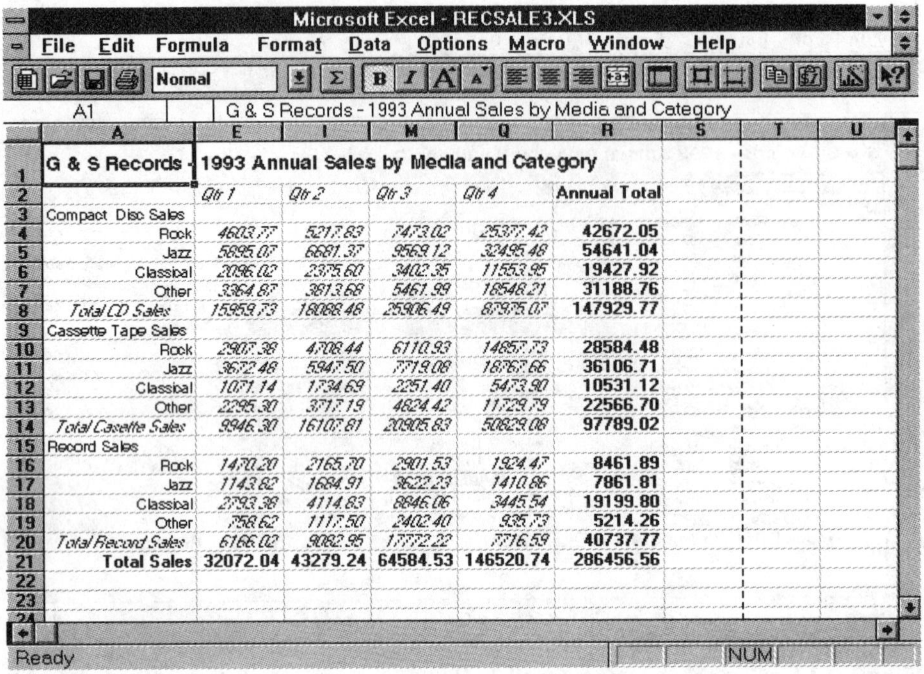

Figure 9.16   RowLvl_3 ColLvl_2 Outline View for the Record Sales
              Worksheet

Printing Summary Reports from the Outline

Once you've created the outline views for your worksheet, you can use them to print summary reports with various levels of detail. To do this, you create a report with the Print Report command on the File menu. (For more information on creating reports, see "Creating a Report Using Different Views" in Chapter 7.) Figure 9.17 shows the contents of a sample report that prints most of the views created for the Record Store worksheet outline.

To use a particular outline view, you simply assign the view as a section of the report in the Add Report dialog box. When creating a report, you decide the order in which the outline views should be printed as well as what page layout settings (including the header and footer) should be used. (Remember to leave the Print Setting check box selected when creating the views of the outline that you want to print.) Also when creating the report, select the Continuous Page Numbers check box in the Add Report dialog box if you want the page numbers for each section of the summary report to be sequential.

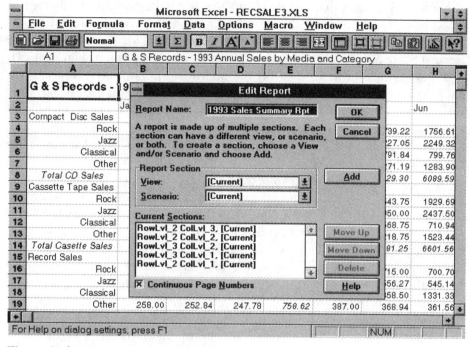

Figure 9.17   Selecting a Summary Report to Print

Copying or Charting Summary Data

As mentioned at the beginning of this chapter, worksheet outlining makes it easier not only to view summary information in a table but also to work with only this data. In this section you will learn how you can select just the summary levels of information that you display in the outline. Once the summary information is selected, you can then copy just these entries to new places in the same worksheet, other worksheets, or even other applications (such as a memorandum created with your word processor). You will also find that selecting just the summary levels in your outline makes charting this information quick and easy.

As you know, when you view different levels of summary rows and columns in an outline, Excel displays the information side by side in the worksheet window by hiding all the subordinate detail rows and columns. Normally, when you select the summary rows and columns, the program selects all the hidden rows and columns between the visible rows and columns as well. You can, however, select just the summary rows and columns that are displayed in your worksheet by clicking the Select Visible Cells tool on the Utility toolbar.

Figure 9.18 illustrates how you can use the Select Visible Cells tool to select only the cell entries that are displayed in the worksheet window. In this figure, I first selected the RowLvl_2 ColLvl_2 view created for the Record Store Sales table (as shown in the Views dialog box in Figure 9.14). This particular outline view shows the quarterly and annual sales totals for each type of media (similar to the view shown earlier in Figure 9.6 only without outline symbols). After selecting this view, I then manually hid the rows containing the media type headings (Compact Disc Sales in row 3, Cassette Tape Sales in row 9, and Record Sales in row 15) and selected the range starting with cell A3 and ending with cell Q20.

Doing this, selected the range A3:Q20, a cell range consisting of 324 cells, all of which are hidden except for the 20 visible cells shown in Figure 9.18. To reduce the selected range from the 324 cells between cells A3 and Q20 to the 20 visibly selected cells shown in the figure, I then clicked the Select Visible Cells tool on the Utility toolbar. When you click this tool, Excel shows you that only the visible cells are selected by restricting the highlighting to each individual cell in the selection instead of highlighting the contiguous range.

Having selected only the quarterly sales figures for each type of media, I then charted just this data in the 3-D column chart shown in Figure 9.19.

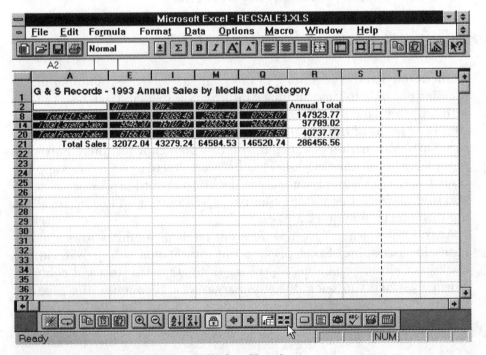

Figure 9.18 Selecting Visible Cells for Charting

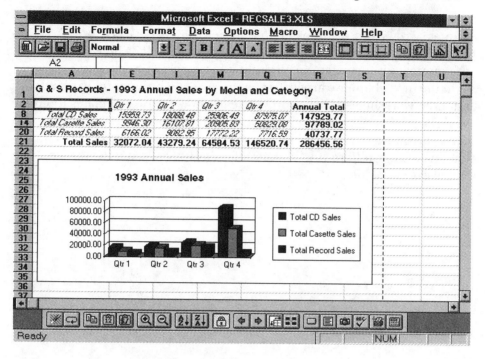

Figure 9.19   3-D Bar Chart Showing Quarterly Sales

(For information on how to create charts like this, see Chapter 12.) If I had needed to, I could also have used the **C**opy and **P**aste commands on the **E**dit menu to copy just these cells to another part of the worksheet or to another worksheet file.

Alert! You can't use the Drag and Drop feature to copy cells that you've selected with the Select Visible Cells tool—you must use the **E**dit **C**opy (Ctrl+C) to copy the information to the Clipboard and then use the **E**dit **P**aste (or press Ctrl+V or Enter) to copy the cell entries to another part of the worksheet or the **E**dit **P**aste **L**ink command to copy and link the cells in another worksheet file.

SUMMARY

In this chapter you learned how to use Excel's unique worksheet outlining feature to organize and view different levels of summary and detail information in a table of data. Specifically, you learned how to create an outline, select the levels you want displayed, and manually adjust the detail and summary rows and columns in an outline. You also learned how to set up outline views and use them in printed reports as well as how to select only the summary information in an outline for copying or charting.

In the next chapter you will learn a variety of techniques for working with multiple worksheets. There you will learn how to use templates to create worksheets that use the same layout, to edit and format such worksheets at the same time as a group, to link data between two worksheet files, consolidate data from different worksheet files, and save related worksheets in a single workbook file.

10

Working with Multiple Worksheets

Some of the worksheets you create will use the same layout and formatting, such as income statements or budget worksheets that you prepare on a quarterly or annual basis. To facilitate the creation of such worksheets, you can make a template and then use it to generate all of these worksheets. The template contains the basic formulas and formatting required in each worksheet; when generating a new worksheet from the template, all you have to do is enter your data. Templates not only make it a great deal faster to create new worksheets but also give all worksheets of a particular kind a consistent look. Their use can also cut down considerably on worksheet errors because you have to troubleshoot the formulas only in each template, not in each worksheet created from it.

At times, you may need to consolidate the information from several similar worksheets, such as totaling revenues and costs from income statements for the last five years or totaling planned expenditures from the budgets prepared by the different departments in your company. If you generate all these documents from the same template, the job of consolidating the information becomes a simple one. Although Excel can consolidate information from worksheets that use different layouts, the task is much more straightforward when all the worksheets share a common arrangement.

At other times, you may need to take information from one worksheet and feed it into another one that does not share a common layout. For example, you might need to transfer the sales totals from a sales worksheet to your labor worksheet so that you can analyze the relationship between your daily or weekly labor costs and earnings. In such cases, you can bring the information from one worksheet into the other in such a way that changes to the data in the original worksheet will be updated automatically in the other worksheet (a technique known as *linking*).

In this chapter we look at Excel's techniques for working with multiple worksheets, both those that share a similar layout and those that do not. You will learn not only how to set up templates and generate worksheets from them, edit and format several worksheets at a time, consolidate data from multiple worksheets, and use linking to share data between worksheets, but also how to save related worksheets together in a special file called a *workbook*. The workbook is a new feature in version 4.0 that enables you to organize different worksheets and save them together as a single file, making it easy to find, work with, and distribute associated worksheets.

However, before we start learning these more sophisticated techniques for working with multiple worksheet files at one time, we should first examine the basics of file management. We'll start by recapping the procedures for managing more than one worksheet file in the Excel window. (You're already familiar with these window techniques from Chapter 7.) Then we'll briefly look at the ways you can manage your disk files from within Excel.

Managing Files on the Screen

In Excel, you can open as many different worksheet files (with the **F**ile **O**pen command or the File Open tool on the Standard toolbar or by selecting the filename directly from the bottom of the **F**ile menu) as the free memory in your computer can accommodate. If your computer is getting low on memory, Excel may have trouble loading the worksheet you select in memory, and you may receive an alert box that says **Not enough system resources to display completely**. If you see this message box, you should close one or more open document windows with the **F**ile **C**lose command before you go about editing any open worksheets. In that way you will have sufficient memory to make and save your changes. (If memory gets too low, Excel may not allow you to save your worksheet until you have closed one or more open windows.)

When you open a worksheet, Excel adds its filename to the bottom of the Window menu. To activate the document window of a particular worksheet and display it in the Excel work area, you select the filename at the bottom of the **W**indow menu or open this menu and type the number assigned to it. (Each file is assigned a number on the menu between **1** and **9**, reflecting the order in which the worksheet was opened.) If you open more than nine worksheet files at a time (a rare but possible occurrence), Excel adds a **M**ore Windows command to the very bottom of the **W**indow menu. To activate a worksheet with a document window a number higher than 9, you choose this **M**ore Windows command. Excel opens an Activate dialog box that contains an **A**ctivate list box showing the names of all open worksheets. To display the desired worksheet window, you simply double-click its name in the **A**ctivate list box or select its name followed by the OK button.

You can also use the keyboard to activate the open worksheet windows in sequence. When you press Ctrl+F6, Excel activates the next open document window (according to the sequence in which you are opening the windows). When you press Ctrl+Shift+F6, Excel activates the previous document window. You can continue to press Ctrl+F6 until the program displays the document window with the worksheet you want to use. If you find that you've gone past the desired worksheet, you can then press Ctrl+Shift+F6 to back up until it is displayed on the screen.

Arranging Windows on the Screen

When working with multiple worksheet windows, it is often important to be able to view more than one worksheet window at a time. In Chapter 7 you learned how to use the **A**rrange command on the **W**indow menu to display multiple windows opened on a single worksheet file. You can use this same command and its options to arrange and display different windows holding the various worksheet files you have open. Remember that the Arrange Windows dialog box contains four arrange option buttons:

- **T**iled to arrange the open document windows side by side above and next to one another.
- **H**orizontal to arrange the open document windows side by side above one another.
- **V**ertical to arrange the open document windows side by side next to one another.
- **N**one to cancel the current window arrangement.

Figure 10.1 shows the Excel window with three tiled document windows, each containing a different document. When the document windows are arranged together in the Excel work area, only the active document window contains scroll bars and sizing buttons. You can activate a new document window in the work area simply by clicking it. Excel shows you that the new window is active by darkening its title bar and adding scroll bars and sizing buttons to it. To make the active window full size in the work area, you click its Maximize button in the upper-right corner. To return the document window

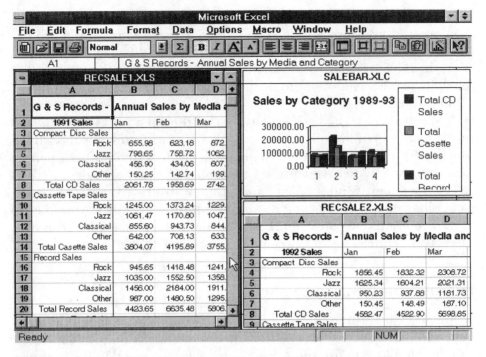

Figure 10.1   Three Tiled Document Windows with Different Files

to its previous size (and restore the current tiled, horizontal, or vertical window arrangement), you then click the Restore button at the far right of the Excel menu bar.

Tip   When you save a worksheet, Excel saves its size and position as it is currently arranged. This means that the worksheet will resume its previous size and position in the work area even when it is the only document you have open. If you want your worksheet to open up full size, choose the None option button in the Arrange Windows dialog box right before you save your worksheet file for the last time before closing the file or exiting Excel.

Managing Files on Disk

Most of the file management tasks, such as initializing floppy disks, creating directories to hold your Excel worksheet files, and copying and/or moving the worksheet files to new directories or disks, are done outside of Excel, using the Windows File Manager or some other Windows file management utility. (For complete information on using the Windows File Manager to perform these types of file maintenance operations, consult your Microsoft Windows User's Guide.) There are, however, a few disk file-related tasks that you can perform from within Excel. For example, you can save a worksheet in a different file format, save the worksheet with a password, create a backup version of your worksheet, delete files from a particular directory or disk, and place the worksheets and macro sheets that you want opened automatically each time you start Excel in a special startup directory.

Using the File Save As Command

When you save changes to an existing worksheet with the File Save command (Shift+F12) or the Save file tool on the Standard toolbar, Excel saves your changes under the same filename. If you want to create a copy of your worksheet (under the same or new filename), save the worksheet in a different file format (such as the one used by Excel 3.0 or 2.1 or Lotus 1-2-3), assign a password to the worksheet, or save the previous version as a backup file, you choose the **File Save As** command (F12) and use the options in the Save As dialog box (shown in Figure 10.2) instead.

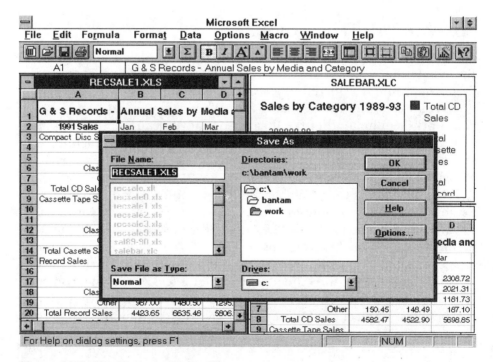

Figure 10.2 The Save As Dialog Box

To save a copy of the worksheet file with a new name, you simply edit the worksheet filename displayed in the Filename text box and select the OK button. If you want to change the file's location (as when making a backup copy on a floppy disk or placing a copy of the worksheet in someone else's directory), you need to choose the appropriate disk drive in the Drives drop-down list box and/or choose the appropriate directory in the Directories list box.

For example, suppose that you have saved the active worksheet with the filename BUDGET92.XLS in the C:\ACCTS directory. To save a copy of this worksheet on a formatted diskette placed in drive A of your computer, you would select the a: drive icon in the Drives drop-down list box before selecting the OK button. (To save the worksheet file with a new name on drive A, you would also edit the document's name in the Filename text box.) To save a copy of this worksheet in your assistant's personal directory, D:\ROGER, you would select the d: drive icon in the Drives drop-down list box, then select the roger folder icon in the Directories list box before you choose the OK button. (Again, to save the worksheet file with a new name in Roger's directory on drive D, you would also edit the document's name in the Filename text box.)

CHANGING THE FILE FORMAT

By default, the program saves all worksheet files in the Excel version 4.0 file format, simply referred to as Normal in the Save File as Type drop-down list box of the Save As dialog box. When you need to save a copy of your worksheet in another file format so that you can use the worksheet with an earlier version of Excel (3.0 or 2.1), Excel on the Macintosh, or another application program, you need to select the desired format in the Save File as Type drop-down list box.

Table 10.1 shows the available file format options and explains their usage. Note that when you save an Excel worksheet in a file format used by an earlier version (2.1 or 3.0), the program does not change the filename extension. (All versions of Excel for Windows uses the same XLS extension.) To avoid overwriting the original (4.0) version of your file when you save the worksheet in an earlier Excel file format, you need to change the location and/or the main filename in the Save As dialog box before you select the OK button to save the document.

Table 10.1   The File Format Options in the Save File as Type Drop-down List Box

File Format Option	Used For
Normal	Saving worksheets in the Excel 4.0 file format.
Template	Saving worksheets as template files (see "Using Worksheet Templates" later in this chapter). When you select this option, Excel changes the XLS filename extension to XLT.
Excel 3.0	Saving worksheets to use with Excel 3.0 for Windows.
Excel 2.1	Saving worksheets to use with Excel 2.1 for Windows.
SYLK	Saving worksheets to use with Multiplan for DOS. When you select this option, Excel changes the XLS filename extension to SLK.
Text (ANSI)	Saving worksheets as ANSI text files to transfer the information to Windows applications such as word processors that can't read Excel files directly. When you select this option, Excel changes the XLS filename extension to TXT.
CSV (Comma Separated Values)	Saving worksheets as comma-delimited files for use with Windows spreadsheets or database management programs that can read CSV files but can't read Excel files. When you select this option, Excel changes the XLS filename extension to CSV.
WKS	Saving worksheets to use with Lotus 1-2-3 version 1A. When you select this option, Excel changes the XLS filename extension to WKS.
WK1	Saving worksheets to use with Lotus 1-2-3 version 2.0, 2.1, 2.2, or 2.3. When you select this option, Excel changes the XLS filename extension to WK1.
WK3	Saving worksheets to use with Lotus 1-2-3 version 3.0, 3.1 or 3 Plus. When you select this option, Excel changes the XLS filename extension to WK3.
DIF (Data Information Format)	Saving worksheets as DIF files for use with spreadsheet programs such as SuperCalc 5 that can't read Excel files directly. When you select this option, Excel changes the XLS filename extension to DIF.

Table 10.1 *(continued)*

DBF 2	Saving worksheets to use with dBASE II. When you select this option, Excel changes the XLS filename extension to DBF.
DBF 3	Saving worksheets to use with dBASE III or III Plus. When you select this option, Excel changes the XLS filename extension to DBF.
DBF 4	Saving worksheets to use with dBASE IV version 1.0, 1.1, or 1.5. When you select this option, Excel changes the XLS filename extension to DBF.
Text (Macintosh)	Saving worksheets as Macintosh text files to transfer the information to Macintosh applications that can't read Excel files directly. When you select this option, Excel changes the XLS filename extension to TXT.
Text (OS/2 or MS-DOS)	Saving worksheets as ASCII text files to transfer the information to OS/2 or DOS applications that can't read Excel files directly. When you select this option, Excel changes the XLS filename extension to TXT.
CSV (Macintosh)	Saving worksheets as comma-delimited files for use with Macintosh applications that can read CSV files but can't read Excel files. When you select this option, Excel changes the XLS filename extension to CSV.
CSV (OS/2 or MS-DOS)	Saving worksheets as comma-delimited files for use with OS/2 or DOS applications that can read CSV files but can't read Excel files. When you select this option, Excel changes the XLS filename extension to CSV.

Note: The file format options in the Save File as **T**ype drop-down list box change when you save a chart or macro sheet with the File Save As command. With charts (which use the XLC extension), the formats are limited to Template, Excel 3.0, and Excel 2.1. (See Chapter 12 for information on saving charts.) With macro sheets (which use the XLM extension), the file formats include Add-In, Int'l Macro, and Int'l Add-In along with the regular format choices such as Template, Text, CSV, and DIF. (See Chapter 17 for information on saving macros.)

SAVING A BACKUP VERSION OF A FILE

You can have Excel save a backup version of your worksheet each time you save changes to your worksheet document. The program does this by saving the previous version of the document on the disk with the extension BAK before saving your changes to the worksheet file on the screen with the same filename and standard XLS extension. For example, if you add a new table to a worksheet named BUDGET92.XLS and then save the file using the backup file option, Excel will save the previous version (without the new table) in a file named BUDGET92.BAK before it saves the new version of the worksheet (with the new table) in the filenamed BUDGET92.XLS.

To have Excel save backup versions of your worksheet each time you save the file, you choose the **F**ile Save **A**s command (F12), then select the Options button. This opens the Save Options dialog box (shown in Figure 10.3) where you select the Create **B**ackup File check box and OK button. When you then choose the OK button in the Save As dialog box, Excel displays an alert box asking you if you want to replace the existing file. As soon as you select the OK button in this alert box, Excel saves your changes with the same filename after saving the previous version of the file with the BAK extension. Thereafter, Excel automatically creates a backup version of the latest disk version before saving the latest screen version of your file. If you decide that you don't need or don't have the room for backup versions of your document, you need to open the Save Options dialog box again and

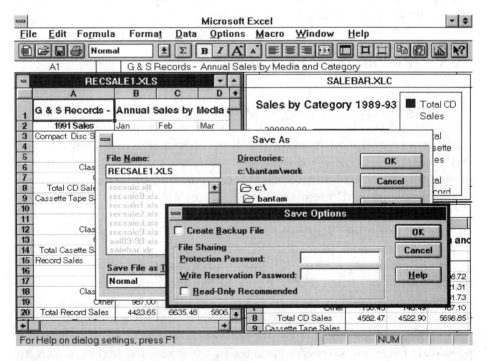

Figure 10.3 The Save Options Dialog Box

remove the X from the Create **B**ackup File check box before you save the worksheet file again in the Save As dialog box.

To open the backup version of a worksheet file instead of the latest version, you need to choose the **File O**pen command (Ctrl+F12) or click the Open file tool in the Standard toolbar, then select the XL* in the File Name text and replace these characters with BAK and press Enter. Excel then lists all of the files using the BAK extension in the current drive and directory. To open your backup, simply double-click its name or select the name and the OK button.

Alert! When using the backup option to make backup versions of different types of Excel files (worksheet, chart, and macro sheets), you need to make sure that the main part of every filename you use is unique in the directory or disk you are working. For example, when you create a chart from a worksheet and save it in a separate chart file, Excel automatically gives the chart file the same main filename as the worksheet file and adds to it the XLC extension. Therefore, you might have, for instance, a BUDGET92.XLS and a **BUDGET92.XLC** file in the same directory, and Excel would save the backup versions for both types of documents in the same **BUDGET92.BAK** file. This would mean that the backup file will contain the previous version of only the file you saved most recently (worksheet or chart).

PASSWORD PROTECTING A FILE

You can assign a password to your Excel document in the File Sharing area of the Save Options dialog box. After you assign a password in the **Protec**tion Password text box, you cannot reopen the document unless you can accurately reproduce the password. When you assign a password in the **W**rite Reservation Password text box, you cannot reopen the file in any mode other than read-only unless you can correctly enter the write reservation password. This means that you cannot save any changes that you make to the worksheet unless you use the **File Save As** command and change the worksheet's filename.

You follow the same procedure to assign either a protection password or a write reservation password. To assign a password, type the password in the **P**rotection Password text box and/or the **W**rite Reservation Password text box exactly as you want it. Keep in mind that Excel distinguishes between uppercase and lowercase letters in a password so that the password shazam does not match the password Shazam. As you type the password, Excel masks each character in the Password text box with an asterisk. When you select the OK command button in the Save Options dialog box or press Enter, Excel displays the Confirm Password dialog box where you must reenter the password exactly as you first typed it. Upon successfully duplicating the password and selecting OK or pressing Enter, Excel returns you to the Save As dialog box. When you choose the OK button or press Enter to save the document in this dialog box, Excel saves your document with the protection password and/or the write reservation password that you assigned.

When you try to open a worksheet that has a protection password assigned to it, Excel displays the Password dialog box where you must be able to enter the password exactly as you assigned it. If you are unable to reproduce the password, you will not be able to open and use the worksheet again. (Be sure that you write the password down and keep it somewhere safe.) As you type the password in the **P**assword text box, Excel once again masks each character that you enter. When you successfully enter the password and choose the OK button, Excel opens the document in the work area. If you mistype the password, Excel displays an alert box, and you must then perform the **F**ile **O**pen procedure again.

When you assign a write reservation password to a worksheet file, Excel displays a Password dialog box indicating that the file is reserved by the author of the worksheet. You can then enter the password in the **P**assword text box to gain write access to the worksheet, or you can select the **R**ead Only command button to open the worksheet up in read-only mode. If you open the document in read-only mode, Excel indicates this by adding the words [Read Only} to the filename shown in the document's title bar. Remember that in read-only mode, you cannot save changes to the worksheet with the same filename. To save changes, you must use the **F**ile Save **A**s command and rename the worksheet.

To remove a protection password from a file, you must open the document (which requires correctly entering the protection password). When you are ready to save the document, you must use the **F**ile Save **A**s command, open the Save Options dialog box, and delete the entire password (displayed by a string of asterisks) in the **P**rotection Password text box before you select OK. Then, when you select the OK button in the Save As dialog box, Excel saves the document without a protection password.

To remove a write reservation password, you must open the document with write access (which requires correctly entering the write reservation password). Then when you save the document, you use the File Save As command, open the Save Options dialog box, and delete the entire password (displayed by a string of asterisks) in the **W**rite Reservation Password text box before you select OK. When you select the OK button in the Save As dialog box, Excel saves the document without the write reservation password.

> *Note:* You can assign passwords to worksheet files that you save as templates (using the Template option in the Save File as Type drop-down list box) or to macro sheets that you save as add-in macros (using the Add-In option in the Save File as Type drop-down list box).

Instead of assigning a write reservation password to a document, you can check the **R**ead-Only Recommended check box in the Save Options dialog box instead. When you use this option, Excel displays a dialog box stating that you should open the document in read-only mode unless you have to save changes to it. To go ahead and open the file in read-only mode, you then choose the **Y**es command button or just press Enter. If, however, you want to override the read-only recommendation, you can open the file with write access mode by selecting the **N**o command button. If you choose the **N**o button, you can save changes to the file as you would normally.

If you open the document in read-only mode, you can save changes to the document only with a new filename. Note, however, that the read-only recommendation will be transferred when you save the file under a new name. This means that Excel continues to display the dialog box suggesting that you open the file in read-only mode. To prevent this dialog box from appearing every time you open the worksheet, you must choose the **File Save As** command, then open the Save Options dialog box and clear the **R**ead-Only Recommended check box. Then select the OK button in the Save Options, the OK button in the Save As dialog box, and the OK button yet again in the alert box asking you to replace the existing file.

Using the AutoSave Add-in Macro

Excel includes an AutoSave Add-in macro that saves your Excel files for you at the frequency you specify. Before you can use the AutoSave command, you must open the **autosave.xla** file. This file contains the AutoSave Add-in macro sheet; this sheet runs the macro that adds the autosave capability and attaches the AutoSave command to the **O**ptions menu. (For more on using customizing Excel with add-in macros, see Chapter 18.)

To use the AutoSave feature as you work, you follow these steps:

1. To run the AutoSave add-in macro and turn on the AutoSave feature, select the **O**pen command on the **F**ile menu instead (or click the Open file tool on the Standard toolbar or press Ctrl+F12). Double-click the library folder in the **D**irectories list box to open this directory, then double-click autosave.xla in the Filename list box to open this macro sheet and run this add-in macro. Excel automatically

turns on the AutoSave feature as soon as the program loads the
autosave.xla file into memory (indicated by the check mark preceding the **Au**toSave command on the **O**ptions menu).

2. To change the frequency with which your files are saved or to change
   the other AutoSave settings, choose the **Au**toSave command on the
   Options menu to open the AutoSave dialog box.

3. By default Excel sets the save frequency to about 9 minutes between
   saves by selecting the **M**edium option button. To change the save frequency to about 3 minutes between saves, select the **H**igh option
   button. To change the frequency to about 30 minutes between saves,
   choose the **L**ow option button. To temporarily turn off the AutoSave
   feature, select the **N**ever option button.

4. By default, the AutoSave feature prompts you before saving your files
   at the save frequency. (Prompting allows you to change the filename
   or other save options in the Save As dialog box.) To have Excel automatically save your files without prompting you, clear the X from the
   Prompt Before Saving check box.

5. By default, the AutoSave feature saves all open files at the same frequency. To have Excel save only the active document you are working
   on, clear the X from the **S**ave All Files check box.

6. Choose the OK button or press Enter to close the AutoSave dialog
   box and put your new AutoSave settings into effect.

Tip The AutoSave command continues to be available on the **O**ptions
menu only until you exit Excel. If you don't want to have to open the
autosave.xla file manually each time you start Excel, use the Windows
File Manager to move this file from the **c:\excel\library** directory to the
c:\excel\xlstart directory. That way Excel automatically opens this add-in
macro each time you start the program.

Deleting Files in Excel

Although you cannot perform file housekeeping tasks such as initializing
diskettes or copying and moving files from within Excel (you must use the
Windows File Manager to perform these tasks), Excel does enable you to
delete unwanted files from your disks with its **File D**elete command. To delete
a file from your disk, you select the document you want to remove in the
file list box in the Delete Document dialog box. When you double-click
the filename or select it and then choose the OK button, Excel displays an
alert box that displays the name of the file that you are about to delete.

To go ahead and delete the document from the disk, choose the **Yes** command button in this alert box. To close this alert box without deleting the selected document, choose the **No** button instead.

Alert! Be very careful when using the **File Delete** command. If you delete the wrong file in Excel, you cannot use the **Edit Undo** command to restore the erased file to the disk. In fact, the only way you can restore the file is by running a utility program such as Norton Utilities that offers an undelete command or, if you are using MS-DOS version 5.0, by returning to the DOS operating system and using its Undelete command.

Using the Startup Directory

When you install Excel, the program automatically creates a startup directory called xlstart. (This directory is located under your Excel directory, as in c:\excel\xlstart.) Any Excel files, such as worksheet files, worksheet templates (discussed below), macro sheets, or macro add-in files, that you place in this directory are opened automatically each time you start Excel. You can place any Excel documents that you routinely use in the **xlstart** directory to have immediate access to them.

Tip To place an Excel document in the **xlstart** directory, open the File Manager from the Windows Program Manager, select the file you want to move, choose the **M**ove command on the **F**ile menu (or press F7), and then type the full path for the **xlstart** directory in the To text box, such as c:\excel\xlstart before you choose the **M**ove command button or press Enter.

SPECIFYING AN ADDITIONAL STARTUP DIRECTORY

You also can specify an alternate startup directory of your own creation to be used in addition to the **xlstart** startup directory. The program automatically opens any Excel document that you save in the alternate startup directory after opening all of the Excel documents located in the **xlstart** startup directory.

To create and specify an alternate startup directory for Excel, follow these steps:

1. To create the alternate startup directory, start Windows and double-click the File Manager program icon to start the File Manager.

2. Click the folder icon in the Directory Tree document window under which you want to place the alternate startup directory. For example, to

create a directory named **altstart** and place it under the Excel program directory **c:\excel**, you would click the folder icon named EXCEL.

3. Choose the Create Directory command on the **File** pull-down menu.

4. Type the name for the directory in the **Name** text box in the Create Directory dialog box. The name can be up to eight characters long with an optional three-character extension. The Create Directory dialog box shows you the name of the current directory (as in C:\EXCEL). The name that you enter for your new alternate startup directory is added to this path (as in C:\EXCEL\ALTSTART).

5. Choose the OK button or press Enter. The File Manager adds a new folder with the name of your alternate startup directory displayed beneath the directories above it in the path.

6. Close the File Manager and return to Excel, then open the altstart.xla macro add-in file. This file is found in the library directory in the directory that contains the Excel program files (such as c:\excel). When the add-in file finishes loading, the Alternate Startup Folder dialog box is displayed on the screen.

7. Type the complete path for the alternate startup directory in the Change to text box. For example, when using alstart in the c:\excel directory as the alternate directory, you would type C:\EXCEL\ALTSTART in the Change to text box.

8. Choose the OK button or press Enter. Excel then displays an alert box informing you that the alternate startup directory has been changed successfully and will be used the next time you start Excel.

9. Select the OK button in the alert dialog box to close it.

After setting the alternate directory in this manner, Excel automatically loads all files in this directory the very next time (and all times after that) that you start the program.

 Tip If you use Excel on a network, all Excel documents placed in the **xlstart** directory (which is located on the server) are available to all Excel users on the network. To make accessible the Excel documents that you use routinely, create your own alternate startup directory as described above and place these documents in this directory.

Using Worksheet Templates

As you learned earlier in this chapter in the section "Changing the File Format," Excel supports a file type called Template. When you save an Excel document such as a worksheet, chart, or a macro sheet as a template, Excel automatically opens a copy of the file rather than the original template file. That way, all the changes you make are saved in a copy and do not affect the original document. For example, if you create a budget template named **budget.xlt** (Excel automatically appends the **xlt** extension onto the main filename when you select Template as the file type) and then open this document with the **File O**pen command, Excel opens a copy of the document to which the program assigns the temporary filename **budget1**. When you save your work with the **File S**ave, **File Save As**, or the Save File tool, Excel opens the Save As dialog box. You can save your document there with this temporary filename or change the name to something more appropriate.

> *Note:* When you create a new chart from a chart template, Excel does not use the data series that you used to create the chart in the template. Instead, the program graphs the current selection in the worksheet that is active at the time you open the new chart from the chart template. See Chapter 12 for more information on charting worksheets.

To create a template, you simply build a document with all the standard text, formulas, range names, styles, and formatting that you need to create a new worksheet, chart, or macro from it. For example, if you want to create a worksheet template for tracking your annual sales, you would build a worksheet that contains all the standard column and row headings as well as all the formulas for summing and analyzing the sales data. You also would assign all of the styles and other types of formatting (including fonts, borders, shading, colors, and the like) to appropriate cells, divide the document window into panes or create different views of the worksheet, and define the desired print settings. If entries are allowed in only certain cells of the worksheet, you could speed up data by naming a nonadjacent cell range that includes all of the input cells. And, if appropriate, you can also unlock the cells in this input range and then turn on the protection in the worksheet template.

Figure 10.4 shows you just such a worksheet template. This template is called **recsale.xlt**, and it will be used to generate the annual sales worksheets for the record store. This worksheet template contains all of the headings, formulas, and formatting needed to generate a new sales worksheet. All you have to do is open the worksheet template, fill in the year in cell A2, then fill in the monthly sales figures for each type of media and each type of music. To help you fill in this information as quickly as possible, the range name *Input* has been assigned to all of the cells where you enter data, and the cells in the range have been unlocked and the document protected. Then, to enter the data for your new sales worksheet,

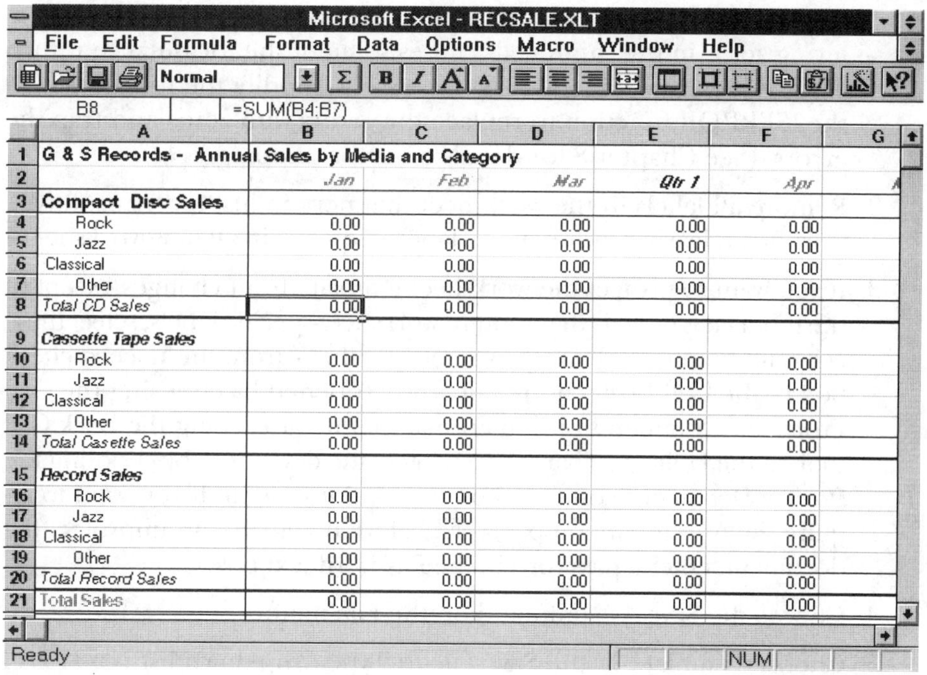

Figure 10.4   Sample Worksheet Template for Generating Sales Worksheets

you can use the **G**oto command on the Fo**r**mula (F5) and select the **Input** range name to restrict the data input to just these cells.

By using a worksheet template to generate new worksheets, you not only save a great deal of time but are also assured of consistency both in the look and the contents of your worksheets. As you will learn later in this chapter, having worksheets with a consistent layout makes it easier to consolidate their data. Also, you will probably find that worksheets generated from a single template contain less worksheet errors. This is because all of your error-checking and error-trapping efforts go into the creation of the single template file. Once you've assured yourself that the formulas in your template file are error-free, you know that the worksheets generated from it will be as well.

Creating a Template from a Document

The easiest way to create a worksheet template is to create an actual working document that contains all of the formulas and formatting you want in all the other worksheets of that type. After you've finished creating, formatting, error checking, and saving your prototype worksheet, you are ready to create a template from it as follows:

1. Replace all of the constant values in the worksheet with zeros. If entering zeros in the input cells causes some of the formulas to return error values (such as the #DIV/0! error), modify the formulas with the ISERROR function to replace the errors with zeros and trap the errors. (See Chapter 8 for details on error trapping.)

2. Remove all labels in the worksheet that pertain just to the prototype worksheet, leaving only generic labels required in all new worksheets.

3. If you want to protect the worksheet template from changes except in the input cells or cells that require worksheet-specific labels, select these cells and then unlock them by removing the X from the **L**ocked check box in the Cell Protection dialog box (opened by choosing the Cell Protection command on the Forma**t** menu) or clicking the Lock Cell tool on the Utility toolbar. Then protect the document by choosing the **P**rotect Document command on the **O**ptions menu. If you want to require the user to enter a password before he or she can unprotect the document, enter a password in the **P**assword text box.

4. Choose the Save **A**s command on the **F**ile menu.

5. Choose Template in the Save File as **T**ype drop-down list box. Excel changes the filename extension from XLS to XLT as soon as you choose **T**emplate as the file type.

6. If necessary, edit the main part of the template's filename in the Filename list box (be sure to leave the XLT extension), then choose the OK button or press Enter.

After creating a template, you can then generate a new document from it simply by opening the file with the File **O**pen command or the Open File tool on the Standard toolbar. When you open a new document from a template, Excel automatically opens a copy and assigns a temporary filename (such as **Recsale1**, **Recsale2**, and the like when the template filename is **recsale.xlt**). For example, Figure 10.5 shows you a new worksheet opened with the **recsale.xlt** template file shown in Figure 10.4.

To edit the template file, you can open the original file instead of a copy by holding down the Shift key as you double-click the template filename in the Open dialog box or by holding down the Shift key, selecting the template filename, and then choosing the OK button or pressing Enter.

You can save changes to the template file as you would any other Excel document. When you save a new worksheet generated from the template, Excel displays the Save As dialog box. You can then save the worksheet file with the temporary filename or modify the filename to something more descriptive before you save the document.

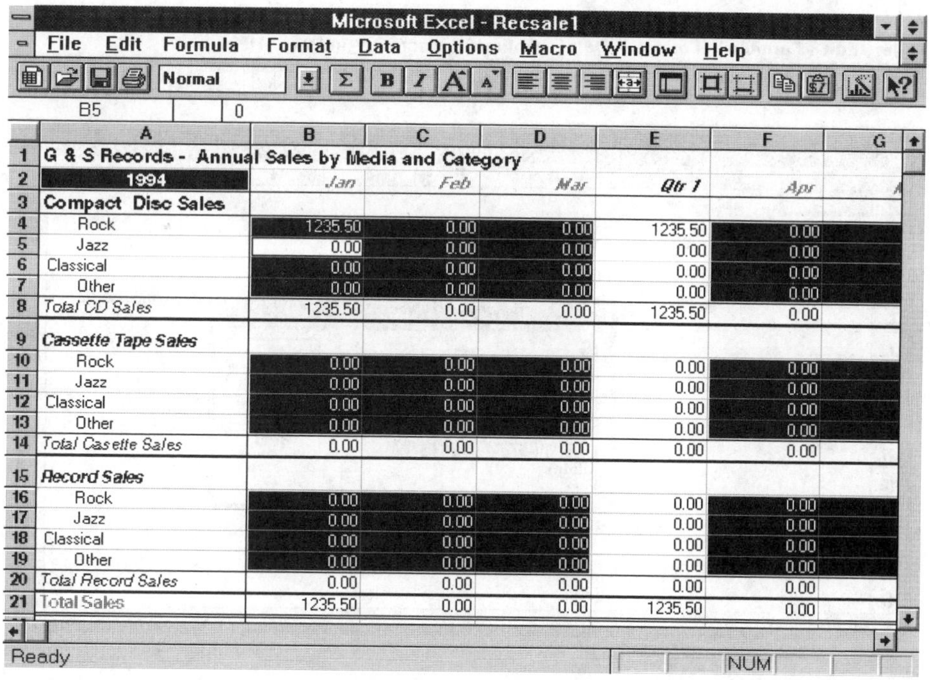

Figure 10.5 Sample Worksheet Generated from the Record Sales Template

Adding Templates to the File New List Box

If you create worksheet templates that you or other workers who share your computer use regularly, you can add the templates to the New dialog box as types of documents that you can create. That way you can open new documents generated from various templates by using the **File New** command rather than the **File Open** command.

To have a worksheet template listed in the New list box of the New dialog box, you need to place the original template file or a copy of it in the **xlstart** startup directory (as described earlier in "Using the Startup Directory") or in the directory specified as the alternate startup directory (as described earlier in "Specifying an Additional Startup Directory").

After moving or copying a template file into the **xlstart** or alternate startup directory, the New dialog box automatically displays the name of the template (*sans* the XLT extension). To open a new document from it, you simply double-click its name in the **New** list box or choose the template name and then select the OK button or press Enter.

Figure 10.6 shows you the New dialog box after adding the **Recsale** template name to its **New** list box. To create a new record sales worksheet, you simply double-click **Recsale** or select the name and choose OK.

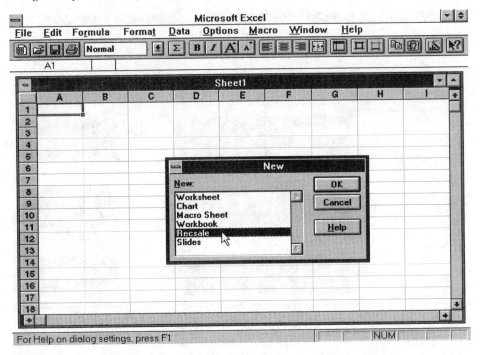

Figure 10.6   The New Dialog Box After Adding the Record Sales Template

> *Note:* Any template file that you move or copy into the **xlstart** or alternate startup directory during an Excel work session will not show up in the New dialog box until the next time you start the program.

Creating a Startup Worksheet

You can create a worksheet template called **sheet.xlt** that defines the cell styles and display settings that Excel should use in each new worksheet that you begin. For example, you might redefine the font in the Normal style from Helvetica to Palatino, remove the color [Red] from the Comma and Currency styles, and make dark blue the new grid and heading color in the Display Options dialog box.

After making these types of formatting changes in a new worksheet, you would then save the file as a template as follows:

1. Open the Save As dialog box with the **File Save**, **File Save As**, or **File Save** tool, then choose Template as the format in the Save File as Type drop-down list box.

2. Edit the filename in the File Name text box to **sheet.xlt** by deleting the sheet number assigned to the new worksheet.

3. If necessary, double-click the **xlstart** folder (or the folder with the name of your alternate startup directory if you're using one) in the **Directories** list box to select and open it. You must save the **sheet.xlt** template file in the **xlstart** or alternate startup directory to have Excel use it as the template from which all new worksheets are generated.

4. Choose the OK command button or press the Enter key.

5. To start using the **sheet.xlt** template to generate your new worksheets, exit Excel, restart the program, and then choose the File New command and press Enter (to select the Worksheet option) or click the New Worksheet tool on the Standard toolbar.

Group Editing

Sometimes you may find that you need to create a series of nearly identical worksheets on a one-time basis that doesn't justify setting up a worksheet template, or you may have a group of worksheets that are similar but use different formatting because they were created before a template was available. In such situations, you can use the **Group Edit** command on the **Options** menu to edit and format the different worksheets as a single group.

To indicate the worksheets you want to edit and format as a group, you follow these steps:

1. Open all of the worksheet files that require group editing.

2. Activate the document window that contains the primary worksheet you want to edit and/or format by clicking its document window or selecting it from the Window pull-down menu.

3. Choose the **Group Edit** command on the **Options** menu to open the Group Edit dialog box shown in Figure 10.7.

4. By default, Excel selects all the open worksheets in the Select **Group** list box. To designate all of them as the group, choose OK or press Enter. If, however, you don't want all of the open worksheets to be included in the group, remove the ones not to be included by holding down the Ctrl key as you click their filenames in the Select **Group** list box before you choose OK or press Enter.

After you define the group in this manner, Excel adds the designation [Group] to the end of the title bar of the active document window. (Actually, you would see this designation appended to the title bars of all document windows in the group if you arranged them in the Excel work area as shown

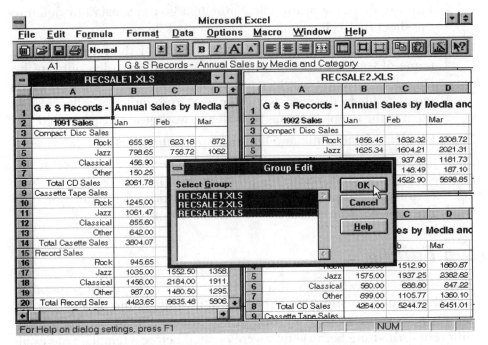

Figure 10.7   Selecting the Worksheets in the Group Edit Dialog Box

in Figure 10.7.) After you designate your worksheets as a group, all editing and formatting changes that you make to the active worksheet in the group affects all of the others equally. In addition, when you save your changes in the active worksheet, Excel saves the changes to all worksheets in the group, and when you close the active worksheet, Excel closes each worksheet in the group in succession. Also, you can print all the worksheets in the group at one time by selecting the **File Print** command (Ctrl+Shift+F12) or clicking the Print tool on the Standard toolbar.

When group editing, any additions, insertions, deletions, or format changes that you make to the cells of the active worksheet are made as well to the corresponding cells of the other worksheets in the group. This enables you to enter and format your data very quickly in several worksheets. Figures 10.8 and 10.9 illustrate how the editing and formatting you do in the active worksheet is applied equally to all other worksheets in the group. In Figure 10.8 the Classic 1 autoformat is being selected and applied to the first table of data in the recsales1.xls worksheet. In Figure 10.9 you can see the result: The first table of data in all three record sales worksheets in the group is now formatted with the Classic 1 autoformat.

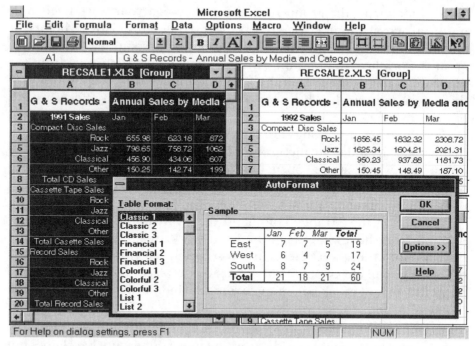

Figure 10.8 Selecting the Classic 1 Autoformat in the Active Worksheets in the Group

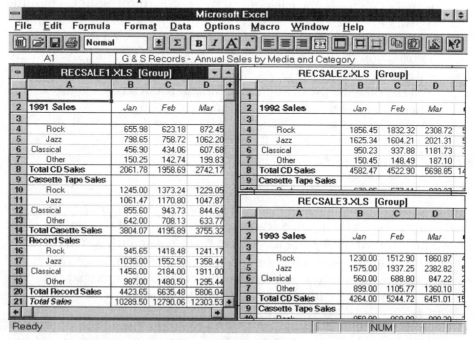

Figure 10.9 Classic 1 Autoformat Applied to all Worksheets in the Group

Excel maintains the group relationship between your worksheets only until you activate another open worksheet. (It doesn't matter whether or not this worksheet is included in the group.) As soon as you switch to another worksheet window, the [Group] designation disappears from the title bars of the worksheets in the former group, and editing and formatting return to normal. (That is, edits and formats you apply affect the cells of the active worksheet only.)

Sometimes when working with a group, you may have worksheets open that are not included in the group. To see which worksheets are in the group and which aren't, open the **Window** pull-down menu. Only the worksheets included in the group will have checkmarks displayed in front of their numbers and names in this menu.

When using the **Arrange** command on the **Window** menu to display multiple worksheet windows in the Excel work area, you can restrict the display to just those worksheets in the group by selecting the Documents of Active Group check box. (This check box replaces the Windows of the **A**ctive Document check box in the Arrange Windows dialog box when you define a group.)

Tip   When you close and save the worksheets in your group, Excel does not preserve the group relationship but merely saves each worksheet individually before closing each one in succession. If you want to continue to work with the same worksheets as a group, you must save them in a workbook. (See "Using Workbooks" later in this chapter for more information on saving worksheets together.) Thereafter, Excel opens each worksheet in the group whenever you open the workbook file. You can then use the Group Edit command as described in this section when you need to edit their contents as a group.

Linking Worksheets

Linking worksheets enables you to copy data from one worksheet to another in such a way that you can change the data in the original or *source* worksheet and Excel automatically updates the copied data in the other worksheet (called the *dependent* worksheet). To create such a link, you build a formula that contains an *external reference*, that is, a reference to a cell, cell range, or range name in a different worksheet file. The external reference shows the name of the file as part of the cell references, as in

    =SALES92!$C$5

which copies the data in cell C5 from the worksheet file **sales92.xls** into the active cell in a different worksheet file. Note that the filename is separated from the cell reference in the external reference by an exclamation point (!). Not surprisingly, linking formulas that contain external references are known as *external reference formulas*. External reference formulas can also contain built-in functions, such as

=SUM(SALES92.XLS!$A$4:$D$10)

which totals the values in the cell range A4:D10 in the worksheet file **sales92.xls** in the active cell of a different worksheet file.

Figures 10.10 and 10.11 illustrate how linking can work between worksheets. In Figure 10.10 you see two worksheets (pricetbl.xls and pricelnk.xls) side by side. The **pricelnk.xls** worksheet contains two linking formulas in cells A5 and B5 with external references to cells A8 and E8 in the **pricetbl.xls** worksheet. The external reference formula in cell A5 of this worksheet is

=PRICETBL.XLS!$A$8

This formula copies and creates a link to the value from cell A8 in the worksheet **pricetbl.xls**. The external reference formula in cell B5 of the **pricelnk.xls** worksheet is

=PRICETBL.XLS!$E$8

which copies and creates a link to the value from cell A8 in the worksheet **pricetbl.xls**.

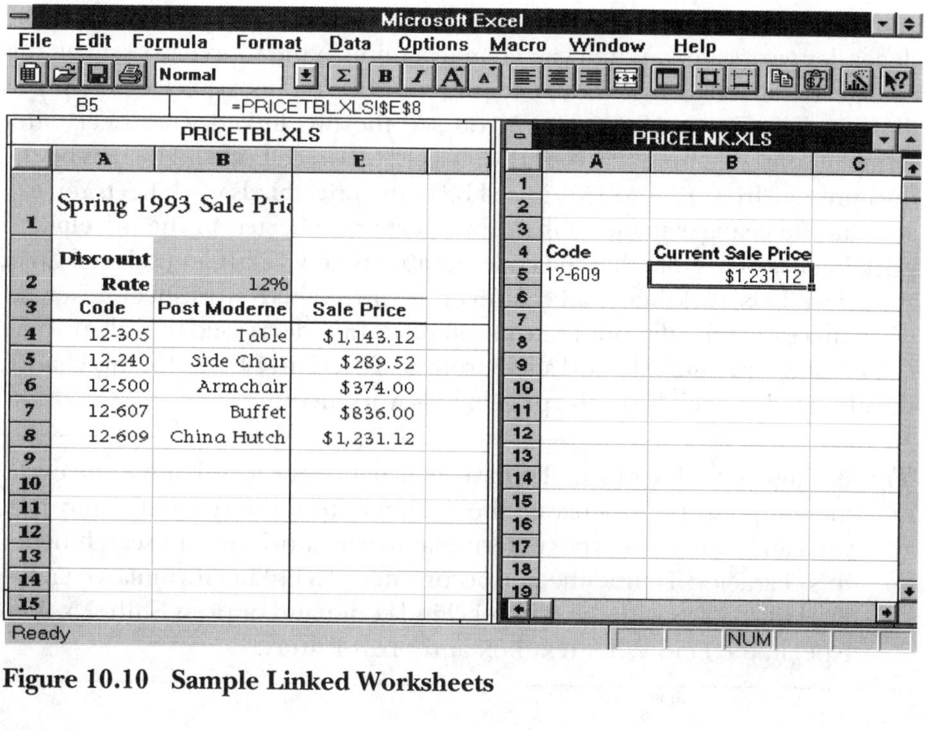

Figure 10.10   Sample Linked Worksheets

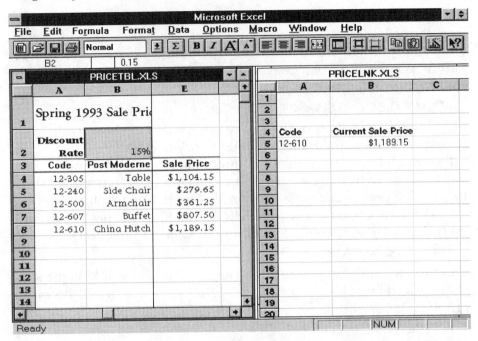

Figure 10.11   Linked Worksheets After Changing Some Values in the Source Worksheet

In this example, **pricetbl.xls** is the source worksheet and **pricelnk.xls** is the dependent worksheet. When you change a value in the source worksheet, this change is reflected in the dependent worksheet. This aspect of linking is illustrated in Figure 10.11. There you see the two linked worksheets after changing the code number from 12-609 to 12-610 in cell A8 and increasing the discount rate from 12% to 15% in cell B2 of the **pricetbl.xls** worksheet. You can see that the changes made to that worksheet are reflected in the **pricelnk.xls** worksheet as well. Note that the code number is now 12-610 in both cell C8 of the **pricetbl.xls** worksheet and cell A5 of the **pricelnk.xls** worksheet. Likewise, when increasing the discount rate in cell B2 to 15% decreased the sale price in cell E8 of the **pricetbl.xls** worksheet from $1,231.12 to $1,189.15, this change was also made to cell B5 of the **pricelnk.xls** worksheet.

 Tip   Because all linking formulas have external references that use the exclamation point (!) to separate the filename from the rest of the formula, you can locate these types of formulas in your worksheet by searching for this character. To find the first occurrence of a linking formula, open the Find dialog box with the Formula Find command or press Shift+F5, then type ! in the Find What text box and press Enter.

Creating Links Between Worksheets

Links are easy to create, especially if you have both the source worksheet(s) and the dependent worksheet open at the same time. When both worksheets are open, you can build the formula with the external reference with pointing or you can use the **C**opy and Paste **L**ink commands on the **E**dit menu.

In building an external reference formula, you use the same general technique as when creating a formula in the same worksheet, with a few variations:

1. Open both worksheets that you want to link. Use the **Arrange** command on the **Window** menu to arrange their document windows in the Excel work area.

2. Make the worksheet that is to contain the external reference formula (that is, the dependent worksheet) the active one .

3. Select the cell in the dependent worksheet where the formula is to appear, then type **=** to start the formula. If you're using a built-in function, type the function name or paste it into the formula bar with the Paste Function command on the Formula menu. If you only want to copy and create a link to a cell in the other (source) worksheet, you simply select the cell in the source worksheet as described in step 4.

4. When you need to select a cell or cell range in the source worksheet to insert the external cell reference into your formula (either as a value to be calculated or an argument of a function), click the source worksheet to activate it, then use the mouse to select the cell, cell range, or nonadjacent selection you want to use. When you make the cell selection in the other worksheet with the mouse, Excel enters the external reference for you.

5. Finish building your formula by entering any other required punctuation and/or cell references (both regular and external), then press Enter to insert the external reference formula into the active cell of the dependent worksheet.

When you need to copy a range of cells from one worksheet to another and create links between the source and dependent worksheets, it is easier to use the **C**opy and Paste **L**ink commands on the **E**dit menu. Figures 10.12 and 10.13 illustrate this situation. In Figure 10.12 you see the **febsal92.xls** worksheet arranged above the **feblbr92.xls** worksheet. You need to copy the daily sales in row 5 of the **febsal92.xls** worksheet into row 17 of the **febsal92.xls** worksheet; this worksheet will use the figures to calculate the percentage of daily wages to sales.

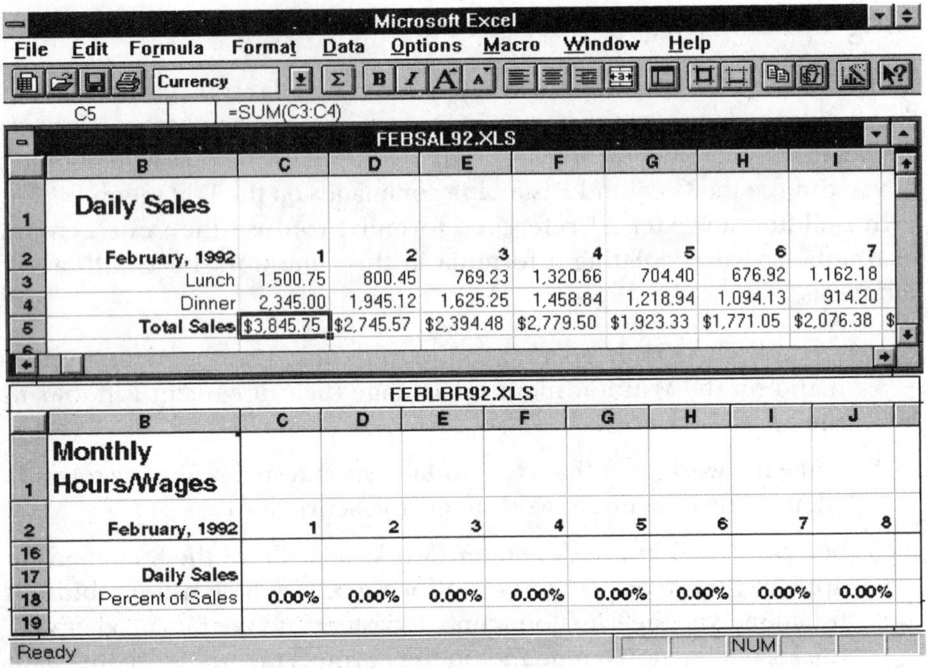

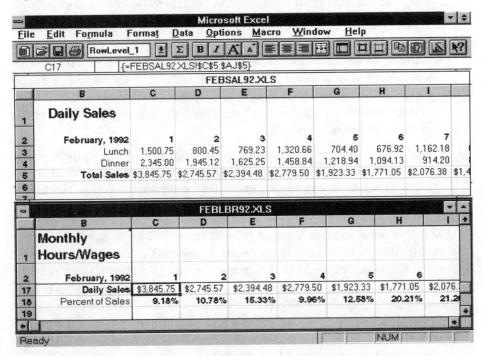

Figure 10.12 Sample Worksheets to Be Linked

Figure 10.13 Worksheets After Linking

To copy the total daily sales from the February sales worksheet into the February labor worksheet and create a link between these two worksheets, you first make the **febsal92.xls** worksheet active, then select the cell range in C5:BAJ, then choose the **C**opy command on the **E**dit menu or click the Copy Cells tool on the Standard toolbar. Next you click the **feblbr92.xls** worksheet and click cell C17 before you choose the Paste Link command on the **E**dit menu. Figure 10.13 shows you the worksheets after pasting the linked values into the cell range C17:AJ17 of the **feblbr92.xls** worksheet (and widening the columns).

Notice the contents of cell C17 in the formula bar in this figure. Excel copied the formulas from the range of cells in the February sales worksheet as an array formula in the February labor worksheet, as in

{=FEBSAL92.XLS!$C$5:$AJ$5}

Because you linked the worksheets, changes in the February sales worksheet that affect the total sales in row 5 will also be updated in the February labor worksheet, causing the labor/sales percentages to change. Figure 10.14 shows this situation. In this figure, the lunch sales on February 2 in cell D3 of the **febsal92.xls** worksheet are increased from 800.45 to 975.45. This

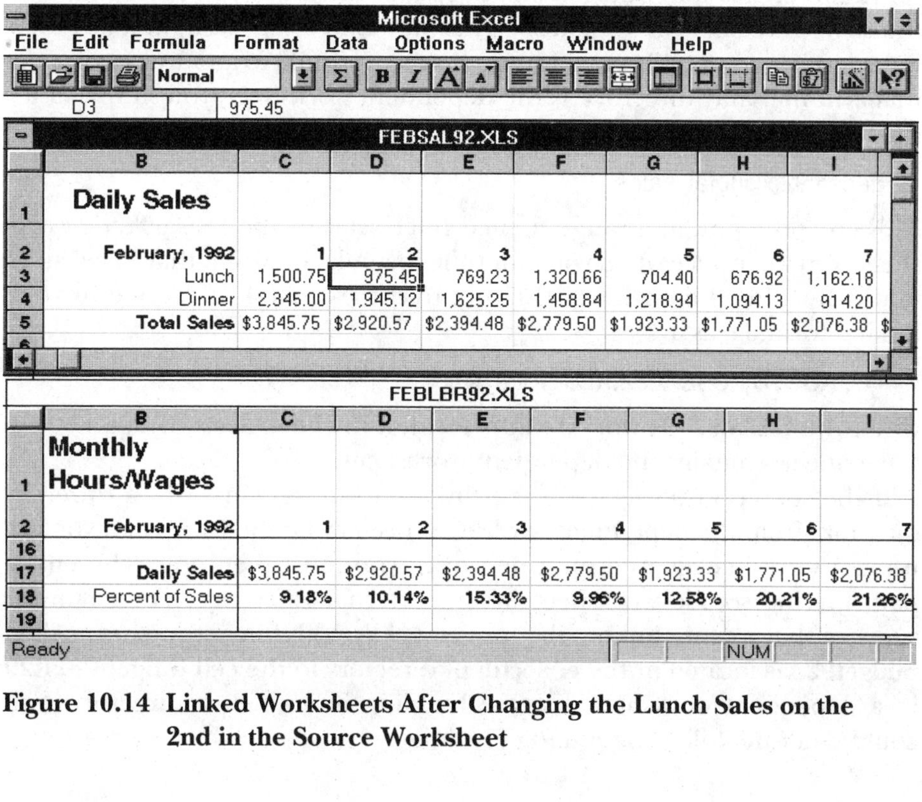

**Figure 10.14 Linked Worksheets After Changing the Lunch Sales on the
2nd in the Source Worksheet**

causes the sales total in cell D5 of this worksheet as well as in cell D17 of the **feblbr92.xls** worksheet to increase from $2,745.57 to $2,920.57. Note too that the percentage in cell D18 of the February labor worksheet has also decreased from 10.78% to 10.14% as a result of this change in the February sales worksheet.

ENTERING THE LINKING FORMULA MANUALLY

You also can type the linking formula with the external reference. Although typing the external reference formula is riskier than building it by pointing (as you could misspell the filename or enter the wrong cell references), it does allow you to link the dependent worksheet to source worksheets on disk. You can use this method when you don't have sufficient computer memory free to open both the dependent and source worksheets at the same time.

When you type the linking formula, you must know the filename of the source worksheet, the location of the source worksheet on the disk if it's not in the same directory as the dependent worksheet, and the addresses or range name of the cell references you want to use in the source worksheet.

Whenever possible, you want to keep all linked worksheets together in the same directory on your disk. That way Excel can easily update their linked information. When building a linking formula to a source worksheet that is in the same directory as the dependent worksheet, you simply enter the filename without the path, as in

    =febsal92.xls!total_sales

This creates a link to a range named **total_sales** in the **febsal92.xls** worksheet. You will notice when you enter the formula, however, that Excel automatically adds the entire pathname to the external reference in your linking formula, as in

    ='C:\ACCTS\FEBSAL92.XLS'!Total_sales

when the **febsal92.xls** worksheet is located in the **c:\accts** directory (the same one as contains the dependent worksheet).

If the source worksheet you are linking to must remain in a different directory from the dependent worksheet (as may be the case when you are using a worksheet shared on a network), you must then enter the entire path for the source worksheet in the external reference. For example, suppose that you are linking the range of cells A3:K3 in a worksheet called **budget92.xls** located in the **e:\acctdept** directory to the cell range A20:K20 in a dependent worksheet you are building in your own directory. You could enter the following linking formula

='e:\acctdept\budget92.xls'!b3

in cell A20. Note that when entering the pathname of a source worksheet file in a different directory, you must enclose the entire pathname including the filename in single quotation marks (').

After entering this external reference formula in cell A20 of the dependent worksheet, you would then copy this formula to the cell range B20:K20 just as you would any other formula (using the Fill handle or the Fill **R**ight command on the Formula menu). Excel adjusts the cell reference B3 in the external reference formula because you did not preface the column and row reference with dollar signs (as in $B$3).

If the source worksheet that you are using is saved in a workbook file (a subject that you will learn about later in this chapter), you must enter the name of the workbook in brackets before the filename. Assume for instance that the **budget92.xls** worksheet in the **e:\acctdept** directory is saved in a workbook filenamed **budgets.xlw**. (Workbooks use the **xlw** extension instead of **xls**.) In that case you would modify your linking formula in cell A20 of the dependent worksheet to

='e:\acctdept\[budgets.xlw]budget92.xls'!b3

If you misspell the filename in the external reference formula, Excel displays a File Not Found dialog box similar to the one shown in Figure 10.15, which contains a **D**irectories and Filename list box. You then can use these list boxes to locate the file and verify the spelling of its name. When you find the filename, double-click it in the Filename list box to select it and close the dialog box. Then return the linking formula to the formula bar and edit the filename so that it now is correct. (Although Excel will use the file you specify in the File Not Found dialog box, the program does not edit the filename for you in the formula—you must do this yourself.)

SAVING LINKED WORKSHEETS

After you have established the links between your worksheets, you must take care to preserve them. When both the dependent and the source worksheets are open at the same time, you always want to save the source worksheets before you save the dependent worksheet. This allows Excel to update any changes that you make to the values that directly or indirectly affect the linked data as well as any changes you make to the filename when saving the worksheet. For example, if you link to a source worksheet that has never been saved, the external link will use the temporary "sheet" name (such as **Sheet1**, **Sheet2**, and so on). When you assign the permanent filename to the source worksheet in the Save As dialog box, Excel then up-

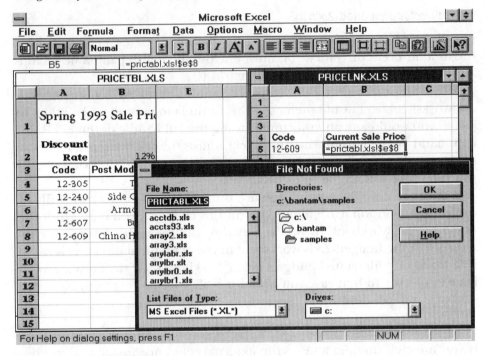

Figure 10.15 The File Not Found Dialog Box

dates the file references in the linking formulas in the dependent worksheet to the permanent filename.

After you have saved all of the source worksheets, you can then save the
changes in the dependent worksheet.

OPENING THE DEPENDENT WORKSHEET

After linking worksheets, when you next open a dependent worksheet
while the source documents are still closed, Excel displays the alert box
shown in Figure 10.16 that asks if you want to update references to unopened documents. If you've changed the source worksheets when the dependent worksheet was closed, some of the values in the dependent
worksheet could be out of date when you next open the document.

In such cases, you can have Excel check the external references and
update any out-of-date links by choosing the **Yes** button in the alert box. To
go ahead and open the dependent worksheet without checking the external references (thereby retaining the values as they were last saved), choose
the **No** command button instead.

When the program locates the source worksheet, it checks all of the
source data used in the linking formulas in your dependent worksheet and

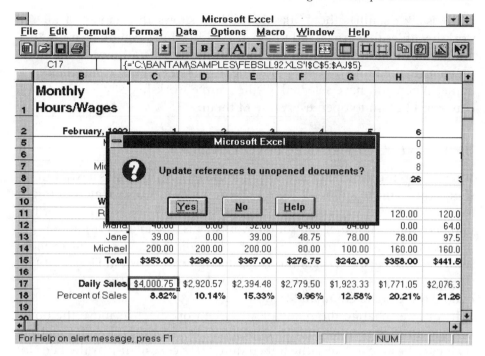

Figure 10.16   Alert Dialog Box for Checking Links

updates any modified values. If the program is unable to locate the source worksheets (which would be the case if you moved them to a different directory), it displays the File Not Found dialog box (shown in Figure 10.15). You can then locate the file using the **D**irectories and File Name list boxes in this dialog box.

OPENING THE SOURCE WORKSHEETS

Once the dependent worksheet is open, you can open a particular source worksheet simply by double-clicking the cell that contains a linking formula with the external reference to that document. For example, if you double-click the cell in a dependent worksheet that contains the formula

   ='C:\ACCTS\FEBSAL92.XLS'!Total_sales

Excel opens up the worksheet called **febsal92.xls** and selects the range name **total_sales** at the same time.

   If you have used several different source worksheets in the external reference formulas in your worksheet and want to open them all up, you can use the **L**inks command on the **F**ile menu to open the Links dialog box (shown in Figure 10.17). When the Link **T**ype option is set to Excel Links (as it is by default), the Links dialog box shows the names of all the worksheet files that are linked to the active worksheet (whether or not they are in the same directory). To open all of these files at once, select each filename in the **Links** list box by holding down the Ctrl key as you click each name. When you have selected all the source worksheets, click the **O**pen command button to open every one of them.

UPDATING AND REDIRECTING LINKS

You can also use the **File Links** to update the linking formulas in your worksheet while you're still working on the dependent worksheet. You might want to do this if you're using Excel on a network and a co-worker has updated one or more of the source worksheets as you are working on the dependent worksheet. To have Excel check the linked values in one or more source worksheets, you open the Links dialog box (shown in Figure 10.17), then select the source worksheets. You should check these before you choose the **U**pdate command button.

  If you ever change the name of a source worksheet or move the document to a new directory while its dependent worksheet is closed, Excel will no longer be able to check the linked values. (Excel will display the File Not

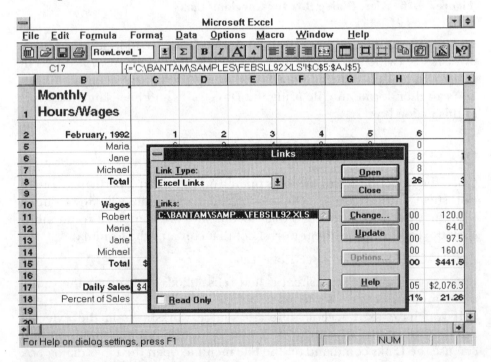

Figure 10.17 The Links Dialog Box

Found dialog box every time you open the dependent worksheet). To enable Excel to update your external reference formulas, you must redirect the worksheet links by indicating the new filename and/or location of the supporting worksheet. To do this, choose the **File Links** command, then select the original name of the source worksheet that has changed and choose the **Change** command button. Excel then opens a Change Links dialog box where you can select the present location in the **Directories** list box and the current filename in the File **Name** before you choose the OK button or press Enter.

CUTTING THE LINKS BETWEEN WORKSHEETS

There may be times when you want to cut the links between worksheets. For example, in the earlier linking example involving the February sales and labor worksheets, you could cut the links between the files as soon as you had verified and closed the books on the February sales. After making any necessary corrections in the sales (source) worksheet and updating the external reference formulas in the labor (dependent) worksheet one last time, you could then sever the links as follows:

1. Activate the dependent worksheet, then select the linking formulas with external references.

2. Choose the **Edit C**opy command or click the Copy tool on the Standard toolbar.

3. Without moving the cell pointer or changing the cell selection in any way, choose the **Edit Paste S**pecial command, then choose the **Values** option button box in the Paste area before you select the OK button or press Enter.

Excel replaces the linking formulas with their currently calculated values, and the worksheet links will be permanently severed as soon as you save the erstwhile dependent worksheet.

Consolidating Worksheets

Excel allows you to consolidate data from up to 255 different worksheets in a single one. With the **Data Consolidate** command, you can easily integrate data from multiple worksheets. For example, you can use the Consolidate command to total all of the budget worksheets prepared by each department in the company or to create summary totals for income statements for a period of several years. If you used a template to create each worksheet you're consolidating, Excel can quickly consolidate the values in the cells you select by virtue of their common position in their respective worksheets. Even if the data is laid out differently in each worksheet you want to consolidate, Excel can still consolidate the worksheets, provided that you've used the same labels to describe the data in their respective worksheets.

Most of the time you will want to add the data that you are consolidating from the various worksheets. By default, Excel uses the SUM function to total all of the cells in the worksheets that use the same cell references when you consolidate by position or use the same labels when you consolidate by category. You can, however, have Excel use any of the other following statistical functions: AVERAGE, COUNT, COUNTA, MAX, MIN, PRODUCT, STDEV, STDEVP, VAR, or VARP. (See Appendix B for more information on any of these functions.)

To consolidate your worksheet, you open a new worksheet to hold the consolidated data. (If you're using a template, open a new worksheet using the template.) Before you begin the consolidation process, you choose the cell or cell range in this worksheet where the consolidated data is to appear. (This range is called the *destination area*.) If you select a single cell, Excel expands the destination area to columns to the right and rows below as needed to accommodate the consolidated data. If you select a single row, the program expands the destination area down subsequent rows of the worksheet, if required to accommodate the data. If you select a single column, Excel expands the destination area across columns to the right, if required to accommodate the data. If, however, you select a multicell range as the destination area, the program does not expand the destination area and restricts the consolidated data just to the cell selection.

Tip If you want Excel to use a particular range in the worksheet for all consolidations you perform in it, assign the name Consolidate_Area to this range. Excel then consolidates data in this range whenever you use the **D**ata **C**onsolidate command.

When consolidating data, you can select data in open worksheets or in worksheets on disk. The cells that you specify for consolidation are referred to as the *source area*, and the worksheets that contain the source areas are known as the *source worksheets*.

If the source worksheets are open, you can specify the references of the source areas by pointing to the cell references. (Even when the Consolidate dialog box is open, Excel allows you to activate different worksheets and scroll through them as you select the cell references for the source area.) If the source worksheets are closed, you must type in the cell references as external references, following the same guidelines you use when typing a linking formula with an external reference (except that you don't type =). For example, to specify the data in range **B4:Q19** in a worksheet named **recsales1.xls** as a source area, you would enter

```
recsale1.xls!$b$4:$q19
```

as the external cell reference.

Note that if you want to consolidate the same data range in all of the worksheets that use a similar filename (for example, **recsale1**, **recsale2**, **recsale3**, and so on), you can use the asterisk (*) or the question mark (?) as a wildcard character to stand for missing characters, as in

```
recsale*.xls!$b$4:$q$19
```

In this example, Excel consolidates the range B4:Q19 in all versions of worksheets that use recsale in the main file whether or not this name is followed by another character (such as 1, 2, A, and so on).

When you consolidate data, Excel uses only the cells in the source areas that contain values. If the cells contain formulas, Excel uses their calculated values; if the cells contain text, Excel ignores them and treats them as if they were blank (except in the case of category labels when you are consolidating your data by category—see "Consolidating by Category" later in this chapter).

Tip When you use the **Data Consolidate** command, you can specify data ranges in Lotus 1-2-3 worksheets to be consolidated as well as data ranges in Excel worksheets.

Consolidating by Position

You consolidate worksheets by position when they use the same layout (such as those created from a template). When you consolidate data by position, Excel does not copy the labels from the source areas to the destination area, only the values. To consolidate worksheets by position, you follow these steps:

1. If you have sufficient memory, open all of the worksheets that you want to consolidate.

2. Open a new worksheet to hold the consolidated data. If you're consolidating worksheets generated from a template, use the template to open the new consolidation worksheet.

3. Select the destination area in the consolidation worksheet. If you want Excel to expand the size of the destination area as needed to

accommodate the source areas, just select the first cell of this range.

4. Choose the Consolidate command on the Data pull-down menu. Excel displays the Consolidate dialog box similar to the one shown in Figure 10.18.

5. By default, Excel uses the SUM function to total the values in the source areas. If you want to use another statistical function, select the desired function in the **F**unction drop-down list box.

6. If necessary, select the **R**eference text box and designate the cell references for the first source area that you want to consolidate. If the source worksheets are open, you can designate the cell references of the source area by pointing. If the document window is not visible, choose the document in the **W**indow pull-down menu, then select the cell selection as you normally would. (Remember that you can move the Consolidate dialog box by dragging it by the title bar.) If the source worksheets are not open, you can use the **B**rowse command button to select the filename in the Browse dialog box to enter it (plus an exclamation point) into **R**eference text box; whereupon you can type in the range name or cell references you want to use. If you prefer, you can type in the entire cell reference including the filename.

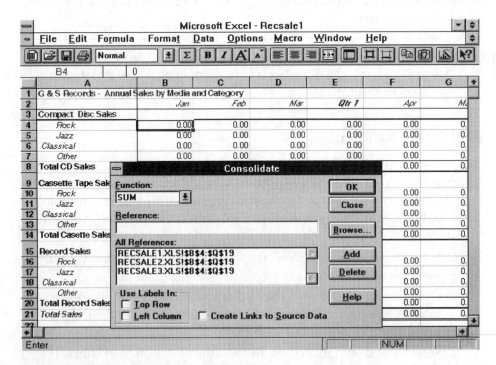

Figure 10.18 The Consolidate Dialog Box

Remember that you can use the asterisk (*) and question mark (?) wild-card characters when typing in the references for the source area.

7. Choose the **A**dd command button to add this reference to the All References list box.

8. Repeat steps 6 and 7 until you have added all of the references for all of the source areas that you want to consolidate.

9. Choose the OK button or press Enter to have Excel consolidate all of the data in the source areas in the destination area. Note that you can use the **E**dit **U**ndo Consolidate command (Ctrl+Z) to undo the effects of a consolidation if you find that you defined the destination and/or the source areas incorrectly.

Figure 10.19 shows you the first part of a consolidation for three years (1991, 1992, and 1993) of record store sales in the **salescon.xls** worksheet in the document window in the upper-left corner. This worksheet consolidates the source area B4:Q19 from the worksheets **recsale1.xls** with the 1991 sales, **recsale2.xls** with the 1992 sales, and **recsale3.xls** with the 1993 sales in the destination area B4:Q19 in the worksheet **salescon.xls**. (However, because all of these worksheets use the same layout, only cell B4, the first cell in this range, was designated as the destination area.)

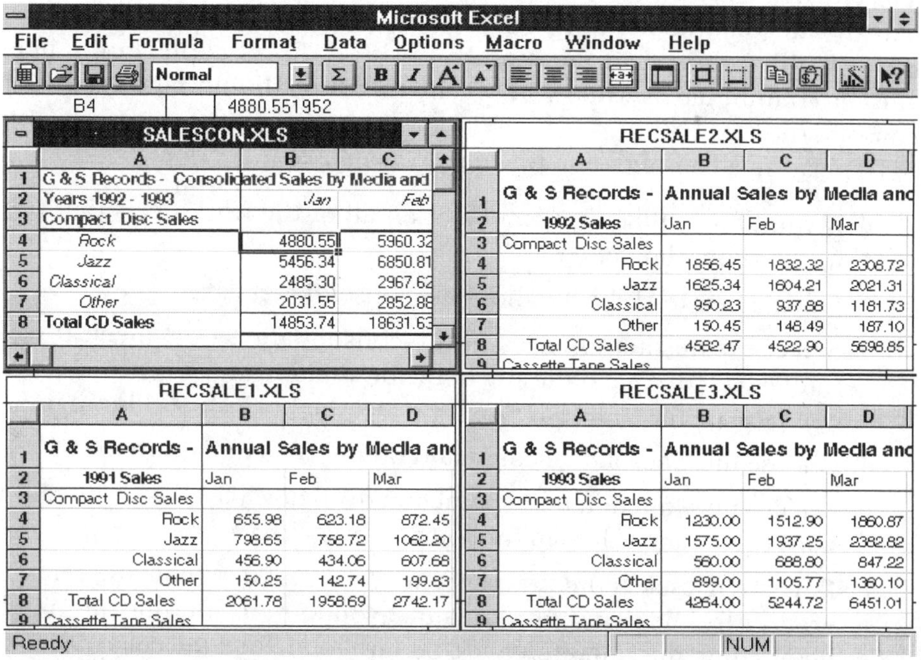

Figure 10.19 Consolidating Worksheets by Position

Note: Excel allows only one consolidation per worksheet at one time. You can, however, add to or remove source areas and repeat a consolidation. To add new source areas, open the Consolidate dialog box, then specify the cell references in the **Reference** text box and choose the **Add** button. To remove a source area, select its references in the All References list box, then choose the **Delete** button. To perform the consolidation with the new source areas, choose the OK button or press Enter. To perform a second consolidation in the same worksheet, choose a new destination area, then open the Consolidate dialog box, clear all the source areas you don't want to use in the All References list box with the **Delete** button, then redefine all of the new source areas in the **Reference** text box with the **Add** button before you perform the consolidation by choosing the OK button or pressing Enter.

Consolidating by Category

You consolidate worksheets by category when their source areas do not share the same cell coordinates in their respective worksheets but their data entries do use common column and/or row labels. When you consolidate by category, you include these identifying labels as part of the source areas. Unlike when consolidating by position, Excel copies row labels and/or column labels when you specify that they should be used in the consolidation.

To perform a consolidation by category, you take these steps:

1. If you have sufficient memory, open all of the worksheets that you want to consolidate.

2. Open a new worksheet to hold the consolidated data.

3. Select the destination area in the consolidation worksheet. If you want Excel to expand the size of the destination area as needed to accommodate the source areas, just select the first cell of this range.

4. Choose the **Consolidate** command on the **Data** pull-down menu.

5. Select a new function in the **Function** drop-down list box if you don't want to sum the values in the source areas.

6. If necessary, select the **Reference** text box and designate the cell references for the first source area that you want to consolidate. When designating the cell references, be sure to include the cells that contain the row and/or column labels that identify the values you are consolidating.

7. Choose the **Add** command button to add this reference to the All References list box.

8. Repeat steps 6 and 7 until you have added all of the references for all of the source areas that you want to consolidate.

9. If the source areas include row headings that identify which data to consolidate, select the **Left Column** check box in the Use Labels In section of the Consolidate dialog box.

10. If the source areas include column headings that identify which data to consolidate, select the **T**op Row check box in the Use Labels In section of the Consolidate dialog box.

11. Choose the OK button or press Enter to have Excel consolidate all of the data in the source areas in the destination area.

Figures 10.20 and 10.21 show you an example of a consolidation performed by category rather than by position. In this example, you have two record store sales worksheets to consolidate that use the same music categories but in different orders (at least for the CD media type). In the 1990 sales worksheet **recsale0.xls**, the row headings identifying the music categories follow the order:

Classical

Jazz

Rock

Other

In the 1989 sales worksheet **recsale9.xls**, the row headings follow a slightly different order:

Jazz

Rock

Classical

Other

When consolidating these two worksheets by category, Excel must use the row headings to identify which values to add to each other.

When setting up this consolidation, you would choose cell A3 as the destination area in the **sal89-90.xls** consolidation worksheet. Note in Figure 10.20 that row headings are not entered in column A of this consolidation worksheet, although column headings in row 2 are (Jan, Feb, Mar, and so on). This is because Excel copies the necessary row labels into the destination area when you consolidate by category. When specifying the cell

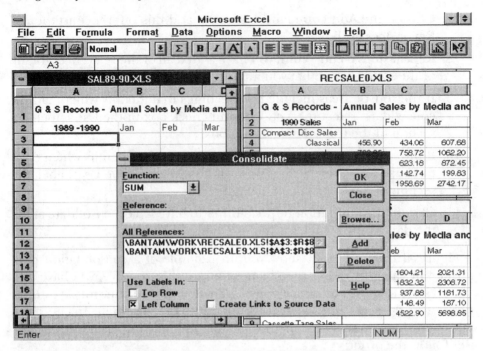

Figure 10.20   Preparing to Consolidate Worksheets by Category

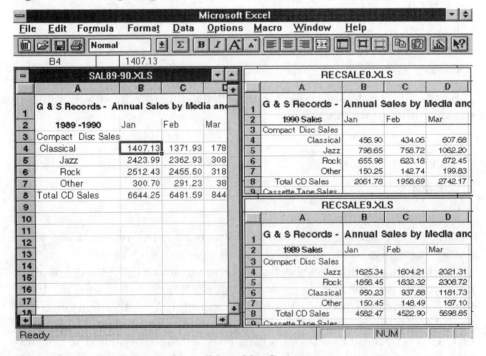

Figure 10.21 Worksheets Consolidated by Category

references of the source areas to be consolidated, you include the row headings along with the data to be consolidated. (In this example, the cell range A3:R8 is the source area in both worksheets.) Finally, because the row headings in the source areas are to be used to identify which values to consolidate, you would select the **Left Column** check box.

Figure 10.21 shows you the result of performing this consolidation by category. In the **sal89-90.xls** worksheet, you see that Excel has ordered the consolidated data according to the arrangement of the row headings used in the **recsale0.xls** worksheet, because the first source area is in this worksheet.

Linking Consolidated Data

Excel allows you to link the data in the source areas to the destination area during a consolidation. That way, any changes that you make to the values in the source area will be updated automatically in the destination area of the consolidation worksheet. To create links between the source worksheets and the destination worksheet, you simply choose the Create Links to **S**ource Data check box when defining the settings for the upcoming consolidation.

When you perform a consolidation with linking, Excel creates the links between the source areas and the destination area by outlining the destination area. (See Chapter 9 for detailed information on outlines.) Each outline level created in the destination area holds rows or columns that contain the linking formulas to the consolidated data.

Figure 10.22 shows an outline created during consolidation after expanding only the Classical level of the outline. There you can see that during consolidation, Excel created two detail rows, Recsale0 and Recsale9. These rows contain the external reference formulas that create the links to the source data. For example, the formula in cell C4 is

    =RECSALE0.XLS!$B$4

This formula links value in cell 4 to the sales in cell B4 in the **recsale0.xls** worksheet. If you change this value, the new value will be updated automatically in cell C4 in the **sal89-90.xls** consolidation worksheet, which will then change the Classical subtotal for January in cell C6.

Alert! You cannot perform a consolidation using the Create Links to **S**ource Data option when the destination area in your worksheet already contains data. Also, keep in mind that unlike when performing a consolidation that doesn't use linking, the Undo Consolidate command is not available after performing a consolidation that creates links to the source data.

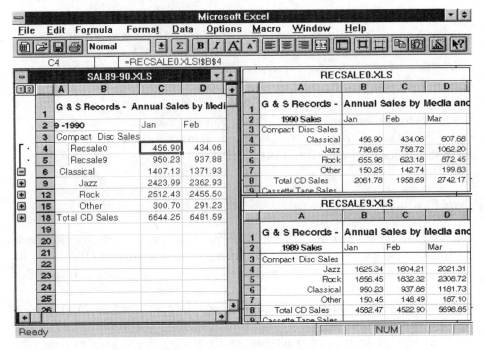

Figure 10.22   Consolidated Worksheets with Links to the Source Data

Using Workbooks

In Excel 4.0 you can combine multiple worksheets that you work with regularly in a special file called a *workbook*. You create a workbook by designating all of the worksheet, macro sheet, and chart files that should be included in it. When you open a workbook file, Excel automatically opens all the documents that are a part of the workbook. Likewise, when you close the workbook file, Excel closes all of the documents that are part of the workbook. A workbook file is given the file extension **XLW** to differentiate it from a standard worksheet file that uses the **XLS** extension.

When adding worksheets to a workbook, Excel differentiates between documents that are actually stored in the workbook file (these are known as *bound documents*) and documents that are listed as part of the workbook but whose files are not actually stored as part of the workbook file (the *unbound documents*). The difference between a bound and unbound document worksheet is significant; a bound document can appear only in the workbook in which it is saved, while an unbound document can appear in any number of different workbooks (provided that the document is unbound in each workbook).

Using workbooks to manage related documents offers several important advantages:

- When using a workbook, you don't have to manually open each work-sheet, macro sheet, and chart you want to work with.

- When using a workbook, you can move quickly between each document either by choosing it on a shortcut menu or by clicking the paging icons that are automatically added to the Workbook Contents sheet.

- When using a workbook, you can include the macro sheets that contain just the macros you use to perform operations in the worksheets stored in the workbook. (See Chapter 18 for more information on creating macros.)

- You can protect all of the bound documents in a workbook by assigning a password to the workbook file.

- When using Excel on a network, you can ensure that your co-workers are always using the most up-to-date version of a document by including it as an unbound document in the workbooks that you distribute to them.

Creating a Workbook

The steps for creating a new workbook are very straightforward. You simply select Workbook as the type of document to open in the New dialog box, then add the documents you want included as follows:

1. Choose the **N**ew option on the **F**ile menu, then double-click Work-book in the **N**ew list box or select this document type and choose OK or press Enter.

2. Click the **A**dd command button at the bottom of the Workbook Contents sheet to open the Add **T**o Workbook dialog box (shown in Figure 10.23). The documents you have open will be listed in the **Se**lect Documents to Add list box.

3. To add documents that are already open to the workbook, select them in the **S**elect Documents to Add list box, then select the **A**dd command button.

4. To add unopened documents to the workbook, select the **O**pen command button, then select the document to open and add to the workbook in the **O**pen dialog box. To select a document in another directory, double-click the folder icon with the directory name in the **D**irectories list box. To open the desired file, double-

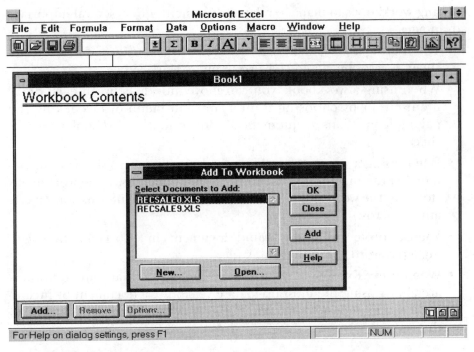

Figure 10.23   Adding Documents to a New Workbook

click its name in the Filename list box or select it and then choose
OK or press Enter.

5. Repeat step 4 until you have opened and added all of the unopened
   documents you want included in the new workbook.

6. To add a new document to the workbook, select the **New** command
   button, then double-click the type of file you want to create in the
   New list box or select the type and choose OK or press Enter.

7. Repeat steps 6 and 7 until you have added all of the unopened and
   new documents you want in the workbook, then choose the OK button or press Enter. Excel creates a workbook in a new document
   window whose title bar contains the temporary filename, such as
   Book1, **Book2**, and the like.

8. Save the workbook with the **File Save** command or by clicking the
   Save File tool on the Standard toolbar. Replace the temporary Book
   filename in the Filename text box with a more descriptive filename,
   taking care not to delete the XLW extension, then choose the OK
   button or press Enter.

At the beginning of each new workbook, Excel places a Workbook Contents sheet that lists all of the documents in the workbook. The order in which the documents appear in the Workbook Contents sheet reflects the order in which you added the documents. Excel displays a different icon for each type of document (worksheet, macro sheet, or chart—see Figure 10.24 for examples of all three icons) followed by the document's filename and an icon indicating whether or not the document is bound or unbound. (By default, all documents that you add are bound documents, so initially only bound icons appear in the Workbook Contents sheet. See "Binding and Unbinding Documents in a Workbook" later in this chapter for examples of unbound icons.)

> *Note:* When you open a workspace saved in Excel version 3.0, Excel 4.0 automatically converts it to a workbook. Likewise, if you open a Lotus 1-2-3 3-D worksheet in Excel 4.0, the program automatically converts it to a workbook as well.

REARRANGING THE CONTENTS OF THE WORKBOOK

The order in which the documents appear in the Workbook Contents sheet determines their order in the workbook. To rearrange the order of

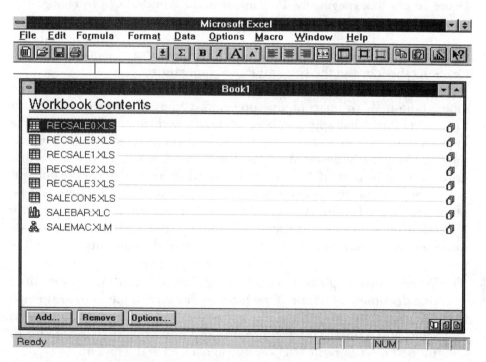

Figure 10.24 Workbook After Adding Documents

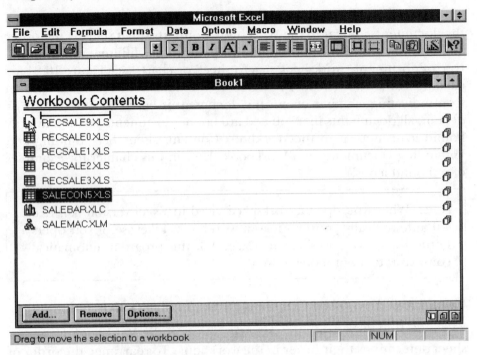

Figure 10.25 Rearranging the Documents in the Workbook by Dragging

your documents, you can drag the document icon to a new position in the Contents sheet or use the Cut and Paste commands.

To move a document by dragging, click the document and hold down the mouse button. As you start to drag up or down, a document icon appears at the pointer and a bar appears above or below the filename. Drag the document icon up or down until the bar is positioned at the place where you want the document to be inserted. If the bar appears above a document, that document will be pushed down in the list and appear right below the one you are moving. If the bar appears below a document, that document will be pushed up in the list and appear right above the one you are moving. Figure 10.25 illustrates moving a document by dragging. There, the **salecon5.xls** worksheet is just about to be inserted at the top of the contents.

Tip When reordering documents by dragging, you can move more than one document at a time. To select two or more sequential documents to move, hold down the Shift key as you drag through the document icons and names. To select two or more nonsequential documents to move, hold down the Ctrl key as you click each document.

You can also move a document in the list with the Cut and Paste commands. Click the document you want to move, then choose **E**dit **C**ut (Ctrl+X). Excel places a marquee around the document's icon and filename. Next select the document that should appear below the one you are about to move, then press the Enter key or choose the **E**dit **P**aste (Ctrl+V) command.

Note that Excel won't allow you to use the Undo command to undo a move made either by dragging or using the Cut and Paste command. The only way to restore the previous order is to move the document that you just finished moving back to its original position.

ADDING AND REMOVING DOCUMENTS

You can always add or remove documents from your workbook after you've created it. To add a document to your workbook, select the **A**dd command button, then select the new, open, or unopened documents just as you did when you first created the workbook. To remove a document from the workbook, simply select the document in the Workbook Contents sheet, then choose the **R**emove command button. Note again that you can't use the Undo command to restore a document removed in error. If you remove a document by mistake, the only way to restore it to the workbook is by adding it back with the **A**dd button.

If the document you want to add is open, you can use the dragging method to add it to the workbook. The easiest way to accomplish this is to display both the workbook and worksheet windows side by side like the ones shown in Figure 10.26. If the document you want to add is a worksheet or macro sheet, click and drag the Select All button (the button at the intersection of the row numbers and column letters) to the Workbook Contents sheet before you release the mouse button. If the document you want to add is a chart, select the entire chart, then drag one of its selection squares to the Workbook Contents sheet before you release the mouse button.

When you release the mouse button, Excel adds the document's icon and filename at the bottom of the list in the Workbook Contents sheet and the window containing the document you just added disappears from the Excel work area (as shown in Figure 10.27). This happens because all new documents are added to a workbook initially as bound documents, which are stored only within the workbook file. After adding the document in this manner, you can then move it to a more preferred order either by dragging its icon or using the Cut and Paste command.

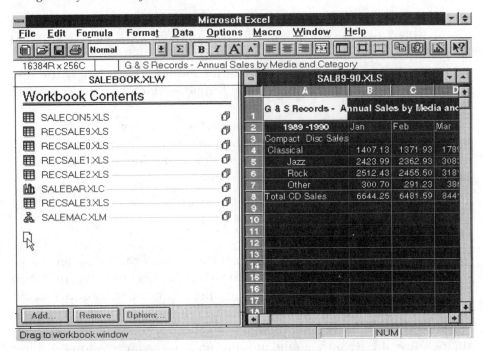

Figure 10.26   Adding an Open Document to the Workbook by Dragging

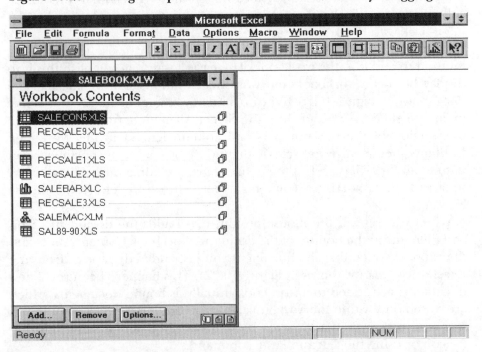

Figure 10.27   Workbook After Adding Document by Dragging

> *Note:* If you have more than one workbook open, you can move a document to a different workbook by dragging its document icon as just outlined. If you want to copy an unbound document to another open workbook, hold down the Ctrl key as you drag its document icon to the new workbook window.

Just as you can add a document to a workbook by dragging, you can also remove a document. Simply drag the document icon for the document you want to delete until you have positioned it outside of the window containing the Workbook Contents in the Excel work area. As soon as you release the mouse button, Excel removes the document from the Workbook Contents listing.

MOVING BETWEEN DOCUMENTS IN A WORKBOOK

Excel adds icons in the lower-right corner of each document window that make it easy to move between the documents in the workbook. To move to the next document in the workbook in sequence, you click the right paging icon (the one with the right corner dog-eared). To move to the previous document in the workbook, you click the left paging icon (the one with the left corner dog-eared).

To move to a particular worksheet in the workbook from the Workbook Contents sheet, you double-click the document's icon or name in the Workbook Contents sheet. To return to the Workbook Contents sheet from any document in the workbook, you click the Contents button (to the left of the left paging icon).

To go to a particular worksheet from anywhere in the workbook, you can open the shortcut menu attached to the Contents button, left paging or right paging icon (by clicking any one of these objects with the *right* mouse button), and then drag to the name of the document you want displayed in the menu (as shown in Figure 10.28). Note that the names of the bound documents in the workbook appear only on this shortcut menu and not on the **Window** menu. (This pull-down menu shows only the name of the workbook file plus any unbound documents or other open documents that are not part of the workbook.) Also in Figure 10.28, note that Excel includes the New command and the Group Edit command at the bottom of the shortcut menu so that you can add a new document to the workbook or turn on group editing when making changes to the multiple documents in the workbook.

When you move to a new document in the workbook, Excel displays each document window the same size and in the same position in the Excel work

	A	B	C	D	E	F	G	H
1	G & S Records - Consolidated Sales by Media and Category							
2	Years 1989 - 1993	Jan	Feb	Mar	Qtr 1	Apr	May	
3	Compact Disc Sales							
4	Rock	7392.98	8415.81	13835.37	29644.17	15154.44	20936.33	3572
5	Jazz	7880.33	9213.74	15736.14	32830.20	17313.90	24142.21	4232
6	Classical	3892.43	4339.55	6981.16	15213.14	7759.48	10450.68	1726
7	Other	2332.25	3144.12	6235.86	11712.23	6741.6		
8	Total CD Sales	21497.99	25113.22	42788.52	89399.74	46969.4		
9	Cassette Tape Sales							
10	Rock	5862.49	6318.20	10415.77	22596.46	8680.6		
11	Jazz	6714.59	7135.17	12598.59	26448.35	10529.0		
12	Classical	3477.51	3648.59	5333.43	12459.53	4578.0		
13	Other	4291.11	4528.96	8018.60	16838.67	6726.8		
14	Total Casette Sales	20345.70	21630.92	36366.39	78343.01	30514.5		
15	Record Sales							
16	Rock	3330.88	4438.15	6498.11	14267.14	4050.4		
17	Jazz	3917.59	6730.40	9022.58	19670.57	6373.0		
18	Classical	6221.13	11706.06	16387.08	34314.28	7026.3		
19	Other	3444.03	5673.75	7349.48	16467.26	12513.1		
20	Total Record Sales	16913.63	28548.37	39257.25	84719.24	29963.0		

SALEBOOK.XLW

√ SALECON5.XLS
SAL89-90.XLS
RECSALE9.XLS
RECSALE0.XLS
RECSALE1.XLS
RECSALE2.XLS
SALEBAR.XLC
RECSALE3.XLS
SALEMAC.XLM

New...
Group Edit...

Figure 10.28   Moving to a Particular Document with the Shortcut Menu

area. To view the document windows full size, click the Maximize button. To view your document windows at less than full size, size them by dragging the lower-right corner of the window (as the Sizing button is replaced by the right paging icon).

As you move to a new document window, the title bar displays the name of the workbook in brackets followed by the document's filename, as in

[SALEBOOK.XLW]RECSALES9.XLS

When creating external reference formulas between bound documents in other documents within the workbook or those outside, the external references in your linking formulas follow a similar format, as in

=[SALEBOOK.XLW]RECSALES9.XLS!$B$4

when you want to set up a formula that copies and links to the value in cell B4 in the bound worksheet **recsales9.xls** in the **salebook.xlw** workbook file.

 Alert! The Contents button and left and right paging icons appear in the document windows of the workbook only when the scroll bars are displayed. If you don't see these objects in your workbook, you need to redisplay the scroll bars by selecting the Scroll Bars check box in the Display area of the Workspace Options dialog box.

DISPLAYING BOUND DOCUMENTS IN SEPARATE WINDOWS

As mentioned in the previous section, bound documents in a workbook do not appear on the **Window** pull-down menu. (Only unbound documents in the workbook use a separate window and appear on this menu.) If you want, however, you can display the Workbook Contents sheet and one of the bound documents in separate windows, which you can then display together on the screen with other unbound documents (or even with other open documents that are not part of the workbook).

To display a bound document in a separate window, move to the Workbook Contents sheet, then hold down the Ctrl key as you double-click the bound document's icon or filename. You can also open a new document window for a bound document by selecting the document's icon and filename in the Workbook Contents sheet or by moving to the document and then choosing the **New** Window command on the **Window** menu.

After you open new windows for all the bound documents you want to work with, the new windows are listed in the **Window** menu along with the name of the workbook file, all unbound documents, and any other documents you have open that are not part of the workbook. You then can arrange the windows listed on the Window menu in the work area with the **Window Arrange** command. To restrict from the window display any documents not part of the workbook, choose the Documents of **A**ctive Workbook check box (which replaces the Windows of **A**ctive Document when a workbook is active) in the Arrange Windows dialog box when you choose the desired Arrange option.

Figure 10.29 shows you a view of the **salebook.xlw** file after creating separate windows for the **recsale0.xls**, **recsale1.xls**, and **salebar.xlc** bound documents and tiling their windows in the work area.

When you are finished using a particular document window, you can close it by double-clicking its Control-menu button. If you want to save the windows and their current arrangement in the Excel work area, save the workbook file with the Save **W**orkbook command on the **File** menu. The next time you open the workbook file, the document windows in the current arrangement will be used to display the workbook.

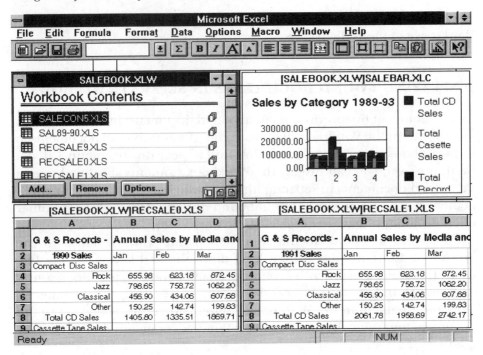

Figure 10.29 Displaying Bound Documents in Separate Document Windows

Tip After creating and arranging the separate windows for the bound documents in the workbook, you can change which bound document is displayed in any one of these document windows. First activate the window, then open the shortcut menu and choose the new document on this menu, or click the left paging or right paging icon until the desired document is displayed in the window.

Binding and Unbinding Documents in the Workbook

Initially, all documents that you add to a workbook are added as bound documents. To unbind a document so that it is not stored as part of the workbook file, you simply click the bound icon opposite the document's icon and filename in the Workbook Contents sheet; or you can select the document and then choose the Options command button at the bottom of this sheet and choose the Separate File (Unbound) option button in the Document Options dialog box.

Excel shows that a document is unbound by displaying the unbound icon (shown in Figure 10.30) across from its document icon and filename in the Workbook Contents sheet. To bind a document again, you click the unbound

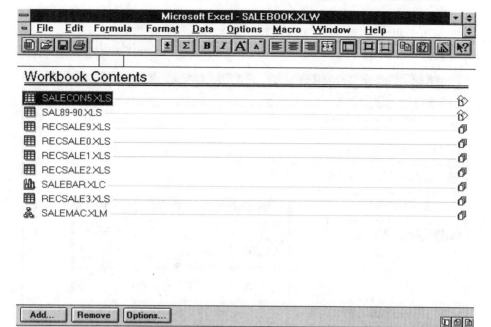

Figure 10.30   Workbook with an Unbound Document

icon across from the document's icon and filename (and the unbound icon immediately changes back to a bound icon); or you can select the document and then choose the Options command button at the bottom of this sheet and choose the **W**orkbook File (Bound) option button in the Document Options dialog box.

When you convert a document to an unbound document in the workbook, Excel no longer saves it as part of the workbook file. This means that you can include the file as part of another workbook or use the file as a single document.

GIVING EXTENDED NAMES TO BOUND DOCUMENTS

One reason for binding documents in a workbook file is that Excel allows you to give them extended names up to 31 characters long (including spaces). These extended names then appear not only in the listing in the Workbook Contents sheet but also in the title bar of each document window when the particular bound document is displayed on the screen.

To change the 11-character DOS filename to an extended name, you select the document's icon and filename in the Workbook Contents sheet, then choose the Options button and type in the extended name in the

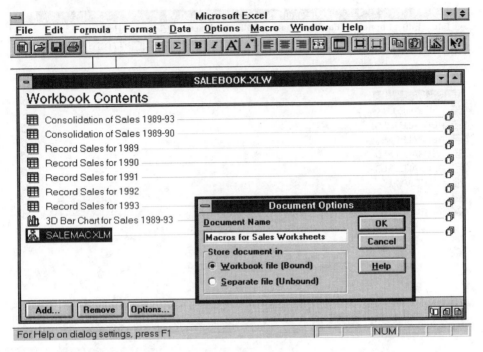

Figure 10.31   Workbook with a Document Option Dialog Box

Document Name text box. (The DOS filename is replaced as soon as you start typing the extended name.)

Figure 10.31 shows you the Workbook Contents sheet of the **sale-book.xlw** workbook after all but the last bound document in the workbook has been given extended names.

Alert! If you change a document's status from bound to unbound after giving a bound document an extended name, you will have to replace the extended name with a legitimate DOS filename (8-character main filename, plus a 3-character extension and no spaces) when the Save As dialog box appears after you choose the Yes button in the alert box asking if you want to save changes in the newly unbound document.

SUMMARY

In this chapter you learned several important techniques for working with multiple worksheet files. You learned how to create template files to generate new worksheets that require the same layout and similar formatting.

You learned how to perform group editing so that the edits that you make to one worksheet will be applied to all of the worksheets in the group. You then learned how to link worksheets so that changes that you make to the source worksheets are reflected automatically in the dependent worksheet. Finally you learned how to consolidate values from a group of worksheets and how to create workbooks to hold related documents that you regularly use together.

In the chapter ahead you will learn advanced techniques for performing extended data analysis. There you will learn how you can perform what-if analysis with data tables and the Scenario Manager. You will also learn how you can perform goal seeking with the Goal Seek and Solver commands.

11

Analyzing Worksheet Data

In an electronic spreadsheet such as Excel, "data analysis" involves several specialized tools for in-depth investigations of the relationships between different key data in a worksheet. The more traditional data analysis tools enable you to perform what-if (or sensitivity) analysis and goal seeking. In what-if analysis, you find out what effect changing various key input values in a worksheet model has on the outcome (that is, the "bottom line"). In goal seeking, you know the outcome you want to realize in the worksheet model and you have Excel find out what input values are required to achieve this outcome. In Excel 4.0 you can perform what-if analysis with the Data Table feature or with its new Scenario Manager. You perform simple goal seeking with the Goal Seek command and more complex goal seeking with the Solver command.

The Excel 4.0 Analysis ToolPak offers you some very powerful and specialized additional tools for analyzing statistical and engineering data. This ToolPak contains a wide variety of different tools for performing complex data analysis (including, among others, Anova, Histogram, F-test, t-test, Regression, Rank and Percentile, and Fourier analysis).

Many types of data analysis require an input range, consisting of a series of values, that are used as the variables in the data analysis. Before we move on to examine the use of the more prominent data analysis tools in Excel 4.0, we should take a moment to review Excel's methods for creating a data series.

> *Note:* Excel 4.0's new Crosstab command also enables you to perform data analysis on data stored in a database using its built-in database functions. See Chapter 16 for details on analyzing and cross-tabulating database data information.

Creating a Data Series

You are already familiar with using the AutoFill feature to create a data series in your worksheet. The AutoFill feature provides the quickest and most direct way to create a data series in Excel 4.0. To use the AutoFill feature, you need to enter the starting value in the data series in the first cell, then drag the Fill handle (the black-cross pointer that appears when you position the pointer in the lower-right corner of the cell) in a single direction (up, down, left, or right). Provided that the first cell contains an entry that Excel recognizes as starting a series (a month such as January, a day of the week such as Sunday, a date such as 5/3/93, a time such as 10:00 AM, or a modified value such as Quarter 1 or Store 1000), Excel then extends the series for you in the range that you select before you release the mouse button.

If you need to create a *linear series,* such as 1, 2, 3, 4, or 10, 50, 100, 150, you need to enter at least the first two values in the series and then select both values before you extend the series with the Fill handle. For example, to create a linear series that starts with the value 200 and then decreases each value by 5 in the cell range C2:A20, you would enter 200 in cell C2, 195 in cell C3, then select the range C2:C3 and use the Fill handle to extend the range down to C20, as shown in Figure 11.1.

> *Tip* You can force Excel to copy values into adjacent rows or columns that the program would otherwise extend as a series by holding down the Ctrl key as you drag the Fill handle to select the cell range into which the initial should be copied. For example, if you want to copy the label June across a row rather than create a monthly series (June, July, August, and so on), you hold down the Ctrl key as you drag the Fill handle. Excel indicates the AutoFill operation will copy rather than extend the series by adding a plus (+) sign to the Fill handle icon.

The AutoFill feature is more than adequate for creating most series you will need when creating and analyzing your worksheets. But in some situations you will need to use the Data Series command rather than the AutoFill feature. These situations arise when you need to create a *growth series* (that is, one where each value is multiplied by a constant) rather than

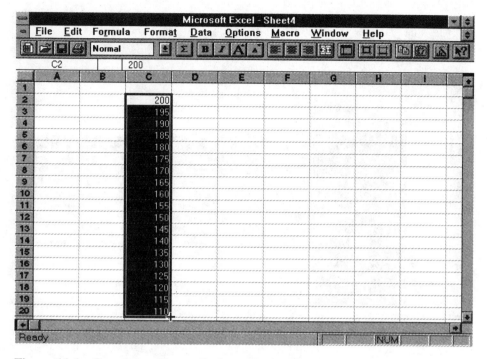

Figure 11.1   Creating a Linear Series with the Fill Handle

a linear series and when you are creating a large series that you want to stop at a particular value.

To build a series with the Data Series command, you follow these steps:

1. Enter the starting value of the series in the cell that you want to be the first in the data series. If you need to build several data series that extend across several adjacent rows of the worksheet, enter starting values in the column at the beginning of the rows you want to fill. If you need to build several data series that extend down several adjacent columns of the worksheet, enter starting values across the row at the top of the columns you want to fill.

2. Select the cell range that you want filled with the series. The cell range for the data series can extend from initial value(s) across row(s) or down column(s) of the worksheet.

3. Choose the Series command on the **D**ata menu. Excel displays the Series dialog box (shown in Figure 11.2).

4. Check to make sure that the option button in the Series in the section of the dialog box matches the way you want Excel to extend the data series. Use the **R**ows option if you have starting values in the cells

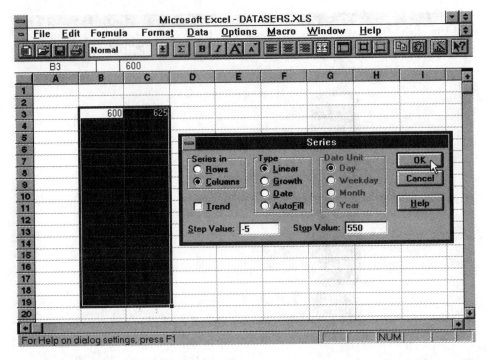

Figure 11.2 The Series Dialog Box

down the first column of the selected range. Use the **C**olumns option if you have starting values in cells across the top row of the selected range.

5. Choose the type of series you want to create in the Type section of the dialog box. By default, Excel selects the **L**inear option, which adds the value in the **S**tep Value text box to the initial value(s) in the selected range. To have the initial value(s) multiplied by the value in the **S**tep Value text box, you would choose the **G**rowth option. To specify that a date unit be added to the starting date value in the **S**tep Value text box, select the **D**ate option, then choose the appropriate unit (**D**ay, **W**eekday, **M**onth, or **Y**ear) in the Date Unit section of the dialog box. To have Excel ignore the step value and fill in the blanks in the range based on the initial value(s) by using the AutoFill feature, select the Auto **F**ill option button.

6. If you entered a single starting value in the selected range, Excel uses a step value of 1. If you entered multiple values across the row or down the column, Excel may display the difference between these values as the step value. To have the program use another step value, enter the value in the **S**tep Value text box. Note that the step value

that you enter here can be positive or negative.

7. Normally, Excel extends the data series until the program has filled the last cell in the selected cell range. To have Excel stop when it has reached a certain value even if the entire range is not filled, select the Stop Value text box and enter the last value of the data series. If you are creating a data series in which each subsequent value in the series decreases instead of increases, be sure that the stop value you enter is smaller than the initial value(s) in the worksheet.

8. Select the OK button or press the Enter key to confirm the data series in your worksheet.

Figure 11.3 shows you an example of two adjacent data series created with the Data Series command. Both these series decrease each value in the column by 5, stopping at the value 550. (Note that adding this stop value prevents Excel from completely filling either column in the cell selection.) To create this data series, you would enter 600 in cell B3 and 625 in cell C3, then select the cell range B3:C19 Next you open the Series dialog box and change the Series in option from **R**ows to **C**olumns, enter the –5 in the Step Value text box and 550 in the Stop Value text box before choosing the OK button.

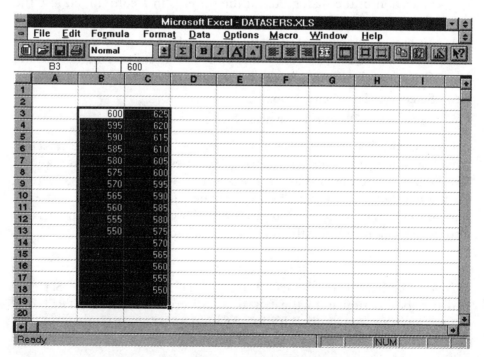

Figure 11.3   Data Entered with the Data Series Command

Creating Trend or Forecast Series

You can create two types of trend or forecast series with Excel 4.0: linear or growth (also known as an exponential trend). To create a linear forecast series, you use the AutoFill feature. To create either a linear or growth best-fit trend series, you use the Data Series command.

To create a linear forecast with the AutoFill feature, enter the first three or more values in the series in an adjacent cell range, then drag the Fill handle to extend the series by extending the cell range, either across adjacent columns or down adjacent rows. When you release the mouse button, Excel fills in the linear forecast series in the cell selection based on the initial values you entered.

To create a linear or growth best-fit trend series with the Data Series command, you follow these steps:

1. Enter all the values you want to fit within the trend in a row or column of the worksheet and then select them.

2. Choose the **S**eries command on the **D**ata menu to open the Series dialog box.

3. If the series is in a row, choose the **R**ows option button in the Series in section of the dialog box. If the series is in a column, choose the **C**olumns option button instead.

4. To create a linear best-fit trend, choose the **L**inear option button in the Type section. To create a exponential best-fit trend, choose the **G**rowth option button instead.

5. Select the **T**rend check box.

6. Choose the OK button or press Enter.

Excel creates the best-fit trend in the range of values you've selected. Note that when you create a linear or growth best-fit trend in this manner, Excel changes the initial value in the selection to produce a best-fit trend for the selected cell range. (When you create a forecast series with the Fill handle, the program never changes the initial values in the range.) Note also that best-fit trends use the method of least squares.

> ***Note:*** The best-fit trend created with the Trend option in the Series dialog box is similar to the best-fit trend created with the TREND function. (See Appendix B for information on using this function.)

What-if Analysis with Data Tables

As you are already aware, you can see the effect of changing an input value on the result returned by a formula as soon as you enter a new input value in the cell that feeds into the formula. Each time you change this input value, Excel automatically recalculates the formula and shows you the new result based on the new value. This method is of limited use, however, when you are performing what-if or sensitivity analysis and need to be able to see the range of results produced by using a series of different input values in the same worksheet so that you can compare them to each other.

To perform this type of what-if analysis, you can use Excel's Data Table command. When creating a data table, you enter a series of input values in the worksheet, and Excel uses each of them in the formula you specify. When Excel is finished computing the data table, you see the results produced by each change in the input values in a single range of the worksheet. You can then save the data table as part of the worksheet if you need to keep a record of the results of a series of input values.

You can create one-variable or two-variable data tables. In a one-variable data table, Excel substitutes a series of different values for a single input value in a formula. In a two-variable data table, Excel substitutes a series of different values for two input values in a formula.

Creating a One-variable Data Table

To create a one-variable data table, you need to set up the master formula in your worksheet and then, in a different range of the worksheet, enter the series of different values that you want substituted for a single input value in that formula. Figures 11.4 and 11.5 show you how this is done.

In Figure 11.4, cell B5 contains a simple formula for computing the projected sales for 1994, assuming an annual growth rate of 3 percent over the annual sales in 1993. The 1994 projected sales in this cell are calculated with the formula

```
=Sales_93+(Sales_93*Growth_94)
```

which adds cell B2 (named Sales_93) to the contents of B2 multiplied by the growth rate of 3 percent in cell B3 (named Growth_94). Cell B5 shows you that assuming an annual growth rate of 3 percent in 1994, you can project total sales of $355,350.

But what if the growth rate in 1994 is not as high as 3 percent, or what if the growth rate is even higher than anticipated? To create the one-variable

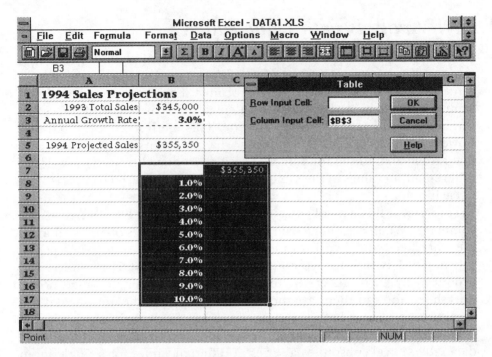

Figure 11.4   Creating a One-variable Data Table

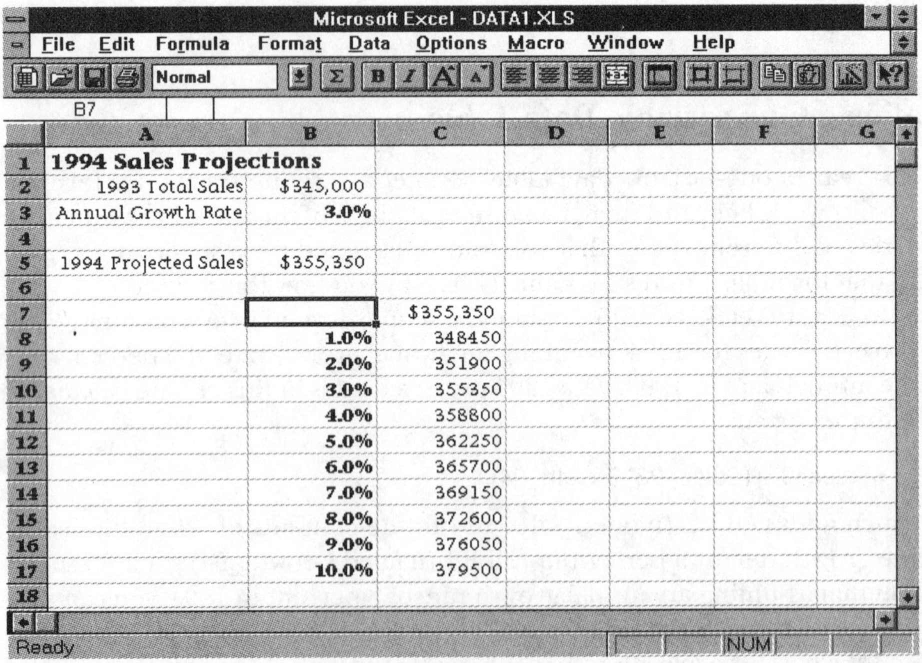

Figure 11.5   Completed One-variable Data Table

table to answer these questions, you first bring forward the master formula in cell B5 to cell C7 with the formula

   =B5

Then you enter the series of different growth rates as the input values in column B, starting in cell B8. (Cell B7, at the intersection of the row with the master formula and the column with the input values, must be left blank in a one-variable data table.) This series of input values for the data table can be created with the AutoFill feature or with the Data Series command. (See "Creating a Data Series" earlier in this chapter.) In this example, a data series that increments each succeeding value by 1 percent is created in the cell range B8:B17, starting at 1 percent and ending at 10 percent.

After bringing the formula in cell B5 forward to cell C7 and entering the growth rate series in the cell range B8:B17, you then select the cell range B7:C17 and choose the **T**able command on the **D**ata menu. The blank cell range C8:C17 is the cell range where Excel put the projected sales figures based on the growth rate entered in the comparable cell in column B.

Excel opens the Table dialog box where you must specify the row input cell in the **R**ow Input Cell text box and/or the column input cell in the **C**olumn Input Cell. The cell that you designate as the row or column input cell in the Table dialog box must correspond to the cell in the worksheet that contains the original input value that is fed into the master formula.

In the data table in this example, you only need to designate B3 as the column input cell. (When you click this cell or use an arrow key to select it, as is the case in Figure 11.4, Excel enters the absolute cell reference as in $B$3.) You choose cell B3 because this is the cell that contains the growth rate value used in the master formula.

After indicating the row or column input cells, Excel computes the data table when you choose the OK button or press Enter. In this example, the program creates the data table by substituting each input value in the data series in the range B8:B17 for the column input cell B3. It is then used in the master formula to calculate a new result, which is entered in the corresponding cell in the cell range C8:C1. When the program is finished calculating the data table, Excel returns the original value to the row or column input cell (3.0% in cell B3 in this case).

Figure 11.5 shows the completed data table. There you can see at a glance the effect on the projected sales for 1994 of changing a single percentage point for the growth rate. After creating the data table, you can then format the results and save the table as part of the worksheet.

If you want to see the effect of using a different range of variables, you need only to enter the new input values in the existing range. By default,

Excel automatically recalculates the results in the output range of a data table whenever you change any of its input values. If you want to control when each data table is recalculated, while still allowing the formulas in the worksheet to be recalculated automatically, choose the **C**alculation command on the **O**ptions menu and then select the Automatic Except **T**ables option button in the Calculation section.

Excel computes the results in a data table by creating an array formula that uses the TABLE function. (For specific information on this macro function, refer to Appendix C.) In this example, the array formula

    {=TABLE(,B3)}

is entered into the cell range C8:C17. The TABLE function can take two arguments, *row_ref* and/or *column_ref*, which represent the row input cell and column input cell for the data table, respectively. In this example, the data table uses only a column input cell, so B3 is the second and only argument of the TABLE function. Because Excel enters the results in a data table using an array formula, you can't clear individual result cells in its output range. If you try to delete a single result in the data table, Excel displays an alert dialog box telling you that you cannot change part of a table.

If you want to delete just the results in the output range of a data table, you must select all of the cells in the output range (cell range C8:C17 in the current example) before you press the Delete key or choose the **E**dit Clear command. If you want to delete the entire data table, you can select the entire array by pressing Ctrl+/ (slash) before you press the Delete key or choose the **E**dit Clear command.

Creating a Two-variable Data Table

To see the effect of changing two of a master formula's input values, you create a two-variable data table. When you do so, you enter two ranges of input values to substitute in the master formula: A single-row range in the first row of the table and a single-column range in the first column of the data table. When you create a two-variable data table, you place a copy of the master formula in the cell at the intersection of this row and column of input values.

Figure 11.6 shows the typical setup for a two-variable data table. This figure uses the projected sales worksheet shown earlier in the section on a one-variable data table. However, here a second variable has been added to projecting the total sales in 1994. This worksheet contains a value in cell B4 (named Expenses_94) that shows the projected percentage of expenses to sales. This formula is used, in turn, in the master formula in cell B5 as follows:

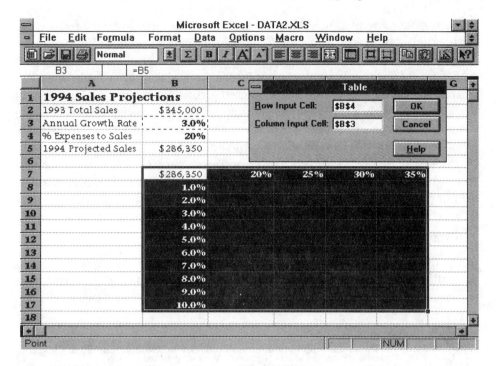

Figure 11.6 Creating a Two-variable Data Table

=Sales_93+(Sales_93*Growth_94)—(Sales_93*Expenses_94)

Note that when you factor in the expenses, the projected sales at an annual growth rate of 3 percent falls in cell B5 from $355,350 to $286,350.

To determine what effect changing both the growth rate and the percentage of expenses to sales will have on the projected sales for 1994, you create a two-variable data table. In setting up this table, you still enter the variable growth rates down column B in the cell range B8:B17. Then you enter the variable expense rates across row 7 in the range C7:F7. This time you bring forward the master formula by entering the formula

=B5

in cell B7, the cell at the intersection of the row and column containing the two input variables.

After setting up the two series of variables in this manner, you are ready to create the table by selecting the cell range B7:F17 and opening the Table dialog box, as shown in Figure 11.6. For a two-variable data table, you must designate both a row input and a column cell in the worksheet. In this example, the row input cell is B4, which contains the original expense-to-sales percentage, while the column input cell remains B3, which contains the original growth rate. Once these two input cells are entered in the Table dialog box, you are ready to generate the data table by choosing the OK button or pressing Enter.

Figure 11.7 shows you the completed two-variable data table with the results of changing both the projected growth rate and the projected expenses. As with a one-variable data table, you can save this two-variable data table as part of your worksheet. You can also have the table updated by changing any of the (two types) of input variables.

The array formula entered in the output range (C8:F17) to create this two-variable data table is very similar to the one created earlier for the one-variable data table, only this time the TABLE function uses both a *row_ref* and *column_ref* argument, as in

   {=TABLE(B4,B3)}

Remember that because this data table used an array formula, you must select all the cells in the output range if you want to delete them. Also, you can select the entire data table (B7:F17) by pressing Ctrl+/ (slash).

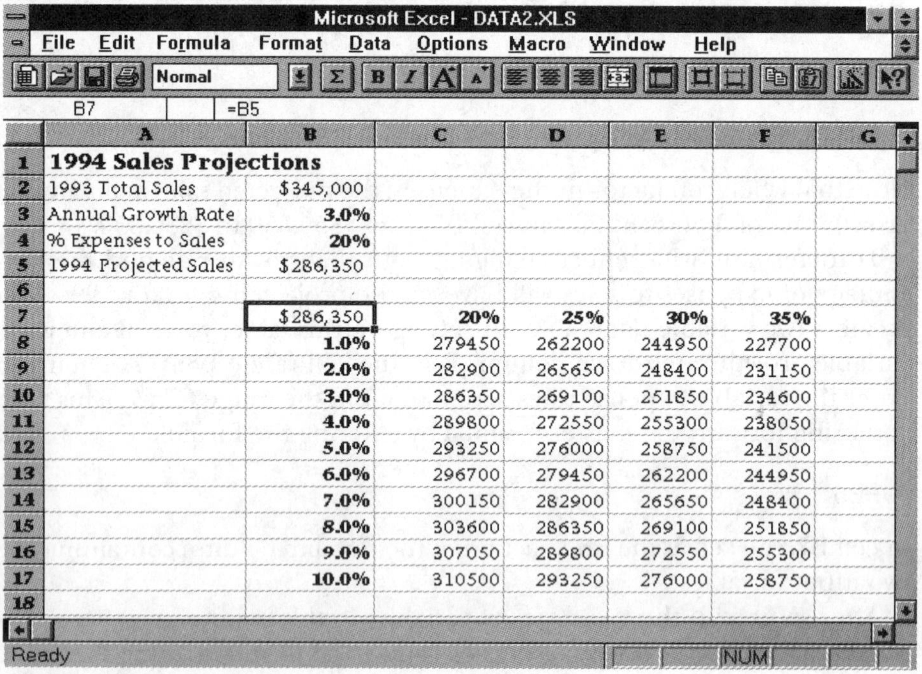

	Microsoft Excel - DATA2.XLS					
File Edit Formula Format Data Options Macro Window Help						
B7	=B5					

	A	B	C	D	E	F	G
1	**1994 Sales Projections**						
2	1993 Total Sales	$345,000					
3	Annual Growth Rate	3.0%					
4	% Expenses to Sales	20%					
5	1994 Projected Sales	$286,350					
6							
7		$286,350	20%	25%	30%	35%	
8		1.0%	279450	262200	244950	227700	
9		2.0%	282900	265650	248400	231150	
10		3.0%	286350	269100	251850	234600	
11		4.0%	289800	272550	255300	238050	
12		5.0%	293250	276000	258750	241500	
13		6.0%	296700	279450	262200	244950	
14		7.0%	300150	282900	265650	248400	
15		8.0%	303600	286350	269100	251850	
16		9.0%	307050	289800	272550	255300	
17		10.0%	310500	293250	276000	258750	
18							

Ready   NUM

Figure 11.7   Completed Two-variable Data Table

Using the Scenario Manager

In Excel 4.0 you can create and save sets of input values that produce different results as *scenarios* with the new Scenario Manager command. A scenario consists of a group of input values in a worksheet to which you assign a name, such as *Best Case, Worst Case*, and the like. To reuse the input data and view the results it produces in the worksheet, you simply select the name of the scenario you want to use. Excel applies the input values stored in that scenario to the appropriate cells in the worksheet. After creating your different scenarios for a worksheet, you can also use the Scenario Manager to create a summary report showing you both the input values stored in each scenario as well as key results produced by each.

The Scenario Manager command is added to the bottom portion of the Formula menu, assuming that you performed a complete installation when installing Excel 4.0. If you open the Formula menu and don't see the Scenario Manager command listed there, you will need to return to the Windows Program Manager and run the Excel 4.0 Setup program again to install this add-in macro. Once installed, this add-in macro sheet is called **scenario.xla** and is located in the **library** directory under the **c:\excel** directory.

Creating Scenarios

When creating a scenario for your worksheet, you must indicate the input cells that you want to change in each scenario (appropriately enough, called *changing cells*.) To make it easier to identify the changing cells in each scenario (especially in any scenario summary reports you generate), you should assign range names to the input cells with the Define Name or Create Names command before you create your scenarios.

To create your scenarios with the Scenario Manager, follow these steps:

1. Choose the Scenario Manager command on the Formula menu to open the Scenario Manager dialog box (similar to the one shown in Figure 11.8).

2. Indicate all the changing cells in the scenarios in the **C**hanging Cells text box. If you've named the changing cells, type in their names separated by commas in the **C**hanging Cells text box. You can also select the cells directly in the worksheet with the pointer. To select nonadjacent cells, hold down the Ctrl key as you click the changing cell you want to add.

3. Choose the Add command button to open the Add Scenario dialog box, similar to the one shown in Figure 11.9. The Add Scenario dialog

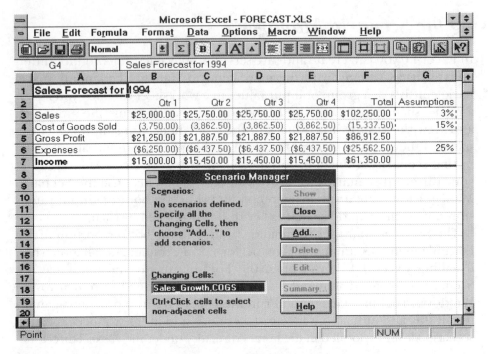

Figure 11.8 The Scenario Manager Dialog Box

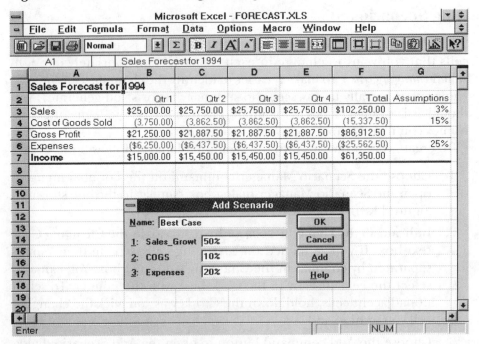

Figure 11.9 The Add Scenario Dialog Box

box contains a **N**ame text box and numbered text boxes for each of the changing cells you identified.

4. Type the name for your new scenario in the **N**ame text box.

5. Enter the values you want to use in this scenario in the numbered text boxes for each of the changing cells that you identified in the worksheet.

6. When you've finishing entering values for all of the changing cells you need to modify in the Add Scenario dialog box, choose the **A**dd command button. Excel adds the scenario to the Scenarios list and clears the **N**ame text box in the Add Scenario dialog box.

7. Repeat steps 5 and 6 to add all the other scenarios you want to create.

8. Choose the OK button in the Add Scenario dialog box to close the dialog box and return to the Scenario Manager dialog box.

When you return to the Scenario Manager dialog box, you will see the names of all the scenarios you added listed in the Scenarios list box. For example, in Figure 11.10, you see that three scenarios, Best Case, Worst Case, and Most Likely Case, are now listed in the Scenarios list box.

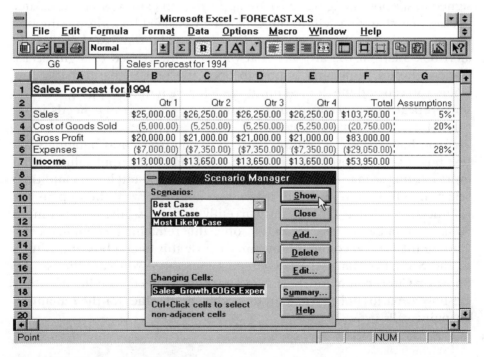

Figure 11.10 Showing Different Scenarios

To show a particular scenario in the worksheet that uses the values you entered for the changing cells, you simply need to double-click the scenario name in this list box or select the name and choose the Show command button. Figure 11.10 shows the results in the sample forecast worksheet after selecting the Most Likely Case scenario.

If, after creating the scenarios for your worksheet, you find that you need to use different input values or want to add or remove scenarios, you can edit the scenarios in the Scenario Manager dialog box. To modify the scenario's name and/or the input values assigned to the changing cells of that scenario, open the Scenario Manager dialog box, select the scenario name in the Scenarios list box, then make the appropriate changes in the Edit Scenario dialog box. To remove a scenario from a worksheet, select the scenario's name in the Scenarios list box and then choose the **D**elete command button. Note, however, that if you delete a scenario in error, you cannot restore it with the Undo Clear command. Instead, you must recreate the scenario using the **A**dd command button as outlined above.

You can also add or delete the changing cells in the **C**hanging Cells text box in the Scenario Manager dialog box. Note, however, that any changes you make to the changing cells (as opposed to changing the values assigned to specific changing cells) are applied to all existing scenarios. After adding new changing cells to the **C**hanging Cells text box, choose the first scenario in the list, then select the **E**dit command button. Excel displays an alert box asking if you are sure that you want the revised changing cells. Choose the OK command button to open the Edit Scenario dialog box where you can add the desired input value for each new changing cell. You must repeat this procedure for every existing scenario that needs input values for the new changing cell(s).

If you have deleted a cell reference or name from the **C**hanging Cells text box, Excel removes this changing cell (and all its input values) from every existing scenario. Simply choose the **E**dit command button and then select the OK button in the alert box that appears. Excel then opens the Edit Scenario dialog box for the currently selected scenario; this time it contains numbered text boxes for only the remaining changing cells. Choose the Cancel command button to close this dialog box and return to the Scenario Manager dialog box. From there you can choose the **S**how or Close command button. (There is no need to edit the other existing scenarios unless you want to modify input values for the remaining changing cells.)

Generating a Summary Report

After creating the different scenarios for your worksheet, you can use the Scenario Manager to create a summary report that shows the changing values used in each scenario and, if you wish, key resulting values each produces. To produce a summary report, you open the Scenario Manager dialog box, then choose the **Su**mmary command button. Excel opens a Scenario Summary dialog box similar to the one shown in Figure 11.11 There you may designate a cell selection of result cells in the **R**esult Cells text box to be included in the report. After selecting the result cells for the report, you simply choose the OK button to have Excel generate the summary report and display it in a new worksheet window.

In the example shown in Figure 11.11, the cell range B7:F7 containing the projected income figures for the sales forecast are designated as the result cells to be included in the summary report. Figure 11.12 shows the actual summary report generated for this sample worksheet in a new document window. Note that because all the changing and result cells in this worksheet were named, the summary report uses their range names in place of their cell references. Also, when the Scenario Manager generates a

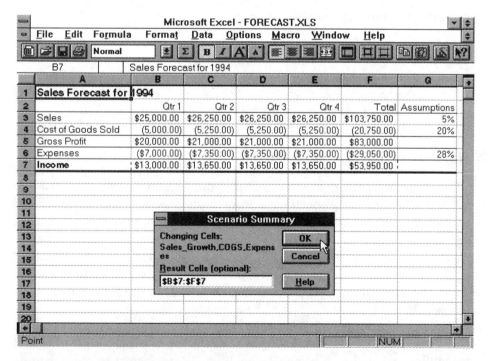

Figure 11.11 The Scenario Summary Dialog Box

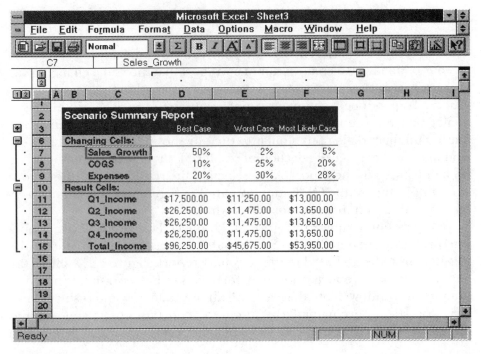

Figure 11.12   Scenario Summary Report

summary report, it automatically outlines the summary data, creating
two vertical levels, one for the changing cells and another for the result
cells.

After generating a summary report, you can save it with the **File Save As**
command and/or print it with the **File Print** command.

Using the What If Add-In Macro

When you don't need to save the individual scenarios, you can use the
What If add-in macro to perform sensitivity analysis on your data instead of
the Scenario Manager. When you use the What **If** command, you can test a
succession of various input values in particular formulas to determine the
different outcomes. To do this, you create a new data sheet that contains all
of the input values that you want to substitute in your worksheet model.
Then the What **If** command applies each of these variable inputs in your
worksheet.

Before you can use the What **If** command, you must open the whatif.xla
file. This What If add-in macro sheet runs the macro that adds the What If
capability to Excel and attaches the What **If** command to the **Formula**
menu. (For more on customizing Excel with add-in macros, see Chapter 20.)

To use the What If add-in macro to create a new data sheet containing the various input values you want tested in a worksheet, follow these steps:

1. Open the Formula menu and choose the What If command. (This command will appear between the **O**utline and **G**oal Seek commands if the What If add-in macro is running.)

2. If the What **I**f command is not displayed on the Formula menu, close this menu and select the **O**pen command on the **F**ile menu instead (or click the Open file tool on the Standard toolbar or press Ctrl+F12). Double-click the library folder in the **D**irectories list box to open this directory, then double-click whatif.xla in the File **N**ame list box to open this macro sheet and run this add-in macro. After you open this file, you can now select the What **I**f command on the Formula menu to open the What If dialog box (shown in Figure 11.13). If this whatif.xla file does not appear in the File **N**ame list box when you select the c:\excel\library directory, you have to run the Excel Setup program to install it.

3. Choose the **N**ew command button in the What If dialog box to create a new data sheet.

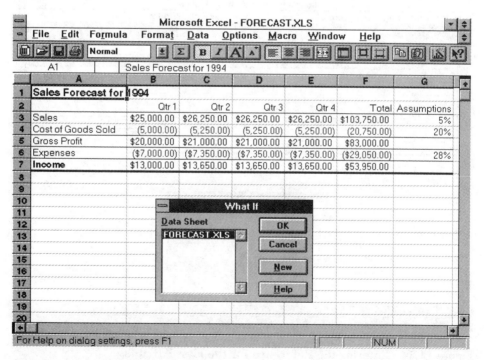

Figure 11.13 The What If Dialog Box

4. Enter the range name or cell reference for the first variable that you want to test in the text box of the What If Variable dialog box as shown in Figure 11.14, then choose the OK button.

5. Enter the first value you want tested for the first variable in the text box of the What If Variable dialog box as shown in Figure 11.15, then choose the OK button.

6. Repeat step 5, each time entering successive values that you want tested for the first variable. After you've entered the last test value as indicated in step 5, choose the **D**one command button.

7. Excel then prompts you to enter the range name or cell reference for the second variable that you want to test in the text box of the What If Variable box. Repeat the procedure outlined in steps 4 through 6 to define the second variable and its input values.

8. Repeat step 7 until you have defined all of the variables that you want tested in your worksheet. After you've finished defining the last variable and its input values, choose the **D**one command button to close the What If Variable dialog box.

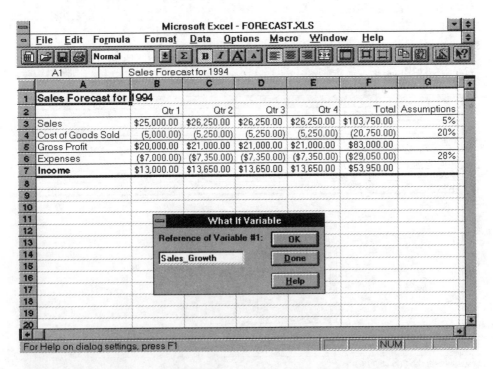

Figure 11.14   Entering the Reference for the First Variable

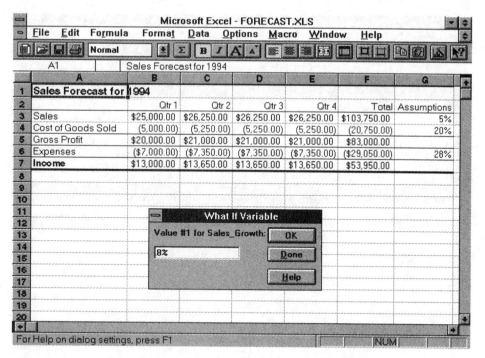

Figure 11.15 Entering the Input Value for the First Variable

After creating a data sheet that holds your various input values, you can then test the values in your worksheet by activating the document window and pressing Ctrl+Shift+T. Figure 11.16 shows you the data sheet created for the sales forecast worksheet introduced earlier. In this example, three different input values were defined for the three variables, Sales_Growth (cell G3) COGS (cell G4), and Expenses (cell G6). These input values are stored in the data sheet placed in the Sheet2 document window (shown below the document window with the forecast worksheet in the figure). As you can see, Excel has arranged the input values for the three variables in the data sheet as a table.

The first cell of this table tells you the number of variables defined in the data sheet (3 in this example). This number is followed by the names (or cell references, if you didn't use range names) of the variables you defined in the data sheet. The numbers in the cells beneath these variable references indicate which input values have been substituted in the active worksheet. The number 1 in Figure 11.16 indicates that the original values are still used in the forecast worksheet. Beneath these numbers, you see the actual input values that you defined for each variable.

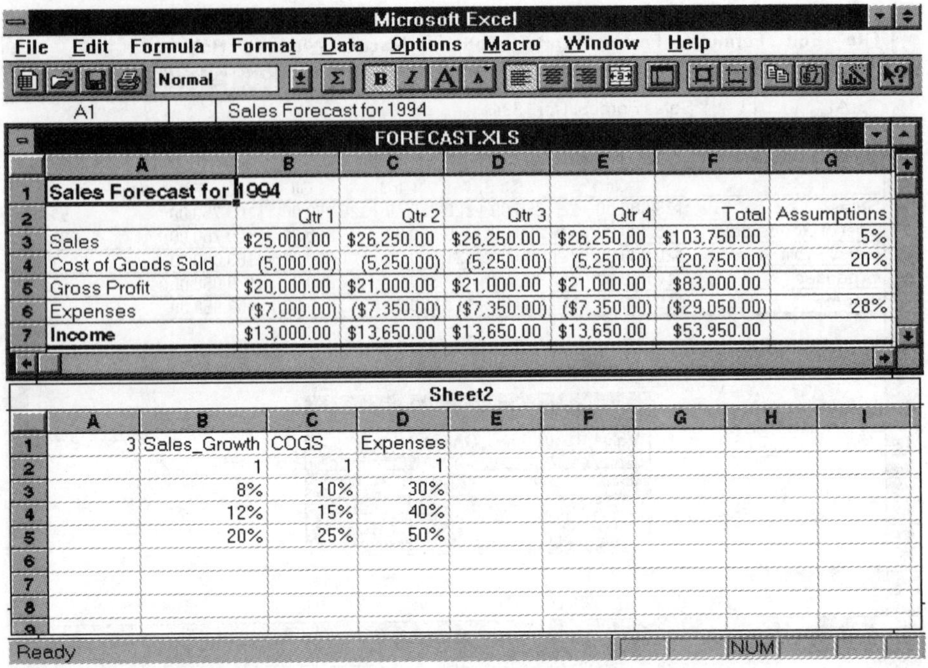

Figure 11.16   Forecast Worksheet with Data Sheet

When you press Ctrl+Shift+T, Excel substitutes the first input value for the Sales_Growth variable in the forecast worksheet (and the number below Sales_Growth changes to 2). When you press this key combination again, Excel substitutes the second input value for the Sales_Growth variable (and its number increases to 3). The next time you press these keys, the program substitutes the third input value for the Sales_Growth variable (and the number changes to 4).

After that, when you press Ctrl+Shift+T, Excel switches to the second column of the table and substitutes the first value for the COGS variable (and its number changes from 1 to 2). The next time you press this key combination, the program switches back to the Sales_Growth variable and substitutes the second input value in the forecast worksheet without changing the value in the COGS cell (as shown in Figure 11.17). After that, Excel substitutes the third Sales_Growth input value, again without changing the input values for the COGS cell.

After testing the first COGS input value with all of the Sales_Growth input values, the program then switches to the second COGS input value. As you continue to press Ctrl+Shift+T, Excel tests this second COGS value with the other two Sales_Growth inputs. You can continue in this manner, pressing Ctrl+Shift+T to test all of the possible input value combinations in your

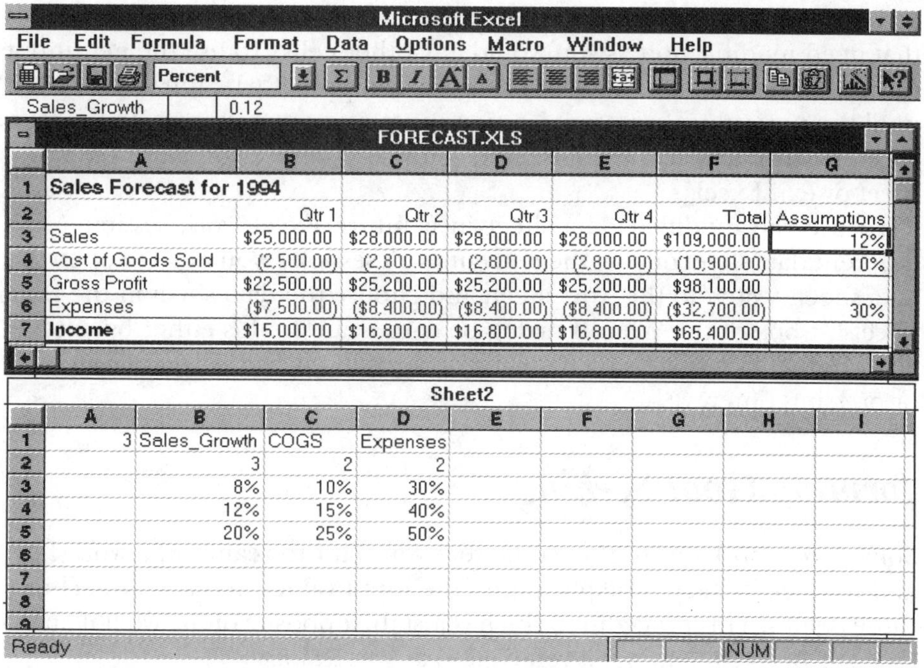

Figure 11.17 **Forecast Worksheet After Substituting Values from the Data Sheet**

worksheet. When you see a combination that you want to save, you can use the **File Save As** command to save the worksheet with those values. If you want to be able to reuse the data sheet with the What If add-in macro at a later time, be sure to activate its document window and use **File Save** to save this worksheet file as well.

Advancing Through the Values for a Single Variable

As you press Ctrl+Shift+T, Excel pairs different input values from different variables defined on the data sheet. If you would rather cycle through the input values for a single variable, you can do this instead. Simply activate the worksheet and select the input cells where the substitutions are to be made. Then press Ctrl+T instead of Ctrl+Shift+T. Excel substitutes each of the input values in the data sheet in succession for just that variable.

Editing a Data Sheet

Once you've created a data sheet using the What If Variable dialog box, you can then change its input values just by editing the data sheet itself. Simply activate the data sheet and then edit the cells containing the input values that need modification as you would any other cells. To use the new input values, activate the worksheet once again and press Ctrl+Shift+T or Ctrl+T until the new values are used. If you want to save your changes to the data sheet, be sure to select the **File Save** command before you close the worksheet or exit Excel.

To use the modified data sheet in a future Excel work session (or a different data sheet during the current work session), you need to open the data sheet, switch to the worksheet, and choose the data sheet in the **Data Sheet** list box of the What If dialog box. You can do this either by double-clicking the data sheet's filename or by selecting it and then choosing OK or pressing Enter.

Performing Goal Seeking

Sometimes you know the outcome that you want to realize in a worksheet and you need Excel to help you find the input values necessary to achieve those results. This procedure, which is just the opposite of the what-if analysis we've been examining, is referred to as *goal seeking*.

When you simply need to find the value for a single variable that will give the desired result in a particular formula, the Goal Seek command is appropriate to use. If you have charted the data and created a two-dimensional column, bar, or line chart, you can also perform the goal seeking by directly manipulating the appropriate marker on the chart. And when you need to perform more complex goal seeking, such as that which involves changing multiple input values to realize a result or constraining the values to a specific range, you can use the Solver command.

Using the Goal Seek Command

To use the Goal Seek command, you simply select the cell containing the formula that will return the result you are seeking (referred to as the *set cell*), indicate what value you want this formula to return, and then indicate the location of the input value that Excel can change to return the desired result. Figures 11.18 and 11.19 illustrate how you can use the Goal Seek command to find how much sales must increase to realize a first-quarter income of $20,000 (given certain growth, cost of goods sold, and expense assumptions).

To do this, first select cell B7, which contains the formula that calculates the first-quarter income, before you choose the Goal Seek command on the Formula menu to open the Goal Seek dialog box (similar to the one shown in Figure 11.18). Because cell B7 is the active cell when you open this dialog

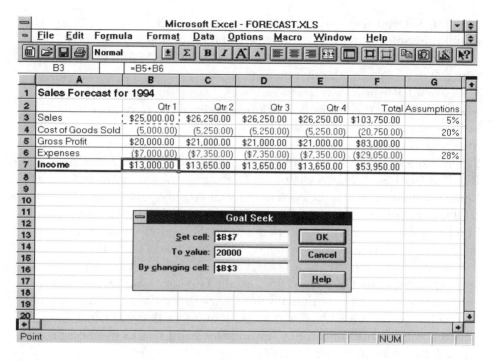

Figure 11.18   The Goal Seek Dialog Box

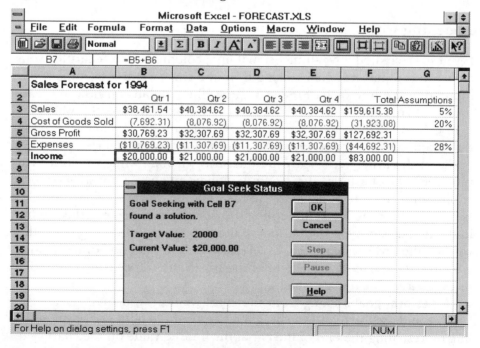

Figure 11.19 The Goal Seek Status Dialog Box

box, the **S**et cell text box already contains the cell reference $B$7. You would then select the To **v**alue text box and enter **20000** as the goal. Then you select the By changing cell text box and select cell **B3** in the worksheet (the cell that contains the first-quarter sales).

Figure 11.19 shows you the Goal Seek Status dialog box that appears when you choose the OK button or press Enter in the Goal Seek dialog box to have Excel go ahead and adjust the sales figure to reach your desired income figure. As you can see, Excel increases the sales in cell B3 from $25,000 to $38,461.54, which, in turn, returns $20,000 as the income in cell B7. The Goal Seek Status dialog box informs you that goal seeking has found a solution and that the current value and target value are now the same. (If this were not the case, the Step and Pause buttons in the dialog box would become active, and Excel could perform further iterations to try to narrow and ultimately eliminate the gap between the target and current values.)

If you want to keep the values entered in the worksheet as a result of goal seeking, choose the OK button to close the Goal Seek Status dialog box. If you want to return to the original values, choose the Cancel button instead. If you change the value by selecting OK, remember that you can still switch between the "before" and "after" input values and results by choosing the Undo Goal Seek command (Ctrl+Z).

Goal Seeking with Charts

If you have created a two-dimensional line, column, or bar chart for your data, you can perform goal seeking from the chart window by directly manipulating the line or bar. (See Chapter 12 for details on how to create these types of charts.) Figures 11.20 and 11.21 illustrate how this works.

In Figure 11.20, you see a two-dimensional bar chart in a chart window that graphs the projected sales and income for all four quarters. The top bar in each cluster represents the quarterly income, while the lower bar represents the quarterly sales. To find out how much sales must increase to realize an income of $20,000 in the first quarter, you hold down the Ctrl key as you click the bar representing the first-quarter income (the top bar in the first cluster near the bottom of the bar chart). When you select this bar with the Ctrl key depressed, Excel selects only this bar and draws handles around it. One handle at the end of the bar in the center handle is a solid black square. (The rest are white.)

To perform goal seeking from the chart window, you then release the Ctrl key and use the pointer to drag the black handle until you position the line representing the end of the bar at the desired value on the chart grid. (In this example, you drag the pointer to the vertical gridline marked

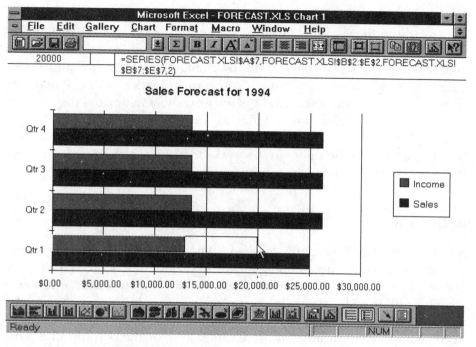

Figure 11.20   Goal Seeking with a Chart

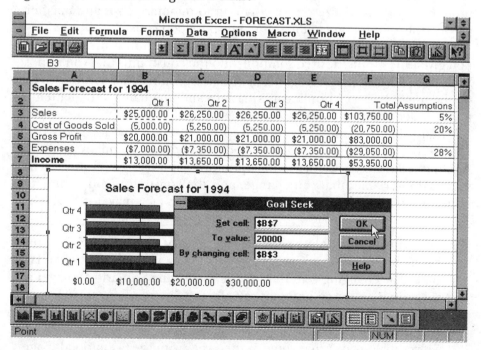

Figure 11.21   The Goal Seek Dialog Box

$20,000.00.) When you release the mouse button, Excel automatically returns you to the worksheet window and opens the Goal Seek dialog box with the **S**et cell and To **v**alue text boxes already filled in. To perform the goal seeking, you simply choose the By **c**hanging cell text box and designate the worksheet cell to change (as shown in Figure 11.21). When you choose the OK button, Excel changes the worksheet values and displays the Goal Seek Status dialog box (similar to the one shown earlier in Figure 11.19). When you choose the OK button in the Goal Seek Status dialog box, Excel changes the values in the worksheet and the chart and automatically returns you to the chart window.

Using the Solver

Although the Data Table and Goal Seek commands work just fine for simple problems that require determining the direct relationship between the inputs and results in a formula, you need to use the Solver when dealing with more complex problems. For example, you would use the Solver to find the best solution when you need to change multiple input values in your model and you need to impose constraints on these values and/or the output value. The Solver can help you with classic resource problems, such as finding the correct product mix to maximize returns, staffing to minimize costs and maximize productivity, and routing to minimize transportation costs.

The Solver works by applying iterative methods to find the "best" solution given the inputs, desired solution, and the constraints that you impose. With each iteration, the program applies a trial-and-error method (based on the use of linear or nonlinear equations and inequalities) that attempts to get closer to the optimum solution.

When using the Solver, you need to keep in mind that for many problems, especially the more complicated ones, there are many solutions. Although the Solver returns the optimum solution, given the starting values, the variables that can change, and the constraints you define, this solution is often not the only one possible and, in fact, may not be the best

Tip You can use the Solver with the Scenario Manager to help set up a problem to solve or to save a solution so that you can view it at a later date. The changing cells that you define for the Scenario Manager are picked up and used automatically by the Solver when you select this command, and vice versa. Also, you can save the Solver's solution to a problem as a scenario (by choosing the **S**ave Scenario button in the Solver dialog box) that you can then view with the Scenario Manager.

solution for you. To be sure that you are finding the best solution, you may want to run the Solver more than once, adjusting the initial values each time you solve the problem.

When setting the problem in your worksheet model to be solved by the Solver, you define the following items:

- The *target cell*, which is the cell in your worksheet whose value is to be maximized, minimized, or made to reach a particular value.

- The *changing cells*, which are the cells in your worksheet whose values are to be adjusted until the answer is found.

- The *constraints*, which are the limits you impose on the changing values and/or the target cell.

After you finish defining the problem with these parameters and you have the Solver solve the problem, the program returns the optimum solution by modifying the values in your worksheet. At that point, you can choose to retain the changes in the worksheet or restore the original values. You can also save the solution as a scenario to view later before you restore the original values.

SETTING UP AND DEFINING THE PROBLEM

The first step in setting up a problem for the Solver to work on is to create the worksheet model. Excel comes with several example worksheets containing classic resource problems that you can use as guides. These sample worksheets are stored in the **\solver** directory, which is located in the **\examples** found in the **c:\excel** directory. They include:

1. **Solver1.xls**, which finds the most profitable profit mix for building products with parts on hand in the inventory.

2. **Solver2.xls**, which finds the least costly shipping routes for shipping goods from production plants to their warehouses.

3. **Solver3.xls,** which finds the most profitable scheduling of staff, using various shift changes.

4. **Solver4.xls**, which finds the maximum interest income from short-term versus long-term investments.

5. **Solver5.xls**, which finds the maximum rate of return for a specific level of risk in a portfolio of stocks.

6. **Solver6.xls**, which contains an engineering problem that determines the appropriate value for a resistor to dissipate a charge to a particular percentage of its initial value within a particular length of time.

In addition to these sample worksheet models, Excel also supplies a sample worksheet in the **\solver** directory called **solverex.xls**. This sample contains a worksheet where you can use the Solver to determine the best advertising budget for maximizing profits.

Note: The Solver command is added to the bottom portion of the Formula menu, assuming that you performed a complete installation when installing Excel 4.0. If you open the Formula menu and don't see the Solver command listed there, you will need to return to the Windows Program Manager and run the Excel 4.0 Setup program again to install this add-in macro and the example Solver files.

To define and solve a problem with the Solver after you have created your worksheet model, take the following steps:

1. Choose the Solver command on the Formula menu to open the Solver Parameters dialog box (similar to the one shown in Figure 11.22).

2. Choose the target cell or enter its cell reference or range name in the Set Cell text box.

3. Choose the appropriate option button in the Equal to section of the dialog box. Select the **M**ax option when you want target cell's value to be as large as possible. Select the **M**in option when you want the target cell's value to be as small as possible. Select the **V**alue option and enter a value in the associated text box when you want the target cell's value to reach a particular value.

4. Choose the changing cells or enter their cell references or range name in the **B**y Changing Cells text box. To select a nonadjacent range, hold down the Ctrl key as you select each range in the selection. To have Excel choose the changing cells for you based on the target cell you selected, choose the **G**uess button to the right of this text box.

5. To add a constraint to a parameter, such as a changing cell or the target cell, choose the **A**dd button to open the Add Constraint dialog box (similar to the one shown in Figure 11.23).

6. When defining a constraint, choose the cell whose value you want to constrain or enter its cell reference or range name in the Cell Reference text box, choose the relationship (=,<=,>=, or **int** for integer) in the drop-down list box to the right and (unless you chose **int**), enter the appropriate value or cell reference in the **C**onstraint text box.

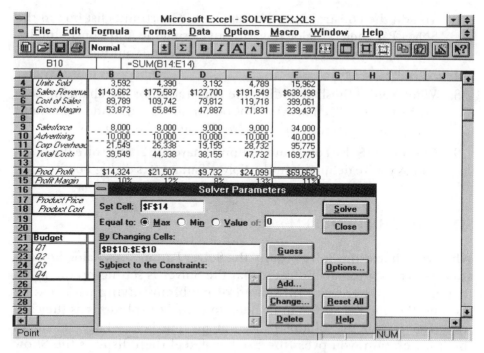

Figure 11.22   Sample Worksheet with the Solver Dialog Box

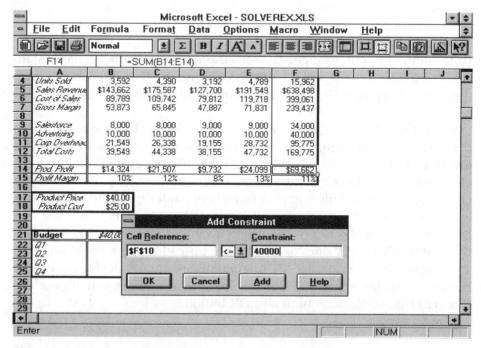

Figure 11.23   The Add Constraint Dialog Box

7. To add the constraint to the **Su**bject to Constraints list box in the Solver Parameters dialog box without closing the Add Constraint dialog box, choose the **Add** button and then define your next constraint as outlined in step 6.

8. When you've finished adding the constraints for the changing cells or the target cell, choose the OK button to close the Add Constraint dialog box and return to the Solver Parameters dialog box.

9. Choose the **S**olve command button to have the Solver solve the problem as you've defined it in the Solver Parameters dialog box.

SOLVING THE PROBLEM

When you choose the **S**olve button, the Solver Parameters dialog box disappears. The status bar indicates that the Solver is setting up the problem and then keeps you informed of problem-solving progress by showing the number of the intermediate (or trial) solutions as they are tried. To interrupt the solution process at any time before Excel calculates the last iteration, you press the Esc key. Excel then displays the Show Trial Solution dialog box informing you that the solution process has been paused.

To continue the solution process, you choose the Continue button. To abort the solution process, you choose the Stop button. To save the current (trial) values in the worksheet as a scenario (see "Using the Scenario Manager" earlier in this chapter for details), choose the **S**ave Scenario button, then enter a new name for the scenario in the Save Scenario dialog box and choose OK.

When Excel finishes the solution process, a Solver dialog box similar to the one shown in Figure 11.24 appears. This dialog box informs you whether or not the Solver was able to find a solution given the target cell, changing cells, and constraints defined for the problem. To retain the changes made by the Solver in your worksheet model, leave the **K**eep Solver Solution option button selected and choose the OK button to close the Solver dialog box. To return the original values to the worksheet, choose the Restore **O**riginal Values option button instead. To save the changes as a scenario before you restore the original values, choose the **S**ave Scenario button and assign a name to the current scenario before you choose the Restore **O**riginal Values option and OK button.

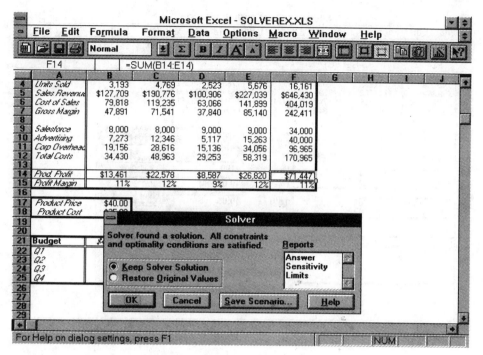

Figure 11.24   The Solver Dialog Box

 Alert!   Unlike when using the Goal Seek command, after selecting the **K**eep Solver Solution option button in the Solver dialog box, you can't use the Undo command to restore the original values to your worksheet. If you want to be able to switch between the "before" and "after" views of your worksheet, you must save the changes with the **S**ave Scenario button and then use the Restore **O**riginal Values option. That way you can retain the "before" view in the original worksheet and use the Scenario Manager to display the "after" view created by the Solver.

CHANGING THE SOLVER OPTIONS

For most problems, the default options used by the Solver will be adequate. In some situations, however, you may want to change some of the Solver options before you begin the solution process. To change the solution options, you choose the **O**ptions command button in the Solver Parameters dialog box. Excel then opens the Solver Options dialog box shown in Figure 11.25, where you can make all the necessary changes. (Refer to Table 11.1 for information on each option.)

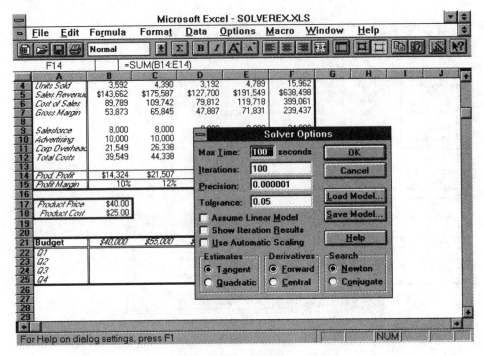

Figure 11.25   The Solver Options Dialog Box

After changing the options, choose the OK button to return to the Solver Parameters dialog box. From there you can then choose the **S**olve button to begin the solution process with the newly changed solution settings.

SAVING AND LOADING A MODEL PROBLEM

The target cell, changing cells, constraints, and Solver options that you used most recently are saved as part of the worksheet when you use the **File Save** command. When you define other problems for the same worksheet that you want to save, you must choose the **S**ave Model button in the Solver Options dialog box and indicate the cell reference or name of the range in the active worksheet where you want the problem's parameters to be inserted.

When you select the **S**ave Model button, Excel opens the Save Model dialog box, containing a Select Model Area text box. This text box contains the cell references for a range large enough to hold all of the problem's parameters, starting with the active cell. To save the problem's parameters in this range, choose the OK button or press Enter. If this range includes cells with existing data, you need to modify the cell reference in this text box before you choose OK to prevent Excel from replacing the existing data.

Table 11.1   The Solver's Option Settings

Option	Function
Max Time	Specifies the maximum number of seconds that the Solver will spend on finding the solution.
Iterations	Specifies the maximum number of times that the Solver will recalculate the worksheet when finding the solution.
Precision	Specifies the precision of the constraints. The number you enter in this text box determines whether the value in a constraint cell meets the specified value or the upper or lower limit you have set. Specify a lower number (between 0 and 1) to reduce the time it takes the Solver to return a solution to your problem.
Tolerance	Specifies the integer tolerance. The number you enter here is the maximum percentage of error allowed for integer solutions when you've constrained some of the changing cells to integers.
Assume Linear Model	Sets the Solver to use the linear programming method using the Simplex method when solving your problem. Selecting this option can greatly reduce the amount of time it takes for the Solver to return a solution to a linear problem.
Show Iteration Results	Pauses the Solver at each trial solution so that you can see the intermediate results in the worksheet.
Use Automatic Scaling	Turns on automatic scaling for finding a solution to a problem where the magnitude of the changing cells differs greatly from the magnitude of the set cell and/or the constraint values.
Load Model	Displays the Load Model dialog box where you can select the reference of saved Solver parameters that you want to load as the current problem into the Solver. (See Save Model that follows.)

Table 11.1   *(continued)*

Save Model	Displays the Save Model dialog box where you specify the reference for storing the current Solver parameters that you want to save in the worksheet so you can reuse them later. You need to use this option to save a problem model only when you've already defined at least one problem for the worksheet and want to save all the problems in it.
Estimates	Specifies the approach used to obtain initial estimates for the basic variables in each one-dimensional search. Choose Tangent to use linear extrapolation from a tangent vector. Choose Quadratic to use quadratic extrapolation (which can improve the results on highly nonlinear problems).
Derivatives	Specifies Forward differencing (the default) or Central differencing for estimates of partial derivatives. (Central requires more worksheet recalculations but can help when the Solver dialog box displays a message indicating that it could not improve the solution.)
Search	Specifies either a (quasi-) Newton (the default) or Conjugate gradient method searching. (Changing to Conjugate can be useful if, when stepping through iterations, you notice little progress between successive trial results.)

After selecting OK, Excel copies the problem's parameters in the specified range. These values are then saved as part of the worksheet the next time you choose the **File Save** command. To reuse these problem parameters when solving a problem, you simply need to open the Solver Options dialog box, choose the **Load Problem** button, and then select the range containing the saved problem parameters. When you choose the OK button or press Enter in the Load Model dialog box, Excel loads the parameters from this cell range into the appropriate text boxes in the Solver Parameters dialog box. You can then close the Solver Options dialog box by choosing OK and solve the problem using these parameters by selecting the **Solve** command button.

Tip Remember that you can use the **R**eset All button when you want to clear all of the parameters defined for the previous problem and return the Solver options to their defaults.

CREATING SOLVER REPORTS

You can create three different types of reports with the Solver: The Answer, Sensitivity, and Limits reports. Excel places each report that you generate for a Solver problem in a separate worksheet window where you can save and/or print the report.

The Answer report (as shown in Figure 11.26) lists the target cell and changing cells with their original and final values along with the constraints used in solving the problem.

The Sensitivity report (as shown in Figure 11.27) indicates how sensitive an optimal solution is to changes in the formulas that calculate the target cell and constraints. The report shows the changing cells with their final values and the *reduced gradient* for each cell. (The reduced gradient measures the objective per unit increase in the changing cell.) If you defined constraints, the Sensitivity report lists them with their final values and the *Lagrange multiplier* for each constraint. (The Lagrange multiplier measures the objective per unit increase that appears in the right side of the constraint equation.)

The Limits report (as shown in Figure 11.28) shows the target cell and the changing cells with their values, lower and upper limits, and target results. The lower limit represents the lowest value that a changing cell can have while fixing the values of all other cells and still satisfy the constraints. The upper limit represents the highest value that will do this.

To generate one (or all) of these reports, you select the report type (Answer, Sensitivity, or Limits) in the **R**eports list box of the Solver dialog box (as shown in Figure 11.24). To select more than one report, hold down the Ctrl key as you click the name of the report. When you select the OK button or press Enter to close the Solver dialog box (after choosing between the **K**eep Solver Solution and Restore **O**riginal Values option), Excel generates the report (or reports) that you selected in a new document window(s). To view, save, and print a report, select the document window containing the report from the **W**indow pull-down menu. (Report windows are listed by report type, as in *Answer Report 1, Sensitivity Report 1,* and *Limits Report 1.*)

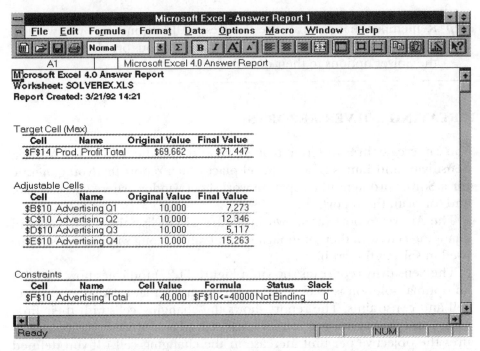

Figure 11.26   Sample Answer Report

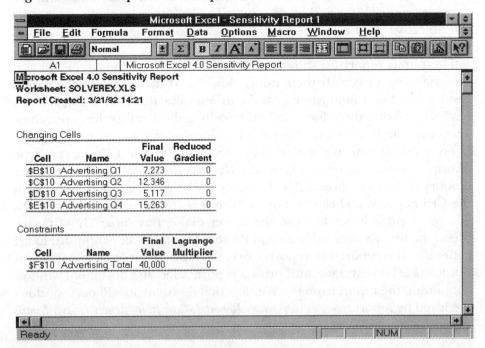

Figure 11.27   Sample Sensitivity Report

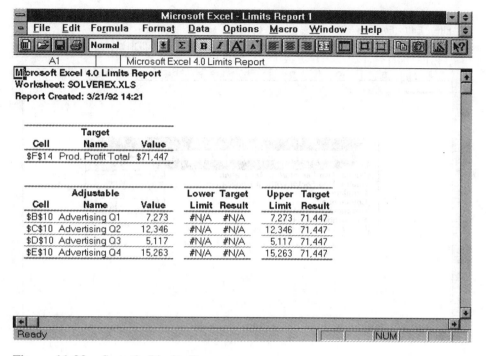

Figure 11.28   Sample Limits Report

Using the Analysis ToolPak

Excel 4.0 offers a diverse set of specialized analysis tools called the Analysis ToolPak that you can use to perform sophisticated statistical analysis on your worksheet data. Table 11.2 lists the analysis tools contained in the Analysis ToolPak with a short description of their functions. (For more specific information on using each tool, refer to Chapter 1, "Analyzing and Calculating Data," in Microsoft Excel User's Guide 2.)

To use one of these tools, you choose the Analysis **T**ools command on the **O**ptions menu. The first time you choose this command, Excel loads the Analysis ToolPak add-in macro to open the Analysis Tools dialog box (shown in Figure 11.29). If you open the **O**ptions menu and don't see the Analysis **T**ools command listed there, you will need to return to the Windows Program Manager and run the Excel 4.0 Setup program again to install this add-in macro.

To quickly select an analysis tool that is not currently displayed in the list box, type the first letter of the tool name (such as r for Regression) to move the first tool whose name begins with that letter and then, if necessary, use the scroll bar to bring the tool into view.

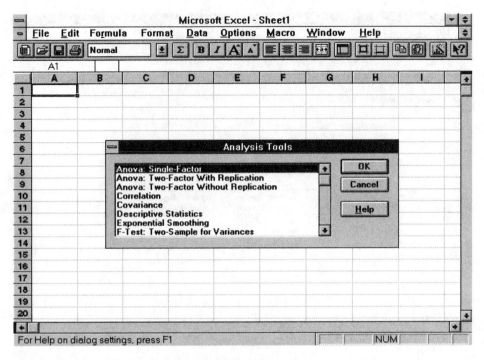

Figure 11.29   The Analysis Tools Dialog Box

Table 11.2   Tools in the Analysis ToolPak

Tool	*Function*
Anova: Single Factor	Performs simple analysis of variance used to determine whether means from two or more samples are drawn from populations with the same mean.
Anova: Two-Factor With Replication	Performs simple analysis of variance that includes more than one sample for each group of data.
Anova: Two-Factor Without Replication	Performs simple analysis of variance that does not include more than one sample for each group of data.
Correlation	Measures the relationship between two sets of data that are scaled to be independent of the unit of measurement.
Covariance	Returns the average of the product of deviations of data points from their respective means.

Table 11.2 *(continued)*

Descriptive Statistics	Generates a report of univariate statistics from the data in the input range (including mean, standard error, median, mode, standard deviation, variance, and the like).
Exponential Smoothing	Predicts a value based on the forecast for the prior period, adjusted for the error in that prior forecast.
F-Test: Two-Sample for Variances	Performs simple *F*-test that compares two population variances.
Fourier Analysis	Solves problems in linear systems and analyzes periodic data, using the Fast Fourier Transform (FFT) method.
Histogram	Calculates individual and cumulative frequencies for a cell range of data and data bins.
Moving Average	Projects values in the forecast period based on the average value of the variable over a specific number of periods.
Random Number Generation	Fills a range with independent random numbers drawn from one of several distributions (Uniform, Normal, Bernoulli, Binomial, Poisson, Patterned, or Discrete).
Rank and Percentile	Creates a table containing the ordinal and percentage rank of each value in a data set.
Regression	Performs linear regression analysis, using the *least squares* method.
Sampling	Creates a sample from a population by treating the data in an input range as a population.
t-Test: Paired Two-Sample for Means	Performs a two-sample student's *t*-test that tests whether a sample's means are distinct. This form of the test does not assume that variances of both populations from which the data are drawn are equal.
t-Test: Paired Two-Sample Assuming Equal Variances	Performs a two-sample student's *t*-test. This form of the test assumes that both data are equal (also known as a *homoscedastic t*-test).

Table 11.2   *(continued)*

t-Test: Paired Two-Sample Assuming Unequal Variances	Performs a two-sample student's *t*-test. This form of the test assumes that variances of both populations from which the data are drawn are equal (also known as a *heteroscedastic t*-test).
z-Test: Two-Sample for Means	Performs a two-sample student's z-test that tests hypotheses about the difference between two population means.

After highlighting the tool that you want to use, double-click it or choose OK or press Enter. Excel then opens that tool's dialog box, where you will specify the parameters pertaining to the type of analysis to be performed. (Normally this includes at least an input range specifying the data in the worksheet to be analyzed as well as an output range that indicates where in the worksheet Excel should place the results of the data analysis.) Remember that you can choose the **H**elp command button in the Analysis Tools dialog box to get on-line help for a particular analysis tool.

SUMMARY

In this chapter you learned several methods for analyzing your worksheet data in Excel 4.0. Specifically, you learned how to perform what-if analysis by creating one-variable and two-variable data tables, using the Scenario Manager, and using the What If add-in macro. You also learned how to perform goal seeking with the Goal Seek command or by manipulating a two-dimensional line, column, or bar chart. Then you learned how to perform complex what-if analysis or goal seeking with the Solver command. Finally you learned about the tools in the Analysis ToolPak that you can use to perform specialized statistical and engineering data analysis.

In the next chapter you will learn the basics of charting your worksheet data. There you will learn how to use the new ChartWizard tool to chart your worksheet data quickly, to use the Chart Toolbar to modify your chart, and edit and format a chart in a Chart window. You will also learn how to save and print your charts, both as separate documents and as part of the worksheet that contains the data they graph.

12

Creating Charts

A chart presents the data from your worksheet visually by representing the data in rows and columns as bars on a chart, for instance, or as pieces of a pie in a pie chart. Charts and graphs have long gone hand in hand with spreadsheets, because they allow you to see trends and patterns that you often cannot see readily from the numbers alone. Which has more consistent sales, the Southeast region or the Northwest region? Monthly sales reports may contain the answer, but a bar chart based on the data shows it more clearly.

In this chapter you will first become familiar with the terminology Excel uses as it refers to the parts of a chart—terms that may be new, such as "data marker" and "chart data series", as well as terms that are probably familiar already like "axis." Once acquainted with the terms, you will begin to put them to use with the ChartWizard, a tool that does not really require much specialized knowledge because it walks you through each of the steps required to create the kind of chart that you want.

Having learned this method for creating charts, you will next learn a faster shortcut. If you want to use default chart types and know the kind of chart you want to create, you can use the Chart toolbar. All you have to do is select the data and click the Chart tool you want. After that, you will learn how to create a chart in the "old-fashioned" way with the pull-down menus.

The heart of preparing a chart (and some of the fun) is matching a chart type to your purposes. To help you with this, you will take a tour through all the chart types available in Excel 4.0, from the old standbys, bar and column charts, to ones that may be new, radar and surface charts. Finally you will learn how to save a chart and how to print one.

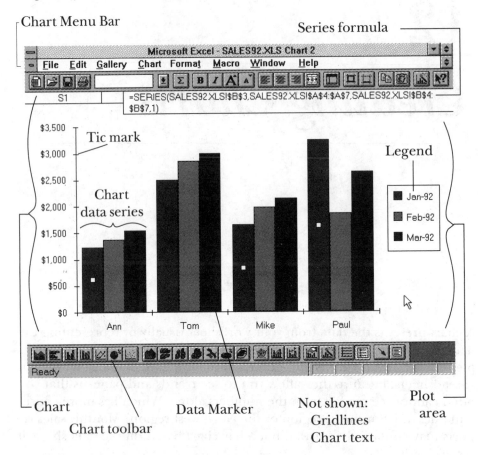

Figure 12.1   The Parts of an Excel Chart

Understanding the Parts of a Chart

There are several distinct parts to the typical Excel chart. Figure 12.1 shows an Excel column chart in a separate document window with labels identifying the parts of this chart. Table 12.1 summarizes the parts of the typical chart.

Creating an Embedded Chart with the ChartWizard

An *embedded chart* is a chart that appears right on the worksheet. When you save or print the worksheet, you save or print the chart along with it. A chart does not have to be embedded. You can also create a chart as a separate document by choosing **New** from the **File** menu and choosing Chart in the New dialog box.

Table 12.1 The Parts of a Typical Chart

Part	Description
Chart	Everything inside the chart window, including all parts of the chart (labels, axes, data markers, tick marks, and other elements).
Chart menu bar	A special menu bar with names of chart menus, such as **G**allery and **C**hart, that appears whenever a chart window is active.
Chart toolbar	The toolbar that displays along the bottom of the screen, just above the status bar. The charting tools correspond to the most commonly used chart types (also available from the Gallery menu).
Data Marker	A symbol on the chart, such as a bar in a bar chart, a pie in a pie chart, or a line on a line chart. The symbol represents ("marks") the worksheet data.
Chart data series	A group of related values, such as all the values in a single row in the chart—all the sales figures listed for Ann in the sample chart, for example. A chart can have just one data series (shown in a single bar or line), but it usually has several.
Series Formula	A formula describing a given data series. The formula includes a reference to the cell that contains the data series name (such as the name Jan-92), references to worksheet cells containing the categories and values plotted in the chart, and the plot order of the series. The series formula also can have the actual data used to plot the chart. You can edit a series formula and control the plot order. For information, see the SERIES function in Appendix B.
Axis	A line that serves as a major reference for plotting data in a chart. In two-dimensional charts there are two axes — the x (horizontal) axis and the y (vertical) axis. In most two-dimensional charts (except, notably, column charts), Excel plots categories (labels) along the x-axis and values (numbers) along the y-axis. Bar charts reverse the scheme, plotting values along the y-axis. Pie charts have no axes. Three-dimensional charts have an x-axis, a y-axis, and a z-axis. The x- and y-axes delineate the horizontal surface of the chart. The z-axis is the vertical axis, showing the depth of the third dimension.

Table 12.1   *(continued)*

Tick mark	A small line intersecting an axis. A tick mark indicates a category, scale, or chart data series. A tick mark can have a label attached.
Plot area	The area where Excel plots your data, including the axes and all markers that represent data points.
Gridlines	Optional lines extending from the tick marks across the plot area, making it easier to view the data values represented by the tick marks.
Chart text	Any text that you add to the chart. *Attached text* is a label linked to an axis, data marker, or other chart object. If you move the object, you move the attached text as well. You cannot move the attached text independently. *Unattached text* is text you add with the Text Box tool on the Chart toolbar. You can also add this type of text directly to an active chart by typing the text and then pressing Enter.
Legend	A key that identifies patterns, colors, or symbols associated with the markers of a chart data series. The legend shows the data series name corresponding to each data marker (such as the name of the red columns in a column chart).

The ChartWizard is the easiest and fastest way to create an embedded chart. It leads you step by step through the most important steps in creating a chart. You just have to "fill in the blanks" as you proceed through a series of dialog boxes. Each ChartWizard dialog box contains the following five buttons at the bottom for navigating in the ChartWizard.

- **Cancel:** to close the ChartWizard and return you to the worksheet.

- **<<:** to return you to the beginning of the ChartWizard, a useful capability if you want to change your selected range or simply start over.

- **< Back:** to take you back to the previous step. Use it, for instance, to try out different chart types, then go back to try out others.

- **Next > :** to take you to the next step. Use it together with the Back button to try out various looks.

- **>> :** to create a chart using the options you have selected to that point and exits the ChartWizard. Alert: Be careful, at first, about using the >> button by mistake instead of the Next button. It creates the chart and takes you out of the ChartWizard.

- **Help:** to display Help information about the options and buttons. It also allows you to access Help for all of Excel.

Suppose, for instance, you wanted to create an embedded chart using some of the data selected in the sample sales worksheet shown in Figure 12.2. To chart this data range with the ChartWizard, you follow these steps:

1. Select the range of cells containing the data you want to plot, including the column and row headings. The labels in the top row of the selected data become category labels in the chart. That is, they appear along the x-axis in most charts to describe the data being charted. The labels in the first selected column on the left are used to name the data series in the chart. Excel assigns values to appear along the y-axis based on the data in those data series.

    Note that you do not have to select the range of cells to plot before choosing the ChartWizard tool, although often it is easier to do so. If you don't preselect a range, you can still type in the cell reference or even select the range after you open the ChartWizard tool. In the sample worksheet shown in Figure 12.2, the cell range A3:D7 is selected for charting.

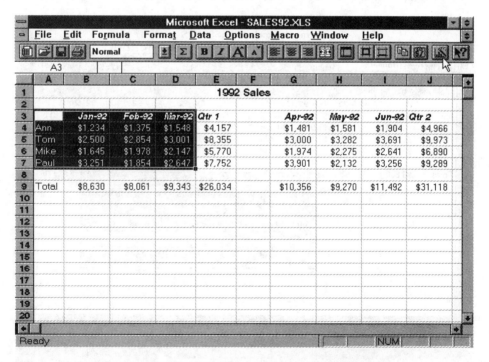

Figure 12.2   Selecting the Data to Chart with the ChartWizard

2.   Click the ChartWizard tool in the Standard toolbar (the tool that is the second from the right). The mouse pointer then changes to a cross hair, and a marquee border appears around the selected range.

3.   Position the cross-hair pointer at the location where you want one corner of the embedded chart to appear. Then drag the pointer until the chart rectangle is the size and shape you want it to be. (To create a square for your chart, hold down the Shift key as you drag. To align the chart to the cell grid, hold down the Alt key as you drag.) When you release the mouse button, the ChartWizard - Step 1 of 5 dialog box appears on the screen, as shown in Figure 12.3, where you can modify the cell range if necessary.

4.   Choose the Next> button to proceed to the ChartWizard - Step 2 of 5 dialog box, as shown in Figure 12.4, where you choose the type of chart you wish to use. By default, the ChartWizard chooses the Column chart, which represents your data with vertical bars.

5.   Choose the Next> button again to display the ChartWizard - Step 3 of 5 dialog box, as shown in Figure 12.5, where you choose a format for the type of chart you selected in the Step 2 dialog box. By default, the ChartWizard chooses the first column chart format.

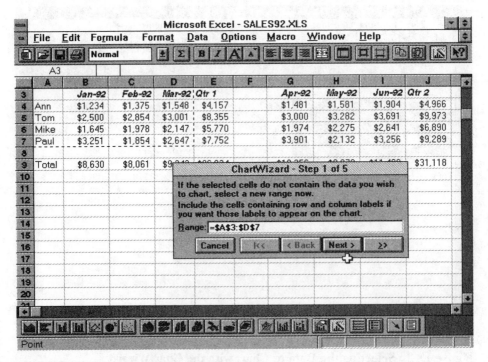

Figure 12.3   First Screen in the ChartWizard

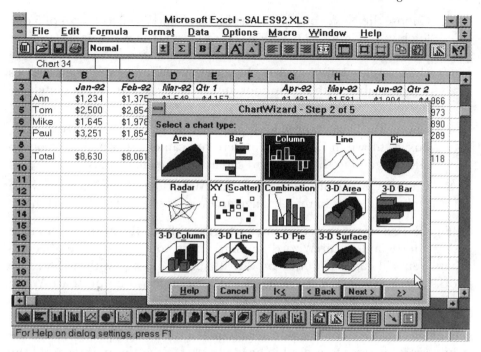

Figure 12.4   Second Dialog Box in the ChartWizard

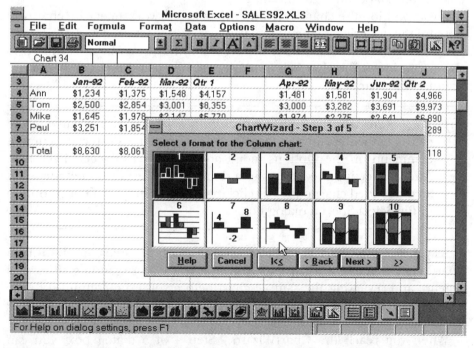

Figure 12.5   Third Dialog Box in the ChartWizard

6.   Choose the Next> button to display the ChartWizard - Step 4 of 5 dialog box, in Figure 12.6, where you can modify how the data is used in plotting the chart. This dialog box also shows you a sample of the chart you are building. Any changes that you make to the data series or chart labels with the options in this dialog box are immediately reflected in the Sample Chart.

7.   Choose the Next> button to display the ChartWizard - Step 5 of 5 dialog box, as shown in Figure 12.7, where you can decide whether or not to add a legend to the chart and can assign the chart titles.

8.   Choose OK to finish using the ChartWizard and have Excel draw the embedded chart in the rectangular area you selected in the worksheet.

Figure 12.8 shows the column chart created from the sample sales data using the default ChartWizard settings. After you create an embedded chart, you still can move it or modify its shape and size within the active worksheet. To move the chart, position the pointer within the chart. When the white cross changes to an arrowhead, drag the outline of the chart to the desired position in the worksheet and release the mouse button. To change its size, position the pointer on one of the sizing squares. When the white cross changes to a double-headed arrow, drag the pointer until the chart is the shape and size you want.

If you position the chart over other data in the worksheet, the chart will obscure the underlying data. When you have the chart sized and positioned the way you want it, click the white cross pointer somewhere in the worksheet (outside of the chart's boundaries) to deselect the chart. The sizing handles will disappear.

Tip   To prevent yourself from inadvertently selecting and modifying the charts embedded in your worksheet, choose the Protect Document command on the Options menu and select the Objects check box. After protecting the objects in a document, you can no longer select an embedded chart either by clicking it or by using the Objects option in the Select Special dialog box.

As you see, the ChartWizard walks you through the steps for choosing a chart type, selecting a format for the type you choose, adding titles or a legend, and reviewing the sample chart before you even commit it to the worksheet. The ChartWizard is so flexible that you may never have to use anything else to create your charts.

When you reach the ChartWizard - Step 4 of 5 dialog box, you can experiment with the options to see what the chart looks like when you

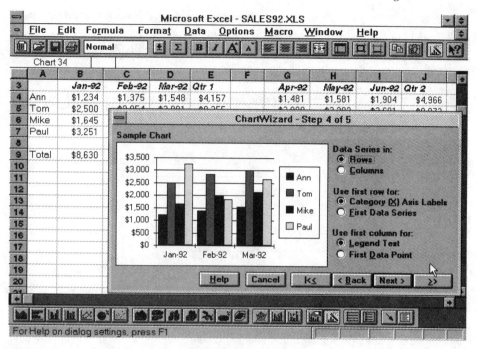

Figure 12.6 Fourth Dialog Box in the ChartWizard

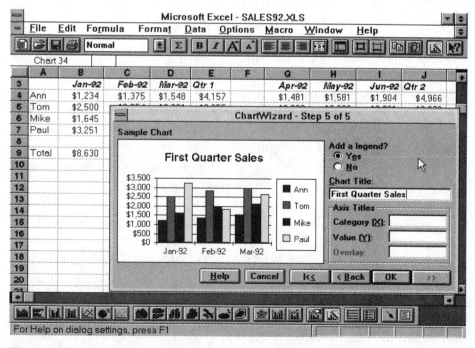

Figure 12.7 Fifth Dialog Box in the ChartWizard

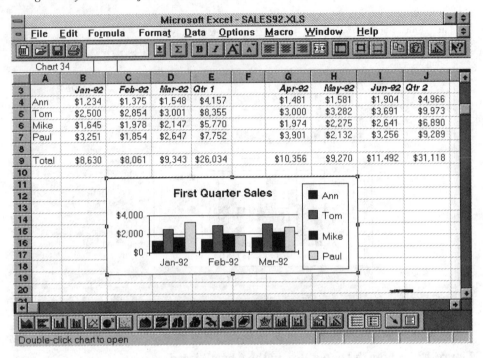

Figure 12.8   Sample Chart Created with the ChartWizard

choose Data Series in Rows, for instance, instead of Data Series in Columns. You can see the result in the Sample Chart section without even exiting from the ChartWizard. The following options are available in the Step 4 of 5 dialog box when creating a column chart. (The options vary slightly depending on the chart type.)

- Data Series in Rows: Excel uses rows from the selected data as the data series for creating data markers on the chart. Rows of data become columns on a chart, for instance.

- Data Series in Columns: Excel uses columns from the selected data as the data series for creating data markers on the chart.

- Use First column for Category (X) Axis labels—Data in the first column (or Row if you have selected Data Series in Rows) becomes labels for the x-axis and is not plotted as a data marker.

- Use First column for First Data Series: Data in the first column (or Row if you have selected Data series in Rows) is plotted as a data marker.

- Use First row for Legend Text: If you have selected Data Series in Columns, you can elect to have Excel create a legend out of the text or data in the first row.

- Use First row for First Data Point: If the first row contains data that you want to plot rather than legend text, choose this option.

Although the ChartWizard gives you a great deal of flexibility, you may need additional control over your charts. You can create a chart without using the ChartWizard, as explained later in the section "Creating a Chart in a Chart Window." If, however, you know the chart you want to create, you can create the chart with the Chart toolbar, as explained in the next section, even faster than you can with the ChartWizard.

Using the Chart Toolbar

When you display the Chart toolbar, Excel normally places it along the bottom of the screen, above the status bar, as shown in Figure 12.1. The Chart Toolbar provides you with a kind of point-and-click charting. You simply select the data you want to chart, then click the appropriate Chart tool for the chart type you want. A marquee appears around the selected data, and a message appears in the status bar saying Drag in document to create a chart. You then use the cross-hair pointer to draw the outline for the chart in the area of the worksheet where you want the chart to appear. When you release the mouse button, Excel plots the selected data in this area. If you want to change the chart type at that point, simply click the Chart tool for the new type you want to see.

Table 12.2 identifies and describes the Chart tools on the Chart toolbar. For a complete description of the various chart types, see "Selecting the Chart Type and Format" later in this chapter. Note that the ChartWizard tool, available on the Standard toolbar, also appears in the Chart toolbar.

Table 12.2 Excel Charting Tools

Tool	Tool Name	Function
	Area Chart	Creates a simple area chart using format 1 in the Chart Gallery for area charts.
	Bar Chart	Creates a simple bar chart using format 1 in the Chart Gallery for bar charts.

Table 12.2   *(continued)*

	Column Chart	Creates a simple column chart using format 1 in the Chart Gallery for column charts.
	Stacked Column Chart	Creates a stacked column chart using format 3 in the Chart Gallery for column charts.
	Line Chart	Creates a line chart with markers using format 1 in the Chart Gallery for line charts.
	Pie Chart	Creates a pie chart using format 6 in the Chart Gallery for pie charts, where the value labels appear as percentages.
	XY (Scatter) Chart	Creates an xy (scatter) chart with markers only, using format 1 in the Chart Gallery for xy (scatter) charts.
	3-D Area Chart	Creates a 3-D area chart using format 5 in the Chart Gallery for 3-D area charts.
	3-D Bar Chart	Creates a 3-D bar chart using format 1 in the Chart Gallery for 3-D bar charts.
	3-D Column Chart	Creates a 3-D column chart with markers using format 1 in the Chart Gallery for 3-D column charts.
	3-D Perspective Column Chart	Creates a 3-D column chart with a 3-D plot area using format 5 in the Chart Gallery for 3-D column charts.
	3-D Line Chart	Creates a 3-D line (ribbon) chart using format 1 in the Chart Gallery for 3-D line charts.
	3-D Pie Chart	Creates a 3-D pie chart with value labels expressed as percentages, using format 6 in the Chart Gallery for 3-D pie charts.
	3-D Surface Chart	Creates a 3-D surface chart using format 1 in the Chart Gallery for 3-D surface charts.

Table 12.2 *(continued)*

	Radar Chart	Creates a radar chart with markers using format 1 in the Chart Gallery for radar charts.
	Line/Column Chart	Creates a combination line and column chart using format 1 in the Chart Gallery for combination charts.
	Volume/Hi-Lo-Close Chart	Creates a combination chart with a column chart and a line chart with three data series for high, low, and closing stock prices using format 5 in the Chart Gallery for combination charts. This combination is useful for showing both stock sales volume and price at the same time.
	Preferred Chart	Creates a chart using the format set with the Set Preferred command on the Gallery menu.
	Chart Wizard	Leads you through the steps to create or edit an embedded chart. See "Creating an Embedded Chart with the ChartWizard" in this chapter.
	Vertical Gridlines	Adds or deletes major gridlines (lines that extend the tick marks on a chart) for the value (y) axis.
	Legend	Adds or deletes a chart legend.
	Arrow	Adds an arrow, equivalent to choosing Add Arrow from the Chart menu.
	Text Box	Adds an unattached text box. Click the tool, then type your text.

So far, then, you've learned two ways to create an Excel chart: Using the ChartWizard or using the Chart tools on the Chart toolbar. Both of these methods create an embedded chart in the active worksheet. You can also create a chart in a separate window, as explained in the next section.

Creating a Chart in a Chart Window

There are advantages to creating a chart from worksheet data in a chart window instead of embedding it in the worksheet. A chart in a separate window does not take up space on the worksheet, although it remains linked to the data in the worksheet. If you change plotted values in the worksheet, Excel automatically changes the chart as well.

You follow these steps when you want to create a chart in a separate document:

1   Select the cells containing the data you want to chart, including the column and row labels. When selecting the data to plot, remember that you can select a nonadjacent selection. For example, to plot the sales totals for the first quarter in the column chart in the separate chart window shown in Figure 12.9, you would select the labels in the cell range B3:D3 and the values in the cell range B9:D9.

2. Choose the New command on the File menu, then choose the Chart option in the New list box as shown in Figure 12.9. Excel creates the chart in a separate window, similar to the one shown in Figure 12.10. You can resize and otherwise manipulate it as you would any other Excel document window.

When Excel plots the selected worksheet data in a new chart window, the program uses the preferred chart format. This format is the default format for the selected chart type that Excel automatically uses unless you tell it to use another. For the column chart type, the first format is the preferred chart format.

Tip To change the preferred chart format for the current session, first create a chart that is the chart type and format you want to use. You can apply custom formatting, as explained in Chapter 13. Then, from the Gallery menu, choose the Set Preferred command. The format of the chart in the active chart window becomes the preferred format for the remainder of your session. Note, however, that Excel does not allow you to change the preferred format permanently (that is, for future sessions).

Note that if Excel does not detect any apparent category names in the selected cells when you create the new chart window, the New Chart dialog box shown in Figure 12.11 appears. In this dialog box, you can indicate whether the first row contains the First Data Series, the Category (X) Axis Labels, or X-Values for XY-Chart.

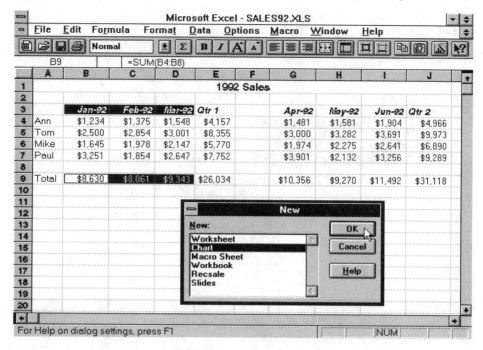

Figure 12.9   New Dialog Box for Creating a Chart in a Chart Window

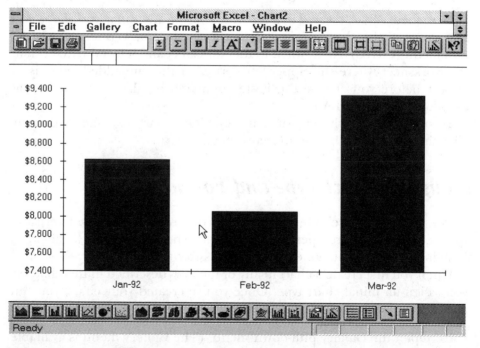

Figure 12.10   Sample Chart Created in a Separate Window

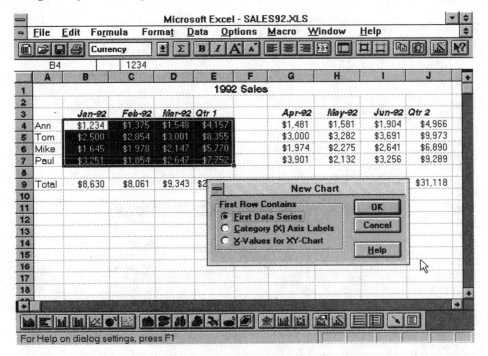

Figure 12.11   New Chart Dialog Box Used by Excel to Set Up Category Names

To embed a chart created in a separate chart window in a worksheet, you first switch to the chart window, then choose the Copy command on the Edit menu (Ctrl+C). Next switch to the worksheet and select the first cell in the worksheet where the upper-left corner of the embedded chart is to appear before you choose the Paste command on the worksheet's Edit pull-down menu (Ctrl+V).

To open a chart window with an embedded chart, you simply double-click the embedded chart in the worksheet.

Selecting the Chart Type and Format

As you are aware, Excel offers a number of different chart types. There are, in fact, fourteen chart types. For each chart type, Excel offers a gallery of built-in formats—a total of eighty eight possible formats.

When you first create a chart in any of the ways described in this chapter, you assign an initial chart type. Once you've created your chart, you can change its type and format by following these steps:

1.   Open the Gallery pull-down menu. (The Gallery menu is available whenever a chart document window is active.) Figure 12.12 shows the

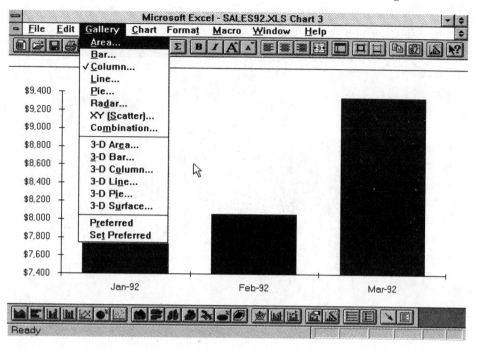

Figure 12.12   Gallery Menu

pull-down Gallery menu listing all 14 chart types.

2. From the Gallery menu, choose the chart type you want. The Chart Gallery dialog box appears, where you can choose a format for the type of chart you've selected. Figure 12.13 shows the Chart Gallery dialog box that appears when you choose the Line command on the Gallery menu. If want to change chart types once the Chart Gallery dialog box is on display, you can use the Next and Previous buttons to move one by one through the available chart types.

3. Once you've selected the format and chart type you want, choose the OK button in the Chart Gallery dialog box or press Enter. Excel then displays your chart in the selected chart type and format in the chart window.

You also can change the chart type from the Format pull-down menu in the chart window. With the document containing your chart active, choose the Main Chart command on the Format pull down menu to display the Format Chart dialog box (similar to the one shown in Figure 12.14). To change the chart type, you can then select the new type in the Main Chart Type drop-down list box before selecting OK or pressing Enter.

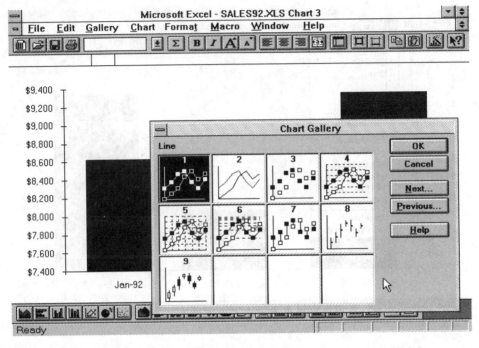

Figure 12.13 Sample Chart Gallery Dialog Box

Tip If you use the Format menu to change your chart type, you can retain any custom formatting you have added. See Chapter 13 for detailed information on custom formatting your charts.

Choosing the Right Chart

In displaying your data visually, choosing the right chart is probably just as important as deciding to use a chart at all. A chart displays data visually, but different charts display data in very different ways. Certain general guidelines may be familiar to you already. Line charts are useful for showing changes over time. Pie charts are useful for showing the relationship of parts to the whole.

As you continue to work with Excel, you may find it beneficial to become more and more familiar with the chart types available and the formats available for those chart types. Using the best chart type and format will help you display your data visually in the most meaningful way. Following is a discussion of the chart types available in Excel, guidelines on when to use each type, and the formats available for each.

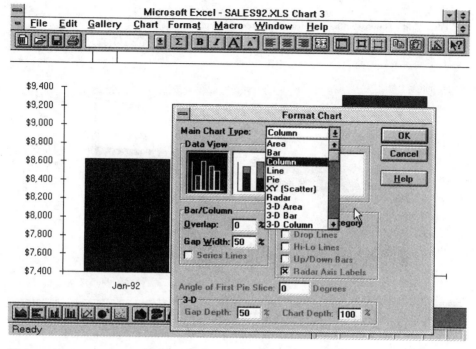

Figure 12.14 Format Chart Dialog Box with Main Chart Type Drop-down List Box Displayed

Area Charts

An area chart shows the relative importance of values over time. The area chart in Figure 12.15, for instance, shows the relative importance of the sales from each person over the first three months in the quarter. An area chart is similar to a line chart. Because the area between lines is filled in, though, the area chart puts greater emphasis than the line chart on the magnitude of values and somewhat less emphasis on the flow of change over time. The area chart is the first charting tool on the left on the charting toolbar.

The Chart Gallery for an area chart (shown in Figure 12.16) offers these five chart formats:

1. Simple area chart

2. 100% area chart

3. Area chart with drop lines

4. Area chart with gridlines

5. Area chart with areas labeled

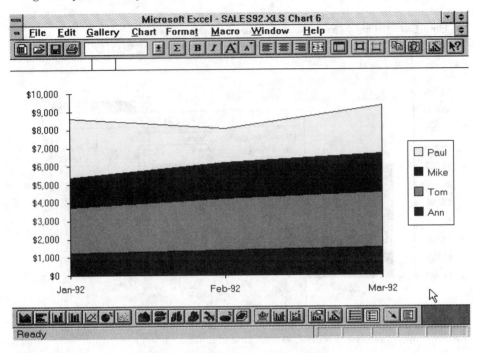

Figure 12.15   Area Chart Comparing Values over Time

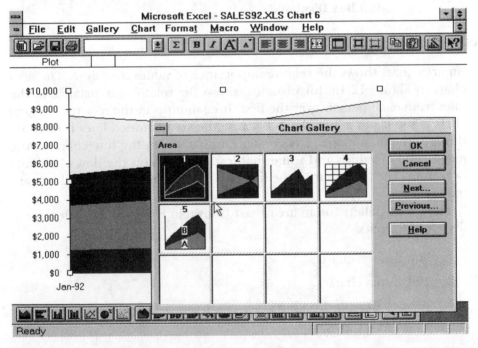

Figure 12.16   Chart Gallery Dialog Box with Chart Types for an Area Chart

Bar Charts

Excel refers to charts with horizontal bars as "bar charts" and those with vertical bars as "column charts." A bar chart (horizontal) emphasizes the comparison between items at a fixed period of time. Figure 12.17, for instance, compares the sales of four salespeople for the single month of January 1992. In a bar chart, categories appear vertically (the names of the salespeople in the example) and values appear horizontally. A stacked bar chart compares different items represented by each bar, while also showing how the parts of each bar relate to the whole bar.

These choices are available:

1. Simple bar chart
2. Bar chart for one series with varied patterns in the bars for each category in the series (each salesperson in the example chart)
3. Stacked bar chart
4. Overlapped bar chart
5. 100% stacked bar chart

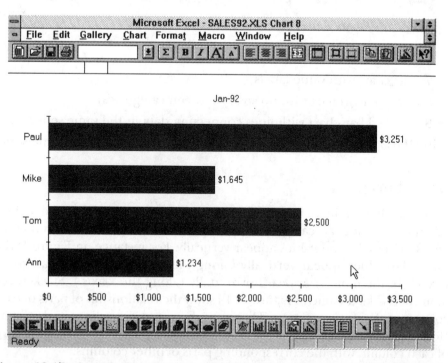

Figure 12.17   Sample Bar Chart Emphasizing Comparison at a Fixed Point in Time

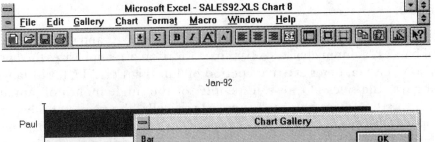

Figure 12.18   Chart Gallery for Bar Charts

6. Bar chart with vertical gridlines

7. Bar chart with value labels

8. Step chart (chart with no space between categories)

9. Stacked bar chart with lines connecting data in the same series

10. 100% stacked bar chart with lines connecting data in the same series

Column Charts

A column chart, unlike a bar chart, emphasizes variation over a period of time. Whereas in a bar chart categories appear vertically, in a column chart they appear horizontally and values appear vertically. For instance, in Figure 12.19, the dollar values appear vertically (along the y-axis.), while the categories (names of the month) appear horizontally (along the x-axis.). Stacked column charts like the one in Figure 12.19 show the relationship of parts of each column to the entire column. Thanks to the comparison lines in the figure (format 9 in the Chart Gallery for Column charts), you can also compare parts of each column with the corresponding parts of other columns.

You can create a column chart and also a stacked column chart (format 3) from the Chart toolbar. Figure 12.20 shows the Chart Gallery for a

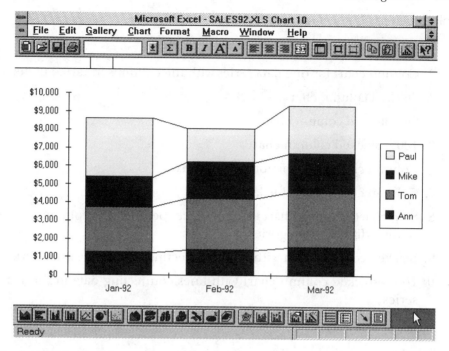

Figure 12.19   Sample Stacked Column Chart with Comparison Lines

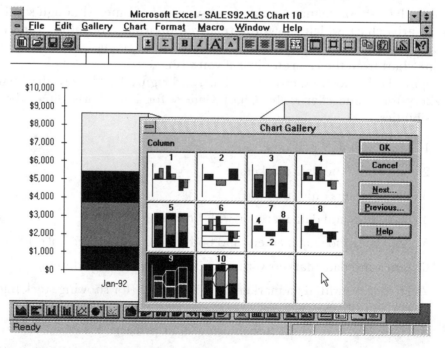

Figure 12.20   Chart Gallery for Column Charts

column chart. These choices include:

1. Simple column chart

2. Column chart for one data series with the columns in varied patterns

3. Stacked column chart

4. Overlapped column chart

5. 100% stacked column chart

6. Column chart with horizontal gridlines

7. Column chart with value labels

8. Step chart (column chart with no spaces between the columns representing different categories)

9. Stacked column chart with lines connecting data in the same series

10. 100% stacked column chart with lines connecting data in the same series

Line Charts

A line chart shows changes in data over a period of time. Although similar to an area chart, which shows the relative importance of values, the line chart emphasizes trends rather than the amount of change. You can create a line chart from the Chart toolbar if you wish.

Figure 12.21 shows a sample line chart, and Figure 12.22 shows the Chart Gallery for a line chart. The Chart Gallery for line charts offers these possibilities:

1. Lines with data markers

2. Lines only (no data markers)

3. Data markers only (no lines)

4. Both lines and data markers, with horizontal gridlines

5. Both lines and data markers, and both horizontal and vertical gridlines

6. Lines and data markers with logarithmic scale and gridlines

7. Hi-lo chart with data markers and hi-lo lines (for showing stock high and low prices)

8. High, low, close chart (for showing stock prices)

9. Open, high, low, close chart (for stock prices)

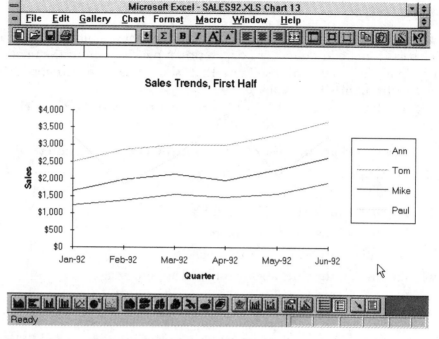

Figure 12.21   Sample Line Chart

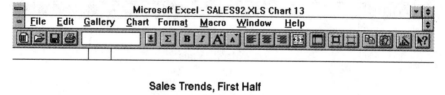

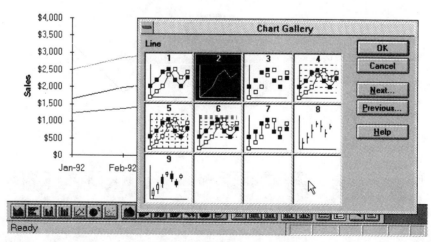

Figure 12.22   Chart Gallery for Line Charts

Pie Charts

Unlike the other charts discussed so far, which can show multiple data series, pie charts contain just one chart data series. A pie chart shows the relationship of the parts to the whole. Figure 12.23 shows a sample pie chart, using format 7 from the Chart Gallery.

Figure 12.24 shows the Chart Gallery for a pie chart. You can choose these chart types from the Chart Gallery for pie charts:

1. Basic pie chart, with each wedge patterned or colored differently.

2. Pie chart with all wedges patterned or colored the same, wedges labeled with categories

3. Pie chart with first wedge exploded

4. Pie chart with all wedges exploded

5. Basic pie chart, with category labels

6. Pie chart, with value labels expressed as percentages

7. Pie chart with category labels expressed as percentages

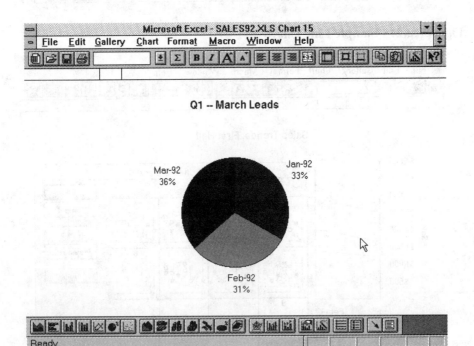

Figure 12.23 Sample Pie Chart

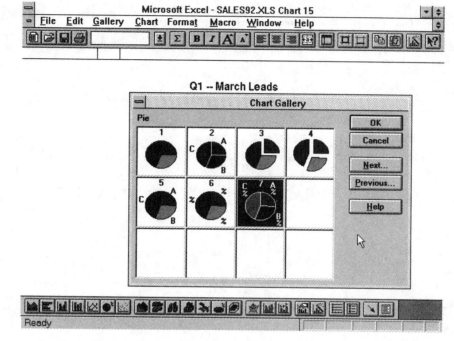

Figure 12.24   Chart Gallery for Pie Charts

 Tip To emphasize the importance of one part, emphasize one "slice" by making it a bright color or broad pattern, "exploding" it out from the rest of the chart, or labeling it clearly.

Radar Charts

 A radar chart shows changes in data relative both to a center point (zero dollars in the sample figure) and to each other. Each category in a radar chart (months in the sample chart) has its own value axis radiating from the center point. Lines connect all the data markers in the same series (all sales by Ann, for instance, in the example).

A radar chart is useful for making relative comparisons among items. The sample chart shows the relative productivity of salespeople. The salesperson whose connected data markers take up the largest area is the one with the highest relative productivity. If you view the sample chart in color on your own monitor, you can see that Tom has the most consistently high productivity, Paul has high productivity but less consistency, and Ann has the lowest productivity.

Figure 12.25 shows a sample radar chart, and Figure 12.26 shows the

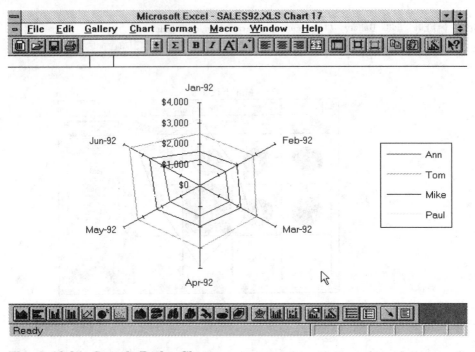

Figure 12.25   Sample Radar Chart

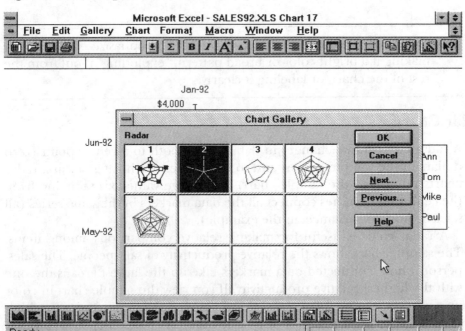

Figure 12.26   Chart Gallery for Radar Charts

Chart Gallery for a radar chart. You can choose from these chart types for radar charts:

1. Radar chart with lines connecting data markers in the same series
2. Radar chart with lines only (no data markers)
3. Radar chart with lines but no axes
4. Radar chart showing lines with axes and gridlines
5. Radar chart showing lines with axes and logarithmic gridlines

XY (Scatter) Charts

Scatter charts are useful for showing a correlation among the data points that may not be easy to see from data alone. You may want to answer such questions as "Does better nutrition mean that athletes have longer careers?" or "Do people with better insurance coverage have fewer accidents?" With an xy scatter chart, you can chart the two data series—in the sample chart, ad expenditures and overall sales—and look for a correlation.

In an xy (scatter) chart, Excel uses numeric values along both axes instead of values along the vertical axis and categories along the horizontal axis. Use a legend to show what the lines represent. If you wish, you can add axis labels of your own.

Figure 12.27 shows a sample xy (scatter) chart, and Figure 12.28 shows the Chart Gallery for an xy (scatter) chart. The chart types for the xy (scatter) charts include:

1. xy (scatter) chart with data markers only
2. xy (scatter) chart with lines connecting data markers from the same series
3. xy (scatter) chart with data markers only (no lines), and horizontal and vertical gridlines
4. xy (scatter) chart displaying data markers with semilogarithmic gridlines
5. xy (scatter) chart displaying data markers with log-log gridlines

Combination Charts

At times you may want to show one data series using one axis scale or chart type and another data series using a different axis scale or chart type. In the xy (scatter) chart just discussed, for instance, it would be helpful to plot advertising dollars spent on a different scale from sales income. You can do

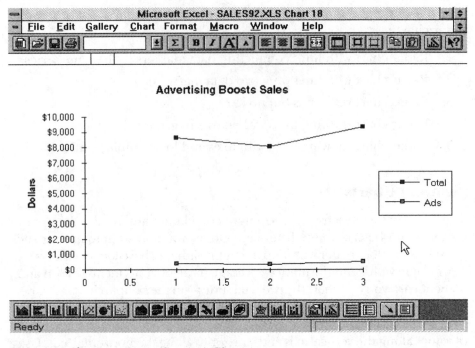

Figure 12.27   Sample xy (Scatter) Chart

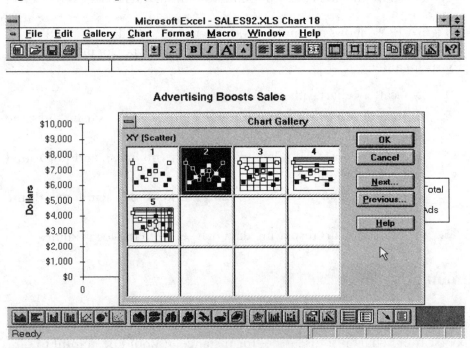

Figure 12.28   Chart Gallery for xy (Scatter) Charts

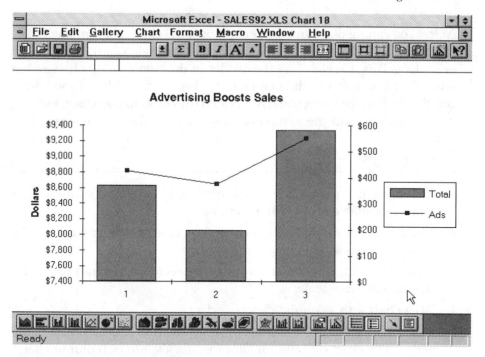

Figure 12.29 Sample Combination Chart

so with a combination chart similar to the one shown in Figure 12.29. A combination chart is a second chart plotted on top of the first chart but using the same chart window. Excel also refers to combination charts as overlay charts.

You can create a combination chart by selecting both the data for the main chart and the data for the overlay chart in the worksheet, then opening a new chart window and selecting either the Combination command on the Gallery menu or the Add Overlay command on the Chart menu. Excel creates the combination chart by dividing the selected chart data series from the worksheet equally between the main chart and the overlay chart. The program plots the first group as the main chart and the second group as the overlay chart. If you have selected an odd number of data series for the chart (such as 7), Excel places one more data series in the main chart than in the overlay chart (4 in the main chart, 3 in the overlay chart, for example).

Figure 12.29 shows a sample combination chart using the same data shown in Figure 12.27. In this combination chart, total sales are displayed in the column chart while the advertising expenditures represented with a line chart overlay. Because this overlay chart uses two scales (one for total sales and another for advertising expenditures), you can readily compare the two data sets.

Figure 12.30 shows the Chart Gallery for combination charts. The following combination chart formats are available:

> **Note:** You cannot place an overlay chart on a 3-D chart. If a combination chart is active and you select 3-D chart type in the Main Chart dialog box or in the gallery, Excel deletes the overlay in the combination chart and returns all data series to the main chart. Also, be aware that if you add additional chart data after you have created the combination chart, Excel does not simply add the additional data series to the overlay chart. It redivides the entire set of data series equally between the main chart and the overlay chart.

1. Column chart with a line chart overlay. This type of combination chart is available on the Chart toolbar.

2. Column chart with a line chart overlay. The line chart has an independent y-axis scale.

3. Line chart with a line chart overlay. The second line chart has an independent y-axis scale.

4. Area chart with a column chart overlay.

5. Column chart with a line chart overlay. The line chart has three data series. The chart is useful for showing stock volumes (column chart)

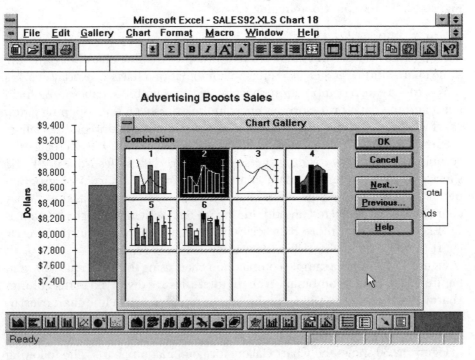

Figure 12.30 Chart Gallery for Combination Charts

compared with high, low, and closing prices (line chart). This type of combination chart is also available on the Chart toolbar.

6. Column chart with a line chart overlay. The line chart has four data series. The chart is useful for showing stock volumes (column chart) compared with open, high, low, and closing prices (line chart).

3-D Area Charts

An area chart, as discussed earlier, shows the relative importance of values over time. A 3-D area chart emphasizes the sum of plotted values rather than simply the plotted values themselves. This type of chart separates the chart data series into distinct layers, which show the differences among the data series.

Figure 12.31 shows a sample 3-D area chart, and Figure 12.32 shows the Chart Gallery for a 3-D area chart. The gallery offers these choices for 3-D area charts:

1. Simple 3-D area chart
2. Simple 3-D area chart with areas labeled
3. 3-D area chart with drop lines

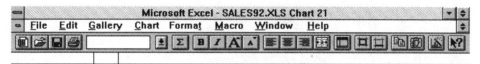

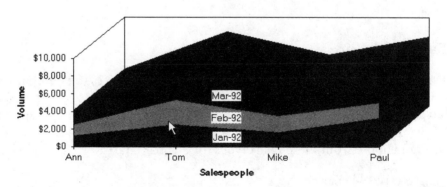

Figure 12.31　Sample 3-D Area Chart

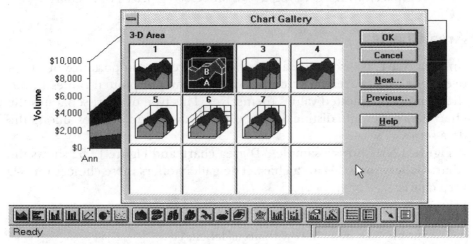

Figure 12.32   Chart Gallery for 3-D Area Charts

4.   3-D area chart with gridlines

5.   3-D plot

6.   3-D plot with gridlines

7.   3-D plot with gridlines for x-axis and y-axis

3-D Bar Charts

A bar chart, as discussed earlier in this section, emphasizes the comparison between items at a fixed period of time. A 3-D bar chart has a similar effect but adds further emphasis to the comparison. Figure 12.33 shows a sample 3-D bar chart, and Figure 12.34 shows the Chart Gallery for a 3-D bar chart. You can choose from these chart types for 3-D bar charts:

1.   Simple 3-D bar chart

2.   Stacked 3-D bar chart

3.   100% stacked 3-D bar chart

4.   3-D bar chart with gridlines

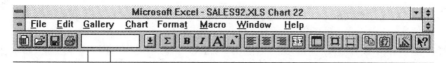

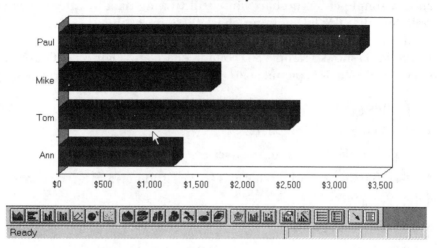

Figure 12.33   Sample 3-D Bar Chart

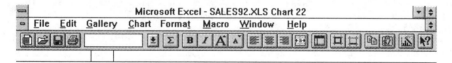

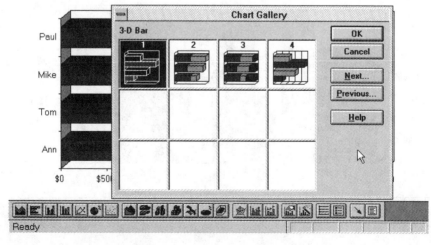

Figure 12.34   Chart Gallery for 3-D Bar Charts

3-D Column Charts

A column chart, as discussed earlier, emphasizes variation over a period of time. A 3-D column chart has the same effect. In a 3-D column chart, you can recognize and compare data within a data series somewhat more easily than in a simple column chart while still viewing data by category. Some people feel that the 3-D column chart (like most other 3-D charts) looks more dramatic than its 2-D counterpart.

Figure 12.35 shows a sample 3-D column chart, and Figure 12.36 shows the Chart Gallery for a 3-D column chart. The gallery offers these chart types:

1.   Simple 3-D column chart

2   Stacked 3-D column chart

3   100% stacked 3-D column chart

4.   3-D column chart with value axis (z-axis) gridlines and 3-D data markers

5.   3-D plot

6.   3-D plot with gridlines

7.   3-D plot with x-axis and y-axis gridlines but no z-axis gridlines

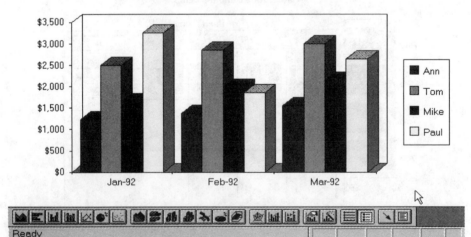

Figure 12.35   Sample 3-D Column Chart

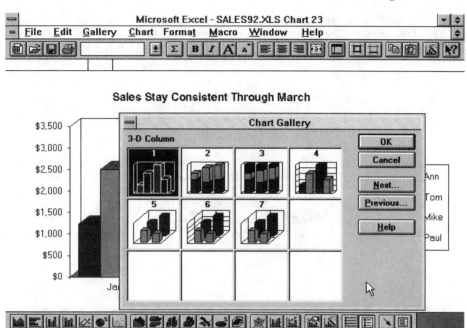

Figure 12.36   Chart Gallery for 3-D Column Charts

3-D Line Charts

A line chart, as discussed previously, shows changes in data over a period of time. A 3-D line chart shows the lines in a line chart as 3-D ribbons, making the lines easier to see. Figure 12.37 shows a sample 3-D line chart, and Figure 12.38 shows the Chart Gallery for a 3-D line chart. The gallery offers four chart types:

1. 3-D plot
2. 3-D plot with gridlines
3. 3-D plot with x-axis and y-axis gridlines only
4. 3-D plot with logarithmic gridlines

3-D Pie Charts

A 3-D pie chart, like a two-dimensional pie chart, shows the relationship of parts to the whole. A 3-D pie chart emphasizes the data values in the front wedges. Figure 12.39 shows a sample 3-D pie chart, and Figure 12.40 shows the Chart Gallery for a 3-D pie chart. These chart types are available:

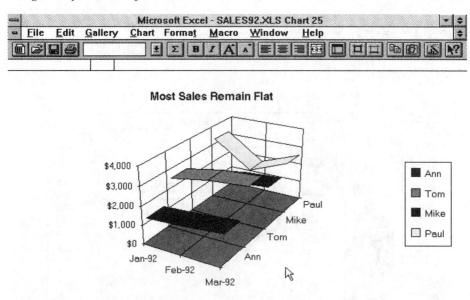

Figure 12.37   Sample 3-D Line Chart

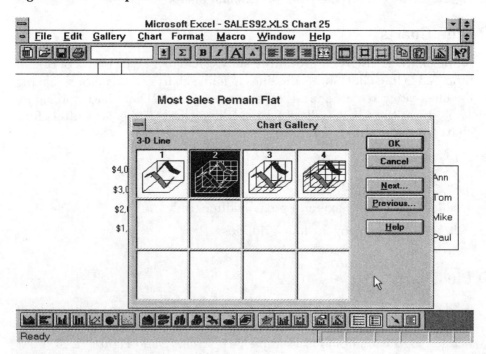

Figure 12.38   Chart Gallery for 3-D Line Charts

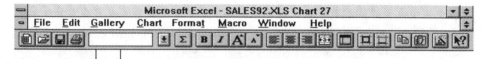

January Holds Its Own

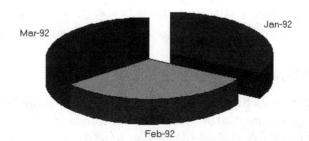

Figure 12.39   Sample 3-D Pie Chart

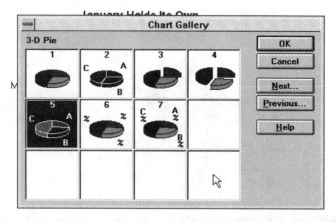

Figure 12.40   Chart Gallery for 3-D Pie Charts

1. Simple 3-D pie chart with each wedge colored or patterned differently.

2. 3-D pie chart with all wedges colored the same and category labels provided.

3. 3-D pie chart with first wedge exploded

4. 3-D pie chart with all wedges exploded

5. Simple 3-D pie chart with category labels provided

6. Simple 3-D pie chart with value labels expressed as percentages

7. Simple 3-D pie chart with category labels expressed as percentages

3-D Surface Charts

A surface chart is useful for finding optimum combinations between two sets of data. With a surface chart you can find optimums that may not be apparent otherwise. The sample chart shown in Figure 12.41, for instance, shows that all the salespeople tend to have monthly sales between $2,000 to $3,000 in goods. Although you could spot such a trend quite readily from the worksheet data, the surface chart can be quite helpful if you are tabulating sales for many salespeople over several months where the monthly totals vary significantly.

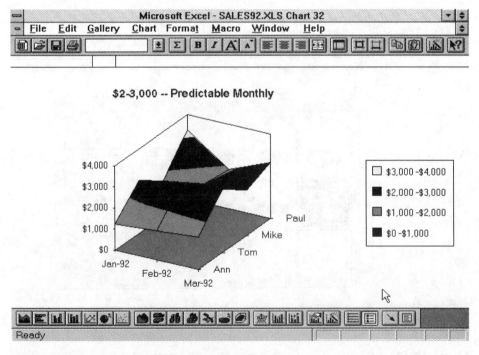

Figure 12.41   Sample 3-D Surface Chart

In a surface chart (as in a topographic map, for example), color does not indicate a data series. Rather, it indicates areas that are at the same height. Surface charts can be colored in or not. Surface charts that are not colored are referred to as wireframe charts.

Figure 12.41 shows a sample 3-D surface chart, and Figure 12.42 shows the Chart Gallery for a 3-D surface chart. These are the choices from the gallery:

1. 3-D surface chart

2. 3-D wireframe chart (same as a surface chart but without color)

3. 2-D color contour chart (a 2-D view of the surface chart from above)

4. 2-D wireframe contour chart (a 2-D contour chart without the color)

Saving Charts

You are already familiar with the steps for saving worksheets. The procedure for saving a chart is almost identical. If a chart is embedded (that is, not displayed in a separate window), you save it along with the worksheet when you save the worksheet.

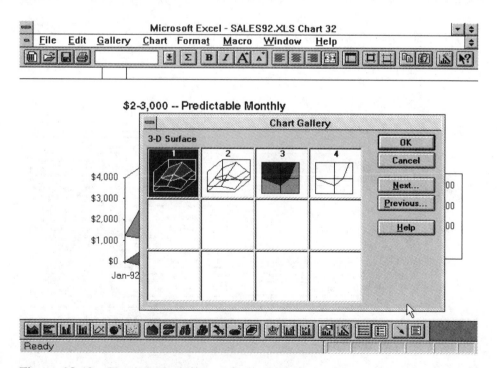

Figure 12.42   Chart Gallery for a 3-D Surface Chart

To save a chart by itself, you first double-click the chart to display it in a separate document window. Then you save the chart in its own file by choosing the Save or Save As command on the File pull-down menu. The Save As dialog box appears (similar to the one shown in Figure 12.43) where you can replace the chart number with a more descriptive filename. Note that Excel automatically adds the extension xlc to a chart to differentiate chart files from worksheet files (with the xls extension).

Once you've saved the chart the first time with the name you want, you can save your changes to the chart by choosing the File Save command when the chart window is active or by clicking the Save File tool on the Standard toolbar.

Printing Charts

To print an embedded chart, print the worksheet in which the chart is embedded with the File Print command or the Print tool on the Standard toolbar. If you've used the Set Print Area command on the Options menu to print a particular cell range in the worksheet, use the Print Preview command on the File menu to make sure that the Print_Area range includes all of the embedded chart. If not, expand the Print_Area range by selecting

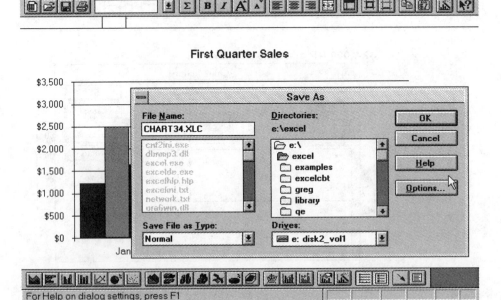

Figure 12.43 Save As Dialog Box for Saving a Chart in a Separate File

the entire range of cells that contain the embedded chart (along with the ranges of data you want printed) and choose the Set Print Area command again. Then print the worksheet with the File Print command or Print tool.

To print a chart that is a separate chart document, make the document window with the chart active, then choose the File Print command from the Chart pull-down menus. The page setup options for printing a chart vary slightly from the standard options for printing a worksheet. In the Page Setup dialog box, you can choose among three Chart Size option buttons, Size On Screen (to print the chart the size it assumes on the screen), Scale to Fit Page (the default, to have Excel reduce the chart so that it prints on the page size you've selected), or Use Full Page (to have Excel expand the chart, if necessary, so that it fills the page size you've selected). The other page setup and printing options are the same as those you use when printing worksheets. (See Chapter 6 for details.)

SUMMARY

In this chapter you learned how to use the basics of charting data in Excel. First you learned how to use the ChartWizard and the chart tools on the Chart toolbar to create embedded charts in your worksheets. Then you learned how to create a chart in a separate chart window. After that you had the opportunity to see all the chart types and formats available in Excel. Finally you learned how to save and print a chart, either as part of the worksheet or in its own chart window.

In the next chapter you will learn how to customize the basic charts that you create in Excel. There you will learn how to select and modify the appearance of individual parts of a chart, including such things as the formatting of the titles and legend in a chart, the scaling and formatting of the chart's axes, and the type of data markers used.

13

Enhancing and Customizing Charts

As you learned in the last chapter, Excel makes it easy to create a finished-looking chart in a few short steps. Often that initial chart is all you need for a presentation. Other times, however, you may feel the initial chart does not sufficiently highlight the most important points about your data, or fully communicate your message. By customizing the chart, you would be able to accentuate these points and keep them from getting lost. For instance, you could add emphasis to certain data markers by changing their colors or patterns (or in the case of a pie chart, by exploding the slices of the pie). You might also accent a part of a chart by annotating it with a text box and using arrows to point directly to the data. And you might modify the formatting or tick marks displayed along the axes of the chart or even delete them altogether.

Excel gives you powerful tools for enhancing charts once you have created them. In this chapter you will learn how to select chart items (a necessary precondition for editing charts in most cases) and modify them. You will also learn to modify the data being graphed by changing the data series they use. Next you will find out how to use the ChartWizard to edit a finished chart quickly.

For those times when you need to get to a fine level of detail, you will learn how to select and modify individual parts of a chart. First you will learn how to annotate your charts with text boxes, titles, and a legend as well as how to change their position, patterns, and fonts. Then you will learn how you can edit the axes of the charts—for instance, by changing the weight of the line or the number and type of tick marks on the axis. You will also learn how to edit chart gridlines—those optional lines stretching across the plot area in some charts. You will find out how to add or remove them with a

517

click of the mouse and how to customize their appearance if you wish. Finally you will learn how to customize the chart data markers and, if you are feeling creative, substitute pictures for them if you wish.

Selecting Chart Items

When you select an item, you tell Excel that you want to perform some editing or formatting upon that item. In most cases you cannot edit an item until you select it. Excel lets you select individual parts of your chart (for a review of the parts of a typical chart, refer back to "Understanding the Parts of a Chart" at the beginning of Chapter 12) such as the x- or y-axis, the legend, or a particular data marker in the chart.

Before you can select a part of the chart, you need to display the chart in its own chart window. If the chart is embedded in a worksheet, double-click the chart to open up a chart window. Then position the pointer on the part of the chart that you want to select (the legend, for example) and click the mouse. Excel shows what item is selected by displaying selection handles (black or white squares around the perimeter of the selected item). Note that you can also select the entire active chart or the plot area (the area of the chart in which Excel plots the data) from the Chart pull-down menu by choosing the Select Chart and Select Plot Area commands, respectively.

If a selected item has black selection handles, you can move or (in most cases, except for legends) size the item directly. That is, you can click on the handle and drag it and apply other techniques explained in the next section. If the item has white selection squares, you cannot move or size it directly. Figure 13.1 shows a selected item marked with white squares, and Figure 13.2 shows a selected item marked with black squares.

To select the entire plot area, click anywhere in the plot area except on a chart item. To select the entire chart, click anywhere outside the plot area except on a chart item. To select a particular chart data series, click one of the markers in the series. Excel automatically selects the whole series, as shown in Figure 13.3. To select a single item in a data series, hold down the Ctrl key as you click the item. Once you have selected a first item, you can cycle through the items in the chart by pressing one of the arrow keys.

Tip If you have developed a chart with overlapping or hidden items, cycling through the items with the keyboard may be easier than using the mouse pointer. To cycle within a class of items —for instance, to choose a single item in a data series—use the left arrow and right arrows, not the up and down arrows.

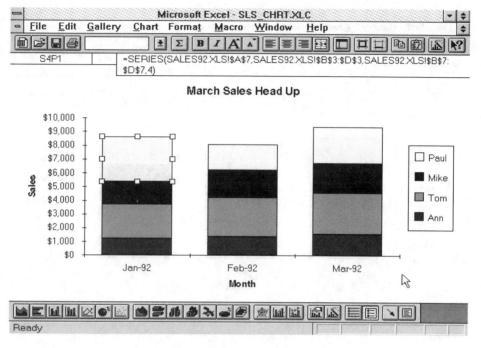

Figure 13.1   Selected Chart Item Marked with White Selection Squares

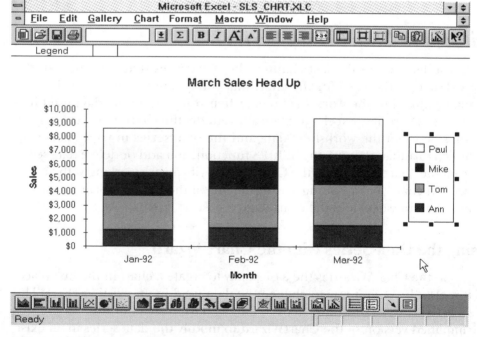

Figure 13.2   Selected Chart Item Marked with Black Selection Squares

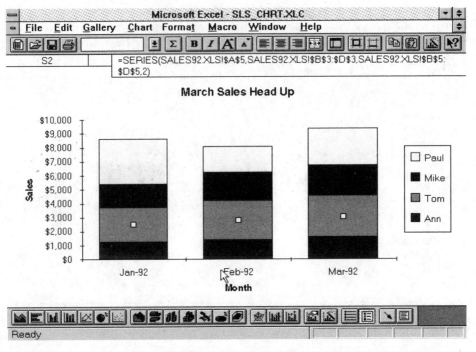

Figure 13.3   Selecting the Whole Data Series by Selecting One Marker in It

Editing the Chart Data Series

As you learned in the last chapter, the data series that you select in the worksheet is the basis for the chart that you create. Because the chart remains linked to the worksheet data, when you change the data used in a chart's data series, Excel automatically redraws the chart. Excel creates the links between the worksheet data and the data series in your chart with linked formulas that use the SERIES function. You add or delete data series from the chart either with the ChartWizard (if you are working with an embedded chart) or by editing the arguments of the SERIES formula used to link the worksheet and the chart data.

Editing the Data Series with the ChartWizard

Just as the ChartWizard is the easiest way to create a chart in the first place, it is also the easiest way to change the data used in an existing chart. The ChartWizard uses just two steps to edit a chart, instead of five. To use this simplified version of the ChartWizard to modify the data series in an existing chart, you follow these steps:

1. Select the chart whose data series you want to edit. If the chart is embedded in the worksheet, click the chart. If the chart is in a separate chart window, make its window active and open the worksheet containing the data used for the chart.

2. Click the ChartWizard tool on the Standard toolbar. If necessary, Excel switches to the worksheet containing the chart data and the ChartWizard - Step 1 of 2 dialog box (similar to the one shown in Figure 13.4) appears along with a marquee around the cell selection you used to plot the chart in the first place. Now you can change the selection by dragging the selection border. If you prefer, you can type in the address of the new selection in the **R**ange text box.

3. Choose the Next> button at the bottom of the ChartWizard dialog box. The ChartWizard - Step 2 of 2 dialog box (similar to the one shown in Figure 13.5) appears. There, you can choose whether to have the data series in rows or columns and make other selections, as explained in Chapter 12. If you wish, you can go back to the first dialog box and change the data selected.

4. Once you are satisfied with the way the chart appears in the Sample Chart area in the Step 2 of 2 dialog box, choose the OK button. Excel

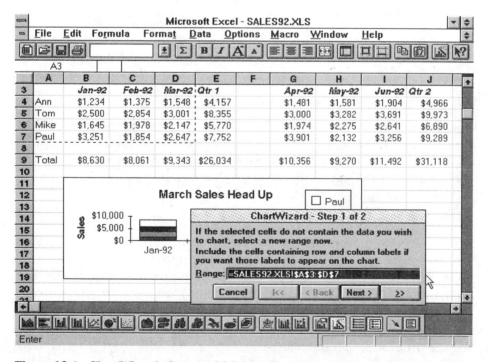

Figure 13.4 ChartWizard - Step 1 of 2 Dialog Box When Editing an Existing Chart

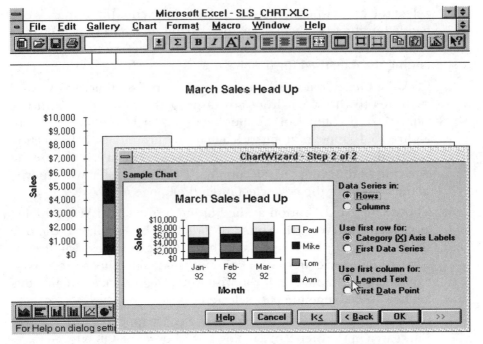

Figure 13.5   ChartWizard - Step 2 of 2 Dialog Box When Editing an Existing Chart

closes the ChartWizard dialog box and redraws the chart using the changed data.

Editing with the Edit Series Command

For each chart you create, Excel creates a linked formula using the SERIES function that you can change if you wish. To see the series formula, open a chart window with the chart, then select one of its series markers. Figure 13.6 shows the series formula for the sample chart used in the previous section.

The SERIES function follows the syntax

=SERIES(name_ref,categories,values,plot_order)

where the *name_ref* argument is the name of the series (an external absolute reference to a single cell), the *categories* argument refers to the range containing the X labels (also an external absolute reference to the cells containing the names of the categories plotted), the *values* argument refers to the range containing the Y values (an external absolute reference to the cells containing the values), and the *plot_order* argument is a number, telling the order in which the data series is plotted in the chart (first, second, third, and so on).

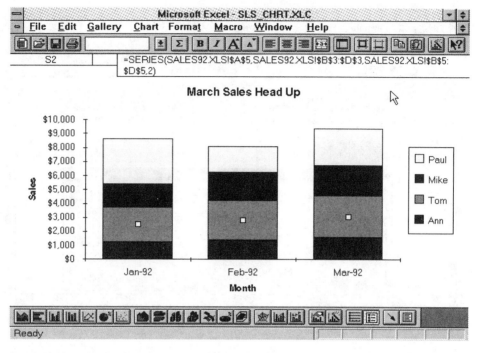

Figure 13.6   Series Formula for a Sample Chart

You can use the **Ed**it Series command on the **C**hart pull-down menu to make it easier to edit any of the arguments used in the SERIES function. When you choose this command, Excel displays the Edit Series dialog box (similar to the one shown in Figure 13.7). If one of the chart's data series is selected when you choose the **Ed**it Series command, Excel selects the name of the data series in the **S**eries list box and displays the current cell reference for the *name_ref* argument in the **N**ame text box, the *categories* argument in the **X** Labels text box, the *values* argument in the **Y** Values text box, and the current value of the *plot_order* argument in the **P**lot Order text box.

Tip   Remember that if you have selected the data series that you want to edit in the chart, you can open the Edit Series dialog box from the shortcut menu attached to that data series by clicking the area with the right mouse button then selecting the **Ed**it Series command from the shortcut menu.

To modify any of the arguments for the SERIES function, you simply select the appropriate text box in the Edit Series dialog box and select the new cell references. Figure 13.7 shows you the Edit Series dialog box after

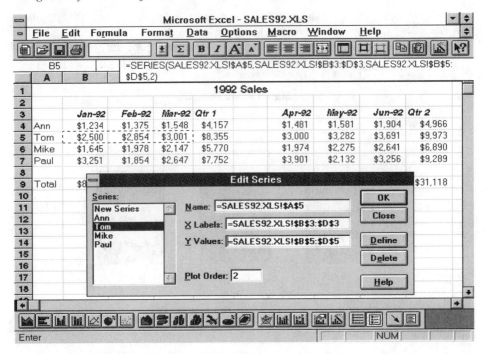

Figure 13.7   The Edit Series Dialog Box After Selecting the X Labels Text Box for Tom's Data Series

selecting the **Y** Values text box for the Tom data series in the chart. When you click the Name, **X** Labels, or **Y** Labels text box in the box, Excel automatically switches to the linked worksheet (assuming that this document is open) and displays a marquee around the current cell reference. You can then modify the cell selection for the argument directly in the worksheet, or you can type in the new cell reference.

If no data series is selected in the chart at the time you choose the Edit Series command, the program selects New Series in the **S**eries list box (as shown in Figure 13.8). You use New Series to add a new data series to the chart. When New Series is selected, Excel selects the next available number for the *plot_order* argument (5 in this example) and retains the external reference for the cell range used as the *categories* argument in the SERIES formulas for the chart. (The text boxes for the *name_ref* and *values* arguments are blank.) To switch to the linked worksheet so that you can select new cell ranges for the *name_ref* and *values* arguments in the new data series, click the **X** Labels text box. After you have defined the cell ranges for these arguments, choose the **D**efine button to add the new data series to the **S**eries list box.

To delete a series, select the series from the **S**eries list box, then choose the **D**elete button. Note that you can also delete a data series by selecting

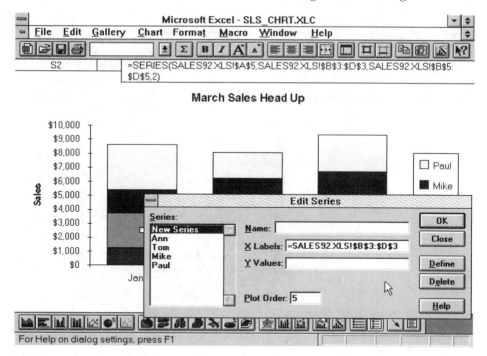

Figure 13.8   The Edit Series Dialog Box After Selecting New Series in the Series List Box

the series on the chart in the chart window and then choosing **E**dit Cl**e**ar command either from the chart menu bar or the data series' shortcut menu and pressing the Delete key and then choosing the Series option button in the Clear dialog box before pressing Enter or choosing OK.

When you've finished editing the SERIES formula in the Edit Series dialog box, choose the OK button to retain your modifications to the selected chart. If you wish to abandon your changes, press the Esc key or choose the Close button instead.

Adding and Formatting Chart Text

As smart as the ChartWizard or Chart toolbar may be when it creates a chart for you, neither one can always anticipate everything that you want to say in the chart. The chart these tools create may be quite satisfactory if you need something quick and easy. Often, though, you will want to embellish the initial chart with text, arrows, and other items.

When you create a chart initially using any of the techniques described in Chapter 12, it does contain some text. The chart shown in Figure 13.9, for instance, is a pie chart based on data from the **deptsales.xls** worksheet

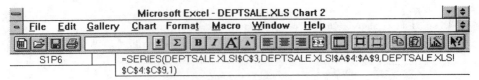

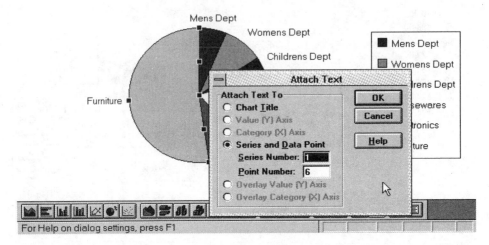

Figure 13.9   Sample Chart with the Attach Text Dialog Box

comparing February sales from the various departments in a department store. The initial text for this chart includes a title, labels for the data series, and legend text.

When editing the text on a chart, you add, edit, and format text of your own. When adding text, you add one of two types: *attached text* or *unattached text*. Attached text is attached to a particular chart object, such as a data marker. In the sample chart in Figure 13.9, for instance, the pie labels are all attached to the data markers (the pie slices). If you select and move a slice, you move the text along with it. If you move the data marker, you move the text. Unattached text can appear anywhere on the chart.

Adding Attached Text

The advantage of attached text is that the text moves automatically when you move a chart element. As you enhance a chart, you are quite likely to drag elements around the screen to display them to better effect. Unless you attach the labels to the chart elements, you can end up moving just the elements or having to make a second move to take along the text.

The easiest way to add attached text is to select the item to which you want to add the text, such as a data marker, before you choose the Attach Text command from the Chart menu bar or from the shortcut menu attached to a data marker. (The Attach Text command does not appear on the shortcut menu attached to the chart title or legend.) Note that you do not have to select the item first, but for a data marker you do have to identify it later by series number and point number which are supplied automatically if the item is selected.

When you select the Attach Text command, Excel displays the Attach Text dialog box similar to the one shown in Figure 13.9. If you have selected an item, Excel automatically selects the appropriate Attach Text To option button for you. After selecting the object to attach the text to, choose the OK button or press Enter.

The current value for the selected object (the number in the linked worksheet cell in the case of a data marker) then appears on the chart, surrounded by white selection squares (the kind that don't enable you to move or resize the selection). At that point, you type the text you want to attach to the selected object in the formula bar. (Entering and editing the attached text on the chart formula bar is the same as entering and editing text for a cell in the worksheet's formula bar.) To insert a line break when typing attached text, press Alt+Enter. When you have the text the way you want it, press Enter or click the Enter button to insert the text in the chart, then press the Esc key to deselect the object.

Adding Unattached Text

The advantage of unattached text is that it is easier and more automatic to create, and you can move it around at will without having to worry about what it may be attached to. You can probably get along quite well creating only unattached text most of the time.

To add unattached text, click the Text Box tool on the Chart toolbar (the very last one on the right). Black selection squares appear around the word Text that is positioned in the middle of the chart, and the word text appears in the formula bar. Type and edit the text just as you would attached text or any cell entry in a formula bar, then press Enter when you are satisfied. Excel inserts your text in the chart. You can then drag any one of the selection handles to move the text to its proper position on the chart.

To delete unattached text, select the text, then press the Delete key.

Tip   When adding attached or unattached text to a chart, you can use an existing label in the worksheet. To do this, select the object or click the Text tool, then type = on the formula bar, use the **Window** menu to activate the worksheet with the text you want to use, select the cell in the worksheet that contains the label to use, then use the **Window** menu to switch back to the chart window and press Enter. Excel creates a linked formula between the worksheet label and the selected object or text box in the chart so that anytime you edit the text in the worksheet cell, the program automatically updates the text in your chart.

Formatting Text

Once you have the text you need in the chart, you still may want to format it. When formatting the text of the chart, the object you select determines which text you format. If you select the entire chart, you can format all the text in it at once. You may do that if, for instance, you want to make all the text to use the same new font. To format the text of a particular object, you select just that object.

To add bold or italics to the font of the selected object, click the Bold or Italic tools from the Standard toolbar, as usual. Likewise, to change the horizontal alignment of the text, click the appropriate alignment tool on the Standard toolbar. To change the font of the selected object, choose the **Font** command on the object's shortcut menu or the Format pull-down menu, then make your choices in the Font dialog box (shown in Figure 13.10).

To change vertical alignment, orientation, or wrap the text, you choose the Text command on the object's shortcut menu or the Format pull-down menu, then make your choices in the Text dialog box shown in Figure 13.11. To change the text borders and the pattern of the area where the text appears, double-click the object or text box and choose the appropriate options in the Patterns dialog box (shown in Figure 13.12) that then appears. (You can also open this dialog box by selecting the **Patterns** command on the object's shortcut menu or the Formula pull-down menu.)

Tip   You can navigate among all the dialog boxes for formatting text once you choose any one of them. From the Patterns dialog box, for instance, you can choose **Font** or **Text**. To have access to all the capabilities for formatting text in the least time, double-click the selected text. From the Patterns dialog box, you can make all the formatting changes you wish to the selected text or to the entire chart.

Furniture is Our Biggest Business

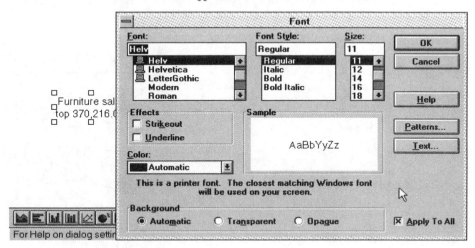

Figure 13.10 Font Dialog Box

Furniture is Our Biggest Business

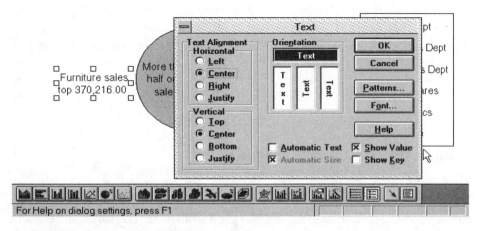

Figure 13.11 The Text Dialog Box

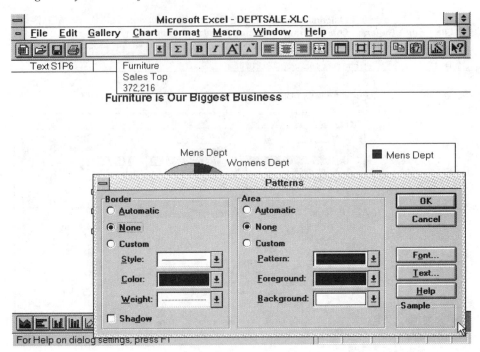

Figure 13.12   The Patterns Dialog Box

Figure 13.13, for instance, shows the sample chart introduced in Figure 13.9 after formatting the title text, the text attached to the Furniture data series, and an unattached note. You will notice that text for the title is now bold and appears in a larger size than the original. Below the title, I have added a text box with the unattached note *More than half our sales.* You will also notice that the attached text *Furniture Sales Top $370,000* has been added to the furniture category label, and this has been enhanced with a drop shadow. I deleted all of the other category labels from this pie chart to make it less cluttered. (The legend identifies the slices anyway, making the labels redundant.) As you can see from this example, a small amount of editing can transform a basic chart into a presentation chart that makes your point clearly.

Customizing the Chart Legend

A legend lists each pattern or symbol used as a data marker in a chart and follows the pattern or symbol with the chart data series name. For instance, the sample chart used in the previous section lists the colors used for each data marker and follows each with the label (Men's Dept, Women's Dept,

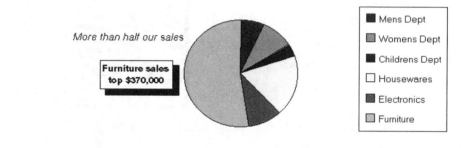

Figure 13.13   Sample Pie Chart with Enhanced Text

and so on). Generally it is good to use a legend when you do not use category labels, and vice versa. Once you have decided to use a legend, you can customize it in various ways.

You can use the Legend tool on the Chart toolbar to add or delete a legend for your chart. Click the legend tool to display a legend if none is showing or to delete a legend if one is showing. You can also add or delete a legend from the **C**hart menu. Choose the Add **L**egend to display a legend or Delete **L**egend to delete it.

When you select a legend, it appears with dark handles around it. These handles enable you to move the legend in the chart. (You cannot, however, resize a legend with the selection handles.) To move the legend, click within its borders, then drag its rectangle to the position you want. If you drag the legend to the edge of the chart window, Excel redraws the legend to make it fit. The program even changes the shape of the legend from horizontal to vertical, or vertical to horizontal.

You can also reposition the legend by selecting a new type for it (**B**ottom, **C**orner, **T**op, **R**ight, or **L**eft) in the Legend dialog box. To open the Legend dialog box shown in Figure 13.14, select the legend, then choose the **L**egend command on the legend's shortcut menu or the Format pull-down menu.

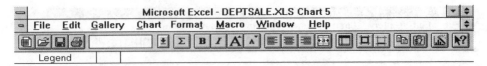

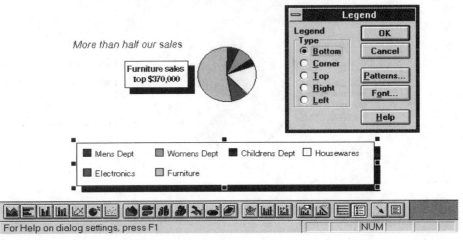

Figure 13.14   Sample Chart with Enhanced Legend Box

As with text, you can change the border around the legend and the pattern within the area of the legend box. The easiest way to make the changes is to double-click the legend itself in the chart. The Patterns dialog box then appears from which you can choose the Font button to display the Font dialog box or the Legend button to display the Legend dialog box.

Figure 13.14 shows a horizontal legend at the bottom of the chart area. This legend uses a custom border and has a drop-shadow. The font has been reduced to 9-point Helvetica.

Customizing the Chart Axes

The axis is the scale used to plot the data for your chart. Except for pie charts and radar charts, all two-dimensional charts have an x- and a y- axis. Three-dimensional charts with a 3-D plot have x, y, and z axes.

When you initially create a chart, Excel sets up the axes for you automatically based on the data you are plotting, which you then can adjust in various ways. To remove the display of any or all the axes in the chart, you simply deselect the check box in the Axes dialog box (similar to the one shown in Figure 13.15) for the particular axis you don't want to see. To open the Axes dialog box, you can select the Axes command on the

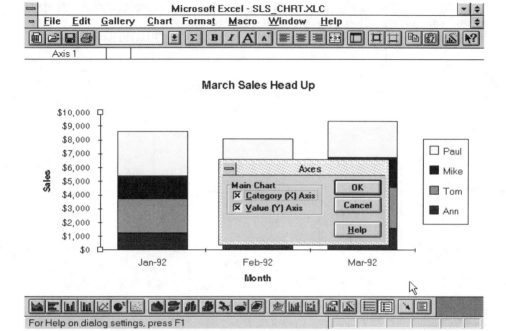

Figure 13.15 The Axes Dialog Box

shortcut menu attached to the chart itself (displayed quickly by pressing Shift+F10) or on the **C**hart pull-down menu. Then clear the check box for the axis or axes you don't want displayed in the chart before you choose OK or press Enter.

Perhaps the most common change you will want to make to the axis is to change its scale. Changing the scale can have a dramatic effect on the results. The sales improvement in the March Sales Head Up chart does not appear to be very great when the chart begins at a scale of 0 for the y-axis, as shown earlier in Figure 13.1 and a number of subsequent figures. When you move the scale up, however, you accentuate the differences among the bars. Figure 13.16 shows the sample chart with the scale for the y-axis set to begin at $7,000 instead of $0.

Depending on which axis you are formatting, different options are available when you change the axis scale. You follow these general steps to change the scale of an axis:

1. Select the axis whose scale you want to change—the y-axis in the current example.

2. From the shortcut menu or the Format pull-down menu, choose the **S**cale command. The Axis Scale dialog box appears, similar to the one shown in Figure 13.17.

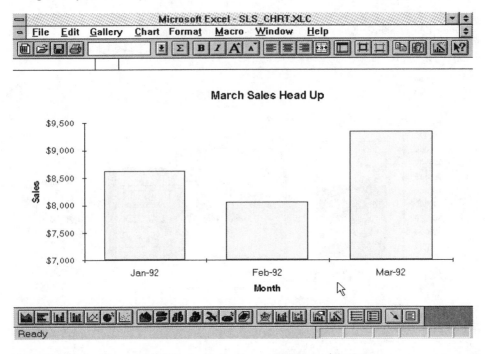

Figure 13.16   Chart with Y Axis Scale Set to Begin at $7,000

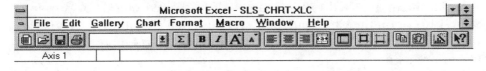

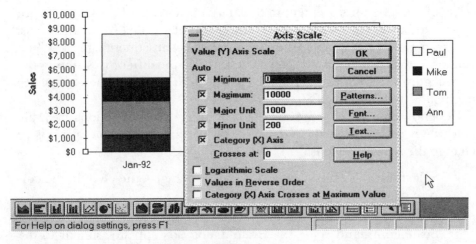

Figure 13.17   The Axis Scale Dialog Box

3. Make your selections in the dialog box, then choose the OK button or press Enter to put them into effect in the chart.

Tip To open the Patterns dialog box, double-click on it. From the Patterns dialog box you can select the command button for other formatting options—**F**ont, **T**ext, and Sca**l**e.

You can choose these options for the value axis (the y- or vertical axis except on 3-D charts).

- **Mi**nimum: to determine the point where the axis begins—perhaps $4,000 instead of the default of $0. If you choose a value higher than 0, smaller data values are not displayed at all. (They do not, for instance, appear as a data marker that goes below the line.)

- **Ma**ximum: to determine the highest point displayed on the vertical axis. Data values greater than the value you specify here simply do not display.

- Ma**j**or Unit: to display the values at the major tick marks.

- Mi**n**or Unit: to display the values at the minor tick marks.

- Category (X) Axis **C**rosses at: to determine the value at which the x-axis crosses the y-axis. If you choose this option, you can have data markers appear below the line.

- **L**ogarithmic Scale: bases the scale on powers of ten and recalculates the Minimum, Maximum, Major Unit, and Minor Unit accordingly.

- Values in **R**everse Order: places the lowest value on the chart at the top of the scale and the highest value at the bottom. Figure 13.18, for instance, shows the sample column chart with the values in reverse order. You might use such a chart if you wanted to emphasize the negative effect of the larger values.

- Category (X) Axis Crosses at **M**aximum Value: places the category axis at the highest value.

Alert! Excel allows you the freedom to combine certain options, but be careful not to confuse your viewer. For instance, you can select Values in **R**everse Order and also select Category (X) Axis Crosses at **M**aximum Value. You then get a chart that looks like the default chart (with the columns heading up) even though the values begin with the largest value at the bottom.

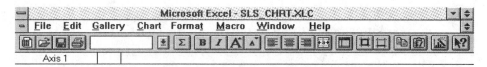

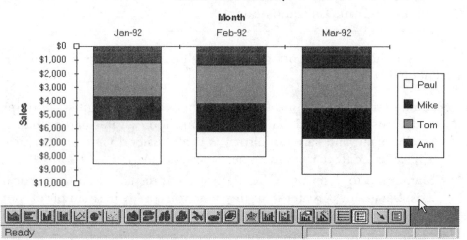

Figure 13.18   Sample Chart with Y-Axis Values in Reverse Order

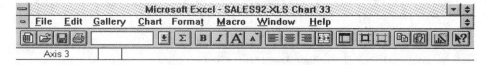

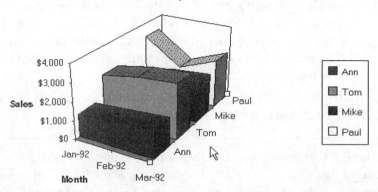

Figure 13.19   Sample 3-D chart with Labels Along the Series Axis

The value axis has these additional options on 3-D charts.

- Floor (XY Plane) Crosses at: to specify the value where the category axis crosses the value axis; it is similar to the Category (X) Axis Crosses at option in a 2-D chart.

- Floor (XY Plane) Crosses at Minimum Value: places the floor (category axis) at the lowest value on the 3-D chart. This option overrides the Floor (XY Plane) Crosses at option.

In a 3-D chart, the x-axis is the category axis, the y-axis is the series axis, and the z-axis is the value axis. For the series axis in a 3-D chart (the y-axis), you can make these choices.

- Number Of Series Between Tick Labels: to specify whether you want to have a label for every data series (an entry of 1), every other series (an entry of 2), and so on. Figure 13.20 shows a sample 3-D chart with labels (Ann, Tom, Mike, and Paul) along the series (y) axis, so that you can relate this option to an actual 3-D chart.

- Number Of Series Between Tick Marks: to change the number of tick marks along the series axis, rather than the number of labels as does the previous option. Again refer to Figure 13.19. For instance, you can choose to have two data series appear between each tick mark along the series axis.

- Series in Reverse Order: to display the chart data series in reverse order— for example, with Paul at the lower left and Ann at the top right in the sample in Figure 13.19.

If you select the category axis (the x-axis in most cases), you can make these choices:

- Value (Y) Axis Crosses At Category Number: to specify the number where you want the value axis to cross the category axis, similar to the Category (X) Axis Crosses at option for the value axis.

- Number Of Categories Between Tick Labels: determines the number of labels that appear on the chart.

- Number Of Categories Between Tick Marks: determines the number of tick marks that appear. Refer to the discussion of Number Of Series Between Tick Labels just above.

- Value (Y) Axis Crosses Between Categories: determines whether the value axis displays at the edge of the category or in the middle of the category in a two-dimensional chart.

- Categories in Reverse Order: changes the order of the displayed categories.

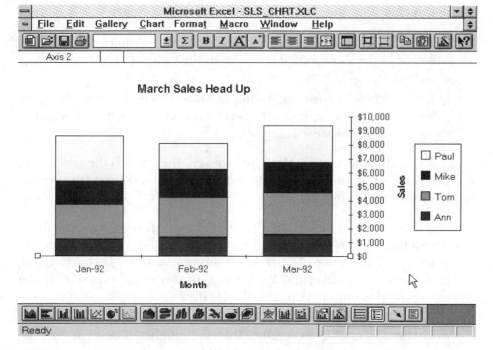

Figure 13.20   Chart Using the Value (Y) Axis Crosses at Maximum Category Option for the Category (X) Axis

- Value (Y) Axis Crosses At Maximum Category: displays the value axis after the last category in a 2-D chart, as shown in Figure 13.20. This option is useful if you have graphical material on the left side of the chart (such as a picture) and want to avoid a cluttered look. It is also helpful if you want the viewer to readily relate values to the last data marker.

If you first select the y-axis (series axis) in a 3-D chart, you have these choices.

- Number of Series Between Tick Labels: specifies whether you have a label for every data series (an entry of 1), every other series (an entry of 2), and so on, similar to the value axis discussed above.

- Number of Series Between Tick Marks: changes the number of tick marks along the series axis, rather than the number of labels. You can choose to have more series between tick marks (resulting in few tick marks) or fewer series between tick marks, similar to the value axis discussed above.

- Series in Reverse Order: displays the series in reverse order from the original (from March to January, for instance, instead of from January to March).

Changing the scale, then, changes the appearance of the chart, sometimes in quite striking ways. You can also change other elements of the axes—the axis patterns, the tick marks, and the tick mark labels—by choosing appropriate options from the axis shortcut menu as described earlier in this chapter.

Customizing the Chart Gridlines

Gridlines are the optional lines that extend from an axis across the plot area to help you relate the data marker to the scale represented on the axis. They can help you relate the values on the value axis to the data markers representing those values. As you may recall from Chapter 12, if you want gridlines to appear when you create a chart, choose a format that includes gridlines.

If you do not put in the gridlines initially, you can add horizontal ones (the ones most commonly used, because they extend the tick marks on the value axis) simply by clicking the Horizontal Gridlines tool on the Chart toolbar. If horizontal gridlines are already displayed in your chart, you can click this tool to delete them.

The Horizontal Gridlines tool is a shortcut for some of the choices from the Gridlines dialog box. To open the Gridlines dialog box (shown in Figure 13.21), choose the **G**ridlines command on the chart shortcut menu

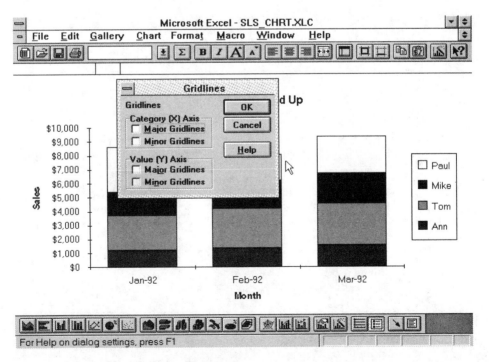

Figure 13.21   The Gridlines Dialog Box

(Shift+F10) or the **C**hart pull-down menu. Make your selections for **M**ajor and **M**inor gridlines for the axes in the chart you are using. To delete gridlines, clear the check boxes for those options you no longer want in the Gridlines dialog box.

You can also work with gridlines individually by clicking one of the type of gridlines you want to work with (major gridlines for the y-axis, for instance). To format them, double-click on any gridline of the type you want to modify. This will display the Patterns dialog box. In the Patterns dialog box, select the **S**tyle, **C**olor, and **W**eight option you want and choose OK. Figure 13.22 shows a sample chart with gridlines formatted in a broken pattern with a heavy weight.

To delete a type of gridlines, select it then choose the **C**lear command on the shortcut menu or **E**dit pull-down menu or press the Delete key.

Customizing Chart Arrows

In Chapter 8 you learned how to add arrows to your worksheet. You can also add arrows to a chart using the Arrow tool on the Chart toolbar or by selecting the Add Arrow command on the **C**hart pull-down menu. As soon as you click the Arrow tool or select the Add Arrow command, Excel inserts

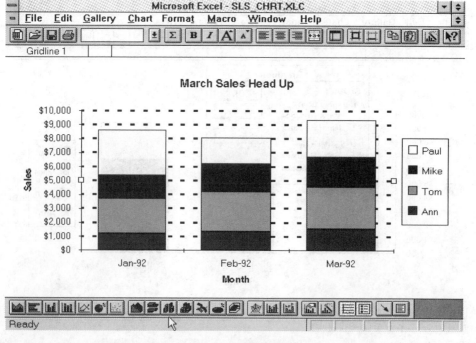

Figure 13.22   Sample Chart with Customized Horizontal Gridlines

a new arrow in your chart pointing toward the center, which remains selected (with black selection handles), as shown in Figure 13.23. You can then immediately move the arrow in the chart, change the direction of its arrowhead, or modify its length by dragging the arrow or one of its selection handles.

To format the arrow, double-click the arrow or choose the **P**atterns command from the arrow's shortcut menu or the Format pull-down menu. Then select your formatting options in the Patterns dialog box (shown in Figure 13.24). You can change the style, width, and length of the arrowhead as well as the style, color, and weight of the line.

Customizing the Chart Data Markers

The options available for formatting chart data markers depend on the type of chart you are working with. For all chart types, you can begin from the **C**hart menu if you wish instead of selecting the data markers. You follow these general steps when you want to customize chart data markers:

1. Choose the **M**ain Chart command from the chart shortcut menu (Shift+F10) or the Format pull-down menu. Excel displays the Format Chart dialog box similar to the one shown in Figure 13.25.

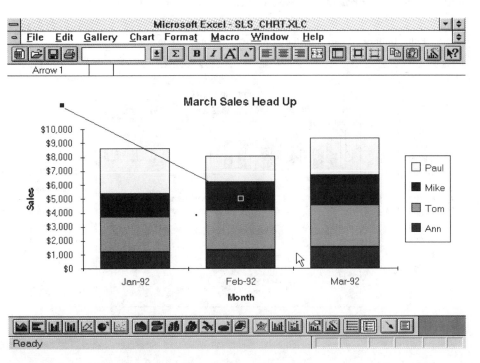

Figure 13.23 Sample Chart After Adding an Arrow

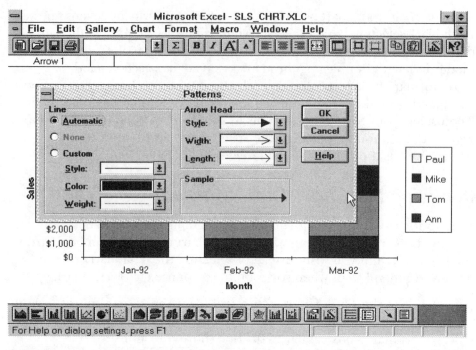

Figure 13.24   Patterns Dialog Box for Line and Arrow Head

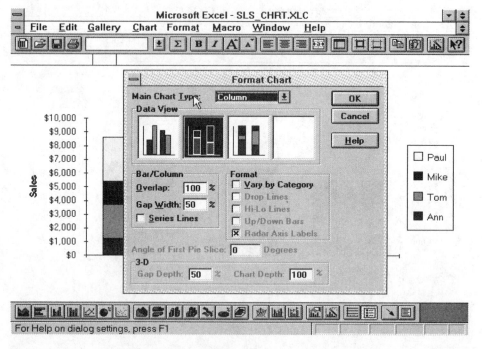

Figure 13.25   The Format Chart Dialog Box

2. From the Main Chart **T**ype drop-down list box, choose the chart type you are working with. The options for that chart type appear in black type. All options that do not apply are in gray.

3. Make your selections in the Format Chart dialog box and then choose OK or press Enter.

You can make these choices in the Format Chart dialog box:

- Data View: to choose the format you want to use, simply click the format you want.

- Bar/Column Overlap: to change the percentage by which markers within a cluster overlap one another in the chart. If the percentage is zero, the markers are touching. If the percentage is negative, there is a gap between the markers.

- Bar/Column Gap Width: to modify the width of the gap between clusters in a bar or column chart. The number you type in the box is a percentage of the column or bar width.

- Bar/Column Series Lines (for stacked bar and stacked column charts): to connect with lines the tops of the data markers for each series.

- Format Vary by Category: to assign a different color or pattern to each data marker for a chart with only one data series.

- Drop Lines: to extend drop lines from each marker to the x-axis in line or area charts.

- Hi-Lo Lines: to insert Hi-Lo lines (that go from the highest to the lowest value in each category) in two-dimensional line charts.

- Up/Down Bars: to insert a rectangle extending from the opening price to the closing price on a given day in open-high-low-close charts.

- Radar Axis Labels: to place labels on the category axes of radar charts.

- Angle of First Pie Slice: to set the angle for the pie slice for the first data series. The angle is measured in degrees clockwise from vertical.

- 3-D Gap Depth: to set the distance between the data series in a 3-D chart (similar to Gap Width in two-dimensional bar and column charts).

- Chart Depth: to set the depth of a #-D chart relative to its width. The depth is a percentage of the chart width.

You can also format the patterns for the data markers in your chart. The options available depend on the type of chart you are working with. Double-click the data markers you want to format to display the Patterns dialog box where you can select your new formats. Figure 13.26 shows the Patterns dialog box for a column chart.

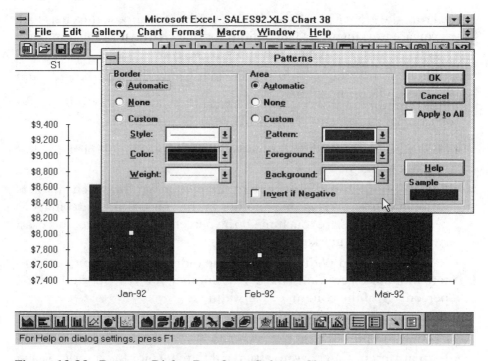

Figure 13.26   Patterns Dialog Box for a Column Chart

As you make changes in the Patterns dialog box, you can see their effect in the Sample box in the lower right. If you choose the Custom option button in the Border section, you can choose a new line **S**tyle, **C**olor, or **W**eight. If you choose the Custom option button in the Area section, you can choose a **P**attern as well as a color for the **F**oreground and **B**ackground. If you choose the Invert if Negative check box, the program reverses the foreground and background colors for a data series marker if the value it represents in the worksheet is negative.

Replacing Markers with Pictures

Graphics has a good deal to do with having fun, and, when working with data markers, there is nothing quite as enjoyable as creating picture charts. Figure 13.27, for instance, shows a picture chart that substitutes cars for the columns in a column chart. It is easier than you might think to create such "fancy" graphics, the kind you used to have to commission from service agencies.

You simply follow these steps to convert a chart into a picture chart:

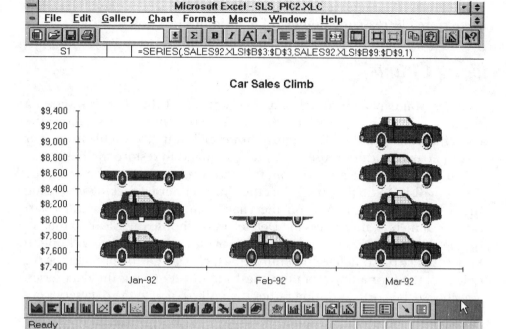

Figure 13.27 Sample Chart Using Stacked and Scaled Pictures

1. Open the application that contains the clip art you want to use. Microsoft PowerPoint offers some excellent clip art, but you can use any source of Windows clip art that you wish.

2. Select the graphic and then use the **C**opy command on the **E**dit menu (Ctrl+C) to copy the picture to the Clipboard. Try to get the clip art to the right size and angle before you copy it to the Clipboard.

3. Switch to the Excel chart where you want to replace the marker with the picture.

4. Select the data marker that you want to replace with the picture.

5. Choose the **P**aste command from the **E**dit menu (Ctrl+V).

Excel offers some special tools for creating picture charts. If you double-click a data marker that uses a picture, a Patterns dialog box with the **Stretch, Stack,** and **Stack and Scale** option buttons appears. The **Stretch** option stretches the picture assigned to the data markers lengthwise. The **Stack** option keeps the picture assigned to the data markers at normal size and stacks copies of the pictures one on top of the other. The **Stack and Scale** option also stacks copies of the pictures, while maintaining the scale displayed in its **Units/Picture** text box. To increase the size of each picture, you increase the number of units in this text box. To decrease the size of the picture, decrease the number of units in this text box.

Deleting Charts

At times, you may want to delete a chart entirely. If the chart is saved in a separate chart file, you can use the **File Delete** command to remove the chart file from your disk. Remember, however, if you delete a file from your disk in error, you cannot use the Undo command to restore the file.

You can also delete a chart from its chart window without removing the file from disk. To do this, you select the chart (either by clicking it or using the Select **C**hart command on the chart's shortcut menu or the **C**hart pull-down menu), then press the Delete key or choose the Cl**e**ar command on the **E**dit menu. Excel displays the Clear dialog box with the **A**ll option button selected. To delete the entire chart, choose OK or press Enter. To delete all the formatting from the chart without removing the data series, you choose the Formats option rather than **A**ll. To delete the data series but leave the formats unchanged, choose the Formulas option instead.

If the chart is embedded in your worksheet, you simply activate the worksheet, select the chart, and press the Delete key or choose the Clear command on the **E**dit menu. Excel immediately deletes the entire chart from the worksheet without displaying the Clear dialog box.

If you delete a chart in the chart window or the worksheet in error, you can restore it to the worksheet by choosing the **E**dit **U**ndo Clear command (Ctrl+Z) right away.

Changing the Viewing Angles of 3-D Charts

There are two methods for changing the viewing angles for a 3-D chart similar to the one in Figure 13.19. If you don't need to be exact in your measurements, you can use the mouse to manipulate the floor and walls directly to change the elevation and rotation angles of the 3-D chart. If you need to be exact (perhaps in accordance with a departmental style sheet or other guidelines), you can modify the viewing angles of a 3-D chart with the **3-D View** command on the Format menu.

To change the viewing angles of a 3-D chart with the mouse, you follow these steps:

1.   If you are changing an embedded 3-D chart, double-click the chart in the worksheet to open a chart window. Otherwise, open the chart window with the 3-D chart you want to modify.

2. Click a corner of the walls or floor of the 3-D chart to select them. When you have selected them properly, that is, by a corner of the 3-D chart, you will see black selection handles instead of white selection handles. Figure 13.28 shows a sample 3-D column chart with the walls and floor selected by clicking a corner.

3. Position the pointer on one of the selection handles, then drag the pointer to create the effect you want and release the mouse button. When dragging the pointer, you can circumscribe a circle around the selection handle to see the outline of the walls and floor of the 3-D chart at all the possible elevation and rotation angles.

Figure 13.29, for instance, shows the sample chart after dragging a right selection handle slightly down to flatten the overall appearance of the chart.

Changing the elevation and rotation with the mouse is like rotating a box inside a sphere. As you will see if you experiment on your own, you can have quite a significant effect on the chart, often more than you want. If you create an effect you do not like, remember you can use the **U**ndo command on the **E**dit menu to return to the original view after you have released the mouse button.

If you choose to work with the **3**-D view command on the **F**ormat menu, you can use the options in the 3-D View dialog box to make precise

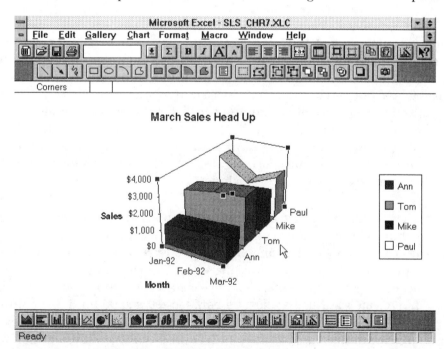

Figure 13.28 3-D Chart with Floor and Walls Selected

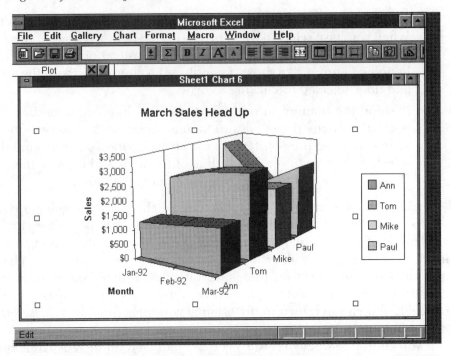

Figure 13.29   Sample 3-D Chart After Changing the Elevation and Rotation with the Mouse

adjustments to the elevation and rotation of your 3-D chart and, in addition, to the perspective, height, and angle of its axes. You can also choose the 3-D View option on the chart shortcut menu to display the 3-D View dialog box. Simply click the *right* mouse button after you have selected one of the chart elements other than the corners of the floor and walls.

Thanks to the sample box in the dialog box, you can preview the effects of changes you make to the options in the 3-D View dialog box before you actually apply them to the chart. Figure 13.30 shows the options in the 3-D View dialog box. These options include:

- **Elevation:** refers to the height at which you view the data markers (the columns in the sample column chart, for instance). Elevation is measured in degrees. The range of choices Excel accepts varies with the type of 3-D chart you are working with. If you attempt to put in an unacceptable number, you see an error message telling you the correct range, such as **Number must be between -90 and 90** for a 3-D column chart. Note that you can click on the arrow buttons in the dialog box to increase or decrease elevation by 5 degrees at a time. If you prefer, you can type a value into the **E**levation text box.

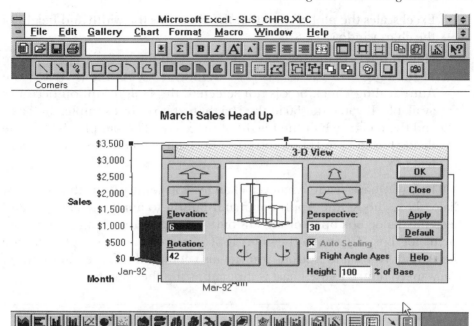

Figure 13.30 3-D View Dialog Box

- **Perspective**: controls how far away the data markers at the back of the chart appear and how close those at the front of the chart appear. The value you specify is the ratio of the front of the chart to the back of the chart and can range from 0 to 100 degrees. The higher the value, the greater the perspective. As with **E**levation, you can click on the arrow buttons to make changes or you can type a value into the **P**erspective text box.

- **Rotation**: the rotation of the plot area around the z- (vertical) axis. Measured in degrees, rotation can vary from 0 to 360 degrees. A rotation of 180 degrees, for instance, displays the chart as you would see it from the back. You can change rotation by clicking on the arrow buttons or by typing the value into the **R**otation text box.

- Select the Right Angle A**x**es check box if you want to show axes at right angles to one another. If you select this check box, the **P**erspective buttons and text box disappear from the dialog box. You can no longer change them.

- While the Right Angle A**x**es check box is selected, the Auto Scaling option then becomes available. If you select the Auto **S**caling check box,

Excel scales the plot area so that the chart fills the width and height of the chart window.

- Height refers to the height of the z-axis and the walls as a percentage of the length of the x-axis. The default is 100 percent. When the Auto Scaling check box is not selected, the Height option becomes available. If you enter 50 in the Height text box, for example, the z-axis and the walls are half the height of the x-axis. The sample chart in the dialog box does not show the effect of changes you make in the Height text box.

When you have made whatever changes you want within the 3-D View dialog box, choose the **Apply** command button to apply the changes and keep the dialog box open or the OK button to apply the changes and close the dialog box. To return the chart to its previous viewing angles, choose the **Default** command button. You can also choose the Close button when you want to return to the chart without applying the changes.

SUMMARY

In this chapter you learned how to edit and enhance the charts you create in Excel. First you learned how to edit the data series used in the chart both with the ChartWizard and Edit Series command. Then you learned how to add and format attached and unattached text that annotates your charts. Finally you learned how to modify chart axes, gridlines, and data markers.

In the next chapter you will learn more about enhancing your worksheets and charts with graphic objects such as pictures, arrows, and geometric shapes that you draw with Excel's own drawing tools. As well as learning how to manipulate the graphic objects you add to your worksheet, you will learn how to create linked and unlinked pictures of parts of a worksheet or a chart.

14

Working with Graphic Objects

For what is, after all, primarily a spreadsheet program, Excel 4.0 offers just about all the graphics power of any presentation graphics package. You no longer have to settle for just plain rows and columns in your worksheets. With Excel's graphics capabilities, you can now place just about any kind of image you want onto a worksheet and manipulate it with just about as much freedom.

In this chapter you will first learn how to create lines and shapes using the tools on the Drawing toolbar. Then you will learn techniques for changing their patterns and shapes and deleting them. You will also learn how to take pictures of parts of the worksheet and use those pictures in a number of ways, including using them as buttons to which you assign macros.

Next you will learn how to import graphics from other applications and how to export and link them if you wish. Finally you will learn how to use Excel's slide show feature to display a series of graphic images on your computer screen.

Understanding Graphic Objects

In Chapter 13 you changed the data markers in a column graph into pictures of automobiles. Pictures are one form of graphic object. One way to create a graphic object, in fact, is to import a picture from another application. The other way to create a graphic object in Excel is to draw it yourself.

To create your own graphic object, you use the tools in the Drawing toolbar while you are in a worksheet or in a macro sheet. Table 14.1 shows you the tools in the Drawing toolbar and briefly explains their use.

Table 14.1 Tools on the Drawing Toolbar

Icon	Tool Name	Function
	Line tool	Draws straight line. Hold down the Shift key while dragging to draw horizontal, vertical, or 45-degree diagonal lines. Double-click this tool to draw multiple lines.
	Arrow tool	Creates an arrow in the active worksheet, macro sheet, or chart. Drag to create an arrow in a worksheet. (The arrow is automatically added to a chart.) Double-click this tool to draw multiple arrows.
	Freehand tool	Draws a freehand line. The line you draw with this tool is automatically selected until you click the Freehand tool again or some other tool or click another part of the worksheet without dragging the pointer.
	Rectangle tool	Draws a transparent rectangle. Hold down the shift key as you drag to draw a square. Functions like the Filled Rectangle tool (see below) if you hold down the Shift key as you click this tool on the Drawing toolbar. Double-click this tool to draw multiple rectangles.
	Oval tool	Draws a transparent oval. Hold down the shift key as you drag to draw a circle. Functions like the Filled Oval tool (see below) if you hold down the Shift key as you click this tool on the Drawing toolbar. Double-click this tool to draw multiple ovals.
	Arc tool	Draws a transparent arc. Hold down the shift key as you drag to draw a segment of a circle. Functions like the Filled Arc tool (see below) if you hold down the Shift key as you click this tool on the Drawing toolbar. Double-click this tool to draw multiple arcs.

Table 14.1 *(continued)*

	Freehand Polygon tool	Draws a transparent polygon composed of freehand and straight lines. Functions like the Filled Freehand Polygon tool (see below) if you hold down the Shift key as you click this tool on the Drawing toolbar. Double-click this tool to draw multiple polygons.
	Filled Rectangle tool	Draws a rectangle filled with the window background pattern and color. Hold down the Shift key as you drag to draw a square. Functions like the Rectangle tool (see above) if you hold down the Shift key as you click this tool on the Drawing toolbar. Double-click this tool to draw multiple filled rectangles.
	Filled Oval tool	Draws an oval filled with the window background pattern and color. Hold down the Shift key as you drag to draw a circle. Functions like the Oval tool (see above) if you hold down the Shift key as you click this tool on the Drawing toolbar. Double-click this tool to draw multiple filled ovals.
	Filled Arc tool	Draws an arc filled with the window background pattern and color. Functions like the Arc tool (see above) if you hold down the Shift key as you click this tool on the Drawing toolbar. Double-click this tool to draw multiple filled arcs.
	Filled Freehand Polygon tool	Draws a freehand polygon filled with the window background pattern and color. Functions like the Freehand Polygon tool (see above) if you hold down the Shift key as you click this tool on the Drawing toolbar. Double-click this tool to draw multiple filled polygons.

Table 14.1   *(continued)*

	Text Box tool	Draws a text box on the active worksheet or chart.
	Selection tool	Selects one or more graphic objects in the active document. Drag the selection to enclose all of the objects you want to select, then release the mouse button.
	Reshape tool	Reshapes a polygon. Drag the selection handles on a freehand line or at the end of straight lines to add, delete, or move vertices.
	Group tool	Groups all selected graphic objects together. (This tool is available only when more than one object is selected.) Functions like the Ungroup tool (see below) when you hold down the Shift key when you click this tool on the Drawing toolbar.
	Ungroup tool	Separates grouped objects into individual graphic objects. Functions like the Group tool (see above) when you hold down the Shift key when you click this tool on the Drawing toolbar.
	Bring to Front tool	Places all selected objects in front of the other objects in the active document. Functions like the Send to Back tool (see below) if you hold down the Shift key as you click this tool on the Drawing toolbar.
	Send to Back tool	Places all selected objects in back of the other objects in the active document. Functions like the Bring to Front tool (see above) if you hold down the Shift key as you click this tool on the Drawing toolbar.
	Color tool	Changes the foreground color of the selected cell or object each time you click this tool. Hold down the Shift key while clicking to reverse the direction of color change.
	Drop Shadow tool	Adds a drop shadow to the selected cells or graphic object.

Alert! You can use only the Arrow, Text Box, and Color tools in the Drawing toolbar when working with a chart as a separate document window. To draw lines and add shapes such as circles and polygons to a chart, you must embed the chart in a worksheet and add the lines and shapes to the worksheet.

With the drawing tools, you can easily enhance a worksheet that you want to use in a presentation. In Figure 14.1, for instance, graphic objects on the page call attention to important points in the worksheet. Creating graphic objects on the worksheet can also have practical consequences: You can create your buttons and assign macros to them and then click the buttons to run the macros.

Drawing Lines and Shapes

With the tools on the Drawing toolbar, you can draw lines, arrows, freehand lines, rectangles, ovals, arcs, and polygons. You can also draw filled versions of the same objects. Note that you must use a mouse to draw lines and shapes with the drawing tools.

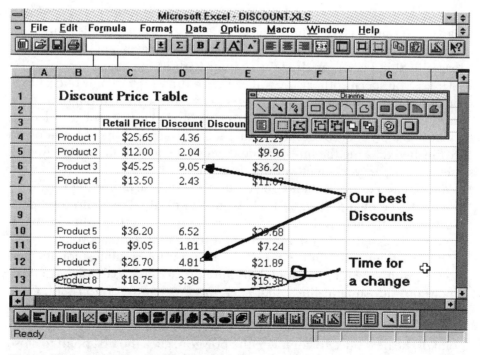

Figure 14.1 Worksheet with Graphic Objects Added

To draw a line or shape with the tools on the Drawing toolbar, you follow these general steps:

1. Click the drawing tool you want to use. For example, to draw a line, you would click the Line tool. When you click the tool, the pointer shape changes to a cross hair.

2. Click the worksheet at the point where you want the object to begin. Do not release the mouse button.

3. Drag the pointer to the position where you want the object to end, and release the mouse button.

When you first draw a graphic object, it is selected automatically. You will find out more about selecting objects in the next section.

Tip   To align an object with worksheet gridlines, hold down the Alt key while drawing the object. The object automatically "snaps to" the closest gridlines. If you draw the object within a single cell, holding down Alt automatically aligns the object with the sides of that cell.

At times, you may want to be sure that an object conforms to a certain shape. You can make certain that a square is a square; a circle is a circle; or a line or arrow is horizontal, vertical, or at a 45-degree angle by holding down the Shift key as you drag the pointer to draw the object.

Unless you specify otherwise, you can use a drawing tool only once. Once you draw an object, the tool is no longer active. If you wish, though, you can draw multiple objects with a tool. Instead of clicking a tool to select it, double-click the tool so that it remains active. To cancel the tool when you are finished drawing the lines or shapes, click the tool again or simply click elsewhere in the worksheet without dragging.

You can also draw freehand objects if you wish. Use either the Freehand tool or the Freehand Polygon tool. To draw with the Freehand tool, click the tool, then click and drag in the worksheet to create the freehand drawing. Release the mouse button when you have the object you want.

Drawing freehand with the Freehand Polygon tool is almost identical to drawing with the Freehand tool, but there are added capabilities. To draw a polygon with straight lines, first click the Freehand Polygon tool. Click where you want the polygon to begin, and *release* the mouse button. Then click the end point for the straight line. Release and click again at the end point of the next line. To complete the polygon, click the first point to close the polygon, or double-click your final point.

Tip You can draw a polygon with a combination of straight and freehand lines. Simply follow the instructions in the previous paragraph for each type of line within a polygon.

Working with Graphic Objects

As with the charts Excel creates for you, initial graphic objects you create often do not end up quite the way you want them. For example, you may want to move an object, fill the object with a pattern or color, change its shape, or even combine it with another object. To make any of these kinds of changes to a graphic object, you first select the object and then make your changes using drawing tools or dialog boxes.

Selecting Graphic Objects

You are already familiar with selecting objects in Excel. To select a graphic object, you position the pointer on it and click the mouse button. Black handles appear on the object when it is selected. You can use these selection handles to resize the object.

Tip Watch the pointer when you are attempting to select a graphic object. When the cross hair changes into an arrowhead, you can click to select the object.

To select multiple objects with the mouse, hold down the Ctrl key as you select the second and any additional objects. You can also select multiple objects using the Selection tool—the dotted rectangle on the Drawing toolbar. First click the Selection tool, then drag the dotted rectangle in the document until it completely encloses all of the objects you want selected. Excel selects all objects that are entirely within the rectangle.

You can use the **Select Special** command on the Formula menu to select all the graphic objects in the active worksheet. To do this, choose the **Objects** option button in the Select Special dialog box (as shown in Figure 14.2) before you choose OK or press Enter.

When you have selected multiple objects, you can deselect a single object without deselecting the others by holding down the Ctrl key, then clicking the object you want to deselect when the pointer changes to an arrowhead.

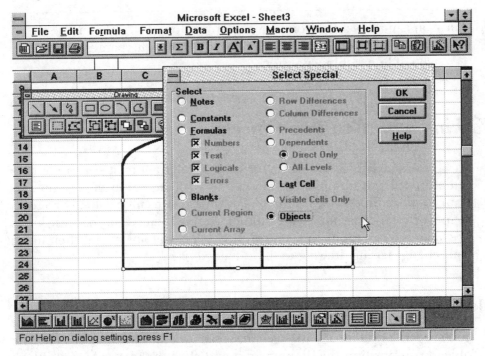

Figure 14.2   Select Special Dialog Box

Grouping and Ungrouping Objects

Once you have selected objects, you can then perform the desired operations on them as a group. If you plan to perform several different operations on the same group of objects, such as change their fill pattern, resize them, and move them, you should first group them into a single object.

To group objects together, you select them, then choose the **G**roup command on the objects' shortcut menu or the **F**ormat worksheet pull-down menu. You can also group objects together by clicking the Group tool if the Drawing toolbar is displayed.

Figure 14.3, for instance, shows a picture of a stadium made up of multiple graphic objects: circles, polygons, an arc, and a line. By grouping these objects together, you can move and format the entire drawing as one object. Figure 14.4 shows you the stadium after grouping its objects together. Now when you select this new "grouped" object, Excel displays fewer selection handles, and only around the edges of the object. You can move or resize all the objects together as a single unit. (That is, you don't move the walls but leave the windows behind, and so on.)

You can ungroup any "grouped" object if you need to format individual items differently. To ungroup an object, select the object, then choose the

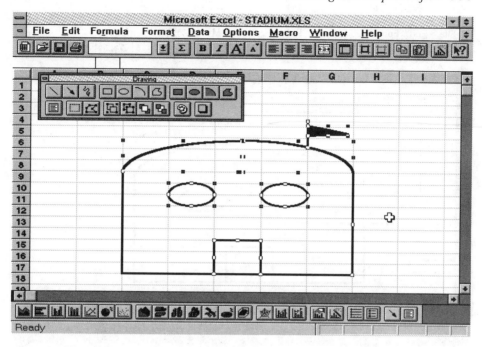

Figure 14.3   Multiple Selected Objects Before Grouping

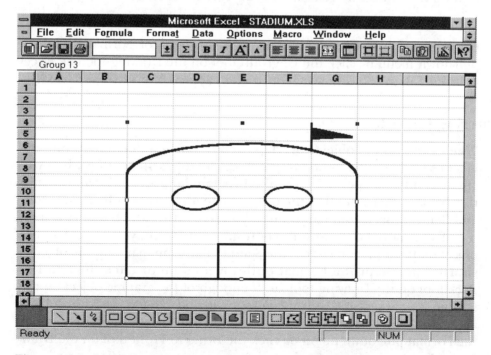

Figure 14.4   Multiple Objects Grouped into a Single Object

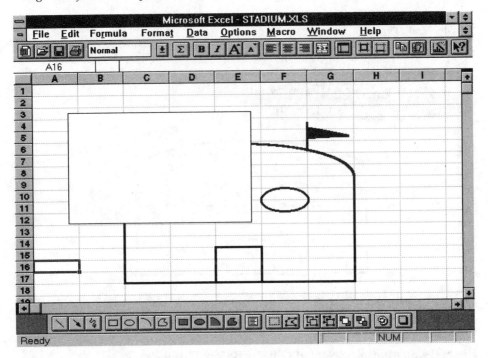

Figure 14.5   Opaque Rectangle Covering Part of the Stadium Drawing

Ungroup command on the object's shortcut menu or Format worksheet
pull-down menu or click the Ungroup tool on the Drawing toolbar. Excel
ungroups all the objects, which once again appear individually selected.

Ordering Objects

When two graphic objects overlap each other in a document, one object lies on top of the other. If the object on top is opaque (as when you
create a filled shape such as a filled rectangle or oval), it will obscure
the display of part or all of the object beneath it. Excel's Bring to Front
and Send to Back commands allow you to control which object lies on
top. To bring the object on the bottom to the front, you can select the
object on the top, then choose the Send to Back command on the object's
shortcut menu or the Format pull-down menu or click the Send to
Back tool on the Drawing toolbar. If enough of the graphic object on the
bottom is exposed so that you can select it, you can also click this object
and choose the Bring to Front command on the object's shortcut menu or
the Format pull-down menu or click the Bring to Front tool on the Drawing toolbar.

Suppose, for instance, you want to place a filled rectangle behind the stadium in the previous figure. Figure 14.5 shows such an opaque rectangle drawn on top of the stadium. Now you cannot select the stadium with the mouse pointer. Nor, of course, can you see what is beneath the rectangle. With the rectangle selected, you choose the Send to Back command. You now have the objects in the order you want them, as shown in Figure 14.6, so that you can both see and select the stadium drawing.

Moving and Sizing Graphic Objects

Unless you specify otherwise, Excel automatically attaches all graphic objects to the underlying cells. This means that when you change the size of the cells or move them, the graphic object moves along with them. Figure 14.7 shows a rectangle drawn around part of a single column in a worksheet to highlight the discount values. As you can see in Figure 14.8, when you resize the column, you resize the rectangle automatically.

If you wish, you can detach a graphic object from the underlying cells. You might want to do so, for instance, for a picture you have drawn that does not bear a direct connection to the underlying cells. Note that pictures imported from other applications are automatically unattached from

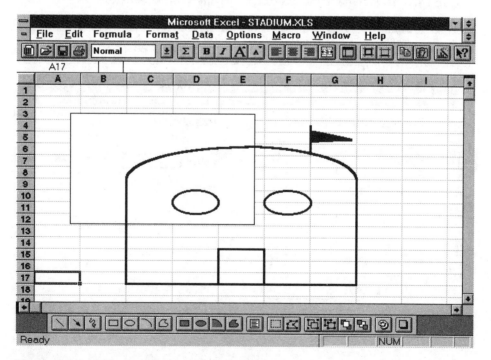

Figure 14.6   Opaque Rectangle Sent to Back

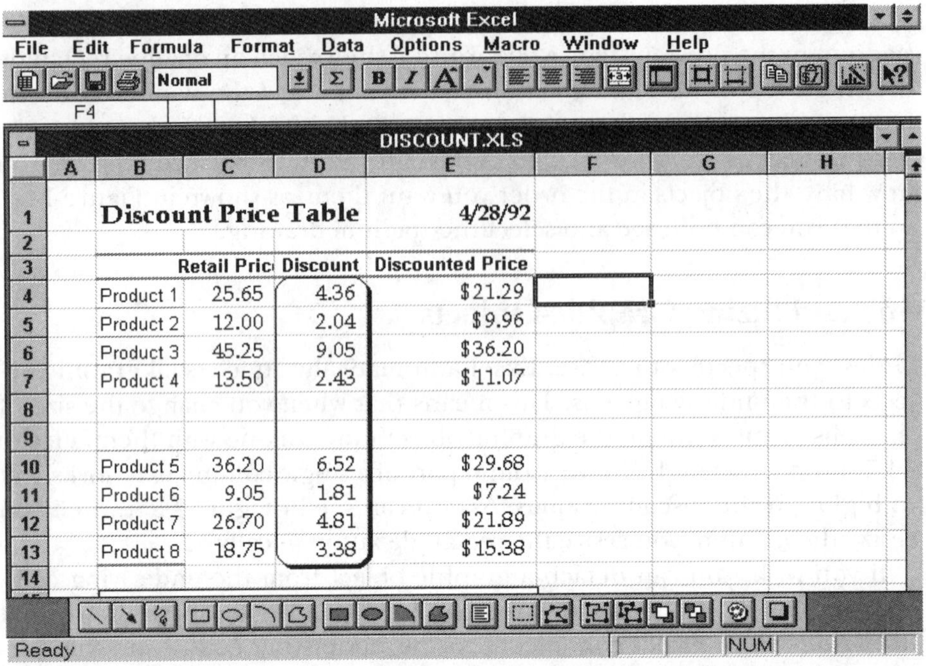

Figure 14.7   Rectangle Attached to Underlying Worksheet Cells

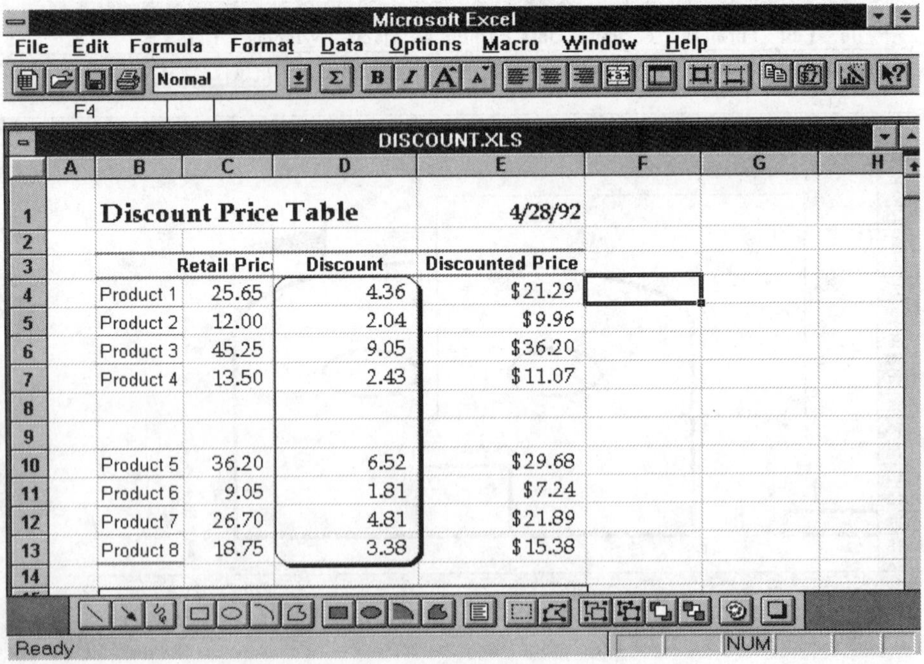

Figure 14.8   Attached Rectangle After Widening the Column

the cells in the active worksheet.

You follow these steps to detach a graphic object from the underlying cells:

1. Select the object you want to detach.

2. Choose the Object Properties command from the object's shortcut menu or from the Format pull-down menu. The Object Properties dialog box appears, as shown in Figure 14.9.

3. To detach the object altogether so that it does not change when you move or size the cells beneath it, choose the **D**on't Move or Size with Cells option button. To move the object with the cells without resizing it, choose the **M**ove but Don't Size with Cells option button instead.

4. Choose the OK button or press Enter.

Sizing graphic objects is very similar to sizing document windows in Excel. To size an object, first select it to display its selection handles. To change the size horizontally or vertically, drag the appropriate side handles. To change the size in both directions at once, drag the appropriate corner selection handle. To maintain the proportions of an object as you

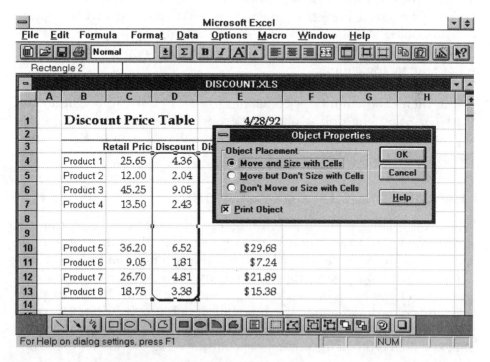

Figure 14.9 Object Properties Dialog Box

size it, hold down the Shift key as you drag a corner handle. If you want to align the object frame with the cell grid, hold down the Alt key as you drag a corner handle.

The technique for moving a graphic object is also familiar to you. When the mouse pointer assumes the shape of an arrowhead, drag the object to its new position and then release the mouse button. To restrain the object to horizontal or vertical movement only, hold down the Shift key as you drag the pointer.

Alert! Watch the pointer shape as you work. If you attempt to move an object when the pointer is a cross hair, you will resize the object instead of moving it.

You can also use the commands on the shortcut or pull-down menus to move a graphic object. Select the object, then use the **Cut** command on the shortcut menu or **E**dit pull-down menu (Ctrl+X) to place it in the Clipboard. Then select the cell or object where you want to place the graphic object and choose the **P**aste menu on the shortcut or **E**dit menus (Ctrl+V) to locate the object in the new position.

To copy a selected object by dragging it, hold down the Ctrl key as you drag the object. A dotted rectangle appears to indicate the position of the copy as you drag. When the dotted rectangle is in the position you want, release the mouse button.

You also can use the Clipboard to copy a selected object. Select the object, then choose the **C**opy command from the shortcut or **E**dit menus (Ctrl+C). Select the cell or object where you want the copied object to appear and choose the **P**aste command from the shortcut or **E**dit menus (Ctrl+V).

CHANGING THE SHAPE OF POLYGONS

When you create a polygon with the Freehand Polygon tool, you can use the Reshape tool to add, delete, or move vertices. With the polygon selected, click the Reshape tool (the icon showing a polygon with selection handles). Selection squares appear along any freehand lines and at the beginning and end of each straight line, as shown in Figure 14.10. Drag the selection squares to change the shape of the object. To delete a vertex, press the Shift key and click its selection square. To add a vertex, press the Shift key, then position the pointer on a line and drag the pointer to the position where you want the new vertex.

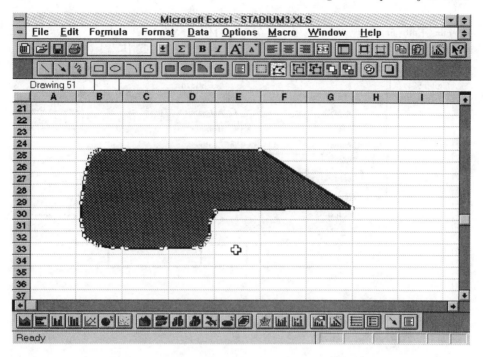

Figure 14.10   A Selected Polygon After You Click the Reshape Tool

Formatting a Graphic Object

You can change the pattern and/or color of an object's border and fill (if the object is filled) with the options in the Patterns dialog box. If the object is transparent (such as a rectangle created with the Rectangle rather than the Filled Rectangle tool), you can also assign a fill pattern or color to the object.

To display the Patterns dialog box (shown in Figure 14.11), double-click the object, or select the object and then choose the **P**atterns command from the object's shortcut menu or the Forma**t** pull-down menu. Choose the Border and Fill pattern options you want to use. Excel shows you the effect of your choices in the Sample box in the lower right corner. When you have the border and fill the way you want them for the selected object, choose the OK button or press Enter.

Creating Pictures of Worksheets and Charts

You can use the Camera tool on the Utility toolbar (the one that uses the camera icon, the fourth from the right) or the **C**opy Picture command on the **E**dit menu (this command appears when you hold down the Shift key—see "Importing and Exporting Graphic Objects" below for information on

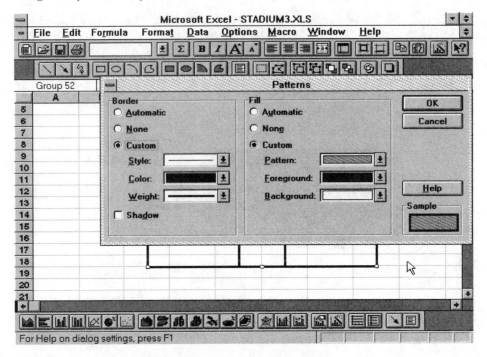

Figure 14.11   Patterns Dialog Box for a Graphic Object

using it) to take a picture of a selected range of cells. You can then place the picture elsewhere in the same worksheet, on another worksheet or macro sheet, or even in a document created in another application. When you use the Camera tool, the picture you create remains linked to the original selected cells. That is, if you change the original cells, the picture of them changes automatically.

To take a picture with the Camera tool, follow these steps:

1. Select the cells you want included in the picture.

2. Click the Camera tool on the Utility toolbar. The message Click in document to create a picture of the selected cells appears on the status bar.

3. Move to the worksheet or macro sheet where you want to place the picture.

4. Click the cell to which you wish to attach the picture. A picture of the cell appears and the new graphic object is selected. You can format and resize this picture as you would any other graphic object. When you have the picture formatted as you want, click outside the picture to deselect it.

Figures 14.12 and 14.13 illustrate how you can use the Camera tool to take a picture of worksheet cells. In Figure 14.12, the cell range D3:D7 containing the Discount prices for the first four products is selected before clicking the Camera tool. Figure 14.13 shows you the picture of these cells after resizing the picture and adding shading and a drop shadow with the options in the Patterns dialog box.

 Tip As with other tools, if you double-click the Camera tool when you select it, the tool remains active, allowing you to take multiple pictures.

Creating Macro Buttons

In Chapter 17 you will learn how to create macros and assign them to macro buttons. Macro buttons are a powerful addition to your worksheets. A macro button, in fact, works just like the tools on any toolbar: Simply click the button to run the macro (a series of commands that can be as lengthy or complex as you wish).

To create a macro button, you take the following general steps:

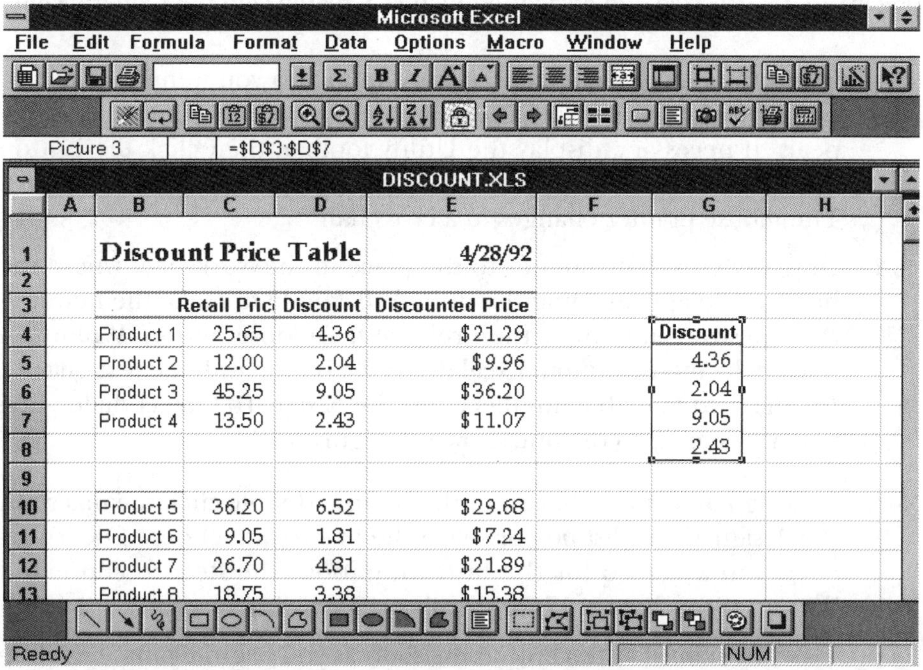

Figure 14.12 Selecting Cells for Picture to Be Taken with the Camera Tool

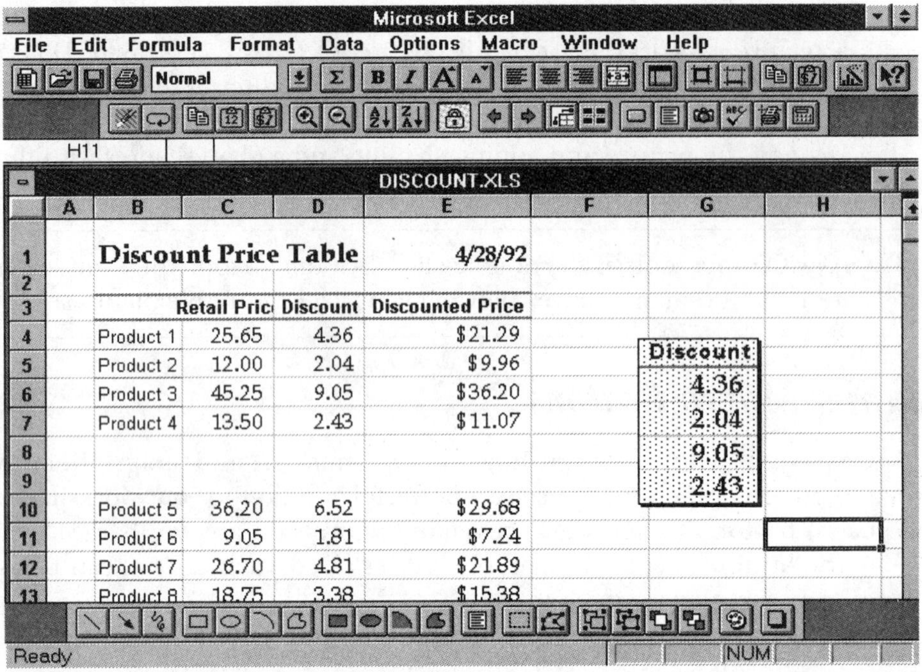

Figure 14.13   Resized and Formatted Picture Created with the Camera Tool

1. Open the macro sheet containing the macro you want to attach to the button, then activate the worksheet where the button is to appear. If necessary, display the Utility toolbar, then click the Button tool (the sixth tool from the right with a picture of a blank button). The mouse pointer changes to a cross hair.

2. Drag the cross-hair pointer to the place in the worksheet where the button is to appear. Drag the dotted rectangle to make the new button the size you want it, then release the mouse button. When you release the mouse button, Excel draws the button with the text Button 1 (or the next available number) and the Assign To Object dialog box appears, similar to the one shown in Figure 14.14.

3. To assign an existing macro to the button, double-click the macro in the Assign Macro list box or select the macro and choose OK. To record a new macro for the button, choose the Record command button. (See Chapter 17 for details on recording macros.)

4. Type the name for the button. As soon as you begin typing, Excel replaces the button number with the name you are entering. Press the Enter key to enter text on a new line in the button.

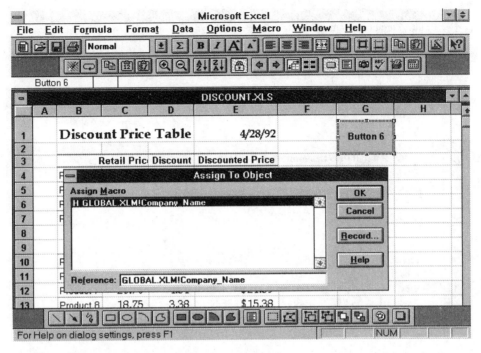

Figure 14.14   The Assign To Object Dialog Box

5. When you are finished naming the button, click the pointer in a cell outside the button to deselect it.

Figure 14.15 shows a sample macro button with edited text.

After creating a button to which you've assigned a macro, you can still edit it. When selecting the button for editing, you must, however, be careful not to end up running the macro instead of selecting the button. To select a button without running the macro, hold down the Ctrl key, then click the button when the pointer assumes the shape of the arrowhead with the plus sign. After selecting the button, you can modify its shape or size with the selection handles or change its formatting or properties with the appropriate commands on the shortcut menu. To modify the text on the button, select the text with the I-beam point and retype the text or delete it with the Delete or Backspace key.

To copy a button, simply drag the arrowhead pointer with the plus sign to a new place in the worksheet and release the mouse button. When moving a button rather than copying it, remember to release the mouse button after selecting the button, then drag the button with the arrowhead (without the plus sign). To delete a macro button, select it and choose the Delete key.

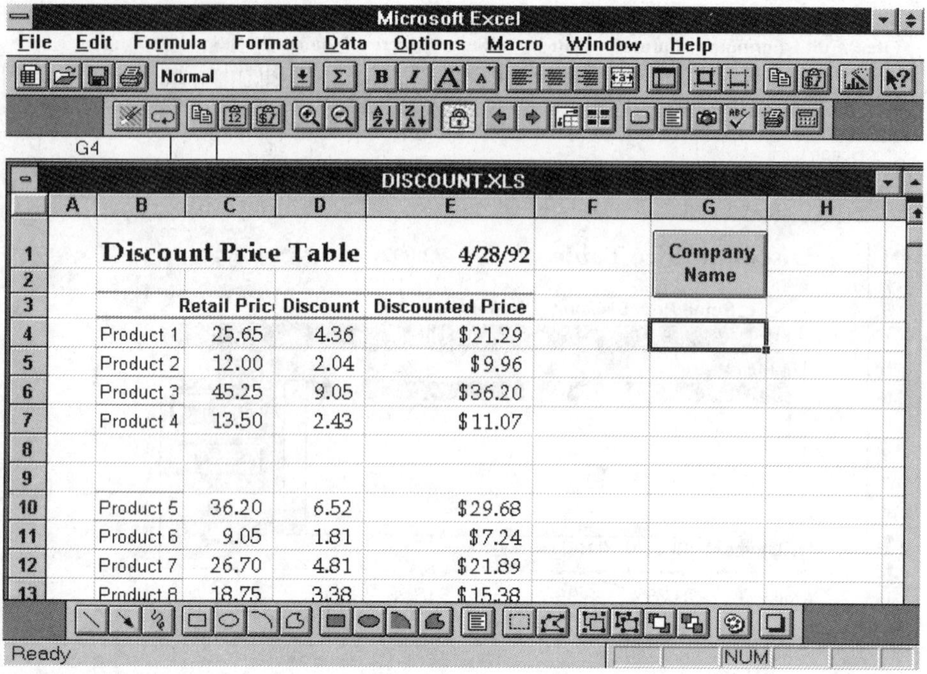

Figure 14.15   Sample Macro Button

Tip Instead of holding down the Ctrl key as you click a button to select it
(as opposed to running its macro), you can also select the object by
first displaying its shortcut menu. Simply click the object with the right
mouse button to display the shortcut menu, then click the pointer in
a worksheet cell outside of the button or menu again with the Right
mouse button. Excel closes the shortcut menu without deselecting the
macro button.

You also can assign a macro to any other graphic object, such as a picture
created with the Camera tool or a circle drawn with the Oval or Filled Oval
tool. To do this, you simply create the graphic object and select it, then
choose the Assign to Object command on the object's shortcut menu or
the Macro pull-down menu and choose or record the macro in the Assign
to Object dialog box.

Importing and Exporting Graphic Objects

It is easy to export pictures that you create of your Excel worksheets or charts
to other Windows applications. Likewise, you can also import graphics from

other Windows applications and use them in your Excel worksheets and charts.

To export a picture from Excel, you follow these steps:

1. Select the worksheet cells or graphic object that you want to export as a picture.

2. Hold down the Shift key, then choose the **C**opy Picture command on the **E**dit menu. The Copy Picture dialog box appears, as shown in Figure 14.16.

3. To copy the picture of the cells with the gridlines and column and rows headings as displayed on the screen, leave the As Shown on **S**creen option button selected under Appearance. To copy the picture without these attributes as the cells would appear in a printout, choose the As Shown When **P**rinted option button instead.

4. To copy the picture in the picture format so that the picture can be scaled proportionally when you change its size, leave the Picture option button selected under Format. To copy the picture in the bitmap format (as colored pixels), choose the **B**itmap option button instead.

5. Choose the OK button or press the Enter key to copy the picture to the Clipboard.

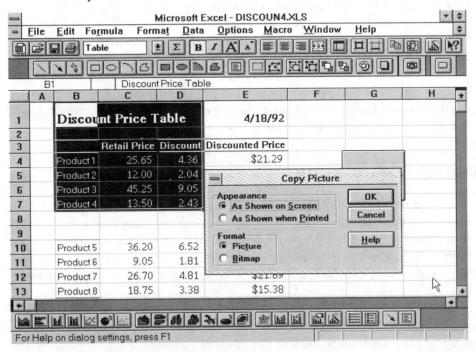

Figure 14.16   Copy Picture Dialog Box

6. Switch to the other Windows application, position the insertion point at the place where you want the graphic object to appear, then choose the **P**aste command on that application's **E**dit pull-down menu to paste the picture at the insertion point. To copy the picture in a different Excel document, switch to the document, select the cell or graphic where the picture is to appear, then hold down the Shift key and choose the **P**aste Picture command on the **E**dit menu.

Tip   When you create a picture of a chart or worksheet with the Camera tool, the picture remains linked to the original data. To create a "static" picture that is not updated when the original data changes, use the **C**opy Picture command on the **E**dit menu with the As Shown when **P**rinted option button selected. When you paste the picture into your Excel document with the **P**aste Picture command on the **E**dit menu, the program pastes a picture without links to the original data.

To import a picture from another application, you again use the Clipboard. Follow similar steps, beginning in this case in the other Windows application. From the application, copy or cut the selected graphic to the clipboard with the **Cut** command (Shift+Del) or **C**opy command (Ctrl+Ins) on the **E**dit menu. Then switch to Excel and select the cell or object where you want to paste the picture and choose the **P**aste command from the **E**dit menu (Ctrl+V). If the application you are importing from supports Dynamic Data Exchange (DDE) or Object Linking and Embedding (OLE), you can paste a linked picture. Instead of just choosing the **P**aste command from the Excel **E**dit menu, choose the Paste **L**ink command. Or hold down the Shift key when you choose Edit. Then choose **P**aste Picture Link.

Creating a Slide Show

Excel 4.0 not only enables you to create powerful individual graphics; it also allows you to display them as a slide show on the computer screen. Your slide show can include Excel worksheets, charts, or graphic objects that you have drawn as well as graphics imported from other applications. In creating a slide show, you determine the viewing order of each image and the time each image is displayed. You can also apply a number of video and audio transition effects to be used as the slide show moves to the next image.

To create a new slide show, you open the **slides.xlt** template file that is stored in the **\slides** directory of the **c:\excel** directory. Excel then opens a new slide show worksheet with the temporary filename **Slides1** (or the next available number), containing a variety of command buttons as shown in Figure 14.17.

To create the slides for the new slide show worksheet, you paste images stored in the Clipboard with the **P**aste Slide button as follows:

1. Choose the **File O**pen command, then double-click the slides folder in the **D**irectories list box to open it and double-click slides.xlt in the File **N**ame list box or select it and choose OK.

2. Switch to the document that contains the data or image you want used as a slide. Select the range of worksheet cells, the chart, or the graphic object(s) that you want in the slide.

3. Choose the **C**opy command on the shortcut menu or the **E**dit pull-down menu (Ctrl+C) to copy your selection to the Clipboard.

4. Select the slide show worksheet in the Window pull-down menu.

5. Choose the **P**aste Slide command button in the slide show worksheet. Excel pastes a miniature picture of the range of cells you've selected into column A of the slide show worksheet and displays the Edit Slide dialog box shown in Figure 14.18.

6. Select your transition options for the slide (as discussed below). To test the transition effect you've chosen, click the **T**est button.

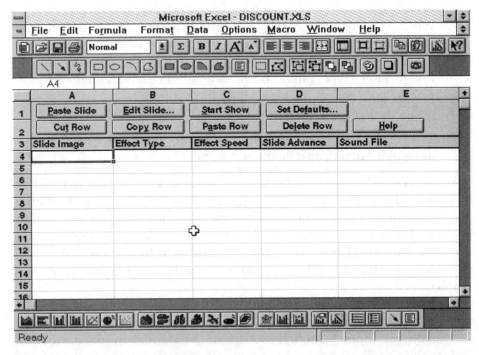

Figure 14.17   Slide Show Worksheet

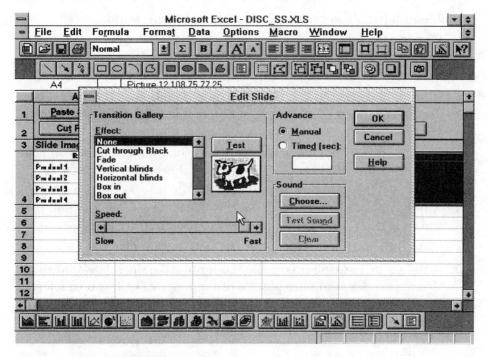

Figure 14.18   Edit Slide Dialog Box

7. When you've finished choosing the effects for the slide, choose the OK button or press Enter. Excel inserts the transition options you selected into the worksheet under the appropriate column headings—Slide Image, Effect Type, Effect Speed, Slide Advance, and Sound File.

8. Repeat steps 2 through 6 for all the other slides you want to include in the slide show.

9. Choose the **File Save** command to save the slide show worksheet under a more descriptive filename.

You can create impressive effects with the options in the Edit Slide dialog box. In the **Effect** list box, you can choose a "special effect" for the transition to the slide you are creating. The slide may appear through vertical or horizontal blinds, for instance, or as a wipe left or right. In general, it is best not to overuse the effects. Use None or a basic transition most of the time, then choose a dramatic effect to lead into a slide you particularly want to emphasize.

In the **Speed** section of the dialog box, you use the scroll box to set the speed of the transition effect. In the Advance box, choose either the **Manual** or Time**d** (sec) option button. If you choose the **M**anual option, move from slide to slide by clicking the mouse button or pressing the space bar.

If you are using Microsoft Windows 3.1 or have the MultiMedia Extensions for Windows 3.0, you can import and record sounds to play during the transition between slides. In the Sound box, select the **C**hoose button, then double-click the sound file in the File **N**ame list box or select it and choose OK or press Enter.

Running a Slide Show

To start a slide show after you have created and edited your slides, click the **S**tart Show button. In the Start Show dialog box (shown in Figure 14.19), select the **R**epeat show to have the slide show run continuously until you press the Esc key. To run the slide show only once, leave this check box empty. By default, Excel displays slide 1 as the first slide in the show. To start with another slide, select its number in the horizontal scroll bar. (For example, if you are developing a new slide and just want to have a look at, say, slide 5, you would choose 5 as the **I**nitial Slide number.) When you choose the OK button or press Enter, Excel clears the screen, and then runs the slide show using the options you've selected in the Start Show dialog box and the effects, advance, and sound options defined for each slide in the show.

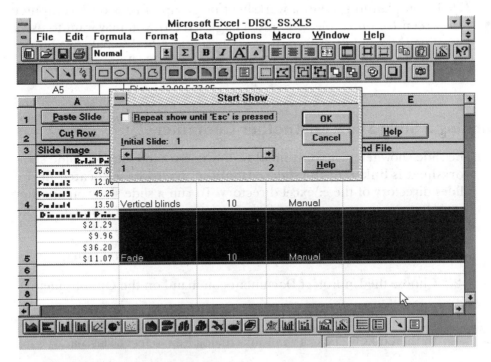

Figure 14.19   Start Show Dialog Box

To interrupt a slide show and stop it before Excel has finished displaying all of the slides, press the Esc key.

Editing the Slide Show

You can use the Set Defaults button to change the default effect, speed, and advance method for each new slide you add to the slide show. To edit any of these options for a slide you've already added to a slide show, select any cell in the row that contains the slide that needs changing, then choose the **E**dit Slide button and make your changes in the Edit Slide dialog box.

To move or copy a slide in the slide show, you can use the Cut Row, Copy Row, and **P**aste Row buttons in the slide show worksheet much as you use the Cut, Copy, and Paste commands on the Edit menu. To move a slide, select one of its cells, then click the Cut Row button. Select a cell in the row where the slide should appear, then click the Paste Row button. To copy a slide to a new place in the slide show, you follow the same procedure except that you initially choose the **C**opy Row button instead of Cut Row. To delete a slide from the slide show, select a cell in the row with the slide and click the Delete Row button.

Tip If you plan to present a worksheet or group of cells on a computer screen (or one projected onto a large screen), you may want to use a slide show simply to show them to best effect. Slides make maximum use of screen space and omit any column heads, buttons, and other distractions that you have not placed directly into them.

Running a Slide Show on Another Computer

The slide show template document with which you create your slide show worksheet is linked to the **slides.xla** add-in macro (also located in the **\slides** directory of the **c:\excel** directory. To run a slide show on another computer, you must modify the links from the slide show template to the slide show add-in macro sheet on the new computer as follows:

1. Open the slide show template slides.xlt on the new computer.

2. Choose the Unprotect Document command on the **O**ptions menu.

3. Choose the **L**inks command on the **F**ile menu.

4. In the **L**inks list box of the Links dialog box, select slides.xla.

5. Choose the **C**hange button.

6.   Double-click slides.xla in the File **N**ame list box or select this file and choose OK.

7.   Close the Links dialog box and save the new links with the **F**ile **S**ave command, then run the slide show with the **S**tart Show command button.

SUMMARY

In this chapter you learned how to create basic graphic objects, both lines and shapes, using the tools on the Drawing toolbar. You then learned how to manipulate and modify these objects. After that, you learned to create pictures of worksheets and charts, create macro buttons, and import and export graphics to and from Excel. Finally you learned how to create your own slide show with special effects, using the slide show template.

In the next chapter you will learn how to store and work with large amounts of data in an Excel database. As you will see, Excel's database management capabilities make it easy to organize and find information stored in the database format.

15

Creating and Using a Database

Excel makes it easy to set up and maintain large amounts of data with its database management tools. In Excel, a *database* is a table of worksheet data that utilizes a special structure. Unlike the other types of data tables that you might create in Excel, a database uses only column headings (technically known as *field names*) to identify the different kinds of items it tracks. Each column in the database contains information for each item you track, such as the client's company name or telephone number (technically known as a database *field*). Each row in the database contains complete information about each entity you track, such as ABC Corporation or National Industries (technically known as a database *record*).

Once you've organized your data into a database following this structure, you can use a variety of Excel's Data commands to maintain the data as well as to retrieve the information you need. As you will learn in this chapter, you can use the **Data Form** command to add new records, find and edit records, or delete unwanted records from the database. You can use the **Data Sort** command to rearrange the records in the database by sorting on one or more of its fields. And you can also set up search criteria in the worksheet that Excel will use to find and/or extract only the information you want when you choose the **Data Find** or **Data Extract** command.

Creating a Database

To create a database, you open a new worksheet and start entering a row of field names in adjacent columns that identify and describe each of the items you need to track. When entering these column headings, be sure each field name is unique and, whenever possible, keep it short. Also, do

579

not use numbers or formulas that return values as field names. (You can, however, use formulas that return text, such as a formula that concatenates labels entered in different cells.) When naming fields, you can align the field name in the cell so that its text wraps to a new line (by pressing Alt+Enter or by selecting the **Wrap Text** option in the Alignment dialog box).

When deciding on what fields you need to create, think of how you will be using the data that you store in your database. For example, in a client database you would split the client's name into separate first name, middle initial, and last name fields if you intend to use this information in generating form letters and mailing labels with your word processor. That way you can address the person by his or her first name (as in *Dear Jane*) in the opening of the form letter as well as by his or her full name and title (as in *Dr. Jane Jackson*) in the mailing label.

Likewise, you would split up the client's address into separate street address, city, state, and ZIP code fields when you intend to use the client database in generating form letters and you want to be able to sort the records in descending order by ZIP code and/or send letters only to clients located in certain states. By keeping discrete pieces of information in separate fields, you will be able to use that field to find particular records and retrieve information from the database, such as finding all the records where the state is California or the ZIP code is between 94105 and 95101.

Figure 15.1 shows you a sample employee database. This database begins in row 3 of this worksheet, which contains the names for the nine fields (ID No through Profit Sharing). Note that employees' names are divided into separate Last Name and First Name fields in this database (columns B and C, respectively). Note too that the first actual record of the database is entered in row 4. When entering your records for a new database, you don't skip rows but keep entering each record one above the other going down successive rows of the worksheet.

When entering the records, you enter the information for each field entry as you normally enter data in any worksheet cell. If you don't have information for a particular field, just leave it blank. When entering values, Excel assigns the General number format unless you include format characters with the values you enter (such as $1,500.00 instead of 1500). When entering dates, Excel assigns the date format closest to the one you use in entering the date.

After you finish entering all your initial records, you can then change the formatting and alignment for any field in the database just as you would modify the formatting for any cell range in a standard worksheet.

Field Names

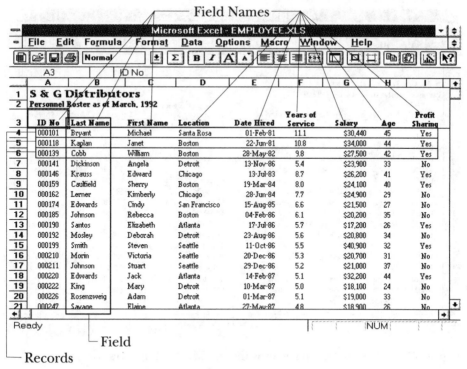

	ID No	Last Name	First Name	Location	Date Hired	Years of Service	Salary	Age	Profit Sharing
1	**S & G Distributors**								
2	Personnel Roster as of March, 1992								
3									
4	000101	Bryant	Michael	Santa Rosa	01-Feb-81	11.1	$30,440	45	Yes
5	000118	Kaplan	Janet	Boston	22-Jun-81	10.8	$34,000	44	Yes
6	000139	Cobb	William	Boston	28-May-82	9.8	$27,500	42	Yes
7	000141	Dickinson	Angela	Detroit	13-Nov-86	5.4	$23,900	33	No
8	000146	Krauss	Edward	Chicago	13-Jul-83	8.7	$26,200	41	Yes
9	000159	Caulfield	Sherry	Boston	19-Mar-84	8.0	$24,100	40	Yes
10	000162	Lerner	Kimberly	Chicago	28-Jun-84	7.7	$24,900	29	No
11	000174	Edwards	Cindy	San Francisco	15-Aug-85	6.6	$21,500	27	No
12	000185	Johnson	Rebecca	Boston	04-Feb-86	6.1	$20,200	35	No
13	000190	Santos	Elizabeth	Atlanta	17-Jul-86	5.7	$17,200	26	Yes
14	000192	Mosley	Deborah	Detroit	23-Aug-86	5.6	$20,800	34	No
15	000199	Smith	Steven	Seattle	11-Oct-86	5.5	$40,900	32	Yes
16	000210	Morin	Victoria	Seattle	20-Dec-86	5.3	$20,700	31	No
17	000211	Johnson	Stuart	Seattle	29-Dec-86	5.2	$21,000	37	No
18	000220	Edwards	Jack	Atlanta	14-Feb-87	5.1	$32,200	44	Yes
19	000222	King	Mary	Detroit	10-Mar-87	5.0	$18,100	24	No
20	000226	Rosenzweig	Adam	Detroit	01-Mar-87	5.1	$19,000	33	No
21	000242	Savage	Elaine	Atlanta	27-May-87	4.8	$18,900	26	No

Field

Records

Figure 15.1   Sample Employee Database

Tip   Remember that you will have to enter numbers as text rather than as values for some fields. For example, ZIP codes should be entered in a ZIP code field as labels rather than as values so that Excel will retain leading zeros, such as 00210 as part numbers or other identification numbers that use leading zeros, as in 00105. To enter a value as text, preface the field entry with the ' (apostrophe), as in '00210 or '00105. Also, remember that you can press Ctrl+" (quotation mark) to copy the entry from the cell above. This is useful when entering a group of records that all use the same city, state, or zip code.

Creating Calculated Fields

When creating a database, you can make full use of Excel's calculating capabilities by defining fields whose entries are returned by formula rather than entered manually. The sample employee database introduced in Figure 15.1 contains just such a calculated field.

Figure 15.2 shows the master formula on the formula bar that was entered in cell F4 to calculate the years of service for the first record (that

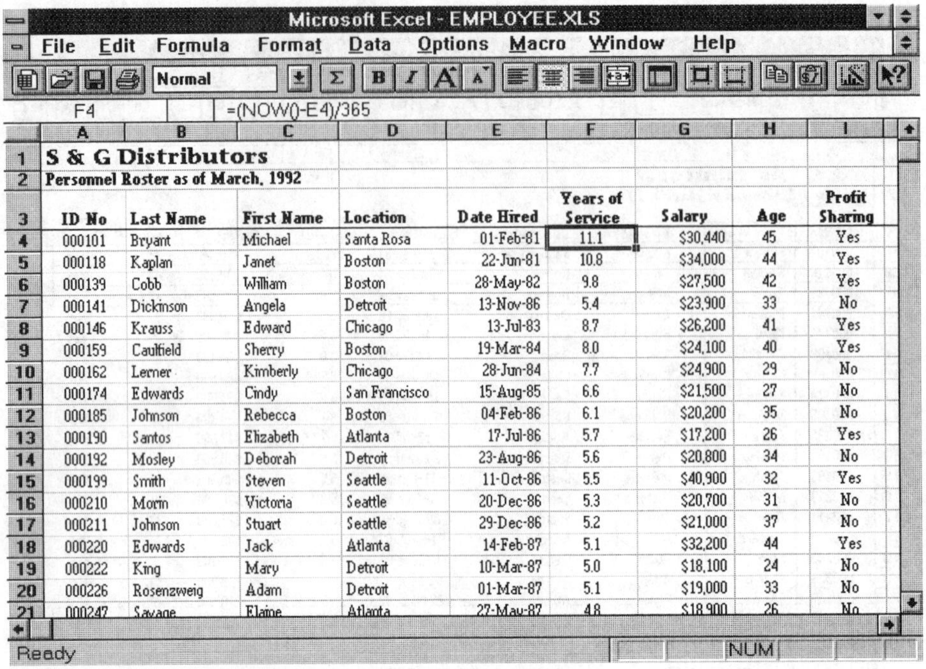

Figure 15.2   Sample Database Showing the Master Formula for the Calculated Years of Service Field

of Michael Bryant) in row 4. This formula

    =(NOW()−E4)/365

subtracts the date in the Date Hired field in cell E4 from the current date (returned by the NOW() function) and then divides the resulting number of days by 365 to return the number of years with the company. After you entered and formatted this master formula in cell F4, it was copied down the column to calculate the years of service for all the other employees with records in the database.

Defining the Database

After entering the row of field names along with your first records for your database, you still need to define the database with the Set Database command on the Data menu (as shown in Figure 15.3). Before you choose this command, select all of the cells in the database (including the row of field names and all records). The easiest way to do this is to make the cell with the first field name of the database active. Then hold down the Shift key and double-click the right side of the active cell as soon as the pointer changes to an arrowhead. (This extends the selection all the way to the last field, assuming that your first

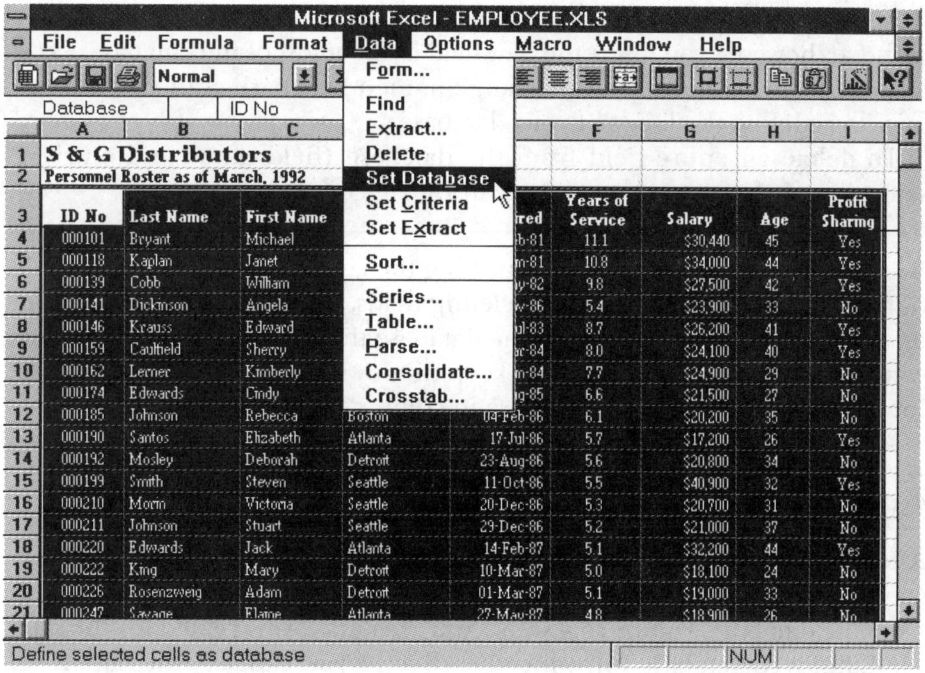

Figure 15.3 Defining the Database

record contains entries for every field.) Then, with the Shift key still depressed, double-click the bottom of the selected row when the pointer assumes the arrowhead shape. (This extends the selection all the way down to the last row, assuming that your last field contains entries for every record.)

When you choose the **D**ata Set Database command after selecting the database, Excel assigns the range name Database to these cells. After that, you then can select the contents of your database simply by choosing the Database in Goto dialog box (opened by choosing the **G**oto command on the Formula menu or by pressing F5).

Modifying the Structure of the Database

After creating your database, you may find that you need to modify its structure by adding or deleting some fields. To add a new field, you select the column (by clicking the column letter) where you want the field inserted, then use the **E**dit **I**nsert command to insert a new column. Enter the name for the new field in the appropriate cell in the row containing the field names, then enter the entries for that field for each record in the database. If you insert the new field as the first or last field of the database, you will have to redefine the extent of the database with the **D**ata Set Database command. If, however, you insert the new field in the midst of the database, Excel automatically includes it in the range named Database, and you will not have to redefine the limits of your database.

To delete an entire field from the database (field name and entries), select its column then choose the **E**dit **D**elete command.

Alert! To avoid losing data or disturbing the layout of data located outside of the database when adding or deleting fields, don't place any data tables or other entries in rows beneath the database that use the same columns as your fields. In other words, always keep the rows beneath the database free for new records. Locate related data in columns to the right.

Using the Data Form

After defining the database, you then can use the data form that Excel generates when you choose the **D**ata **F**orm command to add, edit, or delete records from the database. Figure 15.4 shows you the data form created for the sample Employee database introduced earlier. As you can see, the data form

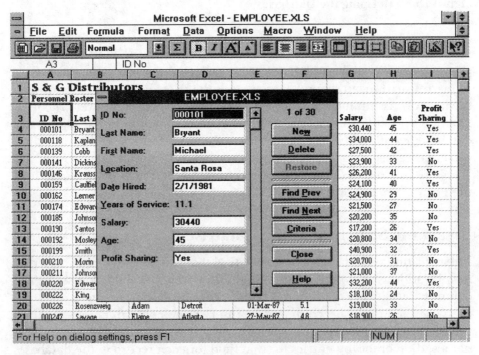

Figure 15.4   The Data Form for the Employee Database

consists of a dialog box (whose title bar contains the name of the worksheet file with the database) that contains a vertical listing of each field defined for the database.

When you choose the **Data Form** command to display the data form, Excel automatically displays the field entries for the first record. On the right side of the dialog box, the data form indicates the current record number out of the total number of records in the database (1 of 30 in this case). This part of the form also contains a number of command buttons that enable you to add a new record, find a particular record for editing, or delete a record from the database.

Once the data form is displayed in the active document, you can use the scroll bar to the right of the fields to move through the records in the database, or you can use various direction keys. (Table 15.1 summarizes the use of the scroll bar and these keys.) For example, to move to the next

Table 15.1 Techniques for Navigating the Data Form

Movement	*Keystrokes or Scroll Bar Technique*
Next record, same field in the database	Press ↓ or Enter key, click ↓ scroll arrow, or click Find **Next** command button.
Previous record, same field in the database	Press ↑ or Shift+Enter key, click ↑ scroll arrow, or click Find **Prev** command button.
Next field in the data form	Press Tab.
Previous field in the data form	Press Shift+Tab.
Move 10 records forward in the database	Press PgDn.
Move 10 records backward in the database	Press PgUp.
Move to the first record in the database	Press Ctrl+↑ or Ctrl+PgUp, drag the scroll box to the top of the scroll bar.
Move to the last record in the database	Press Ctrl+↓ or Ctrl+PgDn, drag the scroll box to the bottom of the scroll bar.
Move within a field	Press ← or → to move one character at a time, press Home to move to the first character and End to move to the last character.

record in the database, you can press the ↓ or Enter key or click the ↓ scroll arrow at the bottom of the scroll bar. To move to the previous record in the database, you can press the ↑ key or Shift+Enter key or click the ↑ scroll arrow at the bottom of the scroll bar. To select a field in the current record for editing, you can click that field's text box or press the Tab (next field) or Shift+Tab key (previous field) until you select the field (and its current entry).

> *Note:* The data form does not allow you to edit calculated fields (such as the Years of Service field in the sample Employee database). To modify the contents of a calculated field, modify the master formula in the appropriate field in the first record and recopy the formula down to the other existing records.

Adding Records

To add a new record to the database, you either can move to the end of the database (by dragging the scroll box to the very bottom of the scroll bar or by pressing Ctrl+↓ or Ctrl+PgDn) or simply choose the New command button. Either way, Excel displays a blank data form (marked New Record at the right side of the dialog box) that you can then fill out. After entering the information for a field, press the Tab key to advance to the next field in the record. (Be careful not to press the Enter key as this inserts the new record into the database.) When creating a new record in the data form, you still can press Ctrl+" (quotation mark) to copy the field entry from the previous record into the current field. You could use this keystroke shortcut, for example, to carry forward entries in the text box for the State field when you are entering a series of records that all use the same state.

When you've entered all the information you have for the new record, press the ↓ or Enter key or select the New button again. Excel then inserts the new record as the last record in the database, redefines the range name called Database to include this last record, and displays a blank data form where you can enter the next record. When you are finished adding records to the database, press the Esc key or choose the Close command button to close the data form dialog box.

> *Note:* You can also add new records to a database by entering the information for each field in the appropriate cells in the first blank row at the bottom of the database. When you add records this way, however, you need to remember to redefine the database with the **Data Set Database** command to include the new records in the Database range name.

Editing Records

The data form makes it easy to edit records in your database. In a smaller database, you can use the navigation keys or the scroll bar in the data form to locate the record that requires editing. In a larger database, you can use the **C**riteria command button to locate the record you need to change quickly (as described below).

Once you've displayed the data form for the record that needs editing, you then can perform your editing changes by selecting the text boxes of the necessary fields and making your changes just as you would edit a cell entry after activating the formula bar.

LOCATING THE RECORD TO EDIT WITH THE CRITERIA BUTTON

You can use the **C**riteria button in the data form to find the records in your database that you need to edit (or delete as described in the next section). When you choose the **C**riteria button in the data form, Excel clears all the field text boxes so that you can enter the criteria to search for. For example, assume that you need to edit Sherry Caulfield's profit-sharing status. You don't have her paperwork in front of you so you can't look up her employee number. You do know, however, that she works in the Boston office and, although, you don't remember exactly how she spells her last name, you do know that it begins with a C instead of a K.

To locate her record, you can at least narrow the search down to all the records where the Location field contains Boston and the employee's Last Name begins with the letter C. To do this, you would open the data form for the Employee database, choose the **C**riteria command button, and then enter

C*

in the Last Name field text box and

Boston

in the Location field text box, as shown in Figure 15.5. When entering the criteria for locating matching records in the data form, you can use ? (question) and * (asterisk) wildcard characters just as you do when using the Formula Find command to locate cells with particular entries. (See "Using the Find Command" in Chapter 4 for a review of using these wildcard characters.)

When you choose the Find **N**ext command button or press the Enter key, Excel locates the first record in the database where the last name begins with the letter C and the location is Boston. This is William Cobb's record, shown in Figure 15.6. Then, to locate the next record that matches your criteria, you would choose the Find **N**ext command

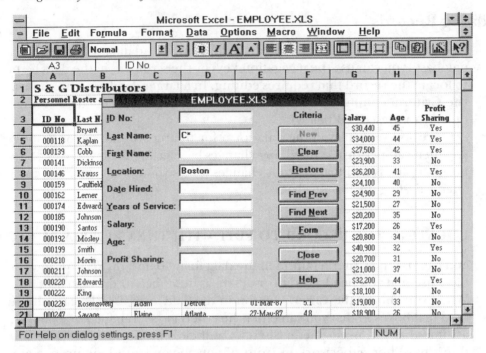

Figure 15.5   Enter the Criteria for Finding a Record

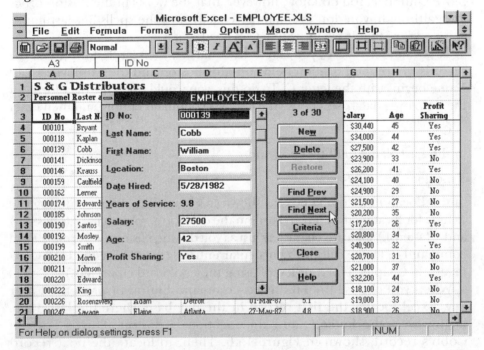

Figure 15.6   Locating the First Matching Record

button or press the Enter key, which would bring you to Sherry Caulfield's record, as shown in Figure 15.7. Having located Sherry's record, you then can change her profit-sharing status by selecting the Profit Sharing text box and replacing **No** with **Yes**. Excel inserts the editing change that you make in the record's data form into the database itself as soon as you close the data form dialog box by choosing the Close command button.

When using the **C**riteria button in the data form to find records, you can use the following logical operators when entering search criteria in fields that use numbers or dates:

=	Equal to	<	Less than
>	Greater than	<=	Less than or equal to
>=	Greater than or equal to	<>	Not equal to

For example, to find all the records where the employee's age is 40, you can enter **=40** or simply **40** in the Age field text box. However, to find all the records for employees who are 40 or younger, you would enter **<=40** in the Age field text box. To find all the records for employees with salaries greater than $35,000, you would enter **>35000** in the Salary field text box. If you wanted to find all of the records where the employees are 40 or younger *and* make more than $35,000, you would enter both **<=40** in the Age field text box and **>35000** in the Salary field text box in the same Criteria data form.

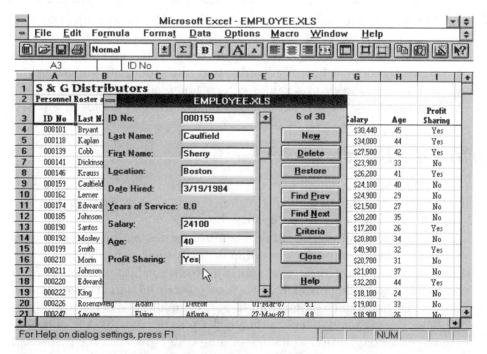

Figure 15.7 Locating the Next Matching Record

When specifying search criteria that fit a number of records, you may have to choose the Find **N**ext or Find **P**rev buttons several times to locate the record you want to work with. If no record fits the search criteria you enter in the Criteria data form, your computer will beep at you when you choose the Find **N**ext or Find **P**rev button. To change your search criteria, select the appropriate text box(es), delete the old criteria, and then enter the new criteria. To switch back to the current record without using the search criteria you entered, choose the **F**orm button. (This button replaces the **C**riteria button as soon as you select the **C**riteria button.)

Deleting Records

In addition to adding and editing records with the data form, you can also delete them. To delete a record, you simply display its data form and then choose the **D**elete command button. Be very careful when deleting records, however, as you cannot restore the records you delete with Excel's Undo command. For this reason, Excel displays an alert dialog box whenever you choose the **D**elete command, indicating that the record displayed in the data form is about to be deleted permanently. To continue and remove the record, you need to choose OK or press Enter. To save the current record, choose **D**elete.

 Tip   Although you can use the **C**riteria data form to locate a group of records that you want to delete, you can only delete one record at a time with the **D**elete button. To delete a group of records that all share the same characteristics (such as all records where the order date is on or before 6/1/89), you need to set up a criteria range and use the **D**ata **D**elete command. (See "Using Data Delete" later in this chapter for details.)

Sorting the Database

Excel's **D**ata **S**ort command makes it easy to rearrange the records or even the fields in your database. You sort the records in your database by rows, while you sort the fields in the database by columns.

In sorting, you can specify either ascending or descending sort order for your data. When you specify ascending order (which is the default), Excel arranges text in A-to-Z order and values go from smallest to largest. When you specify descending order, Excel reverses this order and arranges text in Z-to-A order and values range from largest to smallest. When sorting on a date field, keep in mind that ascending order puts the records in least-recent-to-most-recent date order, while descending order gives you the records in most-recent-to-least-recent date order.

> *Note:* When you choose the ascending sort order for a field that contains many different kinds of entries, Excel places numbers (from smallest to largest) before text (in alphabetical order) followed by Logical values (TRUE and FALSE), Error values, and, finally, blank cells. When using the descending sort order, the program uses the same general arrangement for the different types of entries but numbers go from largest to smallest, text runs from Z to A, and the FALSE logical value precedes the TRUE logical value.

To sort your data, Excel uses *sorting keys* to determine how the records or fields should be reordered in the database. When sorting records, you indicate by cell address which field (that is, column) contains the first or *primary* sorting key. When sorting fields, you indicate which record (row) contains the primary sorting key. Excel then applies the selected sort (ascending or descending) to the data in the key field or row to determine how the records or fields will be reordered during sorting.

When a key field contains duplicate entries, Excel simply lists these records in the order in which they were entered in the database. To indicate how Excel should order records with duplicates in the primary key field, you define a secondary key. For example, if, when organizing the database in alphabetical order by the Last Name field, you have several records where the last name is Smith, you can have Excel order the Smiths' records in alphabetical order by first name by defining the First Name field as the secondary key. If the secondary key contains duplicates (let's say you have two John Smiths in your company), you can define a third key field (the Middle Name field, if your database has one) that determines how the duplicate John Smith records are arranged when the database is sorted.

> *Note:* Although sorting is most often applied to rearranging and maintaining database records and fields, keep in mind that you can use Excel's **Data S**ort command to reorder data in any worksheet table, whether or not the table follows the strict database structure.

Sorting the Records in a Database

To sort the records in your database with the **Data S**ort command, you follow these steps:

1. Select all of the records in the database that are to be sorted. Make sure that you have included all of the fields in each record (not just

the field you want to sort on). Also, be sure that you do *not* include the field names in this cell selection. (Otherwise, Excel reorders the row of field names in with the records.) To make it easy to select all the records in the database, assign a range name, such as Database_Records, to all the records in the database, making sure that this range includes every field without the row of field names. Then you can select all the records simply by choosing this range name in the Goto dialog box (opened with the Formula **G**oto command or by pressing F5).

2. Choose the **S**ort command on the **D**ata menu. Excel opens the Sort dialog box (similar to the one shown in Figure 15.8). By default, the **R**ows option button is selected and the address of the active cell is listed in the 1st Key text box.

3. Select a cell in the field that you want used as the primary key field in sorting the records of the database.

4. To sort the records in descending order, choose the **D**escending option button under the 1st Key text box.

5. If the primary key field contains duplicates and you want to specify how these records should be sorted, choose the 2nd Key text box and select a cell in the field to be used as the secondary key. To sort these

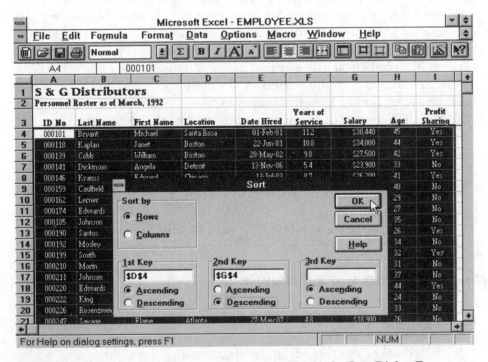

Figure 15.8   Defining a Primary and Secondary Key in the Sort Dialog Box

records in descending order using the secondary key, choose the Descending option button under the **2**nd Key text box.

6. If the secondary key field contains duplicates and you want to specify how these records should be sorted, choose the **3**rd Key text box, and select a cell in the field to be used as the third key. To sort these records in descending order using the secondary key, choose the Descending option button under the **3**rd Key text box.

7. When you've finished defining all of the keys you need to use in sorting your database records, choose the OK button or press Enter to perform the sort.

If, when Excel finishes rearranging the records, you find that you sorted the database using the wrong key fields, choose the **U**ndo Sort command on the **E**dit menu or press Ctrl+Z to restore the database records to their previous order.

Figures 15.8 and 15.9 illustrate how you would go about sorting the employee database first in ascending order by location and then in descending order by salary. To designate the Location field as the primary key in the sort, you select cell D4 (which Excel indicates with an absolute

	A	B	C	D	E	F	G	H	I
1	**S & G Distributors**								
2	Personnel Roster as of March, 1992								
3	ID No	Last Name	First Name	Location	Date Hired	Years of Service	Salary	Age	Profit Sharing
4	000220	Edwards	Jack	Atlanta	14-Feb-87	5.1	$32,200	44	Yes
5	000297	Percival	James	Atlanta	18-Dec-87	4.3	$19,200	36	Yes
6	000247	Savage	Elaine	Atlanta	27-May-87	4.8	$18,900	26	No
7	000190	Santos	Elizabeth	Atlanta	17-Jul-86	5.7	$17,200	26	Yes
8	000348	Reese	Carl	Atlanta	13-Sep-88	3.5	$15,800	23	No
9	000281	Adamson	Joy	Boston	21-Oct-87	4.4	$34,400	46	Yes
10	000118	Kaplan	Janet	Boston	22-Jun-81	10.8	$34,000	44	Yes
11	000139	Cobb	William	Boston	28-May-82	9.8	$27,500	42	Yes
12	000159	Caulfield	Sherry	Boston	19-Mar-84	8.0	$24,100	40	No
13	000262	Bird	Lance	Boston	13-Aug-87	4.6	$21,100	38	Yes
14	000185	Johnson	Rebecca	Boston	04-Feb-86	6.1	$20,200	35	No
15	000367	Fletcher	Amanda	Boston	03-Jan-89	3.2	$16,500	22	No
16	000146	Krauss	Edward	Chicago	13-Jul-83	8.7	$26,200	41	Yes
17	000307	Bjorkman	Robert	Chicago	24-Feb-88	4.1	$25,000	23	Yes
18	000162	Lerner	Kimberly	Chicago	28-Jun-84	7.7	$24,900	29	No
19	000324	Tallan	George	Chicago	20-May-88	3.9	$19,700	27	No
20	000284	Morse	Miriam	Chicago	02-Nov-87	4.4	$19,600	23	No
21	000141	Dickinson	Angela	Detroit	13-Nov-86	5.4	$23,900	33	No

Microsoft Excel - EMPLOYEE.XLS
File Edit Formula Format Data Options Macro Window Help
Normal
A4   000220
Ready   NUM

Figure 15.9 Employee Database Sorted by Location and Salary

reference as $D$4 if you click the cell). To designate the Salary field as the secondary key in the sort, you select cell G4 (entered as $G$4 when you click it). Also, to have the records within each location sorted from highest to lowest salary, you choose the Descending option in the **2**nd Key section. Figure 15.9 shows you the employee database after performing the sort using these two keys. Note how the records are now organized first in ascending order by city listed in the Location field (Atlanta, Boston, Chicago, and so on) and within each city in descending order by Salary (32,200, 19,200, 18,900 and so on).

Tip   You can use the Sort Ascending Tool (the one with A above Z) or the Sort Descending Tool (the one with Z above A) on the Utility toolbar to sort records in the database, using either the first field or the last field in the database as the primary key. To sort the database using the first field as the primary key, make the first entry in the first field active, select all of the records in the database, and then click Sort Ascending Tool or Sort Descending Tool (depending on which order you want to use). To sort the database using the last field as the primary key, make the first cell in the last field active, then select the rest of the database and click either the Sort Ascending Tool or the Sort Descending Tool.

SORTING ON MORE THAN THREE FIELDS

Sometimes you may need to sort on more than three fields (the maximum you can define in one sorting operation). For example, suppose you are working with a personnel database like the one shown in Figure 15.10, and you want to organize the records in alphabetical order first by department, then by supervisor, and finally by last name, first name, and middle name. To sort the records in this database by these five fields, you have to perform two sorting operations.

In the first sorting operation, you define the Last Name field as the primary key, the First Name field as the secondary key, and the Middle Name field as the third key. Figure 15.11 shows you the personnel database after performing this sort. In the second sort, you define the Department field as the primary key and the Supervisor field as the secondary key. Figure 15.12 shows you the personnel database after performing the second sorting operation. As you can see after performing the second sort operation, the records are now arranged in ascending order by department, then by supervisor within the department, and finally by the last name, first name, and middle name under each supervisor.

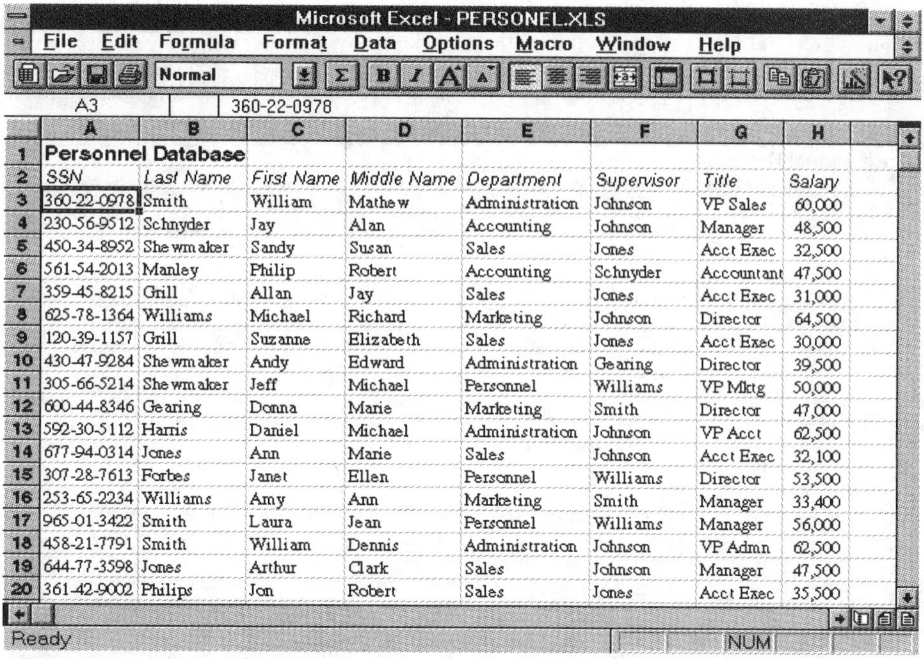

Microsoft Excel - PERSONEL.XLS

File　Edit　Formula　Format　Data　Options　Macro　Window　Help

Normal

A3　　360-22-0978

	A	B	C	D	E	F	G	H
1	Personnel Database							
2	SSN	Last Name	First Name	Middle Name	Department	Supervisor	Title	Salary
3	360-22-0978	Smith	William	Mathew	Administration	Johnson	VP Sales	60,000
4	230-56-9512	Schnyder	Jay	Alan	Accounting	Johnson	Manager	48,500
5	450-34-8952	Shewmaker	Sandy	Susan	Sales	Jones	Acct Exec	32,500
6	561-54-2013	Manley	Philip	Robert	Accounting	Schnyder	Accountant	47,500
7	359-45-8215	Grill	Allan	Jay	Sales	Jones	Acct Exec	31,000
8	625-78-1364	Williams	Michael	Richard	Marketing	Johnson	Director	64,500
9	120-39-1157	Grill	Suzanne	Elizabeth	Sales	Jones	Acct Exec	30,000
10	430-47-9284	Shewmaker	Andy	Edward	Administration	Gearing	Director	39,500
11	305-66-5214	Shewmaker	Jeff	Michael	Personnel	Williams	VP Mktg	50,000
12	600-44-8346	Gearing	Donna	Marie	Marketing	Smith	Director	47,000
13	592-30-5112	Harris	Daniel	Michael	Administration	Johnson	VP Acct	62,500
14	677-94-0314	Jones	Ann	Marie	Sales	Johnson	Acct Exec	32,100
15	307-28-7613	Forbes	Janet	Ellen	Personnel	Williams	Director	53,500
16	253-65-2234	Williams	Amy	Ann	Marketing	Smith	Manager	33,400
17	965-01-3422	Smith	Laura	Jean	Personnel	Williams	Manager	56,000
18	458-21-7791	Smith	William	Dennis	Administration	Johnson	VP Admn	62,500
19	644-77-3598	Jones	Arthur	Clark	Sales	Johnson	Manager	47,500
20	361-42-9002	Philips	Jon	Robert	Sales	Jones	Acct Exec	35,500

Ready　　NUM

Figure 15.10　Personnel Database Before Sorting

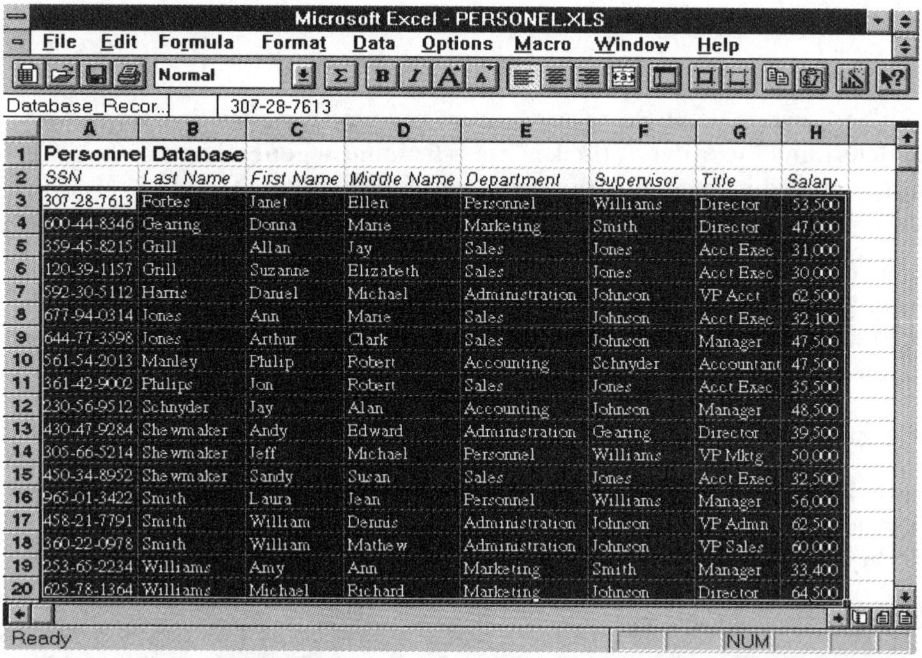

Microsoft Excel - PERSONEL.XLS

File　Edit　Formula　Format　Data　Options　Macro　Window　Help

Normal

Database_Recor..　　307-28-7613

	A	B	C	D	E	F	G	H
1	Personnel Database							
2	SSN	Last Name	First Name	Middle Name	Department	Supervisor	Title	Salary
3	307-28-7613	Forbes	Janet	Ellen	Personnel	Williams	Director	53,500
4	600-44-8346	Gearing	Donna	Marie	Marketing	Smith	Director	47,000
5	359-45-8215	Grill	Allan	Jay	Sales	Jones	Acct Exec	31,000
6	120-39-1157	Grill	Suzanne	Elizabeth	Sales	Jones	Acct Exec	30,000
7	592-30-5112	Harris	Daniel	Michael	Administration	Johnson	VP Acct	62,500
8	677-94-0314	Jones	Ann	Marie	Sales	Johnson	Acct Exec	32,100
9	644-77-3598	Jones	Arthur	Clark	Sales	Johnson	Manager	47,500
10	561-54-2013	Manley	Philip	Robert	Accounting	Schnyder	Accountant	47,500
11	361-42-9002	Philips	Jon	Robert	Sales	Jones	Acct Exec	35,500
12	230-56-9512	Schnyder	Jay	Alan	Accounting	Johnson	Manager	48,500
13	430-47-9284	Shewmaker	Andy	Edward	Administration	Gearing	Director	39,500
14	305-66-5214	Shewmaker	Jeff	Michael	Personnel	Williams	VP Mktg	50,000
15	450-34-8952	Shewmaker	Sandy	Susan	Sales	Jones	Acct Exec	32,500
16	965-01-3422	Smith	Laura	Jean	Personnel	Williams	Manager	56,000
17	458-21-7791	Smith	William	Dennis	Administration	Johnson	VP Admn	62,500
18	360-22-0978	Smith	William	Mathew	Administration	Johnson	VP Sales	60,000
19	253-65-2234	Williams	Amy	Ann	Marketing	Smith	Manager	33,400
20	625-78-1364	Williams	Michael	Richard	Marketing	Johnson	Director	64,500

Ready　　NUM

Figure 15.11　Personnel Database After First Sort by Last Name, First Name, and Middle Name

	A	B	C	D	E	F	G	H
1	**Personnel Database**							
2	SSN	Last Name	First Name	Middle Name	Department	Supervisor	Title	Salary
3	230-56-9512	Schnyder	Jay	Alan	Accounting	Johnson	Manager	48,500
4	561-54-2013	Manley	Philip	Robert	Accounting	Schnyder	Accountant	47,500
5	430-47-9284	Shewmaker	Andy	Edward	Administration	Gearing	Director	39,500
6	592-30-5112	Harris	Daniel	Michael	Administration	Johnson	VP Acct	62,500
7	458-21-7791	Smith	William	Dennis	Administration	Johnson	VP Admin	62,500
8	360-22-0978	Smith	William	Mathew	Administration	Johnson	VP Sales	60,000
9	625-78-1364	Williams	Michael	Richard	Marketing	Johnson	Director	64,500
10	600-44-8346	Gearing	Donna	Marie	Marketing	Smith	Director	47,000
11	253-65-2234	Williams	Amy	Ann	Marketing	Smith	Manager	33,400
12	307-28-7613	Forbes	Janet	Ellen	Personnel	Williams	Director	53,500
13	305-66-5214	Shewmaker	Jeff	Michael	Personnel	Williams	VP Mktg	50,000
14	965-01-3422	Smith	Laura	Jean	Personnel	Williams	Manager	56,000
15	677-94-0314	Jones	Ann	Marie	Sales	Johnson	Acct Exec	32,100
16	644-77-3598	Jones	Arthur	Clark	Sales	Johnson	Manager	47,500
17	359-45-8215	Grill	Allan	Jay	Sales	Jones	Acct Exec	31,000
18	120-39-1157	Grill	Suzanne	Elizabeth	Sales	Jones	Acct Exec	30,000
19	361-42-9002	Philips	Jon	Robert	Sales	Jones	Acct Exec	35,500
20	450-34-8952	Shewmaker	Sandy	Susan	Sales	Jones	Acct Exec	32,500

Figure 15.12   Personnel Database After Second Sort by Department and Supervisor

When sorting database records on more than three key fields, you need to determine the order of the key fields from most general to most specific. In the preceding example, this arrangement would be

Department, Supervisor, Last Name, First Name, Middle Name

After arranging the fields in this manner, you then perform your first sort operation with the more specific key fields at the end of the list. In our example, these fields include the

Last Name, First Name, Middle Name

fields as the primary, secondary, and tertiary keys. Next you perform your second sorting operation with the more general key fields at the beginning of the list. In our example, these fields are

Department, Supervisor

which are used as the primary and secondary keys in the second sorting operation.

Sorting the Fields of the Database

You can use Excel's column-sorting capability to change the order of the fields in a database without having to cut and paste various columns. When you sort the fields in a database, you add a row at the top of the database that you define as the primary sorting key. The cells in this row contain numbers (from 1 to the number of the last field in the database) that indicate the new order of the fields.

Figures 15.13 through 15.15 illustrate how you can use column sorting to modify the field order of a database in the sample employee database. In Figure 15.13 a new row (row 3) has been inserted above the row with the field names for this database. As you can see, the cells in this row contain numbers that indicate the new field order. After the fields are sorted using the values in this row, the ID No field will remain first (indicated by 1), the First Name field will be second (2), the Last Name field third (3), followed by Age (4), Salary (5), Location (6), Date Hired (7), Years of Service (8), and Profit Sharing (9).

Figure 15.14 shows the Sort dialog box to be used in sorting the database according to the numbers in row 3. Before opening this dialog box, you select the cell range A3:I34. This range includes the row with the numbers

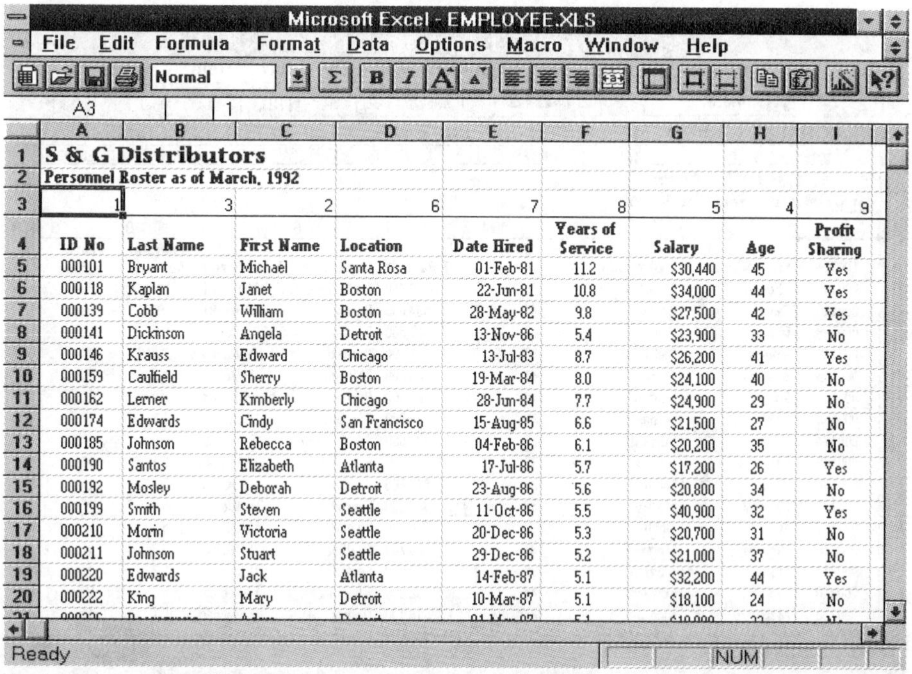

	A	B	C	D	E	F	G	H	I
1	S & G Distributors								
2	Personnel Roster as of March, 1992								
3	1	3	2	6	7	8	5	4	9
4	ID No	Last Name	First Name	Location	Date Hired	Years of Service	Salary	Age	Profit Sharing
5	000101	Bryant	Michael	Santa Rosa	01-Feb-81	11.2	$30,440	45	Yes
6	000118	Kaplan	Janet	Boston	22-Jun-81	10.8	$34,000	44	Yes
7	000139	Cobb	William	Boston	28-May-82	9.8	$27,500	42	Yes
8	000141	Dickinson	Angela	Detroit	13-Nov-86	5.4	$23,900	33	No
9	000146	Krauss	Edward	Chicago	13-Jul-83	8.7	$26,200	41	Yes
10	000159	Caulfield	Sherry	Boston	19-Mar-84	8.0	$24,100	40	No
11	000162	Lerner	Kimberly	Chicago	28-Jun-84	7.7	$24,900	29	No
12	000174	Edwards	Cindy	San Francisco	15-Aug-85	6.6	$21,500	27	No
13	000185	Johnson	Rebecca	Boston	04-Feb-86	6.1	$20,200	35	No
14	000190	Santos	Elizabeth	Atlanta	17-Jul-86	5.7	$17,200	26	Yes
15	000192	Mosley	Deborah	Detroit	23-Aug-86	5.6	$20,800	34	No
16	000199	Smith	Steven	Seattle	11-Oct-86	5.5	$40,900	32	Yes
17	000210	Morin	Victoria	Seattle	20-Dec-86	5.3	$20,700	31	No
18	000211	Johnson	Stuart	Seattle	29-Dec-86	5.2	$21,000	37	No
19	000220	Edwards	Jack	Atlanta	14-Feb-87	5.1	$32,200	44	Yes
20	000222	King	Mary	Detroit	10-Mar-87	5.1	$18,100	24	No

Figure 15.13 Sample Database with New Row for Sorting the Fields

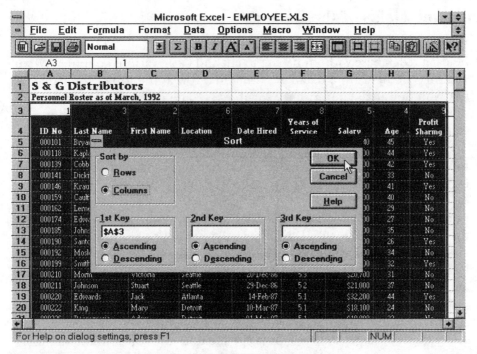

Figure 15.14   The Sort Dialog Box for Sorting Columns

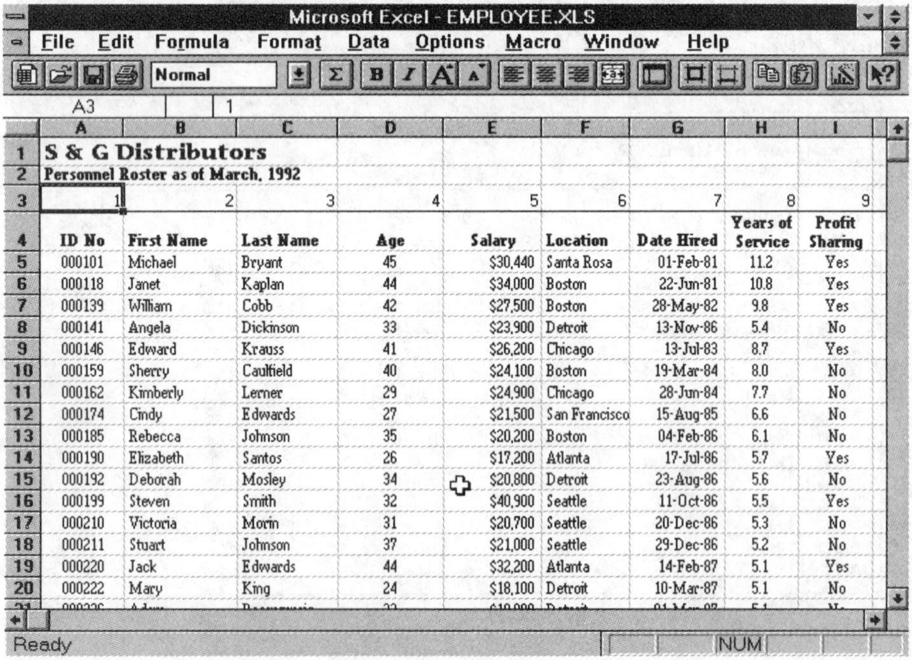

Figure 15.15   Sample Database After Sorting the Fields

for sorting the fields, the row of field names, and all the records in the database. As you can see, the **C**olumns option button is selected and cell $A$3 (the active cell in the selection when the Sort dialog box was opened) is entered as the primary sorting key in the 1st Key text box.

Figure 15.15 shows you the employee database after sorting its fields according to the values in row 3. After sorting the database, you would then delete this row and modify the widths of the columns to suit the new arrangement before you save the database.

Searching the Database

Excel provides you with several tools for locating and retrieving just the information you need from the database. Before you can use these tools to search for information in the database, you need to create a special range of cells in the worksheet called the *criteria range* with the Set **C**riteria command on the **D**ata menu. The criteria range consists of cells containing your selection criteria placed beneath the appropriate field names. For example, to find all of the employees in Boston in the sample employee database, you would enter Boston in the cell below the field name Location and designate these cells as the criteria range. Then Excel uses the Location of Boston as the criteria when you choose the **D**ata **F**ind (to locate each Bostonian) or the **D**ata **E**xtract (to retrieve each Bostonian), or the **D**ata **D**elete command (to remove each Bostonian).

To make it easy to perform a number of consecutive searches using different criteria, you can copy all of the field names to a new section of the worksheet, then place the selection criteria that you want to use under the appropriate field names. When you use the Set **C**riteria command to make this range the criteria range, Excel automatically assigns the name *Criteria* to it. Although you can have only one range named Criteria in the database worksheet at a time, you can create several different criteria ranges (each with its own different selection criteria) and then use the Set **C**riteria command to reassign the range name Criteria to the cell range containing the new selection criteria you want to use.

You normally locate the Criteria range in the worksheet to the right of the database itself instead of below it. That way you can add new records to the database without having to first move the Criteria range, and you can modify the size and shape of the Criteria range without affecting any of the records in your database.

When searching the database, you can display both the Criteria range and some of the database on the same screen by opening a second document window, arranging the two windows horizontally, and then scrolling the Criteria range into view in the top window, while at the same time keeping the first part of the database displayed in the document window below. Figure 15.16 illustrates this kind of arrangement for the employee database. In this worksheet, the criteria range is K3:S4 placed to the right of the database range A3:I33. In this figure, the Criteria range is shown in a second document window placed above the first document window containing the database. With this arrangement, after defining the criteria range with the Set Criteria command, you can enter your selection criteria in the appropriate cells in the top document window, then select the first document window below before you use the **D**ata **F**ind command to locate the matching records. (See "Using Data Find" later in this chapter for details.)

Specifying the Selection Criteria

Entering selection criteria in a Criteria range is very similar to entering criteria in the data form after selecting the **C**riteria command button. There are, however, some differences that you need to be aware of. For example, if you are searching for the last name *Paul* and enter the label Paul in the criteria range under the cell containing the field name Last Name, Excel

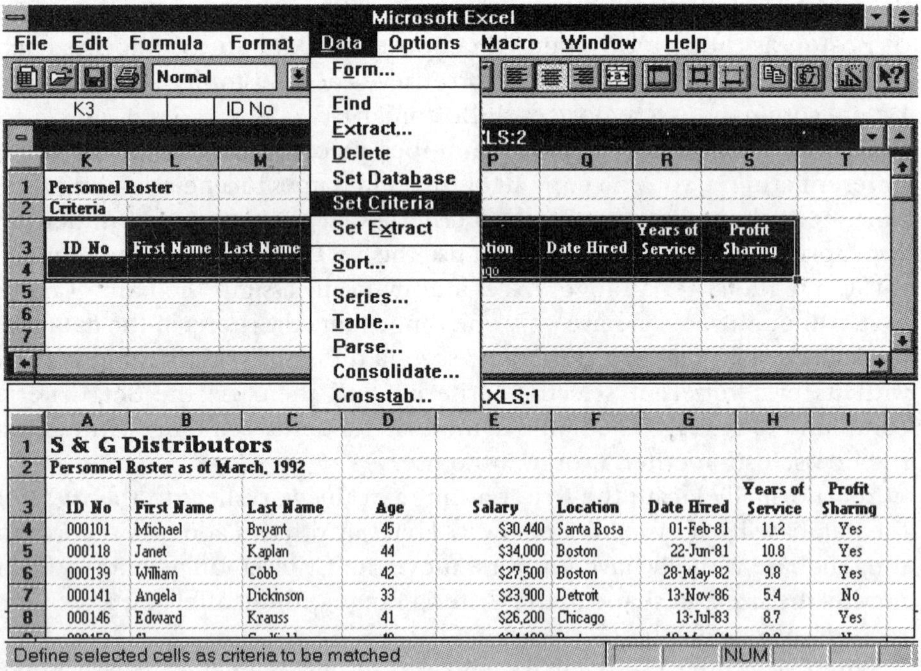

**Figure 15.16 Arranging the Criteria Range in a New Document
Window Above the Database**

matches any last name that begins with *P-a-u-l,* such as **Pauley**, **Paulson**, and so on. To avoid having Excel match any other last name besides Paul, you would have to enter a formula in the cell below the one with the Last Name field name, as in

="Paul"

As when entering criteria in a data form, you can also use the wildcard character of the question mark (?) or the asterisk (*) in your selection criteria. If, for example, you enter the J*n under the cell with the First Name field name, Excel will select any characters between *J* and *n* in the First name field will be a matching including **Joan**, **Jon**, or **John** as well as **Jane**, or **Joanna**. To restrict the matches to just those names with characters between *J* and *n* and prevent matches with names that have trailing characters, you need to enter the formula

="=J*n"

in the cell. When you use a selection formula like this, Excel matches names such as **Joan**, **Jon**, and **John** but not names such as **Jane** or **Joanna** that have characters after the *n*.

When setting up selection criteria, you can also use the other logical operators, including >, >=, <, <=, and <> in the selection criteria. (See Table 15.2 for a description and example of the usage of the logical operators in selection criteria.)

Tip To find all the records where a particular field is blank in the database, enter = and press the spacebar to enter a space in the cell beneath the appropriate field name. To find all the records where a particular field is *not* blank in the database, enter <> and press the spacebar to enter a space in the cell beneath the appropriate field name.

SETTING UP LOGICAL AND AND LOGICAL OR CONDITIONS

When you enter two or more criteria in the same row beneath their respective field names in the Criteria range, Excel selects only those records that meet both of the criteria (referred to as a *Logical AND* condition). Figure 15.17 shows an example of a logical AND condition. There Excel selects only those records where the location is Boston *and* the date hired is after January 1, 1987, because both the criteria Boston and >1/1/87 are placed in the same row (row 4) under their respective field names.

When you enter two or more criteria in different rows of the Criteria range, Excel selects records that meet any one of the criteria they contain (referred to as a *Logical OR* condition). Figure 5.18 shows you an example of a logical OR

Table 15.2   The Logical Operators in the Selection Criteria

Operator	Meaning	Example	Locates
=	Equal to	="CA"	Records where the state is *CA*.
>	Greater than	>m	Records where the name starts with a letter after *M* (that is, N through Z).
>=	Greater than or equal to	>=3/4/92	Records where the date is on or after *March 4, 1992*.
<	Less than	<d	Records where the name begins with a letter before *D* (that is, A, B, or C).
<=	Less than or equal to	<=12/12/94	Records where the date is on or before *December 12, 1994*.
<>	Not equal to	<>"CA"	Records where the state is not equal to *CA*.

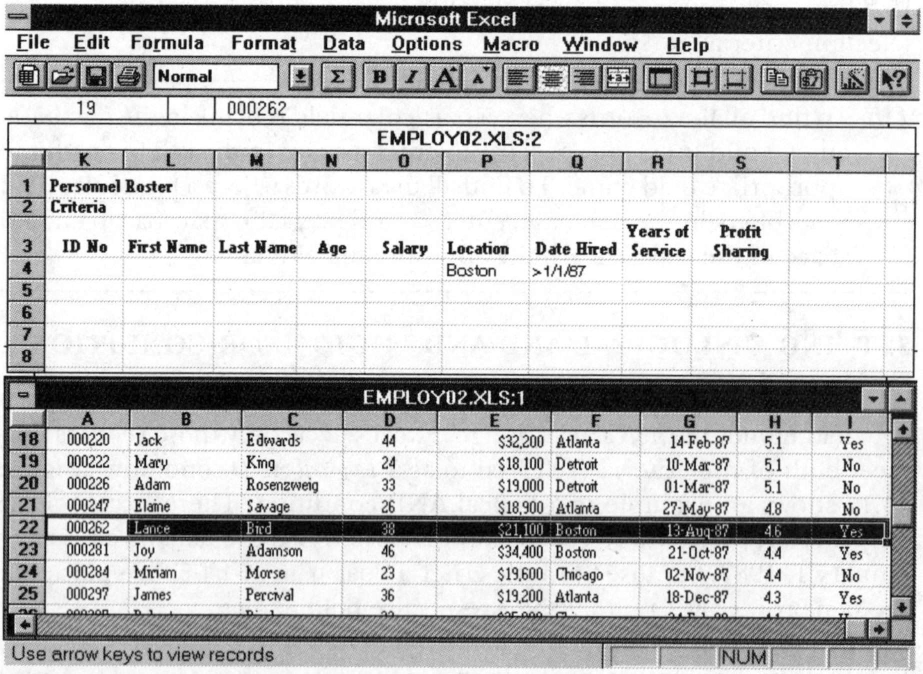

Figure 15.17   Using Logical AND Selection Criteria

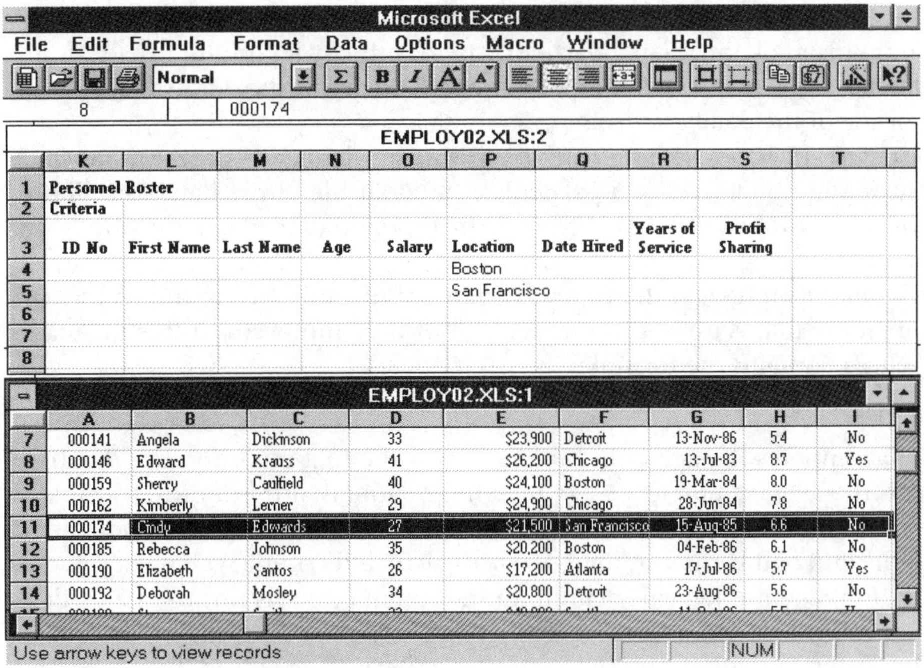

Figure 15.18   Using Logical OR Selection Criteria

condition. In this example, Excel selects records where the location is either Boston or San Francisco because **Boston** is entered in the second row (row 4) of the Criteria range above **San Francisco** in the third row (row 5).

When creating logical OR conditions, you need to remember to redefine the Criteria range with the Set Criteria command to include all the rows that contain criteria. (If you forget, Excel uses only the criteria in the rows included in the Criteria range.)

When setting up your criteria, you can combine logical AND and logical OR conditions (again, assuming that you expand the Criteria range sufficiently to include all of the rows containing criteria). For example, if you enter **Boston** in cell P4 (under Location), >1/1/87 in cell Q4 (under Date Hired), and enter **San Francisco** in cell P5, Excel matches records where the location is Boston and the date hired is after January 1, 1987, or records where the location is San Francisco (regardless of the date hired).

USING CALCULATED CRITERIA

You can use calculated criteria when searching your database. All you need to do is enter a logical formula that Excel can evaluate as either TRUE or FALSE in the criteria range under a name that is *not* used as a field name in the database. Calculated criteria enable you to select records based on a comparison of entries in a particular field with entries in other fields of the database or based on a comparison with entries in the worksheet that lie outside of the database itself.

Figure 15.19 shows an example of using a calculated criterion that compares values in a field to a particular value outside of the database. There, you want to find all of the records in the employee database where the employee's age is above the average age. Cell D2, shown in the lower document window in the figure, contains a formula (using the AVERAGE function) that returns the average age of the employees in this database. Cell T4 contains the formula

    =D4>$D$2

that compares the age entry in cell D4 for the first record in the database with the average employee age in cell D2. Note that this logical formula is placed under the label **Calculated Criteria** in cell T3, which has been added to the end of the criteria range. To use calculated criteria, you must remember to place the logical formula under a name that is not used as a field name in the database itself, and you must include this label and formula in the Criteria range. (In this example, the criteria range is redefined with the Set Criteria command as the cell range K3:T4.)

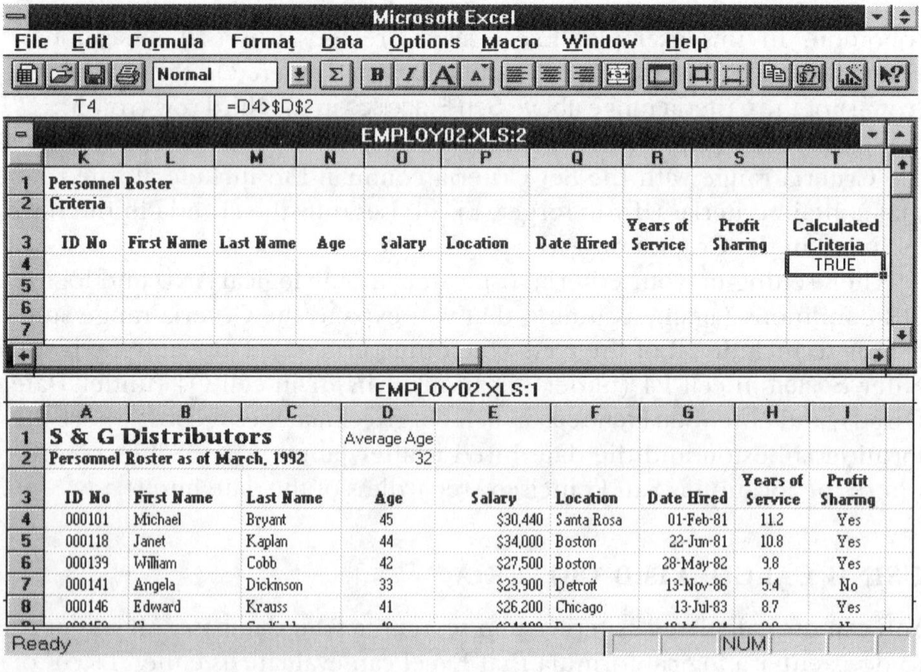

Figure 15.19   Using Calculated Selection Criteria

When you perform a Data Find, Extract, or Delete operation (all described later in this chapter), Excel applies this calculated criteria to every record in the database. Excel does this by adjusting the Age field cell reference D4 (entered as a relative reference) as the program examines the rest of the records below. Note, however, that the reference to the average age cell D2 is entered as an absolute reference ($D$2) in the criteria formula so that Excel will not adjust this reference but rather compare the Age entry for each record to this particular value.

When entering formulas for calculated criteria that compare values outside the database to values in a particular field, you should always reference to the cell containing the very first entry for that field to ensure that Excel applies your criteria to every record in the database.

You can also set up calculated criteria that compare entries in one or more fields to other entries in the database. For instance, to select the records where the Age entry is at least two years greater than the record above it (assuming that you have sorted the database in ascending order by age), you would enter the logical formula

=D5>D4+2

as the calculated criteria under the cell with the label Calculated Criteria. To select the records where the years of service are greater than or equal to half of the employee's age, you would enter the logical formula

=H4>=D4/2

as the calculated criteria under the cell with the label Calculated Criteria.

Most often, you will want to leave the cell references relative to cells within the database itself so that they can be adjusted as each record is examined and the references to the cells outside the database absolute so that they will not be changed when making the comparison with the rest of the records.

 Tip When you enter the logical formula for a calculated criterion, Excel returns the logical value TRUE or FALSE. This logical value applies to the field entry for the first record in the database that you used in the logical formula. By inspecting this field entry in the database and seeing if it does indeed meet your intended selection criteria, you can usually tell whether or not your logical formula is correct.

USING THE AND AND OR FUNCTIONS IN CALCULATED CRITERIA

You can also use the AND, OR, and NOT functions with the logical operators in calculated criteria to find records that fall within a range. For example, to find all of the records in the employee database where the salaries range between $35,000 and $42,000, you would enter the logical formula with the AND function

    =AND(E4>=35000,E4<=42000)

as the calculated criteria under the cell with the label Calculated Criteria, as shown in Figure 15.20.

To find all of the records in this database where the salary is either below $17,000 or above $35,000, you would enter the logical formula with the OR function

    =OR(E4<17000,E4>35000)

as the calculated criteria under the cell with the label Calculated Criteria, as shown in Figure 15.21.

Using Data Find

You use the **F**ind command on the **D**ata menu to select all the records, one at a time, that match the selection criteria in your Criteria range. When you choose this command, the first matching record selected by Excel depends on the location of the cell pointer at the time. If a cell outside the database

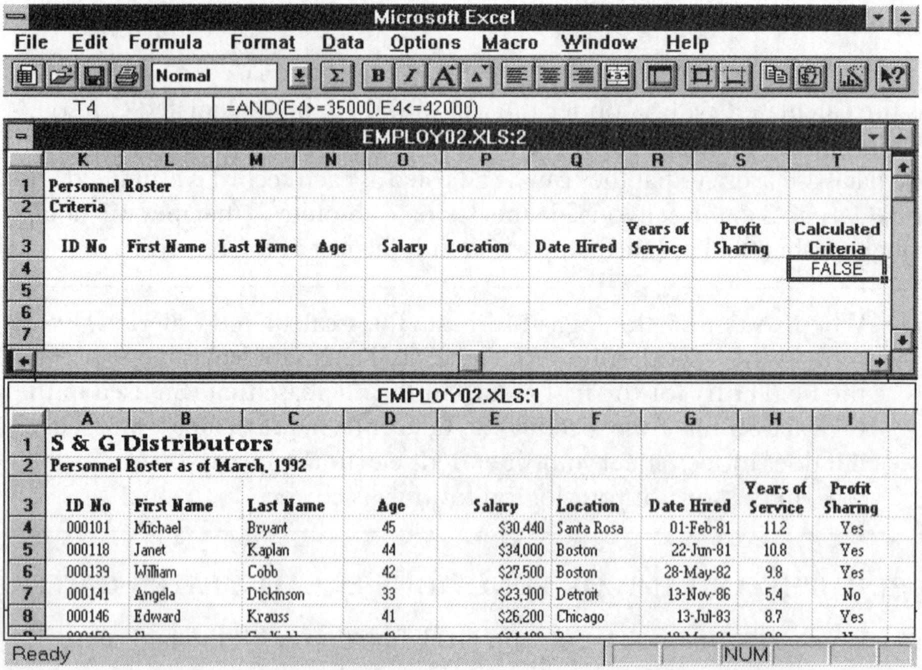

Figure 15.20   Calculated Selection Criteria with the AND Function

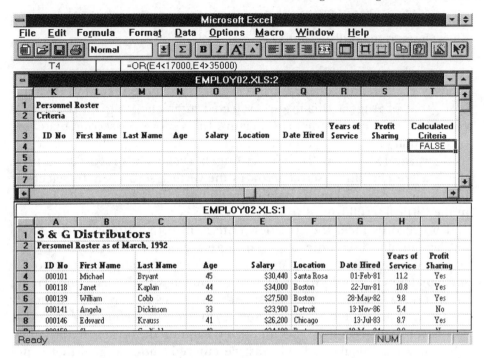

Figure 15.21   Calculated Selection Criteria with the OR Function

or a cell in the row of field names is the active one, Excel selects the first matching record in the database (moving from top to bottom). If a cell within a record is the active one, Excel selects the first matching record that is located below this record.

Tip   Press the Shift key before you choose the **Data Find** command to have Excel search from the active cell up toward the top of the database. This enables you to locate the first matching record above the active cell when the cell pointer is positioned in a record that you know is beneath the one you want to locate.

To move to the next matching record in the database, you can press the ↓ key or ↓ scroll arrow in the vertical scroll bar. (When using the **Data Find** command, the scroll bars become striped, indicating that their function is modified.) To move to the previous matching record, you can press the ↑ key or ↑ scroll arrow in the vertical scroll bar. In a large database, you can drag the scroll box in the vertical scroll bar to skip to the next matching record in a different part of the database. You can use the horizontal scroll bar to scroll left and right to view different fields, but be aware that Excel will not let you scroll the entire database out of sight. (At least the last field must always remain displayed.)

Figures 15.22 and 15.23 illustrate how the **D**ata **F**ind command works. In these figures, the selection criteria are records where the date hired is after January 1, 1984. Figure 15.22 shows the first matching record in the database (that of Angela Dickinson), selected after choosing the **D**ata **F**ind command when cell A3 was active. Figure 15.23 shows the second matching record (that of Sherry Caulfield), selected after clicking the ↓ scroll arrow in the vertical scroll bar. To reselect Angela Dickinson's record, you press the ↑ key or click the ↑ scroll arrow in the vertical scroll bar. To select the next matching record in the database, you press the ↓ key or ↓ scroll arrow in the vertical scroll bar.

If no records meet the selection criteria in your Criteria range, Excel displays an alert box indicating that there are no matching records when you choose the **D**ata **F**ind command. If you were expecting Excel to locate some matching records, you may have a problem with the selection criteria or Criteria range. Check to make sure that you haven't forgotten to modify the size and shape of the Criteria range to include all of your criteria or that you haven't entered the selection criteria under the wrong field names. (Remember, a calculated field must be entered under a label that is not used as a field name.)

When you are finished viewing the matching records, you can exit Find mode and return to normal Ready mode either by selecting the Exit **F**ind command on the **D**ata menu (the **F**ind command changes to Exit **F**ind as soon as you select it) or by simply pressing the Esc key.

If you want to edit a field in the selected record, you only need to click the cell that contains this entry to select it. Doing this automatically exits you from Find mode and returns you to Ready mode so that you can make changes to your entry on the formula bar. If, after editing the record, you still need to search the database for the next matching record, you have to select the **D**ata **F**ind command again.

Using Data Extract

You can use the **E**xtract command on the **D**ata menu to select all of the records that match your selection criteria and copy them as a group to a new part of the worksheet. To extract records from a database, you must define an Extract range (automatically named Extract by Excel) that indicates where the matching records are to be copied, along with the normal Criteria range that contains the selection criteria and the Database range that defines the records to search.

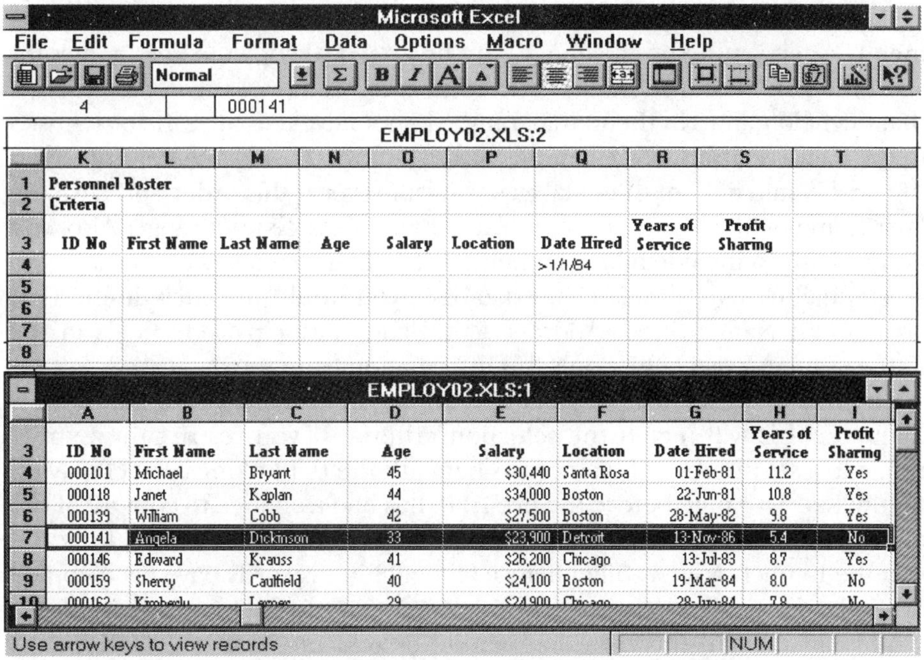

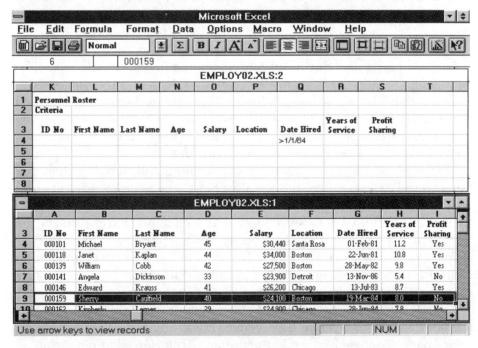

Figure 15.22 Using Data Find to Locate Records in a Database

Figure 15.23 Finding the Next Matching Record in the Database

You define the Extract range with the Set Extract command on the **Data** menu. When setting up this range, you first need to copy the field names for all of the fields that you want extracted to a new range of the database. Note that the field names in the Extract range do not have to match the order used in the database itself. For example, even when the Last Name field precedes the First Name field in the database, you can reverse this order and have the First Name field precede the Last Name field in the Extract range. Also, you do not have to include all of the fields in the Extract range. For instance, to create mailing labels for a client database, you would just include the First Name, Last Name, Street Address, City, State, and Zip Code fields in the Extract range; Excel copies only this information from the database.

Before you perform an Extract operation, you normally don't know how many records will match the selection criteria. If you restrict the Extract range to a set number of blank rows beneath the field names, Excel may fill up the Extract range before the program has had a chance to copy all of the matching records when you perform the Extract operation. Excel indicates that the Extract range is filled before all matching records have been copied by displaying an alert message box indicating that the Extract range is full.

You can prevent this from happening by selecting only the field names that you've copied to the new worksheet. When the Extract range consists only of the field names, Excel uses as many rows beneath these names as is required to copy all the matching records from the database. Be aware, however, that during the Extract operation Excel replaces any existing cell entries with the information copied from the database.

To avoid losing data during an Extract operation, you should locate the field names for the Extract range in an area of the worksheet where there is no possibility of overwriting existing cell entries in the row below. If you have placed the Criteria range in columns to the right of the database, you can usually accomplish this by locating the Extract range in rows below (similar to the arrangement shown in Figure 15.24).

After copying the fields for the Extract range and defining their cell range as the Extract range with the **Data Set Extract** command, you enter your selection criteria in the Criteria range and then choose the **Data Extract** command. When you choose this command, Excel displays the Extract dialog box. (In it you can specify the extraction of unique records only—see the next section for details.) To have Excel extract information from the matching records and copy this information into the Extract range, you click OK or press Enter.

Figure 15.24 illustrates a typical Extract operation. In this example, only the field names First Name, Last Name, Location, Age, Date Hired, and Salary have been used in the Extract range. To ensure that data from all

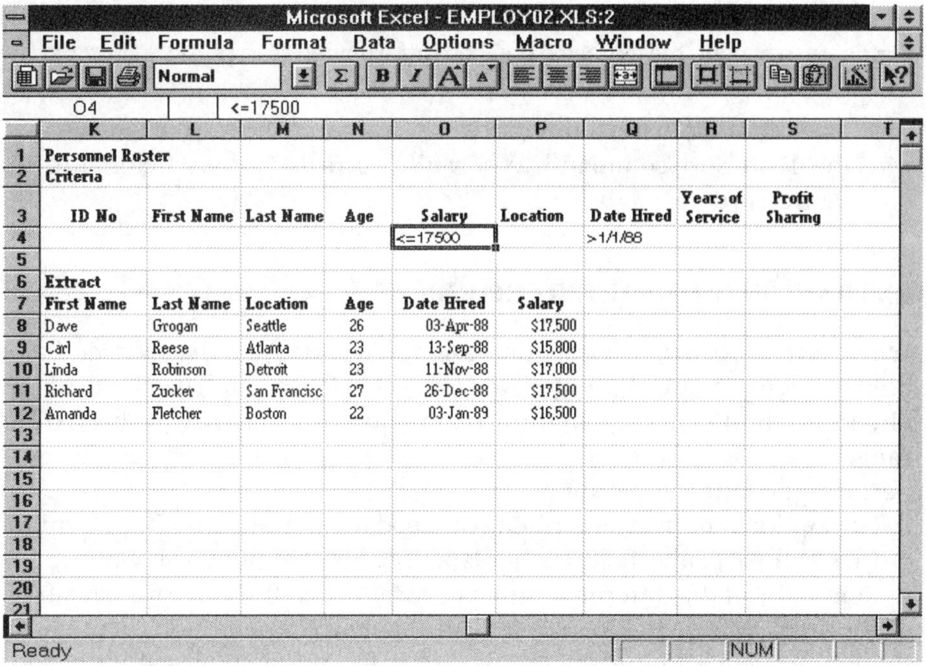

	K	L	M	N	O	P	Q	R	S
1	Personnel Roster								
2	Criteria								
3	ID No	First Name	Last Name	Age	Salary	Location	Date Hired	Years of Service	Profit Sharing
4					<=17500		>1/1/88		
5									
6	Extract								
7	First Name	Last Name	Location	Age	Date Hired	Salary			
8	Dave	Grogan	Seattle	26	03-Apr-88	$17,500			
9	Carl	Reese	Atlanta	23	13-Sep-88	$15,800			
10	Linda	Robinson	Detroit	23	11-Nov-88	$17,000			
11	Richard	Zucker	San Francisc	27	26-Dec-88	$17,500			
12	Amanda	Fletcher	Boston	22	03-Jan-89	$16,500			

Figure 15.24 Extracting Records into the Extract Range

matching records can be copied into the Extract range without filling it up, this range is defined as the single-row range of field names K7:P7. The selection criteria for the extraction (shown in the Criteria range) are Salary less than or equal to $17,500 and Date Hired after January 1, 1988.

You can see the result of performing the Extract operation using these criteria in the Extract range in Figure 15.24. As you can see, there are records in the employee database that match these criteria. Note, however, that Excel does not copy the complete records but only the information specified by the field names in the Extract range.

If you change the selection criteria and perform a subsequent Extract operation without changing the Extract range, Excel deletes the existing contents of the Extract range before copying the new information from the matching records. This means that if you want to save the results of one Extract operation before performing another one, either you need to copy its contents to a new part of the worksheet or to a new worksheet, or you need to redefine the Extract range in a different part of the worksheet that can't affect your original results.

You can save the results of an Extract operation in a new worksheet quite easily. Select the contents of this range (including the field names if you want them in the new worksheet), click the Copy tool on the Standard toolbar, then click the New Worksheet tool to open a new worksheet, activate the first cell of the range to contain the extracted database information, and press the Enter key.

 Tip After copying extracted records to a new worksheet, you can then use the Data Sort command to sort the records and/or fields into the desired order.

EXTRACTING UNIQUE RECORDS

When you perform an Extract operation, Excel displays the Extract dialog box that contains a **U**nique Records Only check box. To have the program eliminate duplicate information from matching records in the Extract range, you select this check box before you choose OK or press Enter to perform the Extract operation.

This option is quite useful when you need to know the number of unique entries in a particular field in the database. For example, you can use this option to list all the different employee locations in the employee database, as shown in Figure 15.25. To perform this Extract operation, you restrict the Extract range to the single-cell range, K7, that contains the Location field name and clear the Criteria range of all selection criteria. Then, after opening the Extract dialog box with the **D**ata E**x**tract command, you choose the **U**nique Records Only check box before you choose OK. When you perform this Extract operation, Excel copies every unique location in the database. Note that when you extract unique records only, you get no idea of how many times a particular field entry occurs in your database, as all duplicates are eliminated from the Extract range.

Using Data Delete

You can use the **D**ata **D**elete command to delete all of the records that meet your selection criteria. When you perform a Delete operation, Excel eliminates all matching records while at the same time closing all gaps in the database and redefining the Database range name. Note that the program safely eliminates records without affecting any data entered outside of the database in the same rows as matching records.

Keep in mind when using the **D**ata **D**elete command, however, that you cannot use the Undo feature to restore records deleted in error. If you should have the wrong selection criteria or, even worse, no selection criteria (which would delete the entire database!) in the Criteria range at the time you choose the **D**ata **D**elete command, you would have to rely on a backup copy of the database to restore the records. If you had no backup copy of

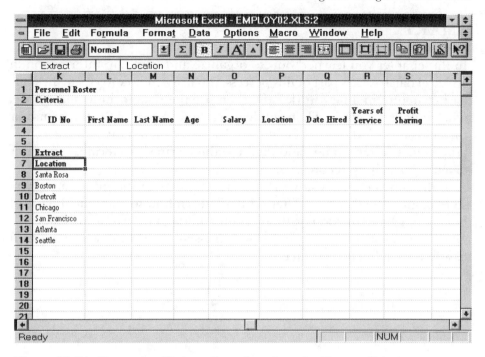

Figure 15.25   Extracting Unique Locations into the Extract Range

the database, you would be forced to reenter all of the deleted records by
hand. Because you cannot undo this type of deletion, Excel displays an
alert dialog box indicating that matching records will be deleted permanently when you select the OK button or press Enter.

To guard against losing records that you still need, you should always save
the database before you perform a Delete operation. You also should
perform a Find or Extract operation after entering the selection criteria in
the Criteria range right before you actually perform the Delete operation.
That way, you can see exactly which records would be eliminated from the
database using your selection criteria before you actually delete them.
Having verified that all the records selected in the Find or Extract operation do indeed need to be deleted, you can then use the **Data D**elete
command in complete confidence.

Tip   You can also delete a single record or adjacent records in the database
by selecting their cell range and then choosing the **E**dit **D**elete command with the Shift Cells **U**p option selected. When you use this
command to remove records, you can use the **E**dit **U**ndelete command
(Ctrl+Z) to restore the deleted record or group of records.

SUMMARY

In this chapter you learned how to organize and maintain information in an Excel database. As part of this process, you learned how to create the database structure in a new worksheet, then use the data form to add, locate, edit, or delete records. Then you learned how to sort the records and/or the fields in your database. Finally you learned how to enter your selection criteria in a Criteria range and then use these criteria to locate, extract, or delete all matching records.

In the next chapter you will learn how to analyze the information you store in an Excel database. There you will learn how to combine the use of built-in database functions with selection criteria to return various statistics. You will also learn how to use the new Crosstab command, which makes it easy to cross-tabulate key data.

16

Analyzing Database Information

Excel offers several tools that make it easy to analyze the data you store in your database. In this chapter you will learn how to use Excel's built-in database functions, both alone and in combination with the Data Table feature, as well as how to use the new Crosstab command to generate complex tables that cross tabulate your data.

As you will see, Excel's database functions allow you to calculate various statistics, such as the total, average, maximum, and minimum for a particular field in the database based on the current selection criteria. For example, with the sample employee database introduced in the last chapter, you could calculate the total salaries for just the employees in the Boston office by using the DSUM database function when the selection criteria is set to Location equal to Boston. So too you could find the average age of the employees who participate in the profit-sharing plan by using the DAVERAGE function when the selection criteria is set to Profit Sharing equal to Yes.

You can also combine the use of the database functions with that of data tables to automate the process of calculating a database function using different selection criteria. For example, you could create a series of ages and then use the DMAX command to calculate maximum salary in the database for each age in this list. By incorporating database functions in a data table, you can calculate a variety of statistics based on different selection criteria in a single operation that would otherwise require several operations of repeatedly editing the selection criteria. Not only does a data table save you from having to edit the selection criteria, it also enables you to view all these statistics together in the worksheet and save them if you so desire.

In addition to the database functions, you can also use the new Crosstab command in Excel 4.0 to analyze your database information. The Crosstab command uses a Crosstab Wizard (similar to the Chart Wizard you learned about in Chapter 12) that walks you through each step of creating a table that cross tabulates various data in your database. By creating crosstab tables, you are able to view at a glance relationships between information in the database that are often not immediately apparent.

Using the Database Functions

The database functions encompass a variety of functions (shown in Table 16.1) that return particular statistics about a database. All the database functions use the same arguments. Once you learn the general syntax

=DFUNCTION(*database,field,criteria*)

you can apply this syntax to any of the specific functions. The *database* argument in the database function refers to the range of cells that contains the database (field names and all records). If you have named this range with the Set Database command on the **D**ata menu, you can enter the range name **Database** as this argument. If you have not used this command, you can enter the cell references of the range holding your database.

The *field* argument in the database function refers to the field in the database whose data is to be used in calculating the function's results. For example, if you want to total the salaries of all the employees in the database who have been with the company five years or longer, you would use Salary as the *field* argument in the DSUM function. When specifying the *field* argument by name, you must remember to place the field name in quotation marks in the database function, as in "Salary" when you want the function to calculate the values in the Salary field. If you wish, you can also specify the field argument by entering its column position in the database when counting from left to right. For example, to specify the Salary field in the sample employee database as the *field* argument in a database function by its column position, you would enter **6** in the function, as the Salary field is in the sixth column to the right of the first field in the database.

The *criteria* argument in the database function refers to the selection criteria that are to be applied when calculating the function result. For instance, in the earlier example of using the DSUM function to total the salaries for all employees who have worked for the company five years or more, the *criteria* argument for this database function would contain cells with the selection criteria Years of Service >=5.

Table 16.1   The Database Functions

Database Function	Usage
DAVERAGE	Returns the average value from the specified field for all records matching the selection criteria.
DCOUNT	Returns the number of numeric entries in the specified field for all records matching the selection criteria.
DCOUNTA	Returns the number of nonblank cells in the specified field for all records matching the selection criteria.
DGET	Returns the value in the specified field for the single record in the database that matches the selection criteria. If no records match the selection criteria, this function returns the #VALUE! Error value. If more than one record matches the selection criteria, the function returns the #NUM! Error value.
DMAX	Returns the largest value from the specified field for all records matching the selection criteria.
DMIN	Returns the smallest value from the specified field for all records matching the selection criteria.
DPRODUCT	Returns the product of the values from the specified field for all records matching the selection criteria.
DSTDEV	Returns the sample standard deviation of the values in the specified field for all records matching the selection criteria.
DSTDEVP	Returns the population standard deviation of the values in the specified field for all records matching the selection criteria.
DSUM	Returns the total of the values in the specified field for all records matching the selection criteria.
DVAR	Returns the sample variance of the values in the specified field for all records matching the selection criteria.
DVARP	Returns the population variance of the values in the specified field for all records matching the selection criteria.

If you used the Set **C**riteria command on the **D**ata menu to name the range with your selection criteria, you can use the range name Criteria for this argument in a database function. If you have not used this command or you want to use a range different from the one defined as the Criteria range for searching the database, you can specify this function argument by cell references. As when using the Criteria range to search for information in a database, the criteria argument in a database function must include the cell with the name of the field or fields to be searched and the selection criteria to be applied to that field or fields.

Because they are statistical functions, most of the database functions can be used only with fields that contain numbers or calculated values. The only exceptions are the DCOUNTA and DGET database functions. You can use the DCOUNTA function to calculate the number of nonblank cells in a field of a database that contains text or numbers. Likewise, you can use the DGET function to return the field entry from a text or numeric field for the one unique record that matches your selection criteria.

Figure 16.1 illustrates how you can use the database functions to calculate various statistics based on different selection criteria. The worksheet shown in this figure uses several different database functions to calculate salary statistics for the men and women in the employee database. (The database was introduced in examples in the last chapter and expanded in this chapter to contain a field identifying the employee's gender.) Cell M7 contains the database function

=DSUM(Database,"Salary",$P$7:$P$8)

which calculates the total of the values in the Salary field in the Database range containing the Employee database based on selection criteria located in the cell range P7:P8 (where Sex is equal to **M**). Cell N7 contains a similar DSUM function

= DSUM(Database,"Salary",$P$9:$P$10)

This DSUM function is the same except for its *criteria* argument, P9:P10, so that this database function totals the salaries for the women in the employee database by setting the selection criteria to Sex equal to **F**.

The formulas in the adjacent cell range below those in cells M7 and N7 use the same *database, field,* and *criteria* arguments but have different database functions. The formulas in cells M8 and N8 calculate the average salary for the men and women in the employee database with the DAVERAGE function. The formulas in cells M9 and N9 return the lowest salary for the men and women with the DMIN function, while the formulas in cells M10 and N10 return the highest salary for the men and women with the DMAX function.

```
─                        Microsoft Excel                      ▼ ◆
 File   Edit   Formula   Format   Data   Options   Macro   Window   Help
 ▦ ▣ ▣ ▣  Comma       ▣ Σ B I A A ▣ ▤ ▤ ▤ ▢ ▢ ▣ ▤ ▣ ▣ ▣?
       M7              =DSUM(Database,"Salary",$P$7:$P$8)
 ▭                           EMPLOY04.XLS:1                   ▼ ▲
```

	L	M	N	O	P	Q	R	S	T
5									
6		*Men*	*Women*	*Both*					
7	Total Salaries	350,840	369,300	720,140	Sex				
8	Average Salaries	23,389	23,081	23,235	M				
9	Lowest Salary	15,800	16,500	15,800	Sex				
10	Highest Salary	40,900	37,500	40,900	F				
11									
12									

```
                            EMPLOY04.XLS:2
```

	A	B	C	D	E	F	G	H	Years of Service	Pr Sha
1	**S & G Distributors**									
2	Personnel Roster as of March, 1992									
3	ID No	First Name	Last Name	Age	Sex	Salary	Location	Date Hired	Years of Service	Pr Sha
4	000101	Michael	Bryant	45	M	$30,440	Santa Rosa	01-Feb-81	11.2	Y
5	000118	Janet	Kaplan	44	F	$34,000	Boston	22-Jun-81	10.8	Y
6	000139	William	Cobb	42	M	$27,500	Boston	28-May-82	9.9	Y
7	000141	Angela	Dickinson	33	F	$23,900	Detroit	13-Nov-86	5.4	I

```
 Ready                                                    NUM
```

Figure 16.1   Calculating Salary Statistics Based on Gender with the Database Functions

Note that the formulas in the cell range O7:O10 return statistics for both the men and the women (that is, all employees in the database) by using standard statistical functions. The table returns the total of the men's and women's salaries in the database with the regular SUM function

=SUM(M7:N7)

in cell O7. This table returns the average of the men's and women's salaries with the standard AVERAGE function

=AVERAGE(M8:N8)

in cell O8. It returns the lowest salary (man's or woman's) in the database with the regular MIN function

=MIN(M9:N9)

in cell O9, and returns the highest salary in the database with the standard MAX function

=MAX(M10:N10)

in cell O10.

Creating Data Tables with Database Functions

By combining the database functions with data tables (covered in Chapter 11), you can have Excel automate the task of substituting different selection criteria in the range use as the function's *criteria* argument. When you use a database function as the data table's master formula, you can view the results of varying the selection criteria in this formula all at once in the same worksheet. Of course, you can also save these results and print them whenever you want.

Figures 16.2 and 16.3 illustrate how you can combine database functions with a single-variable data table to calculate the salary totals for each location in the sample employee database. The cell range L6:L12 contains a list of all the different locations in this database. Cell M5 contains the following formula with the DSUM database function

```
=DSUM(Database,"Salary",R3:R4)
```

This database function calculates the total of all salaries in the employee database because the range R3:R4 defined as the *criteria* argument for this DSUM function contains no selection criteria. (Cell R4 is purposely left blank.)

To create a single-variable data table that will substitute the various cities listed in the range L6:L12 in cell R4, thereby using each of them as the selection *criteria* argument in the DSUM formula, you select the cell range L5:M12, then choose the **Data Table** command and select cell R4 as the Column Input Cell in the Table dialog box, as shown in Figure 16.2.

When you choose the OK button or press Enter, Excel generates the data table shown in Figure 16.3. The program generates this table by substituting each of the cities in the cell range L6:L12 into cell R4 and then calculating the DSUM function using the city as the Location selection criteria. The first time Excel calculates this DSUM function, the program sums the values in the Salary field for the Location equal to Atlanta and places the result of 103,300 in cell M6. After this, Excel replaces Atlanta with Boston (the next city in the list) and then sums the values in the Salary field for the Location equal to Boston and places the result of 177,800 in cell M7. This process of replacing the current selection criteria in cell R4 with the next city in the list, then recalculating the DSUM function and inserting the result in the data table, continues until Excel has used the last city in the list. After calculating the last result for Seattle in cell M12, Excel then returns the original value (a blank in this case) to the Column Input Cell of R4.

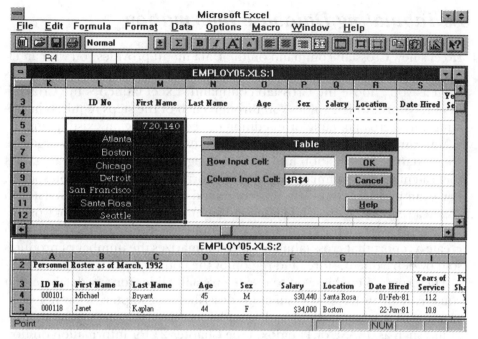

Figure 16.2   Setting Up a Single-Variable Data Table to Total Salaries by Location

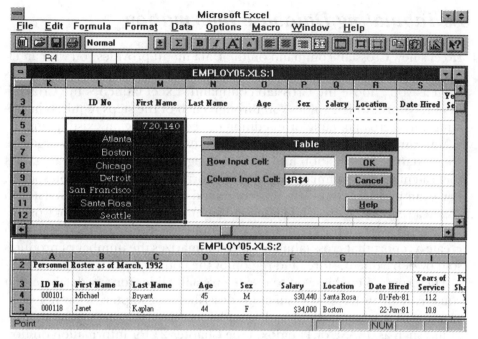

Figure 16.3   Worksheet with Salaries Totaled by Location

Cross Tabulating Database Information

Excel's new Crosstab command on the **D**ata menu provides you with an efficient way to analyze and summarize particular data in your database. As soon as you choose the Crosstab command, Excel launches the Crosstab ReportWizard, which guides you through each of the steps required in creating a new crosstab table or in editing or recalculating an existing one.

You can use the Crosstab command to create tables that simply organize your database information into desired categories, or you can create tables that calculate and summarize database information in the ways you specify. For example, you could use this command with a personnel database to create a report that cross tabulates and summarizes the number of workers at each plant by their job titles. Or you could use it with a sales database to create a report that cross tabulates and summarizes the number of products sold by department, store, and region of the country.

The program enables you to create crosstab tables for any database that you create in an Excel worksheet (as described in Chapter 15) as well as in external databases created with standalone database management programs such as dBASE or Paradox. (See Chapter 21 for information on how to use Q+E to access and search information in external database files.)

When you use the Crosstab command to generate a crosstab table, Excel places the table in a new document window, which you can then save and/or print. In creating the crosstab table, Excel creates a worksheet outline with row and column levels corresponding to the various row and column categories that you define for the crosstab report.

Creating a Crosstab Table with the Crosstab ReportWizard

The best way to learn how the Crosstab command works is to follow along with the steps necessary to create a simple crosstab table for the sample employee database. In this first example, we will create a table that cross tabulates and summarizes the number of men and women at each location in the sample employee database. To create this crosstab report with the Crosstab command, you would take these steps:

1. If you have not already done so, you must first define the database with the Set Database command on the **D**ata menu. (Refer to Chapter 15 for details on creating and defining a database in an Excel worksheet.) Note that if you're creating a crosstab report for an external database, you must open the **qe.xla** add-in macro located in the **\qe** directory of the **c:\excel** directory before you choose the Set Database

command. (See Chapter 21 for details on using Q+E to work with external database files.)

2. If you want to use selection criteria in generating your crosstab report, set up and define a Criteria range that contains your selection criteria using the Set Criteria command on the Data command. (See Chapter 15 for details.) If the cell range named as the Criteria range is empty of selection criteria, Excel uses all of the entries in the fields designated as the row and column categories when generating the crosstab report. If, however, this range contains selection criteria, the row and column categories in the crosstab report generated by Excel will contain data from only those records in the database that match your selection criteria.

3. Choose the Crosstab command at the bottom of the Data menu. Excel displays the Crosstab ReportWizard - Introduction dialog box shown in Figure 16.4.

4. Choose the Create a New Crosstab command button in the Crosstab ReportWizard - Introduction dialog box. Excel displays the Crosstab ReportWizard - Row Categories dialog box similar to the one shown in Figure 16.5.

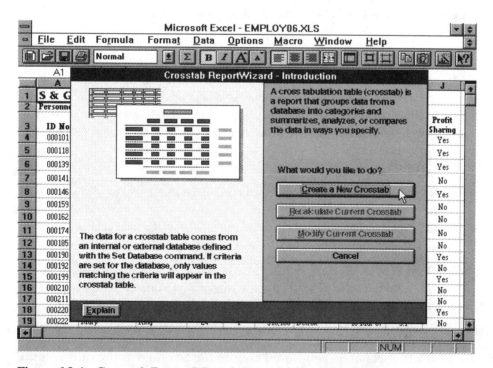

Figure 16.4   Crosstab ReportWizard - Introduction Dialog Box

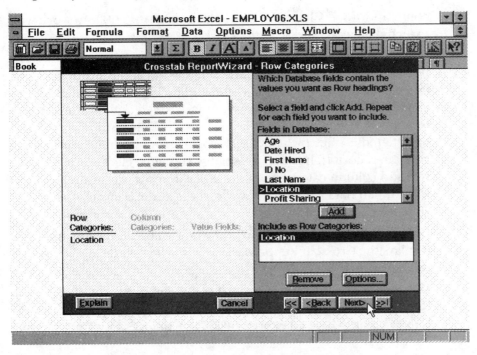

Figure 16.5   Crosstab ReportWizard - Row Categories Dialog Box

5. Double-click the first field in the Fields in Database list box that you want used as the first row category in your crosstab report, or select the field and then choose the **A**dd button to add this field to the Include as Row Categories list box. The fields that you choose for the row categories appear in the leftmost column of the crosstab table. For this example, you would choose the Location field as the sole row category.

6. Repeat step 4 until you have selected all of the database fields that are to make up the row categories in your crosstab report, then choose the Next> button. Excel displays the Crosstab ReportWizard - Column Categories dialog box similar to the one shown in Figure 16.6.

7. Double-click the first field in the Fields in Database list box that you want used as the first column category in your crosstab report, or select the field and then choose the **A**dd button to add this field to the Include as Column Categories list box. The fields that you choose for the column categories appear on the top row of the crosstab table. For this example, you would choose the Sex field as the only column category.

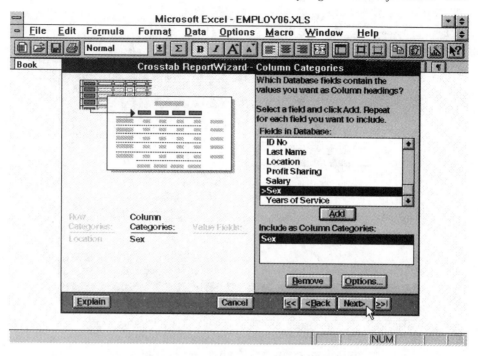

Figure 16.6   Crosstab ReportWizard - Column Categories Dialog Box

8. Repeat step 6 until you have selected all of the database fields that are to make up the column categories in your crosstab report, then choose the Next> button. Excel displays the Crosstab ReportWizard - Value Fields dialog box similar to the one shown in Figure 16.7.

9. Double-click the first field in the Fields in Database list box whose values you want Excel to consolidate in the cells of the crosstab report, or select the field and then choose the Add button to add this field to the Calculate Values from list box. The value field determines which values are summed for every row and column category combination in the database. If you leave the Calculate Values from list box empty, Excel simply counts each row and column category combination in the database. In this example, you would leave this list box blank so that Excel will count the number of men and women at each location.

10. Repeat step 8 for each field whose values you want aggregated until you have selected all of the database fields whose values are to be calculated in your crosstab report, then choose the Next> button. Excel displays the Crosstab ReportWizard - Final dialog box shown in Figure 16.8, where you can check your Row Categories, Column Categories, and Value Fields before you create the crosstab table.

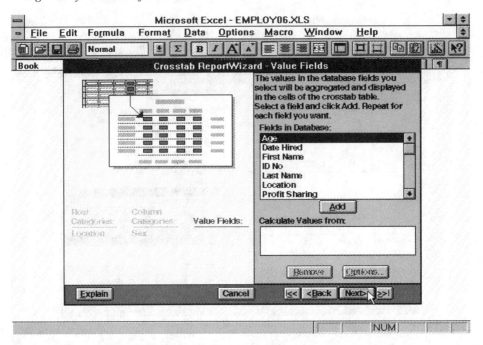

Figure 16.7   Crosstab ReportWizard - Value Fields Dialog Box

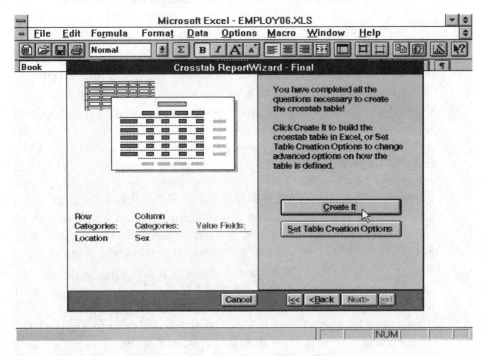

Figure 16.8   Crosstab ReportWizard - Final Dialog Box

11. Choose the **C**reate It command button in the Crosstab ReportWizard - Final dialog box to generate your crosstab report using the Report-Wizard's default settings. After you choose the **C**reate It button, Excel builds the crosstab according to your specifications. The program starts by organizing the row and column categories before calculating the data for the cells in the table. The status bar keeps you informed of Excel's progress in generating the crosstab. Note, however, that this process can be quite time-consuming when you are creating a complex table using several different row and column categories with a large database (especially external databases, which can be quite large).

Figure 16.9 shows the crosstab report created in a new document window when you cross tabulate location and gender in the employee database by selecting the Location field as the row category and the Sex field as the column category. Because you didn't include a value field, Excel uses the COUNT function to count each man and woman at each location in the database.

If you examine the contents of a crosstab table, you will find that it uses the new Excel 4.0 CROSSTAB function (see Database functions in Appendix B for

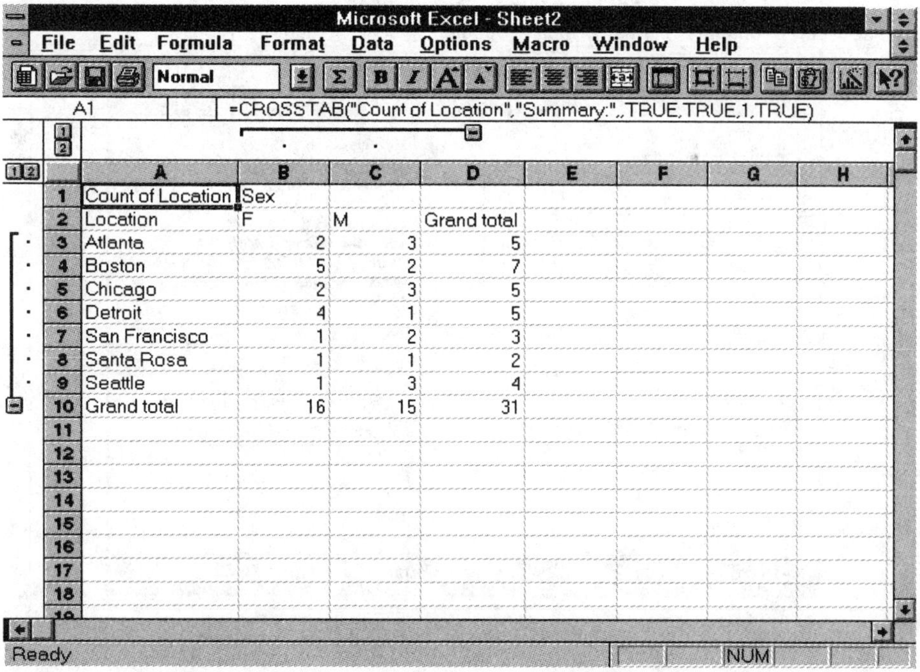

	A	B	C	D
1	Count of Location	Sex		
2	Location	F	M	Grand total
3	Atlanta	2	3	5
4	Boston	5	2	7
5	Chicago	2	3	5
6	Detroit	4	1	5
7	San Francisco	1	2	3
8	Santa Rosa	1	1	2
9	Seattle	1	3	4
10	Grand total	16	15	31

A1 =CROSSTAB("Count of Location","Summary:",,TRUE,TRUE,1,TRUE)

Figure 16.9 Crosstab Report Showing the Number of Men and Women at Each Location

details) to generate the cross-tabulated statistics. If you examine a dialog box such as the Goto dialog box or Paste Name dialog box, you will see that the Crosstab ReportWizard also has assigned multiple range names to the data in the crosstab table that are used in the CROSSTAB functions. Also, as you can readily see, in generating the crosstab table, the Crosstab Report-Wizard has automatically created an outline with two row and column levels. Remember that you can suppress the display of the outline symbols by clearing the Outline Symbols check box in the Display Options dialog box or by clicking the Show Outline Symbols tool on the Utility toolbar. (See Chapter 9 for more information on working with outlines.)

Figures 16.10 and 16.11 illustrate a somewhat more complicated crosstab table. In Figure 16.10, you see the Crosstab ReportWizard - Final Dialog Box for this second crosstab report. In this report, you want to see the total salaries for men and women at each location arranged by whether or not they are participants in the profit-sharing program. To do this, you still use only the Location field as the sole row category, but this time you have to designate both the Sex and Profit Sharing fields as column categories. You also have to define the Salary field as the Value Field for this crosstab report.

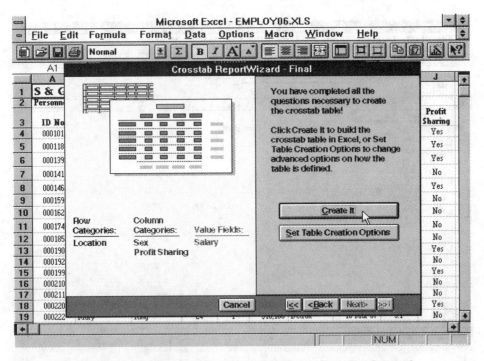

Figure 16.10 Crosstab ReportWizard - Final Dialog Box for Second Crosstab Report

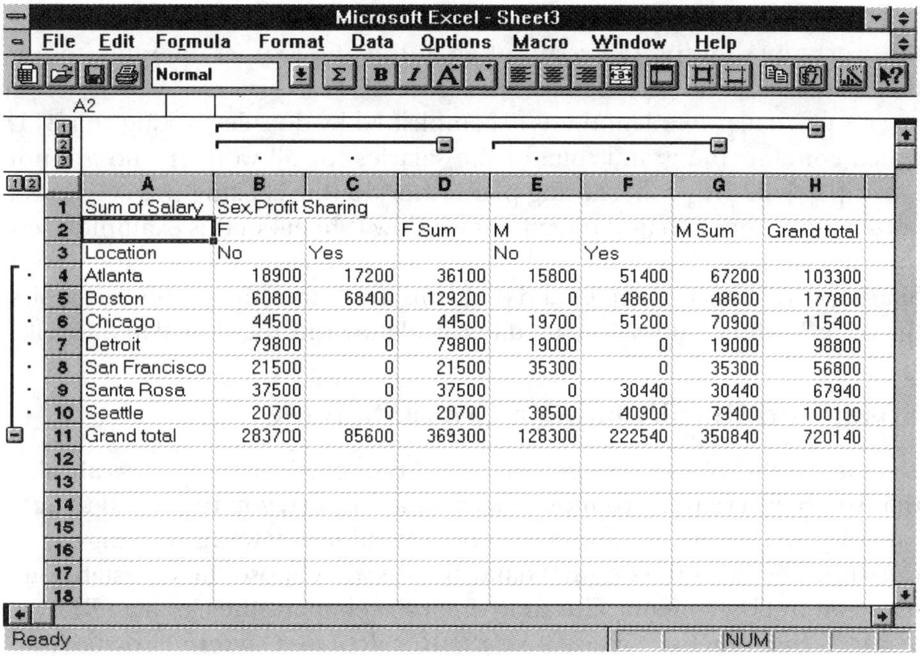

Microsoft Excel - Sheet3

File | Edit | Formula | Format | Data | Options | Macro | Window | Help

Normal

A2

	A	B	C	D	E	F	G	H
1	Sum of Salary	Sex,Profit Sharing						
2		F		F Sum	M		M Sum	Grand total
3	Location	No	Yes		No	Yes		
4	Atlanta	18900	17200	36100	15800	51400	67200	103300
5	Boston	60800	68400	129200	0	48600	48600	177800
6	Chicago	44500	0	44500	19700	51200	70900	115400
7	Detroit	79800	0	79800	19000	0	19000	98800
8	San Francisco	21500	0	21500	35300	0	35300	56800
9	Santa Rosa	37500	0	37500	0	30440	30440	67940
10	Seattle	20700	0	20700	38500	40900	79400	100100
11	Grand total	283700	85600	369300	128300	222540	350840	720140
12								
13								
14								
15								
16								
17								
18								

Ready | NUM

Figure 16.11 Crosstab Report Showing Total Salaries for Men and Women Who Are and Aren't Profit-sharing Participants at Each Location

When you define as a value field a database field such as Salary, which contains values, Excel automatically sums the values for every row and column category combination in the database. If, however, you define as a value field a database field that contains text, Excel simply counts the entries for every row and column category combination in the database. (You can, however, modify the function that is used in tabulating the statistics—see "Changing the Crosstab Table Options" later in this chapter.)

Figure 16.11 shows you the crosstab table generated by using the column and row category and value field settings shown in Figure 16.10. Note how Excel arranges the table when using both the Sex and Profit Sharing fields as the column categories. In this outline, there are three column levels: the first for the grand total of all salaries, the second for the totals of all the men's and all the women's salaries, and the third for total salaries for the men who are and aren't participants in the profit-sharing plan and for the women who are and aren't participants.

Displaying the Source Data

After building a crosstab report, you can have Excel automatically extract the records from the database that were used in calculating a value in the table simply by double-clicking that value. Figure 16.12 demonstrates how this works by showing the result of an automatic Extract operation using the second crosstab report shown in Figure 16.11.

This particular extraction was accomplished by double-clicking cell B11, which contains the grand total of the salaries for all women who are not participants in the profit-sharing plan. After double-clicking this cell, Excel automatically opens a new document window (Sheet4 in this example), sets up the criteria range, enters the selection criteria (Sex = F and Profit Sharing = No in this example) and performs the Extract operation that copies the records whose values were used in calculating the grand total in this cell.

Modifying and Recalculating a Crosstab Table

You can use the Crosstab command to modify or recalculate the crosstab table that you have created. To modify a crosstab report, you first need to activate the worksheet containing the crosstab table you want to change (not the worksheet with the original data) before you choose the Crosstab command on the **D**ata menu. This time when Excel opens the Crosstab Report-Wizard - Introduction dialog box, the **R**ecalculate Current Crosstab and

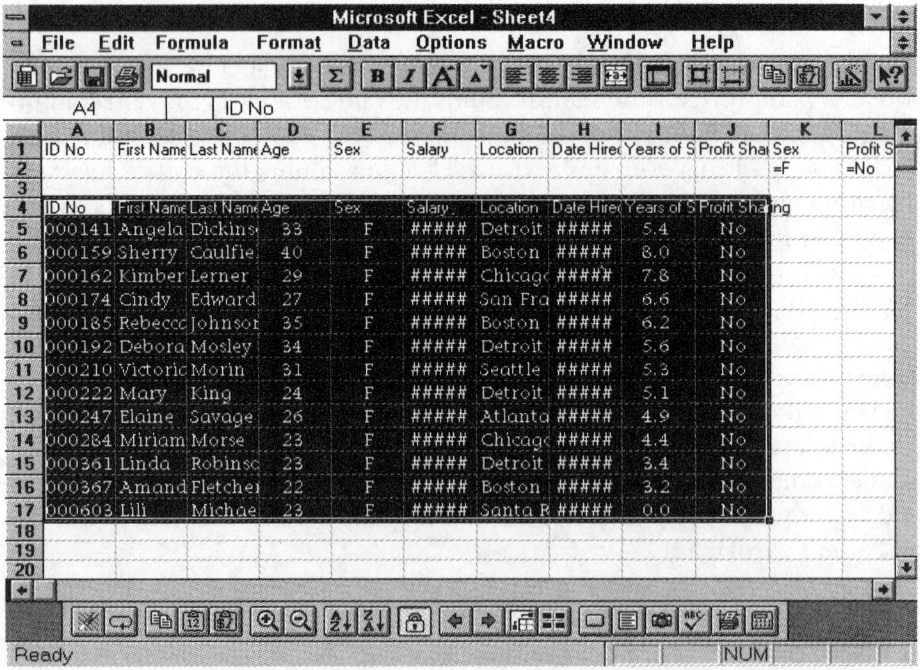

Figure 16.12   Extracted Records Used to Calculate the Grand Total of Salaries for Women Who Are Not Profit-sharing Participants

Modify Current Crosstab command buttons are no longer dimmed. If you have made changes to the records in the database that could affect the calculated values in the crosstab table, you choose the **R**ecalculate Current Crosstab button to have Excel recompute the crosstab table using the new values.

If you want to change the row or column categories or the value fields used in your crosstab report, you need to choose the **M**odify Current Crosstab button. When you do, Excel displays the Crosstab ReportWizard - Row Categories dialog box, where you can change the row categories for the crosstab report. To add a new category, double-click the field in the Fields in Database list box or select the field and choose the **A**dd button. To remove a category, select it in the Include as Row Categories list box, then choose the **R**emove button. To change the row category options, you choose the **O**ptions command button, change the row category options, and select the OK button. (See "Changing the Row and Column Category Options" below.)

Alert! To change the order of the fields used as row or column categories, you have to delete the fields that are out of order and then reenter in the desired order. Excel doesn't allow you to change the field order in the Include as Row Categories or Include as Column Categories list boxes in any other way.

You can make similar changes to the column categories and/or value fields. To move to the next Crosstab ReportWizard dialog box, choose the Next > button. To move to the previous dialog box, choose the <**B**ack button. To move to the Introduction dialog box, choose the |<< button. To move to the final dialog box, choose the >>| button.

After you've finished making your modifications, choose the >>| button to display the Crosstab ReportWizard - Final dialog box, then choose the **C**reate It button to generate. Excel then recreates the crosstab table in the same document window, using your new settings and the same area of the active worksheet.

CHANGING THE ROW AND COLUMN CATEGORY OPTIONS

When first setting up a crosstab table or later modifying it, you can change certain row category, column category, or value field options. Figure 16.13 shows the row category options. (The column category options are identical except that they refer to columns instead of rows.) To change the options for a row or column category, select the field in the Include as Row Categories or Include as Column Categories list box, then select the **O**ptions

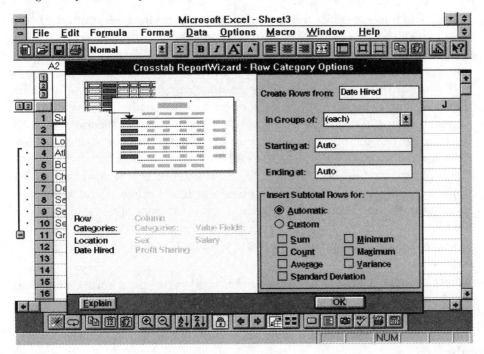

Figure 16.13   Crosstab ReportWizard - Row Category Options Dialog Box

button. When working with fields that contain dates, times, or values, the row and column category options allow you to specify groupings for the dates or values in the crosstab table. To specify a grouping (the default is each), you select the desired grouping in the In Groups of drop-down list box (such as hours for time, weeks for dates, or quarters for financial values), or you can enter the grouping designation in the accompanying text box.

When working with time, date, or numeric fields, you can also specify the range of records to be used by entering the upper and lower limits in the Starting at and Ending at text boxes, respectively. For example, to limit the records for the Date of Sale field grouped by months to the months of June through December, you would enter June in the Starting at text box and December in the Ending at text box. When entering starting and ending values for numeric fields (such as salaries in the Salary field between 35000 and 65000), you must be sure that the value you enter in the Ending at text box is larger than the one you enter in the Starting at text box.

When you are working with row and column categories in groups, you can have the Crosstab ReportWizard provide other statistics besides subtotals. (The crosstab report automatically calculates subtotals and grand totals.) To do this, you simply select all of the check boxes (Sum, Count, Average,

Standard Deviation, **M**inimum, Ma**x**imum, and **V**ariance) in the Insert Subtotal Rows for or the Insert Subtotal Columns for sections of the Row Category or Column Category Options dialog box.

When you have finished changing the row and/or column category options for the selected field, choose the OK button to close the Row Category or Column Category Options dialog box.

CHANGING THE VALUE FIELD OPTIONS

Figure 16.14 shows you the value field options that appear when you display the Crosstab ReportWizard - Value Field dialog box and then choose the **O**ptions button. By default, the crosstab report sums the values in each value field. To have the Crosstab ReportWizard perform a different calculation, open the Calculation Method drop-down list box and select the new calculation method (Count, Average, Minimum, Maximum, Standard Deviation or Variance) in the list.

If you are creating a crosstab table for an external database in your worksheet, you can use a formula as a value field that computes values between fields in the database, such as an Extended Price field created by multiplying the values in the Price field by the values in the Quantity field. To do this, you

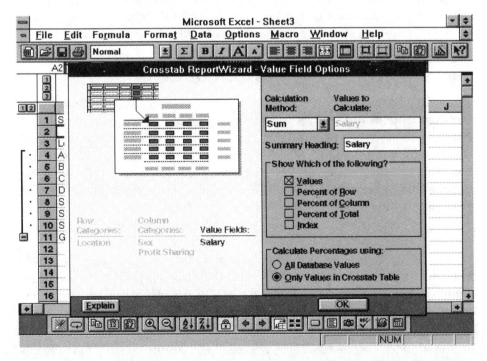

Figure 16.14   Crosstab ReportWizard - Value Field Options Dialog Box

select a field in the database, then open the Value Field Options dialog box and enter the formula in the Values to Calculate text box, as in

    =Price*Quantity

Then, if desired, change the summary heading for the calculated values in the Summary Heading text box. (In this example, you would probably change the heading to Extended Price.)

By default, the crosstab report shows only the values computed according to the selected calculation method. If you desire, you can also have the report show each cell's relationship to the crosstab table either as an index value (by choosing the Index check box) or as a percentage of the row category (Percent of Row check box), column category (Percent of Column check box), or the entire table (Percent of Total). When calculating these percentages, the Crosstab ReportWizard uses only the values in the crosstab table (selected according to the selection criteria in the Criteria range and the Starting at and Ending at values applied to the row and/or column categories). If you would rather have the percentages computed using all the values in the selected value field of the database, choose the All Database Values option button in the Calculate Percentages using section of the dialog box. (The Only Values in the Crosstab Table option is immediately deselected.)

When you have finished making your changes to the selected value field in the Value Field Options dialog box, choose the OK button to record your changes and return to the Crosstab ReportWizard - Value Field dialog box.

CHANGING THE TABLE CREATION OPTIONS

Figure 16.15 shows you the Crosstab ReportWizard - Create Options dialog box that contains the settings you can modify that affect the entire crosstab table. To change the settings for the crosstab table you are creating for the first time or modifying, display the Crosstab ReportWizard - Final dialog box (you can do this in one step by clicking the >>| button), then choose the Set Table Creation Options. When you first create a crosstab table, all of these options are set to Yes. (The Create the crosstab table on a new worksheet? option button is set to No in the figure because this figure was created when modifying an existing crosstab table.)

By default, the Crosstab ReportWizard creates an outline in the Excel worksheet for the crosstab table, creates the crosstab table in a new document window, defines range names for its CROSSTAB formulas, and allows you to double-click the crosstab range to extract the source data in a new worksheet. If you do not want these table options to be applied to your new or modified crosstab table, select the No option button for the appropriate table creation option or options in the Create Options dialog box.

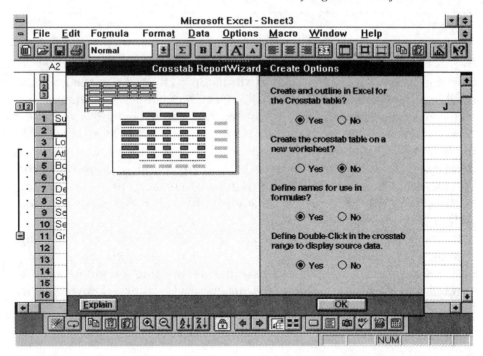

Figure 16.15 Crosstab ReportWizard - Create Options Dialog Box

After making all necessary changes to these report options, select the OK button to close the Create Options dialog box and return to the Crosstab ReportWizard - Final dialog box, where you can create your new or modified crosstab table by selecting the **C**reate It command button.

Tip You can create only one crosstab table per worksheet. However, if you need to display multiple crosstab tables in a single worksheet, you can do so by using the Camera tool on the Utility toolbar to copy pictures of the various crosstab tables to a worksheet that already contains a crosstab table. To take a picture of the crosstab table with the Camera tool, make the worksheet with the table you want to copy active, then select all of the cells in the crosstab table and click the Camera tool. Next, make the worksheet where you want the picture copied to active. Click the cell in the worksheet that should hold the upper-left corner of the picture of the crosstab table and then click the pointer outside of the table to paste its picture in place. Note that Excel automatically updates a picture of a crosstab table pasted in another worksheet whenever you update the source crosstab table with the **R**ecalculate Current Crosstab command button.

SUMMARY

In this chapter you learned how to analyze the information you track in your databases with Excel's database functions. Then you learned how to combine these database functions with data tables to automate the use of a variety of selection criteria. Finally you learned how to generate crosstab tables that cross-tabulate and summarize information in your database with the new Crosstab command. Remember that you can use any of these tools to analyze information in databases that you create in Excel worksheets or in databases created with standalone database management programs such as Paradox or dBASE. (For information on how to use databases created with such programs, refer to Chapter 21.)

In the next chapter you will learn the basics of creating and using macros. There you will learn how to create macros that automate common basic tasks, such as changing print settings for printing a standard report. You will also learn how to enhance your macros by editing them as well as how to debug macros that are not performing properly.

17

Creating and Using Command Macros

Macros enable you to automate almost any task that you undertake in Excel. By creating and using a macro to complete a common task that you perform routinely, you not only speed up the procedure considerably (Excel can play back your keystrokes and mouse actions much faster than you perform them manually), but you are also assured that each step will be carried out in the same way each and every time you undertake the task.

In Excel, you can create two different types of macros: *command macros* which perform a series of actions, such as entering the company name and address in a new worksheet or printing a particular cell range, and *function macros* which perform a customized calculation (or series of calculations) in a worksheet or macro sheet much like Excel's built-in functions. The command macros that you create can run the gamut from those that play back an unvarying action sequence (encompassing data entry as well as the selection of Excel commands) to those which interact with you, playing back different action sequences depending upon your input at the time you run the macro.

You can create command macros in one of two ways: You can have Excel record your actions as you undertake them in a worksheet or chart window or you can write out the instructions that you want included in the macro. Either way, Excel utilizes a special *macro sheet*, which holds the actions and instructions in your macro. The macro instructions in a macro sheet are written (whether by Excel or by you yourself) using special *macro functions* that make up the Excel macro language.

The macro sheet is very similar to the standard worksheet with which you are already familiar, except this type of worksheet uses wider column widths, displays the formulas in the cells, includes the macro functions

637

along with the worksheet functions in the Paste Function dialog box, and saves the file with a temporary macro sheet name (**Macro1**, **Macro2**, and so on) and with an **xlm** file extension (for Excel macro). The macro functions are very similar to the built-in worksheet functions that you learned to use early in Part 1 of this book. Like worksheet functions, macro functions must be prefaced with the = (equal sign), and most macro functions use arguments that indicate what information should be processed. In this chapter you will learn how to create, test, and debug command macros that you use to automate repetitive tasks required when building and using your Excel worksheets and charts. In the next chapter you will learn how to create complex command macros that set up and run custom Excel applications, complete with their own pull-down menus and dialog boxes. In Chapter 20 you will learn how to create and use function macros.

Recording Command Macros

Using Excel's macro recorder, you can create many of the utility-type command macros that help you perform the repetitive tasks necessary for creating and editing your worksheets and charts. When you turn on the macro recorder, it records all of your actions in the active worksheet, chart, or macro sheet as you make them. Unlike some other macro recorders you may have used (such as the one used by Lotus 1-2-3 for DOS and Windows), the Excel macro recorder does not record the keystrokes or mouse actions you take to accomplish an action, but only the action itself. This means that any mistakes that you make while taking an action will not be recorded as part of the macro. If, for example, you make a typing error and then edit it while the macro recorder is on, only the corrected entry will show up in the macro. The original mistakes and steps taken to remedy them are not recorded.

The macros that you create with the macro recorder can be stored either in a *global macro sheet* or on a new macro sheet that you begin. The global macro sheet is automatically named **global.xlm.** Any macros that you store in this worksheet are available whenever you work with Excel, as this file is saved in the **\xlstart** directory of the **c:\excel** directory and is therefore opened each time you start the program. If you store the macros you record in a new macro sheet, you must open that sheet before you can run those macros. For that reason, you always should record the utility-type macros you use routinely in the global macro sheet so that you can run them at any time.

When you create a macro with the macro recorder, you decide not only the macro sheet in which to store the macro but also what range name and shortcut keystrokes to assign to the macro you are creating. When assigning a range name for your macro, you use the same guidelines as when assigning a standard range name to a cell range in your worksheet. When assigning a shortcut keystroke to run the macro, you can assign the Ctrl key plus a lowercase letter between a and z or the Ctrl key plus an uppercase letter between A and Z (the equivalent of Ctrl plus Shift plus the letter). You cannot, however, assign the Ctrl key plus a punctuation or number key (such as Ctrl+/ or Ctrl+1) to your macro.

To see how easy it is to create a command macro with the macro recorder, follow these steps for creating a command macro that enters the Company Name in large, bold type and centers it across rows A through G in the worksheet:

1. Open the Excel document window that contains the worksheet or chart you need to work with, then choose the Re**c**ord command on the **M**acro menu. If no document is currently open in Excel and your macro should open a new document as part of its instructions, choose the Re**c**ord Macro command on the **F**ile menu instead. If the Macro toolbar is displayed, you can click the Record Macro tool (the tool second from the right with the dot in it—see "Using the Macro Toolbar" later in this chapter for more information).

   You can create the macro that centers the company name in the first row of a new worksheet in Sheet1 so you don't have to open a new worksheet before choosing the **M**acro Re**c**ord command. When you choose the **M**acro Re**c**ord command, Excel opens a Record Macro dialog box similar to the one shown in Figure 17.1.

2. If you want your macro to have a more descriptive name, replace the **Record1** temporary range name with a range name of your choice. For this header macro, you would replace **Record1** in the Name text box with the range name **Company_Name**.

3. Select the **K**ey text box, then enter the letter of the alphabet you want to assign to the macro—remember that Excel differentiates between uppercase and lowercase letters. For the header example macro, you would enter **C** (uppercase) to assign Ctrl+Shift+C as the shortcut keystrokes.

4. To make the macro available in any new worksheet you create, you would select the **G**lobal Macro Sheet option button in the Store Macro In section of the Record Macro dialog box. (The **M**acro Sheet option is selected by default.)

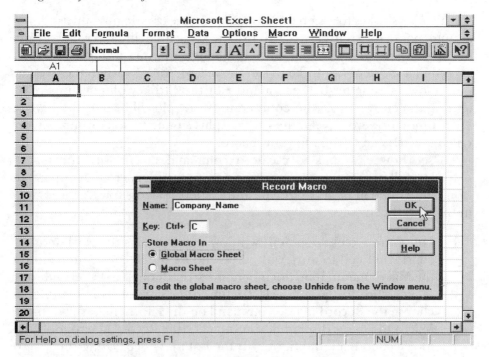

Figure 17.1 The Record Macro Dialog Box

5. Choose the OK command button in the Record Macro dialog box or press the Enter key to close this box and turn on the macro recorder. The message **Recording** now appears on the status bar to remind you that the result of all of the actions you take (including selecting cells, entering data, and choosing commands) will now be recorded as part of your macro.

6. Select the cells, enter the data, and choose the Excel commands required to perform the tasks you want recorded just as you normally would in creating or editing the current document, using either the keyboard or the mouse or a combination of the two. For the example macro, you would press Ctrl+Home to select cell A1 (even when the pointer is already in this cell), then you would enter your company's name in cell A1, select the cell range A1:G1, and click the Center Across Selected Columns tool, the Bold tool, and the Increase Font Size tool in the Standard toolbar before you click cell A1 to deselect the cell range A1:G1.

7. After you've finished taking all of the actions you want included in your macro, choose the Stop Recorder command on the **M**acro menu to turn off the macro recorder. The Recording message on the status bar disappears to let you know that the macro recorder is now turned off.

Running a Command Macro

After recording a command macro, you can run it by pressing the keystroke shortcuts you assigned to it in the Macro Record dialog box (Ctrl+Shift+C in the company name example macro), or by choosing the **R**un command on the **M**acro menu and selecting the macro's range name in the **R**un list box of the Run Macro dialog box. You can select a macro by double-clicking its range name in the **R**un list box or by selecting the name and then choosing the OK button or pressing Enter.

Before running a command macro, you may need to select a new document window or, at least, a new cell range within the active document window. When recording cell references in a macro, the macro recorder always inserts absolute references in the macro sheet. (Unless you choose the Relative Record option—see "Using the Relative Record Option" later in this chapter for details.) This means that your macro will enter its data entries or perform its formatting in the same area of the active document. (Unless the macro itself first selects a new area or opens a new document window.) If you run your macro in a document that already contains data in the cells that the macro uses, you run the risk of having existing data and/or formatting overwritten during the macro's execution. Keep in mind that although you can use the Undo feature to reverse the very last action performed by your macro, most macros perform a series of actions so that you may end up referring to a backup copy of the document, or worse, manually reconstructing the document.

 Alert! Be careful not to run the macro you've just created when the macro sheet that contains its instructions is active. Doing so may overwrite some of the macro functions, which may introduce errors in the macro's command sequences or even make it impossible to run the macro again.

Figure 17.2 shows the Run Macro dialog box after creating the Company_Name macro in the global macro sheet (**global.xlm**). To test out this new macro, you need to open a new worksheet window (Sheet2 in this example) before choosing the **M**acro **R**un command. To run the macro in this new worksheet, you double-click C GLOBAL.XLM!Company_Name in the **R**un list box or simply choose the OK button.

Unhiding the Global Macro Sheet

Excel automatically hides the document window containing the global macro sheet. Before you can display the macros stored in the **global.xlm**

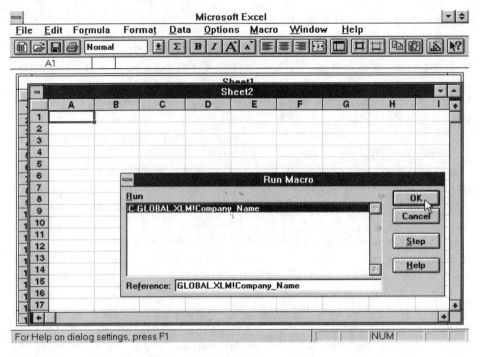

Figure 17.2   The Run Macro Dialog Box

macro sheet, you must first unhide this document window. To do this, select the **Unhide** command on the **Window** menu to display the Unhide dialog box. If no Excel document is currently open, you can display this dialog box by choosing the **Unhide** command on the **File** menu instead.

> ***Note:*** The global macro sheet is not created until you record your first command macro using the **G**lobal Macro Sheet option. If this option is still dimmed when you try to select the **Unhide** command on the **Window** menu, you have not yet recorded a macro with the **G**lobal Macro Sheet option. When you do so, Excel automatically places the document window containing the macro sheet in the background. To display the macro instructions in this macro sheet after you've stopped recording your macro in the active document window, you simply select the name of the macro sheet at the bottom of the **W**indow pull-down menu to activate its document window.

Figure 17.3 shows you the Unhide dialog box after running the Company_Name macro in the Sheet2 document window. To display the macro functions in this macro, you need to unhide the **global.xlm** macro sheet by

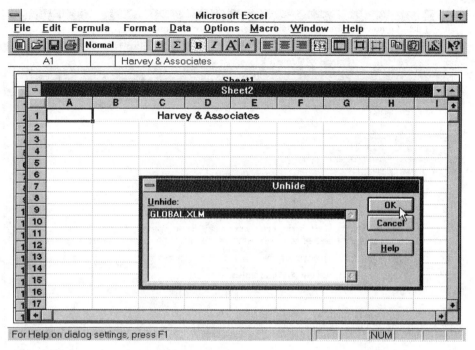

Figure 17.3   Selecting the Global Macro Sheet in the Unhide Dialog Box

double-clicking its name in the Unhide list box or by choosing OK or pressing Enter.

Editing a Command Macro

After opening the macro sheet that contains your macro and making its document window active, you can view the macro's contents and edit them as required. The first time you use the macro recorder to record a macro in either the global or a new macro sheet, Excel places the macro in column A of the macro sheet, using as many rows as are needed to accommodate the actions you have recorded. Figure 17.4 shows you the contents of the Company_Name macro stored in the global macro sheet after unhiding the **global.xlm** window and arranging it on top of the **Sheet2** worksheet window and widening column A.

Note how the macro recorder has located the macro name and instructions for this macro in the cell range A1:A9. Cell A1 contains the range name Company_Name followed by the keystroke shortcut in parentheses (C). Beneath the first cell containing the macro's range name and keystroke shortcut, you find the actual macro functions that Excel used to record each of your actions in the macro. You should notice several things

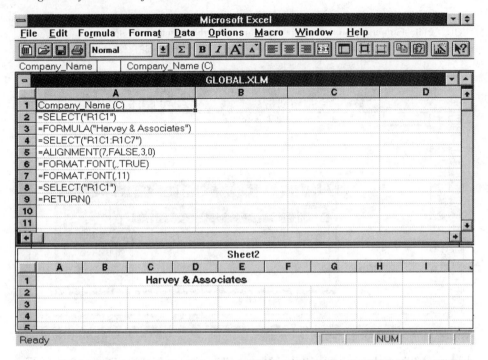

Figure 17.4   Contents of the Company_Name Macro in the Global Macro Sheet

about the macro functions in these cells:

- Each of the macro functions, like the worksheet functions, begins with the equal sign.
- Each places its arguments in a pair of closed parentheses.
- When recording cell references, the macro recorder uses the R1C1 reference system with absolute references.

Documenting a Macro

After recording a command macro or writing the instructions yourself, you should take the time to document each of its steps. Taking the time to document your macros ensures that you will always understand the purpose and function of each part of the macro. Explaining each step makes it much easier for you or someone else in your office to modify the macro at a later date.

Figure 17.5 shows you the Company_Name macro after documenting each of its macro functions in column B of the global macro sheet. Note the usage of each macro function in the macro. The SELECT macro function selects a cell or cell range in the active worksheet; the FORMULA macro

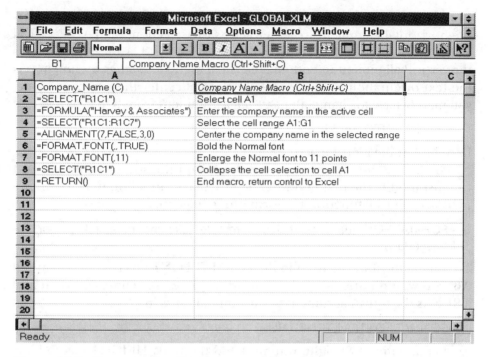

Figure 17.5   Documenting the Company_Name Macro

function enters data in the active cell; the ALIGNMENT macro function aligns the cell selection; and the FORMAT.FONT macro function formats the contents of the active cell. Every macro must end with the RETURN macro function, which indicates the end of the macro instructions and returns program control to Excel.

Using a Command Macro

By editing a macro's instructions in its macro sheet, you can change the functioning of a command macro the very next time you run it. For example, suppose that you want to change the Company_Name macro so that it bolds and italicizes the Normal font, is increased in point size to 14, and vertically centers the company name and increases the row height to 30 points. You could make such changes to the Company_Name by editing its macro instructions in the global macro sheet.

You would begin by modifying the arguments in the ALIGNMENT macro function so that vertical alignment is changed from bottom to center. The ALIGNMENT macro function uses the following syntax:

=ALIGNMENT(horiz_align,wrap,vert_align,orientation)

In the Company_Name macro, the value 7 as the *horiz_align* argument sets the horizontal alignment to center across the selection, the FALSE logical value as the *wrap* argument turns off text wrap, the 3 as the *vert_align* sets the vertical alignment to bottom, and the 0 as the *orientation* argument sets the text orientation to horizontal. To vertical center the company name, you merely have to change the *vert_align* argument from 3 to 2, as in

   =ALIGNMENT(7,FALSE,2,0)

in cell A4 of the global macro sheet.

   To change the font to bold and italics and the size to 14 points, you can just modify the first FORMAT.FONT macro function in cell A6. The FORMAT.FONT function for formatting cells uses the syntax

   =FORMAT.FONT(name_text,size_num,bold,italic,underline,strike, color,out-
   line,shadow)

To change the font size to 14 in the FORMAT.FONT macro function in cell A6, you would enter **14** as the second *size_num* argument and then add TRUE as the fourth argument to turn on italics, as in

   =FORMAT.FONT(,14,TRUE,TRUE)

To increase the row height, you must add the ROW.HEIGHT macro function, which follows the syntax

   =ROW.HEIGHT(height_num,reference,standard_height,type_num)

To increase the row height to 30 points, you simply need to enter **30** as the first *height_num* argument, as in

   =ROW.HEIGHT(30*)*

Because you no longer need the second FORMAT.FONT macro function in cell A7, you can replace this function with the ROW.HEIGHT.

   Figure 17.6 shows you the global macro sheet after making these changes to the macro functions in the Company_Name macro in column A and after modifying the documentation for each edited macro instruction in column B. You can see the effect of running the modified Company_Name macro in the Sheet1 document window beneath the window containing the global macro sheet in the figure.

Tip After editing macros in the global macro sheet, remember to hide this document window with the **Window Hide** command and then select the **Yes** button when asked if you want to save the changes to the **global.xlm** file upon exiting Excel. Otherwise, Excel automatically displays the global macro sheet each time you start Excel.

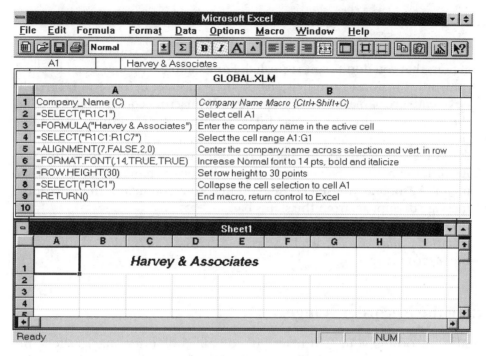

Figure 17.6   The Company_Name Macro After Editing

Using the Relative Record Option

As mentioned earlier, the macro recorder automatically records cell references with absolute references using the R1C1 system of cell notation. Sometimes you may want to have the macro recorded with relative cell references instead. For example, assume that you want to create a macro that enters the company name in whatever cell is active at the time you run the macro and then enters the current date in the cell two columns to the right.

To create such a macro, you must make sure that the macro recorder uses relative cell references instead of absolute cell references. To do this, you open the Excel document required for running through the macro's steps, select the **M**acro Record command, and indicate the macro range name, keystroke shortcut, and sheet to use as usual. Then, before you begin recording the macro, you choose the Rela**t**ive Record command on the **M**acro menu. If during the course of recording your actions, you want to switch back to the default system of recording all cell references using absolute references, you simply choose **A**bsolute Record (which replaces the Relative Record command) from the **M**acro menu.

Pausing the Recording

When performing the tasks to be recorded in a macro, you may have to take actions that you don't want recorded. For example, you may need to check some information in another part of the worksheet before you record the next sequence of macro steps. To prevent the macro recorder from including the actions required to display the new part of the worksheet containing the information you need to review, you turn it off before scrolling the worksheet. To turn off the macro recorder temporarily, choose the Stop Recorder command (which replaces the Record command) on the **M**acro menu. As soon as you select the Stop Recorder command, the Recording message disappears from the status bar.

When you are ready to resume recording actions for your macro, you restart the macro recorder by selecting the **S**tart Recorder command on the **M**acro menu.

Setting the Recorder Range

After recording your first macro in column A of a new macro sheet, the macro recorder automatically places the next macro that you record in that sheet in subsequent empty columns to the right. If you wish, you can use the Set Recorder command on the **M**acro menu to indicate where the macro recorder should place the instructions for the macro you are about to record.

When using the Set Recorder command, you can either restrict the Recorder range to the current cell selection in the macro sheet or leave it open by selecting only the first cell of the Recorder range. When you choose the **M**acro Set Recorder command when a single cell is selected in a macro sheet, the macro recorder inserts the macro's range name in the active cell and places the macro functions required to carry out your recorded actions in rows below this cell. Be aware, however, that the macro recorder will overwrite any existing macro functions that it encounters when adding instructions to this column.

If you are concerned about the possibility of overwriting existing macro functions in the macro sheet, you should restrict the Recorder range to a range of empty cells by selecting them before you choose the **M**acro Set Recorder command. If this Recorder range becomes filled before you've turned off the macro recorder, Excel displays an alert dialog box indicating that the Recorder range is full, and the macro recorder automatically shuts down.

To finish recording your macro, you need to redefine the Recorder range, this time making it larger or leaving it open before you re-record the macro. If your macro is almost complete and you know which macro functions you need to use to finish, you can enter the macro instructions manually at the bottom of the Recorder range. Remember that you must add the

```
=RETURN()
```

macro function as the last instruction for the macro. If you forget to add this command to shut down the macro, Excel will continue to play back all macro instructions in the rows below until the program either encounters a RETURN or HALT macro function in a subsequent macro or reaches the bottom of the column.

If there aren't enough blank rows to finish the macro functions without overwriting the next macro, insert new cells between the macros using the Shift Cells **D**own option in the Insert dialog box.

Saving and Opening Macro Sheets

After recording your macros on a macro sheet, be sure to save the macro sheet with the **File Save** or **File Save As** command. The first time you save a macro sheet, you can give it a permanent and more descriptive filename.

Before you can use the macros you've saved in a macro sheet (other than the global macro sheet), you must open the macro sheet, although you can hide its document window with the **Window Hide** command and still run the macros. You also can open multiple macro sheets at one time and use any of the macros they contain. Be aware, however, in the case of conflicts between keystroke shortcuts in different macro sheets, Excel always runs the macro in the macro sheet whose filename is first alphabetically. Thus if you have two macro sheets open, one named **budget.xlm** and the other named **database.xlm**, and both of these sheets contain macros to which the keystrokes Ctrl+a have been assigned, Excel will run the macro in the **budget.xlm** macro sheet when you press Ctrl+a. In this case, to run the Ctrl+a macro from the **database.xlm** macro sheet while the **budget.xlm** sheet remains open, you must choose the **Macro Run** command and select the macro's range name in the **R**un list box in the Run Macro dialog box.

> *Note:* If you have recorded new macros in the global macro sheet that have not been saved, Excel automatically prompts you to save your changes in the **global.xlm** file when you exit Excel, even when this macro sheet remains hidden.

Adding a Macro Sheet to a Workbook

 If you've created a series of macros in a macro sheet that you use only in conjunction with a particular group of worksheets or charts, you can make all the macros immediately available by placing all the documents (the worksheets, charts, and the macro sheet) together in a workbook file. (See Chapter 10 for specific information on creating workbooks.)

Normally, you will want to add the macro sheet as the last document in the workbook. After adding the macro sheet to the end of the workbook containing the other Excel documents with which you use those macros, you can protect the macro sheet (even adding a password, if you think you need it) with the **P**rotect Document command on the **O**ptions menu. That way, your macros are always available to you whenever the workbook is open without running the risk of being corrupted during the editing of the file.

Assigning Macros to Graphic Objects

Excel makes it easy to assign new or existing macros to graphic objects such as buttons or pictures that you create with the Camera tool on the Utility toolbar or the **C**opy Picture and **P**aste Picture command on the **E**dit menu. (See Chapter 14 for details on how to create buttons and take pictures of the screen.) After you assign a macro to a graphic object, you can run the macro simply by clicking the object with the mouse.

Remember that as soon as you create a button with the Button tool by dragging the crosshair-pointer to size the button, Excel automatically displays the Assign To Object dialog box similar to the one shown in Figure 17.7. To assign an existing macro to the new button, you simply double-click the macro's name in the Assign **M**acro list box or select the name and choose the OK button. If the macro that you want to assign to the new button does not yet exist, you select the **R**ecord command button. Then record the macro with the Record Macro dialog box just as you would after selecting the Macro Record command. (See "Recording Command Macros" earlier in this chapter for details.)

If you choose not to assign a macro to a button at the time you create it or have created a picture in a document to which you want to assign a macro, you can always assign the macro by following these steps:

1. Click the graphic object to select it. (Selection handles will appear around the object's perimeter.)

2. Choose the Assign to **O**bject command on the **M**acro menu (as shown in Figure 17.8).

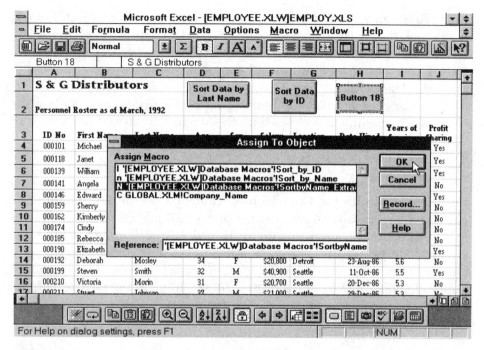

Figure 17.7   The Assign To Object Dialog Box

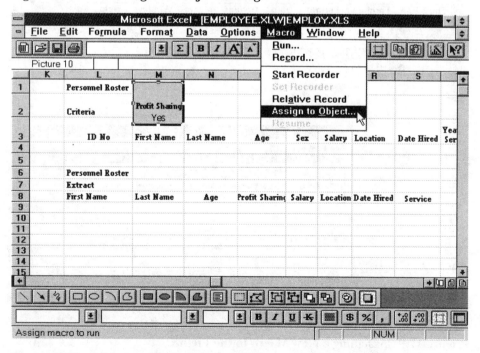

Figure 17.8   Selecting the Picture to Which to Assign the Macro

3. To assign an existing macro to the selected graphic object, double-click the macro's name in the Assign Macro list box or choose the name and select the OK button. To record a new macro, choose the **R**ecord command button and then name and record the macro with the Macro Re**c**ord box as you normally would. When you finish recording the macro and choose the **S**top Recorder command on the **M**acro menu, Excel closes both the Macro Record and the Assign To Object dialog boxes. After assigning a macro to a graphic object, you can run the macro simply by clicking the object.

Figures 17.8 and 17.9 illustrate the assigning of an existing macro to a picture created with the **C**opy Picture command on the **E**dit menu. (See Chapter 14 for details on how to take pictures of part of the screen.) This picture shows the contents of the cells of the Criteria range for the employee database with the Profit Sharing field name above the selection criteria of Yes. To make the picture of these cells look more like a standard button, I added shading and a drop shadow outline to the picture with the Light Shading tool on the Formatting toolbar and the Drop Shadow tool on the Drawing toolbar.

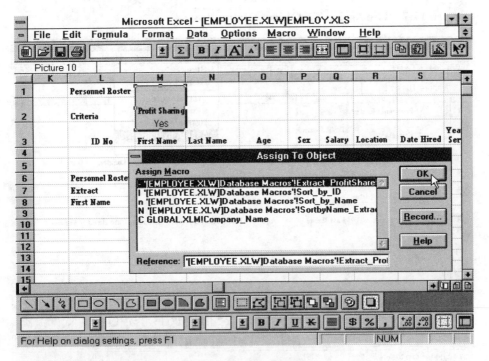

Figure 17.9 Assigning a New Macro to the Picture

To assign the macro that sorts the database by name, then sets the selection criteria in the Criteria range to Profit Sharing equal to Yes and finally performs the Extract operation, you select the picture by clicking before you choose the Assign to **O**bject command on the **M**acro menu (as shown in Figure 17.8). Next you select the macro (the Extract_ProfitSharer macro stored in the Database Macros sheet of the Employee workbook in this example) in the Assign To Object dialog box either by double-clicking the macro name in the Assign **M**acro list box or by choosing the name and selecting the OK button.

After assigning this macro to the Profit Sharing Yes picture, you can extract all of the employees who are participants in the profit-sharing plan sorted alphabetically by last and first name simply by positioning the pointer on the picture and clicking the mouse button when the pointer assumes the shape of the hand, as shown in Figure 17.10.

Note: You also can assign macros to custom tools that you add to one of the toolbars or to an existing tool on a toolbar. See Chapter 19 for details on how to assign macros to tools.

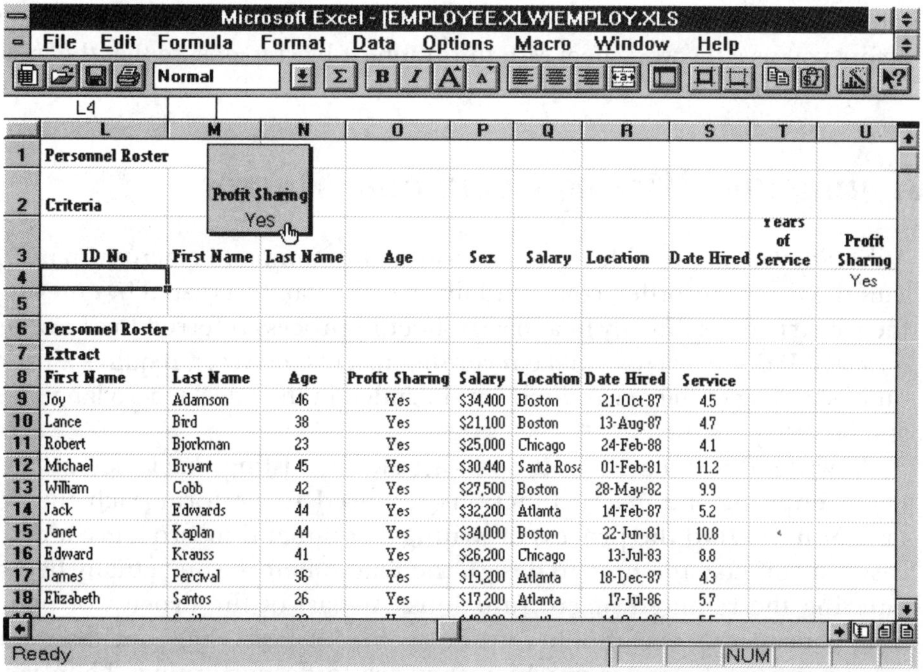

Figure 17.10 Performing the Extraction by Clicking the Profit Sharing Yes Picture Button

Modifying the Links Between a Graphic Object and a Macro

When you use the Assign to Object command on the Macro menu to assign a new or existing macro to a graphic object, Excel creates a link between the graphic object and the macro sheet containing the macro. If you move the macro sheet into a new directory on the disk or move the macro to a new macro sheet, Excel displays an alert message box when you try to run the macro by clicking the button or picture. In such cases, you must modify the link between the graphic object and your macro before you will be able to use it to run the macro again.

To modify the link between a macro and a graphic object, you need to select the graphic object and then choose the Assign to Object command on the Macro menu. Excel then opens the Assign To Object dialog box that shows the current link in the Reference text box. To establish a link to an existing macro, replace the current reference by choosing the macro in the Assign Macro list box, then select the OK button. To establish a link to a new macro, choose the Record command button and name and record the new macro to be assigned the graphic object.

After modifying the link, deselect the graphic object by clicking the pointer in the worksheet and then save the worksheet. If you recorded a new macro in a new macro sheet, be sure to save this file as well. (Save the macro sheet before you save the worksheet with the graphic object to ensure that the links are up to date.)

Designing and Writing Command Macros

Although you may be able to create most of the command macros you need with the macro recorder, command macros also can be created by entering their instructions directly in a macro sheet (a process referred to as *writing a macro*). Writing macros, unlike recording macros, however, requires a basic understanding of the macro functions included in the Excel macro language and how they are used.

To write a new macro, you open a new or existing macro sheet and begin entering the macro functions required to perform each macro task. You will find the process of writing a command macro a great deal easier if you take the time to design the macro before you actually begin entering the required macro functions. As part of the process of planning your macro, you should outline the major tasks that your macro is to perform in the order in which they are to be performed. Then you should detail each of the steps required to perform the major task that you've outlined.

When you actually begin writing the macro, you should structure it in three columns, as shown in Figure 17.11. The first column contains the macro range names that are assigned to each part of the macro, the second column contains the contents of the macro functions used to perform each step, and the third column contains comments that document the purpose of each macro function.

After writing out all of the instructions for your macro in a macro sheet, you must use the **D**efine Name command on the Formula menu to name the first cell of the macro (that is, the one containing the first macro function) before you can run the macro. When you select this command in a macro sheet, Excel opens a slightly altered Define Name dialog box (shown in Figure 17.12) that contains a Macro section at the bottom.

To have Excel add the range name you assign in the **N**ame text box of this dialog box to the **R**un list box of the Run Macro dialog box, you need to select the **C**ommand option in the Macro section. If you wish, you also may assign a keystroke shortcut to your macro by selecting the **K**ey text box and entering a lowercase or uppercase letter. If you enter an uppercase letter there, you can run the macro by pressing Ctrl plus Shift plus the letter. If you enter a lowercase letter there, you can run the macro by pressing Ctrl plus the letter.

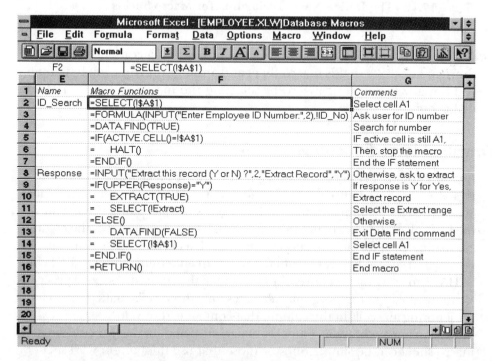

Figure 17.11   Sample Structured Command Macro

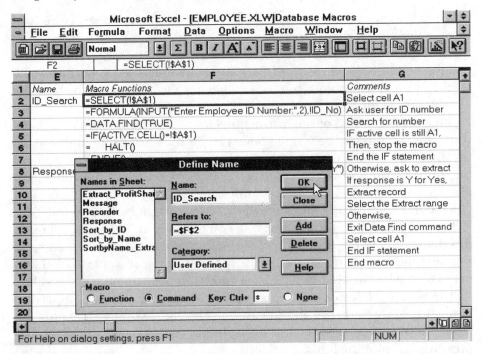

Figure 17.12   The Define Name Dialog Box for Macro Sheets

If you don't assign a keystroke shortcut or you find a conflict between the shortcut keystroke in this macro sheet and another one that you have open, you can always run your macro by selecting the macro in the Run Macro dialog box.

Using the Macro Functions

As you know, Excel performs the actions in your macro by executing a series of macro instructions stored as formulas in the cells of a macro sheet. When you run a command macro, Excel starts by calculating the formula in the first cell of the macro and then automatically proceeds down the column, calculating each formula in succeeding rows. Excel continues calculating the formulas in succeeding rows until the program either encounters a RETURN or HALT macro function or reaches the end of the column. As Excel proceeds down the column, the program calculates only those cells that contain *formulas*, ignoring any cells in the column that contain text or values.

The formulas that you enter as macro instructions in the column of a macro sheet can be simple ones or those that use the built-in worksheet or macro functions. Keep in mind that although you can incorporate any of the worksheet functions (see Appendix B) you use in building your work-sheet in the command macro you are writing, you can use only the macro functions (see Appendix C) in a macro sheet.

Tip Because macros calculate only cells containing formulas, every macro sheet you open automatically displays the formulas in the cells. (This is done by selecting the Formulas check box in the Display Options dialog box.) You can temporarily disable the macros in a macro sheet by displaying the calculated values in the cells of a macro sheet instead of the formulas (done by pressing Ctrl+' [grave accent] or by clearing the Formulas check box in the Display Options dialog box). Then you can enable the macros once again by displaying the formula in the macro sheet (Ctrl+' again or select the Formulas check box in the Display Options dialog box).

Excel's macro functions provide a rich and varied macro command language. You can use macros to accomplish any task that you can perform manually. Table 17.1 shows you the macro function equivalent for the pull-down menu commands in Excel. (For details on the arguments used by each function, refer to the specific macro function in Appendix C.)

For example, if you want your macro to open a new worksheet window, you would use the NEW macro function, which is the equivalent of choosing the **N**ew command on the **F**ile menu. When you use the NEW function, either you can have the macro open the New dialog box so that you can choose which type of document to create each time you run the macro, or you can enter an argument that has the macro do it for you.

For instance, to open the New dialog box and choose Workbook as the default type of document, you would enter

   =NEW?(5)

in the appropriate cell of the macro sheet (5 is the *type_num* argument for selecting the Workbook as the document type). To have the macro open a new worksheet document without displaying the New dialog box, you would enter

   =NEW(1)

instead (1 is the *type_num* argument for selecting Worksheet as the document type). After using this form of the command, the new worksheet window will be open and active, and you can therefore enter subsequent instructions in the macro that performs actions in the new worksheet.

Table 17.1 Macro Function Pull-Down Menu Equivalents

Menu Equivalent	*Macro Function*
File Menu Commands	
New	NEW
Open	OPEN
Close	FILE.CLOSE
Close All	CLOSE.ALL
Links	OPEN.LINKS; CHANGE.LINKS; LINKS; UPDATE.LINKS
Save	SAVE
Save As	SAVE.AS
Save Workbook	SAVE.WORKBOOK
Delete	FILE.DELETE
Print Preview	PRINT.PREVIEW
Page Setup	PAGE.SETUP
Print	PRINT
Exit	QUIT
Edit Menu Commands	
Undo	UNDO
Repeat	EDIT.REPEAT
Cut	CUT
Copy	COPY
Copy Chart	COPY.CHART
Copy Picture	COPY.PICTURE
Copy Tool Face	COPY.TOOL
Paste	PASTE
Paste Picture	PASTE.PICTURE
Paste Picture Link	PASTE.PICTURE.LINK
Paste Special	PASTE.SPECIAL
Paste Link	PASTE.LINK

Table 17.1 *(continued)*

Edit Menu Commands	
Delete	EDIT.DELETE
Insert	INSERT
Insert Object	INSERT.OBJECT
Fill Right	FILL.RIGHT
Fill Left (h)	FILL.LEFT
Fill Down	FILL.DOWN
Fill Up (w)	FILL.UP
Fill Group	FILL.GROUP
Formula Menu Commands	
Paste Name	LIST.NAMES
Define Name	DEFINE.NAME
Delete Name	DELETE.NAME
Create Names	CREATE.NAMES
Apply Name	APPLY.NAMES
Note	NOTE
Goto	FORMULA.GOTO
Find	FORMULA.FIND; FORMULA.FIND.NEXT; FORMULA.FIND.PREV
Replace	FORMULA.REPLACE
Select Special	SELECT.SPECIAL
Show Active Cell	SHOW.ACTIVE.CELL
Outline	OUTLINE
Goal Seek	GOAL.SEEK
Format Menu Commands (Worksheet and Chart)	
Number	FORMAT.NUMBER
Alignment	ALIGNMENT
Font	FORMAT.FONT
Border	BORDER

Table 17.1   *(continued)*

Format Menu Commands (Worksheet and Chart)

Patterns	PATTERNS
Cell Protection	CELL.PROTECTION
Object Protection	OBJECT.PROTECTION
Style	DEFINE.STYLE; APPLY.STYLE; DELETE.STYLE; MERGE.STYLES
AutoFormat	FORMAT.AUTO
Row Height	ROW.HEIGHT
Column Width	COLUMN.WIDTH
Justify	JUSTIFY
Bring to Front	BRING.TO.FRONT
Send to Back	SEND.TO.BACK
Group	GROUP
Ungroup	UNGROUP
Object Properties	OBJECT.PROPERTIES

Format Menu Commands (Chart only)

Text	FORMAT.TEXT
Scale	SCALE
Legend	FORMAT.LEGEND
Main Chart	FORMAT.MAIN
Overlay	FORMAT.OVERLAY
3-D View	VIEW.3D
Move	FORMAT.MOVE
Size	FORMAT.SIZE

Gallery Menu Commands (Chart only)

Area	GALLERY.AREA
Bar	GALLERY.BAR
Column	GALLERY.COLUMN
Line	GALLERY.LINE

Table 17.1 *(continued)*

Gallery Menu Commands (Chart only)	
Pie	GALLERY.PIE
Radar	GALLERY.RADAR
XY (Scatter)	GALLERY.SCATTER
Combination	COMBINATION
3-D Area	GALLERY.3D.AREA
3-D Bar	GALLERY.3D.BAR
3-D Column	GALLERY.3D.COLUMN
3-D Line	GALLERY.3D.LINE
3-D Pie	GALLERY.3D.PIE
3-D Surface	GALLERY.3D.SURFACE
Preferred	PREFERRED
Set Preferred	SET.PREFERRED
Chart Menu Commands (Chart only)	
Attach Text	ATTACH.TEXT
Add Arrow	ADD.ARROW
Add Legend	LEGEND
Gridlines	GRIDLINES
Add Overlay	ADD.OVERLAY
Edit Series	EDIT.SERIES
Select Chart	SELECT.CHART
Select Plot Area	SELECT.PLOT.AREA
Data Menu Commands	
Form	DATA.FORM
Find	DATA.FIND; DATA.FIND.NEXT; DATA.FIND.PREV
Extract	EXTRACT
Delete	DATA.DELETE

Table 17.1   *(continued)*

Data Menu Commands	
Set Database	SET.DATABASE
Set Criteria	SET.CRITERIA
Set Extract	SET.EXTRACT
Sort	SORT
Series	DATA.SERIES
Table	TABLE
Parse	PARSE
Consolidate	CONSOLIDATE
Options Menu Commands	
Set Print Area	SET.PRINT.AREA
Set Print Titles	SET.PRINT.TITLES
Set Page Break	SET.PAGE.BREAK
Display	DISPLAY
Toolbars	CUSTOMIZE.TOOLBARS
Color Palette	COLOR.PALETTE
Protect Document	PROTECT.DOCUMENT
Calculation	CALCULATION; CALCULATE DOCUMENT; CALCULATE NOW; PRECISION
Workspace	WORKSPACE; SHOW.INFO
Spelling	SPELLING.CHECK
Group Edit	WORKGROUP
Macro Menu Commands	
Run	RUN
Resume	RESUME
Assign to Object	ASSIGN.TO.OBJECT
Assign to Tool	ASSIGN.TO.TOOL
Window Menu Commands	
New Window	NEW.WINDOW

Table 17.1 *(continued)*

Window Menu Commands	
Arrange	ARRANGE.ALL
Hide	HIDE
Unhide	UNHIDE
Split	SPLIT
Freeze Panes	FREEZE.PANES
Zoom	ZOOM

In addition to pull-down menu command equivalents, Excel includes several other categories of macro functions. (See Table 17.2 for a list of the major macro function categories.) These categories include Information macro functions for supplying information about the current state of Excel, an Excel document, or entry to the macro; Customizing macro functions for adding custom pull-down menus, toolbars, or dialog boxes to Excel; and Macro Control functions for performing or repeating particular actions when certain conditions exist or cease to exist in Excel.

When writing macros, you can use the Paste Function command on the Formula menu (Shift+F3) or, if the Macro toolbar is displayed, you can click the Paste Name tool in this toolbar (see "Using the Macro Toolbar" later in this chapter for details) to display the Paste Function dialog box from which you can insert the macro function in the active cell of your macro sheet. If the Paste Arguments check box is selected in the Paste Function dialog box, Excel includes names of the arguments as part of the macro function that it pastes in the formula bar when you choose the OK button. You can then select and replace each argument description with the actual information you want used as the argument.

Note, however, that when Excel pastes the names of the arguments in a macro function, the program does not indicate which arguments are required and which are optional and does not show the question-mark form for those macro functions that can display dialog boxes. For this information, you can look up the macro function in Appendix C, where required arguments are shown in bold italics and optional arguments in regular italics, and macro functions that can use the question mark to open a dialog box are shown as alternate forms.

Table 17.2 The Categories of Macro Functions

Category	Description
Information	Includes macro functions that return various types of information about the current state of Excel or an Excel document. This category includes a group of GET macro functions that return specific information about various Excel objects, such as the menu bar, toolbar, active cell, and the like. It also includes the group of IS worksheet functions, such as ISBLANK, ISNONTEXT, and ISNUMBER used to return information about a particular entry.
Commands	Includes the command menu equivalent macro functions (see Table 17.1 as well as commands for performing actions within Excel, such as opening, closing, or activating document windows, or moving around the active worksheet window.
Customizing	Includes commands for adding custom items to Excel, including pull-down menus and commands, toolbars, message dialog boxes, and help information. Also contains a group of ON functions that run other macros only when a certain event occurs, such as selecting a document or pressing a particular key.
Macro Control	Includes the macro commands for branching the macro depending on whether or not a particular condition is met as well as for looping macros a set number of times or until a particular condition exists or no longer exists.

CELL REFERENCES IN COMMAND MACROS

Whenever possible, you should assign range names to the cells in your worksheets and macro that you need to refer to in your macros and then use these range names in the argument of your worksheet and macro functions. That way you can be assured that your macro will continue to run properly even if you change the cell references when modifying the worksheet or macro sheet.

If you need to, you can have your macro name a cell or cell selection in the active worksheet with the SET.NAME macro function. For example, the following SET.NAME macro function assigns the range name *Discount* in the macro sheet to cell B2 in the active worksheet:

=SET.NAME("Discount",!B2)

Note the use of the exclamation point before the cell reference in this example. This indicates that the cell B2 in the active Excel document is to be named *Discount*. If you wanted to use the SET.NAME function in a macro to assign the name *Discount* to cell B2 on the same macro sheet (assuming that this sheet is not active when you run the macro), you would enter

=SET.NAME("Discount",B2)

instead. Note that in either case, the range name *Discount* is always added to the macro sheet containing this macro function and not whatever Excel document happens to be active at the time you run the macro.

You also can combine the SET.NAME macro function with the ACTIVE.CELL or SELECTION function to have the macro assign a range name to the current cell or cell selection in the active worksheet. For instance, the macro function

=SET.NAME("Target_Value",ACTIVE.CELL())

assigns the range name *Target_Value* to the cell that is active at the time the macro calculates this function, whereas the macro function

=SET.NAME("Data_Table2",SELECTION())

assigns the range name *Data_Table2* to the cell selection that is current at the time the macro calculates this function.

Tip When referring to named ranges that exist in the active macro sheet, use the Paste Name command on the Formula menu (F3) or, if the Macro toolbar is displayed, click its Paste Name tool to select the range name you want to use as an argument in the worksheet or macro function you are currently entering in the macro sheet.

When you do use cell references instead of range names in your macro instructions, you can enter the cell references in either the A1 or R1C1 system (for example, as B2 or R[2]C[2]). When entering cell references in macros, you can use the types of references shown in Table 17.3.

Alert! To avoid a macro error, either a worksheet or a macro sheet must be active when your macro calculates the worksheet or macro function that uses a cell reference with an exclamation point.

Table 17.3 Indicating Cell References in Macros

Type of Reference	Examples
Absolute references to a cell in the macro sheet containing the macro.	$A$5 or R5C1
Relative references to a cell in the macro sheet containing the macro.	A5 or R[5]C[1]
Absolute references to a cell in the sheet that is active at the time you run the macro.	!$A$5 or !R5C1
Relative references to a cell in the sheet that is active at the time you run the macro. Note that the cell is relative to the cell in the macro sheet that contains the reference—not the active cell in the active sheet.	!A5 or !R[5]C[1]
Absolute references to a cell in a named sheet.	budget.xlm!$A$5 or budget.xlm!R5C1
Relative references to a cell in a named sheet.	budget.xlm!A5 or budget.xlm!R[5]C[1]

DISPLAYING MESSAGES AND GETTING USER INPUT IN MACROS

Unlike recorded macros that always run uninterrupted from beginning to end, you can have the macros that you write pause and display information or even pause and request information from the user.

To display messages, you can use either the MESSAGE macro function that displays your message in the lower-left corner of the status bar, or you can use the ALERT macro function that displays your message in an alert message dialog box.

The syntax of the MESSAGE macro function is

```
=MESSAGE(logical,text)
```

where the *logical* argument is TRUE to display your message on the status bar or FALSE to turn the display off, and the *text* argument is the text of your message enclosed in quotation marks, as in

=MESSAGE(TRUE,"Processing...One Moment Please!")

which displays the message

Processing...One Moment Please!

on the status bar. When you use the MESSAGE macro function, Excel does not pause the macro but merely displays your message until the macro encounters the

=MESSAGE(FALSE)

macro function, which removes this message from the status bar.

To display an alert message box on the screen, you use the ALERT macro function, which uses the syntax

=ALERT(message_text,type_num,help_ref)

where *message_text* is the text of the message enclosed in quotation marks that you want displayed in the alert box, *type_num* is a number between 1 and 3 that represents the type of alert box, and *help_ref* is the custom help topic that you added to the on-line help in the form

filename!topic_number

When specifying the type of message box, you use 1 as the *type_num* argument to display a dialog box with a question mark as the icon preceding the message text and containing both an OK and Cancel button. When you enter 2 or 3 as the *type_num* argument, Excel displays a message box containing only an OK button. When you enter 2 as this argument, the alert box uses i as the icon preceding the message text (indicating a note that supplies supplementary information). When you enter 3, the alert box uses an exclamation point for the icon (indicating a warning). When you specify a *help_ref* argument in the ALERT function, Excel adds a Help command button that you can use to open the Excel Help window and display the custom help topic that explains the situation.

> *Note:* To add custom topics to the on-line help in Excel for Windows, you must use the Help Compiler version 3.1 or later, which is available directly from Microsoft Corporation.

You can use the INPUT macro function to get information from the user that the macro can then use in performing its subsequent actions. The INPUT function follows the syntax

=INPUT(message_text,type_num,title_text,default,x_pos,y_pos,help_ref)

where *message_text* is the text of the prompt asking the user to enter information, *type_num* is a number indicating the type of data expected from the user (see Table 17.4), *title_text* is the name you want displayed as the title bar for the dialog box, *default* is the entry automatically displayed in the text box that the user can edit, *x_pos* and *y_pos* are the number of points specifying the horizontal and vertical screen positions of the dialog box, and *help_ref* is a reference to the name of the custom help topic added to the on-line help.

	Table 17.4 Type_Num Argument Values for the INPUT Macro Function

Type_Num	*Data Type*
0	Formula
1	Number
2	Text
4	Logical
8	Reference
16	Error

Figures 17.13 and 17.14 illustrate the use of the INPUT macro function in the ID_Search macro (shown in Figure 17.11) to prompt the user for information. The Input dialog box shown in Figure 17.13 prompts the user to enter the employee ID number that he or she wants to look up in the database. The INPUT macro function that creates this dialog box is combined in the macro with the FORMULA function to enter the user's response in the Criteria range in a cell named ID_No

```
=FORMULA(INPUT("Enter Employee ID Number:",2),!ID_No)
```

Only the *message_text* and the *type_num* arguments are specified in this nested INPUT function. As a result omitting the other arguments, the custom dialog box is simply named *Input*, no default value is placed in the text box, and the dialog box is centered on the screen.

Figure 17.14 shows the second custom dialog box created with the INPUT macro function. This custom dialog box appears when the ID number entered by the user in the first Input dialog box is located in the employee database. This second custom dialog box (entitled Extract Record) asks the user if he or she wants to extract the selected record.

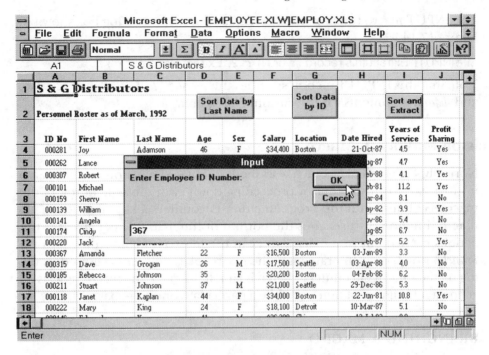

Figure 17.13 Input Dialog Box for Entering the ID Number to Find

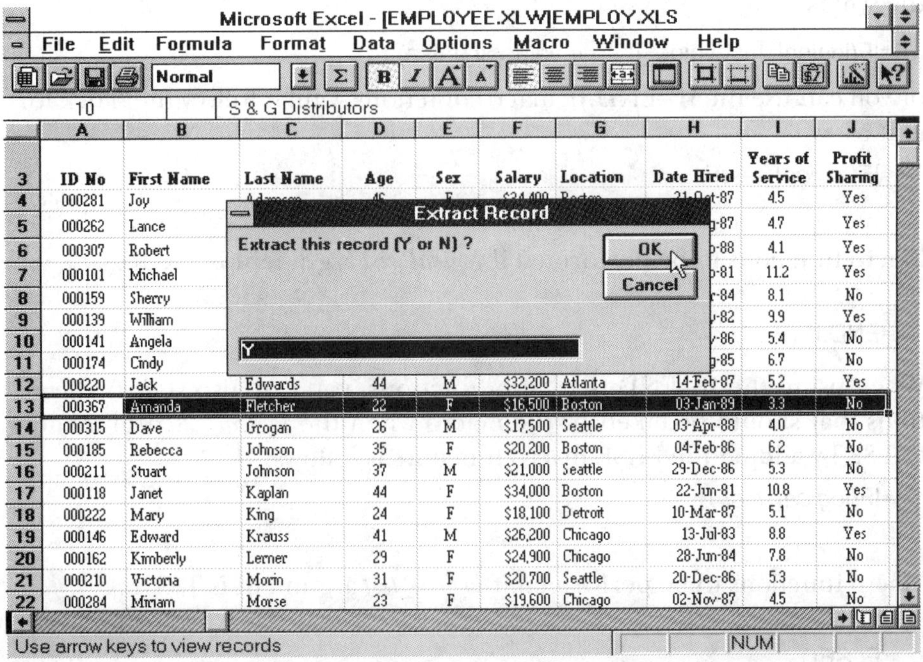

Figure 17.14 Extract Record Input Dialog Box with Default Response

The INPUT macro function used to display the custom dialog box shown in Figure 17.14 is

```
=INPUT("Extract this record (Y or N) ?",2,"Extract Record","Y")
```

Note that this INPUT function specifies the *message_text, type_num, title_text,* and *default* arguments for the custom dialog box.

Decision Making in Macros

Normally, Excel calculates each worksheet and macro function in your macro in strict start-to-finish order by proceeding down each subsequent row of the macro's column until the program either encounters a HALT or RETURN macro function or it reaches the bottom of the macro sheet. To vary the actions carried out by a macro, you can use macro functions that perform *branching* or *looping.* In branching, the macro takes different actions depending on the value it encounters when it is run. In looping, the macro repeats an action a set number of times or while a particular condition exists.

BRANCHING A MACRO

To branch a macro, you can use the standard worksheet IF function with the syntax

```
=IF(logical_test,value_if_true,value_if_false)
```

or you can use the IF–END.IF macro functions, which follow the block format of

```
=IF(logical_test)
:
```

Macro functions to be performed if *logical_test* argument is TRUE.

```
:
=END.IF()
```

When using the IF–END.IF macro functions, you can also specify the actions that should be taken by the macro when the *logical_test* argument is FALSE by adding the ELSE macro function as follows:

```
=IF(logical_test )
:
```

Macro functions to be performed if *logical_test* argument is TRUE.

```
:
=ELSE()
:
```

Macro functions to be performed if *logical_test* argument is FALSE.

```
    :
  =END.IF()
```

When using the IF–END.IF macro functions, you can substitute the ELSE.IF function for the ELSE function when you need to include an additional logical test, using the format

```
  =IF(logical_test)
    :
```

Macro functions to be performed if *logical_test* argument of the IF macro function is TRUE.

```
    :
  =ELSE.IF(logical_test)
    :
```

Macro functions to be performed if *logical_test* argument of the ELSE.IF macro function is TRUE.

```
    :
  =END.IF()
```

When using the IF macro function, you must be sure that you have included an END.IF macro function indicating where the block of actions ends for each IF macro function in the macro.

To make it easier to read IF–END.IF blocks in your macros, it is a good idea to indent the actions to be taken when the *logical_test* argument is TRUE or FALSE in the macro sheet. You can see examples of this kind of indenting in the ID_Search command macro shown in Figure 17.11. The first IF–END.IF block in this macro is

```
  =IF(ACTIVE.CELL()=!$A$1)
  =    HALT()
  =END.IF()
```

This IF–END.IF uses the ACTIVE.CELL function to evaluate the cell reference of the active cell after performing the Find operation in the database with the DATA.FIND macro function. If the cell pointer is still in cell A1, the IF block stops the macro with the HALT function because the ID number input by the user was not found in the database. (If the ID were found, the active cell would no longer be A1 but would be the cell with that ID number.)

·Note how the HALT function is indented in the IF block by inserting a tab *after* the equal sign. (Remember that you insert a tab in the formula bar by pressing Ctrl+Tab.) You must not insert the tab or any spaces before you enter the equal sign or Excel will treat the macro function as text and will bypass the function when you run the macro.

The second IF–END.IF block in the ID_Search macro uses an ELSE macro function and indents both the TRUE and FALSE actions as follows:

```
=IF(UPPER(Response)="Y")
=       EXTRACT(TRUE)
=       SELECT(!Extract)
=ELSE()
=       DATA.FIND(FALSE)
=       SELECT(!$A$1)
=END.IF()
```

If the user has accepted the default response of Y in the custom Extract Record dialog box, the cell named Response (cell F8 in the Database Macros sheet) will contain Y, and the *logical_text* argument in the IF function will be TRUE, causing the macro to evaluate the two macro functions located above the ELSE function. These macro functions extract the selected record to the Extract range and then select the Extract range (so that this range is displayed on the screen). If the Response cell does not contain Y, the macro functions following the ELSE macro function are evaluated instead. These macro functions exit the program from the Data Find mode, then make cell A1 the active cell.

BRANCHING OR RUNNING A SUBROUTINE

When branching a macro, you may want to transfer control to another part of the macro (or another macro entirely) that contains the actions to be performed rather than listing them as individual macro functions in the appropriate position of the IF–END.IF block itself. This is especially true if the actions to be performed are standard ones that are used in several macros (such as sorting a table of data or printing a particular part of the active worksheet). Creating separate macros for commonly used tasks and then branching to them when needed not only makes it easier to test out their steps (debug) but also makes your macro sheets easier to understand.

When transferring control to a new macro, you can either branch to the new macro with the GOTO macro function or *call a subroutine.* The difference between branching with the GOTO function or calling a new macro as a subroutine is significant. When you call a subroutine, control automatically returns to the calling macro when the last instruction in the subroutine is carried out. When you branch to a new macro with GOTO, control does not automatically return to the calling macro when Excel finishes executing its last instruction.

You should use the GOTO macro function only to branch to a new cell or cell range in the same macro sheet and only when you don't want the control to return to the calling macro. To use the GOTO macro function, you enter the range name given to the first cell of the new macro or its cell reference. For example, to transfer control to a macro routine named Error_Trap in the same macro sheet when an Error value is returned to a cell range named Total_Wages in the active worksheet, you could combine the IF macro function with the GOTO function as follows:

```
=IF(ISERROR(!Total_Wages)
=     GOTO(Error_Trap)
=END.IF()
```

In this example, if the *logical_test* argument of the IF macro function is TRUE, the macro immediately begins evaluating the macro functions, beginning with the first cell named Error_Trap in the macro sheet. The macro continues to evaluate the macro functions in this part of the macro sheet until the program encounters a HALT or RETURN command or it reaches the end of the column, whereupon the macro will shut down.

If you want Excel to return control to the calling macro as soon as the macro functions in the new macro have all been evaluated, you call the new macro as a subroutine. This is done by entering the macro name between an equal sign and a pair of closed parentheses. For instance, you could call the Error_Trap macro mentioned in the previous branching example as a subroutine by entering the IF–ENDIF block as

```
=IF(ISERROR(!Total_Wages)
=     Error_Trap()
=END.IF()
```

In this case, Excel jumps to the Error_Trap routine and begins evaluating the macro functions there. This time, however, when the program reaches the end of the Error_Trap instructions, it automatically returns to the macro containing this IF–END.IF block and begins evaluating the macro functions in the cells below the one containing the subroutine call (the =Error_Trap() macro function in this example).

If the macro you want to call is not in the same macro sheet, you need to add the filename to the macro function. For example, if you want to call a macro named Print_Report in a macro sheet named **utility.xlm**, you would enter

```
=UTILITY.XLM!Print_Report()
```

as the subroutine call.

> **Note:** If the macro you want to call is a function macro (as opposed to a command macro) that requires its own arguments, you enter these arguments in the parentheses after the macro name. See Chapter 20 for information on how to create function macros.

LOOPING A MACRO

You add looping to a macro when you want to repeat a series of actions or calculations a set number of times or while a particular condition exists. You use the FOR–NEXT loop to repeat a series of actions a set number of times. You use the FOR.CELL–NEXT loop to repeat a series of actions on each cell in the selected range. You use the WHILE–NEXT loop to repeat a series of actions while a particular condition exists.

The FOR–NEXT loop uses the following format:

```
=FOR(counter_text,start_num,end_num,step_num)
:
```

Macro functions to be performed while the number in *counter_text* argument is less than the *end_num* argument.

```
:
NEXT()
```

In the FOR macro function, the *counter_text* argument is the name of the cell that contains the number of times the loop has run, *start_num* is the initial value placed in the *counter_text* cell, *end_num* is the value at which the loop stops running, and *step_num* is the value by which the macro increases the *counter_text* cell each time the loop runs. The NEXT macro function marks the end of the loop. Excel evaluates all macro functions located in cells between the one containing the FOR macro function and the one containing the NEXT macro function each time the loop is run.

The FOR.CELL–NEXT loop creates a block that follows the format

```
=FOR.CELL(ref_name,area_ref,skip_blanks)
:
```

Macro functions to be performed on each cell in the *area_ref* argument (if area_ref argument is omitted, Excel uses the current selection).

```
:
NEXT()
```

In the FOR.CELL macro function, the *ref_name* argument is the name given to the one cell in the range that is currently being operated on in the loop, *area_ref* is the reference of the cell selection to be operated on each time the loop is run (the current selection is used when this argument is omitted), and *skip_blanks* is a logical value that indicates whether or not blanks in the *area_ref* range or current selection are skipped. (Enter FALSE or omit this argument to skip blank cells or enter TRUE if you want to skip blanks.) As with the FOR–NEXT loop, the NEXT macro function in the FOR.CELL–NEXT loop marks the end of the loop. In this case, however, Excel applies all the macro functions located in the cells between the one containing the FOR.CELL and the NEXT function to each cell specified by the current selection or specified by the *area_ref* argument. The looping ends as soon as actions in the loop have been applied to the last cell in the current selection or the selection specified by the *area_ref* argument.

The WHILE–NEXT loop creates a block that follows the format

```
=WHILE(logical_test)
:
```

Macro functions to be performed while the *logical_test* argument is TRUE.

```
    :
  NEXT()
```

In the WHILE macro function, the *logical_test* argument sets up the condition that is evaluated by the macro. As long as this condition is TRUE, the macro performs all of the actions specified by the macro functions located in the cells between the one containing the WHILE and the NEXT macro function. As soon as the *logical_test* condition is evaluated as FALSE, the looping ends and the program evaluates the macro function in the cell below the one containing the NEXT macro function.

Testing and Debugging Macros

Few macros that you write will run completely error-free the first time you run them. Because the initial testing of a macro can introduce multiple errors in the active worksheet, *ALWAYS* save your worksheet before you test out a new macro on it. If you see that the macro is running amok, press the Esc key to halt it. Excel then displays a Macro Error dialog box similar to the one shown in Figure 17.15. This dialog box indicates the reference of the cell in the macro sheet where the macro is interrupted. To continue running the macro, you would select the **C**ontinue command button. To continue running in step mode so that Excel automatically pauses the macro after evaluating each line, choose the **S**tep command button instead. To stop the macro and return to Ready mode, choose the **H**alt command button.

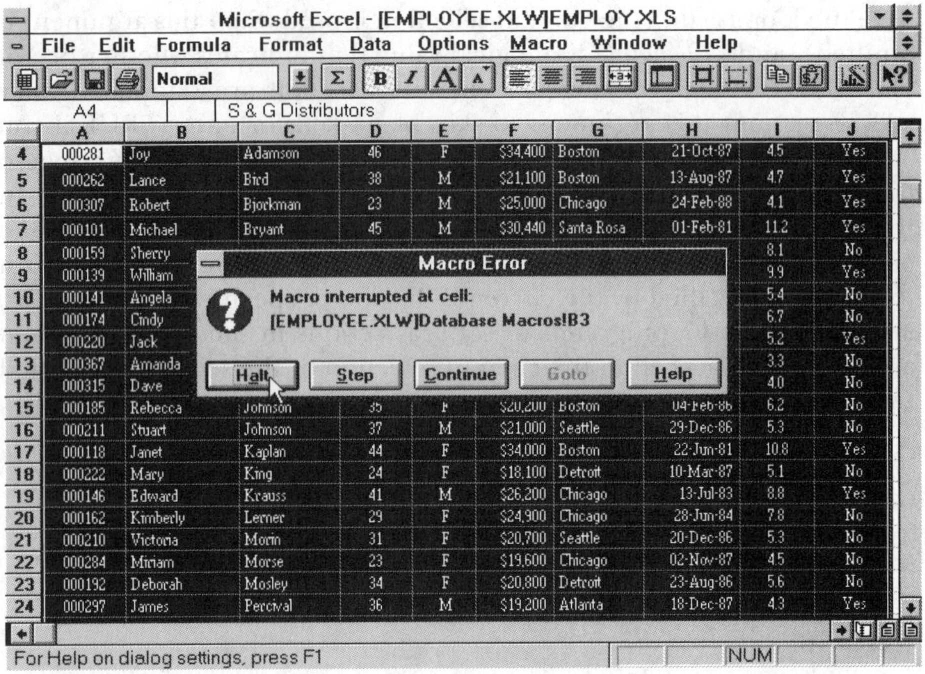

Figure 17.15 The Macro Error Dialog Box

Sometimes when you test a macro for the first time, Excel encounters errors that cause the program to suspend the macro's execution (often referred to as *bugs*). When the macro is unable to evaluate a macro instruction as written because of a bug, the program automatically displays the Macro Error dialog box (like the one shown in Figure 17.15). There are many causes for bugs in your macros; the most common involve improper syntax in the macro functions due to misspellings or improper or missing arguments.

If the bug is not serious and will not adversely affect the running of the rest of the macro, you can choose the **C**ontinue command button to have Excel bypass it and continue running at the next instruction in the macro. If you would prefer to continue running the macro one step at a time, select the **S**tep button instead. If the error must be remedied before you can continue running the macro, you can note the location of the macro error in the Macro Error dialog box, choose the **H**alt button, and then edit the cell in the macro sheet with the error before you try to rerun the macro. If you know your problem and want to fix the bug right away, choose the **G**oto command button to have Excel display the macro sheet and select the cell with the macro bug so that you can edit its contents on the spot.

Running a Macro in Step Mode

Sometimes you will find that your macros contain processing errors rather than actual bugs that prevent Excel from performing all the macro instructions. The causes for processing errors are usually much harder to identify than other types of macro errors. The best way to debug a macro that is working but isn't producing the results you expected is to run the macro in step mode.

To run a macro entirely in step mode, you choose the **R**un command on the **M**acro menu, then select the macro in the **R**un list box and choose the **S**tep command button (as shown in Figure 17.16). Excel then displays the Single Step dialog box (similar to the one shown in Figure 17.17), which shows you the reference of the first cell in the macro as well as its formula. The H**a**lt, **C**ontinue, and **G**oto buttons work the same way in the Single Step dialog box as they do in the Macro Error dialog box.

Note: You also can run a macro in step mode by adding the =STEP() macro command to your macro. Excel runs the macro normally until the program encounters the STEP macro function, whereupon the Single Step dialog box appears. To run the entire macro in step mode, add the STEP function to the first cell of the macro. That way you can run the macro repeatedly in step mode by using its keystroke shortcut instead of having to use the **M**acro **R**un command. After you have successfully debugged your macro, remember to remove the STEP macro function and save its macro sheet again.

To have the macro evaluate each formula in the macro one at a time before going on to the subsequent one, choose the Step **I**nto command button. To have the macro evaluate all the formulas in a subroutine as one step, choose the Step **O**ver button. To pause the macro at the current formula and close the Single Step dialog box so that you can examine something in the active worksheet or the macro sheet containing the macro, choose the **P**ause command button. Whenever you choose **P**ause, Excel displays the Resume Macro tool in its own little dialog box. To redisplay the Single Step dialog box so that you can resume stepping through the macro's formulas, simply click the Resume Macro tool (whereupon the Single Step dialog box reappears and the dialog box with the Resume Macro tool disappears).

When trying to locate processing errors in a command macro, most often you will want to use the **E**valuate button in the Single Step dialog box. When you choose this button, Excel calculates the current formula one

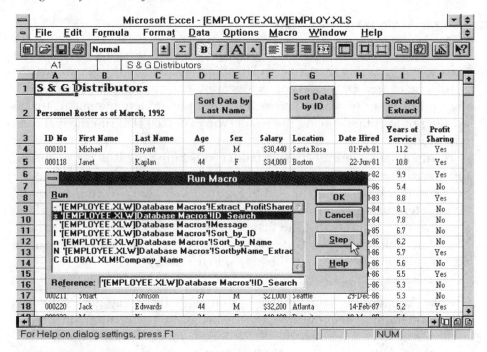

Figure 17.16   Running a Macro in Step Mode

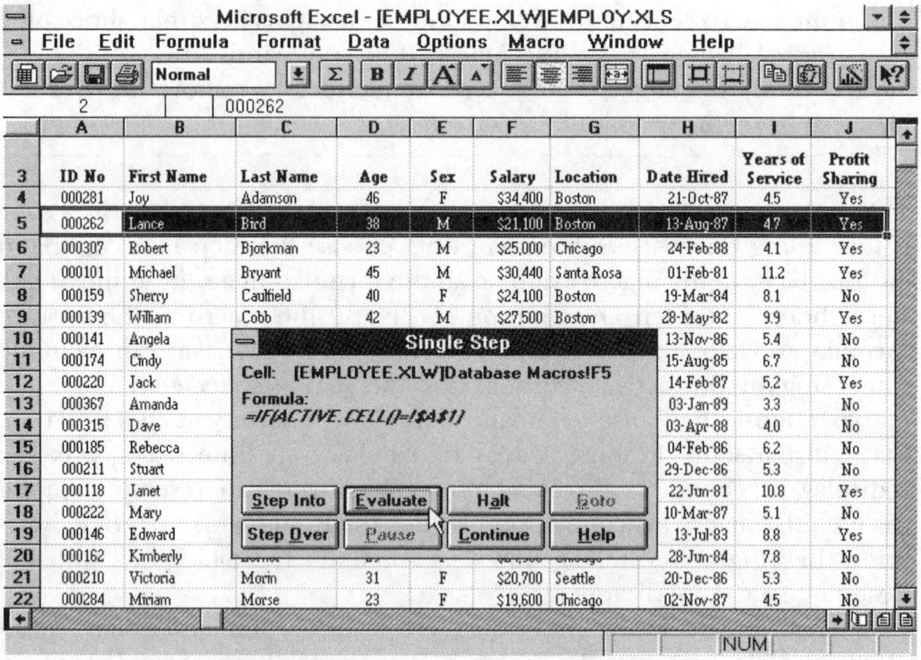

Figure 17.17   Evaluating a Macro Function in Step Mode

function at a time. This enables you to view the intermediate values returned by your worksheet and macro functions. Many times, seeing the intermediate value returned by a function lets you pinpoint exactly where you must alter the working of the macro in order to have it perform according to your expectations.

Figures 17.17 and 17.18 illustrate how the **E**valuate button shows you the intermediate values returned by a macro formula. Figure 17.17 shows the Single Step dialog box after the macro has performed the Data Extract operation and the macro is just about to evaluate the IF function that tests whether or not cell A1 is still the active cell. The first time you click the **E**valuate button, Excel displays the formula in the Single Step dialog box in italics, as shown in Figure 17.17. The second time you click the **E**valuate button, the program displays the calculated result for the italicized formula (again in italics). As you can see in Figure 17.18, the macro has correctly detected that cell A1 is no longer active (cell A5 is active because the program found a match for the ID number that was input) and has returned FALSE as the *logical_test* argument of the IF macro function.

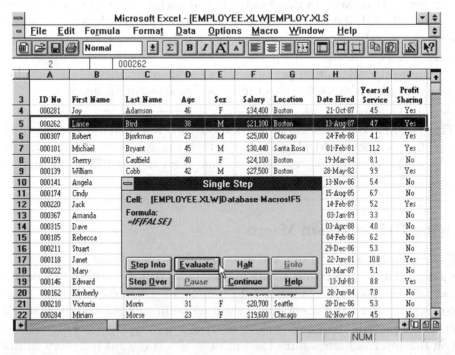

Figure 17.18 Result of a Macro Function Returned in Step Mode

Tip You can always view the values returned by the functions in your macros by activating the macro sheet and then switching from the default of displaying formulas to displaying values—remember that you can toggle between formulas and values in the macro sheet simply by pressing Ctrl+ ' (the accent grave).

Using the Macro Toolbar

 Excel 4.0 includes a Macro toolbar that you can use when working with macros. Table 17.5 shows the tools on this toolbar and briefly explains their usage. Note that you can use only the Run Macro and Step Macro tools from an active macro sheet. To run a macro with the Run Macro tool, position the cell pointer in the first cell of the macro you want to run before you click this tool. To run the macro in step mode, position the cell pointer in the first cell of the macro you want to step through, then hold down the Shift key as you click the Run Macro tool or simply click the Step Macro tool (right next to it).

If you normally run your macros when a particular worksheet or graph window is active, keep in mind that you will *not* be able to run your macros successfully with the Run Macro and Step Macro tools unless the functions in your worksheet contain references to the names of the sheets to be activated. This means that the macros will not run properly if their functions use the exclamation point to refer to the active sheet, because when using these tools the active sheet must be one containing the macro.

 Tip The Macro toolbar has plenty of room for additional tools. If you would like, you can add global macros that you routinely use in creating worksheets and charts to this toolbar. See Chapter 19 for information on how to do so.

Using the Debug Add-in Macro

Excel includes a debugging add-in macro that you can use instead of step mode to locate processing errors in a macro. With this add-in macro, you can add *tracepoints* and *breakpoints* to the macro you need to debug. When you run a macro and it encounters a tracepoint, the macro automatically enters step mode. When the macro reaches a breakpoint, the macro shows you the intermediate values for the variables you want to review at that point. (You also can display your own message in the Breakpoint dialog box.) After displaying the intermediate values at a breakpoint, you can

Table 17.5 The Tools on the Macro Toolbar

Tool	Tool Name	Description
	New Macro Sheet tool	Opens a new macro sheet.
	Paste Function tool	Displays the Paste Function dialog box from which you can select the worksheet or macro function to insert in the active cell of your macro sheet.
	Paste Names tool	Displays the Paste Names dialog box from which you can select the range name you want to use in the formula you're building in the active cell of your macro sheet.
	Run Macro tool	Runs the currently selected macro, starting with the active cell in the macro sheet. This tool functions like the Step Macro tool if you hold down the Shift key at the time you click it. The Run Macro tool is available only when a macro sheet is active.
	Step Macro tool	Displays the Single Step dialog box where you can step through the currently selected macro one step at a time. This tool functions like the Run Macro tool if you hold down the Shift key at the time you click it. The Step Macro tool is available only when a macro sheet is active.
	Record Macro tool	Displays the Record Macro dialog box where you can assign the name to your new macro and begin recording your actions.
	Resume Macro tool	Resumes macro operation after a macro has been paused with the Pause button in the Single Step dialog box or with the =PAUSE() macro function.

then choose a **C**ontinue button to run the macro at normal speed, a **S**tep button to step through the remainder of the macro, or a **H**alt button to stop running the macro altogether.

Before you can use this debugging utility, you must open the **debug.xla** file. This file contains the debug add-in macro sheet that runs the macro that adds the debug utility and attaches the **D**ebug command to the **M**acro menu. (For more on customizing Excel with add-in macros, see Chapter 20.)

To use the **D**ebug command to debug a macro, you need to follow these steps:

1. Activate the macro sheet containing the macro you need to debug. If necessary, turn off the document protection by choosing the Un**p**rotect Document command on the **O**ptions menu. You cannot use the De-bug command on a protected document because the debugging utility must be able to make changes to the formulas in the macro sheet when running. (The formulas are returned to normal when you exit the debugger.) Because the debug utility alters your macro for-mulas at times when running the macro, always save your macro sheet before you use this command to safeguard its contents.

2. Open the **M**acro menu and choose the **D**ebug command. (This com-mand appears below the Re**c**ord command when the debug add-in macro is running.)

3. If this command is not displayed on the **M**acro menu, close this menu and select the **O**pen command on the **F**ile menu instead (or click the Open file tool on the Standard toolbar or press Ctrl+F12). Double-click the library folder in the **D**irectories list box to open this directory, then double-click debug.xla in the File **N**ame list box to open this macro sheet and run this add-in macro. (If this file does not appear in the File **N**ame list box when you select the c:\excel\library directory, you have to run the Excel Setup program to install it.) Af-ter opening this file, you can select the **D**ebug command on the Macro menu. When you choose the **D**ebug command, the menu bar changes. The Debug menu bar contains three menus: **D**ebug, For-mula, and Display.

4. To insert a tracepoint that puts your macro into step mode, select the cell in the macro where step mode should begin, then choose the Set **T**race Point command on the **D**ebug menu.

5. To set a breakpoint that displays your alert message and/or shows you the current values of various variables, choose the cell in the macro where the breakpoint should occur, then choose the Set **B**reakpoint command on the **D**ebug menu.

6. If you want a message displayed when the macro displays the variables at this breakpoint, enter the message in the Alert String text box of the Set Breakpoint dialog box and choose OK. If you don't want to add a message, leave the text box empty and choose OK.

7. To display the intermediate values for certain variables at this breakpoint, choose the Breakpoint Output command on the **D**ebug menu, then choose the **V**ariable text box in the Breakpoint Output dialog box and select the cell with the formula whose value you want to see (or type in its cell reference) and choose the **A**dd button. When you've finished adding all of the variables you want to see in the Variables to **O**utput list box, choose the OK button.

8. Repeat steps 4 through 7 for any other places in the macro that you want identified as tracepoints or breakpoints.

9. To run your macro using the tracepoints and breakpoints you've added, press Ctrl+F6 to display the worksheet or chart window that needs to be active when you run the macro, then choose the **R**un Macro command on the **D**ebug menu.

After running your macro using the tracepoints and breakpoints, the Debug add-in macro restores your formulas to their original condition. To remove a breakpoint or tracepoint before you rerun your macro with the Debug utility, select the cell containing the breakpoint or tracepoint, then choose the **E**rase Debug Point command on the **D**ebug menu. If your macro switches menu bars so that the Debug menu bar is no longer displayed, press Ctrl+R to redisplay the **D**ebug menu.

When you've finished debugging your macro with the Debug utility, choose the **E**xit Debug command on the **D**ebug menu. Excel then replaces the Debug menu bar with the worksheet or chart menu bar (depending on which type of document window is active).

Tip To remove all of the debug points in one operation, choose the Select **D**ebug Points option on the F**o**rmula menu in the **D**ebug menu bar to select all the tracepoints and breakpoints, then choose the **E**rase Debug Point command on the **D**ebug menu.

SUMMARY

In this chapter you learned how to create basic macros that automate common tasks you perform in Excel. First you learned how to use the macro recorder to record all the actions that you want included in the macro as you perform them in a typical worksheet or chart window. Then you learned how to write a macro in a macro sheet using the Excel macro functions. Finally you learned how to test and debug macros that contain either syntax or processing errors.

In the next chapter you will learn how to create macros that customize Excel. There you will learn how to add a macro to the standard Worksheet menu bar as well as how to create your own command menus and dialog boxes.

18

Creating Custom Macro Applications

In Excel you can create macros that do much more than just automate routine tasks that you perform in your worksheets and charts. You can design and create macros that run custom applications as well. For example, you could create a menu-driven application for organizing, consolidating, and printing financial statements or one for updating, searching, sorting, and printing reports from an Excel database. By creating a menu-driven custom application to perform such interrelated tasks, you make it possible for anyone with a basic familiarity with Excel to run your application. Users do not have to understand Excel macros in order to use your custom application and feel comfortable with it.

As part of your custom application, you can create macros that run automatically as soon as the user opens or closes a particular worksheet. You can also add custom commands to the standard worksheet or chart menu bar that enable users to run a particular macro simply by selecting its command from a pull-down menu (just as they choose any other worksheet or chart command in Excel).

For more extensive custom applications, you can create macros that add your own menu bars and toolbars. (See Chapter 19 for information on creating a custom toolbar.) You can also create custom dialog boxes containing your own text boxes, list boxes, drop-down list boxes, option buttons, check boxes, and command buttons. Custom dialog boxes enable your users to input data efficiently and make various selections in your application.

In this chapter you will learn how to create macros that run automatically and to add macros as commands on the standard worksheet, chart, or macro menu bars. You will then learn how to develop a menu bar containing just the commands used by your custom application. After that, you will learn how to use the Dialog Editor to develop a custom dialog box for your application.

Creating Macros that Run Automatically

In your custom application, you may want Excel to run a macro (such as the one that displays a custom menu bar) as soon as the user opens or closes a particular Excel document or switches to another open document. Before you assign a macro to an Excel document that automatically runs as soon as you open the document, be sure that the macro is thoroughly debugged and works exactly as you want it to.

Excel allows you to run a macro when a user opens, closes, activates, or deactivates a particular Excel document. To define a macro that runs automatically, you follow these steps:

1. Create and debug the macros that you want to run automatically.

2. Open and activate the document (workbook, worksheet, chart, or macro) for which you want to define an automatic macro.

3. Choose the **Define Name** command on the Formula menu.

4. To have the macro run when the document is opened, enter a range name that begins with **Auto_Open** in the **Name** text box. To have the macro run when the document is closed, enter a name that begins with **Auto_Close** in the **Name** text box. To have the macro run when the document is activated, enter a name that begins with **Auto_Acti-vate** in the **Name** text box. To have the macro run when the document is deactivated, enter a name that begins with **Auto_Deacti-vate** in the **Name** text box. For example, you might enter the range name Auto_Open_CustMenu for the macro that creates the custom menu bar you want displayed as soon as you open the worksheet, or you might enter the range name Auto_Deactivate_CustDialog for a macro that creates the custom dialog box you want displayed as soon as the user switches to another Excel document.

5. Choose the **Refers to** text box, then switch to the macro sheet and se-lect the first cell of the macro that should run when the document is opened, closed, activated, or deactivated (as the case may be). If the macro sheet is not open, you can type in a formula with an external reference to the macro. (Remember to enter the filename of the

macro sheet followed by the name of the macro separated with an exclamation point.) When the **R**efers to text box contains an external reference to the first cell of the macro, Excel automatically opens the macro sheet containing the macro if the sheet is not already open when you open, close, activate, or deactivate the current document.

6. Choose the **A**dd command button. When you've finished defining the automatic macros for this document, choose the OK button or press Enter.

7. Save the document with the auto-range names.

 Tip To open or close a document without running the automatic macros that you have assigned to the document, hold down the Shift key as you choose the **O**pen or **C**lose command on the **File** menu. Excel will then bypass the macros that normally run automatically. Use the =HALT(TRUE) as part of an IF-END.IF block in an Auto_Close macro to stop the macro and prevent the document from being closed until the user performs a particular action.

Creating Other Event-triggered Macros

You can have your custom application run a macro automatically when other events occur besides just the opening, closing, activating, or deactivating of a particular Excel document. Table 18.1 summarizes the macro functions that you can use to trigger macros and the events that cause them to run. (See Appendix C for detailed information on the arguments required by any of these macro functions.) For example, you can use the ON.KEY macro function to run a macro as soon as the user presses a particular keystroke combination. The ON.KEY macro function uses the syntax

    =ON.KEY(key_text,macro_text)

where *key_text* specifies the keystroke that triggers the macro and *macro_text* specifies the macro to run. For instance, to use this macro function to run a macro named Extract_Data in a macro sheet named **dbase.xlm** when the user presses Ctrl+Shift+F3, you would enter

    =ON.KEY("^+{F3}","DBASE.XLM!Extract_Data")

in the macro (^ in the macro function stands for Ctrl, and + stands for Shift—you use % for Alt.) To return the keystroke combination Ctrl+Shift+F3 to its normal function (of displaying the Create Name dialog box) later on in the macro, you would enter the

    =ON.KEY("^+{F3}")

macro function that specifies just the *key_text* argument. To disable the keystrokes Ctrl+Shift+F3 altogether in the macro, you would enter the

=ON.KEY("^+{F3}","")

macro function that specifies the null string as the *macro_text* argument.

When using one of the automatic macro names or one of the event-triggered macro functions in your application, you can use the CALLER macro function to return the name of the document that made the macro run. The CALLER macro function requires no arguments and is entered simply as

=CALLER()

in the cell where you want the name of the sheet inserted.

Table 18.1 Event-triggered Macro Functions	
Macro Function	*Event That Triggers the Macro*
CANCEL.KEY	Runs a specified macro when the user cancels an operation or macro.
ERROR	Runs a specified macro when the macro function returns an Error value.
ON.DATA	Runs a specified macro when another application sends data to Excel via the Dynamic Data Exchange. (See Chapter 21 for information on DDE.)
ON.DOUBLECLICK	Runs a specified macro when the user double-clicks a cell or object in a particular document.
ON.ENTRY	Runs a specified macro when the user enters data into any cell in a specified document.
ON.KEY	Runs a specified macro when the user presses a particular key or key combined with Shift, Ctrl, or Alt.
ON.RECALC	Runs a specified macro when a document is recalculated.
ON.TIME	Runs a specified macro at a particular time.
ON.WINDOW	Runs a specified macro when the user activates a particular window.

Using the Structured Macro Template

Excel includes a macro sheet template that can help you organize and develop your custom application. This macro sheet template file is called **structm.xlt** and is located in the **\examples** directory of the **c:\excel** directory. When you open this file, Excel opens a copy of this macro sheet and gives it the temporary filename **Structm1** (or the next available number). Figure 18.1 shows you the first part of a macro sheet created with the structured macro template.

As you can see in this figure, Excel automatically adds summary information about the macro sheet including the name of the application, the version number, author, and creation date. (The initial version number, author, corporation, and creation date information are supplied automatically by Excel.) Below the Summary Information section, you find predefined auto_open and auto_close macros that you can modify if your custom application uses macros that should be run automatically whenever the user opens and closes the macro sheet.

When you open a new macro sheet from the structured macro template, your macro sheet includes two utility macros, Indent and Command Window,

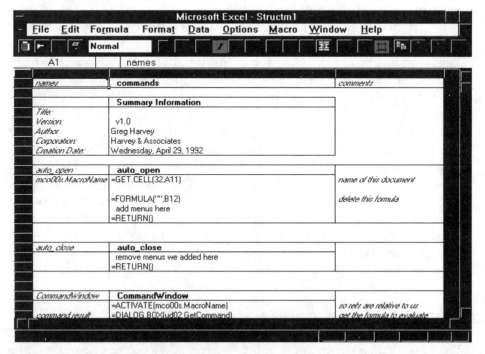

Figure 18.1   Macro Sheet Created with the Structured Macro Template

that help you in writing and debugging the macros in your custom application. The Indent macro automatically indents macro functions used in the following control structures:

- Block IF—END.IF statements
- FOR—NEXT loops
- FOR.CELL—NEXT loops
- WHILE—NEXT loops

To indent the macro functions used in these control structures (which makes the macro much easier to understand), you simply select the cells in the macro sheet that contain them and then press Ctrl+N. Excel then inserts tabs after the equal sign in all the macro functions included in these control structures in the cell selection.

If, for some reason, you decide that you wish to remove the indents from a group of macro functions (whether inserted with the Indent macro or manually with Ctrl+Tab), you can do so by selecting the cells containing the functions and then pressing Ctrl+M.

The Command Window macro that is included in a macro sheet created with the structured macro template enables you to calculate the result of any macro function used in your application. To calculate a particular macro function, press Ctrl+Shift+C, then select the cell that contains the macro function you want to calculate or type it in the **E**xecute Command text box of the Command Window dialog box. To calculate the result of the selected macro function, choose the **R**un command button in this dialog box. Excel then displays the result in the Command Window dialog box.

In addition to these two utility macros, a macro sheet generated with the structured macro template also contains the headings for a dialog box definition table in the cell range E1:L2 and the headings for a menu table in the cell range N1:S2. You can use the headings for the menu table when developing custom menus for your application. (See "Creating a Custom Menu Bar" later in this chapter.) You can use the dialog box definition table headings to identify a definition table created with the Dialog Editor that you paste into the macro sheet. (For complete information on creating a custom dialog box, see "Creating a Custom Dialog Box" later in this chapter.)

Adding a Custom Command to a Menu

When creating a custom application, you can add a custom command to a pull-down menu that runs a particular macro whenever the user selects the command. Assigning macros to pull-down menu commands makes your macros accessible to users of all experience levels. Custom commands are especially useful when you are working with a worksheet or chart document that does not have sufficient open space to permit the addition of buttons for running the macros in your application.

To add a custom command, you first need to set up a *command table* in your macro sheet. A command table consists of five columns: The first column holds the names of the command; the second column, the name of the macros assigned to each command; the third column is for shortcut keys assigned to the command in the Macintosh version of Excel (this column is not used in the Windows version); the fourth column holds the status-bar message that is displayed when the command is highlighted; and the fifth column holds the help topic assigned to the custom command.

You then use the ADD.COMMAND macro function in your macro to add the command described in the command table to a pull-down menu. The ADD.COMMAND function follows the syntax

=ADD.COMMAND(bar_num,menu,command_ref,position)

where *bar_num* is the ID number of the menu bar or shortcut menu (as shown in Table 18.2), *menu* is either the text name of the menu or its number, *command_ref* is an array or a reference to the area in the macro sheet that contains the command table, and *position* specifies the placement of the new command on the menu.

When entering the *menu* argument for a pull-down menu, you can either enter the name of the menu, as in "Data" when adding a command to the Data menu on the worksheet menu bar, or its number. (Menus are numbered from left to right starting with 1, so that the Data menu is number 5 on the worksheet menu bar.) When entering the *menu* argument for a shortcut menu, you enter a number indicating the specific shortcut menu to which to add the command (as shown in Table 18.3). When adding a *position* argument, you either enter the name of the existing command above which you want the custom command to appear (as in "Series..." to add a custom command above the Series command on the Data pull-down menu—note that you must include the ellipsis [...] for this command) or a number describing the command's position on the menu (number 9 to position your custom command above the Series command on the **Data** menu). If you omit the position argument from the ADD.COMMAND macro function, the program adds the menu to the bottom of the pull-down or shortcut menu. Also, note that you can't add custom commands to the middle of either the toolbar shortcut menu (*bar_num* 7, *menu* 1) or the workbook paging icons (*bar_num* 7, *menu* 3).

Tip Whenever possible, enter the names of the menus and menu commands (in quotation marks) rather than their numbers. The numbers
may change if your application customizes the menus by adding and
deleting menus and commands. If you refer to menus and commands
by name instead of number, the macro application will always add your
custom commands to the right menus in the desired position.

Table 18.2   The ID Numbers of the Built-in Menu Bars and Shortcut Menus

ID Number for Bar_num Argument	Menu Bar or Shortcut Menu
1	Worksheet and macro sheet menu bar.
2	Chart menu bar.
3	Null menu bar. (The menu bar displayed when no documents are open.)
4	Info window menu bar.
5	Worksheet and macro sheet menu bar for short menus. (Use the SHORT.MENUS macro function to display short menus.)
6	Chart menu bar for short menus.
7	Cell, toolbar, and workbook shortcut menu.
8	Object shortcut menu.
9	Charting shortcut menu.

Table 18.3 Menu Bar and Menu ID Numbers for the Shortcut Menus

Bar_Num No.	Menu No.	Shortcut Menu Selected
7	1	Toolbars
7	2	Toolbar tools
7	3	Workbook paging icons
7	4	Cells (worksheet)
7	5	Column selections
7	6	Row selections
7	7	Workbook items
7	8	Cells (macro sheet)
8	1	Drawn or imported graphic objects
8	2	Buttons
8	3	Text boxes
9	1	Chart series
9	2	Chart text
9	3	Chart plot area and walls
9	4	Entire charts
9	5	Chart axes
9	6	Chart gridlines
9	7	Chart floor and arrows
9	8	Chart legends

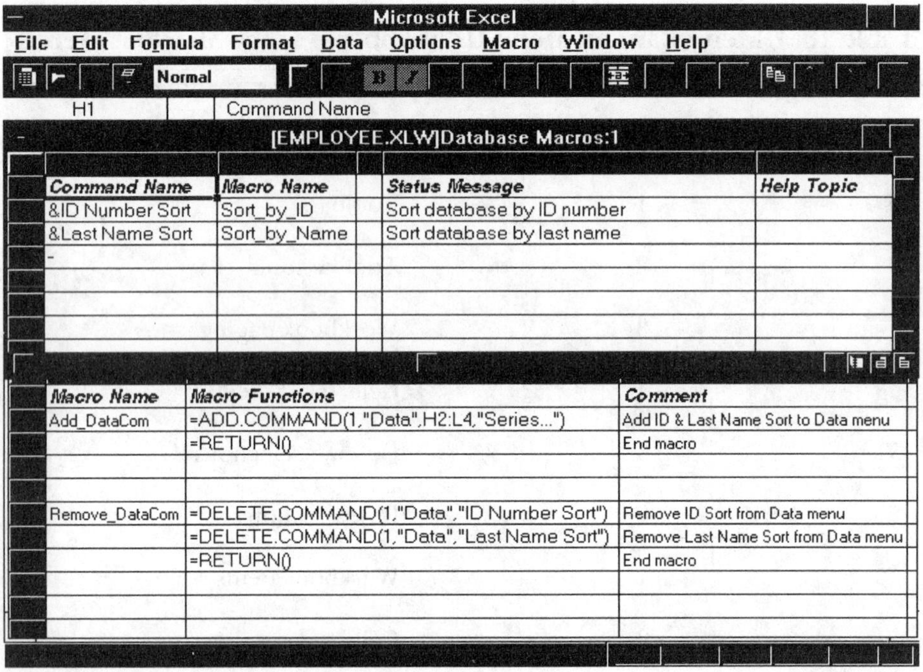

**Figure 18.2   Command Table for Adding Custom Commands to the Data
Menu**

Figure 18.2 shows you the command table (in the top window) and the
Add_DataCom macro containing the ADD.COMMAND macro function
(in the bottom window) for adding two custom commands—ID Number
Sort and Last Name Sort—to the Data pull-down menu (shown in Figure
18.3). Notice the ADD.COMMAND macro function in Add_DataCom is

```
=ADD.COMMAND(1,"Data",H2:L4,"Series...")
```

The *bar_num* argument 1 tells Excel to add the custom commands to the
worksheet and macro menu bar, the *menu* argument "**Data**" tells the program to add custom commands to the Data pull-down menu, the *com-
mand_ref* argument **H2:L4** indicates the cell references of the command
table, and the position argument "**Series...**" indicates that the two custom
commands are to appear above the **S**eries command on the **D**ata menu.

Note that the *command_ref* argument in the ADD.COMMAND function uses
the cell range H2:L4 instead of H2:L3. This is because cell H4 contains a
hyphen (-) that adds a separator line after the second custom command in the
Data menu. You can specify a separator line to appear above the first custom
command you add to a menu. To do so, you enter the hyphen in the first row
of the command table in the column that contains the command name.

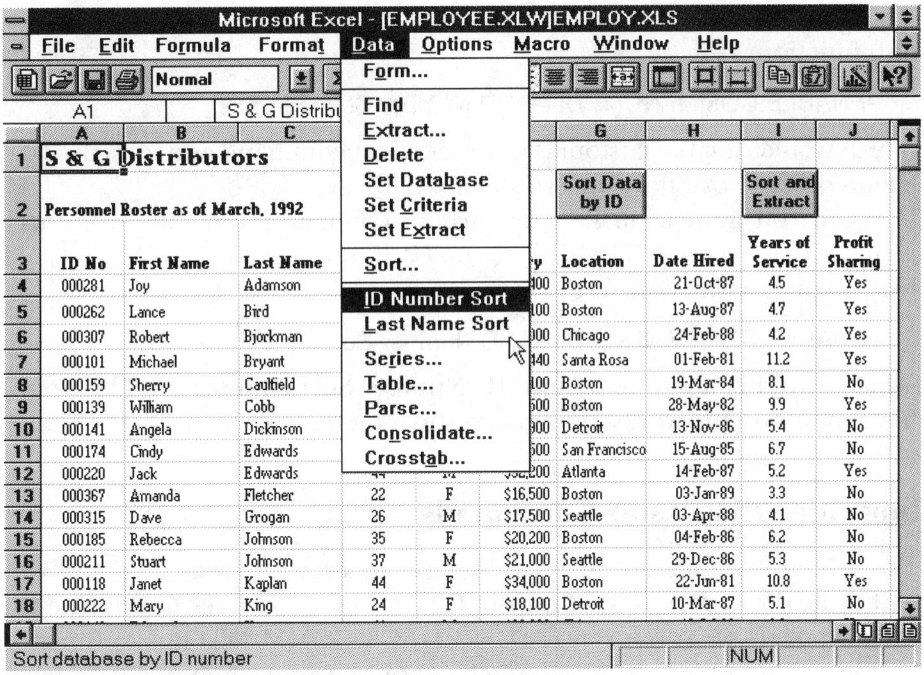

Figure 18.3   Data Menu with Custom Commands

Note too that both of the command names in the command table shown in Figure 18.2 begin with an ampersand (&). You place an ampersand immediately in front of the letter in the command name that should be used as the mnemonic (command) letter. In this example, the *I* in *ID Number Sort* appears underlined and the *L* in *Last Name Sort* appears underlined. This enables the user to press Alt+DI to select the **ID Number Sort** command and Alt+DL to select the **Last Name Sort** command. You can place the ampersand before any character in the custom command name (provided it isn't already used by another command on that menu). If you want to add an ampersand to the command name itself, you need to type && in the command table.

Enabling and Disabling Commands

You can dim commands that you add to a menu when you want to indicate to the user that the commands are not currently available. To disable and enable a command, you use the ENABLE.COMMAND macro function, which follows the syntax

    =ENABLE.COMMAND(bar_num,menu,command,enable)

To dim a particular command, you enter FALSE as the *enable* argument of this function, as in

    =ENABLE.COMMAND(1,"Data","ID Number Sort",FALSE)

which would dim the custom ID Number Sort command added to the Data menu on the worksheet/macro sheet menu bar.

When you want to make your custom command available to the user once again, you enter TRUE as the *enable* argument of the ENABLE.COMMAND macro function, as in

    =ENABLE.COMMAND(1,"Data","ID Number Sort",TRUE)

which would enable the custom ID Number Sort command added to the Data menu on the worksheet/macro sheet menu bar.

Adding Check Marks to Commands

Some menu commands add check marks to show when a command is in effect, as the **G**allery menu on the **C**hart menu bar does to indicate the current chart type. You can use the CHECK.COMMAND macro function to add and remove a check mark before your custom command to indicate when the command is and is not in effect. This macro function follows the syntax

    =CHECK.COMMAND(bar_num,menu,command,check)

where the *check* argument is TRUE when you want the macro to add a check mark to the command and FALSE when you want the macro to remove the added check mark.

Renaming a Command

You can have your application change the name of a custom command to inform your user of which of two possible states is the active one. Perhaps the best example of this in Excel is the **P**rotect Document command on the **O**ptions menu. As soon as you choose this command to protect your worksheet, Excel renames this command Un**p**rotect Document, indicating the document is currently protected.

To rename a command (built-in or custom), you use the RENAME.COMMAND macro function, which follows the syntax

    =RENAME.COMMAND(bar_num,menu,command,name_text)

where the *name_text* argument is the new command name. For example, you could use the following RENAME.COMMAND macro function to rename the

ID Number Sort command on the Data menu of the worksheet/macro sheet menu bar to Last Name Sort after the database has been sorted by ID number:

    =RENAME.COMMAND(1,"Data","ID Number Sort","Last Name Sort")

If you want to change the command name back to ID Number sort after the user sorts the database by last name, you would then add the macro function

    =RENAME.COMMAND(1,"Data","Last Name Sort","ID Number Sort")

to your application.

Deleting a Command from a Menu

To remove a custom command from a shortcut or pull-down menu, you use the DELETE.COMMAND macro function in your application. Figure 18.2 illustrates the use of this function in the Remove_DataCom macro (shown beneath the Add_DataCom macro in the lower window). When you use this macro function to remove a custom command, you only need to specify the bar_num, menu, and command arguments, as in

    =DELETE.COMMAND(1,"Data","ID Number Sort")

to remove the ID Number Sort custom command from the Data menu of the worksheet and macro sheet menu bar.

Note that if your command table includes a hyphen to add a line separator above and/or below your custom command(s), this line separator will remain displayed on the pull-down menu during your work session even after removing the custom command(s) with the DELETE.COMMAND macro function. Line separators added to menus along with custom commands do, however, disappear from the pull-down menus the next time you start Excel.

 Alert! You can use the DELETE.COMMAND macro function to remove built-in as well as custom commands from shortcut and pull-down menus. Do not, however, use this function to remove the **Exit** command on the **File** menu unless your application includes another way to exit Excel. If you remove this command, the user will be forced to power down the computer in order to exit Excel!

Creating a Custom Menu

If your application warrants, rather than just add custom commands to a built-in menu, you can create a custom menu that contains them. To create a custom menu, you need to set up a *menu table* in the macro sheet that defines the contents of the menu. This menu table, like a command table, consists of five columns: The first column contains the menu and command names; the second column holds the names of the command macros that are run when the user selects a command; the third column holds shortcut keys assigned to the command in the Macintosh version of Excel (this column is not used in the Windows version); the fourth column holds the status-bar message that is displayed when the command is highlighted, and the fifth column shows the custom Help topic assigned to each command.

Alert! To add a custom Help topic, create a Help file that contains the Help topic as a text file in your word processor. Begin each Help topic with an asterisk followed by the number of the topic (any integer) and then add the Help text on the lines below. When referring to a custom Help topic in a menu table, enter the filename followed by the topic number, as in cus-tom.hlp!72. Before your application can use custom Help topics, you must convert the Help file from a plain text format to Windows Help format. To do this, you must use the Windows Help Conversion program available directly from Microsoft Corporation.

As with command tables, you can designate a letter in the name of the custom command as the command letter to appear underlined by preceding the letter with an ampersand (&), and you can have Excel insert separator lines in the custom menu by entering a hyphen (-) in a blank cell in the first column of the menu table in the row above or below the command that should precede or follow. Unlike a command table, however, the first cell of a menu table contains the name of the custom menu. The commands that appear on this custom menu are then listed in succeeding rows of the first column of the menu table.

Figure 18.4 illustrates the layout of the menu table. There you see the menu tables for creating four separate custom menus: Add, Sort, Extract, and Quit. The Add menu contains two commands, the Sort menu four commands, while both the Extract and Quit menus contain three commands each. Note the use of the ampersand in both the menu names and the command names to designate which letter is be underlined and can be combined with the Alt key in opening the menu and choosing the command.

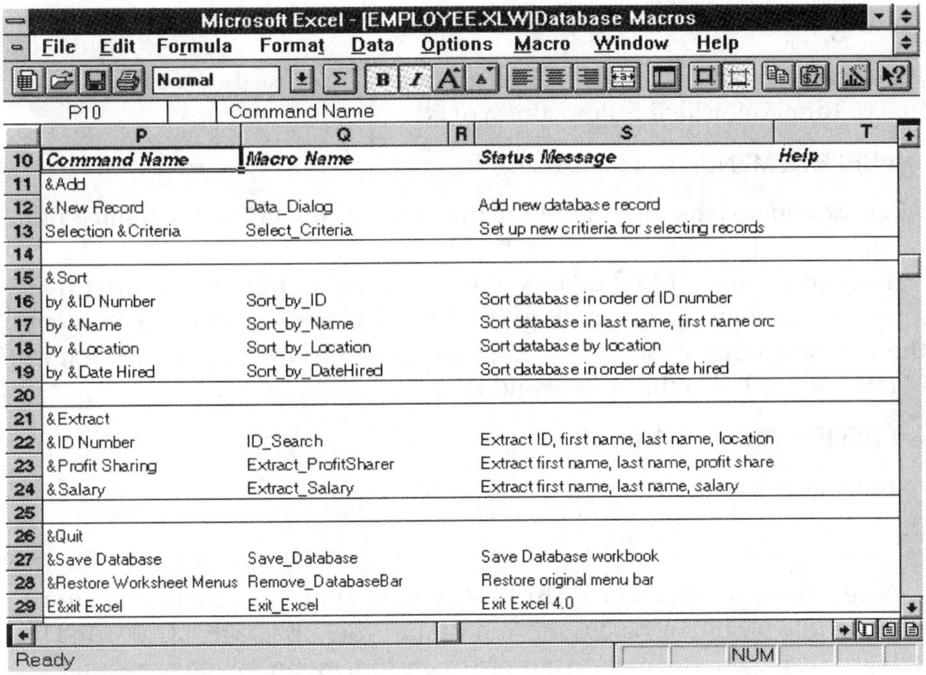
Microsoft Excel - [EMPLOYEE.XLW]Database Macros
File Edit Formula Format Data Options Macro Window Help
Normal
P10 Command Name
P Q R S T
10 Command Name | Macro Name | Status Message | Help
11 &Add
12 &New Record | Data_Dialog | Add new database record
13 Selection &Criteria | Select_Criteria | Set up new critieria for selecting records
14
15 &Sort
16 by &ID Number | Sort_by_ID | Sort database in order of ID number
17 by &Name | Sort_by_Name | Sort database in last name, first name orc
18 by &Location | Sort_by_Location | Sort database by location
19 by &Date Hired | Sort_by_DateHired | Sort database in order of date hired
20
21 &Extract
22 &ID Number | ID_Search | Extract ID, first name, last name, location
23 &Profit Sharing | Extract_ProfitSharer | Extract first name, last name, profit share
24 &Salary | Extract_Salary | Extract first name, last name, salary
25
26 &Quit
27 &Save Database | Save_Database | Save Database workbook
28 &Restore Worksheet Menus | Remove_DatabaseBar | Restore original menu bar
29 E&xit Excel | Exit_Excel | Exit Excel 4.0
Ready
NUM

Figure 18.4 Menu Tables for Four Custom Menus

Adding a Custom Menu to a Menu Bar

You use the ADD.MENU macro function to add the custom menu defined by your menu table either to a built-in or custom menu bar. This macro function follows the syntax:

```
=ADD.MENU(bar_num,menu_ref,position)
```

where *bar_num* is the ID number of the menu bar, *menu_ref* is the reference to the menu table, and *position* is the name of the menu (as quoted text) in front of which the new menu should appear or the number of the new menu's position on the menu bar (counted from left to right). When adding a menu to one of the built-in menu bars, you can use the bar numbers shown in Table 18.2 to determine the *bar_num* argument. When adding a menu to a custom menu bar, you must use the bar number that Excel assigns the new menu bar. (You can use the ADD.BAR macro function to get this number—see "Creating a Custom Menu Bar" later in this chapter for details.) When specifying the *menu_ref* argument, enter the range name assigned to the menu table or the cell references for this table. Also note that if you omit the *position* argument, Excel automatically adds your custom menu to the end of its menu bar.

Removing a Menu from a Menu Bar

When you want to delete a menu from a menu bar, you use the DELETE.MENU macro function, which follows the syntax:

   =DELETE.MENU(bar_num,menu)

where *bar_num* is the number of the menu bar and menu is the name of the menu entered as text.

You can use the DELETE.MENU macro function to remove either built-in or custom menus from a menu bar. For instance, suppose that you want the worksheet menu bar in your custom application to appear without the Macro menu. To do this, you would enter

   =DELETE.MENU(1,"Macro")

in the macro that starts your custom application.

Note: You can use the ENABLE.COMMAND macro function to dim or enable a built-in or custom menu and the RENAME.COMMAND macro function to rename a built-in or custom menu. When using these functions, you enter all the arguments as you would when referring to a command except that in each case you enter 0 for the *command* argument to let Excel know that you want to apply the function to the menu designated by the *bar_num* and *menu* arguments.

Creating a Custom Menu Bar

Some applications require the use of custom menu bars that replace the normal built-in menu bar. To create a custom menu bar, you use the ADD.BAR macro command. This macro function creates a new menu bar and returns its ID number to the cell where the function is entered. After creating a new menu bar with the ADD.BAR function, you then use the ADD.MENU macro function to designate which menus should be added to it. After designating the menus to be included, you then use the SHOW.BAR macro function when you want the custom menu bar to be displayed.

Figure 18.5 illustrates the contents of the Create_DatabaseBar macro that creates and displays a custom Database menu bar. This macro begins in cell Q2 (which is named Database_bar) with an ADD.BAR macro function. This macro function creates a new menu bar and returns the menu

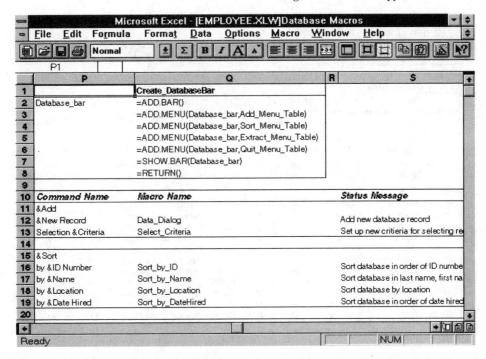

Figure 18.5   The Create_DatabaseBar Macro

bar's ID number to the Database_bar cell. The next four commands in this Create_DatabaseBar macro use ADD.MENU macro functions to add the four custom menus (**A**dd, **S**ort, **E**xtract, and **Q**uit) to this new menu bar. Note that each ADD.MENU function extracts *bar_num* argument from the Database_bar cell and specifies the *menu_ref* argument with the range name assigned to each menu table. (Refer to Figure 18.4 to see the contents of each menu table.)

After specifying what menus are to be added to the Database menu bar, the macro then uses the SHOW.BAR macro function to display this custom menu bar. Again, the Database_bar cell containing the ADD.BAR function is used to specify the *bar_num* argument for the SHOW.BAR function. After displaying the custom Database menu bar with the SHOW.BAR macro function, the RETURN function stops the Create_Database macro.

Figure 18.6 shows you the employee database after running the Create_Database macro. In place of the normal worksheet menu bar, you now see the custom Database menu bar with its **A**dd, **S**ort, **E**xtract, and **Q**uit menus. The **A**dd menu has been opened in this figure so that you can see the **N**ew Record and Selection **C**riteria commands.

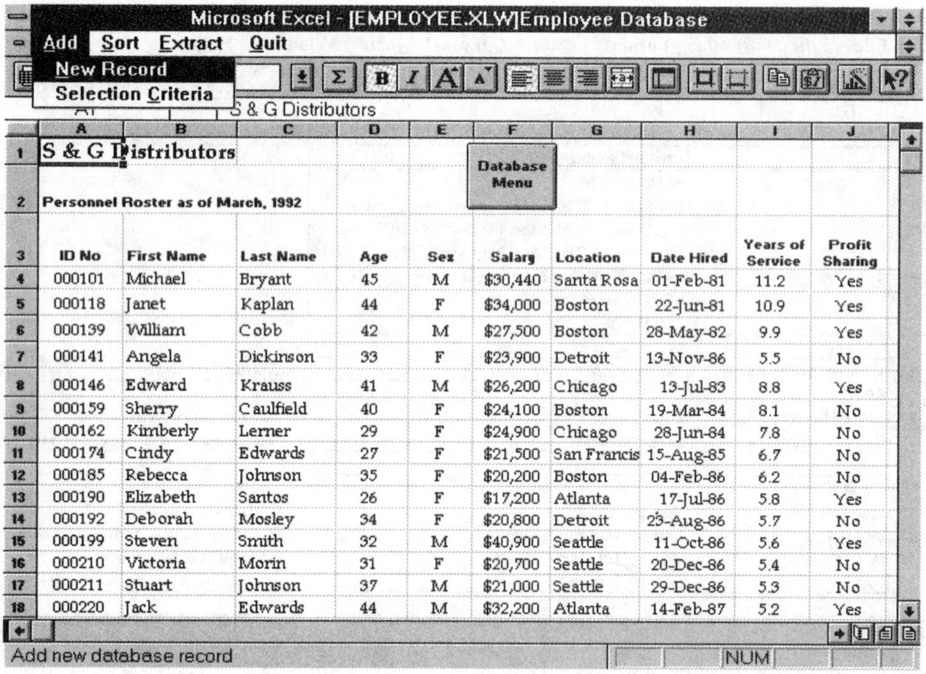

	A	B	C	D	E	F	G	H	I	J
1	S & G Distributors									
2	Personnel Roster as of March, 1992									
3	ID No	First Name	Last Name	Age	Sex	Salary	Location	Date Hired	Years of Service	Profit Sharing
4	000101	Michael	Bryant	45	M	$30,440	Santa Rosa	01-Feb-81	11.2	Yes
5	000118	Janet	Kaplan	44	F	$34,000	Boston	22-Jun-81	10.9	Yes
6	000139	William	Cobb	42	M	$27,500	Boston	28-May-82	9.9	Yes
7	000141	Angela	Dickinson	33	F	$23,900	Detroit	13-Nov-86	5.5	No
8	000146	Edward	Krauss	41	M	$26,200	Chicago	13-Jul-83	8.8	Yes
9	000159	Sherry	Caulfield	40	F	$24,100	Boston	19-Mar-84	8.1	No
10	000162	Kimberly	Lerner	29	F	$24,900	Chicago	28-Jun-84	7.8	No
11	000174	Cindy	Edwards	27	F	$21,500	San Francis	15-Aug-85	6.7	No
12	000185	Rebecca	Johnson	35	F	$20,200	Boston	04-Feb-86	6.2	No
13	000190	Elizabeth	Santos	26	F	$17,200	Atlanta	17-Jul-86	5.8	Yes
14	000192	Deborah	Mosley	34	F	$20,800	Detroit	23-Aug-86	5.7	No
15	000199	Steven	Smith	32	M	$40,900	Seattle	11-Oct-86	5.6	Yes
16	000210	Victoria	Morin	31	F	$20,700	Seattle	20-Dec-86	5.4	No
17	000211	Stuart	Johnson	37	M	$21,000	Seattle	29-Dec-86	5.3	No
18	000220	Jack	Edwards	44	M	$32,200	Atlanta	14-Feb-87	5.2	Yes

Figure 18.6 Employee Database Worksheet with Custom Database Menu Bar Displayed

To restore the original built-in menu bar to the active document (the worksheet menu bar in the case of the employee database), you use the SHOW.BAR macro function again, this time specifying the ID number of the original menu bar as its *bar_num* argument. This is how the Restore Worksheet Menus command on the **Q**uit menu works. This command calls a macro named Remove_DatabaseBar that contains the

```
=SHOW.BAR(1)
```

macro function, which replaces the custom Database menu bar with the standard worksheet menu bar.

Deleting a Menu Bar

Excel supports a maximum of fifteen custom menu bars in any application you create. When your application has defined the fifteenth custom menu bar, you will have to begin deleting menu bars before the application can create any other custom menu bars.

To delete a custom menu bar, you use the DELETE.BAR macro function. This function requires a single *bar_num* argument that specifies the ID number of the custom menu bar you want to delete.

Creating a Custom Dialog Box

In addition to custom menus and menu bars, you can create custom dialog boxes for your application. Unlike the dialog boxes created with the IN-PUT macro function (see Chapter 17), which are limited to a single text box, custom dialog boxes can include all of the types of boxes and buttons used in Excel dialog boxes and in any combination and order you see fit. In fact, a custom dialog box can contain up to 64 different items (32 of which can take or return arguments) with a maximum of 8 list boxes and a total of 1,024 text characters!

As with custom commands and menus, Excel uses a table called a *dialog box definition table* in the macro sheet that indicates the type of items and their arrangement in the custom dialog box. A dialog box definition table contains seven columns in the following order:

1. Item number indicating the type of button or box to use. (See Table 18.4.)

2. X position of the item's upper-left corner measured in points.

3. Y position of the item's upper-left corner measured in points.

4. Width of the item measured in screen units.

5. Length of the item measured in screen units.

6. Text associated with the item.

7. Initial (default) value or the result for the item (selected by the user).

Table 18.4 describes each of the items that you can use in the custom dialog boxes that you create for your application.

Table 18.4 Items in a Custom Dialog Box

Item No.	Type	Description
1	OK button (default)	Closes the custom dialog box and enters the data from the box into the initial/result column of the definition table, then returns control to the macro. To change the name of the button, enter a label other than OK in the text column of the definition table. The button appears with a thick black border around it and is selected when the user presses the Enter key.

Table 18.4   *(continued)*

2	Cancel button (not default)	Closes the custom dialog box and returns control to the macro, ignoring all options selected in the dialog box. To change the name of the button, enter a label other than Cancel in the text column of the definition table.
3	OK button (not default)	Closes the custom dialog box and enters the data from the dialog box into the initial/result column of the definition table, then returns control to the macro. To change the name of the button, enter a label other than OK in the text column of the definition table.
4	Cancel button (default)	Closes the custom dialog box and returns control to the macro, ignoring all options selected in the dialog box. To change the name of the button, enter a label other than Cancel in the text column of the definition table. The button appears with a thick black border around it and is selected when the user presses the Enter key.
5	Text	Enters fixed text used for labeling other items in the custom dialog box or displaying messages.
6	Text edit box	Creates a text box for entering text into the custom dialog box. The text column for this item is ignored. (Use item 5 to label the box.) The initial/result column contains the initial value for this box.
7	Integer edit box	Creates a text box for entering integers (between −32765 and 32767) into the custom dialog box. The text column for this item is ignored. (Use item 5 to label the box.) The initial/result column contains the initial integer for this box.
8	Number edit box	Creates a text box for entering numbers (integers and decimals) into the custom dialog box. The text column for this item is ignored. (Use item 5 to label the box.) The initial/result column contains the initial number for this box.

Table 18.4 *(continued)*

9	Formula edit box	Creates a text box for entering formulas into the custom dialog box. The text column for this item is ignored. (Use item 5 to label the box.) The program converts all cell references in the formula to the R1C1 system in the form of text in the initial/result column but converts these cell references in the custom dialog box to whatever cell reference system is selected in the Workspace dialog box. If the user enters a constant, Excel adds an equal sign before it. If the user enters text, the program encloses it in quotation marks.
10	Reference edit box	Creates a text box for entering cell references into the custom dialog box. The text column for this item is ignored. (Use item 5 to label the box.) Cell references in the initial/result column are entered in the R1C1 cell reference system in the form of text. When these references are displayed in the custom dialog box, Excel converts them to whatever cell reference system is selected in the Workspace dialog box.
11	Option button group (also known as a radio button group)	This item must precede in the row directly above the rows containing the option buttons (item 12—see below). The label entered in the text column becomes the label for the group. Enter the number of the option button to be selected by default in the initial/result column. If no value is entered in this column, Excel selects the first option button as the default. If the initial/result column contains the #N/A value, none of the option buttons in the group is selected. This item does not produce a visible group box. (For this, use item 14.)
12	Option button (also known as a radio button)	Creates an option button with the name entered in the text column.

Table 18.4   *(continued)*

13	Check box	Creates a check box with the name entered in the text column. If you enter **TRUE** in the initial/result column, the check box is selected. If you enter **FALSE**, the check box is empty. If you enter the value **#N/A**, the check box is grayed.
14	Group box	Draws a box around a group of related items. The label entered in the initial/result column is displayed as the group label. Enter this item and its definition in the row immediately above the ones containing the items you want to group.
15	List box	Creates a list box. Enter a reference in the text column to the cell range or array that contains the items to be listed in this list box. Enter the name of the cell range containing the items or cell references as R1C1 text. Enter the number of the default item in the initial/result column. If this column is empty, the first item in the list is selected by default. If the initial/result column contains the #N/A value, no item is selected in the list box. To label the list box, use an item 5. (See above.)
16	Linked list box	Same as item 15 except that the program enters the default item in the list box in a linked text box where the user can edit it. When using this item, you precede it with a text edit box (item 6).
17	Icon	Displays one of three icons. When the initial/result column contains **1**, the icon is the question mark. When the column contains **2**, the icon is the **i** in bold. When the column contains **3**, the icon is the exclamation point.
18	Linked file list box	Lists the files in a directory. This item must precede a linked drive and directory list box (item 19—see below) and must itself be preceded by a text edit box (item 6) where the user can edit the filename. The text column for this item is ignored.
19	Linked drive and directory list box	Similar to item 18 except that it lists the available drives and directories.

Table 18.4 *(continued)*

20	Directory text	Displays the name of the current directory, which doesn't change when the user chooses a new directory. To have the directory updated, use a Text item (item 5) followed by a Linked file list box (item 19). The text and initial/result columns for this item are both ignored.
21	Drop-down list box	Displays a list of items in a drop-down list box. Enter a reference in the text column to the cell range or array that contains the items to be listed in this list box. Enter the name of the cell range containing the items or cell references as R1C1 text. Enter the number of the default item in the initial/result column. If this column is empty, the first item in the list is selected by default. If the initial/result column contains the #N/A value, no item is selected in the list box. The value entered into the height column determines the length of the drop-down list box when it is displayed in the custom dialog box.
22	Drop-down combination edit/list box	Like item 21 except that this item must be preceded by a text edit box (item 6) where the user can edit the selected item in the list.
23	Picture button	Creates a button that works like the OK button but that displays the specified graphic object. A picture button can be any graphic object created with Excel's drawing tools. (See Chapter 14.) Enter the object's identifier in the text column (an object's identifier is displayed in the formula bar when you select it), as in "Rectangle 1." To display a graphic object in a custom dialog box without making it a button that you can press, enter the item number 223.
24	Help button	Displays the custom Help topic for the dialog box. The Help topic reference (Help filename and topic number separated by an exclamation point) can be entered in the first cell in the dialog box definition table or in the Help button's initial/result column. The button's default name is Help. To change this name, enter a label in the button's text column.

Using the Dialog Editor

Although you can set up and enter the values for a dialog box definition table in a macro sheet much as you would set up a menu table, Excel provides a much easier way to create the definition table with its Dialog Editor. The Dialog Editor allows you to add desired dialog box items and position and size them in the dialog box with the mouse. Dragging a particular dialog box item to its correct position in the dialog box is the easiest way to determine its x and y coordinates. And dragging the border of a button or box to increase or decrease its size is the most direct way to decide the optimum width and height for the item.

The Dialog Editor is a separate utility that you can run from Excel (if you have sufficient memory) or directly from Microsoft Excel 4.0 Group window in the Windows Program Manager when Excel is not running. To start the Dialog Editor from Windows, double-click the Dialog Editor program icon or select the icon and press Enter. To start the Dialog Editor from Excel, you follow these steps:

1. Choose the **R**un command on the Excel program Control menu by clicking the Control-menu button. Excel displays the Run dialog box, where you can open the Windows Clipboard, the Control Panel, Excel's Macro Translator, or the Dialog Editor.

2. Choose the Dialog Editor option button in the Run dialog box, then choose the OK button or press Enter.

The Dialog Editor opens in a separate window. When you start this program, the Dialog Editor draws a blank dialog box in the center of the window, as shown in Figure 18.7.

To build your dialog box in the Dialog Editor, you add the items you need to it, arranging them as required. You can resize the dialog box by dragging one of the sides or the corners of the box. When you drag a side, the Dialog Editor moves both sides of the box as you drag. When you drag a corner, the Dialog Editor moves all fours sides of the box (as shown in Figure 18.8).

To add a title bar to your custom dialog box so that the user can move the dialog box around the screen, you simply add a title to the dialog box in the Dialog Info dialog box. The easiest way to display this dialog box is to double-click the new dialog box, although you can also open the Dialog Info dialog box by choosing the **I**nfo command on the **E**dit menu. Figure 18.9 shows the Dialog Info dialog box after double-clicking the new dialog box. To add a title, you choose the **T**ext text box and enter your title there before choosing the OK button.

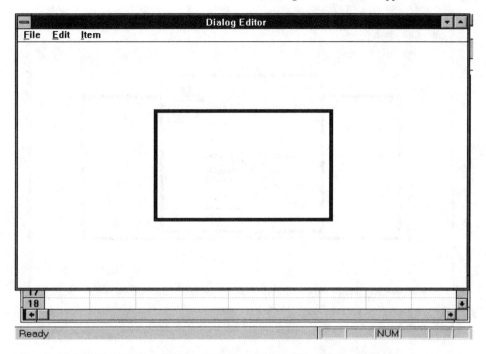

Figure 18.7   The Dialog Editor Window with a New Dialog Box

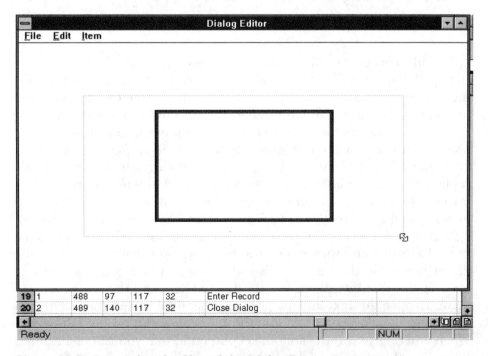

Figure 18.8   Increasing the Size of the Dialog Box

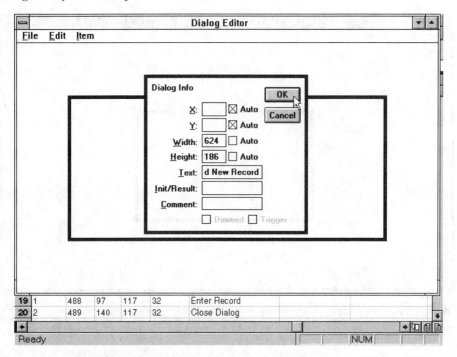

Figure 18.9   Entering the Title for the New Dialog Box

To add items to the dialog box, you choose the type of item from the Item pull-down menu. To add a button, choose the Button command and then the appropriate Button Type (**O**K, **C**ancel, Option, Check **B**ox, **H**elp, or **P**icture). When adding an OK and Cancel button to a custom dialog box, you can make one or the other of these buttons the default (so that the user can choose it by pressing Enter) by selecting its **D**efault check box.

To add a line of fixed text for the custom dialog box as a title or as a caption for a text edit box, you choose the **T**ext command on the **I**tem menu. When you choose this command, the Dialog Editor inserts a text item in the dialog box that contains the word *Text* and is in enclosed in a light gray or dotted box (to show that this item is selected). To replace the word *Text* with your own caption, just begin typing the new caption in the dialog box while the text item is still selected. You can also do this by opening the Text Info dialog box for this text item and replacing the word there. To open the Text Info dialog box, either double-click the text item in your custom dialog box or choose the **I**nfo command on the **E**dit menu. When entering your own caption, keep in mind that you can enter only a single line of text. (The Dialog Editor doesn't allow you to break the line.)

After you add a text item, you can move the item by dragging it to the desired position within the dialog box with the four-headed arrow pointer. If you deselect the Auto check boxes for the **Width** and **Height** boxes in the Text Info dialog box (both are selected by default), the Dialog Editor also allows you to change the width and length of the text item. By manipulating the shape of the text item with the double-headed arrow pointer, you can control the number of lines used and where the lines break. This is very useful when you are working with a long caption that won't fit within the dialog box as one line.

Figure 18.10 shows a new text item right after adding it to the custom dialog box. Figure 18.11 shows you the same text item after you replace Text with the caption Identification Number: in the Text Info dialog box.

To add a text box where the user can input information, you choose the **E**dit Box command on the **I**tem menu, then select the type of edit box to create, depending on the type of information you want from the user. Use the **T**ext option to let the user enter any type of information as text. Choose the **I**nteger option to restrict the entry to whole numbers or the **N**umber option when you want only numbers but will allow decimals as well as whole numbers. Choose the **F**ormula option to accept only formulas or **R**eference to restrict the entry to some sort of cell reference. After choosing the

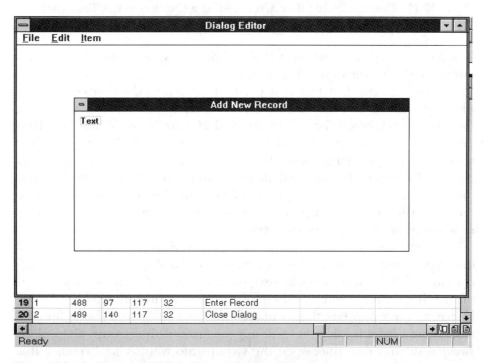

Figure 18.10 Custom Dialog Box with New Text Item

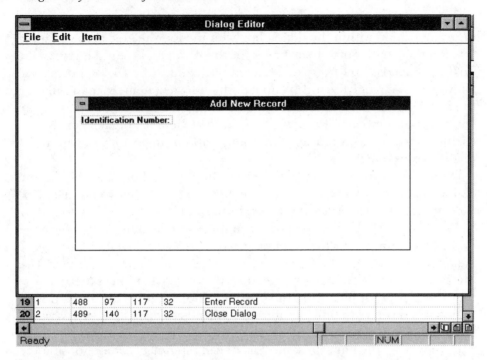

Figure 18.11   Custom Dialog Box After Adding a Caption to the Text Item

Edit Type and OK button, the Dialog Editor inserts a box showing the outline and edit type in the dialog box.

   To move the edit box to a new position, drag it to the desired position within the dialog box with the four-headed arrow pointer. If you deselect the Auto check boxes for the **W**idth and **H**eight boxes in the Edit Info dialog box (only the **H**eight box is selected by default), the Dialog Editor also allows you to change both the width and the height of the edit box. Figure 18.12 shows the custom dialog box after adding an edit text box and moving it to the right of the captioned text item. This edit text box is where the user will enter the employee's identification number when adding a new record to the employee database.

   To group several items together and create discrete sections within a dialog box (just like the Style section in the Font dialog box in Excel, which contains all of the style check boxes), you choose the **G**roup Box command on the **I**tem menu. When you choose this command, the Dialog Editor inserts a new group box that contains the word *Group* and shows the size and shape of the border that will appear around this group. To replace *Group* with your own title, open the Group Info window and replace this word in the **T**ext box.

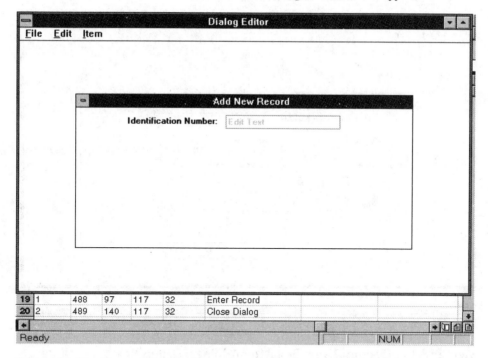

Figure 18.12   Custom Dialog Box After Adding an Edit Text Box

Figure 18.13 shows you the custom dialog box after adding a group box called Location. This group box will eventually contain a dropdown list box from which the user can choose the city where the employee works. (This group box could also contain a series of option buttons.)

If you want to add a list box to your custom dialog box, you choose the **List Box** command on the **Item** menu, then choose the list box type you want to use (**S**tandard, Linked, Linked **F**ile/Directory, **D**ropdown, or Combination Dropdown.) Figure 18.14 shows the custom dialog box after adding a drop-down list box (with the **D**ropdown option) and positioning it within the Location group box.

> *Note:* Although you can create your list boxes with the Dialog Editor, you must enter the list of the user's choices in the macro sheet and then add the reference to this list to the dialog box definition table once you've copied the definition to the macro sheet. See "Editing the Dialog Box Definition Table" later in this chapter for details.

If you want to add an icon or picture to your custom dialog box, you choose the **I**con command on the **Item** menu. Figure 18.15 shows you the

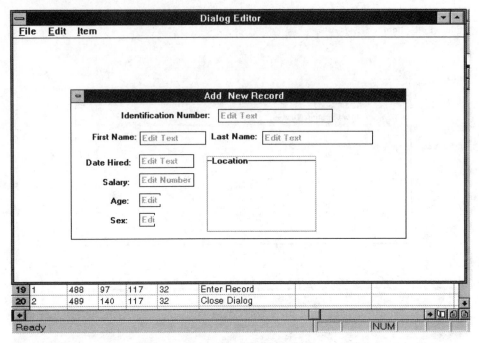

Figure 18.13   Custom Dialog Box After Adding a Group Box

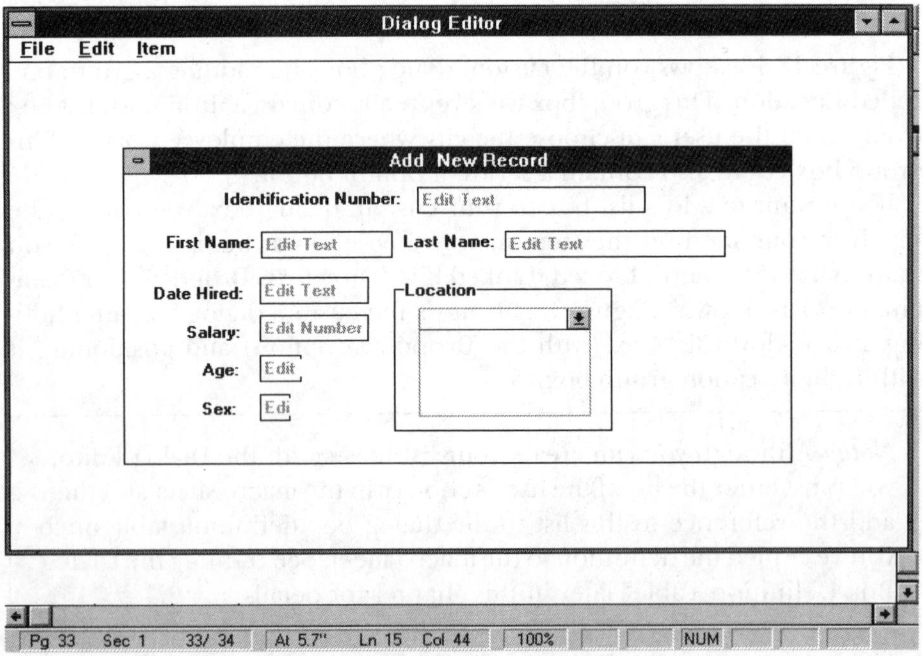

**Figure 18.14   Custom Dialog Box After Adding a Drop-down List Box Item
to the Location Group Box**

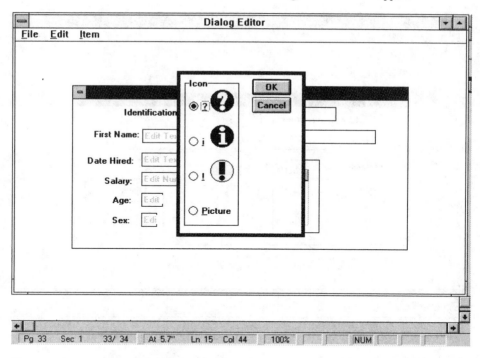

Figure 18.15 Icon Item Dialog Box

dialog box for choosing an icon to add to your dialog box. The first three icons are the standard icons used by Windows programs to indicate different types of message and alert dialog boxes. Choose the **P**icture option if you want to add a graphic object that you've created with Excel's drawing tools. (To indicate what graphic to use for the picture you've added, you enter the object identifier in the text column for this item after pasting the definition table in your macro sheet.)

If you find that you've selected the wrong item from the **I**tem menu at any time while building your dialog box, you can delete the item (provided that it is still selected) by pressing the Del key or choosing the Clear command on the **E**dit menu. If you need to copy an item, select the item and then choose the **D**uplicate command on the **E**dit menu. If you want to create the same type of item as the one you just created, you simply press the Enter key and the Dialog Editor inserts the same type of button or box. Note that you can also use the Cu**t**, **C**opy, and **P**aste commands on the **E**dit menu to move and copy items; be aware, however, that the standard shortcuts, Ctrl+X, Ctrl+C, and Ctrl+P, do not work in the Dialog Editor. (You must use the older Windows shortcuts of Shift+Del for Cut, Ctrl+Ins for Copy, and Shift+Ins for Paste.) Figure 18.16 shows you the completed Add

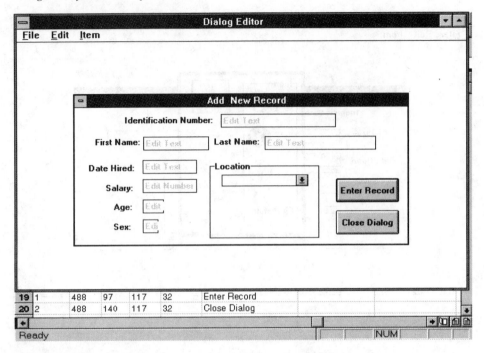

Figure 18.16   Completed Add New Record Dialog Box

New Record dialog box after adding and editing all of the required buttons and boxes.

PASTING THE DIALOG BOX DEFINITION TABLE INTO A MACRO SHEET

After you finish adding and positioning all the buttons and boxes you want in your custom dialog box, you are ready to paste the definition table for the dialog box into an Excel macro sheet. The Dialog Editor is not capable of saving the dialog box directly. To save your work, you must copy the dialog box to the Clipboard and then switch to Excel and paste the contents of the Clipboard into the cells of your macro sheet. When Excel pastes the contents of the Clipboard into your macro sheet, the program inserts the information as a dialog box definition table, following the seven-column layout discussed earlier.

To copy and paste a dialog box definition via the Clipboard, you follow these steps:

1.   Choose the **Exit** command on the Dialog Editor's **File** menu.

2.   Choose the **Yes** button to save the dialog box definition to the Clipboard.

3. If necessary, start Excel and open the macro sheet where you want the dialog box definition table to appear.

4. Select the cell where you want the dialog box definition table to begin. Be sure that there are sufficient blank cells in this area of the macro sheet to accommodate all the Clipboard information without overwriting any of your existing macros.

5. Choose the **P**aste command on the **E**dit menu (Ctrl+V) to paste the dialog box definition table into your macro sheet.

6. Label the columns so that you can identify the values in the table. (Use Figure 18.17 as a guide.)

7. Save the macro sheet with the **F**ile **S**ave command to save the definition table on disk.

Figure 18.17 shows you the dialog box definition table for the custom Add New Record dialog box created with the Dialog Editor after adding column headings in the macro sheet to identify the values. Notice that the first row of the table does not have an item number. This row is used to define the dialog box itself and therefore requires only width and height values.

	Item	x	y	width	height	text	initial/result
1	*Item*	*x*	*y*	*width*	*height*	*text*	*initial/result*
2				624	186	Add New Record	
3	5	95	11			Identification Number:	
4	6	276	9	212		ID Number	
5	5	38	41			First Name:	
6	6	129	40	124		First Name	
7	5	262	41			Last Name:	
8	6	357	40	205		Last Name	
9	5	27	76			Date Hired:	
10	7	128	71	103		Date Hired	
11	5	59	102			Salary:	
12	8	128	97	103		Salary	
13	5	75	128			Age:	
14	8	128	125	40		Age	
15	5	73	155			Sex:	
16	6	128	151	29		Sex	
17	21	275	92	160	90		
18	14	255	74	202	103	Location	
19	1	488	97	117	32	Enter Record	
20	2	489	140	117	32	Close Dialog	

Figure 18.17   Dialog Box Definition Table Pasted into a Macro Sheet

EDITING THE DIALOG BOX DEFINITION TABLE

Once you've pasted a dialog box definition table into a macro sheet, you can make changes to the dialog box simply by editing the values in the table. For example, if you decide that you want to insert default entries for certain items in the table, you would enter their values in the appropriate row of the initial/result column of the definition table. To use the current date as the default value in the date hired Integer edit text box of the Add New Record dialog box, for instance, you would enter the NOW function in the initial/result column for that item (cell AC10) and then format the cell with the date format you want used in the dialog box.

In addition to default values for particular items, you will also want to enter references to the cells containing the list for the list boxes used in the custom dialog box. For instance, to add the list of cities that should appear in the drop-down list box in the Location section of the Add New Record dialog box, you need to enter the list of cities in a range in the macro sheet and then refer to that range in the text column for that item in the dialog box definition table.

To enable the user to select a dialog box item with the keyboard, place an ampersand (&) before the letter you want used as the command letter in the caption that you've entered in the text column of the dialog box definition table. Note that you add the ampersands to the text items that accompany the edit boxes that are actually selected when the user types the letter, rather than to the edit boxes themselves.

Figure 18.18 shows the edited dialog box containing the default values, ampersands denoting the command letters, a list of cities for the drop-down list box, and a reference to this range. In this macro sheet, the range AD12:AD18 contains the list of cities. This cell range has been named Locations and this reference has been entered into the initial/result column for the drop-down item (cell AB17).

EDITING THE DIALOG BOX WITH THE DIALOG EDITOR

To make major changes to a custom dialog box, such as adding new items or rearranging items, you may prefer using the Dialog Editor to editing the values in the dialog box definition table. To edit a dialog box with the Dialog Editor, you first need to copy the dialog box definition table into the Clipboard in the Excel macro sheet and then switch to the Dialog Editor, where you paste the dialog box in from the Clipboard, using these steps:

1.   Make the macro sheet with the dialog box definition table the active one, then select all of the cells in this table (not including the cells with the column headings or the ranges with list box entries).

	Item						
	W	X	Y	Z	AA	AB	AC	AD
	Item	*x*	*y*	*width*	*height*	*text*	*initial/result*	*names*
1								
2				624	186	Add New Record		
3	5	95	11			&Identification Number:		
4	6	276	9	212		ID Number		
5	5	38	41			&First Name:		
6	6	129	40	124		First Name		
7	5	262	41			&Last Name:		
8	6	357	40	205		Last Name		
9	5	27	76			&Date Hired:		
10	6	128	71	103		Date Hired	=NOW()	
11	5	59	102			&Salary:		*Locations*
12	8	128	97	103		Salary	20000	Atlanta
13	5	75	128			&Age:		Boston
14	8	128	125	40		Age		Chicago
15	5	73	155			Se&x:		Detroit
16	6	128	151	29		Sex	M	San Francisco
17	21	275	92	160	90	Locations		Santa Rosa
18	14	255	74	202	103	Location		Seattle
19	1	488	97	117	32	Enter Record		
20	2	489	140	117	32	Close Dialog		

Figure 18.18   Dialog Box Definition Table After Editing

2. Choose the **C**opy command on the **E**dit menu (Ctrl+C).

3. Choose the **R**un command on the Excel program Control menu by clicking the Control-menu button.

4. Choose the **D**ialog Editor option button in the Run dialog box, then choose the OK button or press Enter.

5. Choose the **P**aste command on the **E**dit menu in the Dialog Editor (Shift+Ins). The Dialog Editor replaces the empty dialog box with the one described by the table definition you copied to the Clipboard. Note that all items within the dialog box are selected automatically. To deselect them, click somewhere in the white space within the dialog box.

6. Make your changes to the dialog box, then reverse the process by selecting the **E**xit command on the **F**ile menu and choosing the **Y**es button to copy the table to the Clipboard.

7. Switch back to the macro sheet in Excel and then paste the table from the Clipboard using the **P**aste command on the **E**dit menu (Ctrl+P).

When rearranging the items in a dialog box in the Dialog Editor, you can select more than one item at a time. Simply hold down the Shift key as you click the items you want to select. To select all of the items in the dialog box, you can choose the Select All Items command on the Edit menu. To restrain the movement of the selected items to a single direction (horizontal or vertical), hold down the Shift key as you drag the items.

Tip To precisely align two items with each other vertically so that their tops are aligned, select the item that is positioned correctly in the dialog box. Choose the Info command on the Edit menu and note the value in the **Y** text box for this item. Then, select the second item, choose the Edit Info command again, and enter the same value in its **Y** text box. To align two items horizontally so that their left edges are aligned, repeat this procedure, except this time note and copy the values in the **X** text box.

The custom dialog box always appears in the active Excel document in the same location as it appears in the Dialog Editor. To modify the position of the dialog box, select the dialog box (you can do this by choosing the **S**elect Dialog command on the **E**dit menu or by clicking the dialog box), then choose the **I**nfo command on the **E**dit menu to open the Dialog Info dialog box. Clear the Auto check boxes next to the **X** and **Y** text boxes and choose OK. Then drag the dialog box to the position on the screen where you want it to appear when you run your custom application.

To abandon your changes to a dialog box made in the Dialog Editor, choose the File New or File Exit command and choose the **N**o command button when prompted to save the changes. To save your changes in the Clipboard, choose the **Y**es command button instead.

Displaying the Dialog Box

Once you have your dialog box the way you want and have made all the necessary editing changes to its definition table, you are ready to create the macro that uses the DIALOG.BOX macro function to display the dialog box in your application. The DIALOG.BOX macro function follows the syntax

```
=DIALOG.BOX(dialog_ref)
```

where *dialog_ref* is the reference to the cells that contain the dialog box definition table.

Figure 18.19 shows the Add New Record dialog box displayed in the employee database with a macro that uses the DIALOG.BOX function

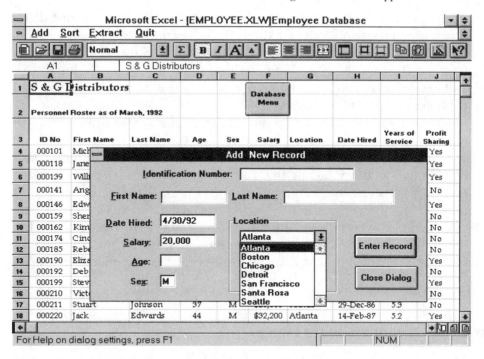

Figure 18.19 The Add New Record Dialog Box Displayed in the Worksheet

=DIALOG.BOX(Database_Dialog)

where Database_Dialog is the range name assigned to the dialog box defi-
nition table in the cell range W2:AC20 of the Database Macros macro sheet.
Note the appearance of the default entries in the **D**ate Hired, **S**alary, and
Se**x** text boxes as well as the list of cities in the Location drop-down list box.

Returning Values from a Dialog Box

When a user enters values into a dialog box and chooses the OK button or
its equivalent (or presses Enter, if you made the OK button the default), the
DIALOG.BOX macro function displays the custom dialog box and places
the values selected for each item in the dialog box in the appropriate row
of the initial/result column in the dialog box definition table. For example,
if the user enters the number **000405** in the Identification Number text box
and then chooses the Enter Record command button (the equivalent of
the OK button in this dialog box), Excel inserts the number 000405 in the
initial/result column for the ID Number edit text box (cell AC4 in this
case). Excel also places the number of the position of the item into the cell
containing the DIALOG.BOX function. For instance, if the Enter Record

command button is the eighteenth item in the Add New Record dialog box, the cell containing the DIALOG.BOX function will contain the value 18. If, however, the user selects the Cancel key or its equivalent in the dialog box, the DIALOG.BOX macro function returns the logical value FALSE, and Excel does not copy the values selected by the user into the initial/result column of the definition table.

After the DIALOG.BOX statement in your macro that displays the custom dialog box, you can add macro functions that evaluate the result in the cell with the DIALOG.BOX function and then perform different tasks depending on the value in this cell. For example, if the cell contains FALSE, the macro may return control to Excel. If the cell contains the position number of the item selected, the macro then can process the information copied into the initial/result column of the dialog box definition table or, depending on the number in this cell, process another routine (perhaps one that displays a different custom dialog box, if the number corresponds to a button such as New Record).

Creating Dynamic Dialog Boxes

The custom dialog boxes that you create can change depending on which option a user selects. You have seen examples of such *dynamic dialog boxes* in Excel itself. For example, the Date Unit section with the **Da**y, **W**eekday, **M**onth, and **Y**ear option buttons remains dimmed in the Data Series dialog box until you choose the **D**ate option button in the Type section. Once you select this option, all of the Date Unit options become available. In this example, the Date option button is the *trigger* that changes the status of the **Da**y, **W**eekday, **M**onth, and **Y**ear option buttons so that they are no longer dimmed.

When creating a dynamic dialog box, you define certain items as triggers that return information to the cell containing the DIALOG.BOX macro function and the initial/result column of the definition table *without* closing the custom dialog box. In other words, a trigger works just by choosing the OK button (or its equivalent) in returning the number of the item's position to the cell with the DIALOG.BOX function and entering the values in the initial/result column of the definition table except that it does all of this without closing the dialog box. This allows your macro the opportunity to modify certain options in the dialog box based on the value in the cell with the DIALOG.BOX function (indicating which item—that is, option—was selected) and/or the values returned to the particular cells in the initial/result column of the definition table.

Tip Instead of altering the options in a dialog box, you can use a trigger to check the values in the initial/result column of the definition table to make sure that the user has entered the required data in one or more items of the dialog box or has entered values within a critical range. If the macro finds that the required data is entered and/or values are within limits, you can then have the macro clear the dialog box by using the macro function =DIALOG.BOX(FALSE).

To designate a dialog box item as a trigger in the Dialog Editor, you open the Info dialog box for the item and select the Trigger check box. To designate a dialog box item as a trigger in the dialog box definition table, you add 100 to the item's type number. For example, to make an option button a trigger in the definition table, you would enter 112 (instead of 12) in the item column for that item.

To make certain dialog box items unavailable when a trigger is selected, you can dim those items. To dim a dialog box item in the Dialog Editor, you open the Info dialog box for the item and select the **D**immed check box. To dim a dialog box item in the dialog box definition table, you add 200 to the item's type number. For example, to dim an option button in the definition table, you would enter 212 (instead of 12) in the item column for that item.

Alert! Certain items in a dialog box cannot be triggers. These items include: fixed text (5), group boxes (14) unless they are option groups (11), icons (17), directory text (20), edit text boxes (6–10, and 22), and help buttons (24).

When entering the macro functions for a dynamic dialog box, you can use the SET.VALUE macro function to turn an item into a trigger or to dim or undim the item. For example, suppose that you've created a dialog box for inputting investments. The box contains an option button that designates that the investments are to be made quarterly, and this button is the fifteenth item (by position) in the dialog box. To make this option button a trigger for making available an integer edit box where you input the beginning quarter, you would enter these macro functions:

```
=SET.VALUE(Quarterly_Button_Item,112)
=SET.VALUE(Start_Qtr_Box_Item,207)
=DIALOG.BOX(Invest_Dialog)
=IF(Invest_Dialog_Box=15)
=SET.VALUE(Start_Qtr_Box_Item,7)
```

```
=DIALOG.BOX(Invest_Dialog)
=END.IF()
```

The first SET.VALUE function makes the Quarterly option button a trigger by adding 100 to its normal item number of 12. The second SET.VALUE function dims the edit integer box by adding 200 to its normal item number of 7. The third macro function displays the dialog box defined by the definition table in the cell range named Invest_Dialog.

The IF—END.IF block contains the commands for undimming the starting quarter edit box when the user selects the option button trigger. When the user selects this option button, the cell containing the DIALOG.BOX macro function (which is named Invest_Dialog_Box in this example) contains the value 15 because this option button is the fifteenth item in the dialog box. When this is the case, the IF function returns TRUE and the macro evaluates the third SET.VALUE function (which undims the edit integer box by returning the item number to 7) and the second DIALOG.BOX function (which redisplays the investment dialog box, this time with the starting quarter text box available). After this IF—END.IF block, you would then put the functions for evaluating and processing the data input by the user into this custom dialog box.

Replacing the Data Form with a Custom Dialog Box

You can replace Excel's built-in data form for entering records in a database with a dialog box of your own design. (Refer back to Chapter 15 for information on using the data form to input records in a database.) For example, you could use a slightly modified form of the Add New Record dialog box shown in Figure 18.19 as the data form for inputting records in the employee database. To do this, you paste the dialog box definition table somewhere in the worksheet containing the database and then assign the range name **Data_Form** to the cells containing the definition table.

In this example, you also must make some modifications to the item types in the dialog box definition table because Excel will accept only fixed text items (5) and edit text boxes (6) in the custom data form. Figure 18.20 shows the dialog box definition table after copying it into the worksheet containing the employee database and modifying some of the items. As you can see, all of the items that accept user input are now edit text boxes (6).

Also, notice that in the initial/result column of the definition table each edit text box item contains the name of the field name to which its information should be linked in the database. When you create the dialog box to be used as a custom data form in the Dialog Editor, you always enter the field name (exactly as it is entered in the database) in the Init/Result box of the

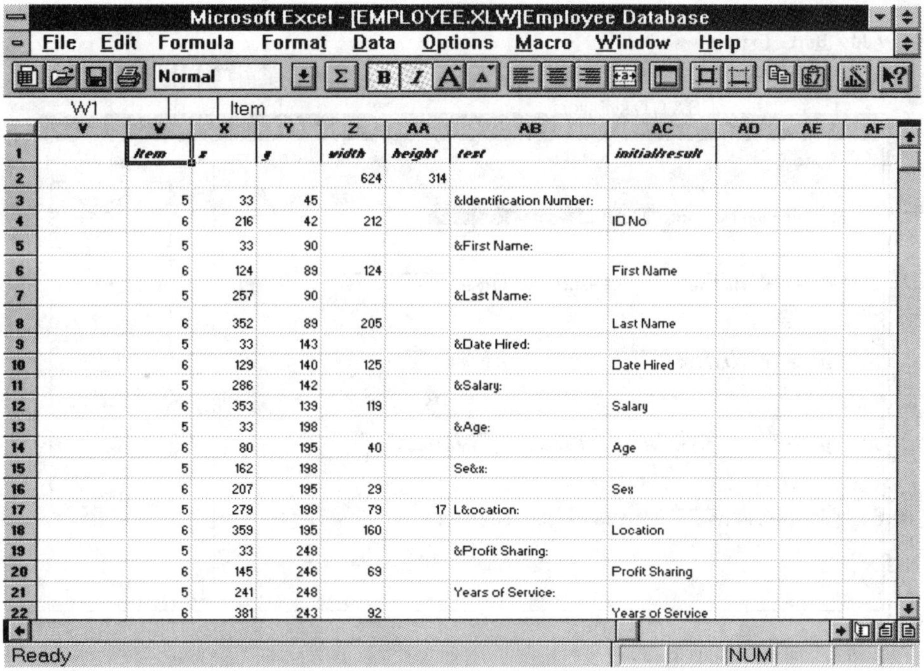

	V	W	X	Y	Z	AA	AB	AC	AD	AE	AF
1		*Item*	*x*	*y*	*width*	*height*	*text*	*initial/result*			
2					624	314					
3		5	33	45			&Identification Number:				
4		6	216	42	212			ID No			
5		5	33	90			&First Name:				
6		6	124	89	124			First Name			
7		5	257	90			&Last Name:				
8		6	352	89	205			Last Name			
9		5	33	143			&Date Hired:				
10		6	129	140	125			Date Hired			
11		5	286	142			&Salary:				
12		6	353	139	119			Salary			
13		5	33	198			&Age:				
14		6	80	195	40			Age			
15		5	162	198			Se&x:				
16		6	207	195	29			Sex			
17		5	279	198	79	17	L&ocation:				
18		6	359	195	160			Location			
19		5	33	248			&Profit Sharing:				
20		6	145	246	69			Profit Sharing			
21		5	241	248			Years of Service:				
22		6	381	243	92			Years of Service			

Figure 18.20 The Dialog Definition Table for the Customized Data Form

Edit Info dialog box for each edit text box you add. By adding the field name to the initial/result column of the definition table, you link the dialog box to the database and indicate where the information in each edit text box should be stored when you use the dialog box to add a new record to your database. This also allows you to arrange the edit text boxes and associated fixed text in any order you see fit—you don't have to follow the order of the fields in the database.

Figure 18.21 shows the customized data form for the employee database displayed in its worksheet. Once you give the name Data_Form to a dialog box definition table in your database worksheet, the customized data form using your dialog box is displayed whenever you choose the F**o**rm command on the **D**ata pull-down menu. Note, however, that the scroll bar, command buttons, and current record information (1 of 31 in this example) are added automatically by Excel to the dialog box defined in your definition table. (You never add command buttons to a dialog box that you intend to use as the data form.)

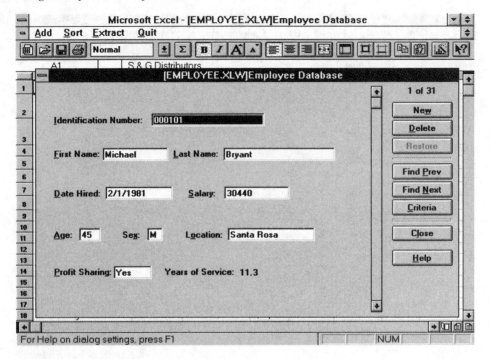

Figure 18.21 The Customized Data Form

SUMMARY

In this chapter you learned how to develop and create custom applications in Excel. Specifically, you learned how to create macros that run automatically when the user opens, closes, activates, or deactivates a particular document. You then learned how to use the structured macro template to help you develop and debug your custom application. Next you learned how to add custom commands to the Excel shortcut and pull-down menus as well as how to create custom menus that you can add to the built-in menu bars or custom menu bars that you create. Finally you learned how to use the Dialog Editor to create custom dialog boxes.

In the next chapter you will learn how to customize the toolbars in Excel. There you will learn how to modify the built-in toolbars that come with Excel as well as how to create toolbars of your own. You will also learn how to assign macros to the toolbars you use.

19

Customizing the Toolbars

Toolbars represent one of the most improved and versatile features in Excel 4.0. Whereas you were restricted to a single toolbar in Excel 3.0, Excel 4.0 provides you with the toolbar introduced in version 3.0 plus six others. Not only can you use these toolbars as they are installed, but you also can easily modify the tools they contain as well as how these tools are arranged. Moreover, you can create your own toolbars that contain only the tools you need to use.

Along with the tools found on the built-in toolbars, Excel 4.0 includes a wide variety of additional tools that you can add to the built-in toolbars or to your new toolbars. If you find that Excel does not already provide a tool for a task that you want to be able to perform from a toolbar, you can create a command macro that performs the task and then assign this macro to a tool.

In this chapter you will learn how to customize the built-in toolbars and create toolbars of your own. If you need information on how to display and work with the built-in toolbars, you should refer to "The Toolbar" section in Chapter 1.

Modifying a Built-in Toolbar

Excel makes it quite simple to modify any of the built-in toolbars. When customizing a toolbar, you can add, remove, or change the order of the tools on a toolbar. Before you can modify a toolbar, you must display it somewhere in the work area. Remember that you can display a toolbar by selecting it on the toolbar shortcut menu (opened by clicking one of the displayed toolbars with the *right* mouse button), as shown in Figure 19.1. If no toolbar is currently displayed in the work area, you can display the toolbar

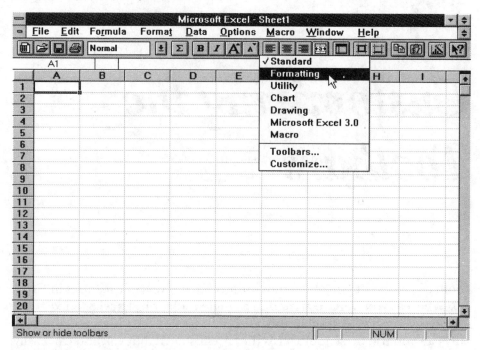

Figure 19.1   The Toolbar Shortcut Menu

you want to customize by choosing the Toolbars command on the Options
menu to open the Toolbars dialog box (shown in Figure 19.2) and then
double-clicking the toolbar in the Show Toolbars list box or by selecting the
toolbar and then choosing the Show command button.

After displaying the built-in toolbar you want to customize, you can
modify it by following these steps:

1. Choose the Customize command on the toolbar shortcut menu or
    choose the Toolbars command on the Options menu and then select
    the Customize command button in the Toolbars dialog box. Excel
    opens the Customize dialog box as shown in Figure 19.3, where you
    can select tools that you want to add to your toolbar. You can also
    make other modifications to the displayed toolbars while this dialog
    box is open, such as removing tools or reordering tools.

2. To add a tool to the toolbar, select the appropriate category in the Cate-
    gories list box, then click the tool in the Tools section of the dialog box,
    drag it to the position on the toolbar where you want the tool to appear,
    and release the mouse button. To get a description of one of the tools
    displayed in the Tools area of the dialog box, click the tool. A brief de-
    scription of the tool's function then appears beneath Tool Description

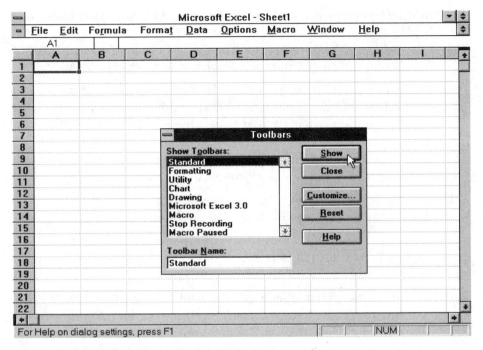

Figure 19.2 The Toolbars Dialog Box

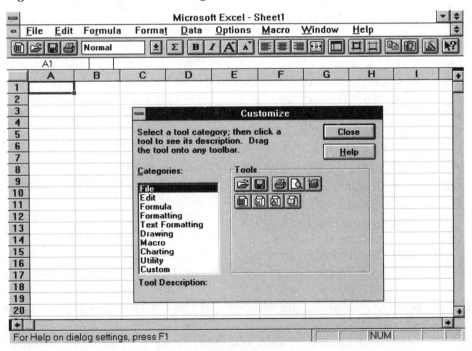

Figure 19.3 The Customize Dialog Box

in the Customize dialog box. When you add a tool, Excel automatically resizes the toolbar to accommodate it. Note, however, that if you add too many tools to a toolbar, you will no longer be able to see the tools at the end of the toolbar when the toolbar is docked.

3. To remove a tool from a toolbar, drag the tool off the toolbar and then release the mouse button. When you delete a tool, Excel closes the gap on the toolbar created by its absence. Note that you cannot use the Undo feature to restore a tool that you remove in error. To restore a tool to a toolbar, you must select the tool in the Tools section and drag it to its original position on the toolbar.

4. To change the position of a tool on a toolbar, drag it to its new position on the toolbar and then release the mouse button.

5. When you've finished modifying the toolbar, close the Customize dialog box by selecting the Close button or pressing the Esc key.

Tip To copy a tool from one displayed toolbar to another (when the Customize dialog box is open), hold down the Ctrl key as you drag the tool to the toolbar where you want it added. When you release the mouse button, Excel adds this tool to the new toolbar without removing it from the original toolbar.

Figure 19.4 shows the modified Standard, Formatting, and Utility toolbars docked around a blank worksheet. The first change that you may notice is that I removed the Style box from the Standard toolbar at the top of the work area. (This box already appears on the Formatting toolbar with the Font and Size boxes.) Other modifications made to the Standard toolbar include moving the Outline Border and Bottom Border tools to the Formatting toolbar (docked at the bottom of the work area) and the Copy and Paste Format tools to the Utility toolbar (docked on the right side of the work area). I also moved the Zoom In, Zoom Out, Lock Cell, Set Print Area, and Calculate Now tools from the Utility toolbar to the Standard toolbar.

In addition to moving tools from one built-in toolbar to another, I also removed some tools and added some others. From the Standard toolbar, I removed the Help tool. From the Formatting toolbar, I removed the Bold, Italics, Underline, Strikeout, Justify Align, and Light Shading tools. From the Utility toolbar, I removed the Sort Ascending, Sort Descending, Promote, Demote, Show Outline Symbols, and Select Visible Cells, Text, and Camera tools.

To the Standard toolbar, I then added the New Chart, New Macro Sheet, and New Workbook tools after the New Worksheet tool at the beginning of

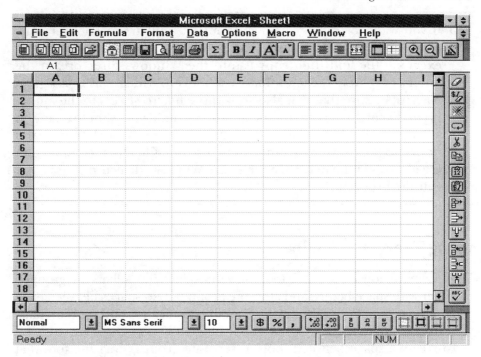

Figure 19.4   Modified Standard, Formatting, and Utility Toolbars

the toolbar; the Print Preview tool in front of the Set Print Area tool; and the Freeze Panes tool after the AutoFormat tool. To the Formatting toolbar, I added the Vertical Text, Rotate Text Up, and Rotate Text Down tools in front of the Light Shading tool and the Bottom Double Line tool between the Outline Border and Bottom Border tools. To the Utility toolbar, I added the Clear Formulas and Clear Formats tools at the beginning of the toolbar; the Cut tool in front of the Copy tool; and the Delete, Delete Row, Delete Column, Insert, Insert Row, and Insert Column tools at the end of the toolbar in front of the Check Spelling tool.

When you exit Excel, the program saves the current arrangement and display of toolbars in a file named **excel.xlb** located in the directory where you installed Windows (**c:\windows** on many computers) so that they are available immediately the next time you start the program. If you want to preserve the previous arrangement and display of toolbars in Excel before you make any modifications, you need to use the Windows File Manager to locate and rename the **excel.xlb** file (such as **excel1.xlb**) before you exit Excel. To switch to a new toolbar arrrangement, you then use the **F**ile **O**pen command to open the toolbar file you want to use in the Windows directory. (Be sure that you save all toolbar files in this directory.)

Tip If you want to transfer your customized toolbars to another computer in the office that uses Excel 4.0, make a backup copy of your **excel.xlb** file and then copy it into the Windows directory on the other computer. If the toolbars use tools to which you've assigned macros, be sure that you also copy those macro sheets to the appropriate Excel directories on the new machine. If you want to abandon all changes you've made to the Excel toolbars in a work session and return to the previous arrangement, use the **File Open** command in Excel to open the **excel.xlb** file in the Windows directory before you exit the program.

Grouping Tools on a Toolbar

You may have noticed how the tools on various built-in toolbars are grouped together with space before and after the group but no spaces between each tool in the group. When modifying a toolbar, you can group tools to make your own arrangements.

To create a space between tools to separate groups, drag the tool that should be preceded by a space to the right so that the tool overlaps the adjacent tool about halfway, then release the mouse button. Excel inserts a space before the tool that you just dragged.

To remove a space in front of a tool to join that tool to an existing group on the left, drag the tool to the left so that it overlaps the adjacent tool at least halfway, then release the mouse button. Excel removes the space in front of the tool that you just dragged.

Restoring a Built-in Toolbar

Sometimes you may make changes to a built-in toolbar that you don't want to keep. No matter what changes you've made to a built-in toolbar, you can always restore it to its original contents and layout. To do this, choose the **T**oolbars command on the **O**ptions menu, then select the toolbar you want to restore to its original condition in the Show Toolbars list box, then choose the **R**eset command button. If the toolbar you restored is not displayed, you then can display it by choosing the **S**how command button. If the toolbar is already displayed, you can close the Toolbars dialog box by choosing the Close button instead.

Creating a New Toolbar

As mentioned, you are not limited to the built-in toolbars that come with Excel. The program makes it easy to create as many of your own toolbars as you like. When creating your own toolbars, you can combine any of the available tools, both those that already are used in the built-in toolbars as well as those that are not. Table 19.1 contains a complete list of available built-in tools arranged by category in the order in which they appear in the Customize dialog box. This table includes all tools displayed in every category except the Custom category. All the tools in this category are blank so that you can assign macros to them. (See "Assigning Macros to Tools" later in this chapter for details on how to assign command macros to these tools.)

Table 19.1 Summary of Available Tools

Tool	Tool Name	Description	Tool Number
File Tools			
	Open File	Lets you open an existing document.	1
	Save File	Saves changes made to the active document.	2
	Print	Prints the active document.	3
	Print Preview	Displays the active document in print preview mode.	4
	Set Print Area	Sets the current selection as the area to print.	5
	New Worksheet	Creates a new worksheet.	7
	New Chart	Creates a new chart.	8
	New Macro Sheet	Creates a new macro sheet.	6
	New Workbook	Creates a new workbook.	9

Table 19.1   *(continued)*

Edit Tools			
	Undo	Undoes last action or command.	10
	Repeat	Repeats last action or command.	11
	Cut	Cuts selection and places it in the Clipboard.	12
	Copy	Copies selection into the Clipboard.	13
	Paste	Pastes contents of the Clipboard.	14
	Clear Formulas	Clears only formulas or values in the selection.	15
	Clear Formats	Clears only formats in the selection.	16
	Paste Formats	Pastes only formats from copied selection.	17
	Paste Values	Pastes only values from copied selection.	18
	Delete	Deletes selected cells.	19
	Delete Row	Deletes selected rows.	20
	Delete Column	Deletes selected columns.	21
	Insert	Inserts blank cells.	22
	Insert Row	Inserts blank rows.	23
	Insert Column	Inserts blank columns.	24
	Fill Right	Copies values, formulas, and formats to cells to the right or left.	25
	Fill Down	Copies values, formulas, and formats to cells down or up.	26

Table 19.1 *(continued)*

Formula Tools

"="	Equal Sign	Inserts the equal sign (=) in the formula bar.	27
"+"	Plus Sign	Inserts the plus sign (+) in the formula bar.	28
"−"	Minus Sign	Inserts the minus sign (−) in the formula bar.	29
"*"	Multiplication Sign	Inserts the multiplication sign (*) in the formula bar.	30
"/"	Division Sign	Inserts the division sign (/) in the formula bar.	31
"^"	Exponentiation Sign	Inserts the caret (^) for exponentiation in the formula bar.	32
"("	Left Parenthesis	Inserts left parenthesis (() in the formula bar.	33
")"	Right Parenthesis	Inserts right parenthesis ()) in the formula bar.	34
":"	Colon	Inserts colon (:) in the formula bar.	35
","	Comma	Inserts comma (,) in the formula bar.	36
"%"	Percent Sign	Inserts percent sign (%) in the formula bar.	37
"$"	Dollar Sign	Inserts dollar sign ($) in the formula bar.	38
Σ	AutoSum	Inserts SUM function and proposes the sum range.	39
=f(x)	Paste Function	Displays dialog box to insert a function.	40

Table 19.1   *(continued)*

Formula Tools (continued)

| | Paste Names | Displays dialog box to insert a name. | 41 |
| | Constrain Numeric | Constrains pen recognition to digits and punctuation. | 42 |

Formatting Tools

	Outline Border	Adds border around outer edge of the selected cells.	43
	Left Border	Adds or removes border along the left edge of the selected cells.	44
	Right Border	Adds or removes border along the right edge of the selected cells.	45
	Top Border	Adds or removes border along the top edge of the selected cells.	46
	Bottom Border	Adds or removes border along the bottom edge of the selected cells.	47
	Bottom Double Border	Adds or removes double border along the bottom edge of the selected cells.	48
	Dark Shading	Applies dark shading to the selected cells.	49
	Light Shading	Applies light shading to the selected cells.	50
	AutoFormat	Applies the last table format you used.	52
	Currency Style	Applies currency number format to the selected cells.	53

Table 19.1 *(continued)*

Formatting Tools (continued)

%	Percent Style	Applies percent number format to the selected cells.	54
,	Comma Style	Applies comma number format to the selected cells.	55
+.0 .00	Increase Decimal	Adds one decimal place to the number format.	56
.00 +.0	Decrease Decimal	Removes one decimal place to the number format.	57
Style	Style Box	Applies or defines cell style.	70

Text Formatting Tools

B	Bold	Applies bold to the selected text.	58
I	Italic	Applies italics to the selected text.	59
U	Underline	Applies underlining to the selected text.	60
K	Strikeout	Applies strikeout to the selected text.	61
	Text Color	Changes the color of the selected text.	62
	Left Align	Left aligns text.	63
	Center Align	Centers text in cells, buttons, or text boxes.	64
	Right Align	Right aligns text.	65
	Justify Align	Justifies text.	66
	Center Across Columns	Centers text across the selected columns.	67

Table 19.1   *(continued)*

Text Formatting (continued)

`10`	Font Size Box	Changes the font size.	68
`Font`	Font Name Box	Changes the font.	69
`Style`	Style Box	Applies or defines cell style.	70
	Increase Font Size	Increases font size of the selected text.	71
	Decrease Font Size	Decreases font size of the selected text.	72
	Vertical Text	Aligns letters one below the other.	73
	Rotate Text Up	Rotates the text sideways bottom to top.	74
	Rotate Text Down	Rotates the text sideways top to bottom.	75

Drawing Tools

	Line	Draws straight lines.	76
	Arrow	Adds an arrow.	77
	Freehand	Draws freehand lines.	78
	Text Box	Adds text box or unattached text.	79
	Button	Adds a macro button.	80
	Selection	Selects graphic objects enclosed in selection rectangle.	81
	Reshape	Changes the shape of polygons.	82
	Rectangle	Draws rectangles or squares.	83

Table 19.1 *(continued)*

Drawing Tools (continued)

	Oval	Draws ovals or circles.	84
	Arc	Draws arc or circle segment.	85
	Polygon	Draws polygons.	86
	Freehand Polygon	Draws freehand and polygon shapes.	87
	Filled Rectangle	Draws rectangles or squares filled with the window background color and pattern.	88
	Filled Oval	Draws ovals or circles filled with the window background color and pattern.	89
	Filled Arc	Draws arc or circle segment filled with the window background color and pattern.	90
	Filled Polygon	Draws polygons filled with the window background color and pattern.	91
	Filled Freehand Polygon	Draws freehand and polygon shapes filled with the window background color and pattern.	92
	Group	Groups selected graphic objects into a single object.	93
	Ungroup	Separates grouped objects into separate objects.	94
	Bring to Front	Places selected objects in front of the others they overlap.	95
	Send to Back	Places selected objects behind the others they overlap.	96

Table 19.1 *(continued)*

Drawing Tools (continued)

	Color	Changes foreground color of selected cells or objects.	97
	Dark Shading	Applies dark shading to the selected cells.	49
	Light Shading	Applies light shading to the selected cells.	50
	Drop Shadow	Adds drop shadow effect around the selected cells or object.	51

Macro Tools

	Record Macro	Records your actions to create a macro.	98
	Stop Recording	Stops recording a macro.	99
	Run Macro	Runs the macro in the active cell of the macro sheet.	100
	Step Macro	Steps through the macro in the active cell of the macro sheet.	101
	Resume Macro	Resumes the running of a macro after it has been paused.	102
	Paste Function	Displays the dialog box to insert a function.	40
	Paste Name	Displays the dialog box to insert a name.	41

Charting Tools

	Area Chart	Creates a simple area chart.	103
	Bar Chart	Creates a simple bar chart.	104

Table 19.1 *(continued)*

Charting Tools (continued)

	Column Chart	Creates a simple column chart.	105
	Stacked Column Chart	Creates a simple stacked column chart.	106
	Line Chart	Creates a simple line chart.	107
	Pie Chart	Creates a pie chart with percentage labels.	108
	3-D Area Chart	Creates a 3-D area chart.	109
	3-D Bar Chart	Creates a 3-D bar chart.	110
	3-D Column Chart	Creates a 3-D column chart.	111
	3-D Perspective Column Chart	Creates a 3-D column chart with a 3-D plot area.	112
	3-D Line Chart	Creates a 3-D line chart.	113
	3-D Pie Chart	Creates a 3-D pie chart with percentage labels.	114
	XY (Scatter) Chart	Creates an XY (scatter) chart.	115
	3-D Surface Chart	Creates a 3-D surface chart.	116
	Radar Chart	Creates a radar chart.	117
	Line/Column Chart	Creates a combination chart with a column chart overlaid by a line chart.	118
	Volume/Hi-Lo-Close Chart	Creates a combination chart for stock prices.	119
	Preferred Chart	Creates an embedded chart in the preferred format.	120

Table 19.1   *(continued)*

Charting Tools (continued)

	ChartWizard	Starts the ChartWizard so that you can create or edit an embedded chart.	121
	Vertical Gridlines	Adds or deletes gridlines for the major category axis.	123
	Horizontal Gridlines	Adds or deletes gridlines for the major values axis.	122
	Legend	Adds or deletes a legend.	124
	Arrow	Adds an arrow.	77
	Text Box	Adds text box or unattached text.	79

Utility Tools

	AutoSum	Inserts SUM function and proposes the sum range.	39
	Text Box	Adds text box or unattached text.	79
	Button	Adds a macro button.	80
	Camera	Pastes a linked picture of the current selection.	125
	Calculate Now	Calculates the formulas in all open documents or in the formula bar if it is active.	126
	Check Spelling	Starts the spelling checker.	127
	Help	Gives you context-sensitive help on the command or option you select.	128
	Promote	Promotes selected rows or columns in an outlined worksheet.	129

Table 19.1 *(continued)*

Utility Tools (continued)

Demote	Demotes selected rows or columns in an outlined worksheet.	130
Show Outline Symbols	Shows and hides outline symbols in an outlined worksheet or creates a new outline for the selection.	131
Select Visible Cells	Selects those cells that are visible in the current selection.	132
Select Current Region	Selects the region in the worksheet containing the active cell.	133
Sort Ascending	Sorts selected rows in ascending order.	134
Sort Descending	Sorts selected rows in descending order.	135
Lock Cell	Locks and unlocks selected cells and objects.	136
Freeze Panes	Freezes and unfreezes split panes in the active worksheet window.	137
Paste Name	Displays dialog box to insert a name.	41
Paste Function	Displays dialog box to insert a function.	40

To create a new toolbar, you follow these steps:

1. Choose the **To**olbars command on the **O**ptions menu to display the Toolbars dialog box.

2. Select the Toolbar **N**ame text box and replace the name of the currently selected toolbar with the name you wish to give to your new toolbar.

3. Choose the **A**dd command button or press the Enter key to open the Customize dialog box. Excel also creates a toolbar dialog box in the upper-left corner of the work area to which you add the tools you want included in your new toolbar.

4. Choose the category containing the first tool you want to add to your new toolbar in the **C**ategories list box, then drag the tool from the Tools section to the tiny toolbar dialog box as shown in Figure 19.5.

5. Select the appropriate category, then drag the tool you want added next to the new toolbar from the Customize dialog box to the desired position in the small toolbar dialog box. As you add tools, Excel automatically widens the toolbar dialog box. (When the dialog box becomes wide enough, the name you assigned to the toolbar appears in the title bar.) If the toolbar dialog box runs into the Customize dialog box, drag the new toolbar down (by its title bar) in the work area until it is clear of the Customize dialog box.

6. Repeat step 5 until you have added all of the tools you want in your new toolbar.

7. Press the Esc key or select the Close command button to close the Customize toolbar.

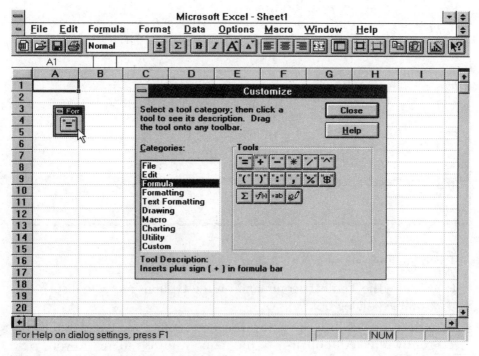

Figure 19.5   Creating a New Toolbar

Figure 19.6 shows you the completed Formula toolbar after closing the Customize dialog box. The tools on this new toolbar enable you to enter the operators and punctuation in your formulas by clicking the appropriate tool.

> ***Note:*** You can also create a new toolbar simply by dragging one of the tools from the Customize dialog box to somewhere in the work area outside of that box. When you release the mouse button, Excel encloses the tool you drag in its own tiny toolbar dialog box to which you can then add other tools. When you start a new toolbar in this way, Excel assigns a default name to it, such as Toolbar1, Toolbar2, and so on, which you cannot replace with a more descriptive toolbar name.

After creating a new toolbar, you can display and hide as well as modify it just as you would any of the built-in toolbars. (The names of your custom toolbars appear below the names of the built-in toolbars in the Show Toolbars list box and on the toolbar shortcut menu.)

To delete a toolbar (Excel won't allow you to delete any of the built-in toolbars), you open the Toolbars dialog box (with the **O**ptions **T**oolbars command), then select the name of the custom toolbar in the Show Toolbars list box, and choose the **D**elete command button. Excel then displays

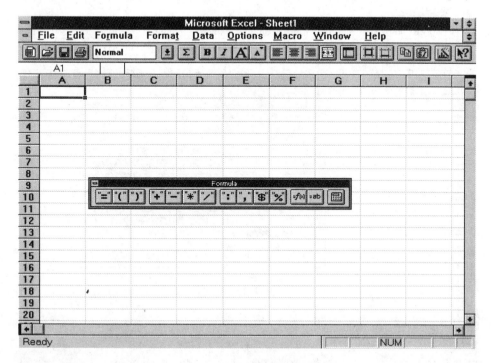

Figure 19.6 New Formula Toolbar upon Completion

an alert box asking you if you are sure that you want to delete the selected toolbar. Choose the OK button to remove the toolbar permanently. Note too that Excel also deletes a custom toolbar when you remove the last tool from its toolbar dialog box. You cannot use the Undo feature to restore a deleted toolbar—you must re-create it from scratch.

Assigning Macros to Tools

Excel makes it easy to assign the command macros that you create to a toolbar. The program provides you with a number of blank tools in the Custom category of the Customize dialog box to which you can assign macros (shown in Figure 19.7). If none of the icons provided by these tools will do, you can use the tool with a blank face (the last tool in the fourth row of the Tools area) and paste your own picture onto it (a technique discussed later in "Customizing Individual Tools").

To assign a macro to one of the Custom tools, you follow these steps:

1. Display the toolbar that is to contain the tool with the macro and, if the macro is not a global one, open the macro sheet containing the macro you want to assign.

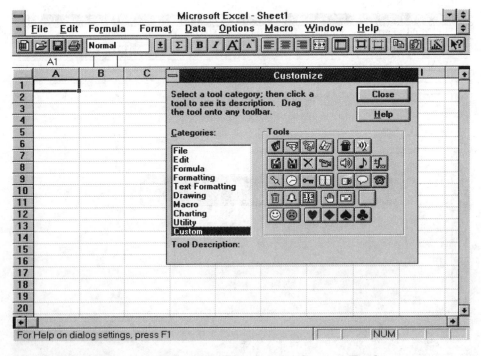

Figure 19.7 Customize Dialog Box Showing the Custom Tools

2. Open the Customize dialog box by choosing the Customize option on the toolbar shortcut menu or select **O**ptions **T**oolbars and choose the **C**ustomize command button.

3. Select the Custom category in the **C**ategories list box.

4. Drag the Custom tool to which you want to assign your command macro to the toolbar where you want the tool to appear. Excel opens the Assign To Tool dialog box, similar to the one shown in Figure 19.8, where you can select or record the macro you want to assign to the tool.

5. To assign an existing macro to the tool, double-click the macro name in the Assign **M**acro list box or select the macro and the OK button. To record a new macro for the selected tool, choose the **R**ecord command button and record this macro as you would any other.

6. Press the Esc key or choose the Close button on the Customize dialog box when you have finished assigning macros to tools and those tools to your toolbars.

After assigning a macro to a tool, you can start the macro at any time simply by displaying its toolbar and then clicking the tool. To delete a tool

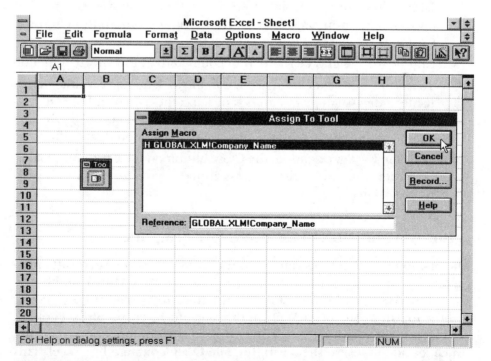

Figure 19.8   The Assign To Tool Dialog Box

to which you have assigned a macro, display its toolbar, open the Customize dialog box, and then drag the Custom tool off the toolbar. Note, however, that you cannot restore a deleted Custom tool with the Undo feature. If you remove a tool in error, you will have to go through all of the steps outlined above to assign your macro and add the tool to the appropriate toolbar.

Reassigning Macros to Tools

If you decide that you would like to assign a different macro to an existing tool (Custom or in some other category), you can do so by taking these steps:

1.   Display the toolbar containing the tool with the macro to which you want to assign a new macro.

2.   Open the Customize dialog box by choosing the Customize option on the toolbar shortcut menu or select **O**ptions **T**oolbars and choose the **C**ustomize command button.

3.   Display the Tool shortcut menu by positioning the pointer on the tool to which you want to assign a new macro and then clicking this tool with the *right* mouse button. Note how this shortcut menu (shown in Figure 19.9) differs from the Toolbar shortcut menu that appears when you click a tool with the right mouse button and the Customize dialog box is not displayed.

4.   Choose the Assign Macro To Tool command on this shortcut menu.

5.   To assign a different existing macro to the tool, double-click the macro name in the Assign **M**acro list box or select the macro and the OK button. To record a new macro for the selected tool, choose the **R**ecord command button and record this macro as you would any other.

6.   Press the Esc key or choose the Close button on the Customize dialog box when you have finished reassigning macros to tools on the displayed toolbars.

Tools for Switching to Other Microsoft Programs

The first four Custom tools can be used to switch to other Microsoft applications. The first tool is used to switch from Excel to Word for Windows, the second to switch to Microsoft Project, the third to Microsoft PowerPoint, and the fourth to Microsoft Mail (in the Macintosh version of Excel only). To assign these switching functions to these custom tools, you open the **switch.xla** add-in macro sheet with the **File O**pen command in Excel. This file is located in the **\library** directory of the **c:\excel** directory.

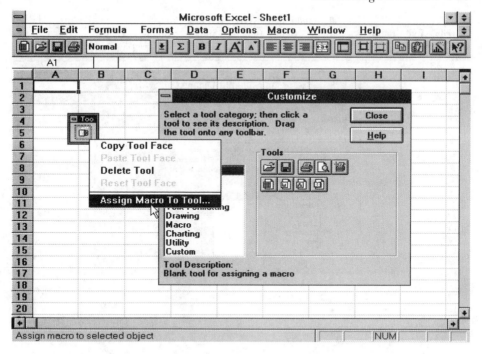

Figure 19.9 The Tool Shortcut Menu that Appears When the Customize Dialog Box Is Open

As soon as you open this add-in macro, the Applications Switching Tools dialog box shown in Figure 19.10 appears. To assign the Microsoft Word tool to a toolbar, choose the toolbar in the **T**oolbar list box, then choose the **A**dd button. To skip to the next tool (the Microsoft Project tool), choose the **S**kip button instead. Continue in this manner either assigning or skipping the remaining switching tools (Microsoft Project, Microsoft Powerpoint, and Microsoft Mail).

After assigning any of these tools to a toolbar, you can switch instantly to the desired Microsoft application by clicking the tool (provided your computer has sufficient memory). If the application is not already open, the macro starts the program. If the application is open, the macro displays its active document.

Customizing Individual Tools

Although Excel provides a variety of icons on the Custom tools, you can use pictures from other sources (either clip art or graphics that you create with a Windows drawing program) and paste them onto copies of the one Custom tool with a blank face. When using pictures from other sources, you have to

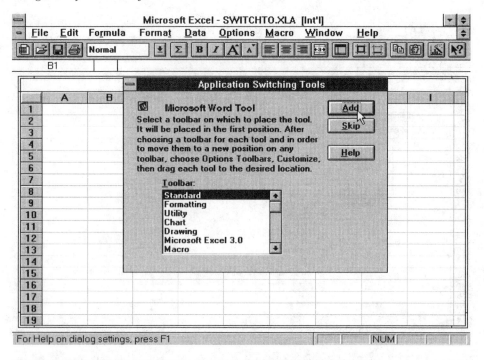

Figure 19.10   The Application Switching Tools Dialog Box

keep in mind the extremely small size of the each tool. (The size of each tool face is only 16 pixels wide by 15 pixels high.) When creating or choosing an icon for a tool, you need to make sure the picture is sufficiently simple to remain visible when reduced to such a small size.

Even though Excel will automatically size any picture that you paste onto the face of a blank tool, the best way to tell if your picture will be too small when it appears on the tool is to paste the face of the blank tool to your graphics application via the Clipboard and then reduce the picture until it fits on the face of the tool as follows:

1. Add the Custom tool with a blank face to the appropriate toolbar and assign the desired macro to this tool as outlined earlier.

2. With the Customize dialog box open, display the Tool shortcut menu and select the Copy Tool Face command on this menu.

3. Switch to the graphics program where you have drawn the picture you want to assign to your tool or are going to manipulate the clip art image you are going to use.

4. Choose the **Paste** command on that program's **Edit** menu to copy the face of the blank tool into the graphics document containing your

picture. Figure 19.11 shows you the blank tool face after copying it into the Microsoft Draw program containing the picture of a star that must be greatly reduced to fit the size of the tool face.

5. Resize the picture until it will fit on top of the rectangle representing the face of the blank tool.

6. If you are satisfied with how the pictures look on the tool face, select the picture, then choose the **C**opy command on the **E**dit menu to copy the picture to the Clipboard.

To paste the graphic that you copied into the Clipboard onto a blank tool in your toolbar, you follow these steps:

1. Switch to Excel and display the toolbar containing the blank tool onto whose face you want to paste the picture.

2. Open the Customize dialog box by choosing the Customize option on the toolbar shortcut menu, or select **O**ptions **T**oolbars and choose the **C**ustomize command button.

3. Display the Tool shortcut menu by positioning the pointer on the blank tool and then clicking this tool with the *right* mouse button.

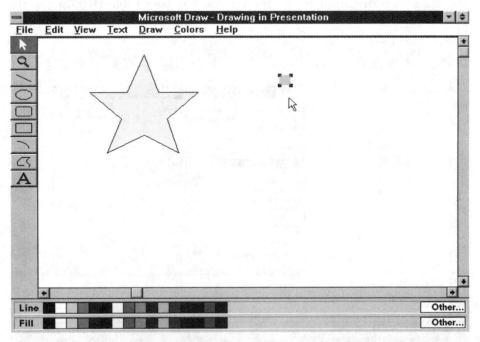

Figure 19.11 Comparing the Size of a Tool Face to That of the Graphic to Be Used as an Icon

4. Choose the Paste Tool Face command on the shortcut menu. Excel pastes the graphic from the Clipboard onto the face of the selected tool, automatically reducing the size of the picture, if necessary. Figure 19.12 shows you the picture of the star after pasting it onto the selected tool in the new toolbar.

5. Press the Esc button or choose the Close button to close the Customize dialog box.

Using Toolbars in Custom Applications

You can use macro functions in your custom applications that create, modify, or delete toolbars. To add tools to your toolbar, create the toolbar, and display it in your applications, you use the macro functions ADD.TOOL, ADD.TOOLBAR, and SHOW.TOOLBAR in much the same way you use the ADD.MENU, ADD.BAR, and SHOW.BAR functions to add a menu to a menu bar, create the menu bar, and then display it in Excel. (See Chapter 18 for details on creating custom menus.)

The ADD.TOOL macro function follows the syntax

=ADD.TOOL(bar_id,position,tool_ref)

where *bar_id* is the number of a built-in toolbar (see Table 19.2 for the ID

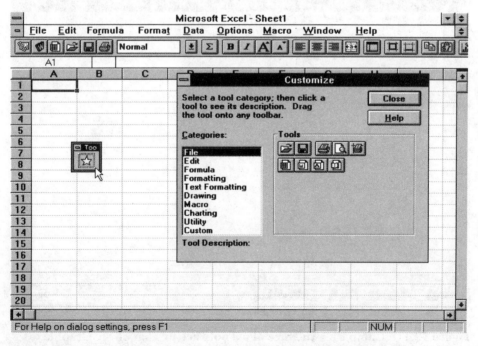

Figure 19.12 Pasting the Picture onto a Tool with a Blank Face

numbers of the built-in toolbars) or the name of a custom toolbar, *position* specifies the number of the position of the tool on the toolbar (starting with 1 at the left side if the bar is horizontal or the top if the bar is vertical), and *tool_ref* is the number of a built-in tool (tool numbers are listed in the last column of Table 19.1) or a reference to a table on a macro sheet or an array that defines a custom tool.

When creating a table for defining custom tools on a macro sheet, you lay the table out in eight columns as follows:

1. In the first column, you place the ID number of the tool. For custom tools, you need to assign a number greater than 140. To create a gap on the toolbar, you enter 0 (zero) as the ID number.

2. In the second column, you enter the name of the macro to assign to the custom tool.

3. In the third column, you enter a Down value of TRUE or FALSE to indicate whether the tool should appear depressed on the toolbar (TRUE) or not (FALSE).

4. In the fourth column, you enter an Enabled value of TRUE or FALSE to indicate whether the tool is available to the user (TRUE) or dimmed (FALSE).

5. In the fifth column, you enter a reference to the object (such as Rectangle 3) that you want used on the face of the custom tool. If this column is left blank for your custom tool, Excel uses a default tool face.

6. In the sixth column, enter the Help text that you want to appear on the status bar when the user selects this tool.

7. In the seventh column, enter the text you want to appear in the Balloon Help for this tool. (This column is used only when building a table in the Macintosh version of Excel running under System 7.0 or higher.)

8. In the eighth column, enter the reference (Help file and topic number separated by an exclamation point) to the custom Help topic, if any, you want to assign to the custom tool.

To create a custom toolbar, you use the ADD.TOOLBAR macro function that follows this syntax:

```
=ADD.TOOLBAR(bar_id,tool_ref)
```

where *bar_id* is a text string identifying your toolbar (such as "Toolbar10") and *tool_ref* is a reference to the definition table in the macro sheet that indicates what tools are to be included on this new toolbar. If you omit the

---

Table 19.2 ID Numbers of the Built-In Toolbars

Bar ID	Toolbar
1	Standard
2	Formatting
3	Utility
4	Chart
5	Drawing
6	Excel 3.0
7	Macro
8	Macro Recording
9	Macro Paused

---

tool_ref argument from this function, Excel adds an empty toolbar (to which you can add tools with the ADD.TOOL macro function).

When Excel evaluates the ADD.TOOLBAR macro function, the program returns the number of the toolbar to the cell containing this function but does not display the toolbar. To display it, you need to use the SHOW.TOOLBAR function, which follows the syntax

=SHOW.TOOLBAR(bar_num)

where *bar_num* is the number of the toolbar you want displayed or a reference to the cell that contains the ADD.TOOLBAR function. (This is the safest way to refer to a toolbar because it will display the correct toolbar even if the toolbar number changes when the user runs your application.)

Note: There are several other macro functions that you may need to use when creating an application that uses toolbars, including DELETE.TOOL, EDIT.TOOL, ENABLE.TOOL, GET.TOOL, LOAD.TOOLBAR, MOVE.TOOLBAR, SAVE.TOOLBAR, SELECT.TOOL, and TOOLBAR.SIZE.

SUMMARY

In this chapter you learned how to customize Excel by modifying the tool-bars. Specifically, you learned how to modify the built-in toolbars by adding, removing, and rearranging their tools. You also learned how to create new toolbars and assign command macros to tools. Finally you learned how to customize individual tools and the macro functions that you can use when you want your custom applications to include toolbars.

In the chapter ahead you will learn how to customize Excel by using add-in macro and custom functions. There you will learn how to convert your command macros to add-in macros and how to create custom functions that perform specialized calculations but work like the built-in functions in Excel.

20

Working with Add-in Commands and Functions

Add-in macros enable you to customize Excel by making their commands and functions appear as if they were a standard part of the program. When you open an add-in macro, Excel automatically hides its macro sheet (and you cannot unhide it), and the commands and/or functions in the macro sheet become immediately available to the Excel user as an integral part of the program. For example, if you open an add-in macro sheet containing custom functions that you have developed, these functions are added to the Paste Function dialog box, where they appear in alphabetical order along with the other built-in functions. Likewise, if you open an add-in macro sheet containing command macros that add custom commands to menus on the worksheet menu bar, these commands appear in the specified order on the pull-down menus as if they were regular worksheet commands.

In this chapter you will learn how to create and manage add-in macros that you use routinely. Before learning more about add-in macros, however, you first need to know how to create custom functions for your worksheets. This is done by creating the second of the two types of macros, function macros.

Creating Custom Functions

A *custom function* (also known as a *user-defined function*) is one that you create in a macro sheet, using formulas and Excel's other built-in worksheet functions. When you create a custom function, you specify the type of result you want the function to return as well as the arguments required when using the function. For example, you could create a Sales_Commission function

757

to calculate sales commissions for your salespeople by entering the weekly or monthly sales figures as the function's argument, or you could create a Discount_Price function that calculates the sales price when you enter the retail price and discount rate as the arguments of this function.

To use a custom function in your worksheet, you must open the macro sheet containing the function (unless you've saved the function macros in the global macro sheet **global.xlm**). When entering the function, you include an external reference to the macro sheet containing the function as well as the function name (separated by an exclamation point) and whatever arguments are required. For instance, if you have created a custom function called Sales_Commission in a macro sheet named **function.xlm** that requires a single argument called Sales, the syntax of the custom function would be

    =FUNCTION.XLM!Sales_Commission(Sales)

where *Sales* is the amount of sales for which you want to calculate commissions. To make it easier to use custom functions, you can have Excel display the function in the Paste Function and then use the Paste Function command on the Formula menu to paste it into a cell of your worksheet.

When creating a custom function, you normally use the RESULT, ARGUMENT, and RETURN macro functions. The RESULT function indicates the type of result you expect the custom function to return. The RESULT function follows the syntax

    =RESULT(type_num)

where *type_num* is the number of the data type you want returned (as shown in Table 20.1). If you want to allow more than one type of data to be returned, you enter the sum of their type numbers. For example, to allow the return of either number or text data, you would enter **3** (the sum of 1 for

Table 20.1   Data Type Numbers

Type Number	Data Type
1	Number
2	Text
4	Logical
8	Reference
16	Error
64	Array

number and 2 for text) as the argument of the RESULT function.

If you omit RESULT from your function macro, Excel assumes a result number of 7 for the custom function, which allows the return of a number (1), text (2), or logical value (4) as the result (1+2+4=7). If you do use RESULT in your function macro, you make it the first function in your macro, and the *type_num* argument you use must be matched in the data types you specify for the ARGUMENT macro functions that follow.

The ARGUMENT macro function is used to specify what type of arguments are required when using your custom function. The syntax of the ARGUMENT macro function is

=ARGUMENT(name_text,data_type_num,reference)

where *name_text* specifies the argument name (as quoted text), *data_type_num* specifies the number of the data type that the argument will accept (refer to Table 20.1 for data type numbers), and *reference* specifies a reference to a cell or cell range where Excel places the argument entered by the user. If you specify a *data_type_num* argument, you don't specify a reference argument and vice versa.

As when specifying the data type for the RESULT function, you can allow the user to enter more than one type of data for an argument by entering the sum of the data type numbers as the *data_type_num* argument. If you omit the data_type_num and reference argument from the ARGUMENT macro function, Excel assumes a default value of 7 and allows the user to enter a number, text, or a logical value for the argument.

When building a custom function, your function macro must include at least one ARGUMENT function. When defining more than one argument for a custom function, you need to pay close attention to the order in which you define them with the ARGUMENT macro function. The order in which the ARGUMENT functions appear in the function macro determine the order in which the user must enter his or her arguments in the custom function itself.

After defining the arguments for your custom function, you need to enter the formula that specifies what calculations are to be performed with them. When defining the formula for a custom function, you enter it just as you would in a worksheet except that you refer to the arguments by their names instead of using cell references. For example, if you want your custom Sales_Commission function to multiply the amount of sales entered for the *Sales* argument by 10 percent, you would enter the following formula in the custom function of the function macro:

=Sales*10%

After entering the formula for the custom function, you then assign a range name to its cell in the macro sheet. Then, in the cell below, you complete the function macro by entering a RETURN function that specifies that range name as the argument. For instance, if you assign the name Commissions to the cell in the macro sheet that contains the sales commissions formula (shown above), you would enter the return function

=RETURN(Commissions)

in the last cell of your custom function.

Figure 20.1 shows you the contents of just such a Sales_Commission custom function in a macro sheet named **function.xlm**. After entering these macro functions in the cell range B3:B6, you still need to name the function with the **D**efine Name on the Fo**r**mula menu command before you can use it. Figure 20.2 shows you the Define Name dialog box when assigning a name to the first cell of this function macro. To have the function macro added to the Paste Function dialog box, you need to select the **F**unction option button in the Macro area of the Define Function dialog box. When you select this option button, the Category drop-down list box, where you indicate in which category the custom function should appear, becomes available. By default, Excel adds the custom function to

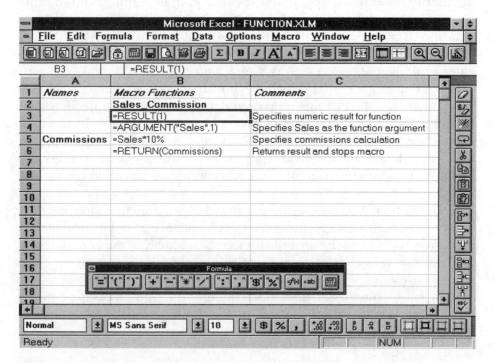

Figure 20.1 The Sales_Commission Function Macro

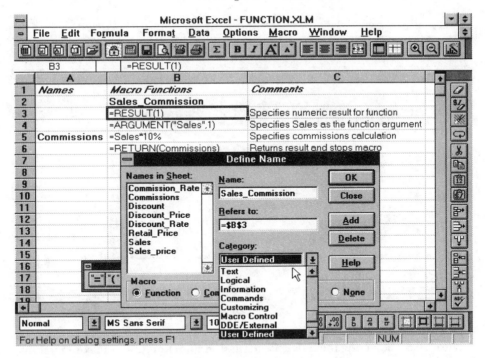

Figure 20.2 Defining the Name for the Sales_Commission Function Macro

the User Defined category, but you can select any another category that you think is more appropriate.

To finish the function macro, you have to assign a name to the cell containing the function's formula (used as the argument in the final RETURN macro function). When you define the name for this cell, you do not select any of the Macro options—simply name the cell as you normally would.

To use a custom function in a worksheet, you need to open its macro sheet then switch to the worksheet document. If you added the custom function to the Paste Function dialog box, you can add the function to a cell by choosing the Paste Function command on the Formula menu. Select the function's category in the Function Category list box, then choose the function in the Paste Function list box. If you want Excel to paste in the arguments along with the function on the formula bar, leave the Paste Arguments check selected when you choose the OK button.

Figure 20.3 shows you the Paste Function dialog box after selecting the Sales_Commission custom function for pasting onto the formula bar along with a description of its single argument. Figure 20.4 shows you the formula bar after pasting this custom function. To complete the entry for this function, you simply replace *Sales* in the function on the formula bar by

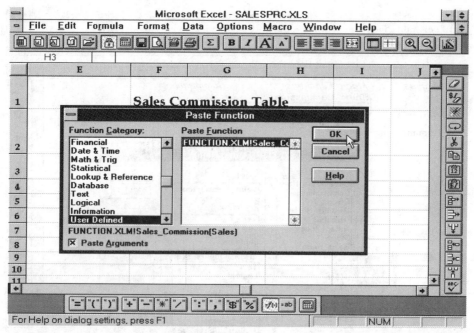

Figure 20.3   Selecting the Sales_Commission Function in the Paste Function Dialog Box

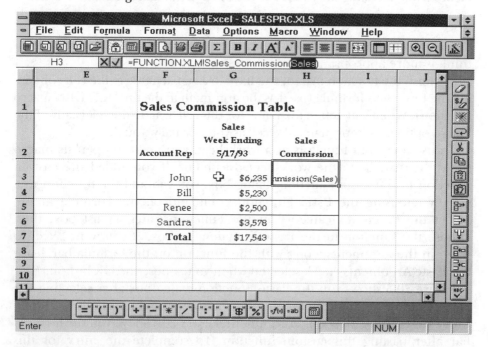

Figure 20.4   Pasting the Sales_Commission Function in a Cell with Its Argument

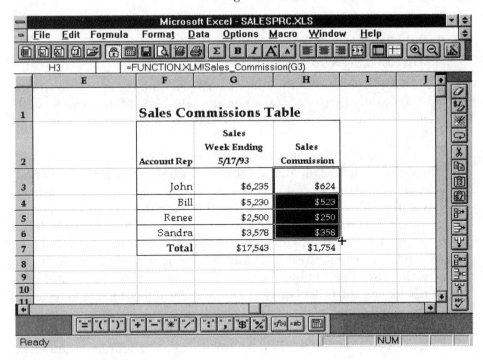

Figure 20.5   Sales_Commission Function After Copying

selecting the cell that contains the weekly sales (cell G3 in this example) and then press the Enter key. Figure 20.5 shows the Sales Commissions Table after entering the function in cell H3 and copying it down the column to the cell range H4:H8.

 Tip   If you open a worksheet containing custom functions before you open the macro sheet that contains their function macros, the cells using these functions will display REF! error values. To prevent this from happening, you can add the worksheet and macro sheet to a workbook file so that the function macros are always opened with the worksheet that uses the custom functions. (See Chapter 10 for details on how to add documents to a workbook.)

Editing a Custom Function

After creating and using a custom function in a worksheet, you can change the way the function works simply by editing its formula in the function macro. Figure 20.6 shows you an example of this type of change. There I have edited the formula for the Sales_Commission custom function by adding an IF function that evaluates the amount of the weekly sales and determines which commission rate to use based on the outcome as follows:

    =IF(Sales>5000,Sales*10%,Sales*8%)

Using this edited version of the formula, the custom function multiplies the amount of sales by 10 percent when the sales are greater than $5,000. Otherwise, the function multiplies the sales by a reduced commission rate of 8 percent.

After you modify the formula for a custom function, Excel does not, unfortunately, automatically update the cells where the custom function has been used in the worksheet. If you switch back to the worksheet containing the Sales Commissions Table that uses the Sales_Commission custom function, you will find that the formulas using this function have not been updated and all still use a straight 10 percent commission rate.

Excel updates formulas using custom functions *only* when you edit the formulas that use the functions or one of the values referred to in them. Not even selecting the Calculate Now command will force Excel to recalculate these formulas and update the custom functions.

When editing formulas to get them recalculated, you simply need to select them, then press F2 or click the formula bar to activate it and click

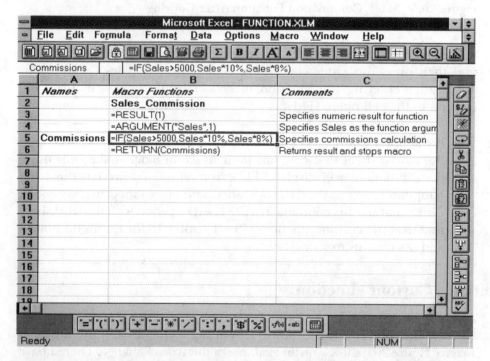

Figure 20.6   Sales_Commission Function After Editing Its Formula

the Enter box. (You can accomplish the same thing by performing this procedure on one of the cells referred to in the argument of the custom function.) As soon as you click the Enter box in the formula bar, Excel recalculates the formula using the latest version in the macro sheet.

Tip You can also get Excel to update the formulas containing edited custom functions by selecting the range containing the formulas and then replacing the = (equal sign) in each formula. To do this, choose the Formula Replace command and enter = in the Find What and Replace With text boxes, then choose the Replace All command button.

If you want Excel to update your custom functions anytime a recalculation occurs anywhere in the worksheet or when you select the cell with the function, activate the formula, and choose the Calculate Now command (F9), you need to add the VOLATILE macro function to the function macro. You add the VOLATILE function to the cell immediately below the one with the last ARGUMENT function in the function macro.

When you add this function, you don't need to specify any arguments. You simply enter

    =VOLATILE()

which is the same as entering =VOLATILE(TRUE). Either form causes Excel to turn on this recalculation function. If you ever need to disable this function, you need to enter **=VOLATILE(FALSE)** in the macro.

Figure 20.7 shows you the worksheet with the Sales Commissions Table after updating the formulas using the Sales_Commission custom function. Note how Renee's and Sandra's commissions have been reduced 2 percent (from 10 percent to 8 percent) because their weekly sales figures are both below $5,000.

Creating Custom Functions with Multiple Arguments

As mentioned earlier, each custom function that you create in Excel must have at least one argument. Many custom functions, however, will use multiple arguments. (A custom function can have up to a total of twenty-nine arguments.) When creating a custom function with multiple arguments, you must define each argument with the ARGUMENT macro function in the order in which the arguments need to be entered in the function. If you include optional arguments (that is, arguments that are not absolutely required in order for Excel to evaluate the custom function successfully), you must be sure to define them after the required arguments.

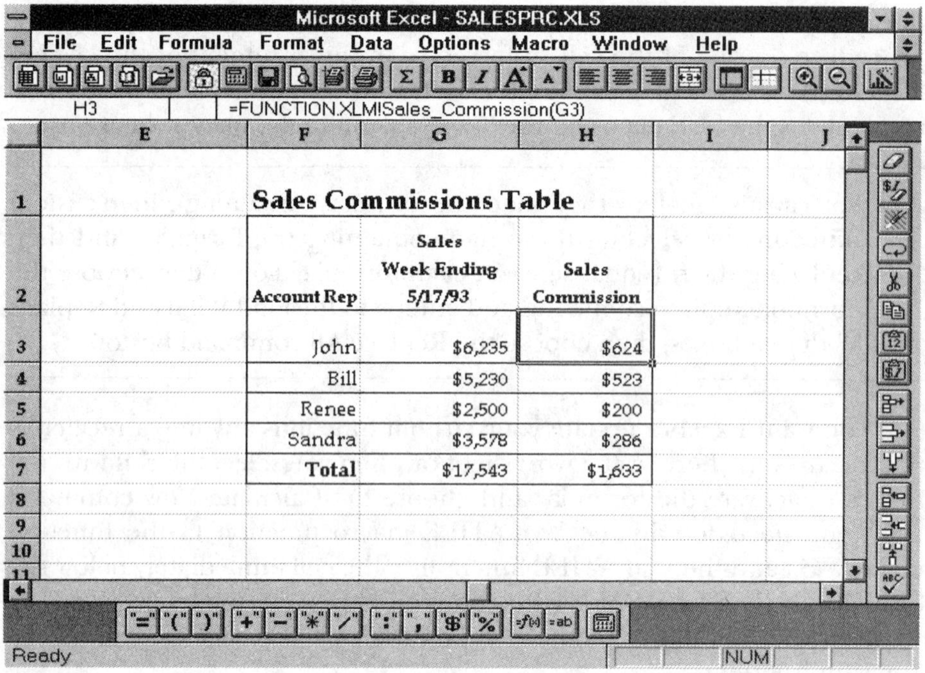

Figure 20.7   Sales Commissions Table After Updating Its Formulas

Figure 20.8 shows a function macro for a custom function called Discount_Price. This custom function requires two arguments: Retail_Price, which specifies the retail price of an item, and Discount_Rate, which specifies the percentage by which the item is to be reduced. Below these two ARGUMENT functions, you see the formula called Sales_Price, which indicates how these arguments are to be used in calculating the sales price. Because the ARGUMENT function that defines the Retail_Price argument is above the one that defines the Discount_Rate, you must always specify the cell reference to the retail price before that of the discount rate when entering the Discount_Price function.

Figure 20.9 shows you a Sales Price Table after entering this custom function in cell D4 and copying down the range D5:D8. As you can see in the formula bar in this figure, cell C4, containing the retail price of item 12-305, is specified as the first argument, and $B$2, containing the discount rate of 12 percent, is specified as the second argument. Because the retail price does change when you copy this formula, this first argument is given as a relative reference. Because the discount rate remains constant, the second argument is given as an absolute reference.

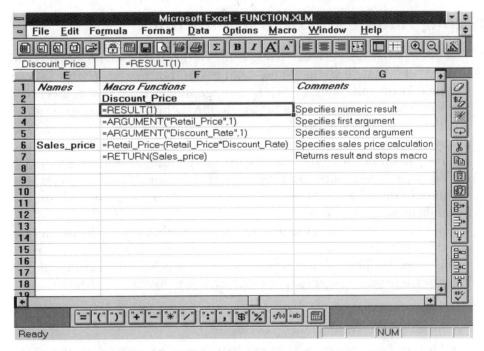

Figure 20.8   The Discount_Price Custom Function

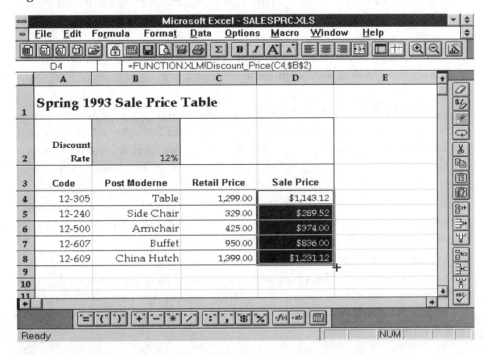

Figure 20.9   Sale Price Table After Updating Its Formulas

Creating Add-in Macros and Functions

You already have experience using some of the add-in macros that come with Excel 4.0, such as the Name Changer add-in macro (**changer.xla** in Chapter 5) for renaming or deleting range names from a worksheet and the Worksheet Auditor add-in macro (**audit.xla** in Chapter 8) for finding and fixing worksheet errors. As you may remember from using these add-in macros, you don't run them with the **R**un command on the **M**acro menu. Rather, you simply open the macro sheet containing the add-in macro with the **F**ile **O**pen command, and Excel adds their commands to the worksheet menu bar (the Change Name and Worksheet Auditor commands on the Formula menu, in this case).

You can save any command or function macro that you create in Excel as an add-in macro. When you open a macro sheet saved in the add-in format (which uses the filename extension **xla**), the following things automatically happen (depending on the types of macro contained in the sheet):

- The add-in macro sheet is hidden and you cannot use the Un**h**ide command on the **W**indow menu to display it.

- Custom functions appear in the Paste Function dialog box alphabetically within their category (instead of all together at the end of the category) and without the external reference to the name of the macro sheet that contains them.

- Command macros no longer appear in the Run dialog box when you choose the **M**acro **R**un command.

- Command macros can be used like built-in functions and no longer need to be preceded by the name of their macro sheet. For example, if you have created a command macro named Sort_by_ID in an open add-in macro sheet, you could use this command in another macro sheet by simply entering =SORT_BY_ID() without including a reference to its macro sheet.

- When you choose the **C**lose All command on the **F**ile menu (displayed by holding down the Shift key when you open the **F**ile menu), Excel does not close the open add-in macro sheets.

- When you choose the **E**xit command on the **F**ile menu, Excel does not prompt you to save changes to the open add-in macro sheets. To have Excel save an add-in macro sheet when you exit the program, you must create an auto-close macro (see Chapter 18) that uses the SAVE macro function.

To save a macro sheet in the add-in format, you follow these steps:

1. Open the macro sheet that you want to save as an add-in macro or make this document active if it is already open.

2. Choose the Save **As** command on the **File** menu.

3. If you would like, enter a new name for the macro sheet in the Filename text box.

4. Select the Add-In option in the Save File as **Type** drop-down list box. Excel changes the filename extension to **xla** in the Filename text box as soon as you select the Add-In file format.

5. Choose the OK button or press Enter to save the file as an add-in macro.

To open an add-in macro sheet, you simply choose **File** **O**pen and double-click the name of the add-in macro sheet in the File **N**ame list box, or choose the name and select the OK button. Figure 20.10 shows the Paste Function dialog box after saving the macro sheet with the Discount_Price and Sales_Commission custom functions as an add-in macro and opening its macro sheet. As you can see, these two custom functions now appear in the Paste Function list box without the external reference to their macro sheet.

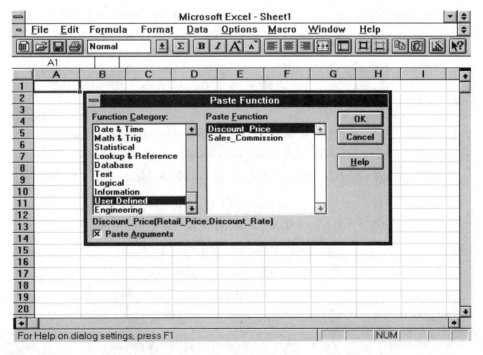

Figure 20.10   The Paste Function Dialog Box with Add-in Macros

Tip To make your command macros and custom functions available each time you start Excel without having to open each add-in macro sheet with the **File O**pen command, save your add-in macro sheets in the Excel start-up directory or alternate start-up directory. (See Chapter 10 for more information on using the Excel start-up directory.)

Editing an Add-in Macro Sheet

To edit a macro sheet saved in the add-in file format, you need to open the macro sheet as a regular macro sheet. To do this, you hold down the Shift key when you double-click the name of the macro sheet in the Filename list box of the Open dialog box or select the filename and choose OK.

After you've finished editing your macros, save your changes and close the macro sheet. As long as you don't change the file format when you save the file, Excel saves the file as an add-in macro and automatically hides the macro sheet once again.

Managing Add-in Commands and Functions

As you are aware, Excel supplies you with a wide variety of add-in macros. Some of these add-in macros form a *working set* of add-ins that are available to you immediately each time you start Excel. (See Table 20.2.) The commands added by the macros in the working set appear on the Excel pull-down menus as if they were an integral part of the menu system, and the program automatically opens their add-in macro sheets the first time you select these commands.

Table 20.2 Add-in Macros Automatically Added to Excel	
Add-in Macro Name	*Commands Added to the Pull-Down Menus*
Add-in Manager	Add-ins command on the **O**ptions menu.
Analysis ToolPak	Analysis Tools command on the **O**ptions menu.
Crosstab	Crosstab command on the **D**ata menu.
Report Manager	Print **R**eport command on the **F**ile menu.
Scenario Manager	Scenario Manager command on the **F**ormula menu.
Solver	Solver command on the **F**ormula menu.
View Manager	View command on the **W**indow menu.

In addition to these add-in macros in the working set, Excel includes many others in the library of add-in macros (located in the **\library** directory of the **c:\excel** directory and subdirectories of the **\library** directory that are automatically installed when you install the complete Excel program). You can use any of the macros in the library that are not part of the working set by opening their macro sheets with the **File Open** command. Table 20.3 lists all of the add-in macros included in the Excel 4.0 macro library and briefly describes their usage.

Table 20.3 Add-in Macros Included in the Macro Library

Add-in Macro	Macro Filename	Description
Add-in Functions	addinfns.xla	Adds five worksheet functions: BASE, DEGREES, FASTMATCH, RADIANS, and RANDBETWEEN. See Appendix B for details.
Add-in Manager	addinmgr.xla	Adds or removes add-in macros from the working set. Add-in macros included in the working set are available automatically when you start Excel.
Alternate Startup	altstart.xla	Specifies or changes the alternate startup directory. Documents located in this directory are opened automatically when you start Excel.
Analysis Toolpak	analysis.xla	Adds financial and engineering functions for performing specialized statistical analysis.
AutoSave	autosave.xla	Saves documents automatically at set intervals as you work in Excel.
Checkup	\checkup \checkup.xlm	Displays a dialog box of technical information about Excel and your computer environment, including the amount of memory available and location of program files.

Table 20.3 *(continued)*

Crosstab	crosstab.xla	Starts the Crosstab ReportWizard for creating cross-tabulated statistics from a database in Excel.
Custom Color Palettes	\color \palettes.xla	Adds the Custom Palettes command to the Options menu, which enables you to select and apply a new color palette for the active worksheet or chart.
Document Summary	summary.xla	Stores the author, title, comments, and creation date with a worksheet or macro sheet.
File Functions	filefns.xla	Adds four macro functions: CREATE.DIRECTORY, DELETE.DIRECTORY, FILE.EXISTS, and DIRECTORIES. See Appendix C for details.
Flat File	flatfile.xla	Parses imported text files with variable length fields and exports data from a worksheet to a space-delimited file. (See Chapter 21 for details.)
Glossary	glossary.xla	Saves frequently used worksheet entries or formulas for pasting into the worksheet or macro sheet you are building.
Macro Debugger	debug.xla	Helps you locate and fix bugs in your command macros.
Name Changer	changer.xla	Changes or deletes names assigned to worksheet cells.
Report Manager	reports.xla	Prints a report that includes views and/or scenarios that you have created for a worksheet.
Scenario Manager	scenario.xla	Saves various what-if scenarios that test the effect of using different sets of values in the input cells you select.

Table 20.3 *(continued)*

Slide Show	\slides \slides.xlt and slides.xla	Works with the Slide Show template to create a slide show that displays various worksheets and charts in the order you select.
Solver	solver.xla	Calculates various what-if scenarios based on the values that can be adjusted as well as those that must be constrained.
Switch	switch.xla and switchto.xla	Adds tools to the toolbars of your choice that enable you to switch to four other Microsoft programs: Word, PowerPoint, Project, and Mail.
View Manager	views.xla	Saves the display of the active document (including formatting) as a view that you select at any time.
What If	whatif.xla	Applies different combinations of input data to your worksheet model.
Worksheet Auditor	audit.xla	Generates reports to help you locate and fix worksheet errors.
Worksheet Comparison	compare.xla	Generates a report that shows the differences between the active version of a worksheet and one saved on disk.

Adding an Add-in Macro to the Working Set

If you frequently use one of the add-in macros not already included in the working set, you can add it to the working set so that it is available to you immediately every time you start Excel. To add an add-in macro to the working set, you follow these steps:

1. Choose the Add-ins command on the **O**ptions menu. Excel opens the Add-in Manager add-in macro sheet and displays the Add-In Manager dialog box shown in Figure 20.11.

2. Choose the **A**dd command button. Excel displays the File Open dialog box, similar to the one shown in Figure 20.12, where you specify

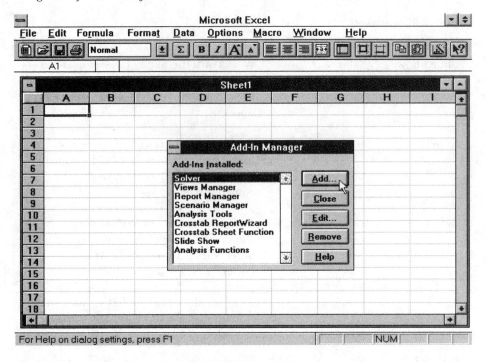

Figure 20.11 The Add-in Manager Dialog Box

the add-in macro file you want to add to the working set.

3. Select the add-in macro file in the Filename text box, then choose the OK button.

4. Repeat steps 2 and 3 until you have added all of the add-in macros that you want included in the working set.

5. Press the Esc key or choose the **C**lose button to close the Add-In Manager dialog box.

After adding an add-in macro to the working set, the add-in macro appears in the Adds-Ins **I**nstalled list box in the Add-In Manager dialog box the next time you open it, and the commands or functions included on its macro sheet are available to you immediately each time you start Excel thereafter.

If you don't need a particular add-in macro that's been included in the working set, you can remove it by selecting it in the Adds-Ins **I**nstalled list box of the Add-In Manager dialog box, choosing the **R**emove command button, and then choosing the OK button in the alert dialog box that appears next.

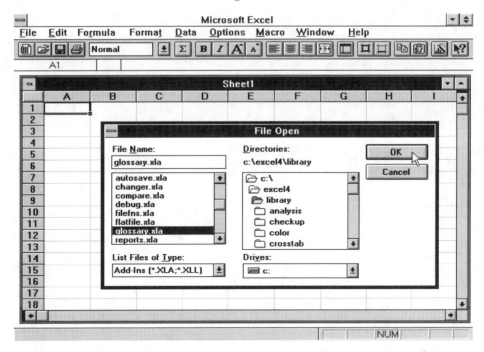

Figure 20.12   The File Open Dialog Box for Selecting Add-in Macros

 Alert! If you move an add-in macro file from its original directory to a new directory, you need to update the working set by choosing the **E**dit command button in the Add-In Manager dialog box, editing the directory path in the **P**ath text box of the Edit Add-In Info dialog box, and then choosing the OK button.

SUMMARY

In this chapter you learned how to customize Excel with add-in commands and functions. First you learned how to create function macros that perform the calculations that you specify. Then you learned how to save macro sheets containing these custom functions and command macros as add-in macros so that they appear as an integral part of the Excel program when you open it. Finally you learned how to add such add-in macros to the working set of add-in macros so that they are immediately available to you each time you start Excel.

In the next chapter you will learn how to use Excel with other applications. There you will learn how to transfer information between Excel and other applications that your office may use. As part of this, you will learn how to link information between applications so that information can be updated automatically.

21

Using Excel with Other Applications

For many people, Excel is only one of several applications they use in the course of doing their job. Even if Excel is the only program that you use, it is probably not the only application co-workers in the office use. Should information generated with Excel be required in some other program or vice versa, you need to be aware of the alternatives available to you for transferring the data between the applications (short of reentering the data).

In this chapter you will learn ways to exchange information between Excel and other applications, including those that run under Windows, DOS, and on the Macintosh. First we will look at how to exchange data using the Clipboard. Then we will look at how to link information between Windows applications so that changes made in a source document are updated automatically in the document where the information is embedded. Next we will look at the ways to exchange documents with other applications, including the programs that can open Excel documents and those that Excel can open, as well as methods for importing and exporting text files. Finally you will learn how to work with external database files created with stand-alone database management programs.

Exchanging Data Via the Clipboard

The Clipboard provides one of the most straightforward ways to transfer charts and worksheet data from Excel to another application as well as text and graphics from other applications into Excel. You can copy worksheet data to all Windows applications and most non-Windows programs. You can copy charts and other graphic objects created in Excel to all Windows applications that can read picture and bitmap graphic file formats. (Very few non-Windows programs can read Excel graphics.)

Copying Excel Worksheet Data to Other Programs

To copy worksheet data from an Excel worksheet to a document in another Windows application using the Clipboard, you follow these steps:

1. Open the worksheet in Excel and select the cells you want to copy.

2. Choose the **C**opy command on the cell shortcut menu or on the **E**dit pull-down menu.

3. Switch to the other application and open or create the document into which you wish to copy the worksheet data stored in the Clipboard.

4. Locate the insertion point at the place where you want the data to appear, then choose the **P**aste command on the **E**dit menu.

Figures 21.1 and 21.2 illustrate copying data from an Excel worksheet to a Word document. In Figure 21.1 the cell range A3:E9 has been selected and copied into the Clipboard with the **E**dit **C**opy command. In Figure 21.2 you see the cell entries after they have been pasted into a new Word for Windows document with the **E**dit **P**aste command. (Note that Word automatically creates a table for the worksheet data that you paste into one of its documents.)

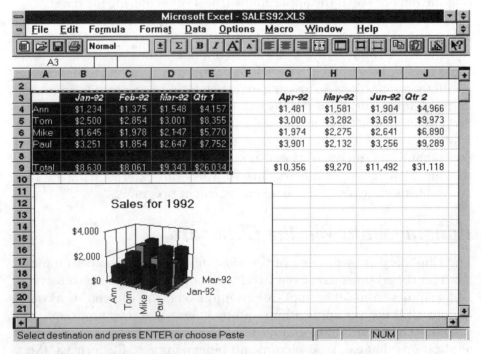

Figure 21.1   Copying the Cell Selection to the Clipboard

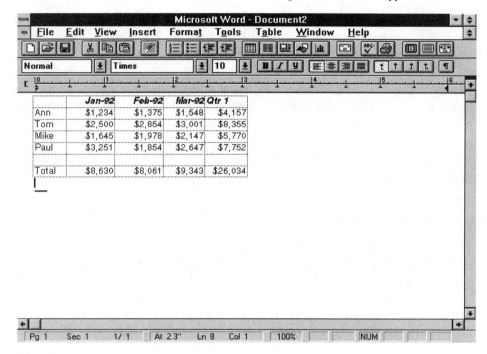

Figure 21.2   Pasting the Contents of the Clipboard into a Word Document

---

Note: You can paste Excel worksheet data stored in the Clipboard into a non-Windows DOS program running in 386 Enhanced Mode. To do this, you need to copy the cells to the Clipboard, switch to the document in the other application that is to contain the information, and then position the cursor at the place in the document where the information is to be pasted. If the application is running in a full-size window, press Alt+Enter to reduce its size, then open the program window's Control menu and choose the **E**dit and **P**aste commands.

Displaying the Contents of the Clipboard

When copying data to and from another application via the Clipboard, you can always check the contents of the Clipboard before you paste the information in the active document. To see the contents of the Clipboard, you need to start the Clipboard Viewer. To do this from Excel, you choose the **Ru**n command on the Excel Control menu, then choose OK or press Enter. (The Clipboard option button is already selected when you open the Run dialog box.) To do this from Windows, you double-click the Clipboard program icon in the Main group window in the Program Manager.

When you copy cells into the Clipboard, the Clipboard Viewer shows you the size of the range you copied (as in 7R times 5C for a range consisting of seven rows and five columns) instead of displaying the contents of these cells (as shown in Figure 21.3). To display the contents of the cell selection copied to the Clipboard, you must choose one of the other Display options besides Auto. Figure 21.4 shows the Clipboard Viewer after selecting the **B**itmap command on the **D**isplay menu to display the contents as a bit-mapped graphic. You can also choose either the **T**ext or **O**EM Text command to see the text. (The **O**EM option usually aligns the columns of worksheet data a little better than the **T**ext option.)

Copying Excel Charts and Graphics to Other Programs

You can also copy charts and other graphic objects created in Excel to other Windows programs you are using. To copy a chart or graphic object, you must first select it before you copy it to the Clipboard. You may need to enlarge an embedded chart if all of the titles and data series markers are not fully displayed in the worksheet. The easiest way to do this is to double-click the embedded chart to open it in a chart window and then, if necessary,

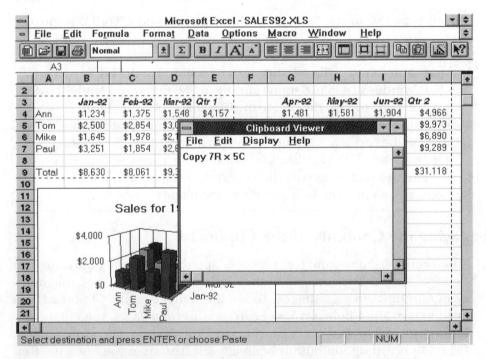

Figure 21.3   The Clipboard Viewer Showing the Dimensions of the Copied Range

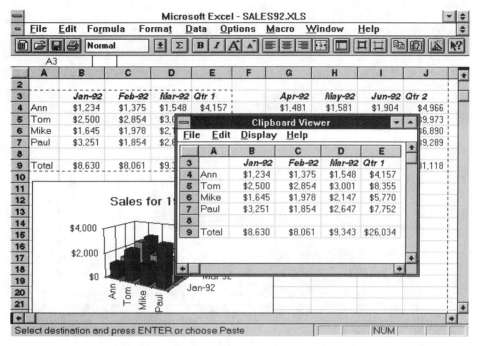

Figure 21.4   The Clipboard Viewer Displaying the Contents of the Copied Range as a Bitmap Graphic

click the chart window's Maximize button. To select the entire chart in the chart window, you can click the background of the chart (white selection handles should appear around the entire chart) or choose the Select **C**hart command on the **C**hart menu.

Figures 21.5 and 21.6 illustrate how easy it is to copy a chart from Excel into Word for Windows. In Figure 21.5 you see the chart embedded in the **sales92.xls** worksheet after it has been copied to the Clipboard. Note that charts and graphic objects that you copy to the Clipboard are properly displayed in the Clipboard Viewer automatically. You do not have to choose a different **D**isplay menu option. In Figure 21.6 you see the chart stored in the Clipboard after it has been pasted into the same Word document that contains the range of worksheet data copied earlier from the **sales92.xls** worksheet.

Copying Data from Other Programs into Excel

You can also copy data created with the other programs that you use into your Excel documents. You can copy text from almost any word processor (both Windows and non-Windows word processors) as well as pictures and graphics from many graphics programs. Table 21.1 shows you a list of the Clipboard formats that are supported by Excel. Data stored in any one of

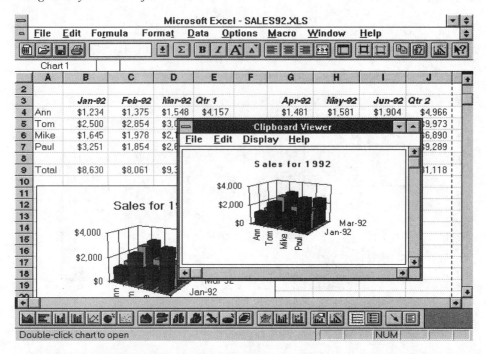

Figure 21.5   The Clipboard Viewer Displaying a Copied Excel Chart

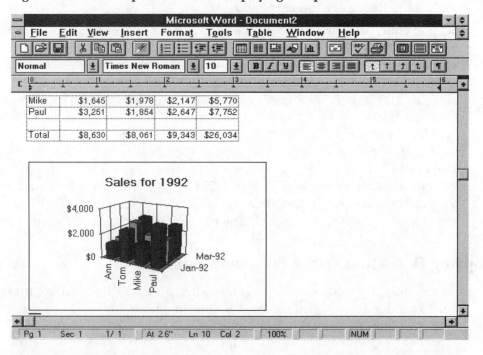

Figure 21.6   Word Document After Pasting the Chart Stored in the Clipboard

Table 21.1 Clipboard Formats Supported by Excel

Format	Clipboard Display Identifier
Picture (metafile)	Picture
Bitmap	Bitmap
Excel file formats	BIFF, BIFF3, and BIFF4
Symbolic Link Format (Multiplan)	SYLK
Lotus 1-2-3 Release 2, 2.2, 2.3, and 2.4 format	WK1
Data Interchange Format	DIF
Text (tab delimited)	Text
Comma Separated Values	CSV
Formatted text	Rich Text Format
Embedded object	Native, OwnerLink, or Picture
Linked object	OwnerLink
Text	Display Text, Text, or OEM Text

these formats can be transferred into an Excel worksheet document without any problems.

Figures 21.7 and 21.8 illustrate the copying of text from a word processor (Word for Windows in this case) to the Excel **sales92.xls** worksheet. In Figure 21.7 you see a table of values entered in a Word document (all the values are separated by a single tab) that has been selected and copied to the Clipboard with the **E**dit **C**opy command. Figure 21.8 shows you the **sales92.xls** worksheet after pasting this table into a blank area of the worksheet with the **E**dit **P**aste command. To paste these values in a range of cells in the worksheet, you have to select only the first cell in the blank range where you want the text to appear (cell L3 in this example).

When pasting text into the worksheet, the area where you want to paste the data must contain sufficient blank rows and columns to accommodate all the text without overwriting any existing data. With Windows programs such as Word, Excel copies text separated by tabs into succeeding columns of the worksheet and text on different lines into succeeding rows. Note, however, that this usually does *not* occur when pasting text from DOS

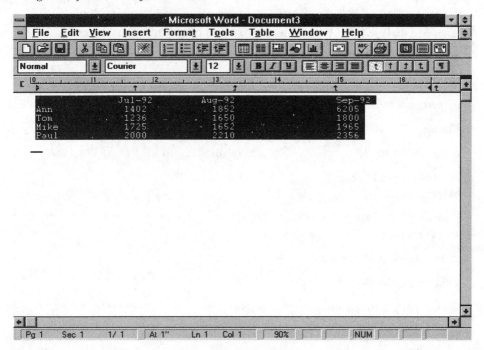

Figure 21.7 Word Document After Copying Selected Text to the Clipboard

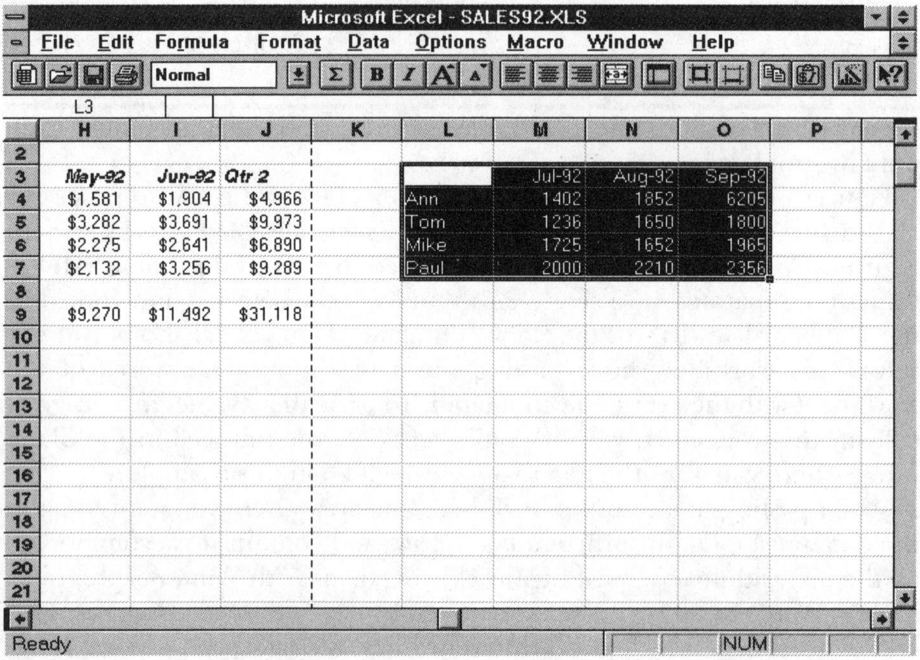

Figure 21.8 Excel Worksheet After Pasting the Text into a New Range

programs such as WordPerfect 5.1. With DOS text, usually all the text in each line of the copied selection is pasted into a single column in succeeding rows of the empty worksheet range. (To split up the long text entries so that the items appear in separate cells, you need to use the **Data Parse** command—see "Parsing Text Files" later in this chapter.)

> *Note:* To paste a picture of the text copied to the Clipboard into your worksheet, hold down the Shift key and choose the **P**aste Picture command on the **E**dit menu. Excel then pastes the Clipboard text into a new text box, which remains selected. Note that Excel automatically copies the text into a new text box when another graphic object is selected in the worksheet at the time you choose the **P**aste command on the **E**dit menu.

Linking to Other Applications

Just as you can link different Excel worksheets so that changes you make to the source data are updated in the linked worksheet automatically, you can link the Excel data that you export to other Windows programs that support DDE (Dynamic Data Exchange) or OLE (Object Linking and Embedding) links. You can also link graphics and text created with other Windows programs that support DDE or OLE links that you paste into Excel documents. For example, you could create a chart in Excel and link it to a word processing report so that any changes you make to the contents or formatting of the chart in Excel are updated automatically in the report. Likewise, you could create a graphic in a Windows drawing program and link it to a worksheet so that changes you make to the graphic object in the drawing program are updated automatically in the linked worksheet.

In order to link data across applications, both Excel and the other application must support the same type of linking (that is, DDE or OLE links). When you use dynamic data exchange, or DDE linking, the linked data pasted in the *dependent document* (that is, the document that depends on the information in the other document) is updated automatically when changes are made to the data in the *source document*. (Updating is immediate when both the dependent and source documents are open at the same time; otherwise, the dependent document is updated the next time you open it.) When you use objecting linking and embedding (OLE), you can open the source document and modify the source data by double-clicking the embedded object in the dependent document. Then, when you've finished editing the source data and close the source document, the changes are reflected in the dependent document automatically.

Whereas DDE linking ensures that your data will always remain up-to-date, OLE linking gives you direct access to the application used to create the linked data or object. You can make your changes using the same commands and functions you used when generating the data or creating the graphic, while at the same time you are assured that changes made with the source program are reflected in the dependent document.

Linking Data and Graphic Objects with DDE Linking

To create a link from an Excel document to another application, you follow these steps:

1. Open the Excel worksheet or chart and select the cells, chart, or graphic object that you want to link. (This becomes the source document.)

2. Choose the **C**opy command on the **E**dit menu (Ctrl+C).

3. Switch to the document in the other application in which you want to paste the linked data or chart. (This becomes the dependent document.)

4. Place the insertion point at the place where you want the linked data or graphic to be pasted.

5. Choose the Paste **L**ink or the Paste **S**pecial command on the **E**dit menu. (The command varies with the Windows application.)

6. If necessary, indicate the type of data you are pasting into the document in the Paste Link dialog box. For example, if you are pasting cells from an Excel worksheet in a Word document, you can choose among Formatted Text, Unformatted Text, Picture, or Bitmap as the data type. Formatted or Unformatted Text is pasted in a Word table that you can edit, Picture or Bitmap is pasted as a graphic that you can move and resize (but cannot edit).

7. Choose the Paste **L**ink button to paste the data or graphics in the active document at the insertion point and establish the link with the Excel source document.

Figures 21.9 through 21.12 illustrate how this type of DDE linking works. In Figure 21.9 the range A3:E8 in the **sales92.xls** worksheet has been selected and copied to the Clipboard with the **E**dit **C**opy command. In Figure 21.10 the Word document has been selected and the worksheet data has been pasted into the memo at the insertion point using the Formatted Text (RTF) option in the Paste Special dialog box. (Word automatically places the pasted data in a table.)

In Figure 21.11 you see the **sales92.xls** worksheet, containing the source data linked to the memo, after changing one of its values. (Paul's February

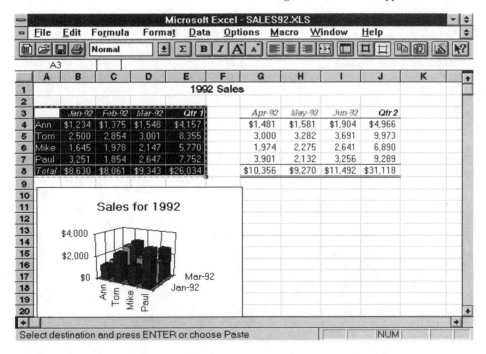

Figure 21.9 Selecting the Worksheet Data to Link to a Word Document

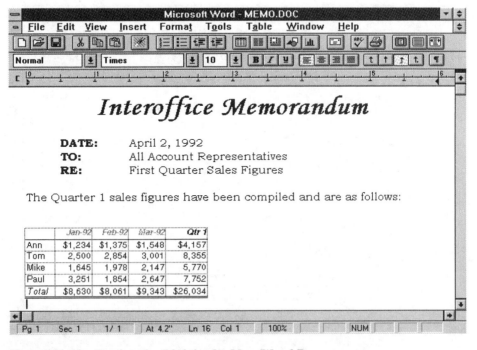

Figure 21.10 Pasting the Link in the New Word Document

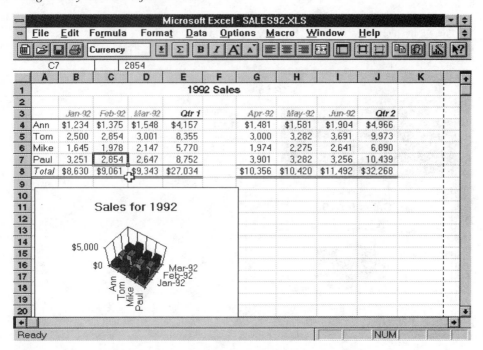

Figure 21.11   Changing the Data in the Excel Source Document

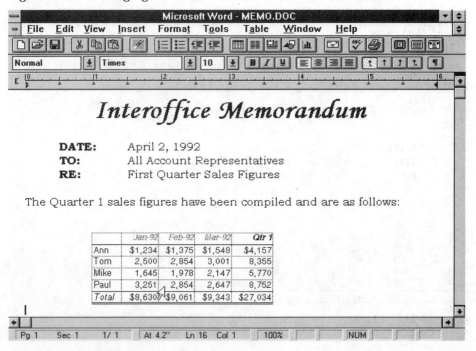

Figure 21.12   The Updated Data in the Word-dependent Document

sales in cell C7 have been increased from $1,854 to $2,854, which increases the February total from $8,061 to $9,061 and Paul's quarterly total from $7,752 to $8,752.) Figure 21.12 shows the linked data after switching to the Word memorandum. Notice that Paul's February sales as well as the February total and his quarterly total are all now up-to-date. If you were to change a value in the table in the **sales92.xls** worksheet when the Word memo was closed, Word would ask if you want to update its table automatically as soon as you open the memo document.

To link information from a document created with another application to an Excel worksheet, you follow these steps:

1. Open the document in the other application that contains the data you want to link to the Excel worksheet. (This becomes the source document.)

2. Choose the **C**opy command on the **E**dit menu (Ctrl+C).

3. Switch to the Excel worksheet in which you want to paste the linked data or chart. (This becomes the dependent document.)

4. Select the cell in the upper-left corner of the area where you want the linked data to be pasted.

5. Choose the Paste **L**ink or Paste **S**pecial command on the **E**dit menu to paste the data into the worksheet. If you're pasting text, you can choose the Paste **L**ink command to paste the text into the cells of the worksheet starting with the active cell. If you're pasting a graphic object, choose the Paste **S**pecial command and then select the Paste Link button to attach the object to the active cell. If the Paste **L**ink and Paste **S**pecial command on the **E**dit menu are dimmed, the application used to create the data you are pasting does not support DDE linking. In such a case, you must select the **P**aste command and paste the data into the worksheet without dynamically linking it to the source document.

To link the data that you paste into the worksheet, Excel creates a *remote reference formula* that contains an external reference to the application and the document as well as a reference to the data. (This can be a cell, range, range name, or the field referred to, depending on the type of source data and its application.) If you paste data into a range of worksheet cells, Excel pastes the remote reference formula into the range as an array formula.

Figures 21.13 and 21.14 illustrate this type of linking between a Word document and an Excel worksheet. In Figure 21.13 you see the table of data in the **qtr3sal.doc** Word document after it has been selected and copied to the Clipboard so that its data can be linked to the **sales92.xls** worksheet. Figure 21.14 shows you the **sales92.xls** worksheet after pasting and linking

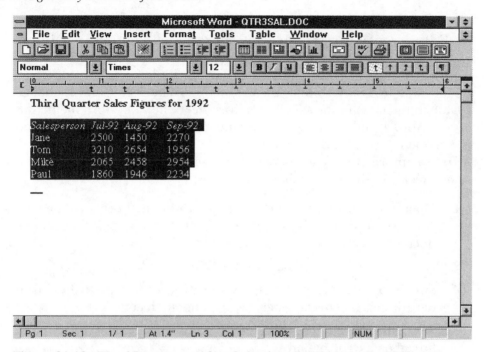

Figure 21.13   Word Document After Selecting the Table to Be Linked to an Excel Worksheet

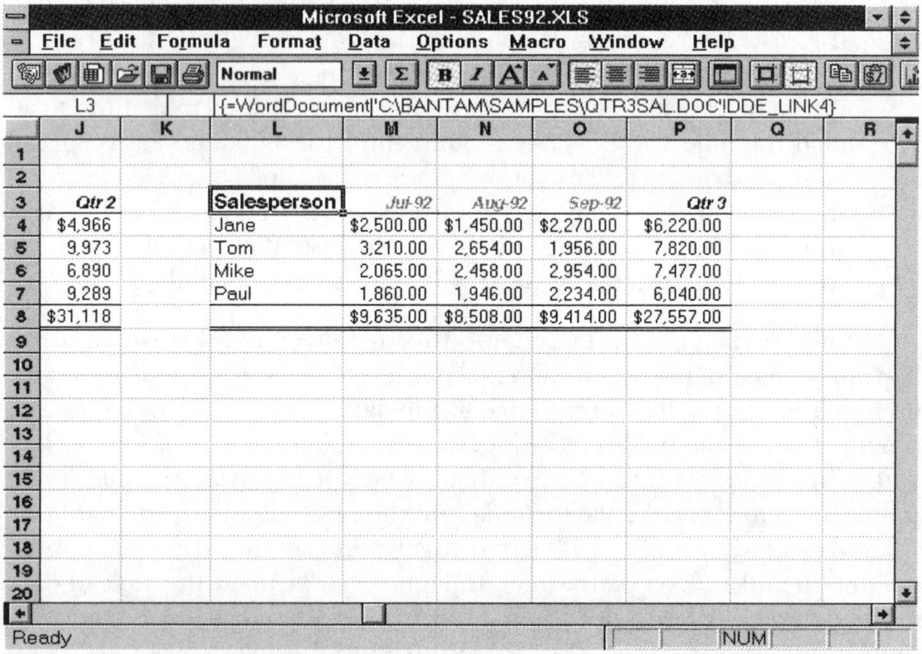

Figure 21.14   Linked Data from a Word Document Pasted into a Worksheet

this table. (This table has also been formatted with the AutoFormat command after creating SUM formulas in Excel for totaling the third quarter sales by month and salesperson.) Note the remote reference formula entered as an array in this figure's formula bar.

 Tip If you paste linked data into a worksheet and both the dependent worksheet and the source document are open at the same time, you can switch to the source document by double-clicking one of the cells containing the remote reference formula.

Controlling Links to Another Application

By default, Excel automatically updates DDE links established between it and another document when you open up the dependent document. This is accomplished by displaying an alert box asking if you want to reestablish the remote links automatically or maintain the automatic links. (The message varies with the application.) To have the program reestablish the links and update any out-of-date information, you simply select the **Yes** button in this dialog box. If you don't want the links updated, choose the **No** button. When two documents are open, changes to the source data in the source document are updated in the dependent document without any prompting.

You can also control when links are updated by changing the links from automatic to manual. To do this, you follow these steps:

1. Choose the **Links** command (located on the **File** menu in some applications, such as Excel, or on the **Edit** menu in other applications, such as Word) to open the Links dialog box.

2. Choose the links you wish to modify in the **Links** list box.

3. If the **M**anual option is available in the Links dialog box, select it. In the Excel Links dialog box, you must make sure that the Link **Type** drop-down text box is set to DDE/OLE Links and then choose the **Op**tions button, deselect the **A**utomatic check box in the DDE/OLE Options dialog box, and choose the OK button.

4. To update the links in the dependent document, choose the **Update** or **Update** Now command button. Otherwise, choose the Close or Cancel button or press Esc to close the Links dialog box.

After changing the links from automatic to manual, you must open the Links dialog box, choose the links in the **Links** list box, and then select the **Update** or **Update** Now command button each time you want the linked information in the dependent document to be updated.

If you change the name of a source document or move the document to a new directory, you must redirect the links in the dependent document so that they include the new directory and/or filename. To do this, you open the Links dialog box, choose the **C**hange or **C**hange Link button, and then edit the remote reference as required (the application and/or pathname). When an Excel document is the dependent document, be careful when editing the remote reference in the **C**hange Links to text box not to inadvertently delete the vertical bar (|) used to separate the application from the document or the exclamation point (!) used to separate the document from the item.

Severing Links Between Applications

If you no longer want the information pasted in the dependent document to be linked to the data in the source document, you can sever the links. For data pasted in an Excel worksheet, you can replace the remote reference formula with its calculated value. To do this, select the cell or cell range containing the formula or array formula, then choose the **E**dit **C**opy (Ctrl+C) and the **E**dit Paste **S**pecial command. Then choose the **V**alues option button before you choose the OK button or press Enter in the Paste Special dialog box. In the case of a graphic object, you need to select the object then delete it with the Del key before you paste it in the worksheet again, this time using the **E**dit **P**aste command instead of the **E**dit Paste **S**pecial command.

In other applications, such as Word, you may not be able to convert the remote reference to its current values. In such cases, you need to delete the field or other items containing the remote reference. (To delete a field in Word, choose the Field **C**odes command on the **V**iew menu to display the fields in the document, then select the field containing the remote reference to your Excel data and press the Del or Backspace key.) If you want, you can then recopy the Excel data or chart and then paste it in the document a second time, this time using the **E**dit **P**aste command rather than the **E**dit Paste **S**pecial or **E**dit Paste **L**inks command.

Embedding Objects with OLE Linking

Some of the more recent versions of Windows applications support object linking and embedding (OLE) as well as dynamic data exchange (DDE) linking. OLE enables you to embed an object created with another (source) application in a (dependent) document and then edit that object in the source application directly from the dependent document. For example, you could create a logo for your company with another Windows drawing program and then embed this picture as a graphic object in an Excel worksheet. That way you can edit the picture from Excel, simply by double-clicking the graphic object containing the logo in the worksheet. Doing this would open the drawing program as well as a document window containing the logo. After editing the picture using the commands and features available in the drawing program, your changes are automatically reflected in the graphic object embedded in the worksheet when you switch back to Excel.

To embed an existing object in an Excel document using OLE linking, you follow these steps:

1. Open the document that contains the information or graphic object you want to embed in your Excel document.

2. Select the information or object, then copy it to the Clipboard using the **E**dit **C**opy command.

3. Switch to the Excel document where the information is to be embedded, then select the cell or graphic object where the embedded information is to appear.

4. Choose the Paste **S**pecial command on the **E**dit menu.

5. Choose the correct data type for the information you are embedding in the Data Type list box, then choose the **P**aste button.

Excel pastes the information and attaches it to either the active cell or the currently selected object. A formula using the EMBED function appears in the formula bar. (The EMBED function always contains at least the name of the application that created the embedded object.)

You can also create a new object with another application and embed the object in an Excel document at the same time. To do this, follow these steps:

1. Open the Excel document and select the cell or graphic object where you want the new embedded object eventually to appear.

2. Choose the Insert **O**bject command on the **E**dit menu to display the Insert Object dialog box.

3. Choose the type of object in the **O**bject Type list box, then choose the OK button or press Enter. Windows starts the application responsible for creating the type of object you selected and opens a new document window in that application.

4. Enter the information or create the graphic in the new document window using that application's commands and features.

5. Close the document window containing the information that will be embedded in your Excel document (using the File **C**lose or File E**x**it

command or by double-clicking the program's or the document Control-menu button). When you switch back to your Excel document, the object you just created appears in the current cell or selected object.

6. Use the **File S**ave command to save the embedded object as part of the Excel document.

You can also embed an object created with Excel, such as a range of cells or a chart, in another application that supports OLE linking. To do this, you follow these steps:

1. Open the Excel worksheet or chart that contains the information or graphic object you want to embed in a document created with another application.

2. Select the cell or object you want to embed, then copy it to the Clipboard using the **Edit C**opy command (Ctrl+C).

3. Switch to the document in the other application where the information is to be embedded, then position the insertion point at the place in the document where the embedded information is to appear.

4. Choose the Paste **S**pecial command on the **E**dit menu.

5. Choose the Microsoft Excel Worksheet Object as the data type in the Data Type list box, then choose the **P**aste button. Excel embeds the object in the active document at the insertion point.

Tip Applications such as Word for Windows 2.0 that support OLE linking also allow you to embed new worksheet, macro sheet, or chart objects in a document by choosing the **O**bject command on the **I**nsert menu and then choosing the type of Excel object you want to embed. Doing this opens Excel with the appropriate type of new document (worksheet, macro sheet, or chart) where you can develop the information you want to embed. When you are finished, close the Excel document and switch back to the application where the embedded information will appear.

Figures 21.15 and 21.16 illustrate the effect of embedding an Excel chart in a Word for Windows document. In Figure 21.15 you see the 3-D area chart after pasting it into the Word document. Because the chart is embedded, when you double-click the chart, Windows starts Excel (if it's not already running) and opens a chart window containing the chart (as shown in Figure 21.16).

You can then modify the chart using the Chart toolbar and any of the other commands on the Chart pull-down menus. Figure 21.17 shows the

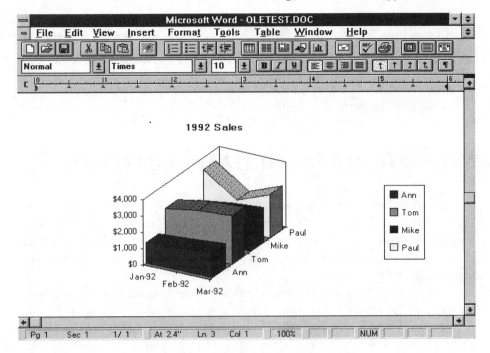

Figure 21.15   Excel Chart Embedded in a Word Document

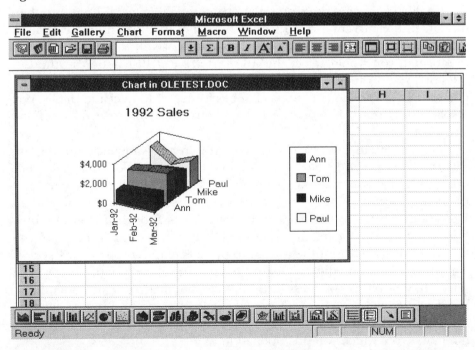

Figure 21.16   Embedded Chart in an Excel Chart Window After Double-Clicking

embedded chart after editing the type of graph, orientation, location of its legend, and adding an arrow and text box. Figure 21.18 shows you the Word document containing the embedded chart after closing its chart window in Excel and switching back to Word. As you can see, all of the changes made in Excel are updated automatically in the selected chart embedded in the Word document.

Exchanging Documents with Other Applications

As you learned in Chapter 10, you can save a copy of your Excel worksheet in a wide variety of different file formats so that the entire document can be opened by other programs that are used in your office. (See Table 10.1 for a list of the file formats in which you can save your worksheets with the **F**ile Save **A**s command.)

In a similar manner, Excel can also open documents saved in any of these file formats. To open a file saved in another compatible file format, you choose the **F**ile **O**pen command or click the Open File tool on the Standard toolbar and then choose the format of the file you want to open in the List Files of **T**ype drop-down list box. When you select a new file format in this list, Excel changes the search pattern in the Filename list box and then displays in the current directory only those files that match the new search pattern. For example, if you are opening a database file saved in the dBASE file format, you would select the dBASE Files (*.DBF) option in the List Files of **T**ype drop-down list box. When you select this option, the search pattern in the Filename text box changes from *.xl* to *.dbf and the list box displays only those files in the current directory that use the **.dbf** file extension.

When you attempt to save changes to a file created with another program with the **F**ile **S**ave or the Save File tool on the Standard toolbar, Excel opens the Save As dialog box. To save your changes using the same file format and filename, select the OK button or press return. To convert the file into an Excel document, select Normal in the Save File as **T**ype drop-down list box. Excel changes the file extension in the File **N**ame list box from the extension used by the current file format to the **.xls** extension used by Excel. If you wish, you can modify the main filename and/or directory before you select the OK button or press Enter to save the file as an Excel document. When you convert the file with the File Save **A**s command in this manner, the original file in the other format remains untouched on the disk or directory from which you first opened it.

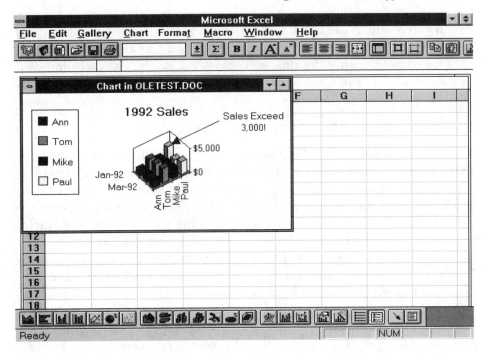

Figure 21.17   Embedded Chart After Editing

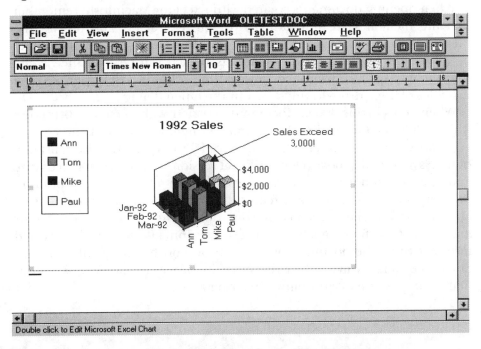

Figure 21.18   Updated Embedded Chart in the Word Document

Tip If you routinely work with a file created in another file format (such as a dBASE database file), you may want to save it as an Excel worksheet file to avoid taking the time to convert the document each time you open the file and save your changes to it.

Compatibility with Other Versions of Excel

As you would expect, Excel 4.0 opens all Excel documents created with Excel 2.1 or 3.0 without losing any of the formatting or functionality. Likewise, Excel documents created with versions of Excel on the Macintosh are completely compatible with Excel 4.0 for Windows. The biggest problem in opening Macintosh documents is transferring the files from the Macintosh file format to a DOS file format. The easiest way to do this is by copying the files across a Mac/PC network or modem. If you're using System 7.0 on your Macintosh, you can also use the Foreign File Access extension. With this utility, the Macintosh will accept a $3\frac{1}{2}$-inch diskette formatted by DOS without trying to reinitialize it. That way you can place a formatted diskette in the Macintosh's floppy disk drive and then copy your Excel for Macintosh documents onto the DOS diskette, which can then be read by your IBM or IBM-compatible computer.

When opening documents created with Excel for Macintosh, remember that the filenames are not limited to eight characters and do not use filename extensions (such as **.xls, .xlc,** or **.xlm**). To display the filenames of your Excel for Macintosh documents (which will be truncated when they include spaces), you need to select the All Files (*.*) option in the List Files of **T**ype drop-down list box in the Open dialog box.

When transferring Excel documents created with version 4.0 for use with earlier versions of Excel, you must remember to select the correct version (Excel 3.0 or Excel 2.0) in the Save File as **T**ype drop-down list box of the Save As dialog box. (Neither Excel version 3.0 nor 2.1 will recognize and open Excel documents created with version 4.0.) Also keep in mind that version 4.0 contains many features and commands that are not available in these earlier versions. If your document contains formulas or macros that use functions introduced in version 4.0, these are converted into text when the document is saved in one of the earlier file formats. Such a conversion may affect the integrity of your worksheet as well as make it impossible to run some of your macros.

Compatibility with Lotus 1-2-3

Excel 4.0 can read and write files created with the 1A, 2.x, 3.x, and Windows version of Lotus 1-2-3 as well as read files saved in Lotus Symphony version 2.1. When you open a Lotus 1-2-3 worksheet file, Excel converts all the formulas, formats, and names it contains to their Excel equivalents.

In the case of number formatting, Excel can read all numeric formats with the exception of +/– and Text, both of which are converted to General. If you are opening a 3-D worksheet file created with 1-2-3 Release 3.0 or 3.1, Excel automatically converts this type of file to a workbook, converting each worksheet in the 1-2-3 file to a bound worksheet document in the new workbook. If your 1-2-3 worksheet contains graphs, Excel displays an alert message dialog box asking if you want to convert them to Excel charts. If you choose the Yes button, the program converts the graphs to comparable charts, which will be embedded in the translated worksheet. If your 1-2-3 worksheet contains formulas that link the worksheet to another file, Excel converts them to formulas with external references. Excel also displays an alert message box asking if you want to update the external references.

RUNNING LOTUS 1-2-3 MACROS IN EXCEL

Excel is equipped with a Macro Interpreter that enables you to run most of the macros stored in a 1-2-3 worksheet file. To run a 1-2-3 macro, you simply open the 1-2-3 worksheet with the **File O**pen command, then press Ctrl plus the letter assigned to the macro name. For instance, if the 1-2-3 macro is named **\a**, you press Ctrl+a to run that macro. While the macro is running, you will see **MI** (for Macro Interpreter) displayed on the status bar. If the macro you are running contains a macro pause command {?}, Excel pauses the macro and displays **MI Pause** on the status bar. When you are ready to resume running the macro, press the Enter key just as you would in Lotus 1-2-3 to resume macro execution.

If the 1-2-3 macros you want to run in Excel have been created and saved in a macro library sheet (with the **.mlb** filename extension), you must copy the macros in the macro library into a regular 1-2-3 worksheet file, then open that worksheet in Excel and run the macros as described above. (You do this by loading the macro library into memory with the Load command on the Macro Library Manager menu and then copying it to your worksheet with the Edit command.)

If your 1-2-3 worksheet file contains an autoexec macro (named \0), this macro automatically runs as soon as you open the worksheet in Excel. To open a 1-2-3 worksheet file without running its autoexec macro, you open it as you normally would except that you hold down the Shift key when you choose the OK button or press Enter after selecting the worksheet's name in the Filename list box.

Excel should have no problem running macros that run successfully in Release 2.01 of Lotus 1-2-3. The program can also run most macros created with the macro command language used in Lotus Release 2.2 except for those that contain keystrokes or command names that start or use add-in programs such as Allways or the Macro Library Manager. You must remove all such references from your macros in order to successfully run them in Excel.

If Excel cannot execute a particular command or keystroke in a 1-2-3 macro, the program displays the Macro Error alert dialog box, displaying the cell reference of the error. To stop a macro before it's finished running, you press Ctrl+Break to halt the macro, just as you do in 1-2-3.

TRANSLATING LOTUS 1-2-3 MACROS

If you decide to convert a 1-2-3 worksheet to the Excel file format, you will want to convert its macros as well. To translate a 1-2-3 macro to an Excel macro, you use the Macro Translation Assistant, a separate utility like the Dialog Editor, except that this program must always be run from within Excel.

To use the Macro Translation Assistant to translate your 1-2-3 macro to an Excel equivalent, you follow these steps:

1. Open the worksheet containing the macros you want to translate, then choose the **Run** command on the Excel Window's Control menu.

2. Select the **M**acro Translator radio button in the Run dialog box, then select the OK button or press Enter. Excel opens the Macro Translation Assistant dialog box containing a single **T**ranslate pull-down menu.

3. Choose the **L**otus 1-2-3 command on the **T**ranslate pull-down menu in the Macro Translation Assistant dialog box. The Macro Translator displays a dialog box where you select the 1-2-3 worksheet containing the macro to be translated.

4. Select the name of the 1-2-3 worksheet containing the macros to translate in the Select Source Sheet list box, then choose the OK button or press Enter. A second dialog box appears similar to the one shown in Figure 21.19, listing all the range names contained in the worksheet you selected.

5. Select the range names of the 1-2-3 macros you want translated, then choose the OK button or press Enter. By default, the Macro Translate

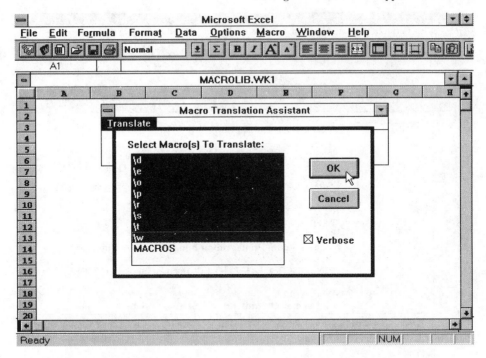

Figure 21.19 Selecting the 1-2-3 Macros to Translate with the Macro Translation Assistant

chooses all the range names whose names consist of a backslash plus a single letter (such as \d or \p). To deselect some of the selected macros, click them. To reselect multiple macros, hold down the Ctrl key as you click their names. When you choose OK, the second dialog box closes and the Macro Translator begins translating the selected macros. As the program works, it keeps you informed of its progress in translating the macros. When the program is finished translating, it displays a message dialog box.

6. To exit the Macro Translation Assistant utility, choose the **Yes** button in the message dialog box asking if you want to close the program. To leave the utility running and return to the Macro Translation Assistant dialog box where you can translate more 1-2-3 macros, choose the **No** button.

Excel puts the translated macros in a new macro sheet. If you left the **V**erbose check box selected when you translated the 1-2-3 macros, Excel includes the 1-2-3 keystrokes and macro commands in italicized text at the beginning of the translated Excel macro (as shown in Figure 21.20). That way you can compare the original 1-2-3 keystrokes and commands to the macro functions inserted in the new Excel macro.

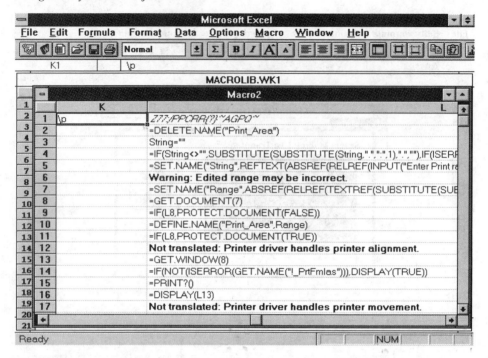

Figure 21.20　New Worksheet Displaying the Translated Print Macro

If the Macro Translator has had trouble translating a particular 1-2-3 keystroke or macro command, the program displays a Warning message in bold indicating the potential problem. If the utility has not bothered to translate a 1-2-3 keystroke or macro command, it displays a Not Translated message in bold that indicates why the particular keystroke or command was not translated.

To run the translated 1-2-3 macros in your new macro sheet, you can select the macro name in the Run Macro dialog box (such as **macro1!\k** or **macro1!\p**) or you can simply press the Ctrl key plus the letter assigned to the name (such as Ctrl+K or Ctrl+P). To save the macro sheet containing the translated macros, choose the **File S**ave or **F**ile Save **As** command and edit the macro sheet name in the **Filename** text box.

Working with Text Files

You may need to use a document that Excel cannot open directly. In such a situation, you need to convert the document to a file format that Excel can read. If the program that created the document cannot convert it into any of the other formats that Excel can read, chances are still good that the program can save the document as a text file that Excel can open.

After converting the document you want to use in Excel to a text file, you can open in a worksheet window by following these steps:

1. Choose the **O**pen command on the **F**ile menu or click the File Open tool on the Standard toolbar.

2. Choose the Text Files (*.TXT;*.CSV) option in the List of Files **T**ype drop-down list box if the text file uses the filename extension **.txt** or **.csv**. If the file uses another extension, choose the All Files (*.*) option instead.

3. Choose the **T**ext command button to display the Text File Options dialog box (shown in Figure 21.21).

4. Choose the appropriate Column Delimiter option, indicating what type of character is used to separate the data in the file (**T**ab, **C**omma, **S**pace, Se**m**icolon, **N**one, or C**u**stom). Excel uses the delimiter character you select to determine where to split up text into different columns in a row of the worksheet. The program automatically inserts text on a new line in the text file into the next row of the worksheet. If your text file uses a nonstandard character, choose the C**u**stom option button and then enter the character in its text box.

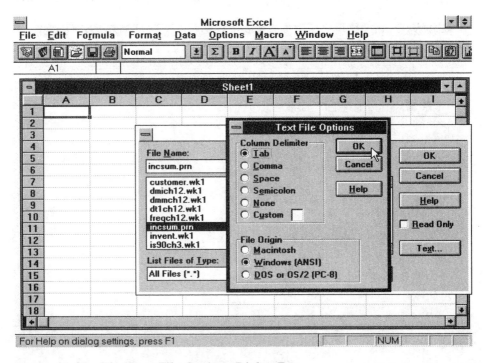

Figure 21.21 The Text File Options Dialog Box

5. Choose the appropriate File Origin option (**Macintosh, Windows** (ANSI), or **DOS** or OS/2 (PC-8)), then select the OK button or press Enter.

6. Double-click the name of the text file to open in the Filename list box or select the filename and choose OK or press Enter.

PARSING TEXT FILES

Whenever possible, you should set up your text files so that each item that you want in a separate column of the worksheet is separated by a particular character, such as a tab, comma, semicolon, or space. This is, however, not always possible. Many programs, such as Lotus 1-2-3, create text files without using a delimiter character. (The space cannot be used because the text file uses multiple spaces to fill out each field.) When you open a text file that doesn't use a delimiter character, Excel copies each line of text in the file as a long text entry in a single column that spills over to adjacent columns to the right (as long as they remain empty in the worksheet).

Figure 21.22 shows you just such a text file. In this figure, cell A2 is active. Note that the contents of this is a long text entry that contains a date (1.Apr-89) followed by a number (58), two text descriptions (Ham Sandwich

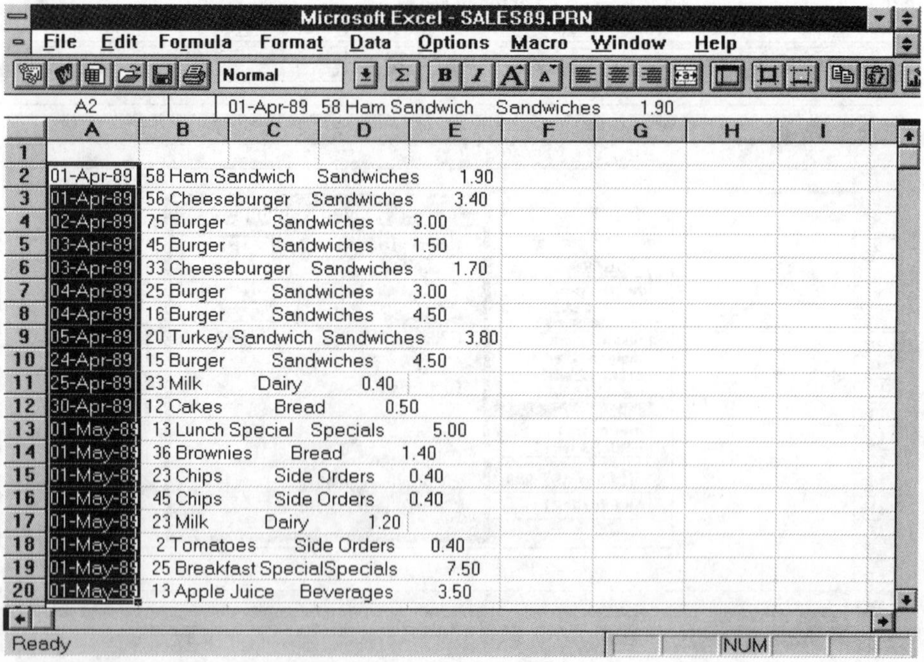

Figure 21.22   Text File with Long Text Entries in Column A

and Sandwiches), and another value (1.90). Each of these five items should be in a separate cell in adjacent columns of row 2 instead of all in cell A2.

You can split long text entries into separate cells in succeeding columns of the worksheet with the **Data Parse** command as follows:

1. Select the column containing the long text entries that you want to break up into separate cell entries. Make sure that you include all of the rows with data. You do not need to select any columns other than the one containing the long text entries.

2. Choose the **Parse** command on the **Data** menu. When you choose this command, Excel displays the Parse dialog box similar to the one shown in Figure 21.23. This dialog box contains a **Parse Line** text box showing how the text in the active cell will be divided when you parse the selection. Brackets are used to indicate column borders.

3. If necessary, edit the location of the brackets in the text that appears in the **Parse Line** text box. To remove all brackets, choose the **Clear** button. To restore the original brackets, choose the **Guess** button.

4. By default, Excel displays the current selection in the **Destination** text box, meaning that the parsed data will overwrite the long entries in the first column and will be inserted into succeeding columns to

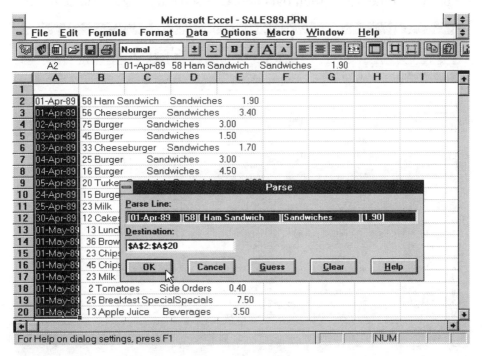

Figure 21.23 The Parse Dialog Box

the right. (Make sure that sufficient columns are blank so that Excel doesn't overwrite any data that you need.) To have Excel insert the parsed data in another range in the worksheet, select the **D**estination text box and select the first cell of the range in the worksheet or enter its cell reference in this text box.

5.   Choose the OK button or press Enter to parse the selection and place the split-up entries in the destination range.

Excel parses the data by splitting up the data items according to the sample line in the Parse dialog box. If some lines are still not split up correctly, you can either split them up manually or select their cells and use the Parse command again.

Figure 21.24 shows you the sample text file after using the Parse command and widening columns C and D. Now that the data items are entered in separate cells in the correct columns, you can format their entries differently and use them in formulas that calculate subtotals and totals.

USING THE FLAT FILE ADD-IN MACRO

Excel provides a Flat File add-in macro (called **flatfile.xla**) that you can use to parse text files when their data items are separated by a variable number

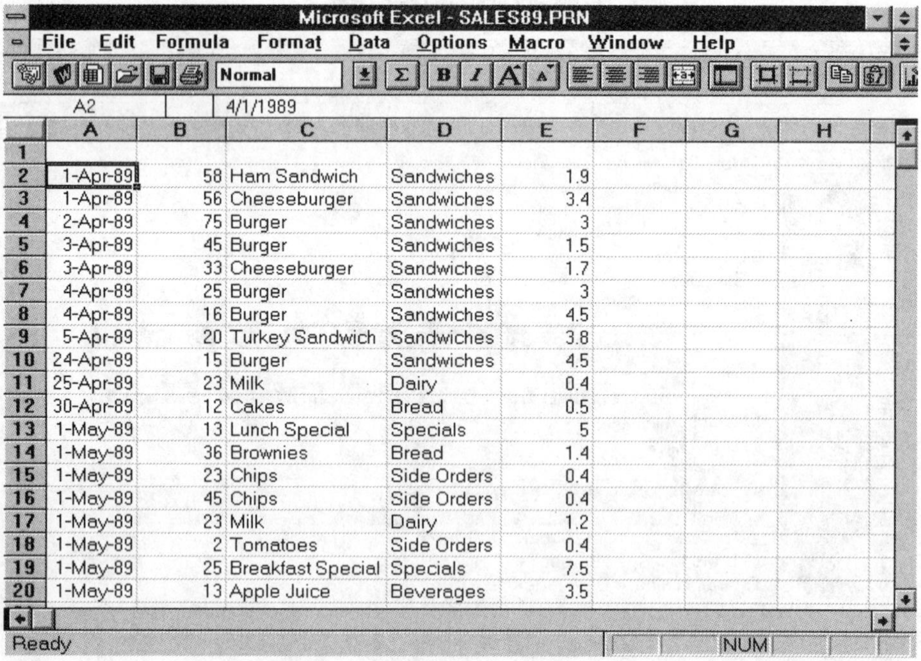

	A	B	C	D	E	F	G	H
1								
2	1-Apr-89	58	Ham Sandwich	Sandwiches	1.9			
3	1-Apr-89	56	Cheeseburger	Sandwiches	3.4			
4	2-Apr-89	75	Burger	Sandwiches	3			
5	3-Apr-89	45	Burger	Sandwiches	1.5			
6	3-Apr-89	33	Cheeseburger	Sandwiches	1.7			
7	4-Apr-89	25	Burger	Sandwiches	3			
8	4-Apr-89	16	Burger	Sandwiches	4.5			
9	5-Apr-89	20	Turkey Sandwich	Sandwiches	3.8			
10	24-Apr-89	15	Burger	Sandwiches	4.5			
11	25-Apr-89	23	Milk	Dairy	0.4			
12	30-Apr-89	12	Cakes	Bread	0.5			
13	1-May-89	13	Lunch Special	Specials	5			
14	1-May-89	36	Brownies	Bread	1.4			
15	1-May-89	23	Chips	Side Orders	0.4			
16	1-May-89	45	Chips	Side Orders	0.4			
17	1-May-89	23	Milk	Dairy	1.2			
18	1-May-89	2	Tomatoes	Side Orders	0.4			
19	1-May-89	25	Breakfast Special	Specials	7.5			
20	1-May-89	13	Apple Juice	Beverages	3.5			

Figure 21.24   Data in the Text File After Splitting Up with the Parse Command

of spaces. When you open this add-in macro, Excel adds a command called Smart Parse to the **D**ata menu. When you use the Smart Parse command, Excel places each group of characters that is separated by one or more spaces (or other delimiter character if you select a different one in the Smart Parse dialog box) into a separate cell.

To use the Smart Parse command, you follow these steps:

1. Open the text file and then select the column containing the long text entries that you want to parse with the Smart Parse command.

2. Open the **flatfile.xla** add-in macro with the **File O**pen command. This file is located in the **\library** directory of the **c:\excel** directory.

3. Choose the Smart Parse command on the **D**ata menu. When you choose this command, Excel displays the Smart Parse dialog box where you specify the delimiter character.

4. By default, Excel uses the **B**lank Space ( ) option as the **C**olumn Delimiter. To use the /, select the **S**lash / option. To use another character, choose the **O**ther option and then enter the character in its text box.

5. If you want Excel to remove the extra blank spaces between the words, choose the **R**emove extra blank space check box.

6. Choose the OK button or press Enter to parse the selection.

Excel splits up each word or group of characters separated by spaces into separate cells, overwriting the current selection and inserting parsed entries into adjacent columns to the right. (Make sure that these columns don't contain data that you don't want to lose.)

 Alert! Don't parse your data with the Smart Parse command when the selection to be parsed contains individual data items composed of a group of characters or words that are separated by spaces. If you do, Excel will split these items up, placing each group of characters or words in a separate column.

Working with External Databases

In addition to being able to open database files either directly (as with dBASE files) or indirectly as delimited text files (most database programs can export their files as text files delimited by commas), you can also work with external database files without opening them in an Excel worksheet. This makes it possible to work with very large database files that contain more records than would fit into the memory of the computer if they were imported into an Excel worksheet because you always work with the files on disk. (To do this, you do not even need to run the database program that created the database file.)

To work with external database files in Excel, you use a separate Windows program called Q+E that you can use either from within Excel or directly in Windows. (This section describes only how to use Q+E from within Excel; consult the "Q+E User's Guide" that came with your Excel documentation for more information on using Q+E as a stand-alone program.) Q+E allows you to work with several different types of database files, such as personal computer databases like those created with dBASE or remote databases like those maintained with the Microsoft SQL Server on a local area network (LAN).

With Q+E you can extract records from the external database file based on selection criteria that you enter in your Excel worksheet. Once the data is extracted into your worksheet, you can then perform any Excel operation that you want on them (such as sorting, adding calculated fields, cross-tabulating data, and printing).

To start Q+E within Excel, you follow these steps:

1. Open a new worksheet or the worksheet where you want to extract data from the external database file.

2. Open the **qe.xla** add-in macro located in the **\qe** directory of the **c:\excel** directory with the **File O**pen command. If the **qe** folder is not listed under the **c:\excel** directory in the Directories list box, you need to install Q+E. (Consult your Excel documentation for information on how to install this program.) When you open the **qe.xla** add-in macro, Excel adds three new commands to the **D**ata menu: Paste Fieldnames to paste the names of the fields in the external database into the active worksheet, SQL **Q**uery to allow you to extract data from the external database by entering an SQL query statement, and Activate Q+E to activate the Q+E program window (or start Q+E if it is not currently running). In addition, the add-in macro modifies the Set Database dialog box so that you can choose between specifying the current selection in the worksheet or an external database file as the database to use.

After you open the **qe.xla** add-in macro, you are ready to specify the external database that you want to work with as follows:

1. Choose the Set Database command on the **D**ata menu.

2. Choose the **E**xternal Database option button in the Set Database dialog box, then choose OK or press Enter. The Set External Database dialog box as shown in Figure 21.25 appears.

3. Choose the source of the external database in the **S**ource drop-down list box. If the source is Oracle, Rdb, or Microsoft's SQL Server,

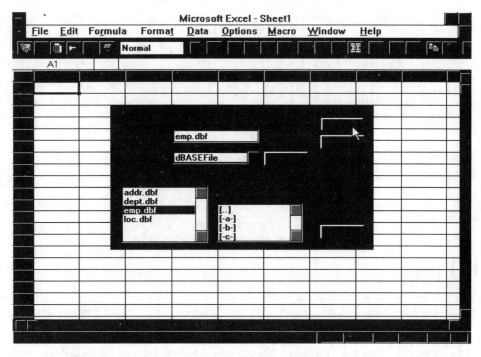

Figure 21.25   The Set External Database Dialog Box

choose the Sources command button, then select the appropriate
option in the **A**vailable Sources list box, choose the **L**ogon button,
and specify the **S**erver, **U**ser Name, and **P**assword as required by the
network in the dialog box.

4. Select the directory containing the database file in the **D**irectories list
   box, then select the database filename in the **F**iles list box. If the filename of your database doesn't appear in the **F**iles list box, edit the
   search pattern in the Filename text box or enter the name of the database file in this text box.

5. Choose the OK button or press Enter.

6. After you select the external database, Q+E expands the Set Database
   (as shown in Figure 21.26) to show the external database you selected. To select a different external database, you choose the
   Change button and select the database in the Set External Database
   dialog box. To add another external database, choose the **A**dd button and select the database in the Set External Database dialog box.

7. When you're finished setting the external database you want to work
   with, choose the OK button or press Enter.

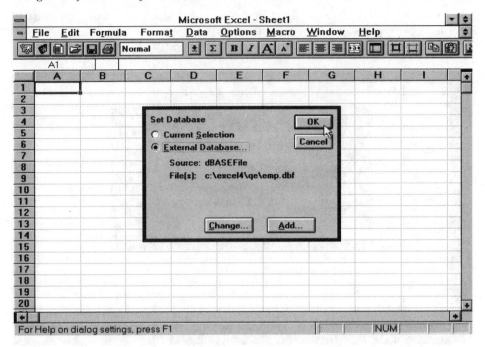

Figure 21.26   The Set Database Dialog Box After Selecting an External Database

 Tip Once you are finished working with a remote external database such as Oracle, you should log off by choosing the Set Database command on the Data menu, then choosing the **C**hange button, the Sources button, and the Logoff button.

After selecting the external database to use, you are ready to paste its field names in the active worksheet. When doing so, you can choose to paste all or just some of the fields from the external file. You can also decide the order in which the fields are to be pasted into the worksheet. As when working with Excel databases, you can use the field names to establish both the Criteria and Extract ranges in the worksheet. (See Chapter 15 for details on how to set up the Criteria and Extract ranges in the worksheet.)

To paste the field names from the external database into the active worksheet, you follow these steps:

1.   Select the first cell in the worksheet where you want the field names to be pasted. Make sure that there are sufficient blank cells to the right in the row with the active cell so that the pasted field names cannot overwrite existing cell entries.

2. Choose the Paste Fieldnames command on the **D**ata menu. Q+E displays the Paste Fieldnames dialog box, which contains an **A**vailable Fields list box containing all the names of the fields in the external database. If you have set more than one external database, Q+E prefaces each field name with the database name, as in addr.CITY for the City field in the **addr.dbf** database file or emp.FIRST_NAME for the First Name field in the **emp.dbf** database file.

3. Select all the fields in the **A**vailable Fields list box that you want to paste in the worksheet. To paste all of the fields, choose the Select **A**ll command button. To paste selected fields, hold down the Ctrl key and click each field.

4. To modify the order in which the field names appear in the worksheet, choose the **O**rder Fields> button. Q+E expands the Paste Fieldname dialog box as shown in Figure 21.27.

5. Select the field in the **A**vailable Fields list box that you want to appear first, then choose the **A**dd button to add this field to the **S**elected Fields list box.

6. Repeat step 5, adding all the rest of the fields you want pasted to the **S**elected Fields list box in the order you want them pasted.

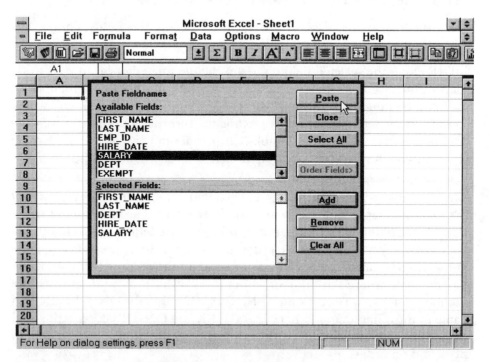

Figure 21.27   The Paste Fieldnames Dialog Box

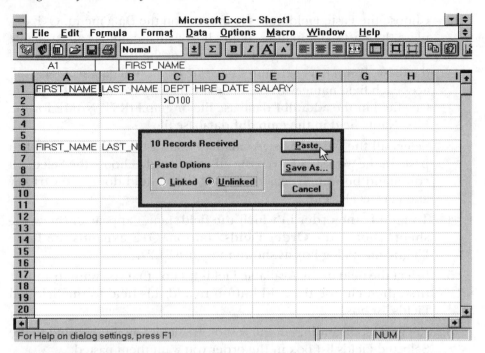

Figure 21.28   Extracting Records in the External Database

7. When you've finished adding and ordering the fields, choose the **P**aste command button.

Q+E pastes the selected field names in the designated order in your worksheet. After pasting the field names in the worksheet, you can use them to set up a criteria range with the Set **C**riteria command on the **D**ata menu where you specify the selection criteria for extracting records. You also can copy the field names and use them to establish an extract range with the Set E**x**tract command on the **D**ata menu where the selected records are to appear.

 Alert! Unlike when searching an Excel database, selection criteria entered in the criteria range when searching an external database are case sensitive. (Uppercase letters match uppercase and lowercase letters match lowercase ones.) Also, if you use computed criteria, you must refer to the fields by name in the criteria formula. For example, to extract the records from an inventory database where the number of items on order is more than twice the number in stock, you would enter >IN_STOCK*2 below the ON_ORDER field name in the criteria range where IN_STOCK and ON_ORDER are the field names assigned to the numeric fields containing the number of the item in stock and on order, respectively.

After setting up the criteria and extract ranges, you can enter your selection criteria and then extract the records with the **Extract** command on the **D**ata menu. When Q+E completes an extract operation on the external database, the program displays a dialog box, similar to the one shown in Figure 21.28, indicating the number of records located that match your search criteria. By default, the **U**nlinked option button is selected. If you want the data extracted into the worksheet to remain linked to the external database (so that changes to the database are updated automatically in your worksheet), select the **L**inked option button. To paste the field entries from the matching records into the extract range, choose the **P**aste button.

Figure 21.29 illustrates an extract operation performed on an external dBASE employee database. The selection criteria in this example is a department number higher than >D100 (with the formula >D100 entered in cell C2 under the DEPT field name). You can see the results of the extraction in the range A7:E16. (The extract range is defined as cell range A6:E6 so that Q+E is not restricted to a set number of blank rows when pasting matching records.)

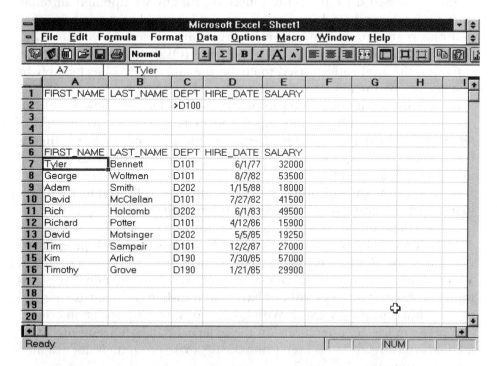

Figure 21.29 Extract Range After Pasting in the Matching Records

Alert! When you repeat an extract operation using the same extract range, Q+E does not automatically clear the entries from the previous extraction (as Excel does when extracting records from an Excel database). Therefore, you always need to clear the previously extracted data from the extract range before you perform your next extraction. Otherwise, Q+E may comingle matching records from your latest extraction with those pasted in the extract range during a previous extract operation.

SUMMARY

In this chapter you learned how to exchange data between Excel and the other applications you use in the office. First you learned how to copy text and graphics between documents created with different programs using the Clipboard. Next you learned how to link the information you exchange between programs using dynamic data exchange (DDE) links so that changes made to the data in the source document are updated automatically in the dependent document. Then you learned how to embed information created in one program in a document created with another program using object linking and embedding (OLE). Remember that you can open the applications used to create the embedded object simply by double-clicking the object in the dependent document.

After learning about linking information, you learned how Excel can open documents saved in different file formats as well as save them in a different file format so that the other application can still open the file. As part of this process, you also learned how to open text files in Excel worksheets. If the text file doesn't contain a delimiter character that Excel can use to divide the individual data items into new cells, you learned how to use the Parse and Smart Parse commands to split up the long text entries and place them in the correct cells of your worksheet.

At the end of the chapter, you learned how to use the Q+E program so that you can work with disk-based database files (both those on a local and a remote disk) created with stand-alone database management programs within an Excel worksheet without having to translate the database file and open it in its entirety in Excel. With Q+E, you can set up selection criteria and perform extract operations on the external database using the Excel methods you already know even when the database program is not installed on your computer.

Keystroke Shortcuts in Excel

Table A.1   Excel Keystroke Shortcuts Grouped by Function

Help Keys

Keystroke Shortcut	Function
F1	Displays the Excel Help window.
Shift+F1	Selects context-sensitive Excel Help.

Moving Through the Worksheet and Selecting Cells

Keystroke Shortcut	Function
Arrow keys ($\leftarrow,\rightarrow,\downarrow,\uparrow$)	Moves left, right, up, down one cell.
Home	Moves to the beginning of the row.
PgUp	Moves up one screenful.
Ctrl+PgUp	Moves left one screenful.
PgDn	Moves down one screenful.
Ctrl+PgDn	Moves right one screenful.
Ctrl+Home	Moves to the first cell in the worksheet (A1).

Table A.1   *(continued)*

Ctrl+End	Moves to the last active cell of the worksheet.
Ctrl+Arrow key	Moves to an edge of a data block.
Shift+Spacebar	Selects an entire row in the current selection.
Ctrl+Spacebar	Select san entire column in the current selection.
Ctrl+Shift+Spacebar	Selects the entire worksheet.
Shift+Arrow key	Extends the selection left, right, up, or down.
Ctrl+Shift+Arrow key	Extends the selection to the edge of a data block.
Shift+Home	Extends the selection to the beginning of the worksheet.
Shift+PgUp	Extends the selection up one screenful.
Shift+PgDn	Extends the selection down one screenful.
Ctrl+Shift+PgUp	Extends the selection left one screenful.
Ctrl+Shift+PgDn	Extends the selection right one screenful.
F8	Turns Extend mode on or off.
Shift+F8	Turns Add mode on or off.
Ctrl+* (asterisk on the numeric keypad only)	Selects the current data block.
F5	Goes to a specific cell or range.
Shift+F5	Displays the Find dialog box.
F7	Finds the cell with the next occurrence of the search string entered into the Find dialog box.
Shift+F7	Finds the cell with the previous occurrence of the search string entered into the Find dialog box.
End	Turns the End mode on and off.
End, Arrow key	Moves to the edge of the worksheet in the direction of the Arrow key (same as Ctrl+Arrow key).
End, Shift, +Arrow key	Extends the selection to the edge of the data block.

Table A.1 *(continued)*

Moving within a Cell Selection

Keystroke Shortcut	*Function*
Enter	Moves the cell pointer down one cell in the selection when the selection consists of more than one row. Moves one cell to the right when the selection consists of a single row.
Shift+Enter	Moves the cell pointer up one cell in the selection when the selection consists of more than one row. Moves one cell to the left when the selection consists of a single row.
Tab	Moves the cell pointer one cell to the right in the selection when the selection consists of more than one column. Moves one cell down when the selection consists of a single column.
Shift+Tab	Moves the cell pointer one cell to the left in the selection when the selection consists of more than one column. Moves one cell up when the selection consists of a single column.
Ctrl+. (period)	Moves to the next corner of the current cell range.
Ctrl+Tab	Moves to the next cell range in a nonadjacent selection.
Ctrl+Shift+Tab	Moves to the previous cell range in a nonadjacent selection.
Shift+Backspace	Collapses the cell selection to the active cell.

Scrolling Through a Document

Keystroke Shortcut	*Function*
Arrow key	Scrolls one row up or down or one column left or right.
PgUp	Scrolls up one screenful.
PgDn	Scrolls down one screenful.
Ctrl+PgUp	Scrolls left one screenful.
Ctrl+PgDn	Scrolls right one screenful.

Table A.1   *(continued)*

Selecting Items in a Chart

Keystroke Shortcut	*Function*
→	Moves to the next item.
←	Moves to the previous item.
↓	Moves to the next class of items.
↑	Moves to the previous class of items.

Formatting a Cell Selection

Keystroke Shortcut	*Function*
Ctrl+S	Selects the style box in the Standard toolbar.
Ctrl+Shift+~	Applies the General number format to the cell selection.
Ctrl+Shift+$	Applies the $#,###0.00_);($#,###0.00) currency format with two decimal places. Negative numbers appear in parentheses in the cell selection.
Ctrl+Shift+%	Applies the 0% percentage format with no decimal places to the cell selection.
Ctrl+Shift+^	Applies the 0.00E+00 exponential number format with two decimal places to the cell selection.
Ctrl+Shift+#	Applies the d-mmm-yy date format with the day, month, and year to the cell selection.
Ctrl+Shift+@	Applies the h:mm AM/PM time format with the hour, minute, and indicating AM or PM with the cell selection.
Ctrl+Shift+!	Applies the number format with two decimal places to the cell selection.
Ctrl +Shift+&	Applies an outline border to the cell selection.
Ctrl+Shift+_ (underscore)	Removes all borders in the cell selection.
Ctrl+1	Applies the Normal font to the cell selection.
Ctrl+B	Applies or removes bold in the cell selection.

Table A.1 *(continued)*

Ctrl+I	Applies or removes italics in the cell selection.
Ctrl+U	Applies or removes underlining in the cell selection.
Ctrl+5	Applies or removes strikeout in the cell selection.
Ctrl+9	Hides selected rows.
Ctrl+Shift+((left parenthesis)	Unhides all hidden rows.
Ctrl+0 (zero)	Hides selected columns.
Ctrl+Shift+) (right parenthesis)	Unhides all hidden columns.
Ctrl+F	Selects the Font Name list in the Formatting Toolbar if displayed; otherwise opens the Font dialog box.
Ctrl+P	Selects the Font Size list in the Formatting Toolbar if displayed; otherwise opens the Font dialog box.

Editing the Worksheet

Keystroke Shortcut	*Function*
Enter	Carries out a command or action.
Esc	Cancels a command or closes the displayed dialog box.
Alt+Enter	Repeats the last action.
Ctrl+Z	Undoes the last action.
Ctrl+Shift+Plus sign (+)	Displays the Insert dialog box.
Ctrl+Minus sign (û)	Displays the Delete dialog box.
Delete	Displays the Clear dialog box.
Ctrl+Del	Clears entries in a cell selection.
Ctrl+X	Cuts a selection to the Clipboard.
Ctrl+C	Copies a selection to the Clipboard.
Ctrl+V	Pastes the contents of the Clipboard.

Table A.1   *(continued)*

Shift+F2	Displays the Cell Note dialog box.
Ctrl+F2	Alternates between displaying the Info window with information about the active cell and the active document window.
F3	Displays the Paste Name dialog box so that you can paste a range name into a formula.
Shift+F3	Displays the Paste Function dialog box so that you can paste a formula and its argument description into a formula.
Ctrl+F3	Displays the Define Name dialog box so that you can assign a range name to the cell selection.
Ctrl+Shift+F3	Displays the Create Names dialog box so that you can assign range names to the cell selection using existing cell labels.
Ctrl+= (equal sign) or F9	Calculates all worksheets.
Shift+F9	Calculates only the worksheet in the active document.
Alt+= (equal sign)	Creates a sum formula (the same as clicking the AutoSum tool on the Standard toolbar).
Ctrl+R	Selects the Edit Fill Right command.
Ctrl+D	Selects the Edit Fill Down command.
Ctrl+8	Toggles the display of outline symbols on and off. If no outline exists, displays the alert dialog box prompting you to create an outline (the same as clicking the Show Outline Symbols tool in the Utility toolbar).
Alt+Shift+→	Selects the Demote tool in the Utility Toolbar if displayed; otherwise displays the Demote dialog box.
Alt+Shift+←	Selects the Promote tool in the Utility Toolbar if displayed, otherwise displays the Promote dialog box.
Alt+;	Selects only the visible cells in the cell selection (same as clicking the Visible Cells Only tool in the Utility toolbar).

Table A.1   *(continued)*

Editing in the Formula Bar

Keystroke Shortcut	*Function*
F2	Activates the formula bar.
Ctrl+; (semicolon)	Inserts the current date in the formula bar.
Ctrl+Shift+; (semicolon—same as Ctrl+:)	Inserts the current time in the formula bar.
Ctrl+' (single quotation mark)	Copies the formula from the cell above the active cell into the formula bar.
Ctrl+Shift+" (double quotation marks)	Copies the value from the cell above the active cell into the formula bar.
Ctrl+Enter	Fills the cell selection with the entry on the formula bar.
Ctrl+Shift+Enter	Enters a formula as an array formula.
Arrow key (↑,↓,←,→)	Moves the insertion point one character up, down, left, or right.
Home	Moves the insertion point to the beginning of the line.
F4	Converts the current cell reference from relative to absolute, from absolute to mixed, and from mixed back to relative.
Alt+Enter	Inserts a new paragraph in the formula bar.
Ctrl+Tab	Inserts a tab in the formula bar.
Backspace	Deletes the preceding character in the formula bar or activates and clears the formula bar when a cell is selected.
Ctrl+Shift+Delete	Deletes the text to the end of the line in the formula bar.

Working with Files

Keystroke Shortcut	*Function*

Table A.1   *(continued)*

Alt+Shift+F1 or Shift+F11	Opens a new worksheet document window.
Alt+F1 or F11	Opens a chart document window.
Alt+Ctrl+F1 or Ctrl+F11	Opens a new macro sheet window.
Alt+F2 or F12	Saves the active file with the Save As command on the File menu.
Alt+Shift+F2 or Shift+F12	Saves the active file with the Save command on the File menu.
Ctrl+F12	Displays the Open dialog box so that you can open an existing Excel document.
Ctrl+Shift+F12	Displays the Print dialog box so that you can print the active document window.

Working with Windows

Keystroke Shortcut	Function
Alt or F10	Selects the Menu bar.
Shift+F10	Opens the Shortcut menu.
Alt+Spacebar	Selects the Control menu for the Excel program window.
Alt+- (Hyphen)	Selects the Control menu for the active document window.
Ctrl+F7, arrow keys	Moves the active document window.
Ctrl+F8, arrow keys	Sizes the active document window.
Ctrl+F10	Maximizes the active document window.
Ctrl+F9	Minimizes the active document window.
Ctrl+F5	Restores the document window.
Ctrl+F4	Closes the active document window.
Ctrl+F6	Switches to the next open document window.
Ctrl+Shift+F6	Switches to the previous open document window.

Table A.1 *(continued)*

Alt+PgDn	Switches to the next document window in a workbook file.
Alt+PgUp	Switches to the previous document window in a workbook file.
F6	Moves to the next pane in a split document window.
Shift+F6	Moves to the previous pane in a split document window.
Alt+F4	Quits Excel.

Working in a Data Form for a Database

Keystroke Shortcut	*Function*
↓	Moves to the same field in the next record.
↑	Moves to the same field in the previous record.
Tab	Moves to the next field so that you can edit in the current record.
Shift+Tab	Moves to the previous field so that you can edit in the current record.
Enter	Moves to the first field in the next record.
Shift+Enter	Moves to the first field in the previous record.
PgDn	Moves to the same field 10 records forward.
PgUp	Moves to the same field 10 records back.
Ctrl+PgDn	Moves to a new record at the end of the database.
Ctrl+PgUp	Moves to the first record in the database.
Home, End, ←, →	Moves the insertion point within the current field.

Moving in Data Find Mode

Keystroke Shortcut	*Function*
↓	Finds the next matching record in the database.

Table A.1   *(continued)*

↑	Finds the previous matching record in the database.
PgDn	Finds the next matching record at least one window down from the selection.
PgUp	Finds the previous matching record at least one window up from the selection.

Viewing a Document in Print Preview (after Zooming)

Keystroke Shortcut	*Function*
Arrow keys	Moves left, right, up, or down on the current page.
Ctrl+Home	Displays the upper-left corner of the current page.
Ctrl+End	Displays the lower-right corner of the current page.
Ctrl+←	Displays the left part of the current page.
Ctrl+→	Displays the right part of the current page.

Appendix **B**

Worksheet Functions in Excel

 Indicates new features in Excel 4.0.

 Indicates Add-in functions separate from Excel's standard package.

Engineering

BESSELI

 Returns the modified Bessel function $I_n(x)$.

Syntax

=BESSELI(*x,n*)

Arguments: X is the value and N is the order of the function. If n is not an integer, it is truncated.

BESSELJ

 Returns the Bessel function $J_n(x)$.

Syntax

=BESSELJ(*x,n*)

Arguments: X is the value and N is the order of the function. If n is not an integer, it is truncated.

BESSELK

 Returns the modified Bessel function $K_n(x)$.

Syntax

=BESSELK(*x,n*)

Arguments: X is the value and N is the order of the function. If n is not an integer, it is truncated.

BESSELY

 Returns the Bessel function $Y_n(x)$.

Syntax

=BESSELY(*x,n*)

Arguments: *X* is the value and *N* is the order of the function. If *n* is not an integer, it is truncated.

BIN2DEC

 Converts a binary number to decimal.

Syntax

=BIN2DEC(*number*)

Argument: *Number* is the binary number to convert. The *number* argument may not contain more than 10 characters (10 bits). The most significant bit of *number* is the sign bit. The remaining 9 bits are magnitude bits. Negative numbers are represented using two's-complement notation.

BIN2HEX

  Converts a binary number to hexadecimal.

Syntax

=BIN2HEX(*number,places*)

Arguments: *Number* is the binary number you want to convert. The *number* argument may not contain more than 10 characters (10 bits). The most significant bit of *number* is the sign bit. The remaining 9 bits are magnitude bits. Negative numbers are represented using two's-complement notation. *Places* is the number of characters to use. If this argument is omitted, the function uses the minimum number of characters necessary.

Notes

- If *number* is not a valid binary number, or if it contains more than 10 characters (10 bits), the function returns the #NUM! error.
- If *number* is negative, the function ignores *places* and returns a 10-character hexadecimal number.
- If the function requires more than *places* characters, it returns the #NUM! error.

BIN2OCT

 Converts a binary number to octal.

Syntax

=BIN2OCT(*number,places*)

Arguments: *Number* is the binary number you want to convert. The *number* argument may not contain more than 10 characters (10 bits). The most significant bit of *number* is the sign bit. The remaining 9 bits are magnitude bits. Negative numbers are represented using two's-complement notation. *Places* is the number of characters to use. If this argument is omitted, the function uses the minimum number of characters necessary.

Notes

- If *number* is not a valid binary number, or if it contains more than 10 characters (10 bits), the function returns the #NUM! error.
- If *number* is negative, the function ignores *places* and returns a 10-character octal number.
- If the function requires more than *places* characters, it returns the #NUM! error.

COMPLEX

 Converts real and imaginary coefficients into a complex number.

Syntax

=COMPLEX (*real_num,i_num,suffix*)

Arguments: *Real_num* is the real coefficient of the complex number. *I_num* is the imaginary coefficient of the complex number. *Suffix* is the suffix for the imaginary component of the complex number. If omitted, *suffix* is assumed to be "i".

Notes

- All complex number functions accept "i" and "j" for *suffix* but neither "I" nor "J". Using uppercase results in the #NUM! error. All functions that accept two or more complex numbers require that all suffixes match.
- If *suffix* is neither "i" nor "j", the function returns the #VALUE! error.

CONVERT

 Converts a number from one measurement system to another.

Syntax

=CONVERT(*number,from_unit, to_unit*)

Arguments: *Number* is the value in *from_units* to convert. *From_unit* is the units for *number*. *To_unit* is the units for the result.

CONVERT accepts the following text values for *from_unit* and *to_unit*:

Measurement	*From_unit or to_unit*
Weight and mass	
Gram	g
Slug	sg
Pound mass (avoirdupois)	lbm
U	u
Ounce mass (avoirdupois)	ozm
Distance	
Meter	m
Statute mile	mi
Nautical mile	nmi
Inch	in
Foot	ft
Yard	yd
Angstrom	ang

Time

Year	yr
Day	day
Hour	hr
Minute	mn
Second	sec

Pressure

Pascal	p
Atmosphere	at

Force

Newton	N
Dyne	dy
Pound force	lbf

Energy

Joule	J
Erg	e
Thermodynamic calorie	c
IT calorie	cal
Electron bolt	ev
Housepower-hour	hh
Watt-hour	wh
Foot-pound	flb
BTU	btu

Power

Horsepower	h
Watt	w

Electricity

Volt	V
Coulomb	C
Ampere	A

Magnetism

Tesla	T
Gauss	ga

Temperature

Degree Celsius	cel
Degree Fahrenheit	fah
Degree Kelvin	kel

Liquid measure

Teaspoon	tsp
Tablespoon	tbs
Fluid ounce	oz
Cup	cup
Pint	pt
Quart	qt
Gallon	gal
Liter	lt

The following unit prefixes can be added to any metric *from_unit or to_unit.*

Prefix	Abbreviation
exa	E
peta	P
tera	T
giga	G
mega	M
kilo	k
deka	e
deci	d
centi	c
milli	m
micro	u
nano	m
pico	p
femto	f
atto	a

Notes

• Unit names and prefixes are case-sensitive.

DEC2BIN

Converts a decimal integer to binary.

Syntax

=DEC2BIN(*number,places*)

Arguments: *Number* is the decimal integer you want to convert. If *number* is negative, *places* is ignored and the function returns a 10-character (10-bit) binary number in which the most significant bit is the sign bit. The remaining 9 bits are magnitude bits. Negative numbers are represented using two's-complement notation. *Places* is the number of characters to use. If *places* is omitted, the function uses the minimum number of characters necessary.

Notes

• If *number* is less than −512 or greater than 511, the function returns the #NUM! error.

• If the function requires more than *places* characters, it returns the #NUM! error.

DEC2HEX

Converts a decimal integer to hexadecimal.

Syntax

=DEC2HEX(*number,places*)

Arguments: *Number* is the decimal integer you want to convert. If *number* is negative, *places* is ignored and the function returns a 10-character (40-bit) hexadecimal number in which the most significant bit is the sign bit. The remaining 39 bits are magnitude bits. Negative numbers are represented using two's-complement notation. *Places* is the number of characters to use. If *places* is omitted, the function uses the minimum number of characters necessary. *Places* is useful for padding the return value with leading 0s (zeroes).

Notes

- If *number* is less than –549755813888 or greater than 549755813887, the function returns the #NUM! error.
- If the function requires more than *places* characters, it returns the #NUM! error.

DEC2OCT

 Converts a decimal integer to octal.

Syntax

=DEC2OCT(*number,places*)

Arguments: *Number* is the decimal integer you want to convert. If *number* is negative, *places* is ignored and the function returns a 10-character (30-bit) octal number in which the most significant bit is the sign bit. The remaining 29 bits are magnitude bits. Negative numbers are represented using two's-complement notation. *Places* is the number of characters to use. If *places* is omitted, the function uses the minimum number of characters necessary. *Places* is useful for padding the return value with leading 0s (zeroes).

Notes

- If *number* is less than minus 536870912 or greater than 536870911, the function returns the #NUM! error.
- If the function requires more than *places* characters, it returns the #NUM! error.

DEGREES

 Converts radians to degrees.

Syntax

=DEGREES(*angle_in_radians*)

Argument: *Angle_in_radians* is the angle in radians that you want to convert.

DELTA

 Tests whether two numbers are equal. Returns 1 if the *number1* argument is equal to the *number2* argument. Otherwise returns 0.

Syntax

=DELTA(*number1,number2*)

Arguments: *Number1* is the first number. *Number2* is the second number. If omitted, *number2* is assumed to be zero.

ERF

 Returns the error function integrated between the *lower_limit* argument and the *upper_limit* argument.

Syntax

=ERF(*lower_limit,upper_limit*)

Arguments: *Lower_limit* is the lower bound for integrating ERF. *Upper_limit* is the upper bound for integrating ERF. If omitted, the function integrates between zero and *lower_limit*.

ERFC

 Returns the complementary error function integrated between *x* and infinity.

Syntax

=ERFC(*x*)

Argument: *X* is the lower bound for integrating function.

GESTEP

 Tests whether a number is greater than a threshold value. Returns 1 if the *number* argument is greater than the *step* argument. Otherwise the function returns 0.

Syntax

=GESTEP(*number,step*)

Arguments: *Number* is the value to test against *step*. *Step* is the threshold value. If you omit a value for *step*, the function uses zero.

HEX2BIN

 Converts a hexadecimal number to a binary number.

Syntax

=HEX2BIN(*number,places*)

Arguments: *Number* is the hexadecimal number you want to convert. *Number* may not contain more than 10 characters. The most significant bit of *number* is the sign bit. The remaining 9 bits are magnitude bits. Negative numbers are represented using two's-complement notation. *Places* is the number of characters to use. If *places* is omitted, the function uses the minimum number of characters necessary. *Places* is useful for padding the return value with leading 0s (zeroes).

Notes

- If *number* is negative, the function ignores *places* and returns a 10-character binary number.
- If *number* is negative, it cannot be less than FFFFFFFE00, and if *number* is positive, it cannot be greater than 1FF.
- If *number* is not a valid hexadecimal number, the function returns the #NUM! error.
- If the function requires more than *places* characters, it returns the #NUM! error.

HEX2DEC

 Converts a hexadecimal number to a decimal number.

Syntax

=HEX2DEC(*number*)

Argument: *Number* is the hexadecimal number you want to convert. *Number* may not contain more than 10 characters (40 bits). The most significant bit of *number* is the sign bit. The remaining 39 bits are magnitude bits. Negative numbers are represented using two's-complement notation. If *number* is not a valid hexadecimal number, the function returns the #NUM! error.

HEX2OCT

Converts a hexadecimal number to an octal number.

Syntax

=HEX2OCT(*number,places*)

Arguments: *Number* is the hexadecimal number you want to convert. *Number* may not contain more than 10 characters. The most significant bit of *number* is the sign bit. The remaining 39 bits are magnitude bits. Negative numbers are represented using two's-complement notation. *Places* is the number of characters to use. If *places* is omitted, the function uses the minimum number of characters necessary. *Places* is useful for padding the return value with leading 0s (zeroes).

Notes

- If *number* is negative, the function ignores *places* and returns a 10-character octal number.

- If *number* is negative, it cannot be less than FFE0000000, and if *number* is positive, it cannot be greater than 1FFFFFFF.

- If *number* is not a valid hexadecimal number, the function returns the #NUM! error.

- If the function requires more than *places* characters, it returns the #NUM! error.

IMABS

Returns the absolute value (modulus) of a complex number.

Syntax

=IMABS(*inumber*)

Argument: *Inumber* is a complex number for which you want the absolute value. If *inumber* is not text, the function returns the #VALUE! error. If *inumber* is not in the form $x + yi$ or $x + yj$, the function returns the #NUM! error.

IMAGINARY

Returns the imaginary coefficient of a complex number.

Syntax

=IMAGINARY(*inumber*)

Argument: *Inumber* is a complex number for which you want the imaginary coefficient. If *inumber* is not text, the function returns the #VALUE! error. If *inumber* is not in the form $x + yi$ or $x + yj$, the function returns the #NUM! error.

IMARGUMENT

Returns the argument θ, an angle expressed in radians.

Syntax

=IMARGUMENT(*inumber*)

Argument: *Inumber* is a complex number for which you want the argument 0. If *inumber* is not text, the function returns the #VALUE! error. If *inumber* is not in the form $x + yi$ or $x + yj$, the function returns the #NUM! error.

IMCONJUGATE

 Returns the complex conjugate of a complex number.

Syntax

=IMCONJUGATE(*inumber*)

Argument: *Inumber* is a complex number for which you want the conjugate. If *inumber* is not text, the function returns the #VALUE! error. If *inumber* is not in the form $x + yi$ or $x + yj$, the function returns the #NUM! error.

IMCOS

 Returns the complex cosine of a complex number.

Syntax

=IMCOS(*inumber*)

Argument: *Inumber* is a complex number for which you want the cosine. If *inumber* is not text, the function returns the #VALUE! error. If *inumber* is not in the form $x + yi$ or $x + yj$, the function returns the #NUM! error.

IMDIV

 Returns the quotient of two complex numbers.

Syntax

=IMDIV(*inumber1,inumber2*)

Argument: *Inumber1* is the complex numerator or dividend. *Inumber2* is the complex denominator or divisor. If *inumber1* or *inumber2* is not text, the function returns the #VALUE! error. If *inumber1* or *inumber2* is not in the form $x + yi$ or $x + yj$, the function returns the #NUM! error.

IMEXP

 Returns the exponential of a complex number.

Syntax

=IMEXP(*inumber*)

Argument: *Inumber* is a complex number for which you want the exponential. If *inumber1* or *inumber 2* is not text, the function returns the #VALUE! error. If *inumber1* or *inumber 2* is not in the form $x + yi$ or $x + yj$, the function returns the #NUM! error.

IMLN

 Returns the natural logarithm of a complex number.

Syntax

=IMLN(*inumber*)

Argument: *Inumber* is a complex number for which you want the natural logarithm. If *inumber* is not text, the function returns the #VALUE! error. If *inumber* is not in the form $x + yi$ or $x + yj$, the function returns the #NUM! error.

IMLOG10

 Returns the common logarithm (base 10) of a complex number.

Syntax

=IMLOG10(*inumber*)

Argument: *Inumber* is a complex number for which you want the common logarithm. If *inumber* is not text, the function returns the #VALUE! error. If *inumber* is not in the form $x + yi$ or $x + yj$, the function returns the #NUM! error.

IMLOG2

 Returns the base-2 logarithm of a complex number.

Syntax

=IMLOG2(*inumber*)

Argument: *Inumber* is a complex number for which you want the base-2 logarithm. If *inumber* is not text, the function returns the #VALUE! error. If *inumber* is not in the form $x + yi$ or $x + yj$, the function returns the #NUM! error.

IMPOWER

 Returns a complex number.

Syntax

=IMPOWER(*inumber,number*)

Arguments: *Inumber* is a complex number you want to raise to a power. *Number* is the power to which you want to raise the complex number.

Notes

- If *inumber* is not text, the function returns the #VALUE! error.
- If *inumber* is not in the form $x + yi$ or $x + yj$, the function returns the #NUM! error.

IMPRODUCT

 Returns the product of two complex numbers.

Syntax

=IMPRODUCT(*inumber1,inumber2*)

Arguments: *Inumber1* is the complex number multicand. *Inumber2* is the complex number multiplier.

Notes

- If *inumber1* or *inumber2* is not text, the function returns the #VALUE! error. If *inumber1* or *inumber2* is not in the form $x + yi$ or $x + yj$, the function returns the #NUM! error.

IMREAL

Returns the real coefficient of a complex number.

Syntax

=IMREAL(*inumber*)

Argument: *Inumber* is a complex number for which you want the real coefficient. If *inumber* is not text, the function returns the #VALUE! error. If *inumber* is not in the form $x + yi$ or $x + yj$, the function returns the #NUM! error.

IMSIN

Returns the sine of a complex number.

Syntax

=IMSIN(*inumber*)

Argument: *Inumber* is a complex number for which you want the sine. If *inumber* is not text, the function returns the #VALUE! error. If *inumber* is not in the form $x + yi$ or $x + yj$, the function returns the #NUM! error.

IMSQRT

Returns the square root of a complex number.

Syntax

=IMSQRT(*inumber*)

Argument: *Inumber* is a complex number for which you want the square root. If *inumber* is not text, the function returns the #VALUE! error. If *inumber* is not in the form $x + yi$ or $x + yj$, the function returns the #NUM! error.

IMSUB

Returns the difference of two complex numbers.

Syntax

=IMSUB(*inumber1,inumber2*)

Arguments: *Inumber1* is the complex number from which to subtract *inumber2*. *Inumber2* is the complex number to subtract from *inumber1*.

Notes

- If *inumber* is not text, the function returns the #VALUE! error.
- If *inumber* is not in the form $x + yi$ or $x + yj$, the function returns the #NUM! error.

IMSUM

Returns the sum of complex numbers.

Syntax

=IMSUM(*inumber1,inumber2,inumber3,...*)

Argument: *Inumber1, inumber2,* and so on are from 1 to 12 complex numbers to add. If any argument is not text, the function returns the #VALUE! error. If any argument is not in the form $x + yi$ or $x + yj$, the function returns the #NUM! error.

OCT2BIN

 Converts an octal number to a binary number.

Syntax

=OCT2BIN(*number,places*)

Arguments: *Number* is the octal number you want to convert. *Number* may not contain more than 10 characters. The most significant bit of *number* is the sign bit. The remaining 29 bits are magnitude bits. Negative numbers are represented using two's-complement notation. *Places* is the number of characters to use. If *places* is omitted, the function uses the minimum number of characters necessary. *Places* is useful for padding the return value with leading 0s (zeroes).

Notes

- If *number* is negative, the function ignores *places* and returns a 10-character binary number.

- If *number* is negative, it cannot be less than 7777777000, and if *number* is positive, it cannot be greater than 777.

- If *number* is not a valid octal number, the function returns the #NUM! error.

- If the function requires more than *places* characters, it returns the #NUM! error.

OCT2DEC

 Converts an octal number to a decimal number.

Syntax

=OCT2DEC(*number*)

Argument: *Number* is the octal number you want to convert. *Number* may not contain more than 10 octal characters (30 bits). The most significant bit of *number* is the sign bit. The remaining 29 bits are magnitude bits. Negative numbers are represented using two's-complement notation. If *number* is not a valid octal number, the function returns the #NUM! error.

OCT2HEX

 Converts an octal number to a hexadecimal number.

Syntax

=OCT2HEX(*number,places*)

Arguments: *Number* is the octal number you want to convert. *Number* may not contain more than 10 octal characters (30 bits). The most significant bit of *number* is the sign bit. The remaining 29 bits are magnitude bits. Negative numbers are represented using two's-complement notation. *Places* is the number of characters to use. If *places* is omitted, the function uses the minimum number of characters necessary. *Places* is useful for padding the return value with leading 0s (zeroes).

Notes

- If *number* is negative, the function ignores *places* and returns a 10-character hexadecimal number.

- If *number* is not a valid octal number, the function returns the #NUM! error.
- If the function requires more than *places* characters, it returns the #NUM! error.

SQRTPI

 Returns the square root of *number* times the constant Pi (π).

Syntax

=SQRTPI(*number*)

Argument: *Number* is the number by which π is multiplied. If *number* < 0, SQRTPI returns the #NUM! error.

Financial

ACCRINT

 Returns the accrued interest for a security that pays periodic interest.

Syntax

=ACCRINT(*issue,first_interest,settlement,coupon,par,frequency,basis*)

Arguments: *Issue* is the security's issue date, expressed as a serial date number. *First_interest* is the security's first interest date, expressed as a serial date number. *Settlement* is the security's settlement date, expressed as a serial date number. *Coupon* is the security's annual coupon rate. *Par* is the security's par value. If you omit *par*, the function uses $1,000. *Frequency* is the number of coupon payments per year. For annual payments, *frequency* = 1; for semiannual, *frequency* = 2; for quarterly, *frequency* = 4. *Basis* is the type of day count basis to use. If *basis* is 0 or omitted, use 30/360. If *basis* is 1, use actual/actual. If *basis* is 2, use actual/360. If *basis* is 3, use actual/365.

Notes

- *Issue, first_interest, settlement, frequency,* and *basis* are truncated to integers.
- If *issue, first_interest,* or *settlement* is not a valid serial date number, the function returns the #NUM! error.
- If *coupon* ≤ 0 or if *par* ≤ 0, the function returns the #NUM! error.
- If *frequency* is any number other than 1, 2, or 4, the function returns the #NUM! error.
- If *basis* < 0 or if *basis* > 3, the function returns the #NUM! error.
- If *issue* ≥ *settlement*, the function returns the #NUM! error.

ACCRINTM

 Returns the accrued interest for a maturity security that pays periodic interest at maturity.

Syntax

=ACCRINTM(*issue,settlement,rate,coupon,par,basis*)

Arguments: *Issue* is the security's issue date, expressed as a serial date number.

Settlement is the security's maturity date, expressed as a serial date number. *Rate* is the security's annual coupon rate. *Par* is the security's par value. If you omit *par*, the function uses $1,000. *Basis* is the type of day count basis to use. If *basis* is 0 or omitted, use 30/360. If *basis* is 1, use actual/actual. If *basis* is 2, use actual/360. If *basis* is 3, use actual/365.

Notes

- *Issue, settlement,* and *basis* are truncated to integers.
- If *issue* or *settlement* is not a valid serial date number, the function returns the #NUM! error.
- If *coupon* ≤ 0 or if *par* ≤0, the function returns the #NUM! error.
- If *basis* < 0 or if *basis* > 3, the function returns the #NUM! error.
- If *issue* ≥ *settlement,* the function returns the #NUM! error.

COUPDAYBS

Returns the number of days from the beginning of the coupon period to the settlement date.

Syntax

=COUPDAYBS(*settlement,maturity,frequency,basis*)

Arguments: *Settlement* is the security's settlement date, expressed as a serial date number. *Maturity* is the security's maturity date, expressed as a serial date number. *Frequency* is the number of coupon payments per year. For annual payments, *frequency* = 1; for semiannual, *frequency* = 2; for quarterly, *frequency* = 4. *Basis* is the type of day count basis to use. If *basis* is 0 or omitted, use 30/360. If *basis* is 1, use actual/actual. If *basis* is 2, use actual/360. If *basis* is 3, use actual/365.

Notes

- All arguments are truncated to integers.
- If *settlement* or *maturity* is not a valid serial date number, the function returns the #NUM! error.
- If *frequency* is any number other than 1, 2, or 4, the function returns the #NUM! error.
- If *basis* < 0 or if *basis* > 3, the function returns the #NUM! error.
- If *settlement* ≥ maturity, the function returns the #NUM! error.

COUPDAYS

Returns the number of days in the coupon period that contains the settlement date.

Syntax

=COUPDAYS(*settlement,maturity,frequency,basis*)

Arguments: *Settlement* is the security's settlement date, expressed as a serial date number. *Maturity* is the security's maturity date, expressed as a serial date number. *Frequency* is the number of coupon payments per year. For annual payments, *frequency* = 1; for semiannual, *frequency* = 2; for quarterly, *frequency* = 4. *Basis* is the type of day count basis to use. If *basis* is 0 or omitted, use 30/360. If *basis* is 1, use actual/actual. If *basis* is 2, use actual/360. If *basis* is 3, use actual/365.

Notes

- All arguments are truncated to integers. Nonnumeric arguments return the #VALUE! error.
- If *settlement* or *maturity* is not a valid serial date number, the function returns the #NUM! error.
- If *frequency* is any number other than 1, 2, or 4, the function returns the #NUM! error.
- If *basis* < 0 or if *basis* > 3, the function returns the #NUM! error.
- If *settlement* ≥ maturity, the function returns the #NUM! error.

COUPDAYSNC

 Returns the number of days from the settlement date to the next coupon date.

Syntax

=COUPDAYSNC(*settlement,maturity,frequency,basis*)

Arguments: *Settlement* is the security's settlement date, expressed as a serial date number. *Maturity* is the security's maturity date, expressed as a serial date number. *Frequency* is the number of coupon payments per year. For annual payments, *frequency* = 1; for semiannual, *frequency* = 2; for quarterly, *frequency* = 4. *Basis* is the type of day count basis to use. If *basis* is 0 or omitted, use 30/360. If *basis* is 1, use actual/actual. If *basis* is 2, use actual/360. If *basis* is 3, use actual/365.

Notes

- All arguments are truncated to integers. Nonnumeric arguments return the #VALUE! error.
- If *settlement* or *maturity* is not a valid serial date number, the function returns the #NUM! error.
- If *frequency* is any number other than 1, 2, or 4, the function returns the #NUM! error.
- If *basis* < 0 or if *basis* > 3, the function returns the #NUM! error.
- If *settlement* ≥ *maturity*, the function returns the #NUM! error.

COUPNCD

 Returns the next coupon date after the settlement date.

Syntax

=COUPNCD(*settlement,maturity,frequency,basis*)

Arguments: *Settlement* is the security's settlement date, expressed as a serial date number. *Maturity* is the security's maturity date, expressed as a serial date number. *Frequency* is the number of coupon payments per year. For annual payments, *frequency* = 1; for semiannual, *frequency* = 2; for quarterly, *frequency* = 4. *Basis* is the type of day count basis to use. If *basis* is 0 or omitted, use 30/360. If *basis* is 1, use actual/actual. If *basis* is 2, use actual/360. If *basis* is 3, use actual/365.

Notes

- All arguments are truncated to integers. Nonnumeric arguments return the #VALUE! error.
- If *settlement* or *maturity* is not a valid serial date number, the function returns the #NUM! error.
- If *frequency* is any number other than 1, 2, or 4, the function returns the #NUM! error.
- If *basis* < 0 or if *basis* > 3, the function returns the #NUM! error.
- If *settlement* ≥ *maturity*, the function returns the #NUM! error.

COUPNUM

 Returns the number of coupons payable between the settlement date and maturity date, rounded to the nearest whole coupon.

Syntax

=COUPNUM(*settlement,maturity,frequency,basis*)

Arguments: *Settlement* is the security's settlement date, expressed as a serial date number. *Maturity* is the security's maturity date, expressed as a serial date number. *Frequency* is the number of coupon payments per year. For annual payments, *frequency* = 1; for semiannual, *frequency* = 2; for quarterly, *frequency* = 4. *Basis* is the type of day count basis to use. If *basis* is 0 or omitted, use 30/360. If *basis* is 1, use actual/actual. If *basis* is 2, use actual/360. If *basis* is 3, use actual/365.

Notes

- All arguments are truncated to integers. Nonnumeric arguments return the #VALUE! error.
- If *settlement* or *maturity* is not a valid serial date number, the function returns the #NUM! error.
- If *frequency* is any number other than 1, 2, or 4, the function returns the #NUM! error.
- If *basis* < 0 or if *basis* > 3, the function returns the #NUM! error.
- If *settlement* ≥ *maturity*, the function returns the #NUM! error.

COUPPCD

 Returns the previous coupon date before the settlement date.

Syntax

=COUPPCD(*settlement,maturity,frequency,basis*)

Arguments: *Settlement* is the security's settlement date, expressed as a serial date number. *Maturity* is the security's maturity date, expressed as a serial date number. *Frequency* is the number of coupon payments per year. For annual payments, *frequency* = 1; for semiannual, *frequency* = 2; for quarterly, *frequency* = 4. *Basis* is the type of day count basis to use. If *basis* is 0 or omitted, use 30/360. If *basis* is 1, use actual/actual. If *basis* is 2, use actual/360. If *basis* is 3, use actual/365.

Notes

- All arguments are truncated to integers. Nonnumeric arguments return the #VALUE! error.

- If *settlement* or *maturity* is not a valid serial date number, the function returns the #NUM! error.

- If *frequency* is any number other than 1, 2, or 4, the function returns the #NUM! error.

- If *basis* < 0 or if *basis* > 3, the function returns the #NUM! error.

- If *settlement* ≥ *maturity*, the function returns the #NUM! error.

CUMIPMT

 Returns the cumulative interest paid on a loan between the *start_period* argument and the *end_period* argument.

Syntax

=CUMIPMT(*rate,nper,pv,start_period,end_period,type*)

Arguments: *Rate* is the interest rate. *Nper* is the total number of payment periods. *Pv* is the present value. *Start_period* is the first period in the calculation. Payment periods are numbered beginning with 1. *End_period* is the last period in the calculation. *Type* is the timing of the payment. If *type* is 0, payment is at the end of the period. If *type* is 1, payment is at the beginning of the period.

Notes

- Be consistent with the units you specify for *rate* and *nper*. For example, if you make monthly payments on a thirty-year loan at 10% annual interest, you would use 10%/12 for *rate* and 30*12 for *nper*. If you were to make annual payments on the same loan, use 10% for *rate* and 30 for *nper*.

- *Nper, start_period, end_period,* and *type* are truncated to integers.

- If *rate* ≤ 0, *nper* ≤ 0, or *pv* ≤ 0, the function returns the #NUM! error.

- If *start_period* < 1, *end_period* < 1, or *start_period* > *end_period*, the function returns the #NUM! error.

- If *type* is any number other than 0 or 1, the function returns the #NUM! error.

CUMPRINC

 Returns the cumulative principal paid on a loan between the *start_period* argument and the *end_period* argument.

Syntax

=CUMPRINC(*rate,nper,pv,start_period,end_period,type*)

Arguments: *Rate* is the interest rate. *Nper* is the total number of payment periods. *Pv* is the present value. *Start_period* is the first period in the calculation. Payment periods are numbered beginning with 1. *End_period* is the last period in the calculation. *Type* is the timing of the payment. If *type* is 0, payment is at the end of the period. If *type* is 1, payment is at the beginning of the period.

Notes

- Be consistent with the units you specify for *rate* and *nper*. For example, if you make monthly payments on a thirty-year loan at 10 percent annual interest, you would use 10%/12 for *rate* and 30*12 for *nper*. If you were to make annual payments on the same loan, use 10% for *rate* and 30 for *nper*.

- *Nper, start_period, end_period,* and *type* are truncated to integers.

- If *rate* ≤ 0, *nper* ≤ 0, or *pv* ≤ 0, the function returns the #NUM! error.

- If *start_period* < 1, *end_period* < 1, or *start_period* > *end_period*, the function returns the #NUM! error.

- If *type* is any number other than 0 or 1, the function returns the #NUM! error.

DB

Returns the real depreciation of an asset for a specified period using the fixed-declining balance method.

Syntax

=DB(*cost,salvage,life,period, month*)

Arguments: *Cost* is the initial cost of the asset. *Salvage* is the value at the end of the depreciation. *Life* is the number of periods over which the asset is being depreciated. *Period* is the period for which you want to calculate the depreciation. *Period* must use the same units as *life*. *Month* is the number of months in the first year. If *month* is omitted, it is assumed to be 12.

Notes

- The fixed-declining balance method computes depreciation at a fixed rate. DB uses the following formulas to calculate depreciation for a period:

    (*cost* - total depreciation from prior periods) * *rate*

  where

    rate = 1 - ((salvage/cost) ^ (1 / *life*)), rounded to three decimal places

- Depreciation for the first and last periods is a special case. For the first period, DB uses this formula:

    cost * *rate* * *month* / 12

  For the last period, DB uses this formula:

    ((*cost* - total depreciation from prior periods) * *rate* * (12 - month)) / 12

DDB

Returns the depreciation of an asset for a specified period using the double-declining balance method.

Syntax

=DDB(*cost,salvage,life,period,factor*)

Arguments: *Cost* is the initial cost of the asset. *Salvage* is the value at the end of the depreciation. *Life* is the number of periods over which the asset is being depreciated. *Period* is the period for which you want to calculate the depreciation. *Period* must use the same units as *life*. *Factor* is the rate at which the balance declines. If *factor* is omitted, it is assumed to be 2 (the double-declining balance method). All five arguments must be positive numbers.

Notes

- The double-declining balance method computes depreciation at an accelerated rate. Depreciation is highest in the first period and decreases in successive periods. DDB uses the following formula to calculate depreciation for a period:

    cost – salvage (total depreciation from prior periods) * *factor* / *life*

- Change *factor* if you do not want to use the double-declining balance method.

DISC

 Returns the discount rate for a security.

Syntax

=DISC(settlement,maturity,pr,redemption,basis)

Arguments: *Settlement* is the security's settlement date, expressed as a serial date number. *Maturity* is the security's maturity date, expressed as a serial date number. *Pr* is the security's price per \$100 face value. *Redemption* is the security's redemption value per \$100 face value. *Basis* is the type of day count basis to use. If *basis* is 0 or omitted, use 30/360. If *basis* is 1, use actual/actual. If *basis* is 2, use actual/360. If *basis* is 3, use actual/365.

Notes

- *Settlement, maturity,* and *basis* are truncated to integers.
- If *settlement* or *maturity* is not a valid serial date number, the function returns the #NUM! error.
- If *pr* ≤ 0 or if *redemption* ≤ 0, the function returns the #NUM! error.
- If *basis* < 0 or if *basis* > 3, the function returns the #NUM! error.
- If *settlement* ≥ *maturity*, the function returns the #NUM! error.

DOLLARDE

 Converts a dollar price, expressed as a fraction, into a dollar price, expressed as a decimal number.

Syntax

=DOLLARDE(*fractional_dollar,fraction*)

Arguments: *Fractional_dollar* is a number expressed as a fraction. *Fraction* is the number in the denominator of the fraction. If *fraction* is not an integer, it is truncated. If *fraction* ≤ 0, the function returns the #NUM! error.

DOLLARFR

 Converts a dollar price, expressed as a decimal number, into a dollar price, expressed as a fraction.

Syntax

=DOLLARFR(*decimal_dollar,fraction*)

Arguments: *Decimal_dollar* is a decimal number. *Fraction* is an integer to use as the fraction's denominator. If *fraction* is not an integer, it is truncated. If *fraction* ≤ 0, the function returns the #NUM! error.

DURATION

 Returns the Macauley duration for an assumed par value of $100. Duration is defined as the weighted average of the present value of the cash flows and is used as a measure of a bond price's response to changes in yield.

Syntax

=DURATION(*settlement,maturity,coupon,yld,frequency,basis*)

Arguments: *Settlement* is the security's settlement date, expressed as a serial date number. *Maturity* is the security's maturity date, expressed as a serial date number. *Coupon* is the security's annual coupon rate. *Yld* is the security's annual yield. *Frequency* is the number of coupon payments per year. For annual payments, *frequency* = 1; for semiannual, *frequency* = 2; for quarterly, *frequency* = 4. *Basis* is the type of day count basis to use. If *basis* is 0 or omitted, use 30/360. If *basis* is 1, use actual/actual. If *basis* is 2, use actual/360. If *basis* is 3, use actual/365.

Notes

- *Settlement, maturity, frequency,* and *basis* are truncated to integers.
- If *settlement* or *maturity* is not a valid serial date number, the function returns the #NUM! error.
- If *coupon* < 0 or if *yld* < 0, the function returns the #NUM! error.
- If *frequency* is any number other than 1, 2, or 4, the function returns the #NUM! error.
- If *basis* < 0 or if *basis* > 3, the function returns the #NUM! error.
- If *settlement* ≥ maturity, the function returns the #NUM! error.

EFFECT

 Returns the effective annual interest rate, given the nominal annual interest rate and the number of compounding periods per year.

Syntax

=EFFECT(*nominal_rate,npery*)

Arguments: *Nominal_rate* is the nominal interest rate. If *nominal_rate* ≤ or if *npery* < 1, the function returns the #NUM! error. *Npery* is the number of compounding periods per year. *Nprey* is truncated to an integer.

FV

Returns the future value of an investment based on periodic, constant payments and a constant interest rate.

Syntax

=FV(*rate,nper,pmt,pv,type*)

Arguments: *Rate* is the interest rate per period. *Nper* is the total number of payment periods in an annuity. *Pmt* is the payment made each period; it cannot change over the life of the annuity. Typically, *pmt* contains principal and interest but no other fees or taxes. *Pv* is the present value, or the lump-sum amount that a series of future payments is worth right now. If *pv* is omitted, it is assumed to be 0. *Type* is the number 0 or 1 and indicates when payments are due. If *type* is omitted, it is assumed to be 0. If *type* is 0, payment is at the end of the period. If *type* is 1, payment is at the beginning of the period.

Notes

- Be consistent with the units you specify for *rate* and *nper*. For example, if you make monthly payments on a thirty-year loan at 10% annual interest, you would use 10%/12 for *rate* and 30*12 for *nper*. If you were to make annual payments on the same loan, use 10% for *rate* and 30 for *nper*.

- In the arguments, cash you pay out, such as deposits to savings, is represented by negative numbers, whereas cash you receive, such as dividend checks, is represented by positive numbers.

FVSCHEDULE

 Returns the future value of an initial principal after applying a series of compound interest rates.

Syntax

=FVSCHEDULE(*principal,schedule*)

Arguments: *Principal* is the present value. *Schedule* is an array of interest rates to apply. The values in *schedule* can be numbers or blank cells; any other value produces the #VALUE error. Blank cells are taken as zeros (no interest).

INTRATE

 Returns the interest rate for a fully invested security.

Syntax

=INTRATE(*settlement,maturity,investment,redemption,basis*)

Arguments: *Settlement* is the security's settlement date, expressed as a serial date number. *Maturity* is the security's maturity date, expressed as a serial date number. *Investment* is the amount invested in the security. *Redemption* is the amount to be received at maturity. *Basis* is the type of day count basis to use. If *basis* is 0 or omitted, use 30/360. If *basis* is 1, use actual/actual. If *basis* is 2, use actual/360. If *basis* is 3, use actual/365.

Notes

- *Settlement, maturity,* and *basis* are truncated to integers.
- If *settlement* or *maturity* is not a valid serial date number, the function returns the #NUM! error.
- If *investment* ≤ 0 or if *redemption* ≤ 0, the function returns the #NUM! error.
- If *basis* < 0 or if *basis* > 3, the function returns the #NUM! error.
- If *settlement* ≥ *maturity*, the function returns the #NUM! error.

IPMT

 Returns the interest payment for an investment for a given period based on periodic, constant payments and a constant interest rate.

Syntax

=IPMT(*rate,per,nper,pv,fv,type*)

Arguments: *Rate* is the interest rate per period. *Per* is the period for which you want to find the interest, and must be in the range 1 to *nper*. *Nper* is the total number of payment periods in an annuity. *Pv* is the present value, or the lump-sum amount that a series of future payments is worth right now. *Fv* is the future value or a cash balance you want to attain after the last payment is made. If *fv* is omitted, it is assumed to be 0. (The future value of a loan, for example, is 0.) *Type* is the number 0 or 1 and indicates when payments are due. If *type* is omitted, it is assumed to be 0. If *type* is 0, payment is at the end of the period. If *type* is 1, payment is at the beginning of the period.

Notes

- Be consistent with the units you specify for *rate* and *nper*. For example, if you make monthly payments on a thirty-year loan at 10 percent annual interest, you would use 10%/12 for *rate* and 30*12 for *nper*. If you were to make annual payments on the same loan, use 10% for *rate* and 30 for *nper*.
- For all the arguments, cash you pay out, such as deposits to savings, is represented by negative numbers; cash you receive, such as dividend checks, is represented by positive numbers.

IRR

Returns the internal rate of return for an investment for a series of periodic cash flows represented by the members in *values*.

Syntax

=IRR(*values,guess*)

Arguments:

- *Values* is an array or a reference to cells that contains numbers for which you want to calculate the internal rate of return.
- *Values* must contain at least one positive value and one negative value to calculate the internal rate of return.
- IRR uses the order of *values* to interpret the order of cash flows. Be sure to enter your payment and income values in the sequence you want.
- If an array or reference argument contains text, logical values, or empty cells, those values are ignored.

Guess is a number that you guess is close to the result of IRR.

- Excel uses an iterative technique for calculating IRR. Starting with *guess*, IRR cycles through the calculation until the result is accurate within 0.00001 %. If IRR can't find a result that works after twenty tries, the function returns the

#NUM! error.

- If *guess* is omitted, it is assumed to be 0.1 (10%).
- If IRR returns the #NUM! error value, or if the result is not close to what you expected, try again with a different value for *guess*.

MDURATION

 Returns the modified Macauley duration for a security with an assumed par value of $100.

Syntax

=MDURATION(*settlement,maturity,coupon,yld,frequency,basis*)

Arguments: *Settlement* is the security's settlement date, expressed as a serial date number. *Maturity* is the security's maturity date, expressed as a serial date number. *Coupon* is the security's annual coupon rate. *Yld* is the security's annual yield. *Frequency* is the number of coupon payments per year. For annual payments, *frequency* = 1; for semiannual, *frequency* = 2; for quarterly, *frequency* = 4. *Basis* is the type of day count basis to use. If *basis* is 0 or omitted, use 30/360. If basis is 1, use actual/actual. If *basis* is 2, use actual/360. If *basis* is 3, use actual/365.

Notes

- *Settlement, maturity, frequency,* and *basis* are truncated to integers.
- If *settlement* or *maturity* is not a valid serial date number, the function returns the #NUM! error.
- If *yld* < 0 or if *coupon* < 0, the function returns the #NUM! error.
- If *frequency* is any number other than 1, 2, or 4, the function returns the #NUM! error.
- If *basis* < 0 or if *basis* > 3, the function returns the #NUM! error.
- If *settlement* ≥ maturity, the function returns the #NUM! error.

MIRR

Returns the modified internal rate of return for a series of periodic cash flows. MIRR considers both the cost of the investment and the interest received on reinvestment of cash.

Syntax

=MIRR(*values,finance_rate,reinvest_rate*)

Arguments: *Values* is an array or a reference to cells that contain numbers. These numbers represent a series of payments (negative values) and income (positive values) occurring at regular periods.

- *Values* must contain at least one positive value and one negative value to calculate the modified internal rate of return. Otherwise, the function returns the #DIV/0! error.
- If an array or reference argument contains text, logical values, or empty cells, those values are ignored; however, cells with the value zero are included.

Finance_rate is the interest rate you pay on the money used in the cash flows. *Reinvest_rate* is the interest rate you receive on the cash flows as you reinvest them.

Notes

- MIRR uses the order of *values* to interpret the order of cash flows. Be sure to enter your payment and income values in the sequence you want and with the correct signs (positive values for cash received, negative values for cash paid).

NOMINAL

 Returns the nominal annual interest rate given the effective rate and the number of compounding periods per year.

Syntax

=NOMINAL(*effect_rate,npery*)

Arguments: *Effect_rate* is the effective interest rate. If *effect_rate* ≤ 0, or if *npery* < 1, the function returns the #NUM! error. *Npery* is the number of compounding periods per year. *Npery* is truncated to an integer.

NPER

Returns the number of periods for an investment based on periodic, constant payments and a constant interest rate.

Syntax

=NPER(*rate,pmt,pv,fv,type*)

Arguments: *Rate* is the interest rate per period. *Pmt* is the payment made each period; it cannot change over the life of the annuity. Typically, *pmt* contains principal and interest but no other fees or taxes. *Pv* is the present value, or the lump-sum amount that a series of future payments is worth right now. *Fv* is the future value, or a cash balnce you want to attain after the last payment is made. If *fv* is omitted, it is assumed to be 0 (the future value of a loan, for example, is 0). *Type* is the number 0 or 1 and indicates when payments are due. If *type* is 0, payment is at the end of the period. If *type* is 1, payment is at the beginning of the period.

NPV

Returns the net present value of an investment based on a series of periodic cash flows and a discount rate.

Syntax

=NPV(*rate,value1,value2,...*)

Arguments: *Rate* is the rate of discount over the length of one period. *Value1,value2*, and so on are arguments representing the payments and income:

- All *value* arguments must be equally spaced in time and occur at the end of each period.
- NPV uses the order of *value1,value2* and so on to interpret the order of cash flows. Be sure to enter your payment and income values in the correct sequence.
- Arguments that are numbers, empty cells, logical values, or text representations of numbers are counted; arguments that are error values or text that cannot be translated into numbers are ignored.

- If an argument is an array or reference, only numbers in that array or reference are counted. Empty cells, logical values, text, or error values in the array or reference are ignored.

Notes

- The NPV investment begins one period before the date of the *value1* cash flow and ends with the last cash flow in the list. The NPV calculation is based on future cash flows. If your first cash flow occurs at the beginning of the period, the first value must be added to the NPV result, not included in the *values* arguments.
- NPV is similar to the PV function (present value). The primary difference between PV and NPV is that PV allows cash flows to begin either at the end or at the beginning of the period. Unlike the variable NPV cash flow values, PV cash flows must be constant throughout the investment.
- NPV is also related to the IRR function (internal rate of return). IRR is the *rate* for which NPV equals zero: NPV (IRR(...),...) = 0.

ODDFPRICE

 Returns the price per $100 face value of a security having an odd (short or long) first period.

Syntax

=ODDFPRICE(*settlement,maturity,issue,first_coupon,rate,yld,redemption,frequency, basis*)

Arguments: *Settlement* is the security's settlement date, expressed as a serial date number. *Maturity* is the security's maturity date, expressed as a serial date number. *Issue* is the security's issue date, expressed as a serial date number. *First_coupon* is the security's first coupon date, expressed as a serial date number. *Rate* is the security's interest rate. *Yld* is the security's annual yield. *Redemption* is the security's redemption value per $100 face value. *Frequency* is the number of coupon payments per year. For annual payments, *frequency* = 1; for semiannual, *frequency* = 2; for quarterly, *frequency* = 4. *Basis* is the type of day count basis to use. If *basis* is 0 or omitted, use 30/360. If *basis* is 1, use actual/actual. If *basis* is 2, use actual/360. If *basis* is 3, use actual/365.

Notes

- *Settlement, maturity, issue, first_coupon,* and *basis* are truncated to integers.
- If *settlement, maturity, issue,* or *first_coupon* is not a valid serial date number, the function returns the #NUM! error.
- If *rate* < 0 or if *yld* < 0, the function returns the #NUM! error.
- If *basis* < 0 or if *basis* > 3, the function returns the #NUM! error.
- The following date condition must be satisfied; otherwise the function returns the #NUM! error:

   maturity > first_coupon > settlement > issue

ODDFYIELD

Returns the yield of a security that has an odd (short or long) first period.

Syntax

=ODDFYIELD(*settlement,maturity,issue,first_coupon,rate,pr,*
redemption,frequency,basis)

Arguments: *Settlement* is the security's settlement date, expressed as a serial date number. *Maturity* is the security's maturity date, expressed as a serial date number. *Issue* is the security's issue date, expressed as a serial date number. *First_coupon* is the security's first coupon date, expressed as a serial date number. *Rate* is the security's interest rate. *Pr* is the security's price. *Redemption* is the security's redemption value per $100 face value. *Frequency* is the number of coupon payments per year. For annual payments, *frequency* = 1; for semiannual, *frequency* = 2; for quarterly, *frequency* = 4. *Basis* is the type of day count basis to use. If *basis* is 0 or omitted, use 30/360. If *basis* is 1, use actual/actual. If *basis* is 2, use actual/360. If *basis* is 3, use actual/365.

Notes

- *Settlement, maturity, issue, first_coupon,* and *basis* are truncated to integers.
- If *settlement, maturity, issue,* or *first_coupon* is not a valid serial date number, the function returns the #NUM! error.
- If *rate* < 0 or if *pr* ≤ 0, the function returns the #NUM! error.
- If *basis* < 0 or if *basis* > 3, the function returns the #NUM! error.
- The following date condition must be satisfied; otherwise, the function returns the #NUM! error:

    maturity > first_coupon > settlement > issue

ODDLPRICE

 Returns the price per $100 face value of a security having an odd (short or long) last period.

Syntax

=ODDLPRICE(*settlement,maturity,last_coupon,rate,yld,redemption,frequency,basis*)

Arguments: *Settlement* is the security's settlement date, expressed as a serial date number. *Maturity* is the security's maturity date, expressed as a serial date number. *Last_coupon* is the security's last coupon date, expressed as a serial date number. *Rate* is the security's interest rate. *Yld* is the security's annual yield. *Redemption* is the security's redemption value per $100 face value. *Frequency* is the number of coupon payments per year. For annual payments, *frequency* = 1; for semiannual, *frequency* = 2; for quarterly, *frequency* = 4. *Basis* is the type of day count basis to use. If *basis* is 0 or omitted, use 30/360. If *basis* is 1, use actual/actual. If *basis* is 2, use actual/360. If *basis* is 3, use actual/365.

Notes

- *Settlement, maturity, last_coupon,* and *basis* are truncated to integers.

- If *settlement, maturity,* or *last_coupon* is not a valid serial date number, the function returns the #NUM! error.
- If *rate* < 0 or if *yld* < 0, the function returns the #NUM! error.
- If *basis* < 0 or if *basis* > 3, the function returns the #NUM! error.
- The following date condition must be satisfied; otherwise the function returns the #NUM! error:

  maturity > *last_coupon* > *settlement*

ODDLYIELD

Returns the yield of a security that has an odd (short or long) last period.

Syntax

=ODDLYIELD(*settlement,maturity,last_coupon,rate,pr,redemption,*
frequency,basis)

Arguments: *Settlement* is the security's settlement date, expressed as a serial date number. *Maturity* is the security's maturity date, expressed as a serial date number. *Last_coupon* is the security's last coupon date, expressed as a serial date number. *Rate* is the security's interest rate. *Pr* is the security's price. *Redemption* is the security's redemption value per $100 face value. *Frequency* is the number of coupon payments per year. For annual payments, *frequency* = 1; for semiannual, *frequency* = 2; for quarterly, *frequency* = 4. *Basis* is the type of day count basis to use. If *basis* is 0 or omitted, use 30/360. If *basis* is 1, use actual/actual. If *basis* is 2, use actual/360. If *basis* is 3, use actual/365.

Notes

- *Settlement, maturity, last_coupon,* and *basis* are truncated to integers.
- If *settlement, maturity,* or *last_coupon* is not a valid serial date number, the function returns the #NUM! error.
- If *rate* < 0 or if *pr* ≤ 0, the function returns the #NUM! error.
- If *basis* < 0 or if *basis* > 3, the function returns the #NUM! error.
- The following date condition must be satisfied; otherwise the function returns the #NUM! error:

  maturity > *last_coupon* > *settlement*

PMT

Returns the payment for an annuity based on constant payments and a constant interest rate.

Syntax

=PMT(*rate,nper,pv,fv,type*)

Arguments: *Rate* is the interest rate per period. *Nper* is the total number of payment periods in an annuity. *Pv* is the present value (that is, the total amount that a series of future payments is worth now). *Fv* is the future value or a cash balance you want to attain after the last payment is made. If *fv* is omitted, it is assumed to be 0.

(The future value of a loan, for example, is 0.) *Type* is the number 0 or 1 and indicates when payments are due. If *type* is 0, payment is at the end of the period. If *type* is 1, payment is at the beginning of the period.

Notes

- The payment returned by PMT includes principal and interest but no taxes, reserve payments, or fees sometimes associated with annuities.

- Be consistent with the units you specify for *rate* and *nper*. For example, if you make monthly payments on a thirty-year loan at 10 percent annual interest, you would use 10%/12 for *rate* and 30*12 for *nper*. If you were to make annual payments on the same loan, use 10% for *rate* and 30 for *nper*.

- To find the total amount paid over the duration of the annuity, multiply the returned PMT value by *nper*.

PPMT

Returns the payment on the principal for a given period for an investment based on periodic, constant payments and a constant interest rate.

Syntax

=PPMT(*rate,per,nper,pv,fv,type*)

Arguments: *Rate* is the interest rate per period. *Per* specifies the period and must be in the range 1 to *nper*. *Nper* is the total number of payment periods in an annuity. *Pv* is the present value (that is, the total amount that a series of future payments is worth now). *Fv* is the future value or a cash balance you want to attain after the last payment is made. If *fv* is omitted, it is assumed to be 0. (The future value of a loan, for example, is 0.) *Type* is the number 0 or 1 and indicates when payments are due. If *type* is 0, payment is at the end of the period. If *type* is 1, payment is at the beginning of the period.

Notes

- Be consistent with the units you specify for *rate* and *nper*. For example, if you make monthly payments on a thirty-year loan at 10 percent annual interest, you would use 10%/12 for *rate* and 30*12 for *nper*. If you were to make annual payments on the same loan, use 10% for *rate* and 30 for *nper*.

PRICE

Returns the price per $100 face value of a security that pays periodic interest.

Syntax

=PRICE(*settlement,maturity,rate,yld,redemption,frequency,basis*)

Arguments: *Settlement* is the security's settlement date, expressed as a serial date number. *Maturity* is the security's maturity date, expressed as a serial date number. *Rate* is the security's interest rate. *Yld* is the security's annual yield. *Redemption* is the security's redemption value per $100 face value. *Frequency* is the number of coupon payments per year. For annual payments, *frequency* = 1; for semiannual, *frequency* = 2; for quarterly, *frequency* = 4. *Basis* is the type of day count basis to use. If *basis* is 0

or omitted, use 30/360. If *basis* is 1, use actual/actual. If *basis* is 2, use actual/360.
If *basis* is 3, use actual/365.

Notes

- *Settlement, maturity, frequency,* and *basis* are truncated to integers.
- If *settlement* or *maturity* is not a valid serial date number, the function returns the #NUM! error.
- If *yld* < 0 or if *rate* < 0, the function returns the #NUM! error.
- If *redemption* ≤ 0, the function returns the #NUM! error.
- If *frequency* is any number other than 1, 2, or 4, the function returns the #NUM! error.
- If *basis* < 0 or if *basis* > 3, the function returns the #NUM! error.
- If *settlement* ≥ *maturity*, the function returns the #NUM! error.

PRICEDISC

 Returns the price per $100 face value of a discounted security.

Syntax

=PRICEDISC(*settlement,maturity,discount,redemption,basis*)

Arguments: *Settlement* is the security's settlement date, expressed as a serial date number. *Maturity* is the security's maturity date, expressed as a serial date number. *Discount* is the security's discount rate. *Redemption* is the security's redemption value per $100 face value. *Basis* is the type of day count basis to use. If *basis* is 0 or omitted, use 30/360. If *basis* is 1, use actual/actual. If *basis* is 2, use actual/360. If *basis* is 3, use actual/365.

Notes

- *Settlement, maturity,* and *basis* are truncated to integers.
- If *settlement* or *maturity* is not a valid serial date number, the function returns the #NUM! error.
- If *discount* ≤ 0 or if *redemption* ≤ 0, the function returns the #NUM! error.
- If *basis* < 0 or if *basis* > 3, the function returns the #NUM! error.
- If *settlement* ≥ maturity, the function returns the #NUM! error.

PRICEMAT

 Returns the price per $100 face value of a security that pays interest at maturity.

Syntax

=PRICEMAT(*settlement,maturity,issue,rate,yld,basis*)

Arguments: *Settlement* is the security's settlement date, expressed as a serial date number. *Maturity* is the security's maturity date, expressed as a serial date number. *Issue* is the security's issue date, expressed as a serial date number. *Rate* is the security's interest rate at date of issue. *Yld* is the security's annual yield. *Basis* is the type of day count basis to use. If *basis* is 0 or omitted, use 3/360. If *basis* is 1, use actual/actual. If *basis* is 2, use actual/360. If *basis* is 3, use actual/365.

Notes

- *Settlement, maturity, issue,* and *basis* are truncated to integers.
- If *settlement, maturity,* or *issue* is not a valid *serial* date number, the function returns the #NUM! error.
- If *rate* < 0 or if *yld* < 0, the function returns the #NUM! error.
- If *basis* < 0 or if *basis* > 3, the function returns the #NUM! error.
- If *settlement* ≥ maturity, the function returns the #NUM! error.

PV

Returns the present value of an investment.

Syntax

=PV(*rate,nper,pmt,fv,type*)

Arguments: *Rate* is the interest rate per period. For example, if you obtain an automobile loan at a 10 percent annual interest, you would enter 10%/12, 0.83%, or 0.0083, into the formula as the *rate. Nper* is the total number of payment periods in an annuity. For example, if you get a four-year car loan and make monthly payments, your loan has 4*12 (or 48) periods, and you would enter 48 into the formula for *nper. Pmt* is the payment made each period and cannot change over the life of the annuity. Typically, *pmt* includes principal and interest but no other fees or taxes. For example, when the monthly payments are $263.33, and you would enter minus 263.33 into the formula as the *pmt. Fv* is the future value, or a cash balance you want to attain after the last payment is made. If *fv* is omitted, it is assumed to be 0. (The future value of a loan, for example, is 0.) If you want to save $50,000 to pay for a special project in eighteen years, then $50,000 is the future value. You could then make a conservative guess at an interest rate and determine how much you must save each month. *Type* is the number 0 or 1 and indicates when payments are due. If type is 0, payment is at the end of the period. If type is 1, payment is at the beginning of the period.

Notes

- Be consistent with the units you specify for *rate* and *nper.* For example, if you make monthly payments on a thirty-year loan at 10 percent annual interest, you would use 10%/12 for *rate* and 30*12 for *nper.* If you were to make annual payments on the same loan, use 10% for *rate* and 30 for *nper.*
- In annuity functions, cash you pay out, such as a deposit to savings, is represented by a negative number; cash you receive, such as a dividend check, is represented by a positive number. For example, a $1,000 deposit to the bank would be represented by the argument –1,000 if you are the depositor and by the argument 1000 if you are the bank.

RATE

Returns the interest rate per period for an annuity. RATE is calculated by iteration and can have zero or more solutions. If the successive results of RATE do not converge to within 0.0000001 after twenty iterations, the function returns the #NUM! error.

Syntax

=RATE(*nper,pmt,pv,fv,type,guess*)

Arguments: *Nper* is the total number of payment periods in an annuity. *Pmt* is the payment made each period and cannot change over the life of the annuity. Typically, *pmt* includes principal and interest but no other fees or taxes. *Pv* is the present value (the total amount that a series of future payments is worth now). *Fv* is the future value or a cash balance you want to attain after the last payment is made. If *fv* is omitted, it is assumed to be 0. (The future value of a loan, for example, is 0.) If you want to save $50,000 to pay for a special project in eighteen years, then $50,000 is the future value. You could then make a conservative guess at an interest rate and determine how much you must save each month. *Type* is the number 0 or 1 and indicates when payments are due. If type is 0, payment is at the end of the period. If type is 1, payment is at the beginning of the period. *Guess* is your guess for what what the rate will be.

- If you omit *guess*, it is assumed to be 10 percent.
- If the function does not converge, try different values for *guess*. The function usually converges if *guess* is between 0 and 1.

Notes

- Be consistent with the units you specify for *rate* and *nper*. For example, if you make monthly payments on a thirty-year loan at 10 percent annual interest, you would use 10%/12 for *rate* and 30*12 for *nper*. If you were to make annual payments on the same loan, use 10% for *rate* and 30 for *nper*.

RECEIVED

 Returns the amount received at maturity for a fully invested security.

Syntax

=RECEIVED(*settlement,maturity,investment,discount,basis*)

Arguments: *Settlement* is the security's settlement date, expressed as a serial date number. *Maturity* is the security's maturity date, expressed as a serial date number. *Investment* is the amount invested in the security. *Discount* is the security's discount rate. *Basis* is the type of day count basis to use. If *basis* is 0 or omitted, use 30/360. If *basis* is 1, use actual/actual. If *basis* is 2, use actual/360. If *basis* is 3, use actual/365.

Notes

- *Settlement, maturity,* and *basis* are truncated to integers.
- If *settlement* or *maturity* is not a valid serial date number, the function returns the #NUM! error.
- If *investment* ≤0 or if *discount* ≤0, the function returns the #NUM! error.
- If *basis* < 0 or if *basis* > 3, the function returns the #NUM! error.
- If *settlement* ≥ maturity, the function returns the #NUM! error.

SLN

Returns the straight-line depreciation of an asset for one period.

Syntax

=SLN(*cost,salvage,life*)

Arguments: *Cost* is the initial cost of the asset. *Salvage* is the value at the end of the depreciation. *Life* is the number of periods over which the asset is being depreciated.

SYD

Returns the sum-of-years' digits depreciation of an asset for a specified period.

Syntax

=SYD(*cost,salvage,life,per*)

Arguments: *Cost* is the initial cost of the asset. *Salvage* is the value at the end of the depreciation. *Life* is the number of periods over which the asset is being depreciated. *Per* is the period and must use the same units as *life*.

TBILLEQ

 Returns the bond-equivalent yield for a Treasury bill.

Syntax

=TBILLEQ(*settlement,maturity,discount*)

Arguments: *Settlement* is the Treasury bill's settlement date, expressed as a serial date number. *Maturity* is the Treasury bill's maturity date, expressed as a serial date number. *Discount* is the Treasury bill's discount rate.

Notes

- *Settlement* and *maturity* are truncated to integers.
- If *settlement* or *maturity* is not a valid serial date number, the function returns the #NUM! error.
- If *discount* ≤ 0, the function returns the #NUM! error.
- If *settlement* > *maturity*, or if *maturity* is more than one year after *settlement*, the function returns the #NUM! error.

TBILLPRICE

 Returns the price per $100 face value for a Treasury bill.

Syntax

=TBILLPRICE(*settlement,maturity,discount*)

Arguments: *Settlement* is the Treasury bill's settlement date, expressed as a serial date number. *Maturity* is the Treasury bill's maturity date, expressed as a serial date number. *Discount* is the Treasury bill's discount rate.

Notes

- *Settlement* and *maturity* are truncated to integers.
- If *settlement* or *maturity* is not a valid serial date number, the function returns

the #NUM! error.

- If *discount* ≤ 0, the function returns the #NUM! error.
- If *settlement* >*maturity* or if *maturity* is more than one year after *settlement*, the function returns the #NUM! error.

TBILLYIELD

 Returns the yield for a Treasury bill.

Syntax

=TBILLYIELD(*settlement,maturity,pr*)

Arguments: *Settlement* is the Treasury bill's settlement date, expressed as a serial date number. *Maturity* is the Treasury bill's maturity date, expressed as a serial date number. *Pr* is the Treasury bill's price per $100 face value.

Notes

- *Settlement* and *maturity*, are truncated to integers.
- If *settlement* or *maturity* is not a valid serial date number, the function returns the #NUM! error.
- If *pr* ≤ 0, the function returns the #NUM! error.
- If *settlement* ≥ *maturity* or if *maturity* is more than one year after *settlement*, the function returns the #NUM! error.

VDB

 Returns the depreciation of an asset for any period you specify, including partial periods, using the double-declining balance method or some other method you specify.

Syntax

=VDB(*cost,salvage,life,start_period,end_period,factor,no_switch*)

Arguments: *Cost* is the initial cost of the asset. *Salvage* is the value at the end of the depreciation. *Life* is the number of periods over which the asset is being depreciated. *Start_period* is the starting period for which you want to calculate the depreciation. *Start_period* must use the same units as *life*. *End_period* is the ending period for which you want to calculate the depreciation. *End_period* must use the same units as *life*. *Factor* is the rate at which the balance declines. If *factor* is omitted, it is assumed to be 2 (the double-declining balance method). Change *factor* if you do not want to use that method. For a description of the double-declining method, see DDB in this appendix. *No_switch* is a logical value specifying whether to switch to straight-line depreciation when depreciation is greater than the declining balance calculation.

- If *no_switch* is TRUE, Excel does not switch to straight-line depreciation even when the depreciation is greater than the declining balance calculation.
- If *no_switch* is FALSE or omitted, Excel switches to straight-line depreciation when depreciation is greater than the declining balance calculation.

Notes

- All arguments except *no_switch* must be positive numbers.

XIRR

Returns the internal rate of return for a schedule of cash flows that is not necessarily periodic.

Syntax

=XIRR(*values,dates,guess*)

Arguments: *Values* is a series of cash flows that correspond to a schedule of payments in *dates*. The first payment is optional, and corresponds to a cost or payment that occurs at the beginning of the investment. All succeeding payments are discounted based on a 365-day year. *Dates* is a schedule of payment dates that corresponds to the cash flow payments. The first payment date indicates the beginning of the schedule of payments. All other dates must be later than this date, but they may occur in any order.

Guess is a number that you guess is close to the result of XIRR.

Notes

- Numbers in *dates* are truncated to integers.
- XIRR expects at least one positive cash flow and one negative cash flow; otherwise the function returns the #NUM! error.
- If any number in *dates* is not a valid serial date number, the function returns the #NUM! error.
- If any number in *dates* precedes the starting date, the function returns the #NUM! error.
- If *values* and *dates* contain a different number of values, the function returns the #NUM! error.
- Excel uses an iterative technique for calculating XIRR. Starting with *guess*, XIRR cycles through the calculation until the result is accurate within 0.000001 %. If XIRR can't find a result that works after twenty tries, the #NUM! error value is returned.
- If *guess* is omitted, it is assumed to be 0.1 (10%).
- XIRR is closely related to XNPV, the net present value function. The rate of return calculated by XIRR is the interest rate corresponding to XNPV = 0.

XNPV

Returns the net present value for a schedule of cash flows that is not necessarily periodic.

Syntax

=XNPV(*rate,values,dates*)

Arguments: *Rate* is the discount to apply to the cash flows. *Values* is a series of cash flows that correspond to a schedule of payments in *dates*. The first payment is optional, and corresponds to a cost or payment that occurs at the beginning of the investment. All succeeding payments are discounted based on a 365-day year. *Dates* is a schedule of payment dates that corresponds to the cash flow payments. The first payment date indicates the beginning of the schedule of payments. All other dates must be later than this date, but they may occur in any order.

Notes

- Numbers in *dates* are truncated to integers.
- If any number in *dates* is not a valid serial date number, the function returns the #NUM! error.
- If any number in *dates* precedes the starting date. the function returns the #NUM! error.
- If *values* and *dates* contain a different number of values, the function returns the #NUM! error.

YIELD

 Returns the yield on a security that pays periodic interest.

Syntax

=YIELD(*settlement,maturity,rate,pr,redemption,frequency,basis*)

Arguments: *Settlement* is the security's settlement date, expressed as a serial date number. *Maturity* is the security's maturity date, expressed as a serial date number. *Rate* is the security's interest rate. *Pr* is the security's price per $100 face value. *Redemption* is the security's redemption value per $100 face value. *Frequency* is the number of coupon payments per year. For annual payments, *frequency* = 1; for semiannual, *frequency* = 2; for quarterly, *frequency* = 4. *Basis* is the type of day count basis to use. If *basis* is 0 or omitted, use 30/360. If *basis* is 1, use actual/actual. If *basis* is 2, use actual/360. If *basis* is 3, use actual/365.

Notes

- *Settlement, maturity, frequency,* and *basis* are truncated to integers.
- If *settlement* or *maturity* is not a valid serial date number, the function returns the #NUM! error.
- If *rate* < 0, the function returns the #NUM! error.
- If *pr* ≤ 0 or if *redemption* ≤, the function returns the #NUM! error.
- If *frequency* is any number other than 1, 2, or 4, the function returns the #NUM! error.
- If *basis* < 0 or if *basis* > 3, the function returns the #NUM! error.
- If *settlement* ≥ *maturity*, the function returns the #NUM! error.

YIELDDISC

 Returns the annual yield for a discounted security—for example, a Treasury bill.

Syntax

=YIELDDISC(*settlement,maturity,pr,redemption,basis*)

Arguments: *Settlement* is the security's settlement date, expressed as a serial date number. *Maturity* is the security's maturity date, expressed as a serial date number. *Pr* is the security's price per $100 face value. *Redemption* is the security's redemption value per $100 face value. *Basis* is the type of day count basis to use. If *basis* is 0 or omitted, use 30/360. If *basis* is 1, use actual/actual. If *basis* is 2, use actual/360. If *basis* is 3, use actual/365.

Notes

- *Settlement, maturity*, and *basis* are truncated to integers.
- If *settlement* or *maturity* is not a valid serial date number, the function returns the #NUM! error.
- If *pr* ≤ 0 or if *redemption* ≤, the function returns the #NUM! error.
- If *basis* < 0 or if *basis* > 3, the function returns the #NUM! error.
- If *settlement* ≥ *maturity*, the function returns the #NUM! error.

YIELDMAT

 Returns the annual yield of a security that pays interest at maturity.

Syntax

=YIELDMAT(*settlement,maturity,issue,rate,pr,basis*)

Arguments: *Settlement* is the security's settlement date, expressed as a serial date number. *Maturity* is the security's maturity date, expressed as a serial date number. *Issue* is the security's issue date, expressed as a serial date number. *Rate* is the security's interest rate. *Pr* is the security's price per $100 face value. *Basis* is the type of day count basis to use. If *basis* is 0 or omitted, use 30/360. If *basis* is 1, use actual/actual. If *basis* is 2, use actual/360. If *basis* is 3, use actual/365.

Notes

- *Settlement, maturity, issue*, and *basis* are truncated to integers.
- If *settlement, maturity*, or *issue* is not a valid serial date number, the function returns the #NUM! error.
- If *rate* < 0, the function returns the #NUM! error.
- If *pr* < 0 or if *pr* ≤, the function returns the #NUM! error.
- If *basis* < 0 or if *basis* > 3, the function returns the #NUM! error.
- If *settlement* ≥ maturity, the function returns the #NUM! error.

Date and Time

DATE

Returns the serial number of a specified date.

Syntax

=DATE(*year,month,day*)

Arguments: *Year* is a number from 1900 to 2078. To specify a year in the range 1920 to 2019, you can enter the last two digits of the year. To specify a year before 1920 or after 2019, enter all four digits of the year. *Month* is a number representing the month of the year. If *month* is greater than 12, then *month* adds that number of months to the first month in the year specified. For example, DATE (90,14,2) returns the serial number representing February 2, 1991. *Day* is a number representing the day of the month. If *day* is greater than the number of days in the month specified, then *day* adds that number of days to the first day in the month. For example, DATE (91,1,35) returns the serial number representing February 4, 1991.

DATEVALUE

Returns the serial number of the date represented by the *date_text* argument.

Syntax

=DATEVALUE(*date_text*)

Arguments: *Date_text* is text that returns a date in a Excel date format. Using the default date system in Excel for Windows, *date_text* must represent a date from January 1, 1900, to December 31, 2078. DATEVALUE returns the #VALUE! error value if *date_text* is out of this range. If the year portion of *date_text* is omitted, DATEVALUE uses the current year from your computer's built-in clock. Time information in *date_text* is ignored. Most functions automatically convert date values to serial numbers.

DAY

Returns the day of the month corresponding to the *serial_number* argument. The day is given as an integer ranging from 1 to 31.

Syntax

=DAY(*serial_number*)

Argument: *Serial_number* is the date-time code used by Excel for date and time calculations. You can give *serial_number* as text, such as "4-15-91" or "15-Apr-1991," instead of as a number. The text is automatically converted to a serial number.

DAYS360

Calculates the number of days between two dates based on a 360-day year (twelve thirty-day months).

Syntax

=DAYS360(*start_date,end_date*)

Arguments: *Start_date* and *end_date* are the two dates between which you want to know the number of days.

- The arguments can be either text strings using numbers to represent the month, day, and year (for example, "1/30/91" or "1-30-91") or they can be serial numbers representing the dates.
- If *start_date* occurs after *end_date*, DAYS360 returns a negative number.

EDATE

Returns the serial number date that is the indicated number of months before or after the *start_date* argument.

Syntax

=EDATE(*start_date,months*)

Arguments: *Start_date* is the serial date number that represents the start date. *Months* is the number of months before or after *start_date.* A positive value for *months* yields a future date; a negative value yields a past date.

EOMONTH

 Returns the serial number date for the last day of the month that is the number of months indicated by the *months* argument before or after the *start_date* argument.

Syntax

=EOMONTH(*start_date,months*)

Arguments: *Start_date* is the serial date number that represents the start date. *Months* is the number of months before or after *start_date.* A positive value for *months* yields a future date; a negative value yields a past date. If *start_date* plus *months* yields an invalid serial date number, the function returns the #NUM! error.

HOUR

Returns the hour corresponding to the *serial_number* argument. The hour is given as an integer, ranging from 0 (12:00 A.M.) to 23 (11:00 P.M.).

Syntax

=HOUR(*serial_number*)

Argument: *Serial_number* is the date-time code used by Excel for date and time calculations. You can give *serial_number* as text, such as "16:48:00" or "4:48:00 P.M." instead of as a number. The text is automatically converted to a serial number.

MINUTE

Returns the minute corresponding to the *serial_number* argument. The minute is given as an integer, ranging from 0 to 59.

Syntax

=MINUTE(*serial_number*)

Argument: *Serial_number* is the date-time code used by Excel for date and time calculations. You can give *serial_number* as text, such as "16:48:00" or "4:48:00 P.M.," instead of as a number. The text is automatically converted to a serial number.

MONTH

Returns the month corresponding to the *serial_number* argument. The month is given as an integer, ranging from 1 (January) to 12 (December).

Syntax

=MONTH(*serial_number*)

Argument: *Serial_number* is the date-time code used by Excel for date and time calculations. You can give *serial_number* as text, such as "4-15-91" or "15-Apr-1991," instead of as a number. The text is automatically converted to a serial number. To display the result of the MONTH function as a month name, use the Number command on the Format menu to format the cell containing the function with the custom number format "mmmm".

NETWORKDAYS

Returns the number of whole working days between the *start_date* argument and the *end_date* argument. Working days exclude weekends and any dates identified as holidays.

Syntax

=NETWORKDAYS(*start_date,end_date,holidays*)

Arguments: *Start_date* is a serial date number that represents the start date. *End_date* is a serial date number that represents the end date. *Holidays* is an optional set of one or more serial date numbers to exclude from the working calendar, such as state and federal holidays and floating holidays.

NOW

 Returns the serial number of the current date and time.

Syntax

=NOW( )

Notes

- Excel for Windows and Excel for the Macintosh use different default date systems. Excel for Windows uses the 1900 Date System, in which serial numbers range from 1 to 65,380, corresponding to the dates January 1, 1900, through December 31, 2078. Excel for the Macintosh uses the 1904 Date System, in which serial numbers range from 0 to 63,918, corresponding to the dates January 1, 1904, through December 31, 2078.

- Numbers to the right of the decimal point in the serial number represent the time; numbers to the left represent the date. For example, in the 1900 Date System, the serial number 367.5 represents the date-time combination 12:00 P.M., January 1, 1901.

- You can change the date system by selecting or clearing the 1904 Date System check box in the Calculation dialog box, which appears when you choose the Calculation command from the Options menu.

- The date system is changed automatically when you open a document from another platform. For example, if you are working in Excel for Windows and you open a document created in Excel for the Macintosh, the 1904 Date System check box is selected automatically.

- The NOW function changes only when the worksheet is calculated or when the macro containing the function is run. It is not updated continuously.

SECOND

Converts a second corresponding to the *serial_number* argument. The second is given as an integer in the range 0 to 59.

Syntax

=SECOND(*serial_number*)

Argument: *Serial_number* is the date-time code used by Excel for date and time calculations. You can give *serial_number* as text, such as "16:48:23" or "4:48:47 P.M.," instead of as a number. The text is automatically converted to a serial number.

TIME

Returns the serial number of a particular time. The serial number returned by TIME is a decimal fraction ranging from 0 to 0.99999999, representing the times from 0:00:00 (12:00:00 A.M.) to 23:59:59 (11:59:59 P.M.).

Syntax

=TIME(*hour,minute,second*)

Arguments: *Hour* is a number from 0 to 23 representing the hour. *Minute* is a number from 0 to 59 representing the minute. *Second* is a number from 0 to 59 representing the second.

TIMEVALUE

Returns the serial number of the time represented by the *time_text* argument. The serial number is a decimal fraction ranging from 0 to 0.99999999, representing the times from 0:00:00 (12:00:00 A.M.) to 23:59:59 (11:59:59 P.M.).

Syntax

=TIMEVALUE(*time_text*)

Argument: *Time_text* is a text string that gives a time in any one of the Excel time formats. Date information in *time_text* is ignored.

TODAY

Returns the serial number of the current date.

Syntax

=TODAY( )

WEEKDAY

Returns the day of the week corresponding to the *serial_number* argument. The day is given as an integer, ranging from 1 (Sunday) to 7 (Saturday).

Syntax

=WEEKDAY(*serial_number*)

Arguments: *Serial_number* is the date-time code used by Excel for date and time calculations. You can give *serial_number* as text, such as "4-15-91"" or "15-Apr-1991," instead of as a number. The text is automatically converted to a serial number.

WORKDAY

Returns the serial number date that is the indicated number of working days before or after the *start_date* argument. Working days exclude weekends and any dates identified in the *holidays* argument.

Syntax

=WORKDAY(*start_date,days,holidays*)

Arguments: *Start_date* is a serial date number that represents the start date. *Days* is the number of nonweekend and nonholiday days before or after *start_date*. A positive value for *days* yields a future date; a negative value yields a past date. *Holidays* is an optional array of one or more serial date numbers to exclude from the working calendar, such as state and federal holidays and floating holidays.

Notes

- If *start_date* is not a valid serial date number, the function returns the #NUM! error.
- If *start_date* plus *days* yields an invalid serial date number, the function returns the #NUM! error.
- If *days* is not an integer, it is truncated.

YEAR

 Returns the year corresponding to the *serial_number* argument. The year is given as an integer in the range 1900 to 2078.

Syntax

=YEAR(*serial_number*)

Argument: *Serial_number* is the date-time code used by Excel for date and time calculations. You can give *serial_number* as text, such as "4-15-91" or "15-Apr-1991," instead of as a number. The text is automatically converted to a serial number.

YEARFRAC

Returns the year fraction representing the number of whole days between the *start_date* argument and the *end_date* argument.

Syntax

=YEARFRAC(*start_date,end_date,basis*)

Arguments: *Start_date* is a serial date number that represents the start date. *End_date* is a serial date number that represents the end date. *Basis* is the type of day count basis to use. If *basis* is 0 or omitted, use 30/360. If *basis* is 1, use actual/actual. If *basis* is 2, use actual/360. If *basis* is 3, use actual/365.

Notes

- All arguments are truncated to integers.
- If *start_date* or *end_date* is not a valid serial date number, the function returns the #NUM! error.
- If *basis* < 0 or if *basis* > 3, the function returns the #NUM! error.
- If *start_date* ≥ *end_date*, the function returns the #NUM! error.

Information

ADDRESS

Creates a cell address as text, given specified row and column numbers.

Syntax

=ADDRESS(*row_num,column_num,abs_num,al,sheet_text*)

Arguments: *Row_num* is the row number to use in the cell reference. *Column_num* is the column number to use in the cell reference.

Abs_num specifies the type of reference to return as follows:

1 or omitted	Absolute
2	Absolute row; relative column
3	Relative row; absolute column
4	Relative

Al is a logical value that specifies the A1 or R1C1 reference style. If *al* is TRUE or omitted, ADDRESS returns an A1-style reference; if FALSE, ADDRESS returns an R1C1-style reference. *Sheet_text* is text specifying the name of the worksheet or macro sheet to be used as the external reference. If *sheet_text* is omitted, no sheet name is used.

CELL

Returns information about the formatting, location, or contents of the upper-left cell in a reference.

Syntax

=CELL(*info_type,reference*)

Arguments: *Info_type* is a text value that specifies what type of cell information you want as follows.

Info_type	*CELL Returns*
"address"	Reference of the first cell in *reference*, as text.
"col"	Column number of the cell in *reference*.
"color"	1 if the cell is formatted in color for negative values; otherwise returns 0.
"contents"	Contents of the upper-left cell in *reference*.
"filename"	Filename (including full path) of the file that contains *reference*, as text. Returns empty text ("") if the worksheet that contains reference has not yet been saved.
"format"	Text value corresponding to the number format of the cell. The text values for the various formats are shown in the next table. Returns "–" at the end of the text value if the cell is formatted in color for negative values. Returns "0" at the end of the text value if the cell is formatted with parentheses for positive or all values.
"parentheses"	1 if the cell is formatted with parentheses for positive or all values; otherwise returns 0.

Info_type	CELL Returns
"prefix"	Text value corresponding to the "label prefix" of the cell. Returns single quotation mark(') if the cell contains left-aligned text, double quotation mark (") if the cell contains right-aligned text, caret (^) if the cell contains centered text, backslash (\) if the cell contains fill-aligned text, and empty text ("") if the cell contains anything else.
"protect"	0 if the cell is not locked, and 1 if the cell is locked.
"row"	Row number of the cell in *reference.*
"type"	Text value corresponding to the type of data in the cell. Returns "b" for blank if the cell is empty, "l" for label if the cell contains a text constant, and "v" for value if the cell contains anything else.
"width"	Column width of the cell rounded off to an integer. Each unit of column width is equal to the width of one character in the currently selected font size.

Reference is the cell that you want information about.

• If *reference* is omitted, it is assumed to be the active cell.

• If *reference* is a nonadjacent selection, the function returns the #VALUE! error.

The following list describes the text values CELL returns when *info_type* is "format" and *reference* is a cell formatted with a built-in number format.

If the number format is	CELL returns
General	"G"
0	"FO"
#,##0	",0"
0.00	"F2"
#,##0.00	",2"
$#,##0_);($#,##0)	"C0"
$#,##0_);[Red]($#,##0)	"C0–"
$#,##0.00_);($#,##0.00)	"C2"
$#,##0.00_);[Red]($#,##0.00)	"C2–"
0%	"P0"
0.00%	"P2"
0.00E+00	"S2"
#?/? or# ??/??	"G"
m/d/yy or m/d/yy h:mm or mm/dd/yy	"D4"
d-mmm-yy or dd-mmm-yy	"D1"
d-mmm or dd-mmm	"D2"
mmm-yy	"D3"
mm/dd	"D5"
h:mm AM/PM	"D7"
h:mm:ss AM/PM	"D6"
h:mm	"D9"
h:mm:ss	"D8"

If the *info_type* argument in the CELL formula is "format" and if the cell is formatted later with a custom format, you must recalculate the worksheet to update the CELL formula.

Notes

- The CELL function is provided for compatibility with other spreadsheet programs. If you need to use cell information in a macro, GET.CELL provides a broader set of attributes.

ERROR.TYPE

Returns a number corresponding to an error type.

Syntax

=ERROR.TYPE(*error_val*)

Argument: Error_val is the error value whose identifying number you want to find. Although *error_val* can be the actual error value, it will usually be a reference to a cell containing a formula that you want to test.

If error_val is	ERROR.TYPE returns
#NULL!	1
3DIV/0!	2
#VALUE!	3
#REF!	4
#NAME?	5
#NUM!	6
#N/A	7
Anything else	#N/A

INFO

Returns information about the current operating environment.

Syntax

=INFO(*type_text*)

Argument: *Type_text* is text specifying what type of information you want returned.

Type_text	INFO Returns
"directory"	Path of the current directory or folder
"memavail"	Amount of memory available, in bytes
"memused"	Amount of memory being used for data
"numfile"	Number of active worksheets
"origin"	Absolute A1-style reference, as text, prepended with "$A:" for Lotus 1-2-3 release 3.x compatiblity
"osversion"	Current operating system version, as text
"recalc"	Current recalculation mode; returns "Automatic" or "Manual"
"release"	Version of Excel, as text
"system"	Name of the operating environment: Macintosh= "mac" Windows = "pcdos"
"totmem"	Total memory available, including memory already in use, in bytes

ISBLANK

Returns TRUE if the *value* argument is blank.

Syntax

=ISBLANK(*value*)

ISERR

Returns TRUE if the value is any error value except #N/A.

Syntax

=ISERR(*value*)

ISERROR

Returns TRUE if the *value* is any error value.

Syntax

=ISERROR(*value*)

ISEVEN

 Returns TRUE if the *value* argument is even, or FALSE if the *value* argument is odd.

Syntax

=ISEVEN(*value*)

Argument: *Value* is the value to test. If *value* is not an integer, it is truncated.

ISLOGICAL

Returns TRUE if the *value* argument is a logical value.

Syntax

=ISLOGICAL(*value*)

ISNA

Returns TRUE if the *value* argument is the error value #N/A.

Syntax

=ISNA(*value*)

ISNONTEXT

Returns TRUE if the *value* argument is not text.

Syntax

=ISNONTEXT(*value*)

ISNUMBER

Returns TRUE if the *value* argument is a number.

Syntax

=ISNUMBER(*value*)

ISODD

 Returns TRUE if the *value* argument is odd, or FALSE if the *value* argument is even.

Syntax

=ISODD(*value*)

Argument: *Value* is the value to test. If *value* is not an integer, it is truncated.

ISREF

Returns TRUE if the *value* argument is a reference.

Syntax

=ISREF(*value*)

ISTEXT

Returns TRUE if the *value* argument is text.

Syntax

=ISTEXT(*value*)

N

Returns the *value* argument converted to a number.

Syntax

=N(*value*)

Argument: *Value* is the value you want converted. If *value* is a number, N returns that number. If *value* is a date in one of Excel's built-in date formats, N returns the serial number of that date. If *value* is TRUE, N returns 1. If *value* is anything else, N returns 0.

NA

Returns the error *value* argument #N/A.

Syntax

=NA( )

TYPE

Returns the type of the *value* argument.

Syntax

=TYPE(*value*)

Arguments: *Value* can be any Excel value, such as a number, text, logical value, and so on. If *value* is a number, TYPE returns 1. If *value* is text, TYPE returns 2. If *value* is a logical value, TYPE returns 4. If *value* is an error value, TYPE returns 16. If *value* is an array, TYPE returns 64.

Mathematical and Trigonometric

ABS

Returns the absolute *value* argument of a number.

Syntax

=ABS(*number*)

Argument: *Number* is the real number of which you want the absolute value.

ACOS

Returns the arccosine of a number.

Syntax

=ACOS(*number*)

Arguments: *Number* is the cosine of the angle you want and must be from –1 to 1. If you want to convert the result from radians to degrees, multiply it by 180/PI( ).

ACOSH

Returns the inverse hyperbolic cosine of the *number* argument. *Number* must be greater than or equal to 1.

Syntax

=ACOSH(*number*)

ASIN

Returns the arcsine of a number.

Syntax

=ASIN(*number*)

Argument: *Number* is the sine of the angle you want and must be from –1 to 1. To express the arcsine in degrees, multiply the result by 180/PI ( ).

ASINH

Returns the inverse hyperbolic sine of the *number* argument.

Syntax

=ASINH(*number*)

ATAN

Returns the arctangent of a number.

Syntax

=ATAN(*number*)

Argument: *Number* is the tangent of the angle you want. To express the arctangent in degrees, multiply the result by 180/PI ( ).

ATAN2

Returns the arctangent from *x*- and *y*-coordinates.

Syntax

=ATAN2(*x_num,y_num*)

Arguments: *X_num* is the *x*-coordinate of the point. *Y_num* is the *y*-coordinate of the point. To express the arctangent in degrees, multiply the result by 180/PI ( ).

Notes

- If both *x_num* and *y_num* are 0, ATAN2 returns the #DIV/0! error.
- A positive result represents a counterclockwise angle from the *x*-axis; a negative

result represents a clockwise angle.

- ATAN2(*a*,*b*) equals ATAN(*b*/*a*), except that *a* can equal 0 in ATAN2.

ATANH

Returns the inverse hyperbolic tangent of the *number* argument. *Number* must be between –1 and 1 (excluding –1 and 1).

Syntax

=ATANH(*number*)

BASE

 Returns the equivalent of a base-10 number into another base as text.

Syntax

=BASE(*number,target_base,precision*)

Arguments: *Number* is a base-10 number. *Target_base* is the base you want to convert the number into. It must be an integer between 2 and 36. If *target_base* is omitted, BASE returns a base-16 number. *Precision* specifies the number of digits you want after the decimal in the returned base. It must be a positive integer. If *precision* is omitted, it is assumed to be 0, and BASE returns an integer.

CEILING

 Returns the *number* argument rounded up to the nearest multiple of the *significance* argument.

Syntax

=CEILING(*number,significance*)

Arguments: *Number* is the value you want to round. *Significance* is the multiple to which you want to round.

Notes

- Regardless of the sign of *number*, a value is rounded up when adjusted away from zero. If *number* is an exact multiple of *significance*, no rounding occurs.
- If *number* and *significance* have different signs, the function returns the #NUM! error.

COMBIN

 Returns the number of ways that the *number_chosen* argument objects can be selected from the *number* argument objects, without regard for order.

Syntax

=COMBIN(*number,number_chosen*)

Arguments: *Number* is the number of objects. *Number_chosen* is the number of objects in each combination.

Notes

- Numeric arguments are truncated to integers.
- If either argument is nonnumeric, COMBIN returns the #NAME? error.

- If *number* < 0, *number_chosen* < 0, or *number* < *number_chosen*, COMBIN returns the #NUM! error.
- A combination is any set or subset of objects, regardless of their internal order. Combinations are distinct from permutations, for which the internal order is significant.

COS

Returns the cosine of the given angle.

Syntax

=COS(*number*)

Argument: *Number* is the angle in radians for which you want the cosine. If the angle is in degrees, multiply it by PI()/180 to convert it to radians.

COSH

Returns the hyperbolic cosine of *number*.

Syntax

=COSH(*number*)

EVEN

 Rounds a number up to the nearest even integer.

Syntax

=EVEN(*number*)

Argument: *Number* is the value to round.

Notes

- Regardless of the sign of *number*, a value is rounded up when adjusted away from zero. If *number* is an even integer, no rounding occurs.

EXP

Returns *e* raised to the power of the *number* argument. The constant *e* equals 2.71828182845904, the base of the natural logarithm.

Syntax

=EXP(*number*)

Argument: *Number* is the exponent applied to the base *e*.

Notes

- To calculate powers of other bases, use the exponentiation operator (^).
- EXP is the inverse of LN, the natural logarithm of *number*.

FACT

Returns the factorial of a number. The factorial of a number is equal to 1*2*3*...* *number*.

Syntax

=FACT(*number*)

Argument: *Number* is the nonnegative number you want the factorial of. If *number* is not an integer, it is truncated.

FACTDOUBLE

Returns the double factorial of a number.

Syntax

=FACTDOUBLE(*number*)

Argument: *Number* is the value for which to return the double factorial. If *number* is not an integer, it is truncated.

Notes

- If *number* is negative, the function returns the #NUM! error.
- If *number* is even:

  $n!! = n(n-2)\ (n-4)...(4)\ (2)$
- If *number* is odd:

  $n!! = n(n-2)\ (n-4)...(3)\ (1)$

FLOOR

Rounds the *number* argument down, to the nearest multiple of the *significance* argument.

Syntax

=FLOOR(*number,significance*)

Arguments: *Number* is the numeric value you want to round. *Significance* is the multiple to which you want to round.

Notes

- If *number* and *significance* have different signs, the function returns the #NUM! error.
- Regardless of the sign of *number*, a value is rounded up when adjusted away from zero. If *number* is an exact multiple of *significance*, no rounding occurs.

GCD

Returns the greatest common divisor of two or more integers. The greatest common divisor is the largest integer that divides both the *number1* argument and the *number2* argument without a remainder.

Syntax

=GCD(*number1,number2,...*)

Argument: *Number1, number2,* and so on are between 1 to 29 values. If any value is not an integer, it is truncated.

Notes

- If any argument is less than zero, the function returns the #NUM! error.
- One divides any value evenly.
- A prime number has only itself and one as even divisors.

INT

Rounds a number down to the nearest integer.

Syntax

=INT(*number*)

Argument: *Number* is the real number you want to round down to an integer.

LCM

 Returns the least common multiple of integers. The least common multiple is the smallest positive integer that is a multiple of all integer arguments.

Syntax

=LCM(*number1,number2,...*)

Argument: *Number 1, number2,* and so on are between 1 to 29 values. If any value is not an integer, it is truncated.

Note

• If any argument is less than one, the function returns the #NUM! error.

LN

Returns the natural logarithm of a number. Natural logarithms are based on the constant *e* (2.71828182845904).

Syntax

=LN(*number*)

Arguments: *Number* is the positive real number for which you want the natural logarithm. LN is the inverse of the EXP function.

LOG

Returns the logarithm of a number to a specified base.

Syntax

=LOG(*number,base*)

Arguments: *Number* is the positive real number for which you want the logarithm. *Base* is the base of the logarithm. If *base* is omitted, it is assumed to be 10.

LOG10

Returns the base-10 logarithm of a number.

Syntax

=LOG10(*number*)

Argument: *Number* is the positive real number for which you want the base-10 logarithm.

MDETERM

Returns the matrix determinant of an array.

Syntax

=MDETERM(*array*)

Argument: *Array* is a numeric array with an equal number of rows and columns. The *array* argument can be given as a cell range, an array constant, or a name for either of these.

MINVERSE

Returns the inverse matrix for the matrix stored in an array.

Syntax

=MINVERSE(*array*)

Argument: *Array* is a numeric array with an equal number of rows and columns. The *array* argument can be given as a cell range, an array constant, or a name for either of these.

MMULT

Returns the matrix product of two arrays.

Syntax

=MMULT(*array1,array2*)

Argument: *Array1* and *array2* are the arrays you want to multiply. The number of columns in *array1* must be the same as the number of rows in *array2*, and both arrays must contain only numbers. The *array1* argument and the *array2* argument can be given as cell ranges, array constants, or references.

MOD

Gives the remainder (modules) after the *number* argument is divided by the *divisor* argument.

Syntax

=MOD(*number,divisor*)

Arguments: *Number* is the number for which you want to find the remainder. *Divisor* is the number by which you want to divide the number. If *divisor* is 0, MOD returns the #DIV/0! error.

MROUND

 Returns a number rounded to the desired multiple.

Syntax

=MROUND(*number,multiple*)

Arguments: *Number* is the value to round. *Multiple* is the multiple to which you want to round *number*.

MULTINOMIAL

 Returns the ratio of the factorial of a sum of values to the product of factorials.

Syntax

=MULTINOMIAL(*number1,number2...*)

Argument: *Number1, number2* and so on are between 1 to 29 values for which you want the multinomial.

ODD

Returns the *number* argument rounded up to the nearest odd integer.

Syntax

=ODD(*number*)

Argument: *Number* is the value to round.

PI

Returns the number 3.14159265358979, the mathematical constant π, accurate to 15 digits.

Syntax

=PI( )

PRODUCT

Multiplies all the numbers given as arguments and returns the product.

Syntax

=PRODUCT(*number1,number2,...*)

Argument: *Number1, number2,* and so on are between 1 to 30 numbers that you want to multiply.

QUOTIENT

 Returns the integer portion of a division.

Syntax

=QUOTIENT(*numerator,denominator*)

Arguments: *Numerator* is the dividend. *Denominator* is the divisor.

RAND

Returns an evenly distributed random number greater than or equal to 0 and less than 1. A new random number is returned every time the worksheet is calculated.

Syntax

=RAND( )

RANDBETWEEN

 Returns an evenly distributed random integer within a given range. A new random number is returned every time the worksheet is calculated.

Syntax

=RANDBETWEEN(*bottom,top*)

Arguments: *Bottom* is the smallest integer the RANDBETWEEN argument will return. *Top* is the largest integer the RANDBETWEEN argument will return.

ROUND

Rounds a number to a specified number of digits.

Syntax

=ROUND(*number,num_digits*)

Arguments: *Number* is the number you want to round. *Num_digits* specifies the number of digits to which you want to round the number.

Notes

- If *num_digits* is greater than 0, *number* is rounded to the specified number of decimal places.
- If *num_digits* is 0, *number* is rounded to the nearest integer.
- If *num_digits* is less than 0, *number* is rounded to the left of the decimal point.

SERIESSUM

 Returns the sum of a power series.

Syntax

=SERIESSUM(*x,n,m,coefficients*)

Arguments: *X* is the input value to the power series. *N* is the initial power to which you want to raise *x. M* is the step by which to increase *n* for each term in the series. *Coefficients* is a set of coefficients by which each successive power of *x* is multiplied. The number of values in coefficients determines the number of terms in the power series.

SIGN

Returns the sign of a number. The function returns 1 if *number* is positive, 0 if *number* is 0, and –1 if *number* is negative.

Syntax

=SIGN(*number*)

SIN

Returns the sine of the given angle.

Syntax

=SIN(*number*)

Argument: *Number* is the angle in radians for which you want the sine. If your argument is in degrees, multiply it by PI()/180 to convert it to radians.

SINH

Returns the hyperbolic sine of the *number* argument.

Syntax

=SINH(*number*)

Argument: *Number* is the angle in radians for which you want the sine. If your argument is in degrees, multiply it by PI()/180 to convert it to radians.

SQRT

Returns a positive square root.

Syntax

=SQRT(*number*)

Argument: *Number* is the number for which you want the square root.

SQRTPI

 Returns the square root of (*number* * π).

Syntax

=SQRTPI(*number*)

Argument: *Number* is the number by which π is multiplied. If *number* < 0, the function returns the #NUM! error.

SUM

Returns the sum of all the numbers in the list of arguments.

Syntax

=SUM(*number1,number2,...*)

Argument: *Number1, number2,* and so on are between 1 to 30 arguments for which you want the sum.

SUMPRODUCT

Multiplies corresponding components in the given arrays and returns the sum of those products.

Syntax

=SUMPRODUCT(*array1,array2,array3,...*)

Arguments: *Array1, array2, array3,* and so on are between 2 to 30 arrays whose components you want to multiply and then add.

SUMSQ

Returns the sum of the squares of the arguments.

Syntax

=SUMSQ(*number1,number2,...*)

Arguments: *Number1, number2,* and so on are between 1 to 30 arguments for which you want the sum of the squares. You also can use a single array or a reference to an array instead of arguments separated by commas.

SUMX2MY2

Returns the sum of the difference of the squares of corresponding values in two arrays.

Syntax

=SUMX2MY2(*array_x,array_y*)

Arguments: *Array_x* is the first array or range of values. *Array_y* is the second array or range of values.

SUMX2PY2

Returns the sum of the sum of the squares of corresponding values in two arrays.

Syntax

=SUMX2PY2(*array_x,array_y*)

Arguments: *Array_x* is the first array or range of values. *Array_y* is the second array or range of values.

SUMXMY2

Returns the sum of the squares of the differences of corresponding values in two arrays.

Syntax

=SUMXMY2(*array_x,array_y*)

Arguments: *Array_x* is the first array or range of values. *Array_y* is the second array or range of values.

TAN

Returns the tangent of the given angle.

Syntax

=TAN(*number*)

Argument: *Number* is the angle in radians for which you want the tangent. If your argument is in degrees, multiply it by PI()/180 to convert it to radians.

TANH

Returns the hyperbolic tangent of the *number* argument.

Syntax

=TANH(*number*)

TRUNC

Truncates a number to an integer by removing the fractional part of the number.

Syntax

=TRUNC(*number,num_digits*)

Argument: *Number* is the number you want to truncate. *Num_digits* is a number specifying the precision of the truncation. The default value for *num_digits* is zero.

Statistical

AVEDEV

Returns the average of the absolute deviations of data points from their mean.

Syntax

=AVEDEV(*number1,number2,...*)

Argument: *Number1, number2,* and so on are between 1 to 30 arguments for which you want the average of the absolute deviations. You can also use a single array or a reference to an array instead of arguments separated by commas.

AVERAGE

Returns the average (arithmetic means) of the arguments.

Syntax

=AVERAGE(*number1,number2,...*)

Argument: *Number1, number2,* and so on are between 1 to 30 numeric arguments for which you want the average.

BETADIST

Returns the cumulative beta probability density function.

Syntax

=BETADIST(*x,alpha,beta,A,B*)

Arguments: *X* is the value at which to evaluate the function over the interval $A \leq x \leq B$. *Alpha* is a parameter to the distribution. *Beta* is a parameter to the distribution. *A* is an optional lower bound to the interval of *x*. *B* is an optional upper bound to the interval of *x*.

Notes

- If *alpha* ≤ 0 or *beta* ≤ 0, the function returns the #NUM! error.
- If $x < A$, $x > B$, or $A = B$, the function returns the #NUM! error.
- If you omit values for *A* and *B*, the function uses the standard cumulative beta distribution, so that $A = 0$ and $B = 1$.

BETAINV

Returns the inverse of the cumulative beta probability density function.

Syntax

=BETAINV(*probability,alpha,beta,A,B*)

Arguments: *Probability* is a probability associated with the beta distribution. *Alpha* is a parameter to the distribution. *Beta* is a parameter to the distribution. *A* is an optional lower bound to the interval of *x*. *B* is an optional upper bound to the interval of *x*.

Notes

- If *alpha* ≤ 0 or *beta* ≤ 0, the function returns the #NUM! error.
- If *probability* ≤ 0 or *probability* > 1, the function returns the #NUM! error.
- If $x < A$, $x > B$, or $A = B$, the function returns the #NUM! error.
- If you omit values for *A* and *B*, the function uses the standard cumulative beta distribution, so that $A = 0$ and $B = 1$.

BINOMDIST

Returns the individual term binomial distribution.

Syntax

=BINOMDIST(*number_s,trials,probability_s,cumulative*)

Arguments: *Number_s* is the number of successes in trials. *Trials* is the number of independent trials. *Probability_s* is the probability of success on each trial. *Cumulative* is a logical value that determines the form of the function. If *cumulative* is TRUE, then the function returns the cumulative distribution function, which is the probability that there are at most *number_s* successes; if FALSE, it returns the probability mass function, which is the probability that there are *number_s* successes.

Notes

- *Number_s* and *trials* are truncated to integers.
- If *number_s* < 0 or *number_s* > *trials*, the function returns the #NUM! error.
- If *probability_s* < 0 or *probability_s* > 1, the function returns the #NUM! error.

CHIDIST

Returns the one-tailed probability of the chi-squared (X^2) distribution.

Syntax

=CHIDIST(*x,degrees_freedom*)

Arguments: *X* is the value at which you want to evaluate the distribution. *Degrees_freedom* is the number of degrees of freedom. If *degrees_freedom* < 1 or *degrees_freedom* 10^{10}, the function returns the #NUM! error.

CHIINV

Returns the inverse of the chi-squared (X^2) distribution.

Syntax

=CHIINV(*probability,degrees_freedom*)

Arguments: *Probability* is a probability associated with the X^2 distribution. *Degrees_freedom* is the number of degrees of freedom.

Notes

- If *probability* < 0 or *probability* > 1, the function returns the #NUM! error.
- If *degrees_freedom* < 1 or *degrees_freedom* 10^{10}, the function returns the #NUM! error.

CHITEST

Returns the test for independence. This function returns the value from the chi-squared (X^2) distribution for the statistic and the appropriate degrees of freedom.

Syntax

=CHITEST(*actual_range,expected_range*)

Arguments: *Actual_range* is the range of data that contains observations to test against expected values. *Expected_range* is the range of data that contains the ratio of the product of row totals and column totals to the grand total.

Notes

- If actual_range and expected_range have a different number of data points, the function returns the #N/A! error.
- If either argument contains a single row or column, the function returns the #NUM! error.

CONFIDENCE

Returns a confidence interval for a population mean.

Syntax

=CONFIDENCE(*alpha,standard_dev,size*)

Arguments: *Alpha* is the significance level used to compute the confidence level.

The confidence level equals $100(1-alpha)\%$, or, in other words, an *alpha* of 0.05 indicates a 95 percent confidence level.

Standard_dev is the population standard deviation for the data range and is assumed to be known.

Size is the sample size.

Notes
- If *alpha* ≤ *0 or alpha* ≥ 1, the function returns the #NUM! error.
- If *standard_dev* ≤ 0,the function returns the #NUM! error.
- If *size* < 1, the function returns the #NUM! error.

CORREL

Returns the correlation coefficient of the *array1* and *array2* cell ranges.

Syntax

=CORREL(*array1,array2*)

Arguments: *Array1* is a cell range of values. *Array2* is a second cell range of values.

COUNT

Counts how many numbers are in the list of arguments.

Syntax

=COUNT(*value1,value2,...*)

Argument: *Value1,value2,* and so on are between 1 to 30 arguments that can contain or refer to a variety of data types, but only numbers are counted.

Notes
- Arguments that are numbers, null, logical values, dates, or text representations of numbers are counted. Arguments that are error values or text that can't be translated in numbers are ignored.

COUNTA

Counts the number of nonblank values in the list of arguments.

Syntax

=COUNTA(*value1,value2,...*)

Argument: *Value1, value2,* and so on are between 1 to 30 arguments representing the values you want to count.

COVAR

Returns covariance, the average of the products of deviations for each data point pair.

Syntax

=COVAR(*array1,array2*)

Arguments: *Array1* is the first cell range of integers. *Array2* is the second cell range of integers.

Notes

- If *array1* and *array2* have a different number of data points, the function returns the #NA! error.
- If either *array1* or *array2* is empty, the function returns the #DIV/0! error.

CRITBINOM

Returns the smallest integer *k* for which the cumulative binomial distribution function is greater than or equal to a criterion value *alpha*.

Syntax

=CRITBINOM(*trials,probability_s,alpha*)

Arguments: *Trials* is the number of Bernoulli trials. *Probability_s* is the probability of a success on each trial. *Alpha* is the criterion value.

Notes

- If *trials* < 0, the function returns the #NUM! error.
- If *probability_s* is < 0 or *probability_s* is > 0, the function returns the #NUM! error.
- If *alpha* < 0 or *alpha* > 1, the function returns the #NUM! error.

DEVSQ

Returns the sum of squares of deviations of data points from their sample mean.

Syntax

=DEVSQ(*number1,number2,...*)

Argument: *Number1, number2,* and so on are between 1 to 30 arguments for which you want to calculate the sum of squared deviations.

EXPONDIST

Returns the exponential distribution function.

Syntax

=EXPONDIST(*x,lambda,cumulative*)

Arguments: *X* is the value of the function. *Lambda* is the parameter value. *Cumulative* is a logical value that determines the form of the function. If *cumulative* is TRUE, then the function returns the cumulative distribution function; if FALSE, it returns the probability density function.

Notes

- If *x* < 0, the function returns the #NUM! error.
- If *lambda* ≤ 0, the function returns the #NUM! error.

FDIST

Returns the *F* probability distribution.

Syntax

=FDIST(*x,degrees_freedom1,degrees_freedom2*)

Arguments: *X* is the value at which to evaluate the function. *Degrees_freedom1* is the numerator degrees of freedom. *Degrees_freedom2* is the denominatior degrees of freedom.

Notes

- If *degrees_freedom1* < 1 or *degrees_freedom1* $\geq 10^{10}$, the function returns the #NUM! error.
- If *degrees_freedom2* < 1 or *degrees_freedom2* $\geq 10^{10}$, the function returns the #NUM! error.

FINV

Returns the inverse of the *F* probability distribution.

Syntax

=FINV(*probability,degrees_freedom1,degrees_freedom2*)

Arguments: *Probability* is a probability associated with the *F* cumulative distribution. *Degrees_freedom1* is the numerator degrees of freedom. *Degrees_freedom2* is the denominatior degrees of freedom.

Notes

- If *probability* < 0 or *probability* > 1, the function returns the #NUM! error.
- If *degrees_freedom1* < 1 or *degrees_freedom1* $\geq 10^{10}$, the function returns the #NUM! error.
- If *degrees_freedom2* < 1 or *degrees_freedom2* $\geq 10^{10}$, the function returns the #NUM! error.

FISHER

Returns the Fisher transformation at *x*.

Syntax

=FISHER(*x*)

Argument: *X* is a numeric value for which you want the transformation. If $x \leq$ minus 1 or if $x \geq 1$, the function returns the #NUM! error.

FISHERINV

Returns the inverse of the Fisher transformation.

Syntax

=FISHERINV(*y*)

Argument: *Y* is the value for which you want to perform the inverse of the transformation.

FORECAST

Returns a predicted value for the *x* argument based on a linear regression of known *x*- and *y*-arrays or ranges of data.

Syntax

=FORECAST(*x,known_y's,known_x's*)

Arguments: *X* is the data point for which you want to predict a value. *Known_y's* is the dependent array or range of data. *Known_x's* is the independent array or range of data.

FREQUENCY

Returns a frequency distribution as a vertical array.

Syntax

=FREQUENCY(*data_array,bins_array*)

Arguments: *Data_array* is an array of or reference to a set of values for which you want to count frequencies. *Bins_array* is an array of or reference to intervals into which you want to group the values in *data_array.*

FTEST

Returns the result of an *F*-test.

Syntax

=FTEST(*array1,array2*)

Arguments: *Array1* is the first cell range of integers. *Array 2* is the second cell range of integers.

Notes

• If the number of data points in *array1* or *array2* is less than 2, or if the variance of *array1* or *array2* is zero, the function returns the #DIV/0! error.

GAMMADIST

Returns the gamma distribution function.

Syntax

=GAMMADIST(*x,alpha,beta,cumulative*)

Arguments: *X* is the value at which you want to evaluate the distribution. *Alpha* is a parameter to the distribution. *Beta* is a parameter to the distribution. *Cumulative* is a logical value that determines the form of the function. If *cumulative* is TRUE, then the function returns the cumulative distribution function; if FALSE, it returns the probability density function.

GAMMAINV

Returns the inverse of the gamma cumulative distribution.

Syntax

=GAMMAINV(*probability,alpha,beta*)

Arguments: *Probability* is the probability associated with the gamma distribution. *Alpha* is a parameter to the distribution. *Beta* is a parameter to the distribution.

Notes

• If *probability* < 0 or > 1, the function returns the #NUM! error.

• If *alpha* ≤ *0* or if *beta* < 0, the function returns the #NUM! error.

GAMMALN

Returns the natural logarithm of the gamma function, $\Gamma(x)$.

Syntax

=GAMMALN(*x*)

Arguments: *X* is the value for which you want to calculate GAMMALN.

GEOMEAN

Returns the geometric mean of an array or range of positive data.

Syntax

=GEOMEAN(*number1,number2,...*)

Argument: *Number1, number2,* and so on are between 1 to 30 arguments for which you want to calculate the mean.

GROWTH

Fits an exponential curve to the data *known_y's* and *known_x's* and returns y-values along that curve for the array of *new_x's* that you specify.

Syntax

=GROWTH(*known_y's,known_x's,new_x's,const*)

Arguments:

- *Known_y's* is the set of y-values you already know in the relationship $y = b*m^x$.
- If the array *known_y's* is in a single column, then each column of *known_x's* is interpreted as a separate variable.
- If the array *known_y's* is in a single row, then each row of *known_x's* is interpreted as a separate variable.
- If any of the numbers in *known_y's* is 0 or negative, the function returns the #NUM! error.

Known_x's are an optional set of x-values that you may already know in the relationship $y = b*m^x$.

- The array *known_x's* can include one or more sets of variables. If only one variable is used, *known_y's* and *known_x's* can be ranges of any shape, as long as they have equal dimensions. If more than one variable is used, *known_y's* must be a vector (that is, a range with a height of one row or a width of one column).
- If *known_x's* is omitted, it is assumed to be the array {1,2,3,...}—that is, the same size as *known_y's*.

New_x's are new x-values for which you want the function to return corresponding y-values.

- *New_x's* must include a column (or row) for each independent variable, just as *known_x's* does. So, if *known_y's* is in a single column, *known_x's* and *new_x's* should have the same number of columns. If *known_y's* is in a single row, *known_x's* and *new_x's* should have the same number of rows.
- If *new_x's* is omitted, it is assumed to be the same as *known_x's*.
- If both *known_x's* and *new_x's* are omitted, they are assumed to be the array {1,2,3,...}—that is, the same size as *known_y's*.

Const is a logical value specifying whether to force the constant *b* to equal 1.

- If *const* is TRUE or omitted, *b* is calculated normally.

• If *const* is FALSE, *b* is set equal to 1 and the *m*-values are adjusted so that $y = m\hat{\ }x$.

HARMEAN

Returns the harmonic mean of a data set.

Syntax

=HARMEAN(*number1,number2,...*)

Argument: *Number1, number2,* and so on are between 1 to 30 arguments for which you want to calculate the mean. You can also use a single array or a reference to an array instead of arguments separated by commas. If any data point ≤ 0, the function returns the #NUM! error.

HYPGEOMDIST

Returns the hypergeometric distribution.

Syntax

=HYPGEOMDIST(*sample_s,number_sample,population_s, number_population*)

Arguments: *Sample_s* is the number of successes in the sample. *Number_sample* is the size of the sample. *Population_s* is the number of successes in the population. *Number_population* is the population size.

Notes

• If *sample_s* < 0 or *sample_s* is greater than the lesser of *number_sample* or *population_s*, the function returns the #NUM! error.

• If *sample_s* is less than the larger of 0 or (*number_sample–number_population + population_s*), the function returns the #NUM! error.

• If *number_sample* < 0 or *number_sample* > *number_population*, the function returns the #NUM! error.

• If *population_s* < 0 or *population_s* > *number_population*, the function returns the #NUM! error.

• If *number_population* < 0, the function returns the #NUM! error.

INTERCEPT

Returns the intercept of the linear regression line through data points in *known_x's* and *known_y's*.

Syntax

=INTERCEPT(*known_y's,known_x's*)

Arguments: *Known_y's* is the dependent set of observations or data. *Known_x's* is the independent set of observations or data.

KURT

Returns the kurtosis of a data set.

Syntax

=KURT(*number1,number2,...*)

Arguments: *Number1, number2,* and so on are between 1 to 30 arguments for which you want to calculate kurtosis.

LARGE

Returns the *k*th largest value in a data set.

Syntax

=LARGE(*array,k*)

Arguments: *Array* is the array or range of data for which you want to determine the *k*th largest value. *K* is the position (from the largest) in the array or cell range of data to return. If $k \leq 0$ or if *k* is greater than the number of data points, the function returns the #NUM! error.

LINEST

Uses the "least squares" method to calculate a straight line that best fits your data and returns an array that describes the line.

Syntax

=LINEST(*known_y's,known_x's,const,stats*)

Arguments: *Known_y's* is the set of y-values you already know in the relationship $y = mx + b$.

- If the array *known_y's* is in a single column, then each column of *known_x's* is interpreted as a separate variable.
- If the array *known_y's* is in a single row, then each row of *known_x's* is interpreted as a separate variable.
- If any of the numbers in *known_y's* is 0 or negative, the function returns the #NUM! error.

Known_x's is an optional set of x-values that you may already know in the relationship $y = mx + b$.

- The array *known_x's* can include one or more sets of variables. If only one variable is used, *known_y's* and *known_x's* can be ranges of any shape, as long as they have equal dimensions. If more than one variable is used, *known_y's* must be a vector (that is, a range with a height of one row or a width of one column).
- If *known_x's* is omitted, it is assumed to be the array {1,2,3,...}—that is, the same size as *known_y's*.

Const is a logical value specifying whether to force the constant *b* to equal 0.

- If *const* is TRUE or omitted, *b* is calculated normally.
- If *const* is FALSE, *b* is set equal to 0 and the *m*-values are adjusted so that $y = mx$.

Stats is a logical value specifying whether to return additional regression statistics.

- If *stats* is TRUE, the function returns the additional regression statistics, so the returned array is
  $$\{m_n, m_{n-1}, \dots, m_1, b; se_n, se_{n-1}, \dots, se_1, se_b; r^2, se_y; F, df; ss_{reg}, ss_{resid}\}.$$
- If *stats* is FALSE or omitted, the function returns only the *m*-coefficients and

the constant *b*.

LOGEST

Calculates an exponential curve that fits your data and returns an array that describes the curve. The equation for the curve is

$$y = (b*(m_1^{\wedge}x_1)*(m_2^{\wedge}x_2)*...) \text{ or } y = b*m^{\wedge}x$$

where the dependent *y*-value is a function of the independent *x*-values. The *m*-values are bases corresponding to each exponent *x*-value. Note that *y*, *x*, and *m* can be vectors. The array that LOGEST returns is

$$\{m_n, m_{n-1},...,m_1, b\}.$$

Syntax

=LOGEST(*known_y's,known_x's,const,stats*)

Arguments: *Known_y's* is the set of *y*-values you already know in the relationship $y = b*m^{\wedge}x$.

- If the array *known_y's* is in a single column, then each column of *known_x's* is interpreted as a separate variable.
- If the array *known_y's* is in a single row, then each row of *known_x's* is interpreted as a separate variable.

Known_x's are an optional set of *x*-values that you may already know in the relationship $y = b*m^{\wedge}x$.

- The array *known_x's* can include one or more sets of variables. If only one variable is used, *known_y's* and *known_x's* can be ranges of any shape, as long as they have equal dimensions. If more than one variable is used, *known_y's* must be a vector (that is, a range with a height of one row or a width of one column).
- If *known_x's* is omitted, it is assumed to be the array {1,2,3,...} that is the same size as *known_y's*.

Const is a logical value specifying whether to force the constant *b* to equal 1.

- If *const* is TRUE or omitted, *b* is calculated normally.
- If *const* is FALSE, *b* is set equal to 1 and the *m*-values are adjusted so that $y = m^{\wedge}x$.

Stats is a logical value specifying whether to return additional regression statistics.

- If *stats* is TRUE, the function returns the additional regression statistics, so the returned array is

$$\{m_n, m_{n-1},...,m_1, b; se_n, se_{n-1},...,se_1, se_b; r^2, se_y; F, df; ss_{reg}, ss_{resid}\}.$$

- If *stats* is FALSE or omitted, the function returns only the *m*-coefficients and the constant *b*.

LOGINV

Returns the inverse of the lognormal cumulative distribution function of *x*, where $\ln(x)$ is normally distributed with parameters *mean* and *standard_dev*. If *p* + LOGNORMDIST (*x*,...).then LOGINV(*p*,...) = *x*.

Syntax

=LOGINV(*probability,mean,standard_dev*)

Arguments: *Probability* is a probability associated with the lognormal distribution. *Mean* is the mean of *x*. *Standard_dev* is the standard deviation of *x*.

LOGNORMDIST

Returns the lognormal cumulative distribution function of *x* where $\ln(x)$ is normally distributed with parameters *mean* and *standard_dev*.

Syntax

=LOGNORMDIST(*x,mean,standard_dev*)

Arguments: *X* is the value at which to evaluate the function. *Mean* is the mean of $\ln(x)$. *Standard_dev* is the standard deviation of $\ln(x)$.

MAX

Returns the maximum value in a list of arguments.

Syntax

=MAX(*number1,number2,...*)

Argument: *Number1, number2,* and so on are between 1 to 30 numbers for which you want to find the maximum value.

MEDIAN

Returns the median of the given numbers.

Syntax

=MEDIAN(*number1,number2,...*)

Argument: *Number1, number2,* and so on are between 1 to 30 numbers for which you want to find the median.

MIN

Returns the minimum value in a list of arguments.

Syntax

=MIN(*number1,number2,...*)

Argument: *Number1, number2,* and so on are between 1 to 30 numbers for which you want to find the minimum value.

MODE

Returns the most frequently occurring value in an array or range of data.

Syntax

=MODE(*number1,number2,...*)

Argument: *Number1, number2,* and so on are between 1 to 30 arguments for which you want to calculate the mode. You also can use a single array or a reference to an array instead of arguments separated by commas.

NEGBINOMDIST

Returns the negative binomial distribution.

Syntax

=NEGBINOMDIST(*number_f,number_s,probability_s*)

Arguments: *Number_f* is the number of failures. *Number_s* is the threshold number of successes. *Probability_s* is the probability of a success.

Notes

- If *probability_s* < 0 or if *probability* > 1, the function returns the #NUM! error.
- If (*number_f* + *number_s* − 1) ≤ 0, the function returns the #NUM! error.

NORMDIST

Returns the normal distribution function for the specified mean and standard deviation.

Syntax

=NORMDIST(*x,mean,standard_dev,cumulative*)

Arguments: *X* is the value for which you want the distribution. *Mean* is the arithmetic mean of the distribution. *Standard_dev* is the standard deviation of the distribution. *Cumulative* is a logical value that determines the form of the function. If *cumulative* is TRUE, the function returns the cumulative distribution function; if FALSE, it returns the probability mass function.

Notes

- If *standard_dev* ≤ 0, the function returns the #NUM! error.
- If *mean* = 0 and *standard_dev* = 1, the function returns the standard normal distribution, NORMDIST.

NORMINV

Returns the inverse of the normal cumulative distribution for the specified mean and standard deviation.

Syntax

=NORMINV(*probability,mean,standard_dev*)

Arguments: *Probability* is a probability corresponding to the normal distribution. If *probability* < 0 or if *probability* > 1, the function returns the #NUM! error. *Mean* is the arithmetic mean of the distribution. *Standard_dev* is the standard deviation of the distribution. If *standard_dev* ≤ 0, the function returns the #NUM! error.

NORMSDIST

Returns the standard normal cumulative distribution.

Syntax

=NORMSDIST(*z*)

Argument: *Z* is the value for which you want the distribution.

NORMSINV

Returns the inverse of the standard normal cumulative distribution.

Syntax

=NORMSINV(*probability*)

Argument: *Probability* is a probability corresponding to the normal distribution. If *probability* < 0 or if *probability* > 1, the function returns the #NUM! error.

PEARSON

Returns the Pearson product moment correlation coefficient, *r*, a dimensionless index that ranges from –1.0 to 1.0 inclusive and reflects the extent of a linear relationship between two data sets.

Syntax

=PEARSON(*array1,array2*)

Arguments: *Array1* is a set of independent values. *Array 2* is a set of dependent values.

PERCENTILE

Returns the value from *array* at the *k*th percentile.

Syntax

=PERCENTILE(*array,k*)

Arguments: *Array* is the array or range of data that defines relative standing. *K* is the percentile value in the range 0...1, inclusive. If *k* < 0 or if *k* > 1, the function returns the #NUM! error. If *k* is not a multiple of $1/(n-1)$, the function interpolates to determine the value at the *k*th percentile.

PERCENTRANK

Returns the percentage rank of *x* among the values in *array*.

Syntax

=PERCENTRANK(*array,x,significance*)

Arguments: *Array* is the array or range of data with numeric values that defines relative standing. *X* is the value for which you want to know the rank. *Significance* is an optional value that identifies the number of significant digits for the returned percentage value. If omitted, the function uses three digits (0.xxx%).

PERMUT

Returns the number of permutations of groups of *number_chosen* objects that can be selected from *number* objects.

Syntax

=PERMUT(*number,number_chosen*)

Arguments: *Number* is an integer that describes the number of objects. *Number_chosen* is an integer that describes the number of objects in each permutation.

Notes

- If *number* ≤ 0 or if *number_chosen* < 0, the function returns the #NUM! error.
- If *number* < *number_chosen*, the function returns the #NUM! error.

POISSON

Returns the Poisson probability distributions.

Syntax

=POISSON(*x,mean,cumulative*)

Arguments: *X* is the number of events. If *x* is ≤ 0, the function returns the #NUM! error. *Mean* is the expected numeric value. If *mean* is ≤ 0, the function returns the #NUM! error. *Cumulative* is a logical value that determines the form of the probability distribution returned. If *cumulative* is TRUE, the function returns the cumulative Poisson probability that the number of random events occuring will be between zero and *x* inclusive; if FALSE, it returns the Poisson probability mass function that the number of events occurring will be exactly *x*.

PROB

Returns the probability that values in *x_range* are between the *lower_limit* and *upper_limit*.

Syntax

=PROB(*x_range,prob_range,lower_limit,upper_limit*)

Arguments: *X_range* is the range of numeric values of x with which there are associated probabilities. *Prob_range* is a set of probabilities associated with values in *x_range. Lower_limit* is the lower bound on the value for which you want a probability. *Upper_limit* is the optional upper bound on the value for which you want a probability.

Notes

- If any value in *prob_range* ≤ 0 or if any value in *prob_range* >1, the function returns the #NUM! error.
- If the sum of the values in *prob_range* = 1, the function returns the #NUM! error.
- If *upper_limit* is omitted, the function returns the probability of being equal to *lower_limit*.
- If *x_range* and *prob_range* contain a different number of data points, the function returns the #N/A! error.

QUARTILE

Returns a quartile from the data points in *array*.

Syntax

=QUARTILE(*array,quart*)

Arguments: *Array* is the array or cell range of numeric values for which you want the quartile value. *Quart* indicates which value to return.

If quart equals	QUARTILE returns
0	Minimum value
1	First quartile (25th percentile)
2	Median value (50th percentile)
3	Third quartile (75th percentile)
4	Maximum value

Notes
- If *quart* < 0 or if quart > 4, the function returns the #NUM! error.
- MIN, MEDIAN, and MAX return the same value as QUARTILE when *quart* is equal to 0, 2, and 4, respectively.

RANK

Returns the rank of a number in a list of numbers.

Syntax

=RANK(*number,ref,order*)

Arguments: *Number* is the number whose rank you want to find. *Ref* is an array of, or a reference to, a list of numbers. Nonnumeric values in *ref* are ignored. *Order* is a number specifying how to rank number. If *order* is 0 or omitted, Excel ranks *number* as if *ref* were a list sorted in descending order. If *order* is any nonzero value, Excel ranks *number* as if *ref* were a list sorted in ascending order.

RSQ

Returns the r^2 value of the linear regression line through data points in *known_y's* and *known_x's*.

Syntax

=RSQ(*known_y's,known_x's*)

Arguments: *Known_y's* is an array or range of data points. *Known_x's* is an array or range of data points.

Notes

If *known_y's* and *known_x's* are empty or have a different number of data points, the function returns the #N/A error.

SKEW

Returns the skewness of a distribution. Skewness characterizes the degree of asymmetry of a distribution around its mean.

Syntax

=SKEW(*number1,number2,...*)

Arguments: *Number1, number2,* and so on are between 1 to 30 arguments for which you want to calculate skewness.

Notes

If there are less than three data points or if the standard deviation is zero, the function returns the #DIV/0! error.

SLOPE

Returns the slope of the linear regression line through data points in *known_y's* and *known_x's*.

Syntax

=SLOPE(*known_y's,known_x's*)

Arguments: *Known_y's* is an array or cell range of numeric dependent data points. *Known_x's* is the set of independent data points.

SMALL

Returns the *k*th smallest value in a data set.

Syntax

=SMALL(*array,k*)

Arguments: *Array* is an array or range of numerical data for which you want to determine the *k*th smallest value. *K* is the position (from the smallest) in the array or range of data to return.

Notes

- If $k \le 0$ or if *k* exceeds the number of data points, the function returns the #NUM! error.

- If *n* is the number of data points in the array, SMALL(*array*,1) equals the smallest value, and SMALL(*array,n*) equals the largest value.

STANDARDIZE

Returns a normalized value from a distribution characterized by *mean* and *standard_dev*.

Syntax

=STANDARDIZE(*x,mean,standard_dev*)

Arguments: *X* is the value you want to normalize. *Mean* is the arithmetic mean of the distribution. *Standard_dev* is the standard deviation of the distribution. If $standard\_dev \le 0$, the function returns the #NUM! error.

STDEV

Estimates the standard deviation of a population based on a sample given as arguments.

Syntax

=STDEV(*number1,number2,...*)

Argument: *Number1, number2,* and so on are between 1 to 30 number arguments corresponding to a sample of a population. *Number* can be a reference to a range.

STDEVP

Calculates the standard deviation based on the entire population.

Syntax

=STDEVP(*number1,number2,...*)

Argument: *Number1, number2,* and so on are between 1 to 30 number arguments corresponding to a sample of a population. *Number* can be a reference to a range.

STEYX

Returns the standard error of the predicted *y* value for each *x* in the regression.

Syntax

=STEYX(*known_y's,known_x's*)

Arguments: *Known_y's* is an array or cell range of numeric dependent data points. *Known_x's* is the set of independent data points.

TDIST

Returns the Student's *t*-distribution.

Syntax

=TDIST(*x,degrees_freedom,tails*)

Arguments: *X* is the numeric value at which to evaluate the distribution. *Degrees_freedom* is an integer indicating the number of degrees of freedom. If *degrees_freedom* < 1, the function returns the #NUM! error. *Tails* specifies the number of distribution tails to return. If *tails* = 1, TDIST returns the one-tailed distribution. If *tails* = 2, TDIST returns the two-tailed distribution.

TINV

Returns the inverse of the Student's *t*-distribution for the specified degrees of freedom.

Syntax

=TINV(*probability,degrees_freedom*)

Arguments: *Probability* is the probability associated with the two-tailed Student's *t*-distribution. If *probability* < 0 or if *probability* > 1, the function returns the #NUM! error. *Degrees_freedom* is the number of degrees of freedom to characterize the distribution. If *degrees_freedom* < 1, the function returns the #NUM! error.

TREND

Fits a straight line (using the method of least squares) to the arrays *known_y's* and *known_x's*. Returns the *y*-values along that line for the array of *new_x's* that you specify.

Syntax

=TREND(*known_y's,known_x's,new_x's,const*)

Arguments: *Known_y's* is the set of *y*-values you already know in the relationship $y = mx + b$.

- If the array *known_y's* is in a single column, then each column of *known_x's* is interpreted as a separate variable.
- If the array *known_y's* is in a single row, then each row of *known_x's* is interpreted as a separate variable.

Known_x's are an optional set of *x*-values that you may already know in the relationship $y = mx + b$.

- The array *known_x's* can include one or more sets of variables. If only one variable is used, *known_y's* and *known_x's* can be ranges of any shape, as long as they have equal dimensions. If more than one variable is used, *known_y's* must be a vector (that is, a range with a height of one row or a width of one column).

- If *known_x's* is omitted, it is assumed to be the array {1,2,3,...}—that is, the same size as *known_y's*.

New_x's are new *x*-values for which you want TREND to return corresponding *y*-values.

- *New_x's* must include a column (or row) for each independent variable, just as the *known_x's* does. So, if *known_y's* is in a single column, *known_x's* and *new_x's* should have the same number of columns. If *known_y's* is in a single row, *known_x's* and *new_x's* should have the same number of rows.
- If *new_x's* is omitted it is assumed to be the same as *known_x's*.
- If both *known_x's* and *new_x's* are omitted, they are assumed to be the array {1,2,3,...} that is the same size as *known_y's*.

Const is a logical value specifying whether to force the constant *b* to equal 0.

- If *const* is TRUE or omitted, *b* is calculated normally.
- If *const* is FALSE, *b* is set equal to 0 and the *m*-values are adjusted so that $y = mx$.

TRIMMEAN

Returns the mean taken by excluding a percentage of data points from the top and bottom tails of a data set.

Syntax

=TRIMMEAN(*array,percent*)

Arguments: *Array* is the array or range of values to trim and average. *Percent* is the fractional number of data points to exclude from the calculation. For example, if *percent* = 0.2, 4 points are trimmed from a data set of 20 (20 x 0.2), 2 from the top and 2 from the bottom of the set.

TTEST

Returns the probability associated with a Student's *t*-Test.

Syntax

=TTEST(*array1,array2,tails,type*)

Arguments: *Array1* is the first data set. *Array2* is the second data set. *Tails* specifies the number of distribution tails. If *tails* = 1, TTEST uses the one-tailed distribution. If *tails* = 2, TTEST uses the two-tailed distribution. *Type* is the kind of *t*-Test to perform.

If type equals	This test is performed
1	Paired
2	Two-sample equal variance (homoscedastic)
3	Two-sample unequal variance (heteroscedastic)

Notes

- If *array1* and *array2* have a different number of data points, and *type* = 1 (paired), the function returns the #NUM! error.
- If *tails* is any value other than 1 or 2, the function returns the #NUM! error.

VAR

Estimates the variance of a population based on a sample given as arguments.

Syntax

=VAR(*number1,number2,...*)

Argument: *Number1, number2*, and so on are between 1 to 30 number arguments corresponding to a sample of a population.

VARP

Calculates the variance of a population based on the entire population as arguments.

Syntax

=VARP(*number1,number2,...*)

Argument: *Number1, number2*, and so on are between 1 to 30 number arguments corresponding to a population.

WEIBULL

Returns the Weibull distribution.

Syntax

=WEIBULL(*x,alpha,beta,cumulative*)

Arguments: *X* is the value at which to evaluate the function. *Alpha* is a parameter to the distribution. *Beta* is a parameter to the distruibution. *Cumulative* determines the form of the function. If *cumulative* is TRUE, the function returns the *cumulative* distribution function; if FALSE, it returns the probability density function.

ZTEST

Returns the two-tailed *P*-value of a *z*-test.

Syntax

=ZTEST(*array,x,sigma*)

Arguments: *Array* is the array or range of data against which to test *x*. *X* is the value to test. *Sigma* is the population (known) standard deviation. If omitted, the sample standard deviation is used.

Lookup and Reference

ADDRESS

Creates a cell address as text, given specified row and column numbers.

Syntax

=ADDRESS(*row_num,column_num,abs_num,a1,sheet_text*)

Arguments: *Row_num* is the row number to use in the cell reference. *Column_num* is the column number to use in the cell reference. *Abs_num* specifies the type of reference to return.

Abs_num	ADDRESS returns this type of reference
1 or omitted	Absolute
2	Ablsolute row; relative column
3	Relative row; absolute column
4	Relative

A1 is a logical value that specifies the A1 or R1C1 reference style. If *a1* is TRUE or omitted, ADDRESS returns an A1-style reference; if FALSE, ADDRESS returns an R1C1-style reference. *Sheet_text* is text specifying the name of the worksheet or macro sheet to be used as the external reference. If *sheet_text* is omitted, no sheet name is used.

AREAS

Returns the number of areas in a reference. An area is a range of contiguous cells or a single cell.

Syntax

=AREAS(*reference*)

Argument: *Reference* is a reference to a cell or range of cells and can refer to multiple areas. If you want to specify several references as a single argument, then you must include extra sets of parentheses so that Excel will not interpret the comma as a field separator.

CHOOSE

Uses the *index_num* argument to return a value from the list of values given as arguments.

Syntax

=CHOOSE(*index_num,value1,value2,...*)

Arguments: *Index_num* specifies which value argument is selected. *Index_num* must be a number between 1 and 29, or a formula or reference to a cell containing a number between 1 and 29.

- If *index_num* is 1, the function returns value1; if it is 2, the function returns value2; and so on.
- If *index_num* is less than 1 or greater than the number of the last value in the list, the function returns the #VALUE! error.
- If *index_num* is a fraction, it is truncated to the lowest integer before being used.

Value1, value2, and so on are between 1 to 29 arguments from which CHOOSE selects a value or an action to perform based on *index_num.* The arguments can be numbers, cell references, defined names, formulas, macro functions, or text.

COLUMN

Returns the column number of the given reference.

Syntax

=COLUMN(*reference*)

Argument: *Reference* is the cell or range of cells for which you want the column number.

COLUMNS

Returns the number of columns in an array or reference.

Syntax

=COLUMNS(*array*)

Argument: *Array* is an array or array formula, or a reference to a range of cells for which you want the number of columns.

FASTMATCH

Returns the relative position of an element in an array that matches the specified value.

Syntax

=FASTMATCH(*lookup_value,lookup_array,type_of_match*)

Arguments: *Lookup_value* is the value you're searching for within *lookup_array*. *Lookup_array* is an array or a range of cells within which you are searching for a match. *Type_of_match* is the number –1, 0, or 1. *Type_of_match* specifies how Excel matches *lookup_value* with values in *lookup_array*.

- If *type_of_match* is –1, the function finds the largest value that is less than or equal to *lookup_value*. *Lookup_array* must be placed in ascending order.
- If *type_of_match* is –1, the function finds the smallest value that is greater than or equal to *lookup_value*. *Lookup_array* must be placed in descending order.
- If *type_of_match* is omitted, it is assumed to be 1.

HLOOKUP

Searches the top row of an array for a particular value and returns the value in the indicated cell.

Syntax

=HLOOKUP(*lookup_value,table_array,row_index_num*)

Arguments: *Lookup_value* is the value to be found in the first row of the table. *Lookup_value* can be a value, a reference, or a text string. *Table_array* is a table of information in which data is looked up. The values in the first row of *table_array* must be placed in ascending order. *Row_index_num* is the row number in *table_array* from which the matching value should be returned. A *row_index_num* of 1 returns the first row value in *table_array*, a *row_index_num* of 2 returns the second row value in *table_array*, and so on.

INDEX

Returns the value of an element in an array, selected by the row and column number indexes. The INDEX function has two syntax forms: reference and array. The reference form always returns a reference; the array form always returns a value or array of values.

Syntax 1 (Reference form)

=INDEX(*reference,row_num,column_num,area_num*)

Arguments: *Reference* is a reference to one or more cell ranges.

- If you are entering a nonadjacent selection for *reference*, enclose *reference* in parentheses.
- If each area in *reference* contains only one row or column, the *row_num* or *column_num* argument, respectively, is optional.

Row_num is the number of the row in reference from which to return a reference. *Column_num* is the number of the column in reference from which to return a reference. *Area_num* selects a range in *reference* from which to return the intersection of *row_num* and *column_num*.

Syntax 2 (Array form)

=INDEX(*array,row_num,column_num*)

Arguments: *Array* is a range of cells in array entered as an array. *Row_num* selects the row in the array from which to return a value. If *row_num* is omitted, *column_num* is required. *Column_num* selects the column in the array from which to return a value. If *column_num* is omitted, *row_num* is required.

- If both the *row_num* and *column_num* arguments are used, the function returns the value in the cell at the intersection of *row_num* and *column_num*.
- If *array* contains only one row or column, the corresponding *row_num* or *column_num* argument is optional.
- If *array* has more than one row and more than one column, and only *row_num* and *column_num* are used, the function returns an array of the entire row or column in *array*.
- If you set *row_num* or *column_num* to 0, the function returns the array of values for the entire column or row, respectively. To use values returned as an array, enter the INDEX function as an array in a horizontal array of cells.

INDIRECT

Returns a reference specified by *ref_text*.

Syntax

=INDIRECT(*ref_text,a1*)

Arguments: *Ref_text* is a reference to a cell that contains an A1-style reference, an R1C1-style reference, or a name defined as a reference. *A1* is a logical value that specifies what type of reference is contained in the cell *ref_text*. If *a1* is TRUE or omitted, *ref_text* is interpreted as an A1-style reference. If *a1* is FALSE, *ref_text* is interpreted as an R1C1-style reference.

LOOKUP

The LOOKUP function has two syntax forms, vector and array. The vector form looks in a vector for a value, moves to the corresponding position in a second vector, and returns this value. The array form looks in the first row or column of an array for the specified value, moves down or across to the last cell, and returns the value of the cell.

Syntax 1 (Vector form)

=LOOKUP(*lookup_value,lookup_vector,result_vector*)

Arguments: *Lookup_value* is a value that LOOKUP searches for in the first vector. *Lookup_vector* is a range that contains only one row or one column. The values must be placed in ascending order: ...–2, –1, 0, 1, 2, ..., A–Z, FALSE, TRUE; otherwise, the function may not give the correct value. Uppercase and lowercase text are equivalent. *Result_vector* is a range that contains only one row or column. It should be the same size as *lookup_vector*.

Notes

- If LOOKUP can't find the *lookup_value*, it matches the largest value in the *lookup_vector* that is less than or equal to the *lookup_value*.

Syntax 2 (Array form)

=LOOKUP(*lookup_value,array*)

Argument: *Lookup_value* is a value that LOOKUP searches for in an array. If the function can't find the *lookup_value*, it uses the largest value in the array that is less than or equal to the *lookup_value*. Array is a range of cells that contains text, numbers, or logical values that you want to compare with *lookup_value*.

- If *array* is square, or covers an area that is wider than it is tall, the function searches for *lookup_value* in the first row.
- If *array* is taller than it is wide, the function searches in the first column.
- HLOOKUP and VLOOKUP allow you to index down or across, but LOOKUP always selects the last value in the row or column.
- The values must be placed in ascending order: ..., –2, –1, 0, 1, 2, ..., A–Z, FALSE, TRUE; otherwise, the function may not give the correct value. Uppercase and lowercase text are equivalent.

MATCH

Returns the relative position of an element in an array that matches a specified value in a specified way.

Syntax

=MATCH(*lookup_value,lookup_array,match_type*)

Arguments: *Lookup_value* is the value you use to find the value you want in a table. *Lookup_array* is a contiguous range of cells containing possible lookup values. *Match_type* is the number –1, 0, or 1. *Match_type* specifies how Excel matches *lookup_value* with values in *lookup_array*.

- If *match_type* is 1, the function finds the largest value that is less than or equal to *lookup_value*. *Lookup_array* must be placed in ascending order: ...,–2, –1, 0, 1, 2, ..., A–Z, FALSE, TRUE.

- If *match_type* is 0, the function finds the first value that is exactly equal to *lookup_value. Lookup_array* can be in any order.
- If *match_type* is –1, the function finds the smallest value that is greater than or equal to *lookup_value. Lookup_array* must be placed in descending order: TRUE, FALSE, Z–A, ...2, 1, 0, –1, –2,..., and so on.
- If *match_type* is omitted, it is assumed to be 1.

OFFSET

Returns a reference of a specified height and width, offset from another reference by a specified number of rows and columns.

Syntax

=OFFSET(*reference,rows,cols,height,width*)

Arguments: *Reference* is the reference from which you want to base the offset. *Rows* is the number of rows, up or down, that you want the upper-left cell to refer to. *Rows* can be positive or negative. *Cols* is the number of columns, to the left or right, that you want the upper-left cell of the result to refer to. *Cols* can can be positive or negative. *Height* is the height, in number of rows, that you want the returned reference to be. *Height* must be a positive number. *Width* is the width, in number of columns, that you want the returned reference to be. *Width* must be a positive number.

ROW

Returns the row number of a reference.

Syntax

=ROW(*reference*)

Argument: *Reference* is the cell or range of cells for which you want the row number. *Reference* cannot refer to multiple areas. If *reference* is omitted, it is assumed to be the reference of the cell in which the ROW function appears.

ROWS

Returns the number of rows in a reference or array.

Syntax

=ROWS(*array*)

Argument: *Array* is an array, an array formula, or a reference to a range of cells for which you want the number of rows.

TRANSPOSE

Returns the transpose of an array. TRANSPOSE must be entered as an array formula in a range that has the same number of rows and columns, respectively, as *array* has columns and rows.

Syntax

=TRANSPOSE(*array*)

Argument: *Array* is an array on a worksheet or macro sheet that you want to transpose. *Array* can also be a range of cells.

VLOOKUP

Searches the leftmost column of an array for a particular value and returns the value in the cell indicated.

Syntax

=VLOOKUP(*lookup_value,table_array,col_index_num*)

Arguments: *Lookup_value* is the value to be found in the first column of the array. *Table_array* is the table of information in which data is looked up. You can use a reference to a range or a range name, such as Database. The values in the first column of *table_array* must be placed in ascending order: ...,–2, –1, 0, 1, 2, ... ,A–Z, FALSE, TRUE; otherwise the function may not give the correct value. *Col_index_num* is the column number in *table_array* from which the matching value should be returned.

Database

CROSSTAB

 Defines the structure and content of a cross-tabulation table.

Syntax 1

For defining row and column headings of the cross-tabulation table.

=CROSSTAB(*label,expression*)

Syntax 2

For defining columns in the cross-tabulation table.

=CROSSTAB(*label,"Columns:",columns_array*)

Syntax 3

For defining rows in the cross-tabulation table.

=CROSSTAB(*label,"Rows:",rows_array*)

Syntax 4

For defining summaries in the cross-tabulation table.

=CROSSTAB(*label,"Summary:",values_array,create_outline,create_names,*
multiple_values,auto_drilldown)

Arguments: *Label* is text that you want displayed in the cell containing the CROS-STAB formula. *Label* is not used by the cross-tabulation table. If *label* is omitted, *expression* determines the value displayed in the cell. *Expression* is a name, formula, or other information that is used to compute the cross-tabulation table. *Expression* varies depending on the type of data in the table. *"Columns:"*, *"Rows:"*, and *"Summary:"* are literal text values that you must enter as shown in the syntax lines. *Rows_array* is a two-dimensional array that specifies a set of fields that appears in each row of the cross-tabulation table. *Columns_array* is a two-dimensional array that specifies a set of fields that appears in each column of the cross-tabulation table. *Values_array* is a two-dimensional array that specifies each field that appears as a value field. *Create_outline* is a logical value that, if TRUE, creates an outline for the cross-tabulation table, or, if FALSE, does not create an outline for the table. *Create_names* is a logical value that, if TRUE, creates names for the values from the table, or, if FALSE, does not create names for the values. *Multiple_values* is a numerical value that specifies how to handle multiple summaries. *Auto_drilldown* is a logical value that, if TRUE, places drilldown formulas in the result cells, or, if FALSE, does not place drilldown formulas in the result cells.

DAVERAGE

Averages the values in the *field* column of records in the *database* that match the *criteria*.

Syntax

=DAVERAGE(*database,field,criteria*)

Arguments: *Database* is the range of cells that make up the database. *Field* indicates which field is used in the function. *Criteria* is the range of cells that contains the database criteria.

DCOUNT

Counts the cells containing numbers that match the *criteria* in the *field* column of records in the *database*.

Syntax

=DCOUNT(*database,field,criteria*)

Arguments: *Database* is the range of cells that make up the database. *Field* indicates which field is used in the function. If *field* is omitted, the DCOUNT function counts all records in the database. *Criteria* is the range of cells that contains the database criteria.

DCOUNTA

Counts the cells that are not blank and that satisfy the *criteria* in the *field* column of records in the *database*.

Syntax

=DCOUNTA(*database,field,criteria*)

Arguments: *Database* is the range of cells that makes up the database. *Field* indicates which field is used in the function. *Criteria* is the range of cells that contains the database criteria.

DGET

Extracts from a database a single record that matches the specified criteria.

Syntax

=DGET(*database,field,criteria*)

Arguments: *Database* is the range of cells that makes up the database. *Field* indicates which field is used in the function. *Criteria* is the range of cells that contains the database criteria.

DMAX

Returns the largest number in the *field* column of records in the *database* that matches the *criteria*.

Syntax

=DMAX(*database,field,criteria*)

Arguments: *Database* is the range of cells that makes up the database. *Field* indicates which field is used in the function. *Criteria* is the range of cells that contains the database criteria.

DMIN

Returns the smallest number in the *field* column of records in the *database* that matches the *criteria*.

Syntax

=DMIN(*database,field,criteria*)

Arguments: *Database* is the range of cells that makes up the database. *Field* indicates which field is used in the function. *Criteria* is the range of cells that contains the database criteria.

DPRODUCT

Multiplies the values in the *field* column of records in the *database* that match the *criteria*.

Syntax

=DPRODUCT(*database,field,criteria*)

Arguments: *Database* is the range of cells that makes up the database. *Field* indicates which field is used in the function. *Criteria* is the range of cells that contains the database criteria.

DSTDEV

Estimates the standard deviation of a population based on a sample, using the numbers in the *field* column of records in the *database* that match the *criteria*.

Syntax

=DSTDEV(*database,field,criteria*)

Arguments: *Database* is the range of cells that makes up the database. *Field* indicates which field is used in the function. *Criteria* is the range of cells that contains the database criteria.

DSTDEVP

Calculates the standard deviation of a population based on the entire population, using the numbers in the *field* column of records in the *database* that match the *criteria.*

Syntax

=DSTDEVP(*database,field,criteria*)

Arguments: *Database* is the range of cells that makes up the database. *Field* indicates which field is used in the function. *Criteria* is the range of cells that contains the database criteria.

DSUM

Adds numbers in the *field* column of records in the *database* that match the *criteria.*

Syntax

=DSUM(*database,field,criteria*)

Arguments: *Database* is the range of cells that makes up the database. *Field* indicates which field is used in the function. *Criteria* is the range of cells that contains the database criteria.

DVAR

Estimates the variance of a population based on a sample, using the numbers in the *field* column of records in the *database* that match the *criteria.*

Syntax

=DVAR(*database,field,criteria*)

Arguments: *Database* is the range of cells that makes up the database. *Field* indicates which field is used in the function. *Criteria* is the range of cells that contains the database criteria.

DVARP

Calculates the variance of a population based on the entire population, using the numbers in the *field* column of records in the *database* that match the *criteria.*

Syntax

=DVARP(*database,field,criteria*)

Arguments: *Database* is the range of cells that makes up the database. *Field* indicates which field is used in the function. *Criteria* is the range of cells that contains the database criteria.

Text

CHAR

Returns the character specified by the code *number.*

Syntax

=CHAR(*number*)

Argument: *Number* is a number between 1 and 255 specifying which character you want.

CLEAN

Removes all unprintable characters from *text*.

Syntax

=CLEAN(*text*)

Argument: *Text* is any worksheet information from which you want to remove nonprintable characters.

CODE

Returns a numeric code for the first character in a text string.

Syntax

=CODE(*text*)

Argument: *Text* is any worksheet information from which you want to remove nonprintable characters.

DOLLAR

Converts a number to text using the currency format, with the decimals rounded to the specified place.

Syntax

=DOLLAR(*number,decimals*)

Arguments: *Number* is a number, a reference to a cell containing a number, or a formula that evaluates to a number. *Decimals* is the number of digits to the right of the decimal point. If *decimals* is negative, *number* is rounded to the left of the decimal point. If you omit *decimals*, it is assumed to be 2.

EXACT

Compares two text strings and returns TRUE if they are exactly the same, FALSE otherwise.

Syntax

=EXACT(*text1,text2*)

Arguments: *Text1* is the first text string. *Text2* is the second text string.

FIND

Finds one string of text within another string of text and returns the number of the character at which the *find_text* argument first occurs.

Syntax

=FIND(*find_text,within_text,start_at_num*)

Arguments: *Find_text* is the text you want to find. *Within_text* is the text containing the text you want to find. *Start_at_num* specifies the character at which to start the search. The first character in *within_text* is character number 1. If you omit *start_at_num*, it is assumed to be 1.

FIXED

Rounds a number to the specified number of decimals, formats the number in decimal format using a period and commas, and returns the result as text.

Syntax

=FIXED(*number,decimals,no_comma*)

Arguments: *Number* is the number you want to round and convert to text. *Decimals* is the number of digits to the right of the decimal point. *No_commas* is a logical value that, if TRUE, prevents FIXED from including commas in the returned text. If *no_commas* is FALSE or omitted, then the returned text includes commas as usual.

LEFT

Extracts the leftmost characters in a text string.

Syntax

=LEFT(*text,num_chars*)

Arguments: *Text* is the text string containing the characters you want to extract. *Num_chars* specifies how many characters you want LEFT to return.

LEN

Returns the number of characters in a text string.

Syntax

=LEN(*text*)

Argument: *Text* is the text whose length you want to find. Note that spaces count as characters.

LOWER

Converts all uppercase letters in a text to lowercase.

Syntax

=LOWER(*text*)

Argument: *Text* is the text you want to convert to lowercase. LOWER does not change characters in *text* that are not letters.

MID

Returns a specific number of characters from a text string, starting at the position you specify.

Syntax

=MID(*text,start_num,num_chars*)

Arguments: *Text* is the text string containing the characters you want to extract. *Start_num* is the position of the first character you want to extract in *text*. The first character in *text* has *start_num* 1, and so on. *Num_chars* specifies how many characters to return from text.

PROPER

Capitalizes the first letter in *text* and any other letters in *text* that follow any character other than a letter. Converts all other letters to lowercase.

Syntax

=PROPER(*text*)

Argument: *Text* is text enclosed in quotation marks, a formula that returns text, or a reference to a cell containing the text you want to partially capitalize.

REPLACE

Replaces part of a text string with a different text string.

Syntax

=REPLACE(*old_text,start_num,num_chars,new_text*)

Arguments: *Old_text* is text in which you want to replace some characters. *Start_num* is the position of the character in *old_text* that you want to replace with *new_text*. *Num_chars* is the number of characters in *old_text* that you want to replace with *new_text*. *New_text* is the text that will replace characters in *old_text*.

REPT

Repeats text a given number of times.

Syntax

=REPT(*text,number_times*)

Arguments: *Text* is the text you want to repeat. *Number_times* is a positive number specifying the number of times to repeat text. The result of the REPT function cannot be longer than 255 characters.

RIGHT

Returns the rightmost characters in a text string.

Syntax

=RIGHT(*text,num_chars*)

Arguments: *Text* is the text string containing the characters you want to extract. *Num_chars* specifies how many characters you want to extract. If *num_chars* is omitted, it is assumed to be 1.

SEARCH

Returns the number of the character at which a specific character or text string is first found, reading from left to right.

Syntax

=SEARCH(*find_text,within_text,start_num*)

Arguments: *Find_text* is the text you want to find. You can use the wildcard character, question mark (?) and asterisk (*), in *find_text*. If you want to find an actual question mark or asterisk, type a tilde (~) before the character. *Within_text* is the text in which you want to search for *find_text*. *Start_num* is the character number in *within_text*, counting from the left, at which you want to start searching. If *start_num* is omitted, it is assumed to be 1.

SUBSTITUTE

Replaces *new_text* for *old_text* in a text string.

Syntax

=SUBSTITUTE(*text,old_text,new_text,instance_num*)

Arguments: *Text* is the text or the reference to a cell containing text for which you want to substitute character. *Old_text* is the text you want to replace. *New_text* is the text you want to replace *old_text* with. *Instance_num* specifies which occurrence of *old_text* you want to replace with *new_text*. If you specify *instance_num*, only that instance of *old_text* is replaced. Otherwise, every occurrence of *old_text* in text is changed to *new_text*.

T

Returns the text referred to by the *value* argument.

Syntax

=T(*value*)

Argument: *Value* is the value you want to test. If *value* is or refers to text, T returns *value*. If value does not refer to text, T returns " " (empty text).

TEXT

Converts a value to text in a specific number format so that the result is no longer calculated as a number.

Syntax

=TEXT(*value,format_text*)

Arguments: *Value* is a numeric value, a formula that evaluates to a numeric value, or a reference to a cell containing a numeric value. *Format_text* is a number format from the Number dialog box in text form. *Format_text* cannot contain an asterisk (*) and cannot be "General".

TRIM

Removes all spaces from *text* except for single spaces between words.

Syntax

=TRIM(*text*)

Argument: *Text* is the text from which you want spaces removed.

UPPER

Converts *text* to uppercase.

Syntax

=UPPER(*text*)

Argument: *Text* is the text you want converted to uppercase.

VALUE

Converts the text argument to a number.

Syntax

=VALUE(*text*)

Argument: *Text* is the text enclosed in quotation marks or a reference to a cell containing the text you want to convert. *Text* can be any of the constant number, date, or time formats recognized by Excel. If *text* is not one of these formats, the function returns the #VALUE! error.

Logical

AND

Returns TRUE if all of its arguments are TRUE; returns FALSE if one or more of the arguments is FALSE.

Syntax

=AND(*logical1,logical2,...*)

Argument: *Logical1, logical2,* and so on are between 1 to 30 TRUE or FALSE conditions you want to test.

FALSE

Returns the logical value FALSE.

Syntax

=FALSE( )

IF

Returns one value if *logical_test* evaluates to TRUE and another value if it evaluates to FALSE.

Syntax 1

Worksheets and macro sheets

=IF(*logical_test,value_if_true,value_if_false*)

Arguments: *Logical_test* is any value or expression that can be evaluated to TRUE or FALSE. *Value_if_true* is the value that is returned if *logical_test* is TRUE. If logical_test is TRUE and *value_if_true* is omitted, TRUE is returned. *Value_if_false* is the value that is returned if *logical_test* is FALSE. If *logical_test* is FALSE and *value_if_false* is omitted, FALSE is returned.

NOT

Reverses the value of its arguments.

Syntax

=NOT(*logical*)

Argument: *Logical* is a value or expression that can be evaluated to TRUE or FALSE. If *logical* is FALSE, NOT returns TRUE; if *logical* is TRUE, NOT returns FALSE.

OR

Returns TRUE if one or more of the arguments is TRUE; returns FALSE if all arguments are FALSE.

Syntax

=OR(*logical1,logical2,...*)

Argument: *Logical1, logical2,* and so on are between 1 to 30 TRUE or FALSE conditions you want to test.

TRUE

Returns the logical value TRUE.

Syntax

=TRUE( )

DDE/External Functions

CALL

Calls a procedure in a dynamic link library (DLL) or code resource.

Syntax 1 (used with REGISTER)

=CALL(*register_id,argument1,...*)

Syntax 2 (used along with Excel for Windows)

=CALL(*module_text,procedure,type_text,argument1,...*)

Syntax 3 (used with Excel for the Macintosh)

=CALL(*file_text,resource,type_text,argument1,...*)

Arguments: *Register_id* is the value returned by a previously executed REGISTER or REGISTER.ID macro function. *Argument1,...* are the arguments to be passed to the procedure. *Module_text* or *file_text* is quoted text specifying the name of the DLL procedure (in Excel for Windows) or the name of the file that contains the code resource (in Excel for the Macintosh). *Procedure* or *resource* is text specifying the name of the function in the DLL (in Excel for Windows) or the name of the code resource (in Excel for the Macintosh). *Type_text* is the text specifying the data type of the return value and the data types of all arguments to the DLL or code resource.

Index

A

ABS function, 203, 870–871
Absolute cell references, using, 155–159
Absolute Record command, 647
ACCRINT function, 837
ACCRINTM function, 837–838
ACOS function, 871
ACOSH function, 871
Activate list box, 375
Activate Q+E command, 808
ACTIVE.CELL function, 671
Active area of a worksheet, 21
Active cell, 40
  locating precedents and dependents of, 336–338
Active option button, 237
Active worksheet window, changing the size of, 36
ADD.BAR macro function, 699, 700–701
ADD.COMMAND macro function, 691, 694
ADD.MENU macro function, 699, 700–701
ADD.TOOLBAR macro function, 752, 753–754
ADD.TOOL macro function, 752
Add Arrow command, 540
Add Color command button, 288
Add command button, 175, 177, 182, 303, 305, 321, 411, 421
Add Constraint dialog box, 460, 461

Add-in commands
  managing, 770–775
  working with, 757–775
Add-in functions
  creating, 768–770
  managing, 770–775
  working with, 757–775
Add-in macros
  adding to the working set, 773–775
  automatically added to Excel, 770
  creating, 768–770
  included in the macro library, 771–773
Add-in macro sheet, editing, 770
Add-In Manager dialog box, 773, 774
Add-ins command, 773
Add-Ins Installed list box, 774
Add Legend option, 531
ADD mode, 16, 42
Add New Record dialog box, 716, 718, 721
Add option button, 168
Add Overlay command, 503
Add Printer command, 236
Add Report dialog box, 306, 368
ADDRESS function, 866, 899–900
Add Scenario dialog box, 443–445
Add to Workbook dialog box, 417, 418
Add View dialog box, 304, 366
Add Words to drop-down list box, 177
Alert boxes, 26

ALERT macro function, 666, 667
Alert String text box, 683
Alignment. *See also* Horizontal alignment; Vertical alignment
  modifying with toolbars, 119–120
  of worksheet data, 118–126
Alignment commands, 118–119
Alignment dialog box, 580
  using, 120–122
ALIGNMENT macro function, 645–646
Alignment option, 66
Alignment tools, 87
All Database Values option button, 634
All Levels option button, 336
All option button, 145, 167
All References list box, 412, 413
Alternate Expression Evaluation option, 230
Alternate Menu Key, 281
Alternate Navigation Keys, 281
Alternate Navigation Keys check box, 50, 51
Alternate Startup Folder dialog box, 387
altstart.xla macro add-in file, 387
altstart directory, 387
Always Suggest check box, 175
Ampersand (&), use of, 69
AM/PM symbol, 98
am/pm symbol, 98
Analysis ToolPak, 216, 431
  tools in, 470–472

926 *Greg Harvey's Excel 4.0 for Windows*